Origins
of the Fifth Amendment,

THE RIGHT AGAINST SELF-INCRIMINATION

LEONARD W. LEVY

NEW YORK
Oxford University Press
1968

Copyright © 1968 by Clio Enterprises Inc.

Library of Congress Catalogue Card Number: 68-15894

PRINTED IN THE UNITED STATES OF AMERICA

ORIGINS OF THE FIFTH AMENDMENT

OTHER BOOKS BY LEONARD W. LEVY

The Law of the Commonwealth and Chief Justice Shaw (1957)

Legacy of Suppression:
Freedom of Speech and Press in Early American History (1960)

Major Crises in American History: Documentary Problems,
2 vols. (1962), editor, with Merrill D. Peterson

The American Political Process (1963), editor, with John P. Roche

Jefferson and Civil Liberties: The Darker Side (1963)

The Presidency (1964), editor, with John P. Roche

The Judiciary (1964), editor, with John P. Roche

The Congress (1964), editor, with John P. Roche

Political Parties and Pressure Groups (1964), editor, with John P. Roche

Freedom of the Press from Zenger to Jefferson (1966), editor

American Constitutional Law: Historical Essays (1966), editor

Judicial Review and the Supreme Court (1967), editor

Freedom and Reform: Essays in Honor of Henry Steele Commager (1967),
editor, with Harold M. Hyman

THIS BOOK IS DEDICATED TO MY FATHER-IN-LAW

MR. ALBERT GITLOW

WITH LOVE AND ADMIRATION

THE *Bill of Rights* epitomizes one of our history's most noble and enduringly important themes, the triumph of individual liberty, yet it has been one of the neglected subjects of scholarship. Although constitutional guarantees of personal liberty go to the heart of American political philosophy, there is no satisfactory study of the origins of the first state bills of rights and there are few studies of particular rights. The courts have assured us, again and again, that our understanding of the right against compulsory self-incrimination is dependent upon history. Chief Justice Warren, for example, noting that the right "was hard-earned by our forefathers," stated that the "reasons for its inclusion in the Constitution—and the necessities for its preservation—are to be found in the lessons of history." Historians have scarcely depicted that history despite the reliance of jurists upon them. This is the first book on the origins of the right.

Although the legal profession customarily refers to the right against self-incrimination as a "privilege," I call it a "right" because it is one. Privileges are concessions granted by the government to its subjects and may be revoked. "In the United States," however, as James Madison observed, "the people, not the government, possess the absolute sovereignty. . . . Hence the great and essential rights of the people are secured . . . not by laws paramount to prerogative, but by constitutions paramount to laws." Although the right against self-incrimination originated in England as a common-law privilege, the Fifth Amendment made it a constitutional right, clothing it with the same status as other rights, like freedom of religion, that we would never denigrate by describing them as mere privileges.

Recently the Supreme Court of the United States reversed its finding of 1908 that the right against self-incrimination is simply a rule of evidence rather than a fundamental principle of liberty and justice. Belatedly the Court has returned to its still earlier and more historically accurate view that the right is indeed such a principle. Those who fought to establish it certainly regarded it as such. They associated it, however inaccurately, with Magna Carta. Today the Court calls it "one of our Nation's most cherished principles," yet still carelessly refers to it as a "privilege."

As far as precedence is concerned, history exalts the right against self-incrimination. It won acceptance earlier than the freedoms of speech, press, and religion. It preceded a cluster of procedural rights such as benefit of counsel. It is older, too, than immunities against bills of attainder, ex post facto laws, and unreasonable searches and seizures. History also exalts the origins of the right against self-incrimination. Its origins are related to the development of the accusatorial system of criminal justice and the concept of fair trial; to the principle that fundamental law limits government —the very foundation of constitutionalism; and to the heroic struggles for the freedoms of conscience and press.

My subject is the history of the right against self-incrimination from its origins to the ratification of the Fifth Amendment in 1791. Accordingly, nothing in this book is intended to prove or disprove any position relating to the contemporary controversy about the right against self-incrimination. I care only for an explanation of its background. Chief Judge Calvert Magruder once said, "Our forefathers, when they wrote this provision into the Fifth Amendment of the Constitution, had in mind a lot of history which has been largely forgotten today." I have tried to tell that story, fully and objectively.

The right or "privilege" against self-incrimination was not a phrase known to the framers of the Fifth Amendment. They spoke more broadly of the right of a person not to be a witness against himself. The first state bills of rights spoke of one's right not to be compelled to give evidence against himself. Earlier it was called a right of silence, a right against self-infamy, and, most commonly by far, the right against self-accusation. The familiar phrase of contemporary usage seems to be of twentieth-century vintage. Nevertheless, I use it, even if anachronistically, as a convenient term that readers will recognize.

Another anachronism in this book is the frequent modernization of spelling and punctuation of very old language. When using manuscript sources I reproduce the material as in the original. But it was impossible to discover the original manuscript of every word quoted; hence when using printed versions of primary sources, I am dependent upon the practice of earlier historians and editors. Some reproduced verbatim; others modernized. Consequently, readers may find me quoting a sixteenth-century document in all its antique flavor, only to discover in the next paragraph a fifteenth-century line rendered in today's English. I did not wish to tamper with the original materials by consistently modernizing everything. The results are sometimes jarring but represent the best possible fidelity to the printed sources. However, I have not followed the originals when dating documents. Until the mid-eighteenth century, the first day of the new year under the Julian calendar was March 25. To avoid confusion, to show temporal relationships more accurately, and for the sake of consistency, I have rendered all dates in accordance with the modern Gregorian calendar. Thus, an event which occurred on March 24, 1590 (old style), becomes March 24, 1591 (new style).

Most of this book is English history, because the origins of the right against self-incrimination are English. Excepting the First Amendment, our Bill of Rights is primarily English in origin. Most of its provisions deal with procedure for the very good reason that the history of both liberty and constitutional government is in large part the history of procedure. The story begins even before Magna Carta, because the English legal system—and therefore the American—owes so much to Henry II, who ruled England in the last half of the twelfth century. Magna Carta itself first became the talismanic symbol and source of individual freedom in connection with the struggle against compulsory self-accusation. Given the fact that English history bulks largest in the history of the right not to be a witness against oneself, the task of depicting its origins would have been better performed by a scholar whose qualifications are more suitable than mine. By training and experience I am a historian of the United States. Yet I enjoyed writing this book because it gave me the opportunity to learn more about a time and place that make American history seem like a mere postscript. But I have few illusions about making much of a contribution to English history—medieval, Tudor, or Stuart; legal or constitutional. I am addressing myself to those who, knowing even less about English history than I, are nevertheless interested in the origins of an important clause in the United States Constitution.

This book has been a long time in the making. In 1957–58 the John Simon Guggenheim Memorial Foundation awarded me a fellowship to aid my research, though I spent most of that academic year writing a related book on the origins of the free-press clause. Similarly, when I enjoyed a fellowship in 1961–62 from the Center for the Study of the History of Liberty in America at Harvard University, my reading diverted me to a book on Jefferson and civil liberties. Nevertheless, much of the research for this present book was undertaken at that time, and the result was intended for publication under the auspices of that Center. It has since become the Charles Warren Center for Studies in American History. I am deeply indebted to its Director, Professor Oscar Handlin, for his encouragement and careful scrutiny of the manuscript. I am also honored to know that the Center regards this book as a product of its program.

I must acknowledge the gracious interest shown in my work by Mrs. Mary Hume Maguire who, in the year of my birth, earned her Ph.D. in history with a dissertation at Radcliffe College on the history of the oath *ex officio*. She very generously lent me her copy of the dissertation, thereby opening the paths of my research. Professor Lawrence H. Leder of the University of Louisiana, New Orleans, a former colleague at Brandeis University, assisted me with the research on the right against self-incrimination in colonial New York, leading to our article on that topic in the *William and Mary Quarterly*. Several of my students over the years have aided by arranging for reproduction of research materials, checking footnotes, and doing other chores that expedited the work. I am particularly thankful to Mr. André Martinsons, Mr. Carl Siracusa, Father William Lichliter, S.J., and Miss Angela Mazzarelli. In the compilation of the Bibliography and Index, Miss Mazzarelli was indispensable; and I am grateful also for Father Lichliter's aid on the Index. Professor Harold M. Hyman of the University of Illinois gave valuable criticism. Professors Alexander Altmann and

Harold Weisberg of Brandeis University gave me very useful suggestions for exploring Hebrew sources; Professor Weisberg and Mr. Sheldon R. Brunswick, formerly Semitics Librarian at Brandeis, sacrificed their own time to provide me with translations from the Hebrew. I am very grateful to Brandeis University and especially to its Dean of Faculty, Peter Diamandopoulos, for a handsome research grant that made it possible for me to photograph many of the sources on which this book is based. The university also gave me sabbatical leave to finish the writing.

My most helpful critic was Professor Norman O. Cantor, my colleague at Brandeis University, who read the early chapters with a sharp eye for errors, checked my Latin translations, and offered dozens of bibliographic suggestions. Professor Morton Keller, another colleague, also reviewed the manuscript for me. Some of their comments indicate that I seem to have rediscovered the truths of libertarianism, which, according to reviewers of two earlier books, I had betrayed. Professor Cantor, on returning the manuscript of this book, observed that I must be "the last of the Victorian liberals." Professor Keller remarked that he felt safer knowing that he was a colleague of someone who dared to come out in print against the Inquisition. He found the manuscript "excessively Whiggish" and added, perhaps a bit maliciously, that it was "even Jeffersonian." I am relieved to think that I may not again have to face the emotional outbursts of reviewers who cannot abide exposure of imperfections in the libertarian tradition. Nevertheless, I remain impenitent, believing that conclusions must always be based on the evidence no matter what it reveals. This seems to be the first occasion that I have worked with evidence that happens—irrelevantly for my purposes—to support libertarian presuppositions.

While expressing acknowledgments I must also reveal a grudge that I bear against the President of the United States. He conscripted into his service as a Special Consultant my dear friend and critic, Professor John P. Roche of Brandeis University, thereby denying me the opportunity of benefiting from his extraordinary knowledge of legal, political, and religious history at a time when I most needed it. Professor Saul Benison, another colleague, offered no help either, but like Professor Roche loves to see his name in print. So do Richard and Rosalind Brown, and Lynn and Elizabeth Gitlow. My daughters, Wendy Ellen and Leslie Anne, who are aging rapidly, assisted on this book in a variety of little ways. As for my wife, Elyse, she could not have rewritten the manuscript without my assistance. Her aversion to excessive adjectives and complicated sentences forces her, out of a sense of professional pride, to disclaim any part of the authorship.

L. W. L.

Brandeis University
Waltham, Massachusetts
August 1, 1967

CONTENTS

ORIGINS OF THE FIFTH AMENDMENT

"Surely, in popular parlance and even in legal literature, the term 'Fifth Amendment' in the context of our time is commonly regarded as being synonymous with the privilege against self-incrimination." Chief Justice Earl Warren in *Quinn* v. *U.S.*, 349 U.S. 155, at 163 (1955).

"Ours is the accusatorial as opposed to the inquisitorial system. Such has been the characteristic of Anglo-American criminal justice since it freed itself from practices borrowed by the Star Chamber from the Continent . . . Under our system society carries the burden of proving it charges against the accused not out of his own mouth." Justice Felix Frankfurter in *Watts* v. *Indiana*, 338 U.S. 49, at 54 (1949).

". . . the American system of criminal prosecution is accusatorial, not inquisitorial, and . . . the Fifth Amendment privilege is its essential mainstay." Justice William J. Brennan in *Malloy* v. *Hogan*, 378 U.S. 1, at 7 (1964).

"The privilege against self-incrimination is a right that was hard-earned by our forefathers. The reasons for its inclusion in the Constitution—and the necessities for its preservation—are to be found in the lessons of history." Chief Justice Earl Warren in *Quinn* v. *U.S.*, 349 U.S. 155, at 161 (1955).

"The privilege against self-incrimination is a specific provision of which it is peculiarly true that 'a page of history is worth a volume of logic.'" Justice Felix Frankfurter in *Ullmann* v. *U.S.*, 350 U.S. 422, at 438 (1956).

THE FIFTH AMENDMENT

"No person shall be held to answer for a capital, or otherwise infamous crime, unless on a presentment or indictment of a Grand Jury, except in cases arising in the land or naval forces, or in the Militia, when in actual service in time of War or public danger; nor shall any person be subject for the same offence to be twice put in jeopardy of life or limb; *nor shall be compelled in any Criminal Case to be a witness against himself,* nor be deprived of life, liberty, or property, without due process of law; nor shall private property be taken for public use, without just compensation." (Italics added.)

CHAPTER I

Rival Systems of Criminal Procedure

In 1537 John Lambert was chained to a stake in Smithfield, England, and roasted in the flames as an obdurate heretic. A priest and fellow of Queen's College, Cambridge, he had had a long record of trouble with the authorities. Five years before his death the Archbishop of Canterbury, instigated by Sir Thomas More, summoned Lambert to Lambeth Palace for an inquisition into his religious beliefs. Suspected of having become a convert to Protestantism, he had to answer by sworn affidavit to forty-five "articles," or charges. Framed as questions, the articles were calculated to expose Lambert's doctrinal convictions. He responded with all the candor of a zealot destined for martyrdom, but refused to answer the first article demanding whether he had ever before been suspected of heresy. His memory was uncertain, he claimed, but "though I did remember . . . yet were I more than twice a fool to show you thereof; for it is written in your own law, 'No man is bound to bewray [accuse] himself' "—to which he appended the Latin expression of that maxim, *"Nemo tenetur prodere seipsum."* [1]

The suspicion that Lambert was a heretic was founded partly on his alleged belief—one of the charges against him—that ecclesiastical judges had no right to compel suspects to swear on the Bible an oath to tell the truth. Lambert replied that he was not opposed to oaths when they were "lawful." What grieved him was the habitual practice by the ecclesiastical judges of forcing a man to swear

> to make true relation of all that they shall demand him, he not knowing what they will demand, neither whether it be lawful to show them the truth of their demands, or no: for such things there be that are not lawful to be showed . . . Yea, moreover, if such judges sometimes, not knowing by any due proof that such as have to do before them are culpable, will enforce them, by an oath, to detect themselves, in opening before them their hearts; in this so doing, I cannot see that men need to condescend to their requests. For it is in the law (but I wot not certainly the place) thus: 'No man is bound to bewray himself.' Also in another place of the law it is written, 'Cogitationis poenam nemo patiatur,' 'No man should suffer punishment of men for his thought.' To this agreeth the common proverb, that is thus: 'Thoughts be free, and need pay no toll.' So that, to conclude, I think it lawful, at the commandment of a judge, to make an oath to say the truth, especially if the judge requireth an oath duly, and in lawful wise . . . and that also for purgation of infamy, when any infamy is lawfully laid against him.[2]

Thus Lambert twice claimed a right not to disclose to ecclesiastical judges information that would place him in criminal jeopardy. He would take no oath that would force him to incriminate himself, because he had not been duly accused. The right against self-incrimination even after due accusation was still more than a century away, but it originated as a defensive claim by the Lamberts who were denied freedom of thought and were victims of the canon law's inquisitorial system.

Several centuries of English experience with an accusatorial system of criminal justice explain Lambert's defiance of his inquisitors. He echoed protests that had been leveled against canon law procedures ever since the Church introduced them into England. His argument on illegality of the proceedings against him was founded on a system of trial that was antithetical to the inquisitorial system and older than Magna Carta. Indeed, accusatorial procedure antedated the Norman Conquest. From the early Middle Ages, civil and ecclesiastical authorities throughout western Europe had employed substantially similar accusatorial procedures. The latter half of the twelfth century and first half of the thirteenth was a period of transition that witnessed profound transformations of procedure. Old forms of trial, once universal, broke down and newer ones emerged. In England, the new forms, presentment and trial by jury, preserved the accusatorial character of the old; on the Continent and in the ecclesiastical courts, inquisitorial procedures were triumphant. By no coincidence the liberties of the subject were to thrive in England and be throttled on the Continent.

Community courts and community justice prevailed in England at the time of the Norman Conquest. The legal system was ritualistic, dependent upon oaths at most stages of litigation, and permeated by both religious and superstitious notions. Legal concepts were so primitive that there was no distinction between civil and criminal cases or between secular and ecclesiastical cases. The proceedings were oral, very personal, and highly confrontative. Juries were unknown. One party publicly "appealed," or accused, the other before the community meeting at which the presence of both was obligatory. To be absent meant risking fines and outlawry. After the preliminary statements of the parties, the court rendered judgment, not on the merits of the issue nor the question of guilt or innocence, but on the manner by which it should be resolved. Judgment in other words preceded trial because it was a decision on what form the trial should take. It might be by compurgation, by ordeal, or, after the Norman Conquest, by battle. Excepting trial by battle, only one party was tried or, more accurately, was put to his "proof." Proof being regarded as an advantage, it was usually awarded to the accused party; in effect he had the privilege of proving his own case.[3]

Trial by exculpatory oath and compurgation, also called canonical purgation, consisted of a sworn statement to the truth of one's claim or denial, supported by the oaths of a certain number of fellow swearers. Presumably they, no more than the claimant, would endanger their immortal souls by the sacrilege of false swearing. Originally the oath-helpers swore from their own knowledge to the truth of the party's claim. Later they became little more than character witnesses, swearing only to their belief that his oath was trustworthy. If he rounded up the requisite number of compurgators and the cumbrous swearing in very exact form proceeded without a mistake, he won his case. A mistake "burst" the oath, proving guilt.[4]

Ordeals were usually reserved for more serious crimes, for persons of bad reputation, for peasants, or for those caught with stolen goods. As an invocation of immediate divine judgment, ordeals were consecrated by the Church and shrouded with solemn religious mystery. The accused underwent a physical trial in which he called upon God to witness his innocence by putting a miraculous sign upon his body. Cold water, boiling water, and hot iron were the principal ordeals, all of which the clergy administered. In the ordeal of cold water, the accused was trussed up and cast into a pool to see whether he would sink or float. On the theory that water which had been sanctified by a priest would receive an innocent person but reject the guilty, innocence was proved by sinking—and hopefully a quick retrieval—guilt by floating. In the other ordeals, one had to plunge his hand into a cauldron of boiling water or carry a red hot piece of iron for a certain distance, in the hope that three days later, when the bandages were removed, the priest would find a "clean" wound, one that was healing free of infection. How deeply one plunged his arm into the water, how heavy the iron or great the distance it was carried, depended mainly on the gravity of the charge.[5]

The Normans brought to England still another ordeal, trial by battle, paradigm of the adversary system, which gave to the legal concept of "defense" or "defendant" a physical meaning. Trial by battle was a savage yet sacred method of proof which was also thought to involve divine intercession on behalf of the righteous. Rather than let a wrongdoer triumph, God would presumably strengthen the arms of the party who had sworn truly to the justice of his cause. Right, not might, would therefore conquer. Trial by battle was originally available for the settlement of all disputes, from debt and ownership to robbery and rape, but eventually was restricted to cases of serious crime. In this particular form of proof there was a significant exception to the oral character of the old procedures. The accusation leading to battle, technically known as an "appeal of felony," had to be written, and nothing but the most exact form, giving full particulars of the alleged crime, would be accepted. The indictment, or accusation, by grand jury would later imitate the "appeal" in this respect.[6]

Whether one proved his case by compurgation, ordeal, or battle, the method was accusatory in character. There was always a definite and known accuser, some private person who brought formal suit and openly confronted his antagonist. There was never any secrecy in the proceedings, which were the same for criminal as for civil litigation. The judges, who had no role whatever in the making of the verdict, decided only which party should be put to proof and what its form should be; thereafter the judges merely enforced an observance of the rules. The oaths that saturated the proceedings called upon God to witness to the truth of the respective claims of the parties, or the justice of their cause, or the reliability of their word. No one gave testimonial evidence nor was anyone questioned to test his veracity.

It was the inquest, a radically different proceeding, which eventually supplanted the old forms of proof while borrowing their accusatorial character. An extraordinarily fertile and versatile device, the inquest was the parent of our double jury system, the grand jury of accusation and the petty jury of trial. Fortunately for the history of freedom, the inquest, a Norman import, was also one of the principal means by which the monarchy developed a centralized government in England. The survival of the inquest was insured by its close ties to royal power and royal prosperity; its particular English form was founded on the old accusatorial procedures. The word "inquest" derives from the Latin *inquisitio*, or inquisition, but beyond the similarity in name shared nothing in common with the canon law procedure, which became, in fact, its opposite and great rival. The inquest was also known as the *recognitio*, or recognition, which meant a solemn answer or finding or declaration of truth. The inquest was just that, an answer or declaration of truth—a *veri dictum*, or verdict—by a body of men from the same neighborhood who were summoned by some official, on the authority of the crown, to reply under oath to any inquiries that might be addressed to them. Men of the same locality were chosen simply because they were most likely to know best the answers to questions relating to it—who had evaded taxes, who owned certain lands, who was suspected of crime, or who knew of misconduct among the king's officers? [7]

At first the inquest was used mainly in administrative and financial inquiries. The Domesday Book, for example, that enormously detailed description or census of landowners, their property down to the last calf and acre, and its cash value, was compiled at least in part by an elaborate inquest for tax assessment purposes. The king's representatives went into the counties in 1086, summoned men from each "hundred," or county subdivision—originally the "hundred" was a hundred households—put them under oath, and demanded their verdicts or truthful answers concerning who owned what and how much. After an abortive attempt by Henry I to establish a system of resident judges, royal commissioners periodically went on circuit, or "eyre," throughout the country to transact the king's business. In the passage of time they undertook duties that became increasingly judicial. They inspected the provinces, gathered revenues and information, occasionally heard lawsuits, and superintended the local details of the king's government. They also aided the exchequer's fiscal business by assessing taxes, holding sheriffs and other revenue collectors to account, and inquiring into the proprietary rights of the crown. Financial and executive business was similarly conducted with the help of inquests, which increasingly involved the itinerant royal commissioners in matters connected with the administration of justice. The king had a stake not only in suits which concerned his royal demesne and his own litigation; he looked to all fines, amercements, escheats, and forfeitures of every sort to contribute to his royal revenues, including the profits that might accrue from purely private suits. He claimed, for example, the goods of felons; not only did he acquire the chattels of a condemned man who had been defeated in battle by private appeal of felony; the king had a right, too, to plunder his lands for a year or sell off that right to a local lord. As Stephen says, "The rigorous enforcement of all the proprietary and other profitable rights of the Crown which the articles of eyre confided to the justices was naturally associated with their duties as administrators of the criminal law, in which the king was deeply interested, not only because it protected the life and property of his subjects, but also because it contributed to his revenues." Thus the king's traveling justices were a major factor in the early centralization of England, and their most useful instrument became the inquest in matters both civil and criminal.[8]

What was long an irregular and in some respects an extraordinary procedure became under King Henry II (1154–89) normal and systematic. A man of powerful will, administrative genius, and reforming spirit, Henry II increased tremendously the jurisdiction of the royal courts, and wherever they traveled on eyre through the kingdom, the inquest followed. Henry II disliked and distrusted the traditional forms of proof. More boldly than his predecessors he regarded breaches of peace or threats to life and limb as offenses of a public nature, warranting more than merely private retribution. Crimes of a serious nature he took to be offenses against the king's peace, requiring settlement in the king's courts by the king's system of justice, whenever possible, rather than by the older proofs only; and the king's system was founded on the inquest, the representative verdict of the neighborhood. What was once only an administrative inquiry became the foundation of the jury of accusation and the jury of trial in both civil and criminal matters.

Older forms of proof or trial were becoming corrupted, their irrationality apparent to the new, university-trained royal administrators. Compurgation, having hardly survived the Conquest in criminal matters, was the most untrustworthy. It had become too easy a proof, almost a certain success for the party, however culpable or liable, who was lucky enough to be awarded the right to resort to his oath with the support of oath helpers. They swore only to their belief that his oath was reliable, no longer to their knowledge that it was in fact true. Compurgators who had become little more than character witnesses could no longer be punished for perjury, making the procedure pretty much a ritualistic farce. Moreover, the oaths of compurgators seemed inconsistent with the oaths of the sworn inquest, a much more impartial body. Henry II placed little more trust in ordeals than he did in compurgation; they were too easily manipulated by the priests who administered them, yet as sanctified ceremonials, proofs were not easily dispensable, and they were both quick and profitable to the crown. Ordeal by battle, however, was too dangerous—not only to life and limb but to the security of vested interests—to endure without providing an alternate form of proof for the settlement of disputes. Battle was also becoming too inequitable and farcical. In civil cases, such as disputes over property, the employment of champions, which was once exceptional, had become routine. Champions were hired to do battle on behalf of a litigant whenever one of the parties was unable, for reasons of age, sex, or physical infirmity, to represent himself. The champion was at first a witness who could prove the case of the litigant, but in time champions became professional fighters available for hire in all civil cases, regardless of the physical capacity of the party. Sometimes champions were used as "approvers" to get rid of gangs of criminals.[9]

Henry II did not abolish older forms of proof; he sought, instead, to supersede them in as many instances as possible, by discrediting them and by making available to litigants an alternative and more equitable form of proceeding. Innovations began in 1164, when the Constitutions of Clarendon prescribed the use of a recognition by twelve sworn men to decide any dispute between laymen and clergy on the question whether land was subject to lay or clerical tenure. The Constitutions of Clarendon provided also that laymen should not be sued in ecclesiastical courts on untrustworthy or insufficient evidence, but that if the suspect were someone whom no one might dare to accuse, the sheriff on the request of the bishop must swear a jury of twelve to declare the truth by bringing the accusation. In the Constitutions of Clarendon, then, there is the glimmering of the civil jury in cases of land disputes and of the grand jury of criminal presentment of accusation.[10]

The Assize, or ordinance, of Clarendon, which Henry II promulgated two years later, on the centennial of the Conquest, provided for the firm foundation of the grand jury and instituted a variety of significant procedural reforms. The king instructed the royal judges on circuit, or eyre, to take jurisdiction over certain serious crimes or felonies presented to them by sworn inquests, the representative juries of the various localities. Twelve men from each hundred of the county and four from each township, or vill, of the hundred were to be summoned by the sheriff to attend the public eyre. They were enjoined to inquire into all crimes committed since the beginning of Henry II's reign, and to report under oath all persons accused or suspected by the vicinage. The parties who were thus presented, if not already in custody, would be arrested and put to the ordeal of cold water. Even if absolved, those of very bad reputation were forced to abjure the realm. In certain cases, then, mere presentment was tantamount to a verdict of banishment, but generally was no more than an accusation which was tried by ordeal. The Assize of Northampton, which was issued in 1176, recodified the Assize of Clarendon, extended the list of felonies, and substituted maiming for hanging as the punishment of the accused felon who was "undone" at the ordeal; he lost a foot, his right hand, and his chattels, and was banished. In actuality, he fled to the forest if he could to live as an outlaw to escape the ordeal or banishment. The Assize of 1176 made permanent, at least at the pleasure of the king, the revised procedure of accusation by twelve knights of the hundred or twelve freemen of the hundred and four of the vill.[11]

The Assizes of Clarendon and Northampton, by establishing what became the grand jury, offered a royally sanctioned option to the old system of private accusations by appeals of felony. Trial by battle, which was begun by an "appeal of felony" in criminal cases, continued; but it was undermined by the king's jury of criminal presentment as the model way of beginning a criminal trial. Henry II also made available an escape from trial by battle in cases begun by an appeal of felony. On the theory that the security of the king's peace could not be safely left to accusations brought by private initiative, many of which were motivated by malice, the writ *de odio et atia,* "of spite and hatred," was provided for appellees. For a price, the writ could be obtained from the king's court by one who claimed that his appellor proceeded from spite and hatred. A jury of recognitors would then be impaneled to render a verdict on this plea; if the jury sustained it, the appeal was quashed and battle avoided. What was in essence a jury's verdict was therefore substituted in some instances for trial by battle. Nevertheless, the trial jury in criminal cases was unknown during the twelfth century. The trial jury in civil cases developed first, providing a model that could be copied later in criminal cases.[12]

Reformation of the machinery of civil justice at the expense of trial by battle was one of Henry II's foremost achievements. Once again his instrument was the sworn inquest or jury. Its use in cases of property disputes contributed to the stability of land tenures, extended the jurisdiction of the royal courts at the expense of the feudal courts, aided the cause of justice at the same time that fees for the privilege of using the royal courts contributed to the exchequer, and sapped trial by battle in civil cases. The Constitutions of Clarendon in 1164 provided the precedent for turning to twelve men of the countryside for a verdict on a question concerning property rights. Such questions, especially in relation to the possession and title of land, produced the most common and surely the most important civil actions. For their solution Henry II gradually introduced what became the trial jury. In 1166 the assize of *"novel disseisin,"* or recent dispossession, established the principle that no one might be evicted or dispossessed of his land without the approval of a jury verdict. This assize created a legal remedy for one who had been dispossessed. He could obtain a writ commanding the sheriff to summon twelve free men of the vicinity who presumably knew the facts of the case, put them under oath, and then in presence of the itinerant royal judges require them to render a verdict on the question whether the tenant had been dispossessed. A verdict in the tenant's favor restored him to possession of his land. If, however, a lord seized the land of a tenant who died before the tenant's heirs might take possession of it, the assize of *novel disseisin* provided no remedy. The assize of *"mort d'ancestor,"* which was instituted in 1176, did so. The heir might obtain a writ which put before a jury the question whether the decedent died in possession of the land and whether the claimant was his rightful heir. In the same reign, the assize of *"darrein prsentment"* provided for a verdict by jury on questions involving rival claims to the possession of certain "advowsons," or ecclesiastical benefices, which were regarded as a form of real estate.[13]

Possession, though often indicative of right, was not synonymous with it. One might be "seissed" of land without having title to it. The dispossesser, not the dispossessed, might be the rightful owner; the heir might have a defective title. Thus, settlement of the question of possession was merely provisional, for it left the main question of ownership undecided, and that question was settled by battle. The claimant obtained a writ of right, the civil analogue to the appeal of felony in criminal cases, and challenged the possessor to a duel, with both parties represented by champions. But Henry II's Grand Assize, which was introduced in 1179, opened the way to peaceable settlement. The challenged party, in any case involving a question of proprietary right, might obtain a counter-writ transferring jurisdiction to the royal courts; he thereby consented to having the question settled by a jury which was chosen with great care to insure disinterestedness. The sheriff selected four knights, who in turn chose twelve others of the same neighborhood where the land was located, and the twelve, mainly from their own knowledge, declared which party had the better right to the land. Glanvill, chief justiciar to Henry II, overpraised the procedure of the Grand Assize as a "royal benefit . . . whereby life and property are so wholesomely cared for that men can avoid the chance of the combat and yet keep whatever right they have in their freeholds." [14]

By the time of Magna Carta, the inquest in civil cases was becoming fairly well established as the trial jury, although in criminal cases it was hardly known at all. The petty or possessory assizes of *novel disseisin, mort d'ancestor,* and *darrein presentment* had proved to be so popular that chapter eighteen of Magna Carta guaranteed that the circuit court would sit several times a year in each county for the purpose of getting verdicts on disputes that they settled. Civil disputes of virtually any description, not merely those named in the petty assizes, might be referred to the verdict of local recognitors if both parties would consent to the procedure. On the criminal side of the law, Magna Carta in chapter thirty-six provided that the writ *de odio et atia,* which by 1215 had become known as the writ of life and limb, should be granted without charge. It was by no means uncommon by then for one accused by private appeal to demand a jury verdict on any number of "exceptions," such as the writ of life and limb, in the hope of getting the appeal quashed. In such cases, however, the jury decided only the question whether the "exception" was valid; the main question of guilt or innocence, which the appeal had raised, was still settled by battle if the exception was not sustained. Criminal accusations, which were presented in accord with the grand inquest provided by the Assize of Clarendon, were tried by ordeal. Magna Carta, in chapter twenty-eight, insured that no one could be put to the ordeal unless formally accused by the jury of presentment before the royal judges on circuit. This was the implication of the provision that "credible witnesses," members of the presenting jury, must corroborate the fact that there had been an indictment. The celebrated chapter twenty-nine did not guarantee trial by jury for the simple reason that its use in criminal cases was still unknown in 1215. At best that chapter insured that indictment and trial by whatever was the appropriate test, whether battle or ordeal, must precede sentence.[15]

The course of history was affected at the same time by events in Rome. The Fourth Lateran Council in 1215 forbade the participation of the clergy in the administration of ordeals, thereby divesting that proof of its rationale as a judgment of God. As a result, the ordeal died as a form of trial in western Europe and some procedure was needed to take its place. While the continental nations and the Church turned to the inquisition, England found in its own form of the inquest, a device at hand that would fill the gap. The absence of heresy in England and therefore of a papal inquisition allowed the alternative.[16]

With the ordeal abolished, battle remained the only means of trying a criminal case. But the movement of the law was away from battle. The same reasons of "equity" which led Glanvill in 1187 to say that the right to a freehold "can scarcely be proved by battle" spurred the search for an alternate means of proving an accusation of crime. Thus Magna Carta had made the writ of life and limb free, but still reflected traditional thinking in terms of ordeals and battle. Battle could never be had, however, in cases where one of the parties was aged, crippled, sick, or a woman. With the ordeal gone, England criminal procedure, in the words of Pollock and Maitland, "was deprived of its handiest weapon." Not only was there no way to try those who could not engage in battle; there was the greater quandary of what should be done with persons who had been accused by the sworn verdict of a grand inquest. Battle was possible only in the case of a private appeal of felony. According to Stephen, "When trial by ordeal was abolished and the system of accusation by grand juries was established, absolutely no mode of ascertaining the truth of an accusation made by a grand jury remained." Nevertheless, compurgation and suit by witnesses lingered for a long time.[17]

The crown's bewilderment was revealed in a writ of 1219 giving instructions to the circuit judges: "Because it was in doubt and not definitely settled before the beginning of your eyre, with what trial those are to be judged who are accused of robbery, murder, arson, and similar crimes, since the trial by fire and water has been prohibited by the Roman Church," notorious criminals should be imprisoned, those accused of "medium" crimes who were not likely to offend again should be banished, and those accused of lesser crimes might be released on "pledges of fidelity and of keeping our peace." The writ concluded, "We have left to your discretion the observance of this aforesaid order . . . according to your own discretion and conscience," a formula that left the judges further perplexed but free to improvise.[18]

Treating an accusation as a conviction, when an accusation was little more than an expression of popular opinion, was a makeshift that fell so short of doing justice that it could not survive. In retrospect it seems natural that the judges on circuit should have turned to a sworn inquest for help. An eyre was a great event, virtually a county parliament. Present were the local nobles and bishops, the sheriffs and bailiffs, the knights and freeholders, and a very great many juries. From every hundred of the county there was a jury of twelve men, and from every township four representatives. Surrounded by the various juries, the judge in a criminal case could take the obvious course of seeking the sense of the community. The original jury of presentment was already sworn, presumably knew most about the facts, and was a representative group. Their indictment had not necessarily voiced their own belief in the prisoner's guilt; it rather affirmed the fact that he was commonly suspected. Although practice varied considerably at first, the judges began to ask the jury of presentment to render a verdict of guilty or not guilty on their accusation. Because the jury of presentment were more likely than not to sustain their indictment, even though they had sworn only that the accused was suspected and not that he was guilty, the judges usually swore in the representatives of the surrounding townships and asked whether they concurred; the jury of another hundred might also be conscripted to corroborate the verdict. In effect a body of the countryside gave the verdict. This practice of enlarging the original jury of presentment or seeking a series of verdicts from different juries was common during the thirteenth century. What became the petty jury was thus initially larger than the grand jury. The practice was too cumbersome, the body too unwieldy. Twelve was the number of the presenting jury and twelve the jury in many civil cases; gradually only twelve jurors were selected to try the indictment, but they always included among their number some of the original jury of presentment. The unfairness inherent in this practice and the theory that the accused must consent to his jury eventually led to a complete separation of the grand jury and the trial jury.[19]

Consent, even if induced by coercion, was an ancient feature of accusatory procedure. In Saxon times the accused party had to appear personally before his accuser and the assembled community, and agreed to submit himself to whatever proof was assigned, or be outlawed. When Henry II introduced the sworn inquest in civil cases, it was available to those who secured a writ requesting it; so, too, parties who sought to escape battle consented to abide by the verdict of a jury under the process of the Grand Assize or of the writ of life and limb. Indeed in such cases where a trial jury was known, it was available only after consent. But no man would be likely to consent to the verdict of his accusers if he thought that they sought his conviction. And no man, it was thought, should be forced to accept the verdict of accusers except freely. While ordeals were still in use, if an accused refused to submit himself to the proof, he was considered to have repudiated the law and might therefore be punished as if he had outlawed himself. But the inquest acting as a trial jury was a novel and extraordinary device, and thus the reasoning that had branded as outlaws those who rejected the ordeal now seemed repugnant when it was applied to a man who refused to put himself to the test of a jury. He might think the jury would not fairly decide, or that his chances of getting a verdict of not guilty, for whatever the reasons, were hopeless.[20]

To cope with such cases the law developed in two completely different ways, one barbaric, the other salutary. Before the judges turned to a second jury to decide the question of guilt or innocence, they would ask the accused whether he would submit to the final verdict of the "country," that is, of the inquest of the countryside or whole county. Most men consented, but some did not, quite likely because conviction meant the forfeiture of chattles and goods. In cases of no consent, some judges proceeded with the trial anyway; others treated the prisoner as if he were guilty; but most felt that it was unreasonable to compel a man to submit unless he consented. If he refused to consent, the law was nonplussed, the proceedings stymied. At length, in 1275 a statute supplied the answer: extort his consent. The statute read, "that notorious felons who are openly of evil fame and who refuse to put themselves upon inquests of felony at the suit of the King before his justices, shall be remanded to a hard and strong prison as befits those who refuse to abide by the common law of the land; but this is not to be understood of persons who are taken upon light suspicion." It is noteworthy that the trial jury, here called the inquest of felony, is described as the common law of the land by 1275. By the same date, incidentally, anyone privately accused of felony might avoid battle if he put himself "upon his country," letting a jury decide the question of guilt or innocence.[21]

The notion of consent to trial by jury incredibly remained the law of the land until 1772. A prisoner who refused to plead to the indictment simply could not be tried, though he was subjected to a peculiar form of torture that was calculated to change his mind. Within a quarter of a century of its introduction in 1275, imprisonment strong and hard (*prison forte et dure*) degenerated into punishment strong and hard (*peine forte et dure*). At first the prisoner was stripped, put in irons on the bare ground in the worst part of the prison, and fed only coarse bread one day and water the next, which was surely cruel enough. Then the refinement of "punishment" was added; he was slowly pressed, spread-eagled on the ground, with as much iron placed upon his body as he could bear "and then more." The punishment by pressing, exposure, and slow starvation continued until the prisoner "put himself upon his country" or died. What made this barbarity so peculiar is that it derived from the admirable though rigid rule that the trial could not proceed without the prisoner's consent; moreover, that the worst felon should have an opportunity to prove his innocence. That is, the purpose of *peine forte et dure* was not to extort a confession but simply to extort a plea; the law did not care whether he pleaded guilty or not guilty, only that he pleaded. In 1772 a new statute provided that a prisoner standing mute to the indictment of felony should be treated as if he had been convicted by verdict or confession, thus ending *peine forte et dure*. Not till 1827 was that rule altered to direct the court to enter a plea of not guilty for a prisoner who stood "mute of malice" and refused to plead.[22]

The other path taken by the notion of consent led to the emergence of the petty jury in criminal cases. This was the outcome of permitting the prisoner to challenge members of the presenting jury who were impaneled to serve on his trial jury. Bracton, writing about 1258, noted that the defendant might object to the inclusion of false and malicious accusers, and Britton, near the end of the thirteenth century, said that he might object if the jurors included enemies who sought his destruction or had been suborned by the lord who sought his land "through greediness of the escheat." In 1305 Prince Edward, later Edward II, acting on behalf of a friend who had been indicted for murder, requested the judge to provide a jury which excluded all members of the accusing jury. With increasing frequency defendants challenged petty jurors who had first served as their indictors, although the king's justices resisted the challenges, because indictors were more likely to convict. For that very reason in the 1340's the Commons twice protested against the inclusion of indictors, but it was not until 1352 that the king agreed to a statute which gave the accused a right to challenge members of the petty jury who had participated in his indictment. As a result of this statute the two juries became differentiated in composition and function. From about 1376 the custom of requiring a unanimous verdict from twelve petty jurors developed; by that time the size of the grand jury had been fixed at twenty-three, a majority of whom decided whether accusations should be preferred.[23]

By the middle of the fifteenth century, criminal trials were being conducted by rational principles that seem quite modern. Although the law of evidence was still in its rudimentary stages, the trial jury was no longer regarded as a band of witnesses, men who of their own knowledge or from knowledge immediately available from the neighborhood, might swear to the guilt or innocence of the accused. The jury was beginning to hear evidence that was produced in court, although the jurors still continued to obtain facts by their own inquiry. As late as the 1450's it was common for the jurors to visit a witness at his home in the country to take his testimony, but they were also beginning to pass judgment on evidence given in their presence in court. More important, they were regarded as a body of objective men, triers of fact, whose verdict was based on the truth as best they could determine it. According to the romanticized view of Chief Justice John Fortescue in the mid-fifteenth century, an innocent man need fear nothing because "none but his neighbours, men of honest and good repute, against whom he can have no probable cause of exception, can find the persons accused guilty." He was no doubt additionally assured because he might challenge without cause as many as thirty-five potential jurors. Witnesses for the crown—the accused was allowed none—gave evidence "in open Court," wrote Fortescue, "in the presence and hearing of a *jury*, of twelve men, persons of good character, neighbours where the fact was committed, apprised of the circumstances in question, and well acquainted with the lives and conversations of the witnesses, *especially as they be near neighbours, and cannot but know whether they be worthy of credit, or not.*" Of course, trial by the local community could be trial by local prejudice, but at least the prisoner knew the charges against him, confronted his accuser, and had freedom to give his own explanations as well as question and argue with the prosecution's witnesses. He suffered from many disadvantages— lack of counsel, lack of witnesses on his own behalf, lack of time to prepare his defense—yet the trial was supremely fair, judged by any standard known in the western world of that day.[24]

The year 1215, which is celebrated in Anglo-American history because of the signing of Magna Carta, is notable too for an ecclesiastical event of sinister import, the regulations of the Fourth Lateran Council in Rome. The one event ultimately symbolized the liberties of the subject; the other, ultimately, the rack and the *auto da fé*. The Council was dominated by that imperious autocrat, Pope Innocent III, who chartered a new course for the criminal procedure of the canon law which would later be opposed by the English common law. The Church in the thirteenth century—and long after—was a world power, the only world power, and Innocent III (1198–1216) was more than its head; he was its master. One of the great legislators of the canon law, he was also the scourge of heretics, the man responsible for the Albigensian Crusade, which slaughtered thousands, and for starting the Holy Inquisition on its bloody path. As John H. Wigmore said, Innocent III—a name scarcely apt—"established the inquisition of heresy, by warrants extending into every corner of Europe—a form of terrorism which served to extirpate those who dissented from the church's dogmas for the next four centuries." The same pope, a maker and breaker of kings, wielded a political authority over the whole of Christendom and sovereignty over its temporal monarchs. It was Innocent III who absolved King John for assenting to Magna Carta, which he thought shameful and detrimental, and for a time reduced England to the status of a vassal of the papacy. Under his leadership the Fourth Lateran Council defined the attitude of the Church toward heretics, the obligations of secular authorities to exterminate them, and a new code of criminal procedures which incorporated both the "*inquisitio*," precursor of the Holy Inquisition, and a new oath that was self-incriminatory in nature.[25]

The *inquisitio*, originating in the decrees of Innocent III at the close of the twelfth century and the beginning of the thirteenth, triggered a steady transition in the canon law from the old accusatorial procedure to the new inquisitional procedures. In English law the inquest had led to the double jury system; in canon law and in the civil law—the secular law of continental nations, which followed the lead of the Church—the inquest took a completely different form, one that left a trail of mangled bodies, shattered minds, and smoking flesh. The inquisitional procedure, which at first was aimed at discovering and punishing misconduct among the clergy, was speedily adapted to the overweening need of preserving the faith against heresy. As late as the twelfth century, however, the Church had an equivocal policy toward heretics, a substantially accusatorial system of criminal procedure, and an abhorrence of some of the very features that shortly proved most characteristic of the Inquisition. Heresy, an error of faith, was not yet a crime of mental state or conscience; or, rather, only external acts of worship or doctrinal differences were punished as heresy, and the Church possessed no special machinery for detecting the guilty, let alone those with guilty thoughts or secret doubts. Back in the fifth century, Saints Chrysostom and Augustine, although urging the suppression of heresy, spoke against the death penalty, against torture, and against forcing men to accuse themselves. One should confess his sins to God said Chrysostom: "I do not say to thee, make a parade of thyself, nor accuse thyself before others. . . ." These views were endorsed by Gratian's *Decretum* in the mid-twelfth century. Gratian espoused the penalties of exile and fine for heretics, repudiated torture, and declared, like Chrysostom, "I say not that thou shouldst incriminate thyself publicly nor accuse thyself before others." As late as 1184 Pope Lucius III merely excommunicated obstinate heretics and turned them over to the secular authority for severe penalties—exile, and confiscation of their properties, destruction of their houses, and loss of all rights—but the penalties did not touch the persons of the guilty; they were neither physically harmed nor imprisoned.[26]

By the mid-thirteenth century, however, all had changed, because of the need of the Church to defend itself from the dangers of mass heresy. St. Thomas Aquinas required truthful answers to incriminating questions and advocated death for heretics in order to save the faith from their corruption; and Pope Innocent IV explicitly sanctioned the use of torture. In the period between Gratian and Aquinas, heresies had spread alarmingly, especially in the South of France among the Cathari, and the faith had found a champion, Pope Innocent III, who used his spiritual sword and administrative genius, however malevolent, to smite the enemies of Christ. Innocent III heralded a new attitude toward heretics. He considered their crime as the most execrable, the most damnable of all, *crimen laesae majestatis divinae* or "high treason against God." In comparison with this crime Sodom and Gomorrah seemed pure, the infidelity of the Jews seemed justified, and the worst sins seemed holy. The Christian's highest duty was to help exterminate heretics by denouncing them to the ecclesiastical authorities, regardless of any familial or human bonds. The son who did not deliver up his parents or the wife her husband shared the heretic's guilt. Faithfulness to a heretic, according to Innocent III, was faithlessness to God. The living must die; the guilty who were already dead, if buried in consecrated ground, must be dug up, cursed, and burned.[27]

The procedures available to the Church for the discovery and prosecution of heretics were archaic and ineffective before the reforms of Innocent III. In the main these procedures were of the same primitive accusatory character as those that were employed by the secular authorities in England and on the Continent during the early Middle Ages. Private accusation led to exculpation by the oath of the party, supported by compurgators (the *purgatio canonica*) or by ordeal (the *purgatio vulgaris*). In addition the Church very early resorted to an inquest by synodal witnesses which, as Adhémar Esmein observed, culminated in an inquisitional procedure which was "the anti-type of the 'inquisitio' from which sprang the English grand jury." In this ecclesiastical inquest, the bishop, who was the ecclesiastical judge, on visiting a parish within his jurisdiction, would convene a synod or gathering of the faithful. He selected some and swore them to denounce all persons guilty of offenses requiring investigation; then he closely interrogated the denouncers, or synodal witnesses, to uncover malefactors and, at the same time, to test the reliability of the testimony. It was but a short step for the ecclesiastical judge to conduct the prosecution against the accused and to decide on his guilt or innocence. Innocent III took that step, which the Fourth Lateran Council confirmed.[28]

The remodeled criminal procedures of the canon law, after 1215, described three modes of prosecution. The first, the *accusatio*, was the traditional form. A private person, on the basis of some information or evidence available to him, voluntarily accused another and thereby became a party to the prosecution, taking upon himself the task of proof. He also took upon himself the risk of being punished in the event that the prosecution failed. The second form of prosecution was the *denunciatio*, which enabled the private accuser to avoid the danger and burden of the *accusatio*. Either an individual or the synodal witnesses played the role of informer, secretly indicting or denouncing someone before the court. The judge himself then became a party to the suit *ex officio*, by virtue of his office, and conducted the prosecution for the secret accuser. The third form was the *inquisitio*, by which the judge combined in his person all roles—that of accuser, prosecutor, judge, and jury. Technically the judge could not institute a suit unless an important preliminary condition had first been met; he must satisfy himself that there were probable grounds for the *inquisitio*. This was the canon law's equivalent of the grand jury of presentment of the English common law. The canon law required that an accusation must rest on *infamia*—infamy or bad reputation—which was established by the existence of either notorious suspicion (*clamosa insinuatio*) or common report (*fama*), which was some sort of public rumor. But the inquisitor himself, supposedly a wise and incorruptible man, was the sole judge of the existence of *infamia*, and his own suspicions, however based or baseless, were also adequate for the purpose of imprisoning the suspect and putting him to an inquisition. The Fourth Lateran Council prescribed no form for the establishment of *infamia* if the judge decided to proceed *ex officio mero*, that is, of his own accord or at his discretion.[29]

One of the "most odious features," as Esmein said, of the whole inquisitional procedure that was introduced by the Fourth Lateran Council was the new oath the suspect was required to swear. It was the oath *de veritate dicenda*, to tell the truth to all interrogatories that might be administered, a seemingly innocuous obligation which in reality was an inescapable trap, a form of spiritual torture, *tortura spiritualis*, calculated to induce self-incrimination. Confession of guilt was central to the whole inquisitional process, and the oath, which was administered at the very outset of the proceedings, was reckoned as indispensable to the confession. The accused, knowing neither the charges against him, nor his accusers, nor the evidence, was immediately placed between hammer and anvil: he must take the oath or be condemned as guilty, yet if he took the oath he exposed himself to the nearly certain risk of punishment for perjury—and his lies were evidence of his

guilt—or condemned himself by admissions which his judge regarded as damaging, perhaps as a confession to the unnamed
crime. The oath *de veritate dicenda* was thus virtually a self-
incriminatory oath. Because it became associated with the Inquisition, it became known as the inquisitional oath; and because it
originated in connection with a proceeding in which the judge
served *ex officio* as indicator, assailant, and convictor, it was also
called the oath *ex officio*.[30]

In the aftermath of the Inquisition, the Church which originated the oath turned against it. In 1698 the pope commissioned a
study of the "expediency of abrogating the custom of requiring
accused persons, prior to interrogation, to take an oath to tell the
truth." Franciscus Memmius, the author of the study, concluded
that the oath was both "violent and unjust" and should therefore
be abolished. He emphasized the difference between the involuntary oath *de veritate dicenda* and either a voluntary oath or the
old oaths of purgation in the medieval *purgatio canonica*. By the
old procedure, the accused party swore an oath to his innocence,
supported by his compurgators, and thereby ended the controversy. The significant character of the old oath, in other words,
was its effect: it won a decision for the oath-taker, because it was
thought to possess a sort of supernatural or divine character which
proved innocence, like a successful ordeal. By contrast, as Memmius pointed out, the oath *de veritate dicenda* thrust the oathtaker
in jeopardy and fear to which he ought not be exposed. It was, according to Memmius, a form of torture more cruel than physical
torture because it tormented one's soul by tempting a man to save
himself from punishment by perjuring himself at the expense of
dishonoring God's name and risking eternal damnation. In 1725, as
a result of such criticism, the Council of Rome abolished the oath
of the criminally accused and declared null and void all confessions that might thereafter be extracted by its use, mainly because
coerced confessions were unreliable.[31]

When the inquisitional oath was first introduced by the decrees
of Innocent III and endorsed by the Fourth Lateran Council, it
signalized, in the words of Wigmore, "an epochal difference of
method." Nevertheless, the accused retained some freedom of defense because the old accusatory procedures did not all die at

once; some lingered for about a century, slowly withering. Originally the accused, when summoned, was acquainted with the testimony which established the *infamia* and was permitted to challenge it by witnesses proving his good repute. But as the Inquisition spread throughout Europe, terrorizing whole populations, this defense proved useless, because no one would dare speak up for anyone unfortunate enough to fall into the inquisitor's hands; to support the victim inevitably came to mean that one shared his guilt and therefore became next in line to share his wretched fate. The defense of proving good repute simply died out. It never was available anyway when the judge proceeded *ex officio mero*, which was initially the exceptional procedure but quickly became the very ordinary, indeed almost the only, procedure, supplanting the *accusatio* and the *denunciatio*. The *accusatio* was systematically discouraged precisely because, being accusatory or litigious, it assured the defendant some means of defense. The *denunciatio* seems to have merged with the inquisitional procedure when a new ecclesiastical functionary, the "promotor," arose to assist the inquisitor in his tasks by denouncing individuals, thereby setting in motion the inquisitional process.[32]

The opportunities for self-defense that were originally available to the accused included a right to be informed of the charges against him, to know the names of the prosecution's witnesses, and to have copies of their depositions. He was then in a position to dispute the charges, to challenge the evidence and even the admissibility of testimony from witnesses who were his enemies. In the ordinary episcopal courts these defenses, as well as the right of counsel, remained unimpaired, but in cases of heresy, which were especially handled by the inquisitors in secret hearings and trials, the accused was denied all the usual rights one by one. The prosecution's witnesses were always examined secretly and out of the presence of the accused. As early as the mid-thirteenth century, Pope Innocent IV empowered the judges to withold the names of witnesses at discretion, and by the end of the century Pope Boniface VIII unreservedly ordered the suppression of their names. Their depositions were no longer produced for the accused's benefit, except at the discretion of his judge, who became a law unto himself, operating in secrecy. Every defense was trammeled, every avenue of escape closed, leaving the accused at the complete mercy of his judge, the inquisitor.[33]

The role of the judicial inquisitor and the nature of the crime which he sought to establish and punish explain the severe procedures of the inquisition as well as its gross atrocities. The judge was commissioned to perform a sacred mission, to avenge God and purify the faith by extirpating the ultimate sin, the heresy of disbelief or doubt. He was not merely a judge of overt acts of crime; as father-confessor to his victim, he also sought to extract from him a confession of his guilt so that his soul might be saved despite his wanton or ignorant errors of conscience which could lead only to eternal damnation. The inquisitor's task, therefore, in the words of Henry Charles Lea, was the nearly impossible one "of ascertaining the secret thoughts and opinions of the prisoner. . . . [T]he believer must have fixed and unwavering faith, and it was the inquisitor's business to ascertain this condition of his mind." The defendant's behavior proved little except outward conformity, and that might be illusory, certainly inconclusive proof of the "most unbounded submission to the decisions of the Holy See, the strictest adherence to orthodox doctrine, the freest readiness to subscribe to whatever was demanded of him. . . ." Despite his verbal professions, his regularity at mass, his punctuality at confession, he might be a heretic at heart, fit only for the stake. His guilt was an unquestioned presumption which could lead only to a foregone conclusion, his condemnation. Legal niceties, procedural regularities, and forms of law counted for little when the objective was to obtain a conviction at any cost in order to fulfill a sacred mission.[34]

On the other hand the canon law, influenced by the Roman law of the later empire, developed a highly sophisticated system of evidence, later known as the theory of legal proofs, which supposedly would help the accused by preventing the conviction of the innocent. The burden of proof, as in the accusatory system of old, was wholly upon the accuser or prosecutor, but the canon law required an unusual degree of proof in both kind and quantity. Innocent III, for example, cautioned inquisitors against convicting on merely "violent presumptions" in a matter as heinous as heresy. What the canon law required was perfect or complete proof which in a later day was specified with considerable complexity and quasi-scientific exactness. Complete proof was proof clearer than the sun at mid-day. It consisted, ideally, of the testimony of two eye-witnesses, neither impeached nor impeachable, to the same fact; they must have seen the prisoner commit the crime in order to complete the proof in a capital case. Proof so stringent and certain was nearly impossible to procure even when the crime was some overt act, certainly impossible in a heresy case when the crime was essentially one of thought. Documentary evidence, such as heretical writings, carried weight but was rarely available. "Proximate indications" or "half proofs," such as many hearsay witnesses, and weighty presumptions or conjectural proofs were insufficient to support a conviction. The prisoner's confession was needed for corroboration.[35]

The tyranny of the system of legal proofs, together with the inquisitor's zeal to snatch a soul from Satan, led irresistibly to the tyranny of the Inquisition, in which the confession became the crux of the trial. The secret interrogation, the requirement of a self-incriminatory oath, and, finally, the employment of torture had as their single objective the confession of the prisoner. "The accused" reported Bernard Gui, one of the leading inquisitors of the early fourteenth century, "are not to be condemned unless they confess or are convicted by witnesses, though not according to the ordinary laws, as in other crimes, but according to the private laws or privileges conceded to the inquisitors by the Holy See, for there is much that is peculiar to the Inquisition." The judge who was convinced of his prisoner's guilt but lacked the necessary proof was driven to extort a confession by any means, however repulsive. In the interest of defending the faith the most unspeakable punishments were sanctioned—the Inquisition was the classic case of the ends justifying the means. In 1252 Innocent IV issued his bull, *Ad extirpanda*, directing the establishment of machinery for systematic persecution and authorizing the use of torture. The bull empowered the civil authorites to torture suspects in order to force them to name their accomplices as well as to confess their own guilt of heresy. Four years later, the pope authorized ecclesiastical judges to absolve each other and mutually grant dispensation for "irregularities," thereby enabling them to administer torture directly.[36]

The rules of the Inquisition prohibited the repetition of torture

in any single case, but by casuistical interpretation a "continuance" rather than a repetition made possible repeated and prolonged applications of the rack, regardless of the intervals between
separate torments. Confessions extorted by torture had to be
"freely" repeated after torture, and in the event of a retraction by
the prisoner, he was returned to the rack for a "continuance."
Torture certainly was an efficacious system of interrogation, saving time and trouble for the inquisitors, but they had other means
of persuading the prisoner to confess. He could be imprisoned indefinitely, often for years, in a dark dungeon, in solitary confinement, and be kept half starved, frozen and sleepless, incapable of
defending himself when brought before the inquisitor for a fresh
interrogation.[37]

The usual course of a trial, which consisted of the secret examination of the accused under oath, was to confront him with the
mass of surmises and rumors and hearsay against him and demand
his confession. The indictment was built from the testimony of
secret informers, malicious gossips, self-confessed victims, and
frightened witnesses who, anxious to save themselves from being
racked, revealed from their frantic imaginations whatever they
thought the inquisitor might wish to hear. Convicted heretics
whose infamy disqualified them as witnesses in all other cases, gave
the most prized testimony in heresy cases, but they could testify
for the prosecution only. A prisoner who confessed, abjured
heresy, and proclaimed his penitence could prove his sincerity—and
escape the stake if not prison—by betraying friends, neighbors,
and family. If he refused, the inquisitor considered him impenitent
and put him to torture again to reveal their guilt—and then dispatched him for execution. By such methods *infamia* was established for an inquisition against fresh batches of victims. With his
dossier of suspicions against the prisoner, the inquisitor cunningly
examined him to obtain from his own lips the final proof of guilt.
Guile, deceit, entrapment, promises, threats, and, if necessary, the
rack managed inevitably to triumph. Lea reported that the entire
history of the Inquisition reveals not a single instance of complete
acquittal. Everyone who appeared before the Inquisition was put
to some form of penance, at the very least. In sum, "Abandon
hope, all ye who enter here" best described the chances of an ac-

cused person under the inquisitorial system of criminal procedure which operated throughout the Continent. The Church had been the first authority to switch to the inquisitorial system from the accusatorial, and its supreme example speedily inspired European nations, excepting England, to reform the procedures of their secular ciminal law in Rome's image. Everywhere the secret examination, the inquisitional oath, and torture became the standard, at first used only in "extraordinary" cases but quickly degenerating into a completely routine procedure for all cases but the most petty.[38]

The English system, which was based on the presentment by grand jury, the written indictment, and trial by jury, differed most markedly from the continental system in the role played by the judge. In the case of a felony, the officers of a French court, like the ecclesiastical judge in a case of heresy, completely dominated the proceedings at every stage from arrest to verdict. The English judge, by contrast, remained essentially a referee of a private fight, enforcing the observance of the rules by both parties. As an appointee of the crown, he was naturally partial to the prosecution and by his conduct often showed his favoritism, but he had neither a personal nor an official stake in the outcome of a criminal proceeding and little ability to command a verdict of guilty. He had no authority whatever to initiate or promote a prosecution, nor to make an accusation of crime against anyone.

In the inquisitorial system, the accusation and prosecution rested entirely with the court, which was also the accuser, to the extent that any accuser was known. He was in a sense nameless and faceless, hidden beneath a hood that was called *"fama"* or *"clamosa insinuatio"*—common report or notorious suspicion. In England the name of the accuser had to be as definite as the accusation itself. The accuser was a witness who instigated the prosecution, and his direct and open participation in the case was indispensable. Unless an officer of the crown of his own knowledge suspected a man's guilt, he could not make an arrest without the sworn complaint or the physical presence of the witness who brought the accusation. The witness himself, as a matter of fact, had virtually the same powers of arrest as a crown officer. Without the accuser there could not even be a prosecution. A suspect might confess his guilt to a justice of the peace at a preliminary examination, be indicted by a grand jury, and yet plead not guilty at his arraignment, perhaps because he planned to retract the confession at his trial. When the trial opened, if his accuser was not present to testify against him or if the justice of the peace, to whom he had confessed, did not testify either, "although the malefactor hath confessed the crime to the justice of the peace, and that it appear by his hand and confirmation," wrote Sir Thomas Smith about 1565, "the twelve men will acquit the prisoner. . . ." The accuser's role was so vital that he even had the same power of prosecution as a crown attorney. In England and in England alone the prosecution of crimes, in Stephen's words, was "left entirely to private persons, or to public officers who act in their capacity of private persons and who hardly have any legal powers beyond those which belong to private persons." By contrast, wherever the inquisitorial procedure prevailed, the court or its officers were alone empowered to institute accusations and prosecutions. Every criminal case was an official inquiry into the guilt or innocence of the accused.[39]

In England the grand jury made the formal presentment of crime against the accused on the basis of information known personally to its members, and the crown attorney framed an indictment accordingly; or the attorney, on the basis of an accusation brought to his attention, drew the bill of indictment for the grand jury's verdict, and if the evidence indicated the suspect's guilt, the grand jury approved of the indictment. Without its approval, however, there could be no prosecution for treason or felony. The judge had no part in the bringing of the presentment, the framing of the indictment, or the verdict of the grand jury. The grand jury not only stood between the suspect and the government which sought to prosecute him; the judge himself subjected the indictment to the most exacting scrutiny. It was the only written document in the entire proceedings, which were in all other respects oral. The indictment inherited the characteristics of the old appeal of felony by private accusers seeking satisfaction by battle. It had to be a rigorously formal document that met every exacting technicality of the law, describing the accusation with the utmost particularity and accuracy. The specific crime charged against the accused and the time, place, and manner of its commission had to be precisely defined. Although the English common law recognized such vague crimes as seditious libel, conspiracy, and compassing the death of the king, it was generally inhospitable to dragnet definitions, which jeopardized personal security, and to crimes of mental state like heresy. The courts demanded strictness in indictments and treated the crown as if it were scarcely more than a private appellor bringing an appeal of felony, although every indictment was framed in the name of the king. Such strictness threw upon the crown the obligation of stating and proving its case in a manner unknown to a court of the inquisitorial system, which knew no such thing as the rule of law enforceable even against the sovereign. There was no security whatever against the arbitrary power of an inquisitor of the Church or a French magistrate. They were not even required to notify a prisoner of the crimes charged against him, let alone when, where, and how he was alleged to have committed them. The English judge had no discretion in such matters; his continental counterpart was governed by discretion alone. In England the entire indictment was read to the prisoner, who was free to make exceptions on grounds of law, though without the aid of counsel. The judge, at least in theory, served as his counsel, and on questions relating to the sufficiency of the indictment or informing him of the charges against him, the theory was realistic.[40]

The English judge presided over a criminal trial that was a symbolic re-enactment of the old trial by battle. The proceeding was adversary in nature, and though the crown possessed several important advantages, its position was like that of the plaintiff in a civil case. Indeed, a criminal prosecution resembled in most respects the most ordinary litigation between private parties disputing the title to an estate. The trial was pre-eminently litigious, following substantially the same rules of procedure and pleadings as a civil trial. The defendant was completely free to make his defense as best he could, and he was tried publicly and before a jury—advantages of inestimable value compared to a secret inquisition. Again, the role of the English judge is most significant. He was in the main an impassive observer. It was not his duty to collect evidence against the prisoner, to evaluate it, to interrogate him—

though he could do so, of course—or to judge him. The English judge was neither accuser nor prosecutor; he conducted no inquest against the defendant, was not a party adverse to him, and rendered no verdicts. Without reason to be powerfully biased against him, to strain for a conviction, or to presume guilt, the judge could afford to be neutral or, at least, relatively fair.

English judges of the Middle Ages tended to be harsh and sometimes abused the defendant by scornful remarks, but they were comparatively just. The crown's attorney had the task of conducting the prosecution and proving his case against the prisoner. The trial was a running argument between prosecution and defense, as if they were engaged in a combat before the jury. The examination of the defendant was the focus of the proceeding. If the defendant had the wit and the tongue, he could give as well as he got from counsel against him, disputing and denying point for point, calling for production of the evidence, criticizing it, demanding to be confronted with the state's witnesses or to see their depositions. As Stephen says, "The trials were short and sharp; they were directed to the very point at issue, and, whatever disadvantages the prisoner lay under, he was allowed to say whatever he pleased; his attention was pointedly called to every part of the case against him, and if he had a real answer to make he had the opportunity to bring it out effectively and in detail. It was but seldom that he was abused or insulted." The judge ruled on points of law, and, when the oral combat was over, summed up the evidence for the benefit of the jury and instructed them on the law that governed the case. The jury was then free to decide as it pleased on the question of guilt or innocence. The entire proceeding stood in merciful contrast to the inquisitorial procedure, which cast the judge in every role and in every one as an implacable enemy of his victim. Lea's remark about the spirit that infected an inquisitor of the canon law applies with equal force to an inquisitor of the French royal court: he conducted himself as if "the sacrifice of a hundred innocent men were better than the escape of one guilty." By contrast, the humanity of the English judge even in an age of cruelty persuaded him that the cause of justice was best served by bending over backwards to avoid convicting the innocent. As early as 1302 it was said that the best course was to relinquish the punishment of a wrong-doer rather than punish the innocent. Chief Justice Fortescue, in the mid-fifteenth century, expressed a standard that became a maxim of English law: "Indeed, one would much rather that twenty guilty persons should escape the punishment of death, than that one innocent person should be condemned, and suffer capitally." A century and a half later even the Star Chamber professed to believe in the maxim that "it were better to acquit twenty that are guilty than condemn one Innocent." [41]

The humanity of the English judge was above all marked by his abhorrence of torture. The horrible punishment meted out to a prisoner who refused to plead either guilty or not guilty was undoubtedly a form of torture, yet *peine forte et dure* was never imposed except to force one to consent to being tried by a jury. It was never employed to extort a confession or to force the prisoner to incriminate himself in any manner. It was the proud boast of the English judge that torture was illegal in a common-law proceeding. Fortescue's panegyric of English law turned him to French law again and again for a chauvinistic comparison. The French, he said, do not think it enough to convict the accused by evidence, lest the innocent should thereby be condemned; they choose, rather, to put the accused to the rack "till they confess their guilt, rather than rely entirely on the depositions of witnesses, who, very often, from unreasonable prejudice and passion; sometimes, at the instigation of wicked men, are suborned, and so become guilty of perjury. By which over cautious, and inhuman stretch of policy, the suspected, as well as the *really* guilty, are in that kingdom, tortured in so many ways, as is too tedious and bad for description. Some are extended on *the rack*, till their very sinews crack, and the veins gush out in streams of blood: others have weights hung to their feet, till their limbs are almost torn asunder, and the whole body dislocated: some have their mouths gagged to such a wideness, for a long time, whereat such quantities of water are poured in, that their bellies swell to prodigious degree, and then being pierced with a faucet, spigot, or other instrument for the purpose, the water spouts out in great abundance, like a whale . . . To describe the inhumanity of such exquisite tortures affects me with too real a concern, and varieties

of them are not to be recounted in a large volume." Other king-
doms, added Fortescue, similarly engaged in torture: "now, what
man is there so stout or resolute, who has once gone through this
horrid trial by torture, be he never so innocent, who will not
rather confess himself guilty of all kinds of wickedness, than undergo the like tortures a second time? Who would not rather die
once, since death would put an end to all his fears, than to be
killed so many times, and suffer so many hellish tortures, more terrible than death itself?" [42]

Torture thrived in dark and secret places, but could not survive
a public trial before a jury. Secrecy, having infected the entire inquisitorial process, brutalized its judges. They cited, arrested, accused, imprisoned, collected evidence, examined, prosecuted, tortured, convicted, and punished—all in secrecy. Only the final sentence was publicized. By contrast publicity bathed the English
common-law procedure, at least through the mid-sixteenth century. Criminal procedure under the Tudors took on a definite inquisitorial cast, though it remained essentially accusatorial. The
unsettling effect of the Reformation in England, intensified by the
conflicting religious policies of succeeding sovereigns, and frequent riots, rebellious factions, and general disorders motivated
the Tudors to increase the surveillance of the central government
over the entire country by stricter police control. Both torture
and an inquisitorial examination of suspects entered into English
practice, although torture was undoubtedly used on a sporadic
basis as early as the fifteenth century. When Sir Thomas Smith
later wrote that torture "to put a malefactor to excessive paine, to
make him confesse of himselfe, or of his felowes or complices, is
not used in England," he meant that it was not used at common
law. Indeed the opinion of the common-law judges was that torture was illegal. But it could be employed, and was, by the special
command or authority of the king in his prerogative courts. It was
an extraordinary power of the crown which might be inflicted in
extraordinary cases, at first only those involving the safety of the
state; but its brutalizing effect on those who practiced it and its
unquestionable efficiency led inevitably to its use in cases of serious crime that were unrelated to state security. Yet the use of torture, which continued until approximately 1640, was always re-

stricted to the Privy Council and its judicial arm, the Court of Star Chamber.[43]

The principal incursion made by the inquisitorial system on the common law itself was the preliminary examination of accused persons. In 1554 and 1555 Parliament enacted statutes that were intended to safeguard against collusion between justices of the peace and criminal suspects whom they too freely bailed. This legislation, as it turned out, had the effect of increasing the efficiency of criminal procedure by filling an important gap. Grand jurors had lost their character as presenters of the names of those who were reputed publicly to be criminals and were losing their character as witnesses who of their own knowledge suspected certain persons of crime. More and more, grand jurors were becoming dependent upon the production of evidence before them by crown officers. Justices of the peace, those county officials who have been called the government's "men-of-all-work" and whose duties included police and administrative functions as well as judicial functions, were authorized by the acts of 1554 and 1555 to take the examination of all persons suspected of crime and of their accusers.[44]

By the close of the sixteenth century these examinations were becoming quite inquisitorial. The suspect was closely and strictly interrogated in private; his accusers and witnesses against him were examined out of his presence and their evidence was withheld from him until the trial. The purpose of examining the suspect was to trap him into a confession. Torture, however, as has been indicated, was never used in any common-law proceeding. Nevertheless, the preliminary examination by the justice of the peace was a common-law equivalent of the secret inquisition used on the Continent. Moreover, any damaging admissions made by the suspect were produced against him at his trial. The record of the examination was usually introduced in evidence at the beginning of the trial, placing the defendant in an unfavorable light, to say the least. Fortunately the trial itself, even before the Star Chamber, remained public, and the defendant could always retract or deny compromising statements made to the justice of the peace. Neither in the preliminary examination nor in the trial was the defendant required or permitted to make statements under oath. The

requirement of a public trial by a jury and the minimal role of the
trial judge saved English procedure from degenerating into an inquisitorial system. That the court was open to all who cared to attend, the interested and the curious, made a difference; but it was
the authority of the trial jury that finally counted, not merely in
the disposition of any case but in the retention of the accusatory
system.[45]

Despite the preliminary examination by the justice of the peace,
the indictment by the grand jury, the evidence submitted by the
crown, and the instructions of the judge, the trial jury when
locked up to reach a verdict were responsible only to their own
consciences. They were completely free to return a verdict of
their pleasure in accordance with what they thought right. The
evidence was not binding upon them; the judge's charge was not
binding; nothing was. The law did not concern itself with the
question how they reached their verdict. This curiously irrational
element in the jury system proved, of course, to be a great protection to accused persons in many cases, whatever their actual
guilt. If a jury, moved by whim, mercy, sympathy, or pigheaded-
ness refused to convict against all law and evidence, the prisoner
was freed, and that was that. The doctrine as Thayer said, was
"ancient that one should not be twice put in jeopardy of life or
limb for the same offence." [46] On the other hand, a jury prejudiced against a defendant might return a verdict of guilty, but the
judge, if convinced of unfairness in such a case, could reprieve the
prisoner and recommend that the king pardon him.

The finality of the jury's verdict of not guilty, in a criminal
case, probably derived from the fact that the jury originated when
the older forms of proof—compurgation, ordeal, and battle—had
not yet died out. The verdict of the inquest took on the same con-
clusiveness as any judgment of God, especially because the jurors
were originally witnesses whose oaths were decisive. By the late
fourteenth century the requirement of a unanimous verdict became settled practice, adding to the authority of verdicts. The rule
of unanimity may have originated, as Pollock and Maitland said,
because the test was the voice of the country and the country
could have but one voice. The origin of the rule may also be
found in the fact that, in early trials by witnesses and compurga-

tors, there was a requirement of unanimity. If one compurgator failed to make the oath by just the right formula or perjured himself, the oath "burst." By the same analogy the failure of a jury to agree "burst" the verdict. A unanimous verdict by the inquest, which was regarded as representative of the country, an expression of its sense, carried a supernatural weight. In any case, the sworn inquest, having succeeded the older forms of proof, inherited many of their characteristics, including that of finality.[47]

In civil cases, but never in the instance of a criminal verdict, when jurors were still regarded as witnesses the court considered a false verdict as a form of perjury, punishable by a special process known as the "attaint." A special jury of twenty-four tried the civil jury that gave the false verdict, and its members, if convicted, could be punished severely. As jurors lost their character as witnesses, the attaint fell into disuse; by the sixteenth century it was rarely employed and then only rarely successful. Juries in criminal cases, though never subject to the attaint, could be threatened with punishment by the Star Chamber for a false verdict, but the threat was more often than not an idle one calculated to intimidate rather than force a verdict of guilty. In the first half of the sixteenth century, almost every term of the Star Chamber saw some grand inquest or jury fined for acquitting felons or murderers, but that practice also died. One of the last examples of its use occurred after the trial of Sir Nicholas Throckmorton in 1554.[48]

Throckmorton was tried for high treason because of his complicity in Wyatt's Rebellion, which grew out of opposition to the marriage of Queen Mary to Philip of Spain. A treason trial, above all others, most directly involved the security of the state, and even a common-law court of that period would conduct the trial in the interests of the sovereign, determined on a conviction. Throckmorton had been imprisoned for fifty-eight days preceding the day of the trial; he had had no opportunity to prepare his case and had been kept in ignorance of the evidence against him. He had to defend himself, and do it extemporaneously; counsel was not permitted in such cases till 1695. He heard the indictment read against him but had no copy of it—not till 1696 did defendants in treason cases have a right to a copy of the indictment. He had no right to call witnesses on his behalf either; when he saw in the courtroom a man whom he wanted to give testimony, the chief justice ordered the man out. With only the slimmest opportunity of making an effective defense, Throckmorton, nevertheless, had the very great advantage of being tried publicly before a jury and the freedom to say whatever he wished, and he made the most of it. Defending himself with astonishing vigor and agility, he engaged in a spirited altercation with the crown's counsel and even with the chief justice, on points of law as well as fact. He was allowed the liberty of correcting the court's summation to the jury and of making a speech to the jury following the summation. He won an acquittal. The jury's verdict certainly proved the comparative fairness of even an imperfect accusatorial procedure.[49]

The jurors, however, were punished for their audacity. The court, unable to touch Throckmorton, imprisoned all twelve jurors. Four who "made their submission, and owned their offence" were freed, but the remaining eight, after six months in jail, were heavily fined by the Star Chamber and then were discharged. Sir Thomas Smith, about a decade later, observed that if a jury "having pregnant evidence" acquitted a defendant, "which they will do sometime," he went free, but the judge rebuked the jurors and threatened them with punishment. "But this threatening chanceth oftener than the execution thereof, and the twelve answer with most gentle words they did it according to their consciences and . . . as they thought right and . . . so it passeth away for the most part." Alluding to Throckmorton's case, he noted the punishment of the jury, yet added, "But these doings were even then by many accounted very violent, tyrannical, and contrary to the liberty and custom of the realm of England. Wherefore it cometh very seldom in use. . . ."

Thus, although the rule was not finally established until Bushell's case in 1670 that a jury could not be punished for having acquitted a defendant against the evidence or the direction of the court, juries were free to render verdicts of their choice, with impunity, after Throckmorton's case. Notwithstanding their sometimes erratic and even inexplicable behavior, their tendency to reflect public prejudice, and their capability of being intimidated by the court, trial juries were England's major barrier against the growth of the inquisitional mode of procedure.[50]

In sum, then, criminal procedure on the Continent, in both ecclesiastical and secular courts was thoroughly inquisitorial, while England's procedure remained essentially accusatorial. The two systems originated in the same source, the inquest, and developed at the same time but in divergent directions. In one there was no definite accuser, lest it be the judge himself whose suspicions were aroused by common report or secret information; in the other, there was a definite accuser whose charges led to a preliminary examination of the suspect by a justice of the peace. The inquisitorial system did not provide for a specification and revelation of the charges; the accusatorial system, utilizing the grand jury to screen the charges, provided them in a detailed indictment. The inquistorial system surrounded every step in the proceedings with secrecy, making unchecked tyranny inevitable; the accusatorial system was substantially public. The former was non-confrontative, revealing not even the names of the witnesses against the accused; the latter was essentially confrontative, naming the witnesses, producing their depositions in court, and with some exceptions in treason trials allowing them to give sworn tesimony before the accused and the jury. One system presumed the guilt of the accused; the other, requiring the prosecution to prove its case, did not. The one forced the accused to submit to a self-incriminatory oath; the other did not even permit the accused to give sworn testimony if he wanted to. One tried the accused by secret interrogatories, the other by public evidence. One was an official prosecution by the judge; the other made the trial an oral combat before a jury of the accused's peers, with the public watching, the crown's attorney prosecuting, and the judge basically passive. One empowered the judge to decide the question of guilt or innocence, while the other permitted a jury to control the verdict. One routinely used torture; the other regarded it as illegal. One utilized a stringent and sophisticated law of evidence, the theory of "legal proofs," while the other was almost casual about the nature of evidence. One made an absolute differentiation between civil and criminal procedure; the other employed essentially the same litigious procedure for both. One, not recognizing the concept of double jeopardy, retried a suspect indefinitely, while the other would not place anyone in jeopardy more than once for the same offense in a capital case. Finally, one was cruel and arbitrary; the other was relatively fair and just.

What accounts for England's singular escape from the fate of the continental nations of Europe? The most likely answer is that the accusatorial system of procedure, based on the inquest, effectively served the needs of the state, making unnecessary the employment of the inquisitorial system. Fortuitous timing seems to have made a great difference. Pollock and Maitland wrote that England had a narrow escape. The old forms of proof were breaking down. "Happily, however, the reforms of Henry II were effected before the days of Innocent III." Just how narrow was the escape is shown by the fact that Henry II died in 1189, only nine years before Innocent III became pope. But the great Angevin's reforms were instituted in the 1160's and 1170's. In something of overstatement, Pollock and Maitland remarked that "the whole of English law is centralized and unified" by the establishment of royal judges, their frequent eyres throughout the land, and "by the introduction of the 'inquest' or 'recognition' and the 'original writ' as normal parts of the machinery of justice." Not only was English law centralized early; the English state itself was centralized earlier than that of any other country, and one of the foremost means of achieving that centralization was the system of royal justice employing the inquest which became the grand and petty juries. Sir William Holdsworth best made the point: "Thus it happened that the delegates of royal power could make their influence felt all over the country, and royal justice everywhere superseded the justice administered by the local courts. One of the most important instruments of the royal power was the inquisition held under the supervision of a royal judge by means of a jury. And, wherever the royal justice was introduced, this method of determining facts accompanied it. Thus the jury system spread as rapidly and as widely as the justice of the royal courts, and as the rules of that common law which those courts were both making and administering. But the rapidity of the development of the common law caused it to produce a set of fixed principles before the ideas of the civil and canon lawyers had time to exercise an overwhelming influence upon the substance of its rules." [51]

Thus English rules of criminal law retained many archaic ideas, keeping the new jury procedure as accusatorial as the older modes of proof. The jury system was a new mode of proof, or at least was treated as if it were a mode of proof. It was therefore based on consent and its results were taken as final. The judges took the path of least resistance by accepting verdicts rather than by making their own inquiries, a step that would have led to an inquisitorial system. The unsophisticated state of the law of evidence, which was indeed in its rudimentary stages, made it additionally easy for the judges to accept the findings of a band of witnesses —the sworn inquest. Not the least result was that the English judge, relieved of the necessity of making his own determination of guilt or innocence, gained enhanced dignity and impartiality. These wholesome benefits would have been impossible had the crown not been able to adapt the accusatorial system of justice to the needs of the state. The sworn inquest, however, did serve to augment the exchequer, control local feudatories, and enforce the king's peace. By contrast the French monarchy, a century after Henry II centralized England, had extended royal jursidiction over the royal demesne only. The inquisitorial system became a powerful instrument for centralizing France, as the accusatorial had in England. England was also less susceptible to the influences of the canon and civil lawyers of the Continent because of its isolation. For the same reason, perhaps, the contagion of heresy scarcely infected England; her orthodoxy in religion until the late fourteenth century was also a settling force, a bulwark against the need for ecclesiastical inquisitions. When heresy became widespread in England, the accusatorial system was well established, and nationalism, anticlericalism, and the weakness of the papacy prevented a papal inquisition.

It would be misleading, however, to say that the inquisitional system became England's road not taken, for England did not escape. True enough, the only inquisitional process that entered the common-law system was the preliminary examination which to this day has not completely shaken its inquisitional cast. However, the common law was not the only law in England; in the later Middle Ages, prerogative courts, such as the Star Chamber, were established which did not employ the ancient common-law writs, forms of action, or procedures. Some of these prerogative courts,

which were erected by royal commission, exercised criminal jurisdiction. Their system of criminal procedure was decidedly inquisitorial, as we shall later see. By special warrant from the king or his
Privy Council, they even used torture, as had already been noted.
Their proceedings were by no means unconstitutional. England's
judicial system, having become extremely complex by the sixteenth century, utilized more than one set of criminal procedures.
To some degree the prerogative courts and the common-law
courts were competing rivals. In any case, the prerogative courts'
employing the oath *ex officio*, the inquisitional oath, provoked the
struggle that eventually led to the creation of the right against
self-incrimination.

Maitland's epigram that the "seamless web" of history is torn by
telling a piece of it,[52] is borne out by any effort to explain the
origins of the right against self-incrimination. The American origins derive from the inherited English common-law system of
criminal justice. But the English origins, so much more complex,
spilled over legal boundaries and reflected the many-sided religious, political, and constitutional issues that racked England during the sixteenth and seventeenth centuries: the struggles for supremacy between Catholicism and Protestantism, between Anglicanism and Puritanism, between King and Parliament, between
arbitrary rule and limited or constitutional government, between
the suppression of heresy and sedition and freedom of conscience
and press. Even within the more immediate confines of law itself,
the history of the right against self-incrimination is enmeshed in
broad issues of great import: the contests for supremacy between
the accusatory and the inquisitorial systems of criminal procedure,
between the common law and the royal prerogative, and between
the common law and its rivals, canon and civil law. The origins of
the concept that "no man is bound to accuse himself" (*nemo
tenetur seipsum prodere*) can be seen only with a view of this
breadth. As noted earlier, when in 1532 John Lambert defied his
inquisitors by refusing to swear an oath that would have forced
him to accuse himself, he stood on several centuries of English experience with an accusatorial system of criminal procedure.

The Oath *Ex Officio*

Before the Norman Conquest, England had no separate ecclesiastical courts, no independent ecclesiastical law. The courts of the hundred and of the shire heard ecclesiastical causes as well as purely secular matters, and the bishops and archdeacons sat side by side with earls and other lay officials, participating in all cases. The "one authentic monument of William's jurisprudence," wrote William Stubbs, was the act "which removed the bishops from the secular courts and recognised their spiritual jurisdictions. . . ." In accordance with Norman custom, separate ecclesiastical courts were established, under the jurisdiction of the bishops and their subordinates, to hear and determine all cases of an ecclesiastical nature "according to the decrees of the sacred canons." To this momentous enactment, which occurred sometime before 1076—the exact year is uncertain—the canon law owes its introduction into England as a distinct *corpus juris*. A complex system of ecclesiastical courts, justice, and legislation developed in succeeding centuries, as the jurisdiction of the clergy expanded and even encroached on the jurisdiction of the secular courts. From the very time of their origin, the ecclesiastical courts clamed jurisdiction over all cases involving the clergy, even over the case of a priest accused of a clearly secular crime such as murder or rape, and over all cases involving a wide range of alleged ecclesiastical or spiritual matters, including sexual conduct, marriage, wills, the correction of sinners, and church properties.[1]

Chaucer described the greatly diversified business of the ecclesiastical courts in *The Friar's Tale:*

> Whilom there was dwellying in my countré
> An erchedeken, a man of gret degré
> That boldely did execucioun
> In punysching of fornicacioun,
> Of wicchecraft, and eek of bauderye,
> Of diffamacioun and avowterye,
> Of chirche reves and of testamentes,
> Of contractes, and of lak of sacramentes;
> And eek of many another meaner crime,
> Which needeth not to reherse at this tyme;
> Of usur, and of symony also,
> But certes lecchours did he grettest woo,
> They should synge, if that they were bent;
> And small tythers, they were foullie schent,
>   If any person would upon him pleyne,
> There might astert him no pecunial peyne,
> For small tythes, and for small offerynge
> He made the people pitously to synge.
> For er the bisschop caught them in his hook,
> They weren in the erchedeknes book;
> And hadde through his jurisdiccioun
> Power to have of them correccioun.

The extensive criminal jurisdiction of the ecclesiastical courts showed how intimately the church reached into the daily lives of the people, regulating their conduct and belief. One important category of cases consisted of offenses against religion, including heresy, atheism, blasphemy, sacrilege, witchcraft, perjury, profanity, schism, failure to attend church, and violation of the sabbath. Another significant category covered sins of the flesh, such as fornication, adultry, incest, procuring and bigamy. Finally, the criminal jurisdiction of the ecclesiastical courts stretched to a miscellany of offenses—usury, defamation, drunkeness, disorderly conduct, and certain breaches of contract—that related vaguely to immorality of a different kind.[2]

More relevant than the criminal jurisdiction of the ecclesiastical courts was their procedure; it was that of the canon law stripped of its most brutal aspects. In his study of the archidiaconal court on which his predecessors sat as magistrates, Archdeacon William H. Hale described their three "methods of indictment," naming first the "Inquisition," then the "Accusation" and the "Denunciation." In the first of these, which Hale said was the "usual mode of proceeding" before the Reformation, the judge was "in fact the accuser," summoning the accused to appear before him for secret examination under oath on the basis of information known to him personally or from "common fame." Sir James Fitzjames Stephen remarked on the difficulty of realizing that for centuries "this system was in full activity amongst us. It was in name as well as in fact an Inquisition, differing from the Spanish Inquisition in the circumstances that it did not at any time as far as we are aware employ torture, and that the bulk of the business of the courts was of a comparatively unimportant kind. . . ." [3]

Even in its rudimentary stages this procedure was a subject of controversy, provoking bitter protests. The earliest protest seems to have been leveled at the ecclesiastical courts' practice of summoning people to answer reckless or unsupported charges. Such is the implication of the sixth provision of Henry II's Constitutions of Clarendon of 1164, which began, "Laymen are not to be accused save by proper and legal accusers and witnesses in the presence of the bishop. . . ." At the bishop's request the sheriff was required to impanel a sworn inquest of twelve men of the neighborhood to give a verdict. Pollock and Maitland regarded this provision as an insistence by Henry II that the ecclesiastical courts utilize the royal "accusing jury" which he established two years later in the Assize of Clarendon for the presentment of secular crimes before his judges on circuit. The 1164 provision, according to Pollock and Maitland, meant that laymen "ought not to be put to answer in those [ecclesiastical] courts upon a mere suggestion that they are of ill fame. Either someone should stand forth and commit himself to a definite accusation, or else the ill fame should be sworn to by twelve lawful men of the neighbourhood summoned for that purpose by the sheriff; in other words, the ecclesiastical judge ought not to proceed *ex officio* upon private suggestions." Although this is an excessively free reading of the provision in the Constitutions of Clarendon, there can be no doubt that the lack of safeguards in the ecclesiastical procedure generated opposition. What is still more certain is that Henry II did not succeed in remodeling the criminal procedure of the ecclesiastical courts. His failure in that respect was as conspicuous as his achievements in reforming the secular law. As time passed, the model of the canon law of Rome increasingly cast the shadow of the Inquisition over the English canon-law procedure.[4]

England's isolation from the Continent and the general absence of widespread heresy on the island, at least until the rise of Lollardry in the closing years of the fourteenth century, diffused that shadow. Above all, the double-jury system of the common law and Magna Carta's guarantee that no man should be condemned save by judgment of his peers or by the law of the land raised a standard by which to gage the deviances of ecclesiastical procedures. As Pollock and Maitland discerningly observed, it was in opposition to canon law that English law became "conscious of its existence." That consciousness was revealed most significantly in the opposition to the introduction and use of the oath *ex officio* in England.[5]

The oath made its debut in English history in 1236, a gift of Pope Gregory IX presented by his legate, Cardinal Otho, whom Henry III received with such bowing and scraping that men said he was a feudatory of the pope rather than king of England. Otho immediately on his arrival convoked a meeting of all the bishops of England and issued decrees or "constitutions" on a number of ecclesiastical subjects, one of which was the proper canon-law procedure to be followed by English ecclesiastical courts. Apparently the English bishops were not familiar with all of the procedural reforms which had been introduced on the Continent by Innocent III and endorsed by the Fourth Lateran Council. One of Otho's constitutions provided for the use of the oath *de veritate dicenda*, the inquisitional oath which in England became best known, later, as the oath *ex officio*, because the judge compelled it by virtue of his office. "We establish," declared the constitution, "that the oath of calumny to tell the truth in ecclesiastical causes, in order that truth may be more easily uncovered and causes more speedily finished, shall henceforth be administered throughout the realm of England, according to the canons and lawful sanctions, notwithstanding any custom to the contrary." The oath itself, which was in part a sworn statement to give true answers to whatever questions might be asked, was objectionable, it should be remembered, because it was taken in ignorance by the accused, that is, without his first having been formally charged with the accusation against him or having been told the identity of his accusers or the nature of the evidence against him. Following the administration of the oath, the accused, still in ignorance, was required to answer a series of interrogatories whose purpose was to extract a confession.[6]

The new oath procedure was first used in 1246 when Bishop Robert Grosseteste conducted "strict Inquisitions" into the sexual misconduct and general immorality of the people in his diocese of Lincoln. To discover all who were guilty of any of the seven deadly sins, the noble and the humble alike were put to the oath *de veritate dicenda*, "an innovation never used in the Realm before," and were questioned about themselves and others "to the enormous defamation and scandal of many." So bitter were the complaints made to the king about "illegal Oaths" which vexed and oppressed that Henry III issued writs to all the sheriffs of Lincoln ordering them not to permit any subjects within their jurisdiction to appear before the bishop or his officials for the purpose of answering any questions under oath, except in matrimonial and testamentary causes. The king described the oath as derogatory to his crown because it was "repugnant to the ancient Customs of his Realm, his peoples Liberties, and hurtfull to their fames." Bishop Grosseteste insolently declared that the king emulated certain baronial conspiritors in France who showed similar audacities in opposing the Church. Defying the crown, the bishop continued with his inquisitions, forcing Henry III to issue new prohibitions which were also willfully defied. King and Council then commanded the sheriff to attach the bishop and his officials and force them to put up bail and sureties to appear personally to answer for various contempts. The failure of these measures to bring the bishop to heel is evident from the fact that in 1251 Grosseteste inaugurated a new inquisition which provoked the chronicler Matthew Paris, who knew him, to record that if one "were to mention all the instances of tyranny which he exercised, he would be considered not severe, but rather austere and inhuman." The bishops of Gloucester and Worcester, encouraged by his example, followed suit in their dioceses, forcing the king to issue prohibitory writs against them too. In 1252 the king, having lost patience completely, enjoined Grosseteste, declaring that the people still complained about being harrassed by his practice of citing them to appear for inquisition under oath, under pain of excommunication for failure, and compelling them to disclose private sins, accusing themselves and others. Unless Grosseteste ceased and desisted, royal punishment would follow. The upshot of this episode is unknown, although the royal injunction which was followed two years later by the death of the zealous prelate, Grosseteste, probably ended the use of the inquisitional oath for the time being—but only for the time being. The oath had a long, notorious history before its final abolition by Parliament in 1641.[7]

In 1272, Boniface, the Archbishop of Canterbury, revitalized Otho's constitution of 1236 which provided for the use of the oath, thereby touching off another controversy. This one widened to pit the common-law courts against the ecclesiastical courts and the king's Council. Boniface promulgated the following canon for the procedure of the ecclesiastical courts: "We establish that whenever the prelates and ecclesiastical judges inquire into the sins and excesses of subjects requiring punishment, laymen shall be compelled by oath *de veritate dicenda,* under sentence of excommunication if necessary." Any person hindering the taking of the oath was also to be excommunicated and interdicted. That the oath procedure of the ecclesiastical courts provoked fresh controversy must be surmised from the fact that Parliament outlawed the oath, for the first time, in the reign of Edward II, sometime before 1326 —the exact year is unknown. The objections of the common-law courts to ecclesiastical procedure have been lost in the jurisdictional clash between them and their ecclesiastical rivals. In 1285 and again in 1316, crown and Parliament respectively sought to delineate the spheres of jurisdiction of each court, and ordered the common-law judges not to issue prohibitions or writs forbidding the ecclesiastical judges from hearing cases that fell within their spiritual ambit. In the struggle of the common-law courts to ward off ecclesiastical encroachments, ecclesiastical procedure, however objectionable, became a target only belatedly. Yielding in all likelihood to popular complaints, Parliament enacted the *Prohibitio Formata de Statuto Articuli Cleri*, which, unlike earlier acts, was directed at the oath procedure of the ecclesiastical courts as well as their jurisdiction. The act, whose date is uncertain, named various causes over which the common-law courts exercised exclusive jurisdiction and expressly prohibited the ecclesiastical judges from hearing those causes in their courts. Another clause commanded the sheriffs to prohibit any laymen from submitting to any examination under oath except in matrimonial or testamentary causes. Heresy trials of the later fourteenth century, however, reveal that the ecclesiastical courts disregarded the statute by persisting in their practice of examining defendants after compelling them to take an inquisitional oath.[8]

That the ecclesiastical courts preserved the inquisitional oath, contrary to the statute, may be attributed to the extraordinary gravity of the crime of heresy and the example of the most powerful political body in the realm, the king's Council. The Council too used the oath, imitating the ecclesiastical courts, which provided a model of great eminence. The membership of the Council included the greatest officers of state, the most powerful nobles and bishops, officers of the king's household, and the foremost lawyers and judges. The Council exercised executive, legislative, and judicial powers which very gradually became differentiated. Offshoots or special committees of the Council developed into the House of Lords and the central courts of the common law, the Court of Common Pleas (civil) and the Court of King's Bench (criminal). During the fourteenth century, while the Council was becoming a distinct body, its relationship with the central courts was still close, especially on the criminal side; even after the King's Bench split away and became the highest court of criminal jurisdiction in the realm, the Council still retained an undifferentiated mass of judicial work; its jurisdiction and procedures were practically discretionary. When acting as a court, the Council, or a branch of it, sat at Westminster in a room whose ceiling was ornamented with stars. References to the "Sterred Chambre" go back to 1348; what became the Court of Star Chamber developed as the judicial arm of the Council. The Council's judicial procedures, rather than its jurisdiction, gave it its special distinction. Its

characteristic modes of procedure began to appear in the fourteenth century, under the influence of the chancellors, who were
invariably churchmen assisted by bishops and doctors of civil law,
that is, professional lawyers who were specialists in the law used
by the continental nations of Europe, rather than England's common law. The canon law of the ecclesiastical courts, in England
and abroad, was strongly influenced by—and, in turn, influenced—the civil law, which owed much to the revival of Roman
law. These influences, particularly through the example of the
English ecclesiastical courts, penetrated the judicial procedures of
the Council.[9]

Unlike the common-law courts, the Council in its judicial capacity used no juries. It took up criminal cases on "information"
or "suggestion" by private accusers on their own initiative or at
the invitation of the Council which welcomed informers. Secret
accusation by information or suggestion bypassed the whole process of presentment and indictment by grand jury and opened the
way to inquisitorial procedure, including the use of the oath
whose object was to entrap a confession. Prosecution by information entered even the common-law process, but it remained completely public, led to trial by jury, and was restricted to crimes
less than felony. In the Council, secrecy prevailed, encouraging
the use of "suggestions" which became "a wide-spread system of
public espionage." The Council could command attendance of
parties and witnesses by the use of special writs of citation, requiring persons to "give information and to do and receive whatever
shall be required by the council." Pending trial, accused persons
could be committed to prison for indefinite periods of time, although "mainprise," a system of bonds similar to bail, was permitted for those who could afford it. In both civil and criminal cases,
parties and witnesses could be put under oath to tell the truth and
then be subjected to inquisitorial examination.[10]

"This method," wrote J. F. Baldwin, "was naturally most effective in criminal prosecutions, although it was not confined solely
to these. It was a feature most clearly derived from the ecclesiastical courts, where it was employed especially, though not exclusively, in the prosecutions of heresy." This procedure began in the
Council early in the reign of Edward II, who became king in

1307. "The oath, which was an essential part of the system, was exacted in the name of the king, who alone had the right to require it." The defendant was required to swear the oath and then was confronted with a series of interrogatories which were based on the information obtained by suggestions and the examination of witnesses. The defendant, who was not allowed counsel, was usually not told the charges against him. He was required to answer in writing as well as orally. Any discrepancies or contradictions in his answers were used against him in an effort to break him down and force a confession of guilt. "Nothing," said Baldwin, not too accurately, "was more antagonistic to the practices of the common law than to require a man thus to incriminate himself. With good reason, therefore, the examinations were assailed as a 'feature of the civil law in subversion of the law of the land.'" [11]

The assailant was Parliament. As a prerogative body exercising executive authority and a judicial procedure which was at variance with that of the common law, the Council provoked fear, jealousy, and suspicion, which was expressed in protests, petitions, and enactments. The very remarkable transformation of Magna Carta in the fourteenth century from a feudal aristocratic document to an embodiment of common-law liberties can be ascribed only partly to the opposition to the oath procedure of the Council and the ecclesiastical courts. Yet it is no exaggeration to conclude that the opposition to inquisitional procedures, of which the inquisitional oath was a part, had a great deal to do with the burgeoning idea that Magna Carta's famous "law of the land" clause of the twenty-ninth chapter guranteed to every subject an indictment by grand jury and trial by jury in a common-law court by common-law procedure. Two centuries later men would claim with as little historical justification "that by the Statute of Magna . . . this othe for a man to accuse himself was and is utterlie inhibited." [12]

In 1331 Parliament condemned all punishments made by proceedings contrary to "the form of the Great Charter and the law of the land." Ten years later, Magna Carta was invoked again to castigate arrest, imprisonment, and forfeitures which had not originated in private appeals or indictment. In 1347 Commons protested to the king against the Council's practice in summoning persons for examination on the basis of suggestions. The king replied only that henceforth it would not be done without reason. Four years later Commons renewed its petition, this time alluding to the twenty-ninth chapter of Magna Carta to fortify its claim that the Council's practice of oral examinations violated the customary law of the land. The king on this occasion yielded a little by granting the petition as regards freeholds but not in matters touching life and limb; that is, he agreed that in civil matters touching property, common-law procedure must be followed, but he reserved his prerogative in criminal matters. Mary Hume Maguire said of this same period that "we read a series of petitions from the Commons to the Crown referring to the distasteful practice of ecclesiastical courts of proving the case against the defendant by 'fishing interrogatories *viva voce*,'" as well as urging the king to prohibit the use of the oath in the Council. If such petitions were made, they were futile, although an act of 1352 made the protections of Magna Carta applicable to the proceedings of the Council. In accord with "the Great Charter of the Liberties of England" that none should be imprisoned nor put out of his freehold nor of his liberties, the statute provided that "from henceforth none shall be taken by petition or suggestion made to our lord the king, or to his council, unless it be by indictment of good and lawful people of the same neighbourhood where such deeds be done, in due manner, or by process made by writ original at the common law. . . ." This was, incidentally, the first restatement of Magna Carta which applied to all men rather than just "freemen." Two years later this broadening of Magna Carta was made explicit in he phrase "no man of whatever estate or condition he may be"; and of even greater significance was the appearance of the phrase "by due process of law," used for the first time in connection with chapter twenty-nine; no man "shall be put out of Land or Tenement, nor taken, nor imprisoned, nor disinherited, nor put to death, without being brought in answer by due process of law." The brevity and breadth of this formulation made it applicable to the ecclesiastical courts as well as to the Council. In effect, the entire oath procedure was outlawed.[13]

Nevertheless, within a decade Commons again had occasion to

complain in another petition to the king about the continued use of accusation by suggestions, contrary to the process of the law of Magna Carta. Still another statute was enacted, but not yet the last. The last of the Magna Carta statutes of the fourteenth century was passed in 1368, providing explicitly that no man should "be put to answer without presentment before justices, or matter of record, or by due process and writ original, according to the old law of the land: and if any thing from henceforth be done to the contrary it shall be void in law, and holden for error." The fact that so many petitions had to be made and statutes enacted proved how ineffective they were, despite the king's apparent approval. At the same time, however, it is equally clear that the inquisitional procedure which was being introduced in England by the Council and ecclesiastical courts was vehemently despised. But if Magna Carta and the accusatorial system of the common law were being honored more by ceremonial reaffirmation than by observance in the prerogative courts, chapter twenty-nine had swelled in importance and meaning. Slowly a constitutional basis was being forged for the assault of a later era on the practice of forcing men to incriminate themselves. Before that constitutional argument could be advanced and respected, however, the English nation cruelly suffered from the fires of religious persecution for two and a half centuries.[14]

Up to the close of the fourteenth century, England had been remarkably free from that supreme crime, treason against God. Catholic orthodoxy blessed the English church which had escaped such horrors of the Continent as the Albigensian Crusade and the Holy Inquisition. Some heresy, of course, existed in England, but the records show very little persecution for several centuries. A band of thirty foreign heretics were whipped, branded, and deported by the government in 1166, after having been condemned by an ecclesiastical council. An Albigensian was probably burned in London in 1210, and a dozen years later a deacon who converted to Judaism for love of a Jewess was condemned by the Archbishop of Canterbury and summarily burned by the sheriff. On the same occasion a couple who represented themselves as Jesus Christ and Mary were thrown into solitary confinement for life. Beyond these isolated instances, England was free of heresy and therefore free of religious persecution. The opportunity for expressing intolerance, apart from the expulsion of the Jews, had simply not presented itself on a scale worth noting until the time of John Wycliffe and his followers, who were called Lollards.[15]

Wycliffe was the principal early precursor of the Reformation in England. He attacked the authority of the pope and the priesthood, repudiated auricular confession, and denied the doctrine of transubstantiation; he also placed full reliance on the sufficiency of the Scriptures, which he translated into English on the theory that they should be available to all men. In many respects Wycliffe anticipated fundamental Protestant convictions. His heresy was clear—Pope Gregory himself pronounced him a heretic in 1378 —but though he was hounded, his pre-eminence and above all the influential support he received from powerful magnates saved him from burning in his lifetime. Forty years after his death in 1384, his remains were dug up, his memory reviled as a heretic's, and his bones given to the flames.[16]

Wycliffe's followers paid the penalty of his heresies. England was a devout Catholic nation in an age that was absolutely convinced of the duty of the state to support the Church's infallible judgments on spiritual matters. The state was responsible, as a partner of the Church, for the souls of its subjects and was obliged to protect them against heresy; its existence threatened eternal damnation for all who were victims of its contagion. There was one fixed body of revealed and absolute truth. To suffer deviations to exist was thought to reflect doubt on the purity of the faith and the sincerity of the convictions of true believers. Moreover, any sovereign who did not bid the command of the Church on matters of faith might himself be condemned as a heretic, suffer excommunication, and expose his nation to interdiction. Another practical consideration against allowing heresy to exist was the fixed conviction that it led inevitably to schism in the Church and social disorder. Heresy must therefore be extirpated by burning its carriers. Alternative courses were unthinkable. William Courtney, Archbishop of Canterbury, procured the condemnation of Wycliffe's deviant opinions as heresy and with the support of the king called upon the bishops to extirpate them, wherever they existed.[17]

Oxford, the seat of the new "pestiferous poison," harbored Wycliffe's leading disciples, the scholars and priests, Philip Repingdon, Nicholas of Hereford, and John Ashton. In 1382 Archbishop Courtney, styling himself "inquisitor of heretical pravity," in violation of the Act of 1368 examined the three on their "corporal oath," the inquisitional oath to tell the truth, called "corporal" because it was sworn with the right hand on the Bible. The three Lollards were reputed to be "notoriously defamed and suspected of heresy." Ashton, having taken the oath, refused to answer questions about his religious beliefs; he was therefore taken *"pro confesso"*—as if he had confessed—and was pronounced guilty of heresy. He was imprisoned, later recanted, made full abjurations, and was restored. At length he relapsed, but his end is not known. Nicholas of Hereford and Philip Repingdon were also condemned, pronounced contumacious, and excommunicated. Repingdon, soon after, confessed his errors. Restored, he turned against Wycliffe and gradually rose in the hierarchy, becoming Bishop of Lincoln. Nicholas fled to Rome to appeal to the pope, who had him thrown in prison, but he escaped, returned to England, and for a while joined forces with Ashton. Finally captured, he recanted again and in due course became chancellor of a cathedral, distinguishing himself as a "zealous hammer of heretics." William Swinderby, a priest "vehemently defamed" of heresy, was also illegally put to the oath to confess his religious beliefs. He was convicted, but the edifying spectacle of dry wood being gathered for his burning persuaded him to recant too. Unlike Nicholas and Repingdon, he relapsed and became a popular Lollard preacher. When cited to appear before the Bishop of Hereford for an inquisition, Swinderby had the good sense not to show up. He replied in writing, alleging that he had been falsely accused on the earlier occasion and had submitted at that time "for dred of death." Excommunicated and damned as a heretic, he escaped to the Welsh borders.[18]

Walter Brute, a lay graduate of Oxford and a close associate of Swinderby, fell into the hands of ecclesiastical inquisitors in 1392. The record makes no mention whether the convocation that was gathered to examine Brute tendered him the oath, but it is clear that he would not have taken it for reasons of conscience. Brute condemned oaths as un-Christian. In one of the documents exhibited in evidence against him he said of oaths that Christ had declared: "Thou shalt not forswear thyself, but shalt perform unto the Lord those things which thou knowest. But I say unto you, Thou shalt not swear at all, neither by heaven, nor yet by the earth, &c. But let your communication be yea, yea, nay, nay; for whatsoever shall be more than this, proceedeth of evil." Many Christians would rely on this passage as their reason for refusing the oath *ex officio*. But the Bible by no means spoke with a single, clear voice on the question of swearing. St. Paul had preached the value of oaths, and Saint Jerome had narrowly interpreted Christ's statement to mean that he had merely prohibited swearing by heaven, earth, Jerusalem, or one's own head, but had not literally prohibited other swearing. This interpretation, which ignored the beginning and ending of Christ's words, was adopted by Gratian in his *Decretum* and approved by the popes. Accordingly, Brute's reliance on the Scriptures did not aid his cause. His argument that a Christian should not swear at all was merely additional proof of his heresy. Overwhelmed by the bishop and some two dozen other divines, including prelates, abbots, and doctors of canon law, Brute finally submitted himself to their authority and correction. He turned up later, however, with Swinderby and still later with Sir John Oldcastle who would be burned in 1418 for his heresies.[19]

The spread of Lollardry inspired the Church to seek the aid of the secular authority in stamping it out. In 1382 the prelates inexplicably committed an act that Stephen said "can probably not be paralleled in the history of England." They "forged" a statute of Parliament. It recited that many heretics preached to the people, endangering the true faith and engendering dissension in the realm; because these evil persons neither obeyed the summons of the Church nor cared for its censures, on certification by the prelates, sheriffs should arrest them and their supporters as well, holding them in strong prison for "the law of the holy church." This fraudulent act proved that the bishops had no lawful power to command arrest and imprisonment. In 1383 Commons in a petition for annulment called the king's attention to the fact that "the statute was never assented to nor granted by the Commons. . . ."

Although the king approved of the petition, the annulment was never published. The prelates continued to issue commissions to the sheriffs ordering compliance in accord with the "bastard statute." In 1386 the recrudescence of Lollardry moved the "Merciless" Parliament to outlaw heretical writings and make the teaching of Lollard doctrines a crime, exposing the offenders to imprisonment and forfeiture. But the Archbishops of Canterbury and York, still not satisfied, sought fuller co-operation from the coercive power of the state. On the advice of Pope Boniface IX, they appealed to king and Parliament in 1397 for the death penalty. Nothing was done, however, until Richard II's tyrannies led to his deposition, and Henry IV succeeded to the crown. Henry, whose orthodoxy was beyond question, had made a tacit agreement with the prelates to persecute the Lollards in return for the support of the Church to his claim to the throne. The death of William Sawtre in the fires of Smithfield and the act for the burning of heretics, *De Haeretico Comburendo*, redeemed the king's pledge.[20]

Sawtre, a priest and Lollard zealot, having been condemned as a heretic in 1399 by the court of the Bishop of Norwich, had made full confession and submission. On his corporal oath never again to preach heresies nor to hear confessions, the court released him. Within two years, however, he was arrested in London for publicly preaching the very criminal doctrines he had renounced. Sawtre was tried before the court of Thomas Arundel, Archbishop of Canterbury, who meant to make an example of him. Arundel had a co-operative victim, one who proudly flaunted his religious convictions and mocked his inquisitors. On February 23, 1401, Arundel condemned Sawtre as a relapsed heretic and committed him to the secular power for burning. While Sawtre was being tried, Parliament was considering a bill, long urged by Arundel, that would make heresy a capital offense. Papal decrees notwithstanding, there was no lawful authority in England for burning heretics. Not since the execution in 1222 of the deacon who had apostasized for the love of a Jewess had there been a burning in England and in that case the sheriff, it seems, had acted unlawfully. Before Parliament could enact its bill, Henry IV hurriedly issued a writ which ingratiated him with the powerful prelates. Proclaiming himself "a cherisher of the Catholic faith, willing to maintain and defend Holy Church . . . and to extirpate radically such heresies and errors from our kingdom of England," the king commanded that Sawtre "be burnt in the flames, according to law divine and human, and the canonical institutes customary in that behalf. . . ." The writ was dated February 26; Sawtre died March 2. Parliament passed its act March 10.[21]

Maitland asked why Archbishop Arundel was in such an "indecent hurry to burn his man," why, that is, Sawtre had to be burned before the passage of the statute *De Haeretico Comburendo*. "Arundel," he wrote, "had obtained from the king and the lords an admission that, statute or no statute, heretics are to be burnt. They are to be burnt, for divine law and the positive law of the church require it. The aid of a statute was extremely desirable. Unless parliament helped them, the bishops would often be unable to procure the arrest and detention of suspects, and there would be frequent friction between spiritual and temporal power. It was equally desirable, however, that at least one Lollard should be burnt, not under any act of parliament, but under *Ut inquisitionis* (c. 18 in Sexto, 5.2), in order that the right of the church to declare that obstinate heresy is a capital crime might be plainly manifested to all men as a right which no statute gave, and no parliament could take away." Sawtre would have been burned anyway under the statute, but the royal writ was "an innovation in English criminal law," intended to demonstrate that the crown and the prelates meant to terrorize the Lollards into submission.[22]

The statute itself showed that Parliament was of the same mind. Denouncing heresy generally and the false doctrines of the new Lollard sect in particular, Parliament warned that the true faith might be subverted and the people seduced into sedition. The ecclesiastical courts could not alone extirpate the evil because itinerant preachers wandered from diocese to diocese, evading summonses, escaping local jurisdiction, and ignoring the censures of the Church. The statute, therefore, enacted that no one might preach without a license, teach anything contrary to Catholic doctrine, or have anything to do with heretical writings or preachers. To put teeth in the statute, the bishops were given the power to arrest and imprison anyone "defamed or evidently suspected" and to proceed against their prisoners "according to the canonical decrees." Obstinate and relapsed heretics were to be turned over to secular authorities for burning. As Maguire noted, "So long as the clause empowering the bishops to 'determine heresy according to the canonical decrees' remained on the statute book, there could be no legal opposition in England to the administration of the *ex officio* oath by ecclesiastical courts." Henceforth the Church need not persistently violate the law nor forge statutes. King, Council, Parliament, and Church were now united on both the policy and the inquisitional oath procedure to be used against heretics. The statute itself, *De Haeretico Comburendo,* was even known as the statute *Ex Officio.* Lest there were doubts, Archbishop Arundel issued a decree in 1408 to the effect that no one should question the legality of oaths used by ecclesiastical magistrates. That decree, in all likelihood, was an aftermath of the Thorpe case of the preceding year.[23]

Willard Thorpe, a priest suspected of Lollardry, was imprisoned and brought before Arundel for examination. The Archbishop demanded that Thorpe kiss the Bible and swear upon it that he would answer truly and obey whatever was commanded of him in the way of religious opinions. Thorpe replied that a book was merely the product of various "creatures, and to swear by any creature, bothe Gods lawe and mans lawe is against it." Before he would swear, moreover, he wanted to know what he would be asked. Arundel replied that Thorpe would have to forsake all Lollard opinions and name all whom he knew of that heretical sect. Thorpe, finding the role of Judas repugnant, retorted, "Sir, if I consented to you thus as yee have herebefore rehearsed to me, I should become an appealer [an informer], or everie bishioppe's espie, somoner of all Englande. For an I should thus put up, and publishe, the names of men and women, I should herein decive full many persons: Yea Sir, as it is likelie, by the dome of my conscience, I should herein be cause of the death both of men and women, yea both bodilie and ghostlie. For many men and women that stand nowe in the waie of salvation, if I should, for the learning and reading of their beleeve, publish them therefore, up to the bishops or to their unpitious ministers, I knowe some deale by experience, that they should be so distroubled and diseased with persecution or otherwise, that many of them (I thinke) woulde rather chuse to forsake the waie of truth then to be travailed, skorned, slaundered, or punished, as bishops and their ministers nowe use, for to constraine men and women to consent to them."[24]

Arundel had to examine Thorpe without his taking the oath. Thorpe spoke freely of his religious beliefs, but stubbornly refused to testify on oath. He told of a conversation he once heard between a master of divinity and a master of law. The master of law, he said, stated that on the command of his sovereign, he would swear upon the Bible only if he knew the charge against him were lawful. The master of divinity, he said, declared that swearing on a book was like idolatry. "Therefore," concluded Thorpe, "this swearing is ever unlawful." An unnamed associate of Thorpe, on his advice, followed his example, refusing also to swear. Thorpe's courage is evident from the fact that Arundel, referring to Sawtre, threatened to send him to "followe thy fellow into Smithfield" unless he swore. Thorpe's punishment was more prolonged than a fiery death. He was degraded and committed to prison for an indefinite period. He probably died a prisoner.[25]

The victory of the Church in 1401 introduced the Inquisition into England, though neither on the scale nor of the severity as on the Continent. From 1401 to 1534, when the act *De Haeretico Comburendo* was repealed, about fifty persons were burned as heretics. For every one who was burned there were many, like Thorp, who suffered lesser penalties which ranged from carrying fagots as a form of penance to long sentences of imprisonment. For every one who was punished there were a great many who were put to the inquisition. In the period from 1428 to 1431 in just the dioceses of Norfolk and Suffolk, one hundred twenty men and women were examined for heresy, three of whom were martyred. In the century and a third of the statute's life, there were undoubtedly thousands persecuted for their religious beliefs. In just the diocese of Lincoln in the early sixteenth century, under the bishops William Smith and John Longland, many hundreds of early Protestants suffered from a continuing inquisition.[26]

Longland's technique of investigation was most efficient. He began with a couple of people who had abjured, put them under the oath, and forced them to detect and betray everyone with whom they had associated. Every person named was forced to take the oath and to confess his guilt and to name his associates. If within the privacy of the home, the Gospels were read in English, or the worship of the images of saints was discouraged, or the doctrine of transubstantiation was criticized, or pilgrimages were discouraged, or friends were received to discuss religion, Longland unferreted the facts by his crafty and searching interrogatories. He compelled the husband to confess his heresy and then to implicate his wife. She was forced to confirm his guilt, to admit her own, and to betray her children. In succession each member of the family was put to the oath and examined, so that father accused son, the son his sister, the children their parents, and friends their neighbors. Between 1518 and 1521 Bishop Longland's inquisition extended to what John Foxe, the martyrologist, described as "an incredible multitude," some three hundred forty-two people, whose consciences were wrested under oath. Foxe published twenty pages of small print summarizing scores of cases in which individuals incriminated themselves, members of their family, and friends. For the crime of "not thinking catholickly," forty-six persons were sentenced to live imprisoned in monasteries for the remainder of their years as mendicant penitents, hundreds were burdened with lesser forms of penance, and four or five were burned as relapsed heretics—in one case the children were forced to set fire to their father. Out of this "incredible multitude" who were persecuted under the oath procedure, the record does not show that a single one refused to take the oath. The resistance which a few put up against answering incriminating interrogatories was broken down; everyone took the oath and confessed.[27]

Within the next decade a widespread inquisition in London had similar results. The records do not show opposition to the oath procedure except in a few cases, and those few were persuaded to change their minds after being thrown in jail. Two cases are notable. Thomas Philip in 1530 freely promised to forswear all heresies and to favor no heretics, after having denied under oath every objection relating to his religious opinions. He admitted only that he possessed a copy in translation of the New Testament. His judges, Sir Thomas More and Bishop John Stokesley, demanded that he confess the truth of all the articles objected

against him on the basis of "fame." Philip, denying that he was defamed, asserted that he was "not bound to make Answer to the
artycles." He flatly refused to abjure. In prison he received a letter from members of his congregation, advising: "Therefore, according both to God's law and man's, ye be not bound to make
answer in any cause, till your accusers come before you. . . ." Silence, the letter stated, insured that his inquisitors "shall not
craftily, by questions, take you in snares." Philip paid the penalty
of following such advice; he probably died in prison. However,
his petition to the Commons, protesting the procedures which
had been employed against him, may have influenced the parliamentary proceedings which led to an enactment of 1534 condemning inquisitional tactics. John Lambert's case has already been
mentioned. In 1532 he was the first person on record who, charged
with heresy, objected to the oath procedure on ground that it
was illegal to force a man to accuse himself. Lambert, it should be
remembered, meant only that he should not be compelled to detect himself or reveal crimes that were either unknown or unproved; he believed that one should answer under oath if first
properly accused by due process of law.[28]

Lambert may have been reflecting the very influential writings
of William Tyndale, who was the first to translate the New Testament from Greek into English. Although Tyndale was hounded
from England and suffered a heretic's death in exile, in 1536, his
Bible went through many editions during the sixteenth century
and was known to every Englishman who could read his own
tongue. Tyndale's religious tracts also earned a great vogue in his
time, thanks partly to the notoriety which he received from Sir
Thomas More, England's Lord Chancellor, who engaged him in
an acrimonious pamphlet warfare. The foremost English Protestant since Wycliffe's time, Tyndale was honored in Elizabethan
England by John Foxe, the incomparably influential martyrologist. Foxe rekindled Tyndale's reputation by eloquently depicting
his spiritual heroism and by editing a collection of his complete
works.[29]

Tyndale's English Bible was first printed abroad in 1525, in an
edition of three thousand copies which were smuggled into Eng-

land; a decade later and frequently thereafter it was reprinted in an expanded version by Miles Coverdale under license from the crown. With Tyndale's Bible, Englishmen for the first time read in black-letter English these words of Christ; "Agayne ye have herde, howe it was said to them of old tyme, thou shalt not forswere thysilfe, but shalt performe thine othe to god. But I saye unto you, swere not at all: nether by heven, for it ys goddes seate: nor yet by the erth, for it is hys fote stole: Nether by Jerusalem, for it is the cite of the kynge: Nether shalt thou swere by they heed [head], because thou canst not make one heer [hair] whyte or blacke: But your communicacion shalbe, ye, ye: nay, nay. For whatsoever is more then that, commeth of evle." In his prologue to the fifth chapter of Matthew, the source of this passage, Tyndale commented—in a modern translation—that neither an oath of office nor an oath to bear witness was objectionable: "But if the superior would compel the inferior to answer that [which] should be to the dishonour of God, or hurting of an innocent, the inferior ought rather to die than to swear: neither ought a judge to compel a man to swear against himself, that he make him not sin and forswear. . . ." [30]

In Tyndale's principal book, *The Obedience of a Christian Man* (1528), there is a passage on tyrants breaking into the heart and consciences of men and compelling them to swear. In 1591 a group of imprisoned Puritan ministers, protesting against the oath *ex officio*, cited this passage and extended it to read that no man should be compelled "to sweare to accuse him selfe." The same ministers, like others of their time, relied on similar statements from Tyndale's book. Tyndale flatly asserted that a man should refuse an oath put to him by a judge to answer all that is demanded of him. He also protested the practice of "antichrist's disciples" in breaking into men's consciences by compelling them to forswear themselves "or to testify against themselves." The latter phrase, incidentally, has the same tone as the provisions in early American state bills of rights and in the Fifth Amendment, enjoining against forcing men to be witnesses against themselves or to give evidence against themselves. In another passage Tyndale explained that it was "a cruel thing to break up into a man's heart, and to compel him to put either soul or body in jeopardy, or to shame himself." This is probably the earliest statement equating self-incrimination with self-infamy.[31]

The protestations of Tyndale and Lambert against the inquisitional oath procedure of the ecclesiastical courts could not have been unique. But if the sources reveal no more, it is because the records are not sufficiently detailed. Excepting rare instances, verbatim responses of defendants in heresy trials are not given. It is beyond belief that the persistent opposition which is found for the fourteenth century vanished, only to reappear suddenly with Tyndale and Lambert. Lambert's invocation of the maxim, *nemo tenetur seipsum prodere*, must have been based on some tradition. In any case his was not a voice in the wilderness in 1532. The opinions which he expressed on the oath procedure were echoed first by one of the foremost champions of the common law of that day, Christopher St. Germain, and then by the House of Commons.[32]

St. Germain was a barrister of the Inner Temple and author of the seminal legal treatise *Doctor and Student*. Reputedly the most learned lawyer of his time, he was a leading advocate of Henry VIII's claims against Rome and became one of the first theorists of parliamentary supremacy. In 1532 he published a tract, possibly at the instigation of the king, which assailed clerical corruption and the canon law, which he thought completely subordinate to the common law in any case of conflict. In the course of his discussion, St. Germain singled out for criticism the *ex officio* or inquisitional procedure of the ecclesiastical courts. Men had been forced to abjure heresy, he wrote, to do penance, and to pay great sums although they had "not known who hath accused them" or knew only the ecclesiastical judges as their accusers, causing many to "thynke great malice and parcialytie" supported the judges' vexations. A man brought *ex officio* before the "ordinary" or bishop on suspicion of heresy must "purge him selfe after the wyl of the ordinary or be accursed. . . . And that is thoughte by many to be a very harde lawe, for a man may be suspected and nat gyltie, and so be dryven to a purgacion without profe or without offence in hym." the word of confessed heretics was accepted in evidence, and "yf a man be sworne to saye the trouthe concernyge heresie, as well of hym selfe as of other and he fyrste confesseth no thynge, and after contrarye to his fyrst sayenge he appeleth [accused] bothe hym selfe and other," his testimony was accepted even though he was also taken as perjured. "This," St. Germain concluded, "is a daungerous lawe, and more lyke to cause untrewe and unlawfulle men to condempne innocentes, than to condempne offenders." [33]

The answer to St. Germain came from the chancellor, Sir Thomas More, England's foremost Humanist. More, in his classic book, *Utopia*, published in 1516, had "advanced a well-defined system of religious toleration" in favor of the right of all men to hold any religious opinions of their choice. As W. K. Jordan pointed out, the *Utopia* was written at a time when More had no personal knowledge of heretics and no knowledge of their threat to the institutions which he cherished. The Lutheran Revolt, the Peasants' Rebellion, and the views of the Anabaptists and other frightening sects that he saw growing all over Europe shocked him into a reversal of his earlier views. In his *Apology* (1533), a response to St. Germain, he described heresy as "the wurste cryme that canne be," one by which a Christian became "a false traytour to God." Expounding the duty of persecuting heretics to save the faith, he recommended the death penalty and stalwartly defended existing ecclesiastical procedures as the best means of convicting the guilty. If the *ex officio* oath procedure were abandoned, he wrote, and no suspect could be examined unless someone openly accused him and made himself a party against him, "the stretys were lykely to swarme full of heretykes" before any were ever accused. A man might be willing to give secret information to a judge but not to become the sworn accuser of a heretic. "And veryle me thynketh that he whyche can not be proved gyltye in heresye" and yet was suspected by his neighbors, deserved to do some penance. If the ecclesiastical courts "sholde putte awaye the processe ex officio, the thynge sholde be lefte undone"; heretics would multiply, the faith would decay, and sedition would spread throughout the realm.[34]

In the same year, 1533, St. Germain replied to More in another tract which More also answered. St. Germain now advocated the virtues of the common law's accusatorial system over the inquisitorial procedures of the canon law. Mauling the *ex officio* proceeding which made the judge accuser, prosecutor, and jury, St. Germain insisted on the need for a definite accuser other than the judge, open accusations, and specification of the charges. Only God, he claimed, "is the sercher of man herte." To put the suspect to answer and condemn him when his testimony was contrary to witnesses or accusers unknown to him "semeth not reasonable to be accepted for a lawe." St. Germain marveled that More could defend the secret informer—"he doth it of some malice or craft" —and punish a man by giving him penance "bicause his neighbours dare not swere that he is no heretyke." The oath, he said, should not be accepted. The innocent must be protected. He concluded that "it were better to suffre an offender to go unpunysshed, than to punyshe him unrightwisely & agenste due order of justyce." More's new tract added nothing new to his original statement. He defended every step of the *ex officio* proceeding on ground that it was "necessary for the preservacyon of the catholyke faythe" and the peace of the realm. Though he denied that "the spyrytuall judges . . . did with mych wronge & cruely mysse handle men for heresye," he concluded that there was no law in the world that did not hurt innocent men.[35]

St. Germain, like Lambert, did not argue for a general right against self-incrimination, that is, for a right to remain silent to an incriminating question on ground that a truthful answer might furnish evidence leading to one's conviction. No such right existed at common law. The argument, rather, was that the inquisitional procedure, which employed the oath *ex officio*, unfairly denied the defendant every vestige of proper accusation, thereby denying him the opportunity to defend himself. The *ex officio* suit, which St. Germain assailed, enabled the ecclesiastical judge, by virtue of his office, to haul a man before him on the basis of secret information, common rumor, "fame," or on whatever suspicions the judge personally might have, to force the suspect to take the oath to tell the truth, and then to examine him by interrogatories calculated to make him incriminate himself. This was the procedure, since 1401 the ecclesiastical law of the land, against which Commons also protested.

The Parliament of 1532, wrote one of its members, "long debated" various grievances of the laity against the "ordinaries" or bishops, especially their "crueltie . . . for calling men before theym *Ex Officio*," accusing them of heresy and examining them inquisitorially, without accusers, "whiche to the Commons was very dredeful and grevous." Finally the grievances were put in the form of a petition or "Supplication" to the king and presented to him by a delegation led by the speaker. The petition declared that obedient subjects were summoned daily before ecclesiastical judges *ex officio*, sometimes for malice and sometimes without any lawful cause of accusation or credible fame having been first proved. The judges compelled men to appear for answer at a certain time and place, "and that secretly and not in open place," and upon their appearance, "without cause or any declaration then made or showed, commit and send them to ward, where they remain without bail or mainprize, sometimes for a year . . . before they may in any wise know either the cause of their imprisonment or the name of their accuser. . . ." In heresy cases the ordinaries or their ministers "put to them such subtle interrogatories, concerning the high mysteries of our faith, as are able quickly to trap a simple, unlearned, or yet a well-witted layman without learning, and bring them by such sinister introduction soon to his own confusion." A man, never knowing that he was a heretic in thought or deed, might answer truthfully only to find himself taken as confessed, summarily condemned, forced to make his purgation, "and so thereby to lose his honesty and credence for ever," or else "some simple silly soul," knowing his conscience to be clear, refused to confess "and so is utterly destroyed." One of the manuscript drafts of the petition of Commons included a passage, not retained in the final version, that begged on behalf of the laity that they should not be liable to the oath *ex officio*, which gave them only the alternatives of abjuration or being burnt for heresy.[36]

Henry VIII passed the petition to the prelates for discussion and answer. Their formal reply, a mass of evasions and denials, claimed that the jurisdiction of the ecclesiastical courts had been exercised "with all charity." If anyone had been grieved by his treatment—"we remember no such"—it was according to the canon law "and also to your grace's laws," no doubt an accurate reminder of the Act of 1401 and of Henry VIII's very harsh policy toward heretics. "He that calleth a man *ex officio* for correction of sin doeth well. . . . He that is called according to the laws *ex officio* . . . cannot complain." The only persons who were held in custody while awaiting for their cases to be heard were suspected heretics; although causing an innocent man to suffer would be blameable, Commons' petition mentioned no specific cases, said the prelates, making answer impossible in that regard. As for entrapping men into confessions by subtle interrogatories, the prelates replied that subtlety ought not to be used, but they had not "known, read, or heard of any one man damaged, hurt, or prejudiced." In any case, the "persecution of heretics" was a duty owed to God and king. The existing procedures could not be improved upon for that task.[37]

On matters of heresy, Henry VIII differed from other men of his time only in his greater severity and intolerance. As orthodox as the pope, he probably cared not one whit for the victims of the ecclesiastical courts and had no repugnance for their procedures. He meant, however, to make himself sovereign of the English church as well as of the state, and to that end, setting aside his probable sympathy for the argument of the clergy, he encouraged all measures that would turn the people against the pope's supporters. Indeed, the king, or those close to him, may have inspired the petition of Commons; Thomas Cromwell, the king's foremost hatchetman, corrected the draft of the petition. Not until 1534, however, did it suit the king's political purposes to approve of the petition. Parliament then enacted one of those high-sounding ineffectual laws of which there had been so many in the fourteenth century. This one, repealing the statute *De Haeretico Comburendo*, condemned the procedure by which not even the most expert and learned man of the realm, "diligently lying in wayte uppon hym selff can eschewe and avoyd the penaltie and daunger of the same acte and canonycall sanctions if he shulde be examymned upon such capcious interrogatoryes" as was customary when the bishops thought they had a heretic in hand. The new act declared that henceforth no one should be convicted or put to loss of name and goods unless by "due accusacion and wytnes, or by presentment," nor could anyone be put to death but by presentment (grand jury), verdict (trial by jury), confession, or out-lawry.[38]

The repeal of the infamous act of 1401 scarcely wrought any changes in policy, practice, or procedure. The inquisition continued in England more intensely than ever. Indeed, from the repeal in 1534 to the death of Henry VIII, in 1547, fifty-one persons were burned for heresy, as many as were burned in the whole period from 1401 to 1533. The Henrician Reformation, of course, explains the unprecedented persecution. Henry VIII staked his crown, his person, and his dynasty on the success of that Reformation. Having made himself "Supreme Head" of the Church of England, he saw in any deviation from the new religious order a threat to royal supremacy. Whether loyalty to the "Bishop of Rome" or conscientious belief in any of the new Protestant doctrines, the expression of dissent blended heresy and treason into indistinguishable crimes. Those who continued to support the authority of the pope, Henry VIII sent to the executioner's chopping block; those who preached new doctrines he sent to the fires at Smithfield. The form of death differed with the belief, but the crime was essentially the same: a religious conviction that differed from the king's. He reserved for himself in the Act of Supremacy (1534) full power to "repress and extirp all errors, heresies, and other enormities" to which ecclesiastical jurisdiction extended, and, of course, a similar power to rid himself of temporal, as well as spiritual, traitors. Toleration simply did not exist in that era and was unthinkable as a matter of statecraft, when nonconformity was believed to threaten the king, who was the spiritual head of the church.[39]

Sir Thomas More, the scourge of heretics, who mercilessly advocated their death, became one of Henry VIII's earliest and most distinguished victims. His crime was, in form, a political one; he refused to swear that the Act of Supremacy, which made the king Supreme Head of the Church of England, was lawful. More had the same problem as the religious reformers who had been his victims: he had conscientious convictions that unshakeably motivated his conduct. The oath of supremacy was unlike the oath *ex officio*; refusal to recognize Henry VIII in the place of the pope was not literally heresy, or at any rate was some new-fangled political heresy which equally new-fangled law technically considered treason. Nevertheless, for all practical purposes More's situation was little different from that of John Lambert or other early Protestant martyrs. Tendered the oath—the oath of supremacy —he refused to swear, saying, "I nothinge doinge nor nothinge sayenge againste the statut it were a very harde thinge to compell me to saye either precisely with it againste my conscience to the losse of my soule, or precisely againste it to the destruction of my bodye." Thomas Cromwell reminded More that he had required heretics to answer precisely on oath whether they believed the pope to be the head of the Church, and demanded of More why the king should not compel him in the same way. There was a difference, replied More, between the universal law of Christendom and the law of the realm which conflicted with it. Cromwell retorted that it was the difference between burning and beheading, to which More replied that the difference rather, in forcing him to answer, was the difference between heaven and hell. At this point, reported More, "thei offred me an othe by which I shoulde be sworen to make true aunswere to suche thinges as shoulde be asked me on the Kinges behalfe, concerning the Kinges owne person." In other words More was asked to swear an oath —the oath *ex officio*—and testify to his beliefs about the king's supremacy. "Whereto I aunswered that verily I never purposed to swere any booke othe more while I lived." Although they pressed him to take the oath and answer incriminating interrogatories, he persisted in his refusal. He would take no oath while he lived, and so he died. A modern canonist, William J. Kenealy, S.J., construed More's refusal to answer questions as having been grounded on the proposition "that no man could be compelled to accuse himself or to furnish evidence upon which an accusation against him could be made by others. He appealed to an old maxim of the Canon Law, *nemo tenetur se ipsum prodere. . . .*" [40]

The criminal procedure for prosecuting heretics under Henry VIII, after the act of 1534, was highly unsettled. Due accusation, presentment, and verdict—the procedure of the common law provided by the statute—was by no means the only procedure followed. The old ecclesiastical courts could not for a while be relied upon, because many of the bishops and lesser clergy, who could not easily break the habits of a lifetime, still owed their loyalty to the pope, secretly if not openly. Henry VIII could scarcely trust them to prosecute themselves, although they remained greatly useful for prosecuting Lutherans, Anabaptists, and other heretics. The king made Cromwell his viceregent and authorized him, by a special commission issued in 1535, to exercise all ecclesiastical jurisdiction and power. Cromwell, in turn, created minor commissions, which included civil lawyers, to assist him, but in the main he operated through reliable bishops and secular officers of the realm for the purpose of coercing doctrinal conformity. Because of these *ad hoc* arrangements, which augmented the statutory endorsement of common-law procedures, there was not procedural regularity. John Lambert, for example, was tried and convicted before the king himself, who appointed and presided over a special commission of bishops and nobles to assist him. In the same year that Lambert was burned, 1538, one Cowbridge seems to have been convicted by ecclesiastical judges and condemned to the flames by Bishop Longland of Lincoln. Cromwell's commission expired, of course, with his own execution in 1540, leaving an act of 1539 as the main directive on heresy proceedings.[41]

The "Six Articles Act" of 1539, which Protestants called "the Whip with Six Strings," had the virtue of defining heresy rather unmistakeably and the ingenuity of producing a curious mélange of common-law and canon-law procedure for its enforcement. The six articles touched religious doctrine from transubstantiation to mass and confession. Publishing, preaching, or holding any opinion against transubstantiation was declared to be heresy, punishable by burning and forfeiture of all properties, without abjuration or possibility of recanting. For first violation of any of the other five articles, the punishment was forfeiture and indefinite imprisonment; for a second offense, death. The enforcement of the statute was put primarily in the care of the clergy. The archbishop or bishop of every diocese, directly or through his clerical representative, must hold inquests into heresy in every shire at least four times a year and take accusations by the oaths and depositions of at least two witnesses, or by presentments of grand juries. Justices of the peace were similarly empowered to inquire into heresy by the oaths of grand jurors. Every commission, con-

sisting of at least three men, was directed to proceed against accused persons "as is used and accustomed in case of felony," that
is, by jury trial. The statute also stripped accused persons of their
customary right to challenge jurors, required the burning of
heretical writings, and ordered priests to give quarterly readings
of its provisions before parishioners assembled in church.[42]

The assimilation of common-law procedures to the episcopal
inquisition was a new departure in English history and certainly a
far less severe mode of prosecution than had prevailed before
1534. The mixture of procedures invariably stimulated irregularities. There were even monumental evasions as in the 1540 cases of
three notorious Lutheran priests, Robert Barnes, Thomas Garret,
and William Jerome, who were condemned to burn by the Council, at the instigation of Stephen Gardiner, Bishop of Winchester.
The three, according to Foxe, received no public hearing or trial.
Bishop Edmund Bonner tried Richard Mekins by jury in 1542,
but seems to have prosecuted him personally. The most remarkable procedure of all occurred in the case of John Marbeck who
was arrested in 1543 for writing an English concordance of the
Bible, in violation of the Six Articles Act. Bishop Gardiner's examination of Marbeck, first in Council and then in prison, was
reminiscent of the inquisitions before 1534. Marbeck was even put
to the oath *ex officio* which appears to have fallen into disuse
after 1534. He took the oath and answered all questions, but denied all heresies imputed to him and refused to name heretics
known to him. In fact, he knew three who shortly after were
tried with him and burnt at Smithfield. When confronted with
their names, he admitted knowing them, but denied having discussed religion with them. When re-examined by a commission of
three bishops, Marbeck carefully avoided incriminating himself or
others. At one point, feeling threatened by a hostile remark, he
burst out, "By my troth, sir, if ye do tear the whole body in
pieces, I trust in God, ye shall never make me accuse any man
wrongfully." Following his interrogation, Marbeck was indicted
and tried by jury. Most astonishingly, he was represented by
counsel who was permitted to speak on his behalf to the jury, an
unheard of privilege. His three co-defendants had no counsel.
They and Marbeck were found guilty and sentenced to be

burned, but at the eleventh hour he alone was saved by a pardon obtained by his counsel. From oath *ex officio* to counsel and pardon, the Marbeck case stood as a most unusual application of the statute.[43]

The statute itself was somewhat softened by amendments of 1543 and 1544 which restored the right to challenge jurors, allowed offenders to recant, and required presentment and indictment by grand jury only, or, in other words, abolished the provision for formal accusation by witnesses. The king's Council, however, was above the law, as the 1546 case of Anne Askew showed. The Council took and retained jurisdiction of her case, possibly because she reputedly had an influence on ladies at the king's court. Denied knowledge of her accusers, she was put to an inquisition and confessed her religious beliefs. After her conviction she was given the opportunity of recanting and naming heretics who shared her opinions. Because she refused, she was stretched on the rack "till I was nigh dead," she recorded. The Lord Chancellor himself, Thomas Wriothesley, administered the torture, assisted by his successor, Richard Rich. Anne Askew soon was dead, burned at Smithfield without ever having had any sort of process guaranteed by statute.[44]

The death of Henry VIII in 1547 passed the crown to his young son, Edward VI, and to the Protestant cause. They founded the Anglican Church, which Elizabeth later established so securely, giving England a *via media* between Catholicism and the more thorough-going Protestant reforms. In an age of unspeakable cruelty, the short period of Edward's sovereignty, 1547 to 1553, was notable for its extraordinary mildness. Religious persecution, which was taken for granted and even counted a duty on the part of believers of whatever persuasion, hardly existed by any comparison with the immediately preceding and succeeding reigns. One of the very first acts of Edward's sovereignty was the abolition of all treason and heresy laws of Henry VIII's time. Treason and heresy remained capital crimes of the greatest horror, of course—no age can transcend itself. In the eight years that Edward was monarch, only two heretics were burned for "crimes" so heinous by sixteenth-century standards that they would have been burned regardless who was king; they would have been

burned anywhere in Christendom: they denied the divinity of
Jesus. We might, today, call them Unitarians. They were condemned by men like Archbishop Thomas Cranmer and Bishop
Nicholas Ridley, who, though scarcely advocates of religious
toleration, had a breadth of viewpoint that set them apart from
such Marian bishops as Gardiner and Bonner, both of whom were
deprived of their ecclesiastical offices and imprisoned while Edward was king. Their treatment is best appreciated by remembering that during the Catholic Restoration, following Edward's
death, Cranmer and Ridley died at the stake.[45]

The Protestant interlude was extraordinarily mild, but only by
comparison. The principle obtained that the religion of the monarch must be the religion of the nation. In 1549 Edward issued letters patent to establish a commission of great authority which he
empowered to examine and inquire concerning all heresies. The
commission removed Catholic priests, enforced the Anglican Book
of Common Prayer, and established uniformity of worship. A
leading Catholic historian, Philip Hughes, searching for evidence
of real persecution under Edward VI, found it necessary to stress
the heresy provisions of a proposed revision of the canon law that
was never enacted, the two burnings which he admitted would
have occurred under Henry or Mary, and the plunder of Catholic
properties.[46]

Of the few cases from this period, one has compelling interest,
the 1549 trial of Edmund Bonner, the Bishop of London, who
would later be called "Bloody Bonner" even by the children of
London. Bonner's accusers, men who had heard his sermons, confronted him openly before his judges, who included Archbishop
Cranmer and Sir Thomas Smith, the king's principal secretary.
There was no indictment, no jury. The proceeding was *ex officio
mero*, an inquisition, and Bonner took the *ex officio* oath to answer truthfully to the articles objected against him. His judges,
finding his answers "obscure and insufficient," directed him to
state clearly whether he had preached as charged. He would say
no more, however. Warned that he would be taken *pro confesso*
—as if he had confessed—if he remained contumacious, Bonner insisted that he was not compelled by law to answer. Permitted to
state in writing his reasons for asserting that his answers could not

be compelled, Bonner claimed, first, that the procedure against him was irregular, and second, that some of the articles, being captious, were intended to bring his answers "within a snare." The "articles" were propositions or charges which served as interrogatories; he was supposed to affirm or deny them, explaining his answers. But he insisted that the articles were "such sort that, by the king's ecclesiastical laws, a subject of this realm is not bound to make answer unto them, but lawfully may refuse and deny to do it. . . ." The record does not show that he offered further explanation, nor that he invoked the maxim, *nemo tenetur seipsum prodere*, but his argument in sixteenth-century terms was that he refused to incriminate himself. His inquisitors favored him with fresh articles, first taking the precaution of freshly administering the oath *ex officio*, which he took without objection, yet he adamantly refused to answer. After several examinations and much wrangling, the court declared him *pro confesso* on all the unanswered articles, removed him as bishop, and imprisoned him. No greater punishment was inflicted on any Catholic during the reign of Edward VI.[47]

The king's death in 1553 heralded a Catholic restoration under Queen Mary. "The facts are," remarked the distinguished Catholic historian, Philip Hughes, "that in the last four years of Mary's reign, between February 4, 1555, and November 10, 1558, something like 273 of her subjects were executed by burning, under laws which her government had revived for the capital crime of obstinately adhering to beliefs that contradicted the teaching of the Catholic Church. . . . In this respect alone, namely of so many executions for this particular offence in so short a time, the event is a thing apart, in English history: never before, nor ever since, was there anything at all quite like it." According to Hughes, the revulsion that one feels must be tempered by the understanding that the Marian period differed, in the main, only quantitatively. Heresy, that is, was everywhere in Christendom counted as the greatest crime. The foremost leaders of the Reformation—Calvin, Luther, Melanchthon, Zwingli, Knox, and Cranmer—believed that the failure to persecute betrayed God's true faith—whatever version of it they professed. "But," wrote another Catholic historian, Lord Acton, "the Papacy contrived murder on the largest and also on the most cruel and inhuman scale. They were not only wholesale assassins, but they made the principle of assassination a law of the Christian Church and a condition of salvation. Rome taught for four centuries and more that no Catholic could be saved who denied that heretics ought to be put too death." If in England the difference between Protestant and Catholic governments on the question of executing heretics was merely quantitative—two burned under Edward and two hundred seventy-three under Mary in less time—it is impossible to explain why church and state under Mary used the fagot and stake not just for fanatical extremists, like the Anabaptists whom Christians everywhere reviled, but for Anglicans like Cranmer, Ridley, and Latimer.[48]

The ghastly statistics on burnings scarcely suggest the extensiveness of the inquisition and terror under Queen Mary. Borrowing from the example of Henry VIII, who issued a commission to Cromwell to conduct an inquisition to enforce Catholicism-*sans*-pope, and from Edward, who had created a commission to uphold the new Anglican creed by cleansing papist heresies from the clergy, Mary also established a commission whose purpose was to enforce the new laws which made Catholicism and the return to Rome the sole path for the nation. The statute *De Haeretico Comburendo* and supplementary legislation were revived in full force. The bishops, given the task of executing the new commissions, operated through the old ecclesiastical courts. But in 1557, Mary established a new and stronger commission to supersede the others, "for a severer way of proceeding against heretics." It was this body which became in time the Court of High Commission, an ecclesiastical arm of the Privy Council and Star Chamber. The commission under Mary was empowered to inquire into all heresies and seditious words, all offenses committed in church and against church property, and all refusals to attend church and to conform. The prerogative letters patent creating the commission also instructed it on proper procedure: "use and devise all such politic ways and means for the trial and searching out of the premises [charges] as . . . shall be thought most expedient and necessary. . . ." The commission, in other words, was invested with arbitrary or completely discretionary power to invent its own procedure, whether "by the confession of the parties, or by sufficient witnesses . . . or by any other ways or means requisite. . . ." Only one procedural device was expressly commanded: the commission must use the oath *ex officio* "to examine and compel to answer, and swear, upon the holy evangelists, to declare the truth in all such things whereof they or any of them shall be examined." The power to fine and imprison all who refused to appear for examination, or refused to take the oath, or were found guilty, was also given to the commission. It was the perfect tool for the job, helping to make "the fires of Smithfield" and "Bloody Mary" clichés of English history.[49]

The Marian inquisition provoked the first widespread attempt by criminal defendants—suspected heretics all—to refuse to answer for fear of self-incrimination. The minister, John Bland, one of the first Protestants to be arrested, refused to give his opinion, as demanded by his inquisitor, on transubstantiation. "Sir," he replied, "I perceive that ye seek matter against me . . . I think thus I am not bound to make you an answer." Urged to answer, he refused because to do so would bring him "into trouble." In 1555, the following year, another Protestant minister, Laurence Saunders, on being confronted with his own writings, replied, "What I have written, that I have written; and further I will not accuse myself." Nicholas Sheterden's formula for refusing reply was, "Nay . . . ye seek my blood, and not justice." Humfrey Middleton refused utterly to answer. Bland, Saunders, Sheterden, and Middleton were all condemned as obstinate heretics and suffered the extreme penalty. Some were burned on suspicion alone, merely for refusing the oath *ex officio*.[50]

The case of John Philpot is a good illustration of the Marian inquisition in operation. Philpot, the Archdeacon of Winchester, had the nerve to advocate the Anglican cause at a convocation of churchmen called by Mary when she became queen. Removed from office and imprisoned, a year and a half later, in 1555, he was examined many times by the queen's commissioners. One of his judges admitted, "we have no particular matter to charge you withal," but demanded that he answer to suspicions of heresy. Philpot, who knew what a heretic was—he had once reviled and spit in the face of a condemned Unitarian on her way to the stake

—vehemently denied the charge. He had hardly expected such treatment, he declared, because his remarks at the queen's convo-cation were uttered after liberty was first given to every man present to speak his conscience freely in response to questions there raised. Disagreeing, his inquisitors relentlessly interrogated him, though with little success. On the third examination, Bishop Bonner asked for Philpot's opinion on transubstantiation. "I cannot show you my mind," he replied, "but I must run upon the pikes, in danger of my life there-fore." He would talk only if Bonner would "take away the law," allowing an informal discussion off the record. Otherwise he would discuss religion only in convocation; he had been a student of law, he said—he had studied civil law at Oxford—and knew when he must answer. Bonner broke off the examination, only to return for a fourth time, reinforced by three other bishops. When Philpot rejected his invitation to speak his conscience, Bonner informed the others that Philpot had said he was a lawyer. "My lord," the prisoner replied, "I said not I was a lawyer, neither do I arrogate to myself that name, although I was once a novice in the same, where I learned something for mine own defence, when I am called in judgment to answer to any cause, and whereby I have been taught, not to put myself further in danger than I need. . . ." Accused of obstinacy, Philpot pleaded that he could not answer the questions, "because I cannot speak without present danger of my life." [51]

On a later occasion, Bonner visited Philpot in his prison cell and demanded that he take the oath *ex officio* to answer certain articles. Philpot refused the oath, povoking Bonner to denounce him as an Anabaptist for being unwilling to swear. Then Bonner turned to Philpot's fellow cellmates, accused heretics all, and demanded that they take the oath and swear to be witnesses against him. One of the prisoners replied, "My lord, we will not swear, except we know whereto: we can accuse him of no evil, we have been but a while acquainted with him." Exasperated, Bonner declared that if they would not swear against him, he would make them take the oath, under pain of excommunication, to answer the very articles charged against Philpot. "My lord," was the reply, "we will not accuse ourselves." Bonner then ordered the sheriff to put them all in stocks, including Philpot. A month later Bonner found him guilty of heresy and sent him to the stake. [52]

The refusal on the part of suspected heretics to accuse themselves became commonplace. Ordinary laymen—weavers, ironmakers, farmers, and hatters—hoping vainly to save themselves from a horrible end, began routinely to balk the proceedings by pleading that they would not incriminate themselves. Their language varied in style. Philpot had said that he would not run himself upon the pikes. Two years later, first Stephen Gratwick and then Matthew Plaise refused to answer articles which they called "a snare, to get my blood." Richard Woodman refused to be sworn to make answer because, he said, similarly, "I perceive you go about to shed my blood." Ralph Allerton declared, "If I cannot have mine accusers to accuse me before you, my conscience doth constrain me to accuse myself before you. . . ." When he implied that Bonner, his inquisitor, was persecuting him, the bishop, according to Foxe, angrily responded, "Now, by Allhallows, thou shalt be burnt with fire for thy lying, thou whoreson varlet and prick-louse, thou!" Richard Gibson simply refused to take the oath and would say nothing. Reinald Eastland, refusing the oath *ex officio* too, argued that an oath was lawful to end strife—like the old oath of purgation—"but to begin a strife an oath is not lawful." In 1558 Elizabeth Young, according to Foxe, was abused by her examiners for refusing the oath. One Dr. Martin called her a "rebel whore and traitor heretic," and threatened her with the rack unless she swore and confessed her guilt for distributing heretical books. "Sir," she replied, "I understand not what an oath is, and therefore I will take no such thing upon me." When Bonner examined her, she still refused to swear and on being threatened again, she is supposed to have answered, "Do with my carcass what ye will." [53]

The accounts of these trials of Brute and Thorpe, of Lambert and Marbeck, and of Philpot and Gratwick, are based on John Foxe's *Book of Martyrs*, for a century and more the most popular and perhaps the most influential book in the English-speaking world, second only to the Bible. The full title of the first English edition, published in 1563, suggests the spirit of the book: *Actes and Monuments of these latter perilous dayes, touching matters of the Church, wherein ar comprehended and described the great persecutions and horrible troubles that have been wrought and practised by the Romishe Prelates, speciallye in this Realme of*

England and Scotlande, from the yeare of our Lorde a thousande, unto the tyme nowe present. The pages of the huge folio volume were interspersed with some fifty woodcuts vividly depicting the burning of various martyrs. In spirit and content the book is a monumental piece of anti-Catholic propaganda, filled with errors, bowdlerizations, and expurgations. Catholic scholars abhor and eviscerate it with their criticism, although Philip Hughes acknowledged that the one element in the *Book of Martyrs* which can be verified, the translated extracts from the episcopal records of the heresy trials where we are given the questions put to the accused and their answers, are "substantially reliable." Foxe's own commentaries may be untrustworthy and prejudiced, but his accounts of the trials are authentic and accurate; he suppressed disagreeable data, but invented nothing. One of his harshest critics, James Gairdner, admitted, "Among the numerous documents in his book there may, possibly, be one or two that are spurious; but it is not to be supposed that he connived at forgery. Where the originals are attainable it does not appear that he ever tampered with the text of one of them; indeed, one might say that he is generally a very careful editor." Hughes rightly observed, however, that the liveliest parts of the narrative, the interchanges between the judges and the prisoners, derive from the prisoners' own accounts: "it is the trial, and the judge, described from the condemned cell. And it is the prisoners' own account, unchecked, uncorroborated, that is also very often the sole authority for the story of the minor horrors inflicted upon them. And where it is not the prisoner's account (or what is alleged to be the prisoner's account), it is, very often, the hearsay account of some eye-witness who remains anonymous." [54]

The question which naturally arises, whether Foxe is a reliable source, must be answered by a resounding affirmative from the standpoint of one interested in the origins of the right against compulsory self-incrimination. That prisoners answered in exactly the words given in the *Book of Martyrs* may be doubted, but there can be no doubting that Lambert did in fact give the opinion that no man should be forced to accuse himself. Whether Bishop Bonner personally scourged Thomas Hinshaw in 1558 with a willow rod for refusing to answer incriminatory interrogatories may be doubted, but there is no doubting that Hinshaw or others of his time objected to the oath *ex officio*. The *Book of Martyrs* would be a significant and reliable source for the origins of the right against self-incrimination, even if every word and every page were a complete fabrication. For Foxe's account was taken as authoritative in his own time and for long after. It was believed by English Protestants, revered as gospel truth, and accorded a place next to the Bible. A revised and enlarged two-volume edition—it eventually became eight thick volumes, three of which covered the brief Marian period—was published in 1570, and in 1571 a convocation of Anglican prelates ordered that every bishop should have a copy of it. It was soon found in nearly every parish church, chained to a desk along with a large edition of the Bible. Sir Francis Drake took a copy with him on his great voyage around the world. The early English settlers in Virginia and Massachusetts, both Anglicans and Puritans, brought the book with them to America. "With the puritan clergy, and in almost all English households where puritanism prevailed, Foxe's 'Actes' was long the sole authority for church history. . . ." In 1641, the year that Parliament abolished the Court of Star chamber, the Court of High Commission, and the oath *ex officio*, the eighth edition of the *Book of Martyrs* appeared, and by then there had also been numerous abridgments. William Haller estimated that over a century after the first edition there were more copies of Foxe in circulation in England than any other book of similar scope except the Bible.[55]

In Haller's recent study of Foxe's book, he described the "lessons of history" which its readers learned. "People were held on suspicion supported only by reports of informers or the tittle-tattle of neighbours and acquaintances. Charged with no specific offence against the law, they were required to answer on oath questions concerning their beliefs and associations which, they apprehended, were designed to make them expose themselves or their friends to prosecution for what offences they could not tell and were not told. They were pressed to save themselves by informing on others. And if they held back, they were required to answer precisely and correctly certain questions concerning the doctrines of the Church, intended, they believed, to entrap them into making statements which would lay them open to accusations of heresy. They for their part demanded to be told what they were being held for and who were their accusers. They demurred at having to swear in advance to testify concerning any matter whatever their inquisitors might choose to ask about them. They complained of being forced into making compromising and incriminating statements. They showed a strong repugnance to inculpating other persons. . . . Threatened with punishment, they appealed to the laws of the realm. Thus every examination, as Foxe reports it, tended to wind up in a dramatic scene in which an honest believer was shown pitting the plain truth of the Word against the super-subtle sophistries of hypocritical churchmen and a loyal subject of the Crown was shown asserting his rights as an Englishman against a popish prelate. In such stories as these Foxe in effect set a pattern for common people to follow whenever government should invade what men were learning to think of as their rights." [56] Whether intended or not, whether its material was literally true or not, the *Book of Martyrs* became a primer which taught the values of freedom of religion and freedom of speech and, too, certain procedural rights that clustered around the accusatory system of criminal justice, such as proper accusation, fair trial, and the right to remain silent to incriminating questions.

CHAPTER III

The Elizabethan Persecution of Catholics

The government of Elizabethan England, abhorring even the appearance of persecution for the cause of conscience, repealed all the Marian legislation against heresy and quenched the fires of Smithfield. Nor were those fires rekindled with fresh fagots during the great Protestant queen's long reign of over two-score years except to consume four Anabaptists—those of a sect execrated by all Christendom.[1] With these exceptions, important though they were, heresy as a capital crime died with Mary. There was an end to persecution for the spiritual purposes of saving souls or maintaining the purity of the established faith; yet persecution was not ended, nor were inquisition and martyrdom either. Nonconformists filled the jails while the gallows of Tyburn replaced the fires of Smithfield. The contradiction between the government's professions and its practices would have bemused a philosophic spirit even as it occasioned grave regrets in high places and anguished cries from the victims of repression.

England had by no means embarked on an official policy of toleration. That was still an impossibility in an age that could not conceive of a state without an established church to which all, without exception, must conform, if not for the greater glory of God, then for the greater security of the queen's person, national independence, and public order. Essentially secular considerations, rather than spiritual, dictated government policy. What once was heresy had become treason for reasons of state, not religion. Al-

83

though state and church were one, the church was subordinate to the state, its instrument rather than its master or equal. Grim determination, defensive and even regretful, marked the proceedings against traitors whose political crimes proceeded from religious conviction. Where once there had been triumphant zeal when a new martyr was executed, there was now a quick and not insincere profession of official aversion to religious persecution, a denial that such a thing existed any longer in England.

Politics, rather than religion, had become the basis of government policy; treason and sedition were the crimes for which Nonconformists died under the Anglican Establishment. The distinction, however nice, theoretically advanced the cause of toleration. To the government it was a distinction of vital concern. It was a distinction, too, which earned for its victims the satisfaction of going to the gallows and the executioner's block only after having enjoyed the full process of the common law's accusatorial system, even though indictment and public trial might follow inquisition and the rack, and, moreover, the jury, so anxious to save the queen and the state from their mortal enemies, was something less than unbiased. The new laws against subversives stretched impartially to cover Puritans as well as Catholics, but struck the Catholics, especially their priests, with by far the greatest capital incidence. The inquisition against Puritans, which was scarcely less widespread and intense, reaped a far more bountiful harvest of protests against compulsory self-accusing; however, the initial protests in Elizabeth's time against being forced to be a witness against oneself criminally were by Catholic prisoners.

The tragedy of the Elizabethan persecution was all the greater because the government had resolved to pursue a remarkably moderate course, in some ways an even tolerant one by any past comparisons. The religious settlement of 1559 was marvelously calculated to capture the loyalties of as many Englishmen as possible and to offend the fewest number. It was a conservative, cautious, and comprehensive settlement, traditional in the organization and government of the church, traditional, too, for the most part in ritual and ceremony, yet Protestant in doctrine. Because it was Protestant, it was naturally repugnant to devout Catholics, and because it was not thoroughgoing in its reformation, it disenchanted and then embittered the Puritans who had expected Elizabeth's accession to bring a new Geneva to England. Yet the intention of the settlement was purposely to blur sharply defined positions and avoid all suggestions of extremism. The compromise on the sacrament of the altar, for example, illustrates the deliberate ambiguity of Anglican doctrine. Although repudiating the Catholic doctrine that the bread and wine were miraculously transubstantiated into the very body and blood of Christ, the new settlement sought to please all Protestants. It simultaneously affirmed the Lutheran principle of the Real Presence and the contradictory Calvinist principle that the bread and wine were merely symbols, the sacrament itself a simple commemoration of the Last Supper. It was a politic solution, making theology play second fiddle to the needs of the state.[2]

The acts of Supremacy and Uniformity, the first two statutes enacted under Elizabeth and defining the new settlement, were of the same comprehensive character. Although the Henrician relation to Rome was re-established, Elizabeth was made the Supreme Governor of the Church, rather than its Supreme Head, and was not endowed, as Henry had been, with virtually papal powers, nor could she exercise strictly spiritual functions. Yet all members of the clergy and all ministers of state, judges, and mayors were compelled to swear an oath acknowledging Elizabeth's supremacy in "all spiritual or ecclesiastical things or causes" as well as temporal. Conventionally severe penalties were adopted for obstinate nonjurors, bloody ones for anyone persistently maintaining the authority of any foreign prince or prelate. After a supplementary act of 1563, the crime of supporting the jurisdiction or power of the "Bishop of Rome" was made punishable by forfeiture of all properties and life imprisonment on the first offense, by death for high treason on the second. The same statute also extended the requirement of the oath of supremacy to all candidates for university degrees, lawyers, sheriffs and other officers of the courts, and all members of Parliament. Harsh though these statutes of 1559 and 1563 were, they were laxly enforced. Where nonconformity or recusancy was concerned, as long as it was unobtrusive, quiet, and respectful, the policy of the government was to look the other way, rather than make windows into men's souls and secret

thoughts, as Elizabeth herself was reputed to say. The Marian
bishops, having refused to acknowledge the queen's ecclesiastical
supremacy, were removed from office, but none were severely
treated except Edmund Bonner, who was kept closely imprisoned
until his death. The Puritans lusted for bloody vengeance, but
Elizabeth, who was no zealot, refused to follow her sister's example. She preferred instead to show, as she said, that her reformation tended to peace rather than cruelty. Even when persecution
became real and was at its worst, in the 1580's, the government of
England was considerably more tolerant than most of its critics,
or its victims, or its foreign counterparts.[3]

The overwhelming majority of the Marian clergy subscribed to
the new religious order, taking the oath which in effect renounced
allegiance to the pope and affirmed loyalty to Elizabeth as head of
the national church. The church included men of a wide spectrum
of religious belief, from conforming Catholics to fervent Calvinists. For a decade and more an astonishing degree of variety,
though officially disapproved, prevailed in church practice on
matters like making the sign of the cross, kneeling at communion,
wearing a surplice, and using a chalice, rings in the marriage ceremony, or organ music. Despite Elizabeth's injunctions of 1559 and
the Thirty-nine Articles adopted by Convocation in 1562, it was
not until 1571, when Parliament formally adopted the Articles,
that the church had a binding body of doctrine. Even after, the
laws were not rigorously enforced. Some clergymen conducted
authorized public services and then privately celebrated Mass.
Catholic laymen, like all others, were required to attend the established church every Sunday and on holy days or risk a twelve-
pence fine for recusancy. Many, perhaps most, complied, yet
many also took Mass in private. The government scarcely knew
the names of recusants—and did not want to know them. All that
was required, however much it bruised the consciences of believing
Catholics or the Puritan minority, was an external conformity.
Thoughts, as John Lambert once put it, were free and need pay
no toll—as long as they were not put into practice. Anyone might
dissent openly, if he acknowledged the queen's supremacy, ecclesiastical and temporal, but factious practices were not allowed, and
pro forma obedience was expected. It was exacted from the

openly contumacious and from those who flagrantly refused even the perfunctory show of conformity that the law required, not for spiritual reasons but to sustain the political supremacy of the crown. On the whole, however, sporadic enforcement prevailed, with now and then a semi-ritualistic crackdown to remind the people that a particular form of worship, and none other, was by law established and compulsory for all.

Then, in 1575 two heretics were burned, against the protests of John Foxe, the martyrologist, and two years later the government prosecuted Cuthbert Mayne, a young Catholic priest, for the crime of high treason. He was the first of an appalling number of priests who met the same fate. His guilt was proved by the fact that he had in his possession a printed bull of the pope—though it was of no significance and had already expired—some religious trinkets, and a tract against the Church of England. In addition he was accused of having conducted Mass. For these crimes he was executed as a traitor to the state, and in 1579 two more priests paid the supreme penalty for similar offenses. The usual punishment for treason was a peculiarly gory one, deliberately intended to be a spectacle of horror that would terrorize the spirits of any contemplating the same crime against the sovereign or her government. The prisoner was drawn on a hurdle to the place of execution where he was hanged, mutilated, and butchered. According to the conventional sentence, he was cut down from hanging while still alive, and then "your privy parts cut off, and your entrails taken out and burnt in your sight; then your head to be cut off, and your body to be divided into four parts, to be disposed of at her Majesty's pleasure. And God have mercy on your soul." The persecution had begun. By 1585 twenty-three priests were martyred and seventy more were in jail, and after the treason act of that year, another ninety-four were executed. In addition some sixty Catholic laymen were also executed for treason, many of them for harboring or assisting their priests. All were guilty of propagating Romanism; that is, they were put to death for their religion, or, rather, because their religion made their political opinions treasonable opinions. But only an insignificant minority, several laymen and a few priests, were guilty of anything more than criminal views; actual conspiracy or treasonous conduct was the exception. On the other hand, Philip Hughes grossly overstated the case when alleging that only religious persecution was involved: "It was a regime where, from the beginning, it sufficed that a man was a practising Catholic; as it sufficed with Hitler to be a Jew, or with the queen's Catholic sister to be a heretic." Politics, not religion, bottomed the executions and the anti-Catholic inquisition.[4]

Protestant England, Anglicanism and Puritanism alike, was united in a not unjustified fear that an international Roman Catholic conspiracy meant to restore the English state and church to its Marian condition. Elizabeth's ministers of state, her parliaments, her gentry, her office-holders, and her churchmen, and surely too the bulk of the common people, who had suffered most from Mary's inquisitions, fervently believed that Elizabeth stood between them and the destruction of their careers, their power and fortunes, their religion, and possibly their lives. The death of the Virgin Queen would mean the accession of Mary Stuart, Queen of Scots, a devout daughter of the powerful Guise dynasty which spearheaded the most militant and intolerant Catholicism in France. She was a Mary Tudor incarnate in the opinion of English Protestants. Should she succeed to the throne, civil war, foreign intervention, and papal supremacy seemed inevitable. The Council of Trent and the Catholic Counter-Reformation threatened destruction and extirpation of all that seemed dearest to the political and religious establishment of England. Mary's entrance into the country in 1568 immediately made her a rallying point of Catholic opposition to Elizabeth. In 1569–70 occurred the rebellion of the pro-Catholic northern earls, a treasonous uprising subsidized by Rome, provoked in part by a papal emissary. As soon as loyalist forces crushed the rebels and executed hundreds, England learned that the papacy had virtually declared war. Pius V, a Dominican friar who rose to power in the service of the Holy Inquisition, conducted a heresy trial against Elizabeth in 1570, found her guilty, and excommunicated her. The papal bull which announced these results explicitly deposed Elizabeth as queen, absolved her subjects from allegiance, commanding them not to obey her or her laws, and pronounced a sentence of excommunication upon all who continued to support her. "No event in English history," wrote Arnold O. Meyer, "not even the Gunpowder Plot, produced so deep and enduring an effect on England's attitude to the catholic church as the bull of Pius V. Englishmen never forgot their queen's excommunication. Whenever in later ages men's minds were stirred up against the Roman church, the remembrance of 1570 was enough to justify their implacable hatred." [5]

The bull of 1570, judged by its effect upon the queen's Catholic subjects, was a tragic blunder, for it trapped them in an inescapable vise which the government had earnestly sought to avoid: it forced them to choose between their religion and their government. No longer was it possible for them to be good Catholics and loyal subjects of the queen. Moreover, the bull had the inevitable effect of proving to the satisfaction of Protestants their worst suspicions: their Catholic countrymen were potential traitors. The bull certainly branded Catholicism as a subversive faith. If additional evidence were needed, the Ridolfi plot, which was uncovered in 1571, provided it. The pope, Mary Stuart, and a Catholic faction supported by the Duke of Norfolk, England's greatest nobleman, entered into a conspiracy to overthrow the government with the aid of a Spanish expeditionary force, seize or assassinate Elizabeth, and place Mary on her throne. The massacre of some five thousand French Protestants, women and children as well as men, on St. Bartholomew's Day, 1572, raised the specter once again of what might befall England in the event of a Catholic restoration. In Rome, the new pope, Gregory XIII, on receiving the news from Paris, ordered the *Te Deum* to be sung at St. Peter's and candles of rejoicing to be lit, and he summoned the artist Vasari to decorate the Vatican with paintings of the massacre. From time to time the English government uncovered political conspiracies emanating from the Holy See and even papal approval for plots to assassinate Elizabeth. [6]

Pope Gregory vigorously supported the bull of 1570 as well as his predecessor's plan to restore England through missionary work against the Elizabethan heresy. In 1568, a seminary had been founded in the Netherlands for young English Catholics, exiles from their native land, to train them as priests; they were ready if need be to die for the faith. The first three seminarians returned to England in 1574; by 1578, there were over fifty; by 1580 there were more than one hundred. The number of English seminaries on the Continent also grew, and in 1580, English exiles trained as Jesuits added reinforcements to the task of augmenting the faith at home. The apostolate of the seminary priests and Jesuits frightened the English government. As early as 1568, on first hearing of the seminary at Douay, William Cecil, later Lord Burghley, the queen's Principal Secretary, warned against an attempt to withdraw her subjects from allegiance and conformity. As the years passed, with one plot following upon another after the bull of 1570, the disguised Catholic missionaries, as seen from Westminster, came to be regarded as ideological shock troops of an international conspiracy; in the language of a later time, the government considered the priests to be a subversive fifth column, traitors all, and every Catholic subject a fellow-traveler.[7]

New definitions of treason proliferated legislatively to defend state and church against the Catholic threat. The threat was real enough, but the new statutes zeroed in on the wrong target: English Catholics, their priests included, paid the price of papal policies. An act of 1559 created the high treason of simply saying that Elizabeth was not queen; a new act of 1571 added the high treason of alleging that she was a heretic or a schismatic. Moreover, the use of or obedience to any papal bull was also made high treason, and the same penalty attached to reconciling any English subjects to the Catholic Church. For good measure importing crosses, beads, pictures, and other religious objects "from the Bishop of Rome" was criminally punishable too. As J. R. Tanner said, "There were political reasons why patriotic Englishmen should hate the Pope, and from this it was only a short step to hatred of the whole religious system which the Pope represented. Men who were in violent hostility to Rome on political grounds soon found themselves in opposition to the worship and practices of the Roman Church on religious grounds. . . ."[8]

Despite the severity of the acts of 1571, which reflected an increasing influence of the Puritan party in Parliament—the pope's political policies aided the spread of Puritanism—Elizabeth resolutely adhered to her refusal to persecute ordinary Catholic laymen. After the papal bull, she ordered the Star Chamber to declare baseless all rumors that "hir Maty. hath caused or will herafter cause inquisition and examination to be had of mens consciences in matters of Religion." No one, declared the order, had been molested except "in not coming at all to the Church" and none would be molested but for the same reason. Her Majesty "meaneth not to enter into the Inquisition of any mens consciences as long as they shall observe hir Lawes by their open dedes." In conformity with the practice of laxly enforcing this remarkably liberal policy, Elizabeth vetoed a bill passed by Parliament in 1571 that would have enabled the government unerringly to identify Catholic recusants—those who refused obedience. The bill had been passed because the twelve-pence fine for non-attendance at Anglican services was neither enforced, nor enforceable, with any regularity; it would have required all Englishmen to receive Communion at least once a year, according to Anglican rites, on pain of prohibitive fines for failure to do so. A Roman Catholic archbishop accurately reported at this time, "The Queen feels no great interest in any faith or any sect, but that she has no other thought than to keep herself on the throne in whatever ways she can, and by means of that religion which may best serve her purpose." The Church of England had become symbol and bulwark not only of the English Reformation, but of national independence against Rome, France, and Spain. Their support of the intrigues against Elizabeth and their subsidies to the seminarist movement made every missionary priest, in turn, a symbol and bulwark of the union of Catholic powers against England.[9]

The arrival in England of the first Jesuits, Fathers Edmund Campion and Robert Persons, in 1580, at the very time an army under papal banners invaded Ireland, marked a turning point in English policy toward recusants. As late as 1579 the queen's ministers of state were still urging that the government should do nothing to force upon Catholic subjects an absolute choice between conflicting loyalties of state and church. Even Francis Walsingham, the Secretary of State, a Puritan sympathizer who hated Catholics and was not above torturing their priests, had advised his agents to deal leniently with recusants so that they would not be pressed to make a desperate choice; however much "Papists who will not conform themselves to resort to public prayer" might deserve punishment for contempt of the laws, "forbear to persecute by means of indictment. . . ." The legislation of 1559, 1563, and 1571, in other words, was still not being enforced rigorously against the laity. But the seminarist movement, when reinforced by the Jesuits, proved to be more than a threat; it began to be successful. There was a notable revival of Catholicism in England and a corresponding increase in recusancy, because, contrary to the widespread belief which the government encouraged, the priests taught that no Catholic might attend Anglican services without imperiling his soul. The drastic measure of 1581 was the government's answer. The use of bulls to bring about reconciliation had been made treasonous in 1571; now reconciliation brought about by any means, with intent to dissolve allegiance to the queen, was also made treasonous. Being a Catholic was not criminal, but practicing Catholicism by saying or hearing Mass was; becoming a Catholic or bringing about conversions was also made criminal. And absence from established services was punished by a crippling fine of twenty pounds monthly.[10]

The statute of 1585, passed after more assassination plots came to light, further extended the law of treason by bringing within its compass the crime of simply being a Catholic priest in England. At that time there were 262 priests in England; half that number paid the extreme penalty. The official line of the government, explained by Lord Burghley himself, was that no one was or would be persecuted for the opinion, however criminal, that the pope was supreme in matters of faith; the crime to be punished was absolving English subjects from their loyalty to the queen in accordance with the papal bull. Burghley, as Arnold O. Meyer wrote, "treated English catholics more or less in the same way as protestants were treated in catholic countries, and, notwithstanding all the inquisitorial severity of his rule, we must not overlook the fact that English history is free from such blots as the massacre of St. Bartholomew and the murders of protestants in Ireland." But as J. B. Black observed, even though one must remember that the pope endorsed assassination, that the queen's life was believed to be in danger from fanatics, and that England was in daily fear of a Spanish invasion, the majority of priests died "because they held opinions that were considered dangerous to the existence of the state—opinions, moreover, from which they could not dissociate themselves without ceasing to be catholics."[11]

The plight of English Catholics in Elizabethan England was virtually designed to provoke repeated refusals by defendants to answer incriminating questions. One reads a passage like the following with a readiness to believe that it is both accurate and representative: "The prisoner lay on his bed of straw in the Tower of London, too weak to move, too ill to speak. He had been stretched on the rack earlier that day in the hope that he would finally confess to complicity in plots against Queen Elizabeth. Three weeks later he could not lift his hand at his trial to take the oath. His finger[nail]s had been torn out in an effort to extract the 'truth.' He stood silent, invoking his right not to give evidence against himself. History knows him as Blessed Edmund Campion." The description is generally accurate. Campion was hideously tortured, though he did not have to lift his hand at his trial to take the oath because no prisoner in a common-law trial was either required or permitted to give testimony on oath; that was a privilege reserved only for the crown's witnesses. Under torture Campion implicated others and "confessed," though not under oath and not to the principal charges specified in the indictment—conspiring the death of the queen, overthrow of the established religion, and subversion of the state. What he admitted, in the words of the indictment—to which he pleaded not guilty—was seeking "to persuade and seduce the queen's subjects to the Romish religion, obedience to the Pope," but he did not admit that by so doing he sought to disaffect Catholics from allegiance to the queen.[12]

The prosecutor at his trial revealed that Campion had refused the oath of supremacy and refused also to answer whether in his opinion the papal bull of 1570 possessed force of law. Campion reported to the court that though he acknowledged Elizabeth as his queen, he could not answer "bloody questions . . . undermining of my life; whereunto I answered as Christ did to the dilemma, Give unto Caesar that is due to Caesar, and to God that to God belongeth!" He reported also that he had been asked whether the papal bull discharged him from his allegiance: "I said this was a dangerous question, and they that demanded this demanded my blood. But I never admitted any such matters, neither ought I to be wrested with any such suppositions." Far from standing silent at his trial, Campion defended himself brilliantly, answering all charges and evidence introduced against him. His defense, that "our Religion was the cause of our Imprisonment," revealed the cause of his conviction. He did not, of course, invoke his "right" not to give evidence against himself, because no such right existed in a common-law proceeding as of 1581. Yet he surely protested against questions that sought to make him incriminate himself. The "right" to make such a claim and have it legally binding, respected by the court, would eventually come into existence precisely because Campion and men like him—the Lamberts who preceded him and the Puritans who followed—charged the unfairness of inquisitions which sought to force their conviction by their own testimony. They had no choice but to refuse answer, when a truthful reply furnished evidence of their guilt because their religion was a crime.[13]

Campion was by no means the first Catholic in Elizabethan England to refuse to incriminate himself. The earliest record showing any Catholic so refusing goes back to 1535 when Sir Thomas More was interrogated by Henry VIII's officers. Bishop Bonner followed his example when he was tried in the Protestant reign of Edward VI. Under Elizabeth more Catholics came to appreciate the justice of repeated Protestant refusals in Mary's time to take the oath *ex officio* or to respond to damaging interrogatories. In 1562 the Bishops of London and Ely, acting as inquisitors, reported to the Council that they had been unable to extract information from a priest named Haverd who was suspected of saying Mass in a private home. Some think, reported the bishops, that if the priest were "putt to some kynde of Torment," he might be "driven to confesse what he knoweth." They had examined the members of the household with as little effect, for "neyther the Priest nor anye of his Auditours, nott so moche as the Kitchen Mayde will receive any Othe before us to answer to Articles, but stoutly saye they will nott sweare and say also they will neyther accuse themselves nor none other." John Whitgift, the Archbishop of Canterbury, apparently understated his point when he told the House of Lords in 1585 that the oath *ex officio* was "misliked first by Jesuits and Seminaries. . . ."[14]

Priests and kitchen maids may recalcitrantly object to oaths and to self-accusing, but lawyers, we may presume, know their "rights" and will assert them when the need arises. Deep interest, therefore, especially attaches to the case of a criminally suspected Catholic lawyer: surely he would be aware of a canon-law tradition, if one existed, endorsing the maxim *nemo tenetur seipsum prodere*, or a common-law principle, if one existed, barring self-incrimination when criminal jeopardy threatened. In 1568 the queen's commissioners for ecclesiastical causes, later known as the Court of High Commission, summoned Thomas Leigh, an attorney of the Court of Common Pleas, to answer for hearing Mass in the house of the Spanish ambassador. Leigh, it was said, "loved mass as well as he loved his life," but he would not give the commissioners any information about his religious conduct. The commissioners, whose authority derived from royal letters patent which were copied from the Marian model of 1557, demanded his confession on oath. Their authority to do so was seemingly indisputable. Parliament itself, in the very Act of Supremacy annexing to the crown all ecclesiastical jurisdiction, empowered the queen to delegate that jurisdiction to commissioners.

She vested in her commissioners "full power and authority . . . to visit, reform, redress, order, correct and amend in all places within this our realm of England all such errors, heresies, crimes, abuses, offences, contempts and enormities spiritual and ecclesiastical" by the "most expedient" means at their discretion. She specifically empowered them to examine suspects "upon their corporal oath, for the better trial and opening of the premises." Although the regular ecclesiastical courts might punish only by ecclesiastical censures which graduated to excommunication, the letters patent creating her Majesty's commissioners for ecclesiastical causes authorized them to punish "by fine, imprisonment or otherwise." When, therefore, Thomas Leigh, the Catholic attorney, refused to take the oath demanded by the commissioners—the Bishop of London and two others were his judges—they promptly clapped him in prison for his contempt.[15]

Leigh's defense for refusing oath and answer is not known. The jurisdiction, procedure, and punishment meted out by the ecclesiastical commissioners seemed unchallengeable. And, had Leigh pleaded *nemo tenetur seipsum prodere*, they could have replied that he was protected only against the necessity of having to come forward to detect or inform against himself by confessing to a hidden crime, one whose existence was unknown and therefore uncharged. Yet once that crime had been revealed and the prisoner stood accused by vehement suspicion or was commonly reputed to be guilty, he must answer truthfully to the accusation because he was bound to show his innocence, if he could, and clear himself under oath. Such was the canon-law rule derived from St. Thomas Aquinas and followed by the ecclesiastical commissioners and all other ecclesiastical courts, throughout Christendom as well as in England.[16] In Leigh's case, if there was not already proof of his guilt, there was *fama* enough to put him to his oath. Yet one of the high courts of the common law, the Court of Common Pleas before which he practiced, issued a writ of habeas corpus to inquire into the cause of his imprisonment. The ecclesiastical commissioners objected that the common-law judges could not have "exposition" of the Act of Supremacy because it was purely a matter of ecclesiastical law within their exclusive jurisdiction; but Chief Justice James Dyer, speaking for a unanimous bench, resolved that the statute was "temporal meerly." Although the judges did not challenge the jurisdiction of the ecclesiastical commissioners to try Leigh, according to later reports of the case based on Dyer's unpublished records, "yet they ought not in such case to examine upon his oath." Dyer said, "quod nemo tenetur seipsum prodere, and so for this cause they then delivered him. . . ."[17]

This is the earliest known use of the *nemo tenetur* maxim by a common-law court, and clearly something more than merely the canon-law meaning was intended. Unlike the common law, the canon law never abstracted from their qualifying context the words "*nemo tenetur seipsum prodere*" and never vested a right against self-incrimination. From Aquinas to the Court of High Commission, the rule meant that a suspected person, when questioned by proper authority, must answer pertinent questions however incriminating: "*Licet nemo tenetur seipsum prodere; tamen proditus per famam, tenetur seipsum ostendere, utrum possit suam innocentiam ostendere, et seipsum purgare.*" Literally translated, this meant: "No one is bound to produce against himself, but when exposed by common report he is bound to show whether he can show his innocence and is permitted to purge himself." Chief

Justice Dyer apparently wrenched the *nemo tenetur* clause out of context and gave it independent life. Although the canon-law maxim was clear enough in meaning, what was not clear was the common-law meaning. Leigh's case might have only meant that no man was bound to incriminate himself without first having been properly accused by common-law standards. What was at stake may have been the old common-law principle, in the words of the statute of 1368, that no man should "be put to answer without presentment before justices, or matter of record, or by due process and writ original, according to the old law of the land." In other words, the common-law judges may have been aiming at the conditions antecedent to putting a man to answer, rather than at the fact that incriminating interrogatories were addressed to him. Leigh's case was the first shot in a long war between the common-law courts and the Court of High Commission on the issue of the oath *ex officio*. It was a dangerous war for the common-law judges to wage, because the queen's prerogative explicitly supported her ecclesiastical commissioners.[18]

In 1569, the following year, the commissioners summoned barristers from the Inns of Court for an examination into their religious practices, demanding answers to three interrogatories—whether the lawyers had attended established religious services, whether they had received Communion according to law, and "whether they and every of them have not heard other forms of prayer or service then is appoynted by the Lawe, viz. masse mattens or evensonge in Latten, or have byn shreven or howseled after the popish maner." Unlike the first two questions which sought to reveal negligence, the last was intended to discover criminal conduct. The record does not reveal that the commissioners required any of the fourteen lawyers whom they examined to take the oath. Leigh's case may have had some impress, if only temporary. Six of the fourteen respectfully declined, however, to answer the incriminating third question. Of Roger Corham, whose remarks were typical of the six, the record merely says, "he beleveth he is not bound by Lawe to answer to the same, bycause there is a penall Lawe, for offendinge in matters concernyd in this Interr." We may surmise that if the commissioners were simply fishing around for something chargeable, without even common report to support a suspicion, the six rested safely on the canon-law rule. Whether "fame" existed, or perhaps something even more substantial, is unknown, and so too is the fate of the six.[19]

It is surprising not to discover repeated and massive protests by Catholics who were victimized by inquisitorial tactics. So occasional, indeed, are their objections against compulsory self-accusing that the few instances seem to intrude upon the record. Men and women summoned before the High Commission courageously defended their religion or silently acquiesced to persecution, but did not challenge the legality of the proceedings against them nor cry out against the unjustness of being compelled to disclose evidence against themselves. Many of the priests and their accomplices were physically tormented and on release from the rack found no respite when thrown in a totally dark dungeon below the high-water mark, infested with rats. The leading authority on the use of torture in England observed that "there is no period of our history at which this instrument [the rack in the Tower of London] was used more frequently and mercilessly than during the latter years of Elizabeth's reign." Yet if the case of Campion and his confederates is representative, the prisoners when publicly tried complained hardly at all about their treatment.[20]

Campion's famous declaration may have steeled English Catholics to be fatalistic about their treatment: the Jesuits of the world, he wrote, had made a league "cheerfully to carry the cross that you shall lay upon us, and never to despair your recovery while we have a man left to enjoy your Tyburn, or to be racked with your torments, or to be consumed with your prisons." Though the age was doubtlessly cruel and many Englishmen thought the priests got no more than they deserved for fomenting rebellion and schism against the queen, Puritan victims of persecution, far less stoic than their Catholic counterparts, never lost an opportunity to stir public sympathy, if they could, by exposing their mistreatment and by denouncing the oath procedure by which their persecutors sought to force them to incriminate themselves. The martyr complex was notably missing from the make-up of the Puritan minister. Not so the Catholic priest of this period. As A. O. Meyer wrote, "Love for their country and their religion, longing for high achievements, ever noble enthusiasm—all were fused together into one burning desire to die for England's conversion. Not only death itself lost its terrors—that was as nothing —but the lingering and painful tortures which went before were lit up by a halo of glory. There was only one thing on earth worth anything—the martyr's sacrifice." [21]

Catholic laymen, spiritually heroic though they may have been in holding to the faith against desperate adversity, suffered incriminating questions silently, truthfully, evasively, or equivocally, but with little protest against the questions. In the summer of 1580, for example, on an inquisition into recusancy by the High Commission in York, only one out of 170 suspected Catholics refused the oath *ex officio*. The minute in the record on this particular case suggests that the oath was routinely administered to all and intransigently rejected by Baynes alone: "Christopher Baynes of Norton, gent., being required to take an oath to answer as by law he was bound refused twice so to do," and for his contempt the High Commission fined him twenty pounds and imprisoned him for obstinacy in matters of religion. Had he taken the oath, they would have asked him, as they asked the others, why he had not attended the established church and received Communion. Those who promised to conform were set free on bond; those who would not conform joined Baynes in prison. The priests, when taxed with interrogatories that aimed at their undoing, often conducted themselves artlessly: they remained silent, though not in protest against the nature of the questions, or blunderingly answered, or denied that they had learning enough to answer. What was rare was Father Alexander Briant's response to the question whether the queen should be obeyed if the pope commanded the contrary: "And he saith, that this question is too high, and dangerous for him to answer." Equally rare was the answer given to the same question by Father Ralph Sherwin—like Briant, another priest tortured, tried, and butchered with Campion: "He prayeth to be asked no such question, as may touch his life." [22]

Protestant historians have made much of the fact that Pope Greogry XIII in 1580 issued a secret *Explanatio*, copies of which the missionary priests might show to English Catholics, declaring that the 1570 bull against Elizabeth was not binding on them until such time as circumstances made its public execution possible. This new order has been taken as additional proof of Rome's "double dealing," as Conyers Read said, "a clear revelation of the treasonable purposes of the missionary priests." Yet another effect of the *Explanatio* was that it permitted English Catholics to swear truthfully their loyalty to Elizabeth not only as queen but as spiritual head, with the mental reservation that she was queen and spiritual head *pro tempore*—only until such time as the bull of deposition could be executed. The government printed the pope's new dispensation in both the original Latin and in translation, thereby giving it far greater publicity than it might have received by circulation in the Catholic underground. The difficulty with this explanation is that the priests, at any rate, simply did not take the oath which acknowledged the queen's spiritual supremacy.[23]

Although Catholics did not mount a concerted and insistent assault on the oath *ex officio* and against compulsory self-incrimination, the most significant legal development up to its time occurred in a 1580 case involving Catholic defendants. This was a Star Chamber proceeding for contempt against William Lord Vaux, his brother-in-law, Sir Thomas Tresham, and five others charged with refusing to swear that they had not harbored Campion. The tyranny and excessive cruelty which is associated with the Court of Star Chamber belongs to a later era, that of Charles I and Archbishop Laud. In 1580 and for long after, the Star Chamber was a greatly respected court whose reputation had not yet been blemished. It was nothing more than the Privy Council sitting judicially to try cases of disobedience to royal orders and a variety of related offenses such as riots, contempts, libels, forgery, counterfeiting, and fraud. As a prerogative court it had virtually discretionary jurisdiction over any acts which it chose to regard as offenses, excepting treason and felonies. It could torture, imprison, fine, and punish in any way it pleased—by whipping, pillorying, branding, nose-slitting, ear-severing—but it could not dismember limbs or body, nor inflict death, which was the sentence for treason and all felonies; cognizance of these crimes belonged exclusively to the common-law courts. As the judicial arm of the Privy Council, the Star Chamber was composed of the greatest ministers of state and lords of the realm, plus the leading common-law judges. The court that tried Lord Vaux and his confederates included the Lord Chancellor, the Lord Chamberlain, the queen's Treasurer, the Chancellor of the Exchequer, the Chief Justice of Common Pleas, the Lord Chief Justice of England, the Lord Chief Baron, and five great noblemen. As of 1580 their procedure, like that of the Court of High Commission, was still somewhat fluid, though distinctively different from the common law's. Star Chamber procedure savored more the inquisitorial than the accusatorial system. Although its sessions were public, there was a marked trend toward a secret, preliminary examination of the defendants. The practice, which allegedly became routine, was to put the accused to the oath *ex officio* and then administer a set of interrogatories which would expose the guilty. Sometimes the oath was not used; sometimes it was required but there were no set interrogatories, the accused being let alone to tell his story in his own way and then answer questions. The Star Chamber could use any procedure it wished and dispense with its usual procedure when it wished.[24]

The case of Lord Vaux and the others involved what privy councilors described as a "matter of state," the secret mission of the Jesuit Campion, then in the Tower awaiting trial. Under excruciating torture, he had betrayed the names of several Catholics who had given him shelter, although there is evidence that he acknowledged only those names already known to the government. Vaux and the other prisoners, having been named by Campion, were called before the Privy Council and tendered the oath *ex officio* as a preliminary to interrogation. Walter Powdrell, the only one of the seven prisoners who confessed to harboring Campion, was willing to take the oath if he might first see the interrogatories; the others refused the oath outright. For these contempts of the royal prerogative the seven were imprisoned. Two months later they were tried by the Court of Star Chamber for having refused to swear to the offense of having harbored Campion. The trial was technically an *ore tenus*, or word-of-mouth, proceeding, very similar to a common-law trial except that there was no jury. The Attorney-General stated the accusation against the prisoners, and members of the court questioned them each in turn. The court allowed each full opportunity to say whatever he wanted on his own behalf, and neither bullied nor interrupted any of them. The trial was fair and public.[25]

Lord Vaux, acknowledging his refusal to swear, stated that he could not take the oath in a matter of conscience for fear of offending his conscience. He would, however, swear to any interrogatories concerning his loyalty to the queen or in matters of state. Campion, he added, had not been at his house. Lord Chancellor Bromley interposed, "You have denied it unsworne; why do you refuse to sweare it? Naye, you were but required to saye it upon your honour . . ."—a favor shown to him because he was a peer. Vaux replied simply that to a nobleman, affirmation upon his honor was the same as swearing an oath to others. The other defendants, excepting Powdrell and Tresham, also chose to speak briefly and similarly offered conscience as the sole ground of their refusal. As Sir William Catesby put it, he would not "discover matters of conscience, which I maye not doe without offence of my conscience. . . ." Powdrell confessed to the charge that he had refused the oath because he had not been shown the interrogatories first.[26]

Tresham's defense was the highpoint of an otherwise dull trial. He was articulate, quick-witted, and zealous on his own behalf. He spoke at considerable length, even debating his judges on disputed points and correcting them. And he had something worthwhile to say. His position was fundamentally the same as that of the others, conscientious objection to the oath in matters of religion, but in addition he would neither accuse himself nor others. When Lord Leicester summed up his testimony by stating that Tresham "will accuse no catholique in cases of conscience," he replied that his position "breiflie" was that he would swear "to all thinges of alleageance and state, but not to accuse any catholique in cases of conscience onlie, which I still affyrme. . . ." Unlike the others, he not only argued this position with force, but in the course of doing so expressly invoked the maxim, *nemo tenetur seipsum prodere*.[27]

The case, Tresham asserted, was a criminal one. His contempt consisted of refusing to swear whether Campion had been in his house, preached, or said Mass, and in refusing to say who had been present. "All which tendeth to the discoverie of the practise of a contrary religion, other than is warrantable in this state, and which, by the lawes now in force, is penall. . . . Wherefore I making no question but that it is unlawfull in this case to accuse, and most unlawfull to sweare. . . ." He thought it necessary to explain his understanding of the circumstances which rendered his refusal to take the oath not contemptuous. An oath ought never be taken without justice to the party involved, he argued; in his case, justice to himself was impossible because he was condemned by every alternative if he swore: "For, if I sweare falselie, I am perjured; if by my othe I accuse myselfe, I am condemned to the penaltie of the law and displeasure of my prince, which is contrarye to the law of nature *seipsum prodere*. If I sweare trulie, then I laye myself wyde open to perjurie, because Mr. Campion hath oppositely accused me in the affirmatyve. Lastlie, if I sweare as he hath confessed I thereby should recorde myselfe, before no meaner wytnesses then your honours, to be an egregious lyer; to affirme one thinge before your honours unsworne, and by othe before your honours to sweare the contrarye. Secondlie, I should greatlie synne uncharitablye to belye hym, to make hym and myselfe both, guyltie by my othe, who to my knowledge ar most innocent, which I am by Gods worde expreslie forbidden. Lastlie I should committ a grevous synne to sweare against the knowledge of my owne conscience. . . ." [28]

Sir Walter Mildmay, the Queen's Treasurer, objected that Tresham's argument would enable every suspect to refuse to swear on the basis of his own judgment whether swearing and justice were compatible. Tresham answered that he had no doubt that the party ought to refuse to swear at the risk of incurring a temporal contempt rather than swear to even a lawful act which was against his conscience. Accused by the Lord Chancellor of refusing to swear in any case, Tresham replied that he would swear if taking an oath concurred with truth, judgment, and justice. It was at this point that Leicester claimed and Tresham admitted that he would not accuse a Catholic in cases of conscience. He would take the oath on matters of loyalty to the sovereign or duties to the state, "but in this, yet being no mere temporall demaunde but a matter of conscience, and thereby concerneth my soule, I am to have such speciall regarde hereto in this my othe before your

honors, as I maye be abled to make my accompt before the majestie of almightie God at the dredfull daie of judgment." When
Lord Hundson twisted his meaning by saying that he would not
swear for fear of perjury, Tresham explained once again why taking the oath was a trap that left him unacceptable alternatives
only, and once again declared, "And, if I dyd accuse myselfe by
my owne othe, I should condemne myselfe, against the lawe of nature and Gods lawe." [29]

Intending, he said, to teach Tresham a lesson, the Lord Chancellor blunderingly asked him how he could perjure himself by
contradicting Campion when Campion had not "deposed." This
was the first admission that Campion had refused the oath and
confessed without swearing, and Tresham was momentarily
stunned. He finally concluded that he would not swear anyway in
a case of conscience. The Lord Chancellor retorted that this was a
"civil" cause only, that is, did not involve conscience; the position
of the government in all prosecutions against Catholics was that
political crime, rather than religion, was at issue. But Tresham
would not let the point pass unanswered. He reminded the court
that he had been examined on many questions of religion, such as
whether Campion had said Mass at his house, "and never of causes
of state or mere temporall demaundes, unto which I never refuse
to depose, nor yet doe." Leicester replied that the Council had not
asked him more than whether Campin was at his house, to which
Tresham reminded them that he had first been examined by Mildmay, by virtue of a warrant from the Council, on seven articles
bearing on religion. Mildmay denied having asked questions about
Mass and preaching, whereupon Tresham caught him in the lie by
reciting chapter and verse of the seven articles. Leicester lamely
asked what difference it made if he had been asked whether Campion said Mass, "what relygion is in this case?" Tresham's answer
to that apparently persuaded the court to turn to the next defendant rather than permit the audience to hear the government's
case against political crime turned into a persecution of religion.[30]

When the last defendant had had his say, the Attorney-General
summed up the evidence and the court gave judgment without rising. One by one each member stated his opinion, and though the
unanimous judgment of the court was that the prisoners were

guilty of contempt, several of the opinions marked a legal mile-
stone in the development of the right against self-incrimination. In
time the argument based on conscience, which all the prisoners
but Powdrell had advanced, would have tremendous force in
bringing about the abolition of the oath *ex officio*. But it was
Tresham's invocation of the "law of nature *seipsum prodere*"
which had immediately telling effect. Four members of the court,
including, most significantly, the three common-law judges, endorsed the principle advanced by Tresham; yet they qualified it so
that it did not apply to a Star Chamber proceeding. Sir Roger
Manwood, Lord Chief Baron of the Court of Exchequer, declared, "Thoughe the lawe dyd forbydd a man to accuse hymselfe
where he was to loose lyfe or lymme, yet in this case it was not
so." What he meant was that the Star Chamber, by not having
jurisdiction of treason or felony cases, could not punish capitally
or by dismemberment. Sir James Dyer, Lord Chief Justice of the
Court of Common Pleas—the author of the opinion of that court
in Leigh's case—said that in a case involving life or limb, "the lawe
compelled not the partie to sweare, and avouched this place,
'nemo tenetur seipsum prodere.' . . ." Sir Christopher Wray,
Lord Chief Justice of England—head of the King's Bench, the
supreme criminal court—also began his opinion by asserting "that
no may by lawe ought to sweare to accuse hymselfe when he
might loose lyfe or lymme, shewying that he was of opynion that
they ought in this case to swear. . . ." He added that in his court
witnesses were sworn to give evidence between parties and when
the queen was a party, that is, in a criminal prosecution; his point
was that witnesses, unlike the accused, did not stand in criminal
jeopardy by giving sworn testimony. Sir Walter Mildmay, a Puritan, was the only other member of the court to note that the defendants might swear "without danger of life or member." For
their contempts the court sentenced them to imprisonment until
they conformed or until her Majesty's pleasure was known; in addition the court imposed heavy fines ranging from five hundred
marks in Powdrell's case to one thousand marks in Tresham's and
one thousand pounds in Lord Vaux's. Twenty months later
Tresham and Vaux were the last of the prisoners to be discharged.[31]

The case had slight effect upon Star Chamber procedure because its jurisdiction did not extend to cases in which the new doctrine could be operative. For all practical purposes the judges had ruled that the Star Chamber might always require the oath *ex officio* because it could not punish by death or loss of limb. The oath became routine in all cases, and in the notorious heyday of the Star Chamber it was the opening wedge for a devastating inquisition. William Hudson, a Star Chamber lawyer who wrote the most important book about that court, said that the power of examining the parties under oath "was used like a Spanish inquisition to rack men's consciences, nay to perplex them by intricate questions, thereby to make contrarieties which may easily happen to simple men; and men were examined upon 100 interrogatories, nay, and examined of the whole course of their lives." Yet the same source tells us that the defendant was examined on a written complaint or bill which had to state the matter charged with specificity; and, in his written reply, he might, with the advice of counsel, demur for many reasons, among them "that the matter in charge tendeth to accuse the defendant of some crime which may be capital; in which case *nemo tenetur prodere seipsum.* . . ." Hudson even stated, "neither must it question the party to accuse him of crime," indicating that the court respected the principle enough, at least on occasion, to extend it. That extension had only such meaning, however, as the court chose to give it, for at its discretion, whether in matters involving the state or in any ordinary case when the prisoner was disrespectful or unco-operative, the court might browbeat and trap him into a confession. On the other hand the rule *nemo tenetur* was faithfully extended to witnesses. They must be sworn, but they could not be compelled to incriminate themselves or even to answer a question that was prejudicial to themselves or revealed infamy which could not be the basis of a prosecution.[32]

The prime significance of the opinions of the common-law judges in the trial of Vaux and Tresham is to be found in the breadth with which they stated the general principle, not in the exceptions to it in Star Chamber practice. The law forbade a man to accuse himself in a case of life or limb and, therefore, would not compel him to swear against himself. The law of which they spoke was obviously not Star Chamber law; it could only be common law, embodying, very generally, what Tresham had called "the lawe of nature and Gods lawe." Yet common-law procedure gave little more force to the nebulous maxim than Star Chamber procedure. Felony and treason trials remained characteristically an altercation between the accused and the prosecution, with every bit of evidence, every question, and every assertion a means of bringing the prisoner to his confession or throwing him on his defense to rebut the crimination. Even a constitutional right, explicitly recognized and ritualistically reaffirmed, may have merely parchment vitality. Yet, genuine substance and practical application, however much they lag behind, can never evolve without prior recognition of the principle itself. Chief Justice Dyer's opinions in Leigh's case and in Tresham's showed that the principle, even if hollow, was coming to the surface of legal consciousness. At this very time, the preliminary examination of suspects before justices of the peace, which had been authorized by acts of 1553 and 1554, was becoming quite inquisitorial in nature. While the prisoner was not put to his oath when placed on trial, we do not know whether justices of the peace used the oath at the very initiation of a common-law prosecution. If the practice ever existed, it was unauthorized and regarded as improper; it soon came to be regarded as illegal. In 1583, Sir Anthony Fitzherbert's manual for justices of the peace declared that no man should be examined on oath on matters sounding to his reproach, such as whether he had committed a crime, because the law assumes that no man is obliged to accuse himself. The first edition of William Lambard's very popular *Eirenarcha, or the Office of the Justice of the Peace,* 1581, had nothing on this subject, but the second edition, in 1588, carried the *nemo tenetur* maxim, popularizing it for every petty magistrate and lawyer in England.[33]

Although the anti-Catholic inquisitions and persecutions of the Elizabethan period provoked some modestly fruitful protests against compulsory self-incrimination, generally speaking the law was changed in no fundamental way. The effect was little more than a ripple on the Thames from a stone that is skipped across its surface and then sinks. As long as England believed that its national security and the personal security of the queen depended upon the maintenance of a single religion by law established, as long as complete conformity was thought to be indispensable for the support of that religion, and as long as Catholicism was regarded with political overtones directly menacing the sovereign's spiritual supremacy, there could not only be no forbearance in the government's policy against recusants and priests; the law would be made to bend to the state's needs. The slight value attached to the *nemo tenetur* maxim at this period is nowhere better illustrated than by an act of Parliament in 1593 against "Popish recusants." By an act of 1585 Parliament had banished all priests and by an unprecedented inflation of the law of high treason had attainted every English priest as a traitor. The act of 1593, whose main provisions restricted recusants to an area within five miles of their homes, contained a vicious clause of compulsory self-incrimination to supplement the act of 1585. It declared that any person suspected of being a "jesuit, seminary or massing priest" who on examination refused to answer "directly and truly whether he be a Jesuit or a seminary or massing priest," should be imprisoned without bail until he did answer. Because the state deemed Catholics its enemies, priests especially, Catholic opposition to compulsory self-incrimination could not possibly have the effect of similar opposition from Protestant victims of the established church.[34]

CHAPTER IV

Whitgift and the High Commission

Although the Anglican Church under Elizabeth kindled no flames to burn men's bodies—Anabaptists always excepted—it ignited no fires in their hearts either. The Puritan minority charged quite accurately that the ritual, doctrine, and government of the established church had been dictated by political considerations as much as by religious ones. They would not submit to the destruction of true religion simply to uphold royal supremacy, nor would they permit a political church to compel them in matters of faith. The scepter, they believed, could not and should not command conscience—not theirs, anyway. Such views embarrassed and perplexed the government, although the queen herself, a Tudor autocrat who was personally conservative in matters of religion—she kept a crucifix and candles in the royal chapel—had enough cold steel in her makeup to overcome any scruples against persecution. In 1566, for example, when Archbishop Matthew Parker advised her that the Puritans would rather go to jail than conform, she replied coldly, "imprison them." [1]

The problem of the Puritans could not be remedied so summarily. The queen's resolution was weakened by the fact that for a Protestant state, threatened at home and abroad by Romanists, the suppression of Protestants was impolitic. Suppression might depreciate popular support for the religious settlement of 1559, give aid and comfort to the enemy, deprive the government of the services of the most frenetic anti-Catholics in the country, and distress their sympathizers in the government itself. Church and state were, in fact, honeycombed with Puritan sympathizers, who included members of the ecclesiastical hierarchy, Parliament, and even the Privy Council. William Cecil, later Lord Burghley, the queen's most trusted advisor and powerful minister, had Puritan kinfolk and tempered anti-Puritan policies by his personal intervention in behalf of Puritan ministers. Francis Walsingham, Walter Mildmay, Francis Knollys, the Earls of Leicester, Huntington, and Warwick, and other councilors were even closer to the Puritan movement. They preoccupied themselves with the problem of Catholic recusants and turned a blind eye toward the Puritan fox in the Anglican chicken-coop. They were men who prided themselves on their broadmindedness. They could turn up the rack a notch to stretch a priest and walk away from the Tower satisfied in the belief that justice was done in England for the preservation of public and Christian peace, against "Stirrers of Sedition, and Adherents to the Traytours and Enemies of the Realme, without any Persecution of them for Questions of Religion." Desperately wishing never to have to persecute, they believed that they were quite successful in that objective. Lord Burghley summed up the government's position, in 1583, when he wrote that many subjects of the realm differed in religious opinions from the Church of England and did not hesitate to profess their differences, "yet, in that they doe also professe loyaltie and obedience to her majestie, and offer readily, in her majesties defense, to impugne and resist any forreine Force, though it should come, or be procured, from the pope himself; none of these sort are, for their contrary opinions in religion, prosecuted, or charged with any crymes or paines of Treason, nor yet willinglie searched in their consciences for their contrarie opinions, that favour not of treason." [2]

The government's policy inadvertently nourished the steady growth of Puritanism, though its adherents, especially outside of London and Cambridge, were numerically an insignificant minority. The Archbishop of Canterbury in 1584 estimated that only slightly more than 6 per cent of the ordained ministers in the Church of England were Puritan recusants, but his figures were misleading and did not reveal the influence or importance of the Puritans. Although they formed no distinct party, were few in numbers, and embraced a variety of discontents, they constituted a grave threat to the establishment, in political as well as religious terms. As A. G. Dickens said, "Whereas the Catholics were dangerous to Elizabeth through external forces, the Puritan problem remained internal, not only to English society but to the English Church itself. And that Puritanism contained heavier explosive charges than Catholicism, the history of the seventeenth century was to demonstrate." [3]

There were, generally, three groups to whom the name "Puritan" might apply—the low-church Episcopalians who desired greater liturgical reforms, the Presbyterian theocrats who would subordinate the state to a Calvinist sanhedrin, and the Separatists who would secede altogether from the national church to form independent congregations. The first group, which was by far the largest, included many bishops of the establishment, even Edmund Grindal, the Bishop of London who, after Parker's death in 1575, became Archbishop of Canterbury. Out of obedience to his sovereign, he grudgingly conformed by wearing a surplice and cope which he regarded as "Romish dregs." Such men deplored the excesses of the intransigent Presbyterians, but in many respects sympathized with them, favoring a policy of leniency and reasoning in place of a harsh crackdown. For simplicity's sake the name "Puritan" as used here will refer henceforth to the two Nonconformist groups only, the Presbyterians and the Separatists. Only they were a source of such anguish and apprehension to the government, destroying its hope that no Protestants would disturb the waters of the establishment by making ripples of seditious factionalism. They did it "not of contempt," as one Puritan told the Court of High Commission in 1574, "but of conscience"—and that was exactly what made them so formidable, so intractable, and so impossible to deal with, except by coercion.[4]

The archetypal Anglican cleric was, by comparison with his Puritan counterpart, a rather easy-going, practical man of affairs, more this-worldly than other-worldly. He had little of the self-righteousness, militancy, and doctrinal rigidity of the Puritan, tending rather to a latitudinarianism in viewpoint and temperament. He could be reasonable and realistic, able to compromise even on matters of religion, to tolerate differences, and to yield gracefully to the needs of the state. The Puritan, with his arrogant certainty that he and he alone knew the ultimate truth and sole way of salvation, was insufferable to all but another true believer. His faith was a seven-day-a-week, not just a Sunday, affair; he was seized by religious compulsions that penetrated to the depths of his being and barred all other considerations. To an Anglican, he was in a most literal sense a disagreeable person, something of a fanatic and a bigot to boot. The Puritan had a passion, a fierce dedication, and a sense of his own absolute infallibility that passed all Anglican understanding. Incapable of compromise, the Puritan made the slightest deviation from his own exact shade of belief an occasion of contention, and he argued his holy cause so aggressively that he was probably unaware that his language was abusive, rasping, and even libelous. He was, as the name implied, a literal-minded purist who must emancipate the church from every vestige of papistry until there remained only the pure essence of the scripturally approved religion. Church polity, forms of worship, and articles of belief must exactly conform with the Word, as the Puritan understood it. In his view the Anglicans had taken out the stump, but left the root of Catholicism. Anything short of total reformation was not only un-Christian; it was the work of the devil or the pope, and a man of God compromised with neither.

The pamphlet war between Thomas Cartwright and John Whitgift during the 1570's pitted against each other two men who would become rival leaders in the critical years ahead. Their respective styles and thought epitomized the establishment and its principal Protestant opposition. The controversy, showing that a collision course was inevitable, illuminated the government's reasons for believing that it had no alternative to outright suppression. Not the least of the results of that controversy was the emergence of the claim that forcing a man to accuse himself abridged the great charter of English liberties.[5]

Cartwright's biographer called him the "Master Puritan." He almost gave his name to the entire movement; for a while, the Puritans were known as Cartwrightians. Richard Bancroft, who became Bishop of London and Archbishop of Canterbury, when charged with the task of detecting Puritan conspiracies for the

Court of High Commission, described him as "the Patriarche" of the Puritans and "their cheifest counsaylor." Years later the Massachusetts patriarch, John Cotton, remarked that the "form of Church-government wherein we walk doth not differ in substance from that which Mr. Cartwright pleaded." In 1570, before Cartwright reached his great prominence, John Whitgift, the Vice Chancellor of Cambridge University, deprived him of his post as Lady Margaret Professor of Divinity for having advocated presbyterian views, and two years later drove him out of the university for the same reason by depriving him of his Trinity College fellowship. When the Admonition Controversy was touched off in 1572 by a Puritan manifesto calling on Parliament to introduce a Calvinist reformation of the national church, it was Whitgift who was called upon by the Anglican divines to reply and Cartwright who responded for the Puritans. Their controversy continued, flaring up again and again, through 1577, even after Cartwright was driven into exile.[6]

The controversy had begun over externals such as proper clerical attire—"indifferent" matters as Whitgift called them, but to Cartwright who took his religion so seriously, nothing was indifferent. He railed and thundered in a way that mystified Whitgift. The prayer book, which Cartwright found to be an abomination, was admittedly not perfect, but though it could be improved, Whitgift thought it was a godly book. Whatever "imperfections, or rather motes, that you say to be in it," Whitgift added, were not such "that any godly man ought to stir up any contention in the church for them, much less to make a schism and least of all to divide himself from the church." Kneeling at communion, which Cartwright denounced as a "show of papistry," was in Whitgift's mind merely an appropriate way of receiving the sacrament. "The only peril," he said sensibly, "is adoration, which may as well be committed sitting as standing." The Church of England, he declared, had abandoned many Catholic rites and ceremonies, but those which were "godly and pertain to order and decency" did not have to be rejected also. Nor could Whitgift understand Cartwright's claim that a particular form of liturgy and a presbyterian governance of the church were necessary for salvation. The argument that the Scriptures sanctioned only one ecclesiastical polity, one form of worship, and one set of ceremonies was in Whitgift's mind simply unsound; the Bible was silent on many controversial matters, leaving to the church a wide latitude of discretion. The differences between the two men reflected the literalism and rigidity of the one, the comparative tolerance and imprecision of the other. Anglican tolerance, like Anglican doctrine, was equivocal, however. Whitgift was capable on the one hand of offering the Puritans "all kinds of friendliness" —on Anglican terms—"if you could be content to conform yourselves; yea, but to be quiet and hold your peace." On the other hand the Puritans gave the Anglicans the uneasy feeling that they had best do unto the Puritans before they were done unto. For the security of church and state, it seemed to be wise policy not to be overtolerant to the intolerant.[7]

If the wheel of fortune turned, bringing the Puritans into power, the Anglicans believed that they might be treated with as little mercy as the Puritans proposed for the Catholics, blasphemers, heretics, and idolators. Cartwright advocated that heretics and schismatics should be "beaten into the dust." He proposed a reconstruction of the state along Old Testament lines, as he understood the Old Testament, making the state an instrument of church policy, obligated to execute the will of ecclesiastical leaders. In accordance with the old punitive laws, blasphemers and idolaters, that is, Catholics, as well as murderers and adulterers were to be put to death by the secular arm at the command of God. All who "contemn the worde," meaning all who resisted the Puritan discipline, must be put to death; all who neglected the word must die also. Cartwright and his followers would have executed the Catholic priests not because they were traitors but because they were priests. False prophets and teachers, he argued, must pay the capital penalty. If his views "be bloudie and extreme," he wrote grimly, "I am contente to be so counted with the holie goste." Repelled by Cartwright's bloody view of the scriptures, Whitgift would let the civil magistrates interpret the Mosaic laws. As for himself, he thought the law of God, like God himself, was merciful, preferring always that sinners be purged by repentence than be condemned. Cartwright replied, "I denie that uppon repentance, ther owghte to followe any pardon off death, whiche the Judiciall lawe dothe require." Interspersed with such views were epithets against the establishment, describing its prelates as "Romish" and "un-Christian," its prayer book as a "popish dunghill," and its rites as "papistical idolatry." [8]

The Puritans would have tried the patience of a saint. When the Anglicans, who were too practical to be saintly, remembered that the Puritans regarded them as scarcely better than Catholics, they could envision their fate if Cartwright and his followers had the power to try them. Had Cartwright's views prevailed, oppressors and victims would have changed places, with this difference: as Cartwright's sympathetic biographer acknowledged, "If in power, the Elizabethan Puritans would doubtless have excelled in intolerance the authorities whose regime they denounced." [9]

Intolerence, inflexibility, and insult widened the breach between Puritanism and the establishment, but did not make it irreparable. Insubordination did that, willful and contumacious insubordination that appeared to be disloyalty. What had begun as opposition to things "indifferent"—the crucifix, organ music, and the surplice—became seditious, ending with a repudiation of the royal supremacy. The Puritan stance openly affronted the queen. If nothing was indifferent to the Puritans in matters of religion, nothing was indifferent to her in matters of politics, above all when her sovereignty seemed to be at issue. To be sure, Cartwright and his followers professed the utmost allegiance, disavowing all imputations of subversion, no doubt with the utmost sincerity. Although they advocated radical changes in the ecclesiastical polity, they did so by peaceable, constitutional means. But the queen looked at the ends as well as the means, and realized that the triumph of Puritanism promised the subordination of state to church. The relationship of state and church was indeed at the bottom of the conflict, making the political implications of Puritanism a menace to the crown. As Elizabeth explained to King James of Scotland, who was destined to become her successor, it was best to "stop the mouthes" of those who pretended merely religious differences and dissembled devotion while they really aimed at the throne: ". . . let me warne you that ther is risen, bothe in your realme and in myne, a secte of perilous consequence, suche as wold have no kings but a presbitrye, and take our place while the[y] injoy our privilige, with a shade of godes word, wiche non is juged to folow right without by ther censure the[y] be so demed." [10]

The Puritan assault on the Erastian character of the Church of England did unmistakably assault the sovereign. Anglican authorities immediately understood this when Cartwright, in his Lady Margaret lectures, had first advanced the propositions that Whitgift catalogued for the Council's inspection—that the offices of archbishops and archdeacons should be suppressed, that the church should be restored to its apostolic condition, that its government should be lodged in the control of its ministers and elders, and that the ministers should be free from ordination by bishops and should be chosen by their congregations. William Chaderton, the Regius Professor of Divinity, summed up the matter by reporting to Lord Burghley that Cartwright intended "to overturne and overthrow all ecclesiasticall and civill governance that now is, and to ordeyn and institute a new founde pollicie. . . ." A few years later, when Cartwright had further explained the Puritan position during the Admonition Controversy, Bishop Edward Sandys, bringing Whitgift's list up to date, ticked off the first ruinous demand as, "The civil magistrate has no authority in ecclesiastical matters." [11]

Assailing the prelates and the governance of the church necessarily brought the logical Puritans into conflict with the Supreme Governor of the Church. Elizabeth and her prelates believed that the state should control the church chiefly in the interests of secular policy. Cartwright, however, argued that the "commonwealth must agree with the church, and the government thereof with her government." Sovereigns or civil magistrates, he contended, should govern only "according to the rules of God prescribed in his word . . . they be servants unto the church, and as they rule in the church, so they must remember to subject themselves unto the church, to submit their sceptres, to throw down their crowns before the church, yea, as the prophet speaketh, to lick the dust of the feet of the church." The church alone could construe the Scriptures, fix ceremonies, and determine ecclesiastical policy; the function of the civil government was to enforce what the church commanded in religious matters, not to dictate matters of faith to the faithful. Christ alone was head of the church; the queen was but the titular head and a member of it, subject to its discipline like any member, even to censure and excommunication. When Whitgift rejoined that Cartwright would strip the queen of all authority "both in ecclesiastical and civil matters," Cartwright admitted that though her authority was the greatest on earth, it was not infinite; rather, it was "limited by the word of God"—as the presbytery defined that word. Men were beginning to say the same thing even on the floor of Parliament. In 1571, for example, during the debate on a bill to reform the Book of Common Prayer along Puritan lines, Christopher Yelverton, one of the Puritan supporters, attacked the episcopacy and had the effrontery to declare that it was "treason" to say that Parliament could not limit the crown: "He shewed it was fit, princes to have their prerogatives; but yet the same to be straitened within reasonable limits. The prince, he shewed, could not of herself make laws. Neither might she by the same reason break laws." The menace of such logic was self-evident.[12]

Whitgift read Cartwright on the duty of the sovereign to submit crown and scepter to the presbyterian discipline, and immediately recognized something all too familiar: "I have read it in the books of the papists." The similarity, however paradoxical, between Roman Catholic and Puritan doctrine was startling to the establishment. Papists and Puritans, reported Archbishop Parker to Lord Burghley, "have one mark to shoot at, plain disobedience." Both agreed on the supremacy of church over state and the duty of the latter to promote the true religion as determined by the former, whose word was final. Both claiming to know the sole path of salvation found it outside the national church. Both affirmed the authority of the church to censure and excommunicate its Supreme Governor. Both abused her ecclesiastical polity as that of the anti-Christ. Both engaged in recusant conspiracies. When Parliament again considered reformation of the church along Puritan lines, Whitgift declared that passage of the bill would overthrow the government in some respects, shake it in others, and greatly endanger it in still others. The injury would be "especially to her Majesty . . . to her supremacy, to her strength, and to her person." Elaborating his point, he asked, rhetorically, "For, I pray you, wherein differ these men, in this case, from the Papists? The Pope denyeth the supremacy of princes: so do, in effect, these. The Pope yieldeth to them only *postestatem facti, non juris, non causas* [power to execute but not to make laws]. No more do our Reformers in this point. The Pope where he entreth, doth abrogate al such laws as any prince hath made in Church matters, to his dislike. And so would these men. . . ." That the government was harsh with the Puritans, as with the Catholics, was the result of their political, not their religious, doctrines, although to the victims, there was no distinction between the two.[13]

In 1572–73 the government curbed and muzzled the Puritans. Elizabeth issued a proclamation against "despisers" and "breakers" of the Book of Common Prayer; the Privy Council ordered Archbishop Parker to enforce uniformity and, in Parker's words, "to cause diligent inquisition to be made"; and the Ecclesiastical Commission issued warrants for the arrest of Puritan leaders. Their secret press was discovered and smashed, some ministers were deprived, others imprisoned. Cartwright himself fled into exile to escape the wrath of the government. For a time the Puritans were scattered and intimidated, but not silenced; they continued their struggle against the establishment by underground organization and answered the episcopacy from abroad. Their most effective tactic was to spread the word during meetings of the local clergy which were held for purposes of group study and discussion, ostensibly to correct clerical ignorance. These meetings or "prophesyings" soon came to the government's attention, and Elizabeth demanded their suppression. But she lacked a prelate of iron to enforce her will.[14]

Archbishop Parker, whom the Puritans had offended, had recognized that under color of reformation, they not only "cut down the ecclesiastical state, but also give a push at the civil policy." He might have aided the queen, but he died in 1575. Edmund Grindal, the new Archbishop of Canterbury, did his best to regulate the prophesyings, ordering, for example, that no one should "glance" against the state or "invect" against the established church. But Grindal was ineffective. He was a gentle person who believed in the value of debate and reasoned conviction; suppression was contrary to his nature, the prophesyings a means, in his view, of reforming the clergy. Seeing some good in Puritanism, he thought he could control it in the best interests of the church. Elizabeth, wanting only obedience and uniformity, had no patience with Grindal's temporizing and moderate course. She ordered him to end the prophesyings at once, whereupon Grindal appalled her by replying as a Puritan divine might. In an elaborate letter in 1576 he lectured to her interminably on religion and on her duty to the church, reminding her that in religious matters she must defer to her bishops as she deferred to her judges on legal matters. Worse still he reminded her that in religious matters she should not make pronouncements "too resolutely and peremptorily," for it was "the antichristian voice of the Pope" to command as if mortal will should take the place of reason or the will of God. "Remember, Madam, that you are a mortal creature," he advised, "And although ye are a mighty Prince, yet remember that he which dwelleth in heaven is mightier." He was forced, he concluded, by his conscience and the fear of offending God, to withhold consent from the suppression of the prophesyings. Elizabeth, in a fury, confined Grindal to Lambeth Palace and suspended his authority; he remained obdurate till he died in 1583.[15]

During that anomalous period when the church had an Archbishop of Canterbury in name only, the energies of the government were given over to the task of suppressing Catholic recusants and the missionary priests. Puritanism, nourished by popular hatred of Rome, regained its lost ground and threatened to undermine the authority of the English church. Grindal's power having devolved on various subordinates, the queen's ecclesiastical commissioners were bereft of effectual leadership. The Bishop of London, John Aylmer, whom Elizabeth made head of the Commission, was a mortal enemy of Puritanism; but he was also a weak and corrupt sycophant who was despised by the Privy Council. Burghley, who was not keen on suppressing the Puritans when the Romanist crisis was most acute, outfoxed and stymied Aylmer who feared him. As Marshall M. Knappen wrote, Aylmer's proposals to purge London of the Puritan ministers and institute a system of espionage by the Ecclesiastical Commission were "lost in the bottomless depths of Burghley's chests," and when Aylmer sought to exercise the powers of the Commission, Burghley scared him off, warning him not to meddle or do anything that would create in the Privy Council displeasure against him or his ecclesiastical commissioners. Aylmer, abjectly and with much fawning, submitted; and the Commission remained a tool of the Council's anti-Catholicism, toothless against the Puritans. Elizabeth knew what policies she wanted her government to follow against them, but without aggressive support from her leaderless church and commissioners, her Council subtly thwarted her. In 1583 the death of Grindal, who had been recommended by Burghley, gave her the opportunity of chosing as his successor a primate to her own liking: John Whitgift, since 1577 the formidable Bishop of Worcester.[16]

Whitgift was one of those rare men of whom it may truly be said that he had a palpable effect upon the course of history in his own time. He saved the Elizabethan religious settlement by ruthlessly doing what had to be done to break the Puritan movement. He was perfectly equipped for the task. He knew the Puritans better and had greater experience with them than any other man in the establishment. More important he had a grim sense of mission, convinced as he was that the Puritans, if not crushed, would overthrow his church, his state, and his queen. Although remorseless, choleric, and humorless, Whitgift was neither an intolerant fanatic by conviction, nor a cruel tyrant by nature. He had been entrusted by his beloved queen with a responsibility which he meant to discharge with his usual single-minded devotion to purpose, unflinching resolution, and unbelievable industry. A man of keen intelligence and superb administrative talents, he was bold in the use of power. No man was more efficient, nor less vulnerable to personal attack. A bachelor who gave his life to the service of the queen's church, he was utterly incorruptible and led a blameless private life. He saw eye to eye with Elizabeth who fondly called him her "little black husband." She favored him in many ways, with visits to Lambeth Palace, with an unprecedented appointment to her Privy Council, and with unflagging endorsement despite his detractors among her courtiers and councilors. Whitgift had the courage to stand against them, almost alone, bulwarked by the queen's support. Other men respected or feared him, but they did not like him nor want him as an enemy.

The Puritans, enemies of the establishment, saw Whitgift as their foremost persecutor and understandably hated him. A distinguished Anglican historian alleged that during the Archbishop's lifetime he was "consistently misrepresented by his enemies, so he has been persistently misjudged by posterity." Henry Barrow, the Separatist leader, described Whitgift as "a monster, a miserable compound, I know not what to make him; he is neither ecclesiastical or civil, even that second beast spoken of in the Revelation." "Martin Marprelate," the pseudonymous Puritan pamphleteer, wrote that "John of Kankerbury" and his "swinish rabble" of bishops, "are petty Antichrists, petty Popes, proud Prelates, enemies to the Gospel, and most covetous wretched Priests." Reserving for Whitgift alone other choice denunciations, the Puritans claimed that he was more tyrannous than Bloody Bonner, a brother to Haman, Lucifer incarnate. Whig historians sound little different, one calling Whitgift "an inquisitor as merciless as Torquemada," another describing him as "narrow-minded to an almost incredible degree," and a third holding him up as a "mean and tyrannical priest, who gained power by servility and adulation, and employed it in persecuting both those who had agreed with Calvin about Church Government, and those who differed from Calvin touching the doctrine of Reprobation." [17]

Even discounting the hyperbolic quality of these characterizations, the principal criticism to be made of them is not that they were wrong, but that they were not to the point. Whitgift should not be faulted for having done his job exceedingly well, but, rather, for having misconceived his job. Like his queen he lacked a statesman's vision where the Puritans were concerned. He knew how to crush, but not to build; he knew how to cope with an emergency, but not how to provide for the future; he knew how to best the enemy by draconian means, but not how to siphon off its popular support and render it impotent; and he knew how to spot a genuine enemy—the Separatists, who, unlike the Presbyterians, rejected the national church—but he did not know how to ignore their pipsqueak claim to the discovery of a heaven below as well as above. Whitegift was no fool; on the contrary he was a crafty politician. But as a statesman seeking a solution that would be durable after he and Elizabeth were dust-unto-dust, his judgment was bad. Worse still he had learned too little from Foxe's

Book of Martyrs. He should have learned that heresy can not be permanently suppressed. Yet few had learned that.

Whitgift should have stolen the Puritan's thunder, leaving the Presbyterians, like the Separatists, an extremist sect of crabbed ministers without a constituency worthy of the government's attention. All the "popish dregs" that Whitgift had admitted were "indifferent" matters, and there were a score or more—the matrimonial ring, the organ music, the sign of the cross in baptism, kneeling at communion, the priestly garments, the unleavened bread, and the like—should have been expunged from the Church of England. That is, the reformation should have been extended as to liturgy, ceremonials, and symbols, if in fact they were indifferent. The Anglican *via media*, being far to the right of continental varieties of Protestantism, left many English Protestants uneasy conformists and an influential minority of them disaffected. Stern puritanism in matters indifferent would have solidified the Protestant character of the Church of England, setting it off more sharply from Roman Catholicism. If the fear of an international conspiracy of the Catholic powers was so great, if the dread of a Catholic restoration was so real, and if the question of the succession was so unsettled, particularly as long as Mary Stuart of Scotland lived (she was not executed until 1586, after being held prisoner for eighteen years), self-interest called for further reformation of the national church. The clergy had shown themselves to be wholly unreliable; under Henry VIII, Edward VI, Mary, and Elizabeth, the clergy donned and shed their religion at the dictates of the crown. By contrast, Parliament and people preferred further reformation, and no one was more eager to live and die for Protestantism than a Puritan. Half measures made the religious settlement unstable, liable to regression; more thorough measures would have enlisted greater commitment. Had the government supported further reformation in things indifferent, drawing the line against Presbyterian polity and intolerance, it could have removed the fangs of Presbyterianism. Popular sympathy for Cartwright's demand for purified church rites did not extend to his demand for a reformed church polity. Because the Elizabethan settlement was primarily political, it would have been politic to yield in indifferent matters, for the greater security of the realm, the queen, and the national church. But Whitgift and Elizabeth were of a different mind.

Even before his solemn confirmation in September 1583 as the seventy-second Archbishop of Canterbury, Whitgift busied himself with plans for ferreting out Puritans and expelling them from the ministry of the Church of England. With the queen's approval he framed a series of injunctions calculated to enforce uniformity in accord with the Book of Common Prayer. The sixth was the sticking point: no one would henceforth be permitted to preach, minister the sacraments, or perform any ecclesiastical function unless he first subscribed to three articles before the ordinary—the bishop or archdeacon—of his diocese. The second of these articles was utterly obnoxious to the Puritans, because it declared that that repository of so many indifferent matters, the Book of Common Prayer, like the episcopal structure, "containeth nothing in it contrary to the word of God." The same article also provided that all ministers should use only that book for prayer and the administration of the sacraments "and none other." No Puritan could subscribe without being "killed in his soul," yet anyone not subscribing would lose his living and his ministry. Within a month of Whitgift's enthronement as primate, he instructed his bishops that with the queen's gracious assent and allowance, his injunctions were to be enforced. A few weeks later, on the silver anniversary of Elizabeth's coronation as queen, the archbishop preached in St. Paul's, before a magnificent state assemblage, on the text "Put them in rememberance to be subject unto principalities and powers, to obey magistrates." Classifying the wayward, contentious persons within the church as a disobedient group not unlike Papists and Anabaptists, he declared that they contemned magistrates, obeyed only whom they pleased and what they wanted, "and al because they cannot be governours themselves." [18]

Whitgift was too able an administrator simply to make speeches, issue injunctions, and rely on subordinates to execute them. Others had done the same with little effect. He realized that he needed a centralized engine of enforcement which he himself might direct. Precedent provided the device of a special commission from the crown. Under authority of the Act of Supremacy, Elizabeth had issued letters patent in 1559, 1562, 1572, and 1576, creating commissioners for ecclesiastical causes who had rendered invaluable assistance to the Privy Council and Court of Star Chamber by policing the Elizabethan religious settlement. The ecclesiastical commissioners, although vested with independent and virtually discretionary authority over offenses of religion, functioned under orders of the Privy Council. Exercising little discretion in practice, the commissioners possessed jurisdiction, followed procedure, and fixed penalties as directed. When the Privy Council wanted an investigation conducted into the activities of a suspected nest of Catholic recusants, or wanted to know why members of the Inns of Court failed to attend Sunday services, the ecclesiastical commissioners acted. They supervised the administration of the oath of supremacy under the Act of Supremacy and the collection of fines for recusancy under the Act of Uniformity. They also "deprived," or removed from office, clerics who failed to conform. The main target of the various ecclesiastical commissions under Elizabeth had been the Catholic recusant, although there had also been a few notable cases involving Puritan Nonconformists. The repression of 1572–73, following the "Admonition to Parliament," had, for example, been conducted by the ecclesiastical commissioners. In addition to such duties, the Privy Council increasingly directed them to decide certain ecclesiastical cases which occasionally came before the Council, involving such matters as divorce, fornication, adultery, assault, perjury, wills, and disorderly conduct.[19]

Until Whitgift's time the Ecclesiastical Commission was less an institution than an *ad hoc* instrument of state policy on ecclesiastical affairs. Although chiefly an executive agency of discipline and suppression, it was nevertheless developing a distinct judicial character. The Commission of 1572 was the first to include more clergymen and civil lawyers than state dignitaries like the Lord Mayor, the Chancellor of the Exchequer, the Treasurer of the Queen's Household, the Recorder of London, the common-law judges, and privy councilors. By the time Whitgift became Archbishop of Canterbury, the commissioners, under the influence of members who were bishops and civil lawyers, were developing a somewhat regularized procedure, which followed that of the ordinary ecclesiastical courts, and the bulk of their work was made up of suits between private persons who sought relief that could not be obtained as efficiently or authoritatively in the ordinary ecclesiastical courts.[20]

As early as 1570 the Privy Council referred to the commissioners as a court of law, and the letters patent creating the Commission of 1576 were the first to mention its "judgments" as well as its orders and decrees. By that time the Commission was being referred to as "the High Commission" and the phrase denoted a court of law. Eventually it evolved into a permanent institution, the Court of High Commission for Ecclesiastical Causes, with regularized sessions and a fixed procedure. By 1583, however, it had not achieved either permanence or regularity, nor was it powerful in its own right either as a court or as an executive agency charged with the suppression of nonconformity, schism, recusancy, or heresy. It was still very much a creature of the Privy Council, subject to its will and dominance. While Grindal was titular Archbishop of Canterbury and Aylmer headed the High Commission, Burghley was its real master. Puritan victims of the High Commission successfully appealed to the Privy Council for relief from its vexations, detentions, fines, and deprivations, with the result that the Council hobbled the Commission, leaving it demoralized. When Whitgift became archbishop he found a languishing body.[21]

Whitgift saw in the High Commission the instrument which he might convert to suit his needs and execute his policies. It offered the possibility of independence from the Council, the machinery of enforcement, and mastery of a court of law which was becoming England's supreme ecclesiastical court. Accordingly, he recommended the issuance of new letters patent creating a fresh commission. He argued that it was needed because it could punish criminally, by fines and imprisonment, while the ordinary ecclesiastical courts could merely employ ecclesiastical censures. The High Commission, moreover, had jurisdiction over the entire realm, so "if any such notorious offender fly the diocese of his Ordinary, he cannot be gotten to be punished but by the said commission." A third reason for renewing the High Commission, Whitgift argued, was that it searched for unlawful books and examined their writers, printers, and sellers "upon their oaths."

Another reason was, "Disordered persons (commonly called Puritans) contemn the censures ecclesiastical. So that the realm will swarm with them, if they be not met withal by the commission." It alone could punish notorious faults in members of the clergy. "The whole ecclesiastical law," concluded Whitgift, was "a carcasse without a soul," if its wants were not remedied by a new commission.[22]

Before 1583 came to an end, Whitgift had what he wanted. The new High Commission, like its recent predecessors, included about forty-four men; but the canon and civil lawyers for the first time overwhelmingly outnumbered the usual state dignitaries and representatives of the common law by more than three to one. Backed up by a dozen bishops and a score of deans, archdeacons, and civil lawyers, Whitgift, the new President of the High Commission, was in complete control. The archbishop and only two others constituted a quorum for conducting business; in practice only a few others attended meetings regularly. The influence of Whitgift, a couple of bishops, and several civil lawyers of unusual ability—Richard Bancroft, Gabriel Goodman, William Aubery, Richard Cosin, and Edward Stanhope—was predominant. Others sometimes attended when Whitgift, who decided the time of meetings and the agenda, summoned them.[23]

The new High Commission possessed an ecclesiastical jurisdiction and authority that was fettered only by its discretion. Its competence extended to violations of any statutes passed for the maintenance of religion and to all offenses punishable by ecclesiastical law. All such offenses might be tried by the ordinary ecclesiastical courts, but there were many circumstances warranting trial by the High Commission. The ordinary ecclesiastical court might be negligent in its duty, making redress possible only in the High Commission. Its intervention might be requested by a party or by a lower court Christian. The accused might have moved out of its jurisdiction or witnesses might live in different jurisdictions. Offenders might delay justice by frequent and frivolous appeals, or might require more severe treatment than ordinary ecclesiastical censure. An aggrieved party who had no remedy, or the credible information of some great personage, might move the Commission to take jurisdiction. It might do so on common report, or "fame," established by the information of persons taking offense, or if notorious suspicion (*clamosa insinuatio*) existed against someone. In addition to its jurisdiction over statutory crimes concerning religion and all usual cases of ecclesiastical law, the Commission was specifically empowered by its letters patent to act punitively against heretical opinions; seditious writings, contempts, and conspiracies; false rumors; and slanderous words. It was also enjoined to reform and restrain all religious errors, schisms, and recusancy, and to deprive any cleric who maintained any doctrine contrary to the Book of Common Prayer and the Thirty-nine Articles.[24]

The letters patent prescribed any procedure which the High Commission might wish to follow: it could operate with or without a jury (it never employed a jury), summon witnesses, or resort to "all other means and ways you can devise." According to their "wisdoms, consciences, and discretions," the judges might devise "all such lawful ways and means for the searching out of the premises," as they thought necessary. The one and only procedure that was recommended was examination of all suspects "on their corporal oaths, for the better trial and opening of the truth." Finally, the High Commission might punish by ecclesiastical censures, by fines "according to your discretions," or by imprisonment for indefinite periods. The penalties applied not only to those whom the High Commission found guilty, but to anyone not obeying its orders. Failure to appear when summoned, or to take the oath, or to answer truthfully, or to conform, could mean a crippling fine and jail. There the prisoner would remain until he yielded to the Commission's wishes or until it decided to release him.[25]

Even before the High Commission could get under way, complaints poured into the Privy Council from ministers who had been suspended or deprived because they refused to subscribe to the archbishop's three articles. One supplication was signed by twenty Norfolk ministers, another from Essex by twenty-seven, one from Kent by seventeen, and that from Lincolnshire by twenty-one. They all protested their loyalty to the queen and their reverence for the established church. Bemoaning that their consciences had been distressed, their livings taken away, and their parishioners left without shepherds, they declared their readiness to subscribe to all points of doctrine. They also pledged that they would make no disturbance in the church nor separate from it if only they were not forced to subscribe that all rites and ceremonies and the episcopal polity accorded with the word of God. They complained bitterly at their severe treatment under Whitgift, which they thought unwarranted since they were neither heretics nor schismatics. They and their parishioners besieged Burghley and other members of the Council with petitions for relief. Burghley, forwarding the petitions and protestations to the new archbishop—he had been primate for only three months—summoned him to appear before the Council to justify his conduct.[26]

Whitgift was not the sort of man who backed down or deferred. Instead of appearing in person, he wrote a long letter in which he justified his conduct by chiding the Council for its interference. Expressing resentment that the suspended ministers should have gone over his head by troubling the Council with a matter not "incident" to its business, he reminded Burghley and the others that the queen had been pleased to commit all ecclesiastical causes to him; he would "make answer to God and to her Majesty" as his office required. Nevertheless, he favored the Council with an explanation of his reasons for believing that the ministers were contentious, schismatic, and dangerous to the church, concluding that no encouragement should be given to their conspiracy. He could not be persuaded that their lordships had such an intent or that they meant to call his own doings into question. Having no judge but God and her Majesty, he would defend his three articles against anyone in England. The Council did not reply.[27]

Turning his attention to the High Commission, Whitgift quickly fixed upon a procedure which remained constant in dealings with the Puritans. It was, of course, the inquisitorial procedure of the canon law—*sans* torture—which had been gradually developing as the Commission's procedure for some years. Whitgift accelerated and regularized the trend which had been most pronounced in the strictly judicial work of the Commission when deciding suits between private parties. If a woman wished to prefer charges against her husband for adultery or someone wanted his neighbor punished for slander, the plaintiff, acting through counsel or the court's proctor, framed and signed a careful specification of his case. A member of the High Commission, on certifying the plaintiff's "articles," issued a writ commanding the defendant's appearance before it. If the crime alleged was "publikely offensive," or if the defendant was notorious or was a fugitive, the Commission issued a warrant for his arrest; after apprehension he would lie in Clink prison until his case came up, which might be weeks or years. When it did, he had to swear with his hand on the Bible to answer truthfully to any questions that might be asked. This, of course, was the oath *ex officio,* administered before the accused was told the identity of his accuser or the accusation. Richard Cosin, the Dean of Arches and a member of the Commission, explained that it required the defendant to take the oath to answer articles and interrogatories before they were revealed to him, because he might otherwise "answere cautelously, indirectly, or wholly to refuse to make answere; perhaps because he sees they touch him over neerely, as conjecturing by whom they may be prooved." The High Commission always proceeded *ex officio,* Cosin explained, so that it might exact the oath *ex officio,* as Cosin put it, "to the intent, he [the defendant] may not be privileged to say, that he is not bounde to answere; being at the suite of the *Office,* and duetie of the *Judge* (for the publique interest of the Church and Common-weale) as perhaps he might; if it were at first preferred and prosecuted by *a partie.*" [28]

As a matter of fact, most ordinary suits were first preferred and prosecuted by a party, but the procedure was more like the *denunciatio* than the *accusatio.* The High Commission termed it the *ex officio promoto,* a prosecution by the court at the instance and petition of someone who voluntarily will "stirre up and sollicite the Judge unto his duetie." After the defendant took his oath, he answered the articles in writing and without the advice of counsel. At that point, the person who had promoted the case re-entered it and took upon himself the burden of proof by witnesses; they too gave their evidence in writing. The defendant, at this stage acting through counsel, might submit interrogatories for the plaintiff and his witnesses, questioning their evidence. After all evidence was in, counsel on each side drew up briefs and the case went before the High Commission for a hearing, which consisted of a reading of the briefs and speeches by counsel. The opinions of the commissioners, given seriatim, were based on the canon-law system of legal proofs. Such, roughly, was the *ex officio promoto* proceeding.[29]

Related but quite different was the *ex officio mero* proceeding that Whitgift and the Commission employed mainly for Nonconformists. The accuser in this proceeding was the court itself which took the initiative of prosecuting without a private promoter. Such a proceeding had to be founded upon a presentment of some sort. It could be established by the court, to its own satisfaction, on suspicion aroused by the personal knowledge of the judges. It could also be established by "fame," by witnesses secured by the court, or by "notoritie of the facte"—the statements of informers, who must be "credible persons," touching the suspect's reputation. When the judge had such information "brought often to his eares," the presentment was said to be based on *clamosa insinuatio*. The suspect, on being cited for examination, was immediately put to his oath and could be required to answer touching the crime itself; but if the presentment had been founded upon *clamosa insinuatio*, the interrogatories could be aimed only at the circumstances of the crime but not the crime itself, unless the judge first examined neighbors and others to establish fame.

The court might, however, proceed with the oath and require answers to interrogatories touching the crime itself whether or not the requisite degree of suspicion existed, "albeit not warranted by lawe," admitted Cosin. If the defendant did not object, his consent was implied; if he did object, the court must be prepared to show the basis of the presentment. If the basis was "fame," the proof consisted in the fact that it was "blowen abroad" or "bruited about" by the locality. However, if the crime were of such a nature that only a few could know about it, as in the case of adultery, the few were sufficient to establish the fame. Mere rumor was insufficient, except in three instances: in the case of heresy, any sort of suspicion was adequate; when the government or any of its agencies, such as the High Commission itself, conducted a semi-executive inquiry, its disinterestedness and service to the public good justified its procedure; and when the purpose of the inquiry was not to punish but to reform the party spiritually "for his soules health." [30]

In effect, the High Commission operated on the principle that it never investigated a secret or "undreamed of" crime. In the case of such a crime, no man, generally speaking, would or could be put to the oath to furnish evidence of his own guilt. As the Commission reasoned, the mere fact that it was conducting an inquiry proved that its *ex officio mero* proceeding must be properly grounded on a suspicion supporting a presentment. If the defendant's complicity in the crime were really unknown, there could not be an inquiry. However, certain exceptions existed to the general principle, endorsed by St. Chrysostom, that a secret sin need not be published but, rather, could be left to God. A minister of God, for the good of his own conscience, must come forward to detect himself; if required by an ecclesiastical inquiry to take the oath and reveal whether he was guilty of any crime, he must submit. He had no right to refuse the oath even in the case of secret crime. The other exception was in any instance when by concealment of the offense "great perill doth growe, to the *church*," as in heresy, schism, or nonconformity. In such a case, when the Commission inquired into the state of the church, it could require oath and answer even from one whose crime was secret.[31]

Whitgift's rules requiring oath and answer were an iron-clad guarantee that no one, least of all a suspected Puritan, could make good a claim that he was not obligated to comply with the Commission's demands. Not only was Whitgift responsible for the stringency of the rules, although he had the aid, of course, of his civil and canon lawyers; his contribution also consisted in the fact that he regularized the Commission's procedure, making the oath *ex officio* compulsory. Previously, as Roland G. Usher, the historian of the Commission wrote, there were "very few traces of anything resembling a fixed procedure of any kind at the trials or hearings. The commissioners sat down before the culprit and questioned him as searchingly as their combined ingenuity could suggest. He replied as best he could, and the debate soon degenerated into a series of recriminations and insults in which the commissioners were not ordinarily victorious, if the Puritan version of these trials be correct. . . . No oaths were tendered to the Puritans. . . ." Usher referred to trials of 1567 and 1574 which made no mention of the oath. A trial of 1570 was even more revealing. The defendant, a Puritan clergyman named Axton, was asked what he thought of the episcopacy. "I may fall into danger by answering this question," he replied. A bishop said, "I may compel you to answer upon your oath," to which Axton rejoined, "But I may choose whether I will answer upon oath or not." The court made no further reference to the oath, continuing the examination without it. Trials just before and after 1580 mention its tender to the accused, but also made it clear that it was omitted if the defendants objected to it. The Commission claimed the right to use its discretion as to procedure, doffing its judicial robes at will and resuming its garb as inquisitorial visitors or quasi-executive inquirers who might freely improvise. "But," Usher added, "after 1583 we find the oath insisted upon as the cardinal point of procedure without which no trial could begin." Whitgift's innovation touched off the long and acrimonious struggle which eventually resulted in the right against self-incrimination.[32]

If the defendant refused to take the oath *ex officio*, the Commission found him guilty of the crime charged, according to Commissioner Cosin. Oaths to testify truthfully, he wrote, were "necessarie to be taken for if they be refused, being so tendered, he is overthrowen (in his cause) that refuseth; and is holden *pro confesso* and *convicto*," that is, as if he confessed and was convicted. In practice, however, refusal to swear the oath was punished as contempt of court. Cosin was more accurate, though inconsistent, when stating that for refusal the defendant was taken as "contumacious." Refusal to answer a "criminous interrogatory" was also, in practice, punishable as a contempt, though Cosin said that the defendant "may be proceeded against as convicted of so much, as he wilfully refuseth to answere." The distinction, perhaps, is without meaning since contempt could be punished by imprisonment for an indefinite period, at the pleasure of the Commission, or until the prisoner yielded.[33]

Insistence upon the oath, which was made the crux of the entire proceeding, was doubtless the result of the fact that under ecclesiastical law, unlike common law, conviction was extraordinarily difficult because of the need for "complete" proof of guilt in accordance with the stringent rules of "legal proof." As Cosin said, "For without the parties confession, or two witnesses; none may be absolutely convicted." Since the guilt of the Puritans for schism and nonconformity, and possibly for heresy, was an unquestioned article of faith in the minds of the commissioners, requiring, at the very least, suspension from the ministry under jeopardy of criminal penalties for violation, to admit to Puritan beliefs and practices was to convict oneself by providing the Commission with a confession. "And very often," wrote Cosin, "it falleth out, that by such oathe, the partie is drawn to discover his owne *dolum malum* [evil deeds], *covine* [secret conspiracies], *fraude*, or *mal-engine* . . . penall to himselfe." [34]

In the *ex officio promoto* proceeding, after the defendant took the oath and made written answer to the articles and interrogatories, he was virtually a nonparticipant during the remainder of the trial. By contrast, in the inquisitorial proceeding conducted by the Commission *ex officio mero*, which was the form always followed if the crime of Puritanism was alleged, the examination of the defendant was virtually the entire trial, and the main evidence consisted of his answers. Usher's description of a trial in the period before Whitgift's primacy applies with equal accuracy to the period after 1583. Refusal to take the oath would lead to a wrangle about its morality or legality, with the Commission attempting to overawe the defendant into submission by threats of dire consequences. If the defendant remained obstinate, they threw him in prison to reconsider the wisdom of his course. If he took the oath, they read the articles to him, demanding answer and seeking to bully him into response should he refuse, dissemble, or equivocate. His failure to satisfy them met with imprisonment. His answers led to further questions, often resulting in heated exchanges of a recriminatory nature and an altercation on the godliness of rites and church polity. Anyone drawn into such disputations was certain to convict himself by his own testimony.

An innocent man might have nothing to fear by taking the oath and answering all questions truthfully, but a Puritan was as innocent to the High Commission as a Jesuit priest to the Privy Council. The Commission might have only the vaguest suspicions about his religious convictions and activities, not nearly enough to suspend him from the ministry let alone convict him of a penal offense. Yet, once summoned, he was ruined. He could refuse the oath and rot in jail, or having taken it, refuse to answer and meet the same fate. If he took the oath and lied, he committed the unpardonable and cardinal sin of perjury which was simply not an option for a religious man; he was incapable of forswearing God and damning his soul. If he took the oath and told the truth, he foreswore himself, supplying his enemy with legal proof of his guilt, and, what was equally appalling, he forsook his co-religionists, necessarily betraying them. The sole route of escape from all personal punishment was unthinkable: to repudiate one's conscience, apostatize by becoming a conformist, and in earnestness of repentence play Judas by turning state's evidence. One alternative was more cruel and sinful than the next. The only honorable choice for a decent, God-fearing Puritan was some form of martyrdom, ranging from the loss of his ministry—a soul-wrenching deprivation of his calling—to crushing fines and imprisonment. His only meaningful choice was to decide on the means most suited to bring about his personal disaster by defending his faith. Individuals differed on whether that was best done by refusing the oath, by remaining silent to interrogatories, or by vigorous championship of Presbyterian or Congregationalist beliefs without naming others.

In May of 1584, Whitgift, having decided that his three articles requiring subscription were not enough to cleanse the church of its enemies within, devised an infallible net for the High Commission to catch them. He drew up twenty-four articles for use by the Commission against all Puritan suspects. Complex and detailed —a printed version runs almost six pages—the articles constituted a set of charges framed in the old inquisitorial style, covering belief and practice respecting the Book of Common Prayer, clerical vestments, baptism, the sign of the cross, the matrimonial ring, the litany, the burial service, communion, preaching, attendance at conventicles, and the episcopacy. Each article, beginning with the formula, "We do object, assert, and declare," made an accusation of a fishing nature, for example, "That within the tyme aforesaid you have advisedly and of sett purpose preached, taught, declared, sett downe, or published by writinge, publique or private speeche, matter against the said Booke of Common Praier, or of some thing therein conteined. . . ." Each accusation was of a generalized nature and was followed by a demand for confession of all the particulars—the time, place, number of instances, content, reason, circumstances, and the like. Whitgift's strategy for revealing the Puritan conspiracy against church and state was to summon a suspect before the Commission, require him to take the oath, and then order answers to the twenty-four articles. Widespread contumacious behavior on the part of the suspects might result in failure to reveal the conspiracy; but it could not fail to break the back of the Presbyterian movement by jailing its ministry.[35]

Puritanism Versus the High Commission

One of the earliest victims of the oath procedure, perhaps the first, was Edward Brayne, a minister of Cambridge. He and another minister, having refused to subscribe to Whitgift's three articles as contrary to Scriptures and the dictates of conscience, stood in imminent danger of suspension. They appealed to Lord Burghley to intercede in their behalf, and he, influenced by other councilors to defend the Puritans, recommended to Archbishop Whitgift that they be charitably treated. The ministers of state viewed the ministers of religion as a means of keeping the Jesuits "fenced," as Sir Francis Knollys told Whitgift. The Puritans would "stir up true obedience to her Majesty," Knollys claimed, and he beseeched Whitgift to "open the mouths of al zelous preachers," even if they refused to subscribe, for they were "not compellible by law," that is, Parliament had not required subscription. Although Burghley did not share Knollys's enthusiasm for the Puritans and would not countenance schism, he saw the advantage of using the Puritans to hedge a Catholic resurgency. He told Whitgift that counsilors "dayly assayled" him to stay his "vehement" measures against the queen's antipapist preachers. Whitgift replied sharply that Brayne and his kind were "contentious, seditious, and persons vagrant." Brayne himself complained to Burghley of harsh treatment by the archbishop, notwithstanding the Lord Treasurer's commendation. The High Commission had summoned him, Brayne reported, and ordered him to take the oath *ex officio* as a preliminary to answering the twenty-four articles. He had offered to answer unsworn to the articles if he might see them in advance, but Whitgift, after "grave speeches," had canonically admonished him and registered him for contempt. Burghley, on interviewing Brayne, asked why he had not answered truthfully, and Brayne replied that the articles were so numerous and diverse that he was "afraid to answer to them, for fear of captious interpretation." At that point, the Lord Treasurer obtained for himself a copy of the articles. Appalled by what he read, he wrote a scathing letter to the Archbishop of Canterbury.[1]

He found the articles "so curiously penned, so ful of branches, and circumstances, as I think the Inquisitors of Spain use not so many questions to comprehend and to trap their preyes." He knew that canonists could defend the articles in all particulars, "but surely under your Graces correction this judicial and canonical sifting of poor Ministers is not to edify or reform. And in charity, I think, they ought not to answer to al these nice points, except they were very notorious offenders in Papistry or heresy." Burghley desired peace and unity in the church, he told Whitgift, and would favor no recusants. "But I conclude, that, according to my simple judgment, this kind of proceeding is too much savouring of the Romish inquisition: and is rather a device to seek for offenders, than to reform any. This is not the charitable instruction that I thought was intended." [2]

Two days later Whitgift replied at considerable length, yielding not an inch. Accused of vehement treatment of the Puritans, he argued that his only mistake was in being too lenient with them. Accused of encouraging papists by stopping the mouths of Puritans, he retorted that, on the contrary, the papists benefited when the Puritans, who "after a sort joyne with them," were befriended in high places despite disordered doings against their civil and ecclesiastical governors. As for his twenty-four articles "smelling of the Romish inquisition," wrote Whitgift in a pointed *tu quoque*, he was amazed that Burghley should think so, "Seeing it is the ordinarie cowrse in other courts likewise: as, in the Starchamber, the Court of the Marches, and other places." Indeed his articles were, he thought, more tolerable and less captious than those in other prerogative courts which examined private men concerning private actions, whereas the High Commission examined the public actions of men of a public calling. "And therefore I see no cause, why our judicial and canonical proceadings in this poynt should be misliked." His own conscience was clear, regardless of what others thought, and he would persevere in his duty in accordance with the charge from her Majesty, remembering that though he was unworthy, she had, next to herself alone, committed "the cheafe care" to him.[3]

No man had ever dared speak to Burghley in such a manner, but out of allegiance to the queen he did not challenge Whitgift's authority. He did, however, challenge his procedure. Had the archbishop charged the ministers with violation of order the case would have been different. "But your Grace," said Burghley, "not charging them with such faults, seeketh by examination to urge them to accuse themselves; and then I think you will punish them." Nevertheless, he would not interfere; Whitgift and Bishop Aylmer might use Brayne as their wisdoms directed, however uncharitably.[4]

Resolute yet wary of alienating Burghley and other magnates, Whitgift turned to persuasion. Trusting that the Lord Treasurer would not cast off old friends for any of the "new fangled and factious *sectaries*," the archbishop sent him two documents. The first was entitled, "Reasons why it is convenient that those which are culpable in the articles, ministered generally by the Archbishop of Canterbury, and others her Majesty's Commissioners for causes ecclesiasticall, should be examined of the same upon their oathes." Only one of the many reasons spoke to Burghley's point that by use of the inquisitorial oath, the High Commission compelled men to accuse themselves and then punished them for their confessions. Whitgift realized that the great councilor, who was an adept racker, was not opposed to the procedure in principle; his opposition was to the use of the procedure against Puritans. Whitgift, after pointing out that the oath *ex officio* had been used "synce there hath bene any lawe ecclesiasticall in this realme," stressed that the Privy Council had supported the High Commission's oath procedure against papists.[5]

That procedure could not be regarded as uncharitable, Whitgift argued, when it was warranted by law—presumably the provision

in the letters patent—and by the need to reform disturbers of the
unity of the church, those who by "their own speeches or actes"
defamed themselves. That the "form of such proceeding by articles *ex officio mero* is usuall" appeared in the records of all former ecclesiastical commissions, including those of her Majesty's
reign. "If it bee sayd, that it is against law, reason, and charitee,
for a man to accuse himself, *quia nemo tenetur seipsum prodere,
aut propriam turpitudinem revelare* [or to reveal his own infamy]:
I aunswere, that by lawe, charitee, and reason, *Proditus per de-
nuntiationem alterius, sive per famam, tenetur seipsum ostendere,
ad evitandum scandalum, et seipsum purgandum* [whoever is accused by the denunciation of others or by common report is
obliged to reveal himself, to avoid scandal, and to clear himself]."
Continuing in Latin, Whitgift added that it was not necessary to
establish the prior existence of "fame" if the prelate examined for
deviations and errors among the clergy, since they were accountable to the church. He then defended the twenty-four articles as a
means of ferreting out schismatics, concluding that the procedure
could not be compared to any "bloudie inquisition" of the past.
Death was not the object now, only "deprivation from ecclesiastical lyving." Whitgift's second paper was an expediential argument on the "inconveniences of not proceeding *ex officio mero*
. . . but only upon presentment and conviction by witnesses."
He began with the proposition that papists, "Brownistes" or Separatists, and other sectaries "spreade their poison in secrete, making it nearly impossible to produce witnesses against them; he
ended with complaint that the High Commission would be taxed
with too burdensome a task to get witnesses even when it might
be possible.[6]

Neither of Whitgift's papers convinced, or even quieted,
Burghley or the Privy Council, least of all its fiery clerk, Robert
Beale. Beale was, as a hostile writer acknowledged, "a man of parts
and some learning." An experienced diplomat used often by the
queen on important foreign missions, he served on several occasions as acting Secretary of State in the absence of his powerful
brother-in-law, Sir Francis Walsingham. Beale sat in six successive
Parliaments from 1576 through 1593, always an aggressive champion of the Puritan cause and of Magna Carta, which he con-

scripted into service against the oath *ex officio* and all the inquisitorial proceedings of the High Commission. He was a common lawyer and, by his own boastful statement, a student of the canon law, too, for twenty-six years. He could quote Scriptures and engage in theological disputation as easily as he could dash off a legal treatise. Contentious, outspoken to the point of indiscretion, and implacable in his opposition to the High Commission, Beale could nettle Whitgift as no one else could. Though he was but a secondary figure in his own time, he looms as a giant in the history of the right against self-incrimination. He invented the fiction, which grew in time to the stature of an article of constitutional faith, that Magna Carta outlawed forcing a man to be a witness against himself. His first treatise, according to Whitgift, was "a book against oaths that be ministered in the courts of ecclesiastical commission from her Majesty, and in other courts ecclesiastical." The book was published abroad in 1584 and imported into England, but most regrettably no copy of what was probably an original constitutional argument has survived, though we do have his later restatements.[7]

Beale also wrote what Whitgift called "another great book" in 1584, which was never published, defending his first book against oaths, impugning the High Commission, and above all defending the Puritan view on ceremonies, vestments, and the Book of Common Prayer. He presented a copy of the manuscript to Whitgift who thought it to be so subversive that he sent it to Burghley together with a digest of it and his own reply. According to the archbishop, Beale derogated from Elizabeth's title as *Fidei Defensor* by picturing her as "a defendress of beggerlye, Popish, Antichristian rites and ceremonies." Placing all the blame on the prelates for "foul abuses" of her authority, Beale argued that "many thinges bear the cloke and colour of the law which are not law," including the Book of Common Prayer itself as enforced by Canterbury. What made this contention, otherwise without special interest, so significant is that Beale founded upon it an argument for religious toleration. Himself an arch-persecutor of Catholics, though only for their "treasons," of course, he claimed that princes and magistrates had no authority to make laws "in things indifferent, to bynde men to the observation thereof." To prescribe rules for men's consciences in things indifferent—which excluded Catholicism—was "a doctrine fit for Antichriste. . . . But the Lord hath reserved the conscience of man to be settled by hym self in his good time, as he thinketh meete in these indifferent thinges. . . ." The very matters that Whitgift's twenty-four articles were calculated to expose as schismatic and disloyal were "indifferent" to Beale. In Parliament a year later, in 1585, he would combine this plea with an assault on the oath *ex officio*, bringing together a claim for religious toleration and one for freedom from self-accusing imposed by law.[8]

After delivering a copy of his book to Whitgift, Beale went to Lambeth Palace and in "a great passion" remonstrated with the archbishop against the enforcement of his twenty-four articles. Affronted by Beale's shouting and contempt, Whitgift ended the interview with a warning that he might complain to the queen; instead, he complained to Burghley. Beale, who was not easily intimidated, carried on the controversy in an angry letter, informing Whitgift scornfully that he would "be not by the nose ledde with anye Pythagorical or Papall *ipse dixit*, knowinge, as I knowe, the writinges and use of the best learned men in Europe, to be to the contrarie." Whitgift got no satisfaction from the Lord Treasurer to whom he sent Beale's letter with his own bitter complaint; but the archbishop knew how to reply to contumely in kind. He did not in the slightest divert from his course against the Puritans. By mid-1584 he had "deprived" forty-nine ministers and suspended nearly five times as many. Holding the trump cards, the queen's support and the church's control over the ministry, Whitgift reduced the Privy Council to a supplicant. It could only ask that he proceed charitably toward zealous preachers so that the people would not be deprived of their services. Although the Privy Council could not restore a minister to good standing with the church, it could restore him to freedom, as it did in the case of Barnaby Benison. Benison had refused the oath *ex officio*, and for "non-conformity" Bishop Aylmer threw him into the Clink. The Council ordered his release, but it had not been able to prevent his harsh treatment.[9]

One of the suspended ministers, Humphrey Fenn, complained that "these proceedings are not according to law; but an inquisition into our hearts and consciences, for which there is no law." An associate of Fenn observed that a poor preacher caught by the proceeding *ex officio mero* would lose his living, his liberty, and "lie by the heeles," for the bishops, employing tricks of the canon law, entrapped all who did not serve under their yoke. In the summer of 1584, a Puritan conference discussed the question of the oath *ex officio* in the hope of finding some means of coping with the High Commission. Brethren who had been victimized by the oath reported their stories, and the judgment of legal counsel was also reported "that the othe offered by the Bishops is not to be allowed." The Puritans concluded that they must avoid the oath if possible, but that in the event that they must swear, they should mislead their inquisitors if they could. God's will, they decided, could not require them to deliver themselves into the hands of the enemy. They would report some facts, no doubt undamaging ones, and deny the rest or conveniently suffer a lapse of memory, ever ready, however, to fall back on conscience as a mainstay for refusing answer.[10]

When David Blake, a schoolmaster, fell into the clutches of the High Commission, he declared, "upon myne othe I am not bounde to aunswere to matters criminall or captious—or to accuse myself." Giles Wigginton, the pastor of Sedbrugh in Yorkshire and a man of uncommon learning, told a tale which John Field, a co-author of the "Admonition to Parliament" and general secretary of the movement, circulated among the faithful as a warning. In 1584, Whitgift, learning that Wigginton was in London to preach, had him arrested and brought before the High Commission. The archbishop reviled and threatened his victim unmercifully if Wigginton's account is believed, and then imprisoned him for nine weeks without cause or further legal proceeding "save only that I would not speake and answer before him to certaine Articles being against my selfe. . . ." Wigginton's account suggests that the Puritans had circulated the advice of counsel. The archbishop, he later reported, "urged me the same time to swear and answer to certaine written Articles, and other questions being against my selfe, without giving me any knowledge of mine accusers, and a Copy of the Articles, and without Bill of Complaint or Due Process of Law &c. Whereto I refused to sweare and to answer unto him, and thereupon he committed me to close prison in the Gatehouse at Westminster." [11]

Wigginton's case being by no means unusual, the Puritans, on finding no relief from the Privy Council, turned to Parliament, which met near the close of 1584. There were good reasons for expecting a sympathetic response. The country at that time was acutely apprehensive about the danger from an international Catholic conspiracy. The leading Protestant monarch on the Continent, William of Orange, had recently been assassinated by a Catholic fanatic, giving further credence to the dread belief that Elizabeth's life was also in danger. The government did, in fact, uncover assassination plots with almost regular frequency. The Throckmorton conspiracy of 1583, implicating the ambassador of his Catholic Majesty, Philip of Spain, was only the most recent episode. As Parliament convened, Lord Burghley was readying a stern bill for the better security of the queen's person, imposing new restraints upon Catholics, recusants and priests alike, and providing for a Protestant interregnum in the event of regicide. Even before the bill could be enacted, Burghley learned that Dr. William Parry, one of his own agents and a man who, being in favor at court, had immediate access to the queen, was a double agent planning to murder her. Parliament, normally sympathetic to Puritanism, was all the more disposed to strengthen the hand and voice of its most anti-Catholic preachers. The Puritans, moreover, were superbly prepared for religio-political action. They had begun the *classis* movement, looking toward an independent presbyterian organization within the Church of England. Each congregation was to have its cell composed of ministers and elders; the cells of a dozen or so neighboring churches formed a *classis* or clandestine conventicle; the *classis* would send representatives to a provincial synod which, in turn, would send representatives to a national synod. This ecclesiastical polity, following the Genevan model, would govern the church, enforce uniformity of ceremony and doctrine, and direct political action in the interests of the church. At the Parliament which opened in November of 1584, for example, there was a Puritan lobby whose agents solicited at the door of the House of Commons by day, and by night pushed their cause in the private chambers of members of Parliament.[12]

When Parliament opened, Dr. Peter Turner, a Calvinist member, presented a bill and a book—the Genevan Prayer Book—which would have revolutionized the national church by introducing the Presbyterian system and rites. There were many fellow-travelers in the House of Commons, but few would go so far or dare to admit it. Turner's bill and book died for lack of support. A more moderate course, however, mustered majority support. Among the various petitions to Commons, one, joining the cause of religious reform with that of the High Commission's victims, objected that the prelates "by inquisition upon oathe, information they care not from whome," punished conscientious ministers by suspension and deprivation and reviled them most reproachfully as schismatics, heretics, and factious seditionists. Another petition, also pleading for restoration of the deposed ministers, requested, "That the ministring of the articles *ex officio* lately used may be forborn, seing they are against the law and libertie of the land; upon no occasion of suspicion of misdemeanor to make a man accuse himself." The House of Commons entrusted such petitions to the consideration of a special committee, which included Robert Beale and James Morice, a Puritan lawyer whose contribution to the development of the right against self-incrimination would match Beale's.[13]

The committee framed "The humble Petitions of the Commons" which, with House approval, was sent to the Lords Spiritual and Temporal. This document requested that the ministers who had been "molested by some exercising ecclesiastical jurisdiction" should be set at liberty to preach, that none hereafter be required to subscribe, and that the ecclesiastical courts and the High Commission in particular should abandon "their examinations *ex officio mero,* of godly and learned preachers, not detected unto them for open offense of lyfe, or for publicke maynteyning of apparent error in doctrine. . . ."[14]

The Lords' answer came at the close of February in 1585. Burghley informed a deputation from the Commons that the queen had seen their petitions, discussed them with the Archbishop of Canterbury and his bishops, and wanted Parliament to drop the matter. The Bishop of Winton objected that without the *ex officio* proceeding the church would be unable to cope with "a great nomber of disordered causes." Whitgift himself, scornfully rejecting each of sixteen requests, also warned against schismatics; the Commons, he declared, "would not have them examyned *ex officio*. Whereby should bee taken from us an usuall, lawfull, and ordinary kinde of proceeding, without which wee cannot performe that which is looked for at our handes. . . ." He said that it was a "mere surmyse, proceadinge of ignoraunce" that the *ex officio* procedure was a recent innovation, as alleged, for it had been practiced "from the beginninge, not only in this Court of the High Commission, but in the Star-chamber alsoe. . . ." Indeed, he added, it had never been "gaynesayed or mislyked, till of late by the Jesuites and Seminarie Priestes, of whom I thought that our men also had borrowed their exceptions against that maner of proceeding." [15]

Beale and the members of the Commons were "nothing satisfied" by the prelates' cavalier treatment. In an interminable address—the manuscript runs 114 pages—Beale delivered a summary of his two angry books of the preceding year. He began by extolling "the greate charter of the libertie of Englande," reviewed its reconfirmations, and asked the House to endorse the principle that the queen's subjects "maye be no otherwise dealt with in causes Ecclesiastical, than maye stande with the said charter, and lawes and liberties of this realme." Going back half a century, he quoted St. Germain, Parliament's supplication of 1532 against *ex officio* proceedings, and its act of 1534 condemning "captious interrogatories" and declaring that no one should be convicted or subject to loss of good name and goods without common-law accusation. Beale even found in the "Register of Writs" copies of Henry III's thirteenth-century writs of prohibition against Grosseteste, the Bishop of Lincoln, enjoining an end to his inquisitions and ordering that no one answer questions under oath except in matrimonial and testamentary cases. To the same effect he quoted the *Prohibitio de Statuto Articuli Cleri* of the fourteenth century. The situation in our own time, said Beale, was worse than at any other in the past. The clergy, by extending their ecclesiastical commissions further than the laws of the realm warranted, had fastened a heavy yoke upon the necks of loyal subjects and were strangling the liberties of the land. The church abounded in an unlearned clergy, yet the more godly and learned, "for a refusall to a certayne subscription" were "examyned by corporall oths" upon captious articles, copies of which could not be obtained. Some were "putt to silence; some (as it is sayd) imprisoned without bayle; some suspended and deprived from their livings and ministerie," contrary to English liberties.[16]

The High Commission, Beale continued, was being used "as a cloke for the maintenance of these said abuses and enormities." Parliament controlled the ecclesiastical law of the land, and its Act of Uniformity did not authorize the prayer book to be illegally enforced by the bishops. The Act of Supremacy authorized the establishment of commissioners in ecclesiastical causes, but did not empower them to fine, imprison, compel subscription, or use the oath *ex officio* whereby suspected persons were forced to accuse themselves in indifferent matters which should be left to conscience. The commissioners had "no authority to minister any oaths unto subjects of this land, unless it be in a cause of testament or matrimony," and no one need answer on oath. The *ex officio mero* proceeding was a product of the "Inquisition in Spayne and Rome," and should be stopped by prohibitions from the common-law courts. The only proper procedure was by indictment and trial by jury. "I take it to be contrarie to the lawes and liberties of this lande for I think it not appoynted to any Ecclesiastical power to restrain or remitt a free man from his libertie which the greate charter granteth hym: *Nullus liber homo capiatur vel imprisonetur nisi per legem terrae* but only in those cases . . . warranted by the lawes of this realme." Beale then launched a long disquisition on religion, upholding Puritan views on matters touched by Whitgift's twenty-four articles.[17]

It was a daring performance from a high-placed royal official. Commons had gotten out of hand, and the queen's own privy councilors, Knollys and Mildmay among them, far from controlling the situation, had contributed to the opposition. Elizabeth intervened personally. First she held an audience with Archbishop Whitgift and three bishops, in the presence of her principal officers of state. She went out of her way to protect Whitgift from Burghley's criticism and to show her favor to the prelates. "We understand," she said, "that some of the Nether House have used divers reproachful speeches against you . . . which we will not suffer." As for her own councilors who had been parties to the incident, "we will redress or else uncouncil some of them." She would permit no interference from Parliament in ecclesiastical matters. Charging her officers of state and church to bring about "conformity and unity" so that all ministers preached "one truth," she added, in chastisement of Burghley, "And we require you that you do not favour such men, being carried away with pity, hoping of their conformity, and inclining to noblemen's letters and gentlemen's letters, for they will be hanged before they will be reformed." Comparing the Puritans with the Catholic recusants, since both rejected her supremacy in the church, she recalled an Italian proverb, "From mine enemy let me defend myself; but from a pretensed friend, good Lord deliver me. Both these," she declared, "join together in one opinion against me, for neither of them would have me to be Queen of England." [18]

That day, a Saturday, the committee of Commons prepared recommendations for proceeding with measures to protect Puritan ministers. On Monday morning the queen routed the speaker out of a sick bed and gave him his orders. The following morning he reported to the House: Her Majesty absolutely commanded them not to "meddle with matters of the Church, neither in reformation of religion or of discipline." When Parliament closed a few weeks later, Elizabeth personally addressed the assembly, saying that one subject touched her so closely she could not overlook it, "religion, the ground on which all other matters ought to take root, and, being corrupted, may mar all the tree." Fault-finders with the clergy slandered her and her church, "whose overruler God hath made me," and it would be negligence on her part, she averred, to suffer schism or heretical errors. She saw many "overbold" with presumption so great she would not tolerate it. She would not "animate Romanists . . . nor tolerate new-fangledness," for in both here were perils, but in the latter, in Puritanism, she saw something "dangerous to kingly rule." [19]

Thus ended the Parliament of 1584–85. Although the queen had stymied both redress and reform, and had given unstinting endorsement to Archbishop Whitgift, a spark had been kindled which the scepter could smother but not snuff out altogether.

Men were beginning to talk again about Magna Carta and English liberties, and some even wondered whether their beloved sovereign should be obeyed in all respects, particularly when she trod on the freedom of the House of Commons. Others were beginning to question whether God-fearing, loyal subjects, guiltless of real crime, should be exposed to inquisitions and be forced by a prerogative court to accuse themselves.

After the Parliament of 1584–85, Archbishop Whitgift was unstoppable. Once he had bested both the Privy Council and the House of Commons, there was no fettering the High Commission. In 1585 Elizabeth publicly showed her esteem for Whitgift by appointing him to the Privy Council, an honor which she had not bestowed on previous primates. Whitgift was now able to deal politically with Burghley, Walsingham, Mildmay, Knollys, and the others on equal terms. They could rebuff him only when he sought to extend his aggressions outside of the ecclesiastical or spiritual realm, as when he sought revenge on the Clerk of the Privy Council, Robert Beale.

Whitgift drew up a schedule of fourteen charges against Beale, and although nothing came of them, they are a curious revelation of the archbishop's mind. The first several charges dealt with the same point: Beale had written a book against oaths, distributed manuscript copies, and then got the book printed abroad and imported it by a Scottish ship. Another charge was that he had written a second book which attacked the High Commission's jurisdiction and its procedure. Then followed charges that Beale had disputed the Commission's authority to apprehend anyone, "what malefactor soever he be," not even Jesuits or Seminary Priests, or to imprison anyone, or to impose fines, or to force answers under oath "albeit the offences touch neither lives nor limbs." The last two charges are the most interesting: "13. He condemneth (without exception of any cause) *racking* of grievous offenders, as being cruel, barbarous, contrary to law, and unto the liberty of English subjects." Whitgift apparently thought that the Privy Council would be outraged by criticism of its frequent torturing of Catholic priests. What nettled the archbishop most, however, was Beale's explicit criticism of him for his own use of the rack. When Whitgift was Bishop of Worcester, he had also served as Vice

President of the Council of the Marches of Wales, which was both a court of law and an executive instrument of government, similar to the English Privy Council and Star Chamber. In 1579, when confronted with a nest of Catholic recusants who refused to confess, Vice President Whitgift sought and received permission from the Privy Council to use torture. Beale, as Clerk of the Privy Council, knew about the incident. Whitgift's fourteenth charge against Beale, in 1585, was: "He thereupon giveth a *caveat* to those in the Marches of Wales, that execute torture by virtue of instructions under her Majesty's hand, according to a statute, to look unto it, that their doings be well warranted." [20]

Although Whitgift got no satisfaction against Beale on this occasion, he had a free hand against Puritan ministers. Nearly every case resulted in bitter complaints against compulsory self-incrimination. One celebrated case—the victim's account was circulated among the Puritan ministry—involved Thomas Carew, an Essex preacher whom Bishop Aylmer had suspended in 1584. Defiant, Carew established a local presbytery, continued preaching, and notoriously defamed the Book of Common Prayer. Aylmer summoned Carew before the High Commission in 1585, and there was a scene about whether he could be forced to take the oath *ex officio*. The court committed him for his refusal, but on re-examination he relented and swore the oath. Yet he would not answer the interrogatories, arguing that it was illegal to make a man accuse himself by asking him incriminating questions under oath. The Commission's proceeding, he asserted, "is meere contrary to the Lawes of England . . . For no man is to be adjudged but upon due proofe by witnes or otherwise, not to be forced to accuse himself, as their Articles of Inquisition draw men unto." The bishops ought not put men to the oath except in cases of matrimony. The articles, Carew declared, had been "cunningly drawne to entrapp me, and therefore to many of them which touched my selfe I would not answer. . . ." His patron, a laymen named Edmond Allen who had turned the locality against the orthodox minister whom Alymer had sent to replace Carew, was tried at the same time; he was equally obstinate. The High Commission imprisoned both and denied them bail. After eight weeks in Fleet prison, the Privy Council released them. [21]

Among the many cases of the following year, 1586, two merit notice because of the identities of the defendants. One was Giles Wigginton, in trouble again for having made the same mistake; he came to London to preach against "popish prelates and usurpers" in defiance of Whitgift's command never again to preach in his diocese. The pursuivant of the High Commission arrested Wigginton in his lodgings and hauled him before the archbishop. Furious because the Puritan would not submit to his authority, Whitgift "threatened me rotting in prison," reported Wigginton, "and burning, as if I were an Hereticke." He attempted to "entrap me as guilty of some capital charge." Yet Wigginton would neither submit, take the oath *ex officio*, nor answer questions "which were against my selfe." The High Commission deprived him and confined him in the White Lion prison where he was kept in irons for five weeks before being released.[22]

John Udall was another leading Puritan who was persecuted at this time. Like Wigginton he was also educated at Cambridge and was an exceptionally gifted man, noted for his Hebrew scholarship. His religious beliefs eventually led to his conviction for a capital felony. James VI of Scotland prized Udall's Hebrew grammar and dictionary, and on arriving in England to succeed Elizabeth inquired for him. On learning that he was dead, the king is said to have exclaimed, "By my soul, then, the greatest scholar of Europe is dead." Udall's troubles began in 1586, when he was deprived for refusing to take the oath *ex officio*. Seeking to be restored, he requested a rehearing of his case. The Bishop of Winchester opened the inquiry with the remark that he had heard Udall would submit. Udall replied that he had always been willing to submit to anything "godly." "What you will do now," answered the bishop, "I know not, but you have not done it heretofore; for you refused to swear according to Law." Offering to swear only if he might first see the articles against him, Udall stood firm despite abuse which brought him to tears. Finally the commissioners relented, showed him the articles, and Udall took the oath *ex officio*, reserving to himself the right to answer in writing, "so far as it appeareth to me that by Law I ought." His answers, however, furnished enough evidence against him to cause further examination before the High Commission at Lambeth,

Whitgift presiding. Udall candidly replied to questions concerning his doctrine, and at the end naïvely remarked that he thought he had purged himself by his answers. "Nay, by your leave that you have not," was the reply, "your Answers do accuse you. . . . You have confessed sufficient against your selfe." They refused to restore him, though they punished him no further. The lesson was clear, however, and Udall never forgot it. The report of "Mr. Udall's Troubles" which circulated among the Puritan ministry was a warning against taking the oath or confessing religious beliefs.[23]

At the close of 1586 the Puritans turned once again, for relief, to Parliament, which was then convening. As before, the House of Commons was a place for venting Puritan discontent and promoting the cause of perfect reformation, and never were the Puritans better prepared. They had successfully electioneered for members who would place the sovereignty of God over that of the queen. Their lobbyists were everywhere, efficient and persuasive; and they prepared a huge petition, "A General Supplication Made to the Parliament," to which they annexed an enormously detailed survey of nearly ten thousand churches, to prove the lamentable state of the Anglican establishment and the need for Parliamentary adoption of their program. Among the grievances catalogued in the petition, they mentioned that the High Commission cruelly treated many ministers, depriving them, imprisoning them, and holding them in irons. "But in the proceeding to these extremities there is one thing more grievous than all the rest, which is that an oth ex officio, as thei call it, is tendred them, to awnser to all Interrogatories. . . ." The petition described how the oath, "which to a conscience that feareth God is more violent then anie racke," forced a man to answer "though it be against himself and to his most grievous punishment," and his "confession being so gotten, is their ground wherupon thei proceede to punishment of them with all rigor against all law of God and of this land, and of all nations in Christendome except it be in Spaigne by the Inquisition. . . ." Devout ministers suffered whether they confessed truthfully under the oath or refused to take it. Such was the result of following the "bloudie" example of the "Antichristian tirrany" of the pope.[24]

Left to its own impulses and the influence of the Puritan cau-
cus, the Commons would have swallowed the Puritan program
hook, line, and sinker. Once more, however, Elizabeth interceded
via the speaker of the House, speedily and drastically, aborting Sir
Anthony Cope's bill and book for the Genevan system. Robbed
of its legislative agenda, the Commons rebelliously debated
whether the condition of the Church required reformation. Then
Peter Wentworth rose, on March 1, 1587, to deliver his celebrated
address on freedom of speech, questioning the right of the speaker
to enforce the queen's injunctions against the House. His questions
may, in the words of J. E. Neale, have been "comparable, in the
secular sphere, with the theses posted on the church door at Wit-
tenberg by Martin Luther," but Luther was not promptly clapped
into the Tower. A day later, Cope and three others followed
Wentworth there. Nevertheless, the House adopted a motion for
"amendment of some things whereunto ministers are required to
be sworn," and they appointed a committee, which included Beale
and Morice, to frame a petition. Once again Elziabeth intervened,
this time with a message on the subject, "Why you ought not to
deal with matters of religion." The message concluded with the
statement that the queen viewed the action of Commons as violating "the prerogative of her crown." Given the choice of showing allegiance or contempt of the crown, members dropped the
project to do something about compulsory swearing. Two years
later, in another Parliament, there was another futile effort to assault the whole *ex officio* process and prevent imprisonment except after due course of the common law. But a bill to this end
was not even read, for the same reason that comparable measures
in 1584–85 and 1586–87 had failed.[25]

In 1587 Archbishop Whitgift and the High Commission executed a stunning coup by discovering a secret conventicle of Separatists in London. Twenty-two persons were arrested, including
their preacher, John Greenwood. Before the year was up the
leader of the sect, Henry Barrow, was seized when he daringly
visited Greenwood in the Clink. The Separatists, who were called
Brownists or Barrowists, were a prize catch, for they were truly
subversive. They were Puritans with a difference: they found the
national church so abominable that they withdrew from it com-

pletely. Cartwright and the Presbyterians believed in the medieval notion of one church and one state, every member of the commonwealth belonging to both. Although they subordinated state to church, they did not question the need for a national church. On the contrary, they affirmed the duty of the civil magistrate to plant a true church and enforce obedience to it on all subjects. The Separatists, by contrast, saw religion as a private relationship between man and God, the church as a company of true believers convenanting with the Lord to obey his commandments and Scriptures in return for salvation. They did not believe, therefore, that the secular power could make a church or maintain the gospel. Because a church, in their view, was the result of a covenant between the elect and God, they did not believe that it could encompass the entire nation. They regarded the Church of England as so corrupt and peopled with so many unregenerates that they seceded to form their own self-governing, independent congregations. Personal salvation could not wait until the civil magistrate saw the light.

On the other hand, the Separatists of the sixteenth century, like the Presbyterians and the Anglicans—and the Catholics, too—believed that it was the duty of the state to suppress and root out everything contrary to the true worship. They differed from each other on what true worship was, but the Separatists differed from all the others by denying the principle of a uniform national church. They were a living contradiction to that principle, a unique species of religious thought and practice. Notwithstanding their inconsistent endorsement of intolerance toward others, the Separatists heralded the coming of a time when pluralism in religion necessitated an official policy of state toleration for all. Historically, the existence of one religion in a state has meant a policy of persecution, two religions have occasioned a form of civil war, while many resulted in freedom for all. The road to freedom has been paved with as many intolerant intentions as the road to hell with good ones. However, from the standpoint of a national establishment of religion, committed to a single form of worship under one sovereign requiring conformity from all, separatism represented an internal threat that could not be ignored. The Separatists, though insignificant in number, were genuine rebels who clearly repudiated the supremacy of the sovereign in the ecclesiastical realm; by implication they sought the overthrow of the state. In self-defense, it must obliterate them.

In 1583 the queen issued a royal proclamation against the seditious books of Robert Browne who provided the theological underpinnings of the new sect, and in that year three men were hanged for the crime of circulating Browne's books. Browne himself, who donned and doffed religions with remarkable alacrity, was like a falling star in the history of separatism; for a brief time he blazed a path and then burned out. In 1585 he made his peace with the establishment and lived the remainder of his life in quiet conformity. Henry Barrow, a gentleman lawyer, and John Greenwood, a deprived minister, perpetuated the new sect by founding an independent congregation in London. Their work led their church to congregationalism and brought them to the gallows.[26]

As soon as Barrow was recognized and arrested late in 1587, a pursuivant of the High Commission took him to Whitgift for examination. Barrow promptly proved himself to be the most exasperating man the archbishop ever confronted. Straight off, Barrow demanded to know the cause of his imprisonment. "That yow shal know upon yowr oath," replied Whitgift, "wil yow sweare?" When Barrow asserted that he held it lawful to swear, Whitgift reached for a Bible, and Barrow began with his objections. He would not swear the oath *ex officio* by the Bible, whether his hand was on it or off it. Nor would he swear with his hand on the table or holding the archbishop's hand. He would swear with his hand toward heaven, but only if not commanded. Then it turned out that he would not swear until he knew the cause of his arrest. When Whitgift informed him that he was reported to be unwilling to attend the services of the established church, rejected it outright, and was disobedient to the queen, the following exchange occurred:

> BARROW: These are reportes. When yow produce yowr testimonie I wil answer.
> WHITGIFT: But I wil better beleeve yow upon yowr oath than them: how say you, wil yow sweare?
> BARROW: I wil know what I sweare to before I sweare.
> WHITGIFT: First sweare: and then if any thing be unlawfully demaunded, yow shal not answer.

BARROW: I have not learned so to sweare. I wil first know and
consider of the matter before I take an oath.

Whitgift was so eager for Barrow's testimony that he was willing
to waive formalities, but he finally lost patience. When Barrow, in
reply to the question, "Wel, when were yow at church?," told
the archbishop it was none of his business, Whitgift called him a
schismatic, a recusant, a seditious person, and a heretic. But Whitgift regained his temper and tried again, asking whether Barrow
had spoken against the Church of England.

BARROW: When yow produce your witnesse I wil answer.
WHITGIFT: But upon your oath I wil beleeve you.
BARROW: But I wil not accuse my self.

The examination ended when the archbishop ordered Barrow's
imprisonment for refusal to take the oath *ex officio*.[27]

Eight days later Barrow was taken before the High Commission
which he described as a "synode" of bishops, deans, and civil lawyers who had the appearance of "wel-feede silken preistes, as I
suppose might wel have bessemed the Vaticane." The archbishop,
"with a grimme and an angrie countenance," denounced him for
having refused to swear the oath and asked whether he had reconsidered. Barrow was intransigent, yet won the point. "Wel," said
Whitgift, "I wil thus far satisfie your humour." Whitgift then
produced the charges against Barrow, drawn from a Separatist
manuscript attributed to him, on the reasons for forming a separate church. Barrow, who was indeed the author, had described
the Church of England as idolatrous, its ministry un-Christian,
and its prelates anti-Christs. Whitgift also declared that Barrow
had condemned Calvin, Cartwright, and Wigginton, and added,
with a rare streak of humor, "This fellow deales indifferently, he
makes us al alike." Bishop Aylmer interjected that the prisoner
should appreciate the rare favor shown to him by the archbishop:
the charges against him had been read before the oath was required. Yet Barrow still refused to swear or to accuse himself.
Whitgift then exploded: "Where is his keeper? Yow shal not
prattle here. Away with him: clap him up close, close, let no man
come at him: I wil make him tel an other tale, yet I have done
with him." Six months later, Barrow and Greenwood were taken
from prison to be tried for violation of an act of 1581 which had

been passed originally to penalize recusant Catholics: they had failed to pay £20 monthly for failure to attend established services. Found guilty and unable to produce the sum of £260 which each was adjudged to owe, they were returned to jail.[28]

The High Commission, meanwhile, had been energetically and successfully prosecuting its campaign to lock up all Separatists. Since the discovery of the first conventicle in October of 1587, there had been further arrests. The authorities hounded and punished them with unusual severity. From a petition of early 1589 we learn that there had been "daily spoilinge, vexing, molestinge, hurtinge, pursuyinge, imprisoninge, yea, barringe and locking them up close prisoners in the most unholsome and vyle prysones, and their deteyninge them, without bringinge them to their answers, untyll the Lord by death put an ende to their myseries." Some were never examined; others, for refusing the oath, were punished by denial of food or beds, or even straw, to sleep on. Others were kept in fetters of iron in unheated prisons. Some were thrown in "Little Ease," a hole too small to stand in or stretch out. Others were kept in solitary confinement. "All this barbarous havocke they make without regard of age, sexe, estate, or degree, as may appear by the lamentable estate of those which remayne, and by the deaths of others"—six died by March, 1589—"by them murthered in the prisons whose bloud cryeth out. . . ." Another grievance, somewhat naïve, was that many did not know the cause of their imprisonment, unless it be "for refusinge to take an othe ministred by them *ex officio*. . . ."[29]

In a "Pastoral Letter from Prison," which Barrow addressed to his congregation shortly after his arrest, he also attributed his imprisonment to the fact that he had refused to take an oath to answer truly and directly to accuse himself. His refusal, which captured Barrowists copied, did in fact become a charge against the sect generally, but their crime, of course, which they knew as well as their judges, was their religion. What they meant, in their frequent complaints that they did not know the cause of their imprisonment, was that they had not been formally charged by an indictment. Barrow claimed that he and his followers would swear by the name of God "before a lawfull magestrat uppon just occasion." Presumably such an occasion would be in a proper court

—the Barrowists never recognized the lawfulness of any of the ecclesiastical courts, least of all the Court of High Commission —after grand jury proceedings and confrontation by the witnesses against them. Barrow would not even take the oath before a special commission appointed by the queen to examine him, although the members of the commission included the two Lord Chief Justices, the Master of the Rolls, the Lord Chief Baron, and another Baron of the Exchequer—five of the greatest judges of England —as well as Whitgift and two bishops. The queen had specifically empowered this august body to examine Barrow on the oath *ex officio*. Sir Christopher Wray, the Chief Justice of England, informed him that if he took the oath, he need not answer "if any unlawful thing be demaunded," yet Barrow refused to answer on oath. Notwithstanding his frequent references to the injustice of requiring him to accuse himself, and his allegation that he would give sworn testimony "uppon just occasion," his recalcitrance seems to have been equally founded on a conscientious objection to swearing. In his fullest statement on the matter, expressed in a secretly written and published book which the government eventually used as evidence to hang him, he stressed the unfairness of the oath-procedure by constantly comparing it with the "Romish" or "Spanish" inquisitions; and he emphasized, too, how unnatural and inequitable it was to drive men to accuse themselves, thereby furnishing their adversaries with abundant evidence to convict them. Yet he gave equal attention to Biblical injunctions against swearing, mentioning especially the provision in Matthew 5:34, 35, where Jesus said, "Do not swear at all. . . ." [30]

Presbyterian ministers, though lacking Barrow's legal training, were giving reasons as legalistic as he for refusing the oath. John Wilson, in 1587, told the commissioners that he would take an oath if the law required, "but I thinke it doth not compell a man to be sworne to accuse himselfe for that is very dangerous for a man will hazard much rather than confesse any thing against himselfe, and I hope I shall not be urged further then the Law appointeth." The commissioners inexplicably waived the oath *ex officio* in his case, although they demanded his confession which he adamantly refused to give. Later in the same year when Wilson had the temerity to seek from Whitgift himself permission to preach in London, the archbishop demanded that he take the oath. He refused on ground that he had a right first to see the questions that might be asked. Dr. Stanhope, a civil lawyer who was a member of the Commission, asked Wilson to explain himself, to which he replied that it was a violation of the common law that a man should be sworn to accuse himself. "That is in Causis criminalis in criminal causes as you terme them." He added, too, that they might urge him to reveal "privities of mine own heart, or of my neighbours or friends secrets," which was unlawful. Although they waived the oath once again, Wilson would not testify. His punishment was mild: they refused to license him to preach.[31]

Giles Wigginton, who was as experienced as any in dealing with the Commission, when examined again in 1588 for information which he might have concerning the writing of certain seditious books, informed Whitgift, "We do follow the instructions of learned Counsellors [James Morice above all] in these matters, who we trust will stand by us when we neede shall require. And you be ready, when you shall be called to an account to answer on the contrary touching the course of your dealings, you know whence your examination ex officio came"—a reference to papal canons. In spite of this anti-Catholic allusion, when Whitgift condemned Wigginton's persistent refusal to incriminate himself by alleging that he answered like the papists, Wigginton had the good sense to reply, "If the Papists eat brown bread so would he and not fear to doe as they did in any good thing."

Wigginton's responses on this occasion reflect the fact that the Puritans were better prepared to cope with the High Commission than a few years earlier. Whitgift accepted Wigginton's answers on his word only, probably because the Commission wanted his testimony at any price, but his objections to the oath procedure had substance as well as indignation. Even though he testified without being sworn, Wigginton would not remotely incriminate himself. Indeed his answers were variations on the same theme, incensing the archbishop who had a "glowringe countenance." Had Wigginton read any of these seditious books? "I will not answer to accuse my selfe." How had he gotten these books? "I would rather accuse my selfe then others, but I will accuse neither of both, let mine accusers, and due witnesses according to the Lawes of God and of this Realme proceede against me. . . ." Had Wigginton bought or sold any of the books? "I account it as unnaturall a thing for me to answer against my selfe, as to thrust a knife into my thigh, the matter I understand is dangerous and doubtfull, and I will neither accuse my selfe nor others. . . ." Whom did he suppose was the author? The printer? The distributor? Where did he think the press might be located? The questions were systematic, the answers always the same. Whitgift tried to convince Wigginton that he was obligated by law to answer because he was vehemently suspected and *publica fama* was against him. Wigginton scorned the archbishop's canon law and claimed the benefit of the good laws of the realm, that is, the common law. When the archbishop tried to convince him that it was lawful for him to answer, the preacher replied, "it was no English Law, he meant it was a Popish Law." After a further diet of the same sort of answers, Whitgift's only satisfaction was in sending Wigginton to prison for contempt of the High Commission.[32]

Dr. Richard Cosin, speaking for the Commission, explained that no one who knew the law and the facts could respect Puritan objections to the oath. He proved in detail, at least to his own satisfaction, that neither the Scriptures, the Church Fathers, nor the early practices of the Christian Church, supported the Puritan position; on the contrary, all were on the side of the Commission. The Puritans abhorred and avoided the oath, if they could, for the simple reason that they were guilty as suspected. Truthful answers under oath could not possibly trap or hurt an innocent man. The oath, being no more than an instrument for revealing the truth, and therefore not being an engine of oppression, was the best means for an innocent man to clear himself. His denial of the charges could not possibly furnish evidence on which to convict him. Only a guilty conscience would protest. Puritan talk about conscience was simply part of the whole design by which they covered their criminal conspiracies with the raiment of religion; they traded on respect for godliness and the Gospel even as they polluted the Bible by refusing to swear on it. They refused to swear not only to hide their guilt, but also because they knew that the Commission would examine them as witnesses against their accomplices. It properly sought to make them confess under oath concerning the criminal actions of their brethren. They affirmed that conscience bound them not to inform against those whom they believed to be harmless, yet the Church Fathers, whom Cosin quoted in abundance, required disclosure. As St. Augustine said, a heretic can be trusted only if he proves his repentence by revealing all whom he knows to be of the same opinion. The discovery of secret accomplices glorified God. Even Plato, a pagan, in his *Laws* commanded the citizens to tell everything to the magistrates.[33]

In his effort to persuade the Puritans to co-operate, as well as to justify the High Commission, Cosin argued that disclosing the crimes of others did not make the informer guilty or reproachful; since he was obligated by law, when duly charged, he need not feel that he consented to their punishment. Informing was a patriotic duty, too. Private judgment in such matters was nothing less than disobedience to the sovereign, a jeopardy to the safety of the realm. The arguments of the Puritans, in this regard, were like those of the papists, and their guilt was equal. A dutiful man, mindful of the good of the church and of the state, was bound to reveal even private conversations between friends seeking to resolve their consciences. "I can not see, howe it may stand with any mans dutie to *God*, unto the *Prince*, unto *Lawes*, and to the *Common wealthe* to conceale it, being charged to the contrary." The Puritans might dredge up from Foxe's *Book of Martyrs* stories of Willard Thorpe and John Lambert who refused to disclose the errors of friends, or they might recall the persecutions of Bishop Longland who forced children by oath to accuse their parents of heresy. For all their history, Cosin asserted, the Puritans were simply trying to divert attention from the fact that the High Commission required them to discover their criminal accomplices in the *classis* movement. In such cases the oath *ex officio* was indispensable. "For if the matter do concerne treason against the *Prince*, or the common wealth; I make no doubt, but that, a man may & ought to be tortured, even against his *natural father*, and others, howe neere soever. But if this be lawful for *treason* against man, much more then, for that which is heresie indeede; being no lesse then *treason* against the *devine majestie* of God himselfe, who is King of kings, and Lord of lords." [34]

Cosin as easily disposed of the Puritan argument that the oath abridged the common-law principles, *nemo tenetur seipsum prodere* and no one need answer till he knew the particulars against him. As for the former, they "would have much a doe to finde it (by any booke of the *common lawe*) to be the *common custome of England*." Though secrets need not be voluntarily disclosed, when they were suspected by common report, or "fame," one must confess. As for not answering until the particulars were revealed, the fact was that few took the oath when given that favor, unless they first found the charges could not be proved—in which case they would deny them. That was why the Puritans would not promise by their word to take the oath and reply to the interrogatories if first the particulars were revealed to them. Their demand to see the articles first was merely a deliberate quibble not involving a serious matter of scruple. Moreover, there were practical reasons for denying them the right to see the articles first and letting them then decide whether they would or would not take oath and answer. They would abuse the favor by instructing confederates how to conceal or disguise the truth, while they themselves remained as obstinate as ever. Also the oath could not be constrained to the initial articles, for one answer gave rise to new interrogatories. Finally, the High Commission did not require answer to questions that put life or limb in jeopardy; therefore one might take the oath, sight unseen, and reserve the right to challenge questions of life and limb as they arose. The simple fact, Cosin reiterated, was that the Puritans were afraid of the truth, because they were guilty. Such was the High Commission's attitude toward refusal to swear the oath and respond to incriminating interrogatories.[35]

By the eventful year of 1588 the Commission was on the threshold of sapping the Puritan movement. Purging the pulpits and occasionally filling the jails was beginning to silence the Puritan ministry or drive them underground; their measures of desperation would provoke stern retaliation. Literary skirmishes between Separatists and Presbyterian nationalists reflected a schism that also weakened the movement. External events contributed to the same end. The defeat of the Spanish Armada in 1588 minimized the frightful danger—England's defeat by the Catholic powers of continental Europe—which had stalked the country since Elizabeth's accession. The missionary priests and Catholic recusants, whose existence had been a foil for the growth of Puritanism, were an acute threat only in the context of a foreign assault. After the victory over Spain the usefulness of the Puritans as an internal countervailing power against the possibility of Catholic subversion was greatly reduced. The queen was never one to put much credence in the argument that the Puritans were needed to keep down the Catholics, and after 1588 there were fewer around her to advance that argument or other claims for leniency toward those whom she had always loathed. At about this time death took several of the most influential Puritan sympathizers at court, among them the Earls of Leicester and Warwick, Sir Francis Walsingham, and Sir Walter Mildmay. Their places were filled by more compliant men who were closer to Archbishop Whitgift, like Christopher Hatton, a stanch Anglican, who became Lord Chancellor. Hatton's chaplain, Dr. Richard Bancroft, who quickly became Whitgift's right arm, enormously strengthened the Commission itself. He was a tough polemicist, an expert in the canon and civil law, and by singular concentration made himself a specialist without peer on the Puritan movement. Most important, perhaps, he masterminded a system of secret intelligence and detection. Through a network of spies, informers, and pursuivants, Bancroft, who was particularly adept at interception of the mails, systematically built up a file on almost every Presbyterian *classis* and Barrowist conventicle. With Bancroft on the Commission, precise articles and pinpoint interrogatories eventually supplemented general fishing expeditions.[36]

At this point, "Martin Marprelate"—a pseudonym taken from the author's threat that a young Martin Luther would arise in every parish to mar the prelates of England—published the first of his sensational and daring tracts toward the close of 1588, touching off the government's most systematic inquisition against the Puritans. The government rightly regarded the Martinist literature as the most seditious stuff since the first "Admonition to Parliament" in 1571. Although Martin added nothing to conventional Presbyterian arguments, his immense readability, a vivid contrast to the usually turgid, grave treatises, made him especially dangerous. Scurrilous beyond compare, he could express himself in a gay and rustic dialect enlivened by japing badinage and a ribald wit. He was facetious, pungent, satirical, and vicious in turn, as he regaled his readers with tales of the episcopacy. His lampoons enraged the bishops and made them wince. Such a man had to be silenced. The queen directed Hatton and Burghley to instruct Whitgift that nothing should be spared on the part of the High Commission in finding the secret press and capturing all connected with it, for it tended to subvert all government under her charge, "both in the Church and commenweale." Elizabeth herself issued a proclamation against the "seditious and evill disposed persons" who had issued the libels which worked to "overthrowe her Highnesse lawfull Prerogative." Agents of the High Commission, under Bancroft's immediate direction, fanned out into the countryside to search for "Martin Marprelate" and his confederates. To this day Martin's identity remains a mystery although he doubtlessly was one of those who were captured. Within a year the secret press was discovered and smashed, and all connected with it—harborers, managers, printers, proofreaders, bookbinders, paymasters, suppliers, distributors—were in custody, with the sole important exception of John Penry. He was captured and hanged three years later.[37]

Many of those arrested not surprisingly refused to incriminate themselves or others. Whitgift's first suspect, for example, had been Giles Wigginton, whose examination on this occasion, in December of 1588, has been discussed. His complicity in the Martinist conspiracy is beyond question, for he lived in the house of Mrs. Elizabeth Crane when she harbored the press that printed the first two tracts, and he distributed copies. Like Wigginton, Mrs. Crane, when examined before the High Commission, refused to answer any question concerning herself, because, she said, "she would not be her own Hangman," nor would she implicate confederates because "she could not in her conscience, be an Accuser of others." Most of the evidence against the Martinists derived from the confession of Henry Sharpe, the bookbinder, who turned state's evidence, and the confessions of John Hodgkins, the printer, and his two assistants, extorted from them on the rack.[38]

Among those taken in the round-up was John Udall, the silenced minister and Hebrew scholar. He too had frequented Mrs. Crane's house, and was a close friend of Penry and Wigginton. Both Mrs. Crane's servant and Henry Sharpe implicated Udall. Although he was not the author of any of the Martinist tracts, in 1588 he had written two books, *A Dialogue* and *Demonstration of Discipline*, which Sir John Puckering, the Lord Keeper, described as "the ring-leader" of those tracts. Early in January of 1590, pursuivants of the High Commission arrested Udall and brought him for examination before a special board of inquisitors, consisting of several ecclesiastical commissioners augmented by members of the Privy Council whom Elizabeth had assigned to aid the High Commission in its search for the Martinists. Lords Cobham and Buckhurst, who had been appointed privy councilors on Whitgift's suggestion, were included. Thomas Egerton, the Solicitor General (later the great Lord Chancellor Ellesmere), and Edmond Anderson, Chief Justice of the Court of Common Pleas, were also present.[39]

Udall denied his authorship and all knowledge of the Martinist tracts, but when Anderson asked him whether he had written *A Dialogue* and *Demonstration of Discipline*, he replied, "I cannot answer to that question, my lord." The chief justice taking this to be a virtual admission of Udall's authorship, urged him to confess outright and asked whether he was ashamed of his own work. Udall replied that though he admired the books, he would not answer whether he had written them. Besides, he added, "if I were the author, I think that by law I need not answer." "That is true," replied Chief Justice Anderson prophetically, "if it concerned the loss of your life." Whether he was acknowledging a right against self-incrimination in capital cases generally, or was merely mindful of the fact that the right existed as to questions jeopardizing life or limb in cases before such prerogative tribunals as the High Commission or Star Chamber, is not at all clear. Udall pressed the point. He was not merely protesting against the unfairness of incriminating interrogatories; he was claiming a legal *right* against self-incrimination at least in cases where the procedure did not comport with Magna Carta. "I pray your lordship," he asked, "doth not the law say generally, no man shall be put to answer without presentment before justices, or thing of record, or by due process, or writ original? &c. Anno 42 Edw. 3. cap. 5 [a 1368 reconfirmation of Magna Carta; chapter 3, not chapter 5, is the correct reference]." Anderson replied most evasively, "That is law, and it is not law." Udall pressed him, professing not to understand why the statute was not law if not repealed. The chief justice merely insisted that the law required Udall to answer "in this case," leading the prisoner to plead that he be told where he might find the law, for, he said, he understood Latin, French, and English "wherein all the laws be written." They told him that he was "very cunning" and abruptly changed the subject.[40]

Later in the examination, they returned to the authorship of the two books, and for the first time the question of the oath arose, although Udall knew, of course, the charges against him. Then occurred this exchange:

ANDERSON: I pray you let us make short work with him, offer him a book; will you swear to answer to such things as shall be demanded of you in the behalf of our sovereign lady the queen?

UDALL: I will take an oath of allegiance to her majesty, wherein I will acknowledge her supremacy according to statute, and promise my obedience as becometh a subject; but to swear to accuse myself or others, I think you have no law for it.

ANDERSON: Mr. Solicitor, I pray you tell him the law in this point.

EGERTON: Mr. Udall, I am sorry that you will not answer, nor take an oath, which by law you ought to do; I can assure you, your answers are like the seminary priests answers; for they say, there is no law to compel them to take an oath to accuse themselves.

UDALL: Sir, if it be a liberty by law, there is no reason why they should not challenge it; for (though they be very bad ones) they are subjects, and until they be condemned by law, may require all the benefits of subjects; neither is that any reason, that their answering so, should make the claim of less value for me, seeing that herein we are subjects alike, though otherwise of a most contrary disposition.

BUCKHURST: My lord, it is not standing with him thus; what sayst thou, wilt thou take the oath? [41]

At that point, almost every member of the commission urged Udall either to take the oath or confess, promising him, in return, the queen's mercy, yet threatening harsh treatment if he remained obstinate. They could not budge him. Dr. Aubery, one of the High Commission's canon lawyers, reminded Udall that he had taken the oath *ex officio* in an examination before Archbishop Whitgift two years earlier, "and why will you not take it now?"

> UDALL: Indeed you call to remembrance a good reason to refuse it; I was called to answer to certain articles upon mine oath heretofore, which I voluntarily did, and freely confessed that against myself, concerning my judgment and preaching of the points of discipline, which could never have been proved; and when my friends laboured to have me restored to my place, the archbishop answered, that there was sufficient matter against me, by mine own confession, why I should not be restored: whereupon I covenanted with mine own heart, never to be mine own tormentor in that sort again. . . .
>
> BISHOP OF ROCHESTER: The day is past, and we must make an end: will you take the oath?
>
> UDALL: I dare not take it.
>
> ROCHESTER: Then you must go to prison, and it will go hard with you, for you must remain there until you be glad to take it.
>
> UDALL: God's will be done! I had rather go to prison with a good conscience, than to be at liberty with an ill one.[42]

After six months of solitary confinement, Udall was examined again by Sergeant John Puckering. When he continued in his refusal to incriminate himself, Udall was taken to the assizes at Croydon, fettered in irons like a dangerous criminal, and was indicted for seditious libel against the queen under a statute of 1581 making that offense a capital felony. The crime specified was writing *Demonstration of Discipline*. Puckering, who had been one of the commissioners against him, was one of his judges; the other was Baron Clarke. The prosecutor was James Dalton, an apostate from Puritanism. Udall never had a chance. Although he was guilty, that is, was the author of the book—a fact which he never admitted—he was tried for his life by a court which followed the principle of off-with-his-head and on-with-the-trial. The government appeared to be determined to secure his conviction from an intimidated jury regardless of forms of law. It was a common-law trial influenced by High Commission procedure. No defendant was ever permitted to give sworn testimony in a common-law court, yet the judges, acting like inquisitors, helped in several ways to procure a conviction. They urged Udall to take an oath and answer directly to the question whether he wrote the book. Dismissing his protests as a "shift," they told the jury that his refusal to clear himself by oath argued his guilt. The defendant could only answer that the prosecution was supposed to prove it. Denial of his request for counsel was routine for that time, but in theory the judges were supposed to be neutral, offering to the defendant counsel on matters of law when requested. At the outset of the trial, when Udall requested an explanation about the challenging of jurors, the court refused him, saying: "Nay, I am not to tell you that; I sit to judge, and not to give you counsel." [43]

The statute explicitly stated that no one could be indicted for any offense under it unless the offense were proved by two witnesses at the time of the indictment, "which said witnesses . . . shall be brought forth in person before the party so arraigned face to face, and there shall openly declare all they can say against the said party so indicted. . . ." Yet the prosecution did not produce a single witness against Udall. Depositions by three men, sworn under oath before the High Commission, constituted the evidence against him. All three were absent from court. One offered merely hearsay; another claimed to have seen papers in Udall's study "tending as he supposed, to the making of such a book as this," while the third flatly said that Udall himself told him of his authorship. Udall denied that he had said any such thing, offered to swear to it, and offered too to produce witnesses who were present in court to impeach the creditability of the absent accuser. Yet the judges ruled that because such witnesses were "against the queen's majesty," they could not be heard.[44]

The statute punished the writing or publication of a seditious libel when made with "a malicious intent" against the queen and "encouraging" insurrection or rebellion against her. Its original purpose had been to punish Catholics who called Elizabeth a heretic, denied her supremacy, or questioned her legitimacy. Udall claimed that such a statute could not apply to loyal Protestants, adding that the author of the book had not libeled the queen, that malicious intent must be proved, and that the book had not remotely raised an insurrection, nor even individual disobedience, since its appearance in 1588. The court, however, took all these questions away from the jury, ruling that as a matter of law the intent was malicious even if it was not malicious in fact! That the book mentioned the bishops only and the queen not at all did not alter the case, for the assault on them was equivalent to an assault on her in view of her position as Supreme Governor of the church. The book, summarized Judge Clarke, was felonious within the meaning of the statute. Udall protested: "When I was before the lords of her majesty's Council at the time of my commitment, amongst other things that I alledged against the taking of an Oath to accuse myself, I said, that the thing was accounted criminal, and therefore by law I was not to answer: My lord Anderson said, that I said true, if the case had concerned either the loss of life or limb; whereby it is manifest, that then my case was not esteemed felony." Clarke then made the astonishing admission that "the violent course of others since, hath caused your case to be more narrowly sifted." After Clarke had made a hanging charge to the jury, the foreman inquired, "What can we find?" The answer: "Find him Author of the Book, and leave the Felony to us." Twice, before reaching their verdict, the jury sent messages to Udall exhorting him to submit himself as the judges commanded. He answered in his old refrain: his conscience was clear and he "was not to accuse himself." The verdict was guilty.[45]

Udall had conducted his own case with extraordinary ability, exposing the distortions and irregularities of both court and prosecution (the two were indistinguishable). He was probably the first defendant in a common-law trial who claimed a right against self-incrimination, at least in a capital case, even though he had been duly indicted. But his cause was lost from the start. The government did not, however, want a martyr on its hands. What it wanted was the confession, humiliation, and submission of one of the foremost Puritan spokesmen. Notwithstanding the verdict, the judges did not promptly pronounce sentence upon him. When they brought him back the next day, they asked him to admit his guilt, express remorse, fall to his knees, and crave her Majesty's mercy. As if the bizarre trial had never occurred, there was a long wrangle about the law and the evidence, the judges emphasizing the dangers of Puritanism—"this presbytery which these men seek for, would overthrow all. . . ." In the end, when Udall promised to submit, Clarke at last revealed the government's objective; Udall would have to submit in writing: that would provide a public record to use against Puritanism.[46]

The prisoner was returned to jail, without sentence having been passed. Seven months later his supplication to the queen was rejected as unsatisfactory, because he had not acknowledged his crime. In February 1591 the court cautioned him that a proper submission was expected. He yielded not at all, presenting instead an elaborate legal appeal against the verdict. After he and the judges fought the case over again, Puckering tired of fencing with his victim. "We shall make short work of you," he threatened, "will you here acknowledge all the Laws Ecclesiastical and Temporal of this land, to be agreeable to the Word of God?" Udall refused, and they sentenced him to the gallows.[47]

Execution was postponed. Dr. Bond, Elizabeth's chaplain, came from the queen herself to seek Udall's signature to a prepared statement of confession and submission that would serve the government's purposes. There was no dealing with the man. Refusing, he offered an unsatisfactory counter-statement. Sir Walter Raleigh urged him to submit, as did the very eminent Anglican divines, Lancelot Andrews and Alexander Nowell, who were sent by the Privy Council. Nowell reasoned with him for hours on end, but Udall was a flinty monument to conscience and seemed determined to die for it. When it looked as if there was nothing left but to hang him, a way out appeared. Some merchants who were leaving for Turkey offered to take him along as minister. Whitgift agreed and promised to get the queen's pardon if Udall would pledge never to return to England without her permission. He refused to accept the condition. Meanwhile his imprisonment had ruined his health. By the time Whitgift agreed to withdraw the condition, Udall was ill and the merchants had to leave for Turkey. Before the queen could sign the pardon, the ship left without him. Near the end of that year, 1592, Udall died in prison.[48]

Two years earlier John Penry, the "hot Welshman" and Martinist, wrote his bitter denunciation of the High Commission, *The Appellation to Parliament* (1590). Penry, who had earlier spent a month in jail, knew the Commission's oath procedure from personal experience. Following his description of that procedure, he demanded to know whether Parliament would "suffer this bloodie and tirannous inquisition, to be practized any longer within the kingdom? What can the murthering inquisitors of Spaine do more, then by this snare, inveigle mens consciences, and contraine them to spill their owne blood?" The laws of the land, he added, "inforce no man to be his owne accuser" in criminal causes. With increasing frequency others, besides Penry, were beginning to publish similar sentiments.[49]

Robert Beale was the most prolific critic of all, yet as Clerk of the Privy Council he dared not publish his writings. A Star Chamber ordinance of 1586 had centralized the censorship system under Whitgift who would license nothing by Beale or anyone else against the High Commission. Beale's prominence as an officer of the government and his well-known views made even anonymous publication abroad too risky. In 1588 or 1589 he wrote "certain notes against the manner of proceeding *ex officio* by oath" which he forwarded to Burghley for approval. The Lord High Treasurer, though shielding Beale from punishment, passed his manuscript on to Whitgift. Although nothing said or written outside of Parliament could be protected by the privilege of the House, Beale rewrote his manuscript in 1589–90.[50]

One of his prominent themes, still novel in 1590 and potentially dangerous to the royal prerogative, was based on Magna Carta. Although Parliament had authorized the queen to appoint ecclesiastical commissioners with vast jurisdiction, the Commission's oath procedure and its terrible power to punish temporally derived wholly from the queen's letters patent. Supporters of the Commission, therefore, relied on the royal prerogative against critics who would have restricted the Commission to the letter of Parliament's act. By his 1585 speech in the Commons, as well as by his earlier books, Beale had made himself the principal lay critic of the Commission. Insisting upon Parliamentary supremacy in matters of religion, he led the way for common lawyers of a later day to rest their constitutional case against an unlimited prerogative on historic precedents, above all on Magna Carta as the source of the liberty of the subject. Beale found old writs restricting the oath *ex officio* to cases of wills and marriage, and other writs by which common-law courts prohibited ecclesiastical courts from taking jurisdiction over any matter of temporal cognizance. He clinched his argument with the following point: "But to shewe that the said wrytte in the Register and Fitzherberte is a lawe and ought to be esteemed as a Lawe, this may be truelie said, that it conteynethe nothing els then that which is conteyned in the lawe of Lawes, that is the greate Charter of Englande touching the othe now unlawfully used by the Clergie and sought to be mainteyned with the overthrowe of the authoritie or the Lawe, and discredite of the authenticall bookes and reverent Judges of our Lawe." After quoting chapter twenty-eight of Magna Carta, which prohibited bailiffs from putting a man to his oath without witnesses against him, Beale rehearsed reconfirmations of the charter and concluded: "Whereby I doe inferre that by the Statute of Magna Charta and the olde lawes of this realme, this othe for a man to accuse himself was and is utterlie inhibited." [51]

He relied on chapter twenty-nine, containing the law of the land clause, to show the illegality of the power of the High Commission to fine and imprison as well as to search and seize indiscriminately. In one outburst he asked indignantly, "What is become of the great Charter of England which saith that no freeman shall be taken or imprisoned or disseised of his freehold or liberties or free customes, or be outlawed or exiled or otherwise be distrayned but by lawfull judgment and by the lawes of the land . . . when every warrant pursuivant by a warrant under the hande of the Commissioners shall enter into mens houses, break upp their chests and chambers . . . carry away what they list, and afterward pick matter to arrest and committ them, whereof there is no other proofe, but that the partie must be compelled by oth to answer unto the same."

That Beale's argument was in many respects historically unsound is unimportant. What matters is that he took a feudal document stating the liberties of the great magnates and converted it into a constitution for the liberties of all. Creative glosses like Beale's would make Magna Carta a talismanic symbol of freedom, subjecting authority, even the royal prerogative, to the rule of law. He confused the oath *ex officio* with the oath of compurgation; he expanded the meaning of the word "bailiff" to cover even ecclesiastical judges; he read chapters twenty-eight and twenty-nine as if they outlawed the oath *ex officio;* he construed writs which limited the oath to testamentary and matrimonial cases as applicable to members of the clergy as well as to laymen; he found in chapter twenty-nine a bar against general search warrants; and he gave the impression that one had a constitutional right not to incriminate himself involuntarily. He did not know it, but he was making myths that would live. Although his manuscript was never published, it was more than a soliloquy. The original version which passed from Burghley to Whitgift, was turned over to Dr. Cosin for reply. A manuscript book by James Morice, the Puritan lawyer, traveled the same route. Cosin quoted generously from both Beale and Morice in the process of rebutting them in his *Apologie,* in 1593, thus giving their ideas public circulation. Both, moreover, were members of the Commons in 1593 when the question of the oath *ex officio,* raised at their instigation, occasioned fiery speeches that spread their views and resulted in their being punished. Before then, however, the High Commission scored other major victories. The imprisonments of Greenwood, Barrow, Wigginton, and Udall were preliminaries to the main event.[52]

CHAPTER VI

Cartwright, Barrow, and Morice

Thomas Cartwright, the master Puritan and old antagonist of Archbishop Whitgift, returned to England in 1585 after nearly a dozen years in exile. Bishop Aylmer immediately imprisoned him, but he was free in little more than a month. Powerful men on the Privy Council favored his petition for pardon, which he coupled to a pledge that he would live in peace with the church. Even Whitgift, to his credit, was willing to let the past die; he treated Cartwright with such charity and consideration that Cartwright himself spoke well of him for his favors.[1]

Although Cartwright, true to his word, engaged in no public controversies against the church, he took a leading role in the secret movement to presbyterianize the church. This was the period, from about 1586 to 1590, for which Richard Bancroft described Cartwright as "the Patriarche" of the Puritans and "their chiefest counsaylor." "When great matters are to bee handled," said Bancroft, "he must needs be one in every place: Coventry, Cambridge, London etc." Cartwright completed the task, begun by Walter Travers, of writing "the Book of Discipline," a compendious guide for a Presbyterian polity, to which he and his brethren subscribed. He was the leader of the Warwick *classis* and attended general conferences and synods whose purpose was to enforce Presbyterian discipline and reorganize the governance of the church. By interception of letters, Bancroft kept a watchful eye on the *classis* movement for the High Commission. In 1590 he and Whitgift resolved that the time had come to strike. They suspected that Cartwright, because of his importance, must know something about "Martin Marprelate"; moreover, they had accumulated enough evidence to accuse the leaders of the *classis* movement, which they meant to crush.[2]

Arrests began in the spring of 1590. In May, a pursuivant of the High Commission placed Cartwright on notice to ready himself for examination. Determining not to take the oath when the time came, he expressed anxiety about the likelihood of being committed for his refusal. The High Commission kept him in suspense while it built a case against him. Meanwhile, nine of his confederates took the oath, answering freely to the interrogatories. They believed that having done nothing illegal, they ought to stand upon the integrity of their actions. Refusal to co-operate, they thought, would cast the suspicion of sedition upon the movement. Moreover, they saw no practical value in concealing from the Commission what it had already learned from intercepted letters and captured documents. Such men were not necessarily less honorable than Cartwright, but they were not the stuff from which martyrs or new rights were made. Whitgift, in an elaborate report to Burghley on the *classis* movement, mentioned that the synods had agreed that "an oath whereby a man might be tyed to reveal any thing which may be penal to himself, or his faithful brethren," should not be taken. Those who breached such an agreement, invoked the universal Puritan justification: the dictates of private conscience. The *classis* movement aimed at the overthrow of the episcopacy and governance of church affairs by the presbytery rather than by the sovereign. Accordingly the authorities were not likely to appreciate the dictates of private conscience when used to obstruct the High Commission's investigation.[3]

In October 1500, the time of reckoning for Cartwright arrived. Burghley advised Whitgift not to sit with the commissioners in order to avoid the appearance of acting revengefully against an old enemy. The ecclesiastical members of the Commission were supplemented by three of the leading common-law judges, Attorney-General John Popham, and Sergeant John Puckering. Thirty-one articles were objected against Cartwright, among them that he had renounced his Episcopal ordination and had been re-ordained Presbyterian style; he had formed a Presbyterian church among English merchants abroad; he had preached unlicensed since his return to England, criticizing the church and bringing others to his persuasion; he knew the authors, printers, and dispersers of "Martin Marprelate"; he wrote all or part of the Presbyterian "Book of Discipline" and had taken an active part in the *classis* movement; and he and his followers had decreed that no man should incriminate himself or others, or, having taken the oath, should not reveal the truth. In accordance with the Commission's routine procedure, the oath *ex officio* was tendered to Cartwright at the outset of the examination, before he knew any of the charges against him. He immediately took issue with the oath, refusing to swear to tell the truth, sight unseen, to whatever might be demanded of him. Eager for his testimony and not unwilling to expose Cartwright's objections as a sham, the Commission read to him the "heades and generalls" of the articles against him, thus apprising him of the charges in advance, and then demanded that he swear the oath. He answered that although he did not feel bound by the law of God or the law of the land to swear as required, he was so innocent of some of the crimes objected against him that he would take the oath under certain conditions: he must have a copy of the articles, time to deliberate, the advice of counsel, and the freedom to answer only to specific articles, with the ununderstanding that he would explain why he would not answer the others. If this course did not suit the Commission, he would submit to their punishment.[4]

The Commission, having appeased Cartwright by telling him the general charges, was angered by his refusal to swear generally. A second examination failed to budge him. His testimony was so essential, although his unsworn answers could not be used to convict him, that they appeased him further. They did not give him the privilege of consulting counsel, but they handed him a special set of articles to answer in writing in the privacy of his cell. Each of the dozen articles had several questions, and every one dealt with the *classis* movement. They had dropped the nonsense about deeds long dead and about complicity in the "Marprelate" affair. As Cartwright noted in his replies, the purpose of the inquiry seemed to be to determine whether the Puritans sought further reformation of the church by "forcible and violent meanes." He answered that he stood ready to swear on the Bible that he "never intended any such seditious and rebellious disorder," nor had any other minister of his acquaintance. They had used and would continue to use only lawful means, such as petitions to the Privy Council, Parliament, and the queen herself, to achieve their ends. As for the various *classes* and synods, Cartwright said, he was not aware that it was unlawful for dutiful subjects to assemble and confer together. Their purpose was to consider ways of keeping their congregations from being infected with "Poperie," heresy, or the Barrowist schism. The "Book of Discipline," which had never been put into practice, was simply an ideal model of the form of ecclesiastical polity deemed to be most consonant with the word of God. To all of this Cartwright offered to swear on oath. He was completely evasive, however, on all "particulers" respecting times, places, and names, and he avoided answer to many of the articles.[5]

Cartwright's imprisonment, in the words of his biographer, "was in itself a staggering blow to the Presbyterian cause," but his answers did not serve the government's purpose. Having seen the articles, he would take an oath only on his own terms, merely to deny selected charges, and would admit nothing. In effect he offered to take the oath of purgation, not the oath *ex officio*. Moreover, eight other ministers, all close associates of Cartwright who were also in custody, were of the same mind. They were Humphrey Fenn, Andrew King, Daniel Wight, John Payne, Edward Lord, Edmund Snape, William Proudlove, and Melancthon Jewel. Whitgift had tried Burghley's way, the way of moderation, charity, and appeasement. Now he was eager to try his own way, but Burghley, knowing that Cartwright took very badly to imprisonment—he was not, like a Campion, a Barrow, or a Udall, impervious to pain and privation—played a waiting game, certain that a few months in prison would crush his obstinacy. But Burghley had misjudged his man. Cartwright complained piteously, yet prison fortified his resolve, aided, doubtlessly by the example of the other eight prisoners.[6]

Late in 1590 or early in 1591, Cartwright and the eight others drafted a statement of their views on the oath *ex officio*. Remarkably lacking in legal perspicuity, this statement was clearly the product of clergymen who saw the issue in religious terms. They did not need to mention, as they did in passing, that they had been denied legal counsel. No lawyer would have so stressed the sacred nature of an oath, the fear of taking the name of God in vain, or the repugnance of the oath to "the lawe of righteousnesse and of love." Soon after, the nine prisoners composed a more meaty statement on the oath, this time a sizable essay of some nine thousand words. Nine men of God were confronted by an acute problem of conscience. Inevitably their words possessed great moral force and conviction.[7]

The oath, they contended, lacked Biblical sanction, "put the conscience uppon the racke," and violated scriptural injunctions. No prudent man would ignore the danger of swearing generally to answer to whatever might be inquired of him, nor would a devout man forswear God so casually. If, in accord with the scriptural requirement for a presentment, two or three witnesses should accuse someone to his face, he might swear his innocence, in the name of God, thus clearing himself and ending the controversy. In an *ex officio* proceeding, however, where there were no witnesses, the oath was merely the beginning of a controversy, thus a perversion of its sacred purpose, dishonoring God. No God-fearing man could take it, nor would a sensible man make himself an instrument of his own hurt by informing against himself. "Much more is it equall that a mans owne private faults should remayne private to God and him selfe till the lord discover them. And in regard of this righte consider howe the lord ordained wittnesses whereby the magistrate should seeke into the offences of his subjects and not by oathe to rifle the secretts of theare hearts. So that this oathe in this respect cannot be held other then injurious to a mans owne private righte, makinge him to discover his owne secret offence, which in conscience should not discover the secretts of another." By "putting them to declare against them selves," the oath destroyed the excellent privilege of calling for one's accusers, even as it shipwrecked a man's conscience "betwene desire to save himselfe from danger and the reverence of an oath in which feare manye tymes it is not a little strained."[8]

The oath was also a wrong because it damaged in other and

not so obvious ways the one who took it. It made him a "false brother betrayinge others," to their hurt and that of the church, as well as to his own. It was also a destroyer of human relationships, for by forcing a man to become an informer, "then the nearest frend in religion or nature will fall into a jellousey and for feare one of another dowting least at one tyme or other the secretts which pass between them shall be discovered this waye." Thus the pastor dared not trust his people nor they him except in matters he would be willing to have the world know. "And this mischeife at lenth enter even into the famylie that the husband shall not dare to use his wife, the father his sonne nor the master his servant anie thinge which maye come in publick question. And the tymes maye prove such (as often they have) that by this meanes a man by taking this oathe maye spoile him selfe of all the comforts of this life causing all those in whose fellowshippe his harte rejoyseth to fall from him and not to trust him." In much the same way Cartwright and the others contended that if the *ex officio* proceeding could be used against them, under color of the royal prerogative, it might be used in other cases where the sovereign's authority was much more absolute. Anyone might be forced to swear against himself in penal cases to the great prejudice of the subject's liberty granted by ancient laws prohibiting the oath *ex officio* from being taken by laymen except in certain cases of marriage and wills.[9]

To this moral argument, extensive lessons from history were added, drawn mainly from Foxe's *Book of Martyrs*. From the persecution of Wycliffe, William Thorpe's refusal to swear, and Longland's inquisitions turning friends and family members against each other, to John Lambert, William Tyndall, and the martyrs under Bloody Mary, history taught that men should neither accuse themselves nor others, and that "oathes have in them a slaughter and torment of conscience." Robert Beale had built his case on Magna Carta, which he called "the law of laws." To Cartwright, the law of laws was conscience. On these two, Magna Carta and conscience, was founded what would become the right against compulsory self-incrimination.[10]

No such right was recognized in Cartwright's case. Whitgift contemptuously wrote that the ministers' paper against the oath was filled with "very frivolous and childish cavils," but he took no chance that it might influence sympathetic members of the Privy Council. Nine of the High Commission's lawyers framed a reply. They agreed that no man was bound to accuse himself of a hidden crime, but if it was discovered or vehemently suspected, the culprit might be put to oath to reform him and discourage others. Suspicion might come to the ears of an ecclesiastical court by many rumors passed on by credible persons or by common fame. In such a case the supect must answer directly and truly on his oath, "clearing or convicting himself." The *nemo tenetur* doctrine, concluded the learned doctors of the civil law, applied only to the case of a secret crime.[11]

At about the same time, the High Commission sent a formal report of its findings to the Privy Council, under the heading, "The doctrine, with some practices of sundry troublesome Ministers in England, tending to the erecting a new pretended discipline, and to the overthrow of her Majesty's government and prerogative, as well in causes civil as ecclesiastical." The theme of the report was the subversive nature of the *classis* conspiracy of the Cartwrightian Puritans to presbyterianize the English church and state. The report stated the refusal of the imprisoned ministers to take the oath on ground that it tended to accuse them or their brethren and was against the laws both of God and of the land. Such objections were regarded as mere obstructions, refusal to take the oath as part of the general conspiracy: "Which course is the overthrow of the *common justice* of the land in all causes, both *civil* and *ecclesiastical.*" The culprits had been deposed from their ministries by the Commission and committed, "Which is all that by that authority may be inflicted upon them." This was an admission by the Commission that refusal to take the oath had blocked the proceedings completely, for the simple reason that unsworn testimony in an ecclesiastical court was legally worthless. The prisoners could be punished for their contempt by incarceration for the remainder of their lives; but they could not be convicted of the crimes charged.

The Commission, continued the report, had therefore consulted with the two Chief Justices, the Chief Baron, the Attorney-General, and the Queen's Solicitor. All agreed "that this matter is of as great and dangerous consequence to the commonwealth, as any that of long tyme hath happened." In order to reveal the conspiracy, declared the Commission, and impose exemplary punishment "to the terror of others," only one course remained: a speedy, public hearing upon bill and interrogatories in the Star Chamber against the principal offenders, with a punishment as great as precedent showed that court had ever inflicted. For much lesser crimes, there were precedents showing "*banishment* and *condemnation* to the *gallies*." In this case perpetual banishment in some remote place might be most fitting and in the best interests of the quiet of the realm. So recommended the High Commission.[12]

While the Privy Council deliberated on the recommendation, the prisoners sent to the councilors and to Elizabeth a long supplication whose tone suggested that they had somehow managed to obtain the advice of counsel, probably James Morice or Nicholas Fuller, who was also a Puritan lawyer of distinction. The supplication, protesting that the charges against the prisoners were unfounded and their imprisonment unjustified, argued that their activities were consistent with the duties of faithful, obedient subjects. What is so intriguing is their first two pages, a criticism of the procedural shortcomings of the High Commission's course against them. They mentioned conscience and charity, but stressed their right to common-law procedures and statutory guarantees based on a 1534 reaffirmation of the principles of chapter twenty-nine of Magna Carta. The "oath of inquisition," they declared, next to their alleged but unproved crimes, was the "immediate" cause of their troubles. They were entitled to be charged by "due and ordinary course of proceeding, by open accusation and witnesses." Instead, an illegal oath had been demanded for the purpose of forcing them to reveal "private speeches and conference with our dearest and nearest friends; yea, of the very secret thoughts and intents of our hearts, that so we may furnish both matter of accusation, and evidence of proof against ourselves. . . ." Recalling the enactment in Henry VIII's time against "captious interrogatories," they claimed that no person should be convicted, or be put to loss of life, good name, or goods, except by due accusation and presentment; and, to avoid malicious and

anonymous accusations, the law provided that none should be put
to answer but upon indictment by grand jury.[13]

Whitgift, meanwhile, continued to press for a Star Chamber
trial. He wrote another paper summarizing the prisoners' crimes,
including their refusal to take the oath, and urged the need for
further exposure. "Seeing this cannot be effected by any means,
but by the confession of such as were partakers of their conferences (if they and others shall persist in refusal), what course
were best to be taken for the terror of others? Whether by
praemunire [forfeiture of all property and life imprisonment], if
they have incurred it by law; or by some exemplary corporal punishment, to be inflicted by the Lords of the Star-chamber, or
otherwise." The Star Chamber, incidentally, could punish corporally by public whipping, ear-cropping, nose-slitting, branding,
and similar refinements. [14]

A Star Chamber proceeding was agreed upon. About a week
before it was scheduled to begin in mid-May 1591, the High
Commission made one last effort to break down Cartwright's resistance to taking the oath. The obstinacy of the Puritan ministers
had completely stymied the Commission, bringing its authority
into serious question and its proceedings to a dead halt. While
anyone declining the oath could be punished for contempt, he
might nevertheless take satisfaction in knowing that he had crippled the Commission's legal process. It could investigate but could
not legally try and convict in its capacity as an ecclesiastical court
except for contempt. Its revenge against the Cartwrightians for
flouting its authority in no way enhanced that authority, for it not
only failed to make its charges stick; it could not even prosecute
them. Like the Puritans, the Commission was a victim of its procedures. Cartwright, as the leader of the Puritans, was the man to
break. Turning the case over to the Star Chamber might serve the
cause of public justice, but it was also a measure of desperation,
virtually announcing that the High Commission itself was ineffective to serve that cause.

Bishop Aylmer presided at the critical meeting with Cartwright.
Attorney-General Popham represented the secular arm of the
state. Richard Bancroft was present and two of the Commission's
lawyers who had framed and signed the Commission's answer to

the ministers' conscientious objections against taking the oath. The examination dealt with the oath only. Conducted by men who lacked all understanding, who sought to overawe, demand, and intimidate, it was a futile venture. Cartwright, though constantly stopped when he sought to discuss the charges, doggedly resisted. They would talk only about the oath, while he was by now as articulate and fixed in his opinion about it as a man could be. Nothing new, of course, remained to be said. When Popham insisted how dangerous it was that men "should upon the conceits of their own heads, and yet under colour of conscience, refuse the thinges that have bene recyved for lawes of long time," Cartwright imperturbably dropped any effort to justify himself by the law of the land and rested his case on the one ground where his expertise yielded to none, "the law of God." Finally, having harangued and badgered him with many "long speaches," they realized that they were simply dashing themselves on the rock of his immoveable conscience. He had defeated the Commission. Nothing remained but to turn him over to the Star Chamber.[15]

Ten years earlier in the trial of Vaux and Tresham for harboring Campion, the Star Chamber had made the monumental ruling that the *nemo tenetur* maxim applied only in cases involving life or limb. Because that great court—the Privy Council sitting judicially, augmented, usually, by the chief justices of the common-law courts—could not punish capitally or by dismemberment, it could exact the oath *ex officio* in its own proceedings. By implication, the ruling in the case of Vaux and Tresham meant that the High Commission might lawfully employ the oath, too. Although generalizations about Star Chamber procedure are always dangerous because the court might at will exercise its prerogative of altering procedure, there were, nevertheless, significant differences in the Star Chamber's use of the oath as compared to the High Commission's.[16]

James Morice, shortly after the Cartwright case, wrote a treatise against the oath *ex officio* in which he acknowledged that both the Court of Star Chamber and the Court of Chancery used the oath, a point which its proponents frequently made to justify its use by the High Commission. "But," Morice asked, "Who hath ever seene in these Courtes [Star Chamber and Chancery] any subject of this lande, in a cause concerning him selfe, brought forth and compelled to depose or make aunswere uppon his oath, no bill of complainte or information formerlie exhibited against him [?] Nay on the contrarie, these Courtes observing the due form of Justice, enforce no man to answere, but where hee hath a knowne accusor, and perfect understandynge of the cause or cryme objected, and therewithall is permitted to have a coppie of the bill of complainte or information (being not *ore tenus*). And allowed moreover both tyme convenient, and counsell learned well to consider and advise of his oathe and answere." In the Star Chamber, Morice continued, the defendant might demur either to the jurisdiction of the court or to the form or matter of the complaint; and he need not answer impertinent interrogatories. The High Commission afforded none of these procedural protections. It prosecuted words and thoughts, while the Star Chamber, which unlike the Commission compelled no man to be "his owne accusor and condemner," prosecuted facts and deeds.[17]

Morice's description of the use of the oath *ex officio* by the Star Chamber goes a long way toward explaining why common lawyers like him and Nicholas Fuller could with consistency assault the High Commission and not the Star Chamber. Beale, indeed, as Clerk of the Privy Council, was also Clerk of the Star Chamber. In a state prosecution before the Star Chamber, the Attorney-General framed a bill of complaint which, like a common-law indictment, specifically stated the charges. The defendant received a copy of the bill—he got no copy of his indictment from a common-law court—and with the advice of counsel had plenty of time to reply to the charges in writing. At that point he had to take the oath *ex officio*, swearing not only that his reply was true but that he would answer truthfully to all relevant interrogatories which might be demanded of him. The inquisitorial feature of a Star Chamber proceeding was reflected in the next step. With no advance knowledge of the interrogatories and without counsel, the defendant was privately examined, under oath, on a series of questions to which his answers were taken in writing and subscribed by him. On the other hand, he might then have witnesses on his behalf, just as the crown might produce witnesses against him, but all witnesses were examined separately and privately, under oath, in writing, and without benefit of counsel. When all the evidence was taken, there was a public trial before the court; it never sat with a jury. The Lord Chancellor presided, and on a vacant chair were displayed the royal arms, a mace, and a purse to symbolize the presence of the sovereign and the fact that the court was vested with royal authority. At the trial, the written record was read, giving the defendant full knowledge of the evidence and of his accusers. He was represented by counsel who answered for him.

On the other hand, the Star Chamber might scrap all procedural regularity and do just as it pleased, and it did just that in so-called extraordinary cases, those involving matters of state and any others deemed by the Star Chamber, in its prerogative discretion, to be extraordinary. Many cases were tried by a summary oral procedure, called *ore tenus*, as in the trial of Vaux and Tresham. The oath, elaborate preliminaries, witnesses, written record, and counsel were all dispensed with. The suspect was simply "grilled" or put to a "third degree" type of examination whose only purpose was to trap him into a confession and conviction.[18]

Cartwright and his confederates received the full formal treatment from the Star Chamber. Nicholas Fuller, who later became a heroic figure in the history of English liberty, represented them. He, Morice, and Beale were a triumvirate of outstanding lawyers who laid the groundwork for the right against self-incrimination, although Fuller's principal contribution came in the next reign when he went to prison for the cause. Regrettably we know little of his part in Cartwright's case. Nor do we know whether the Star Chamber demanded that Cartwright and the others must swear their answers to the bill of complaint, and if so, whether they complied or answered unsworn. The government's case was based on the sworn depositions of nine Puritan ministers who had been close to the defendants in the *classis* movement and who had taken the oath *ex officio* when examined before the High Commission. Yet four of the nine also deposed on behalf of the defendants. They had by no means turned state's evidence. For all practical purposes their testimony was enough to indict but not enough to convict.[19]

The main charge was seditious conspiracy, by writing, preaching, and assembly, to overthrow the established church and erect a Presbyterian system in its place. The prisoners admitted favoring a new ecclesiastical polity, yet denied that they had ever put it into execution. They had utilized only lawful means, they contended, always observing the laws of the land and never disturbing the public peace. In effect they demurred to most of the charges, admitting facts—such as their subscription to the "Book of Discipline," holding conferences, and denial of the oath—but asserting the legality of everything done or proposed. Under Fuller's guidance, the answers to the twenty-one charges in the bill of complaint were wary, evasive, and full of indignant objections to the aspersions on their loyalty. At certain points they "take not themselves bound to aunswere." Defying an order from the court to answer more "particularly and directlie," they reaffirmed their belief that they "ought not to aunswer" some of the questions. On the matter most to the point, the refusal of the prisoners "to answere upon their corporal oathes" even though they had been "acquainted" with the articles, they gave their standard reply. They also denied the charge alleged, that their refusal was merely a guise to "cover" their seditious purpose to presbyterianize the church by force "to the utter overthrow of . . . governmente." Again and again they flatly denied such a purpose or the use of unlawful means. Their only unhedged reply that could have exposed them to a perjury charge was the denial that they had ever dissuaded any one from taking the oath. One of the nine prisoners, Edward Lord, later confessed that he had done so, and only John Johnson, of the nine witnesses deposing for the government, supported the charge. Johnson was also the only one alleging that his brethren in the *classis* movement had privately practiced the "Book of Discipline" and sought to convert others to it, knowing there was no way to get their program established by law.[20]

The prisoners' answers to the bill of complaint became the basis of written interrogatories which sought to draw from them detailed information about their beliefs and practices. Cartwright's replies to forty-three interrogatories were described by Whitgift as grossly unsatisfactory. He and the others "aunswer not all the most part." At the first hearing before the Star Chamber, the oath issue was debated in detail, the prisoners recalcitrantly adhering to

their position and to their refusal to reply to "the principal interrogatories." The court, on the advice of its common-law judges,
brought the prisoners back for a second hearing and commanded
them to reply directly to certain interrogatories which were central to the issue: Where did their assemblies meet? When and how
often? Who else attended? What matters were discussed? Who
wrote the "Book of Discipline"? Which parts of it were carried
into execution? Was the sovereign the head of the church and was
it lawful for her to ordain its sacraments and ceremonies? Was the
ecclesiastical government of England lawful and conformable to
the word of God? To all these questions which the court ordered
the prisoners to answer, Whitgift reported to Burghley, they
"notwithstanding stil refuse to aunswer." [21]

They could hardly justify their contempt by claiming that the
questions were not relevant to the inquiry or the charges.
Whether they were simply silent or attempted to justify their behavior is unknown. Their lawyer, Nicholas Fuller, had been
present at the assizes in Croydon a year earlier, when John Udall
was tried and convicted for the capital crime of seditious libel
under an act of 1581. Fuller had tried unsuccessfully to address
the jury on Udall's behalf. At the time of the Star Chamber trial
of Cartwright and the others, Udall, their friend, was in prison
awaiting execution of the death sentence. The "Book of Discipline" was far more seditious than Udall's *Demonstration of Discipline*. It is tempting to speculate that Fuller advised his clients to
answer no questions concerning the "Book of Discipline" or the
classis movement to which it was a guide. The Star Chamber, to
be sure, could not punish capitally, but a confession before it
might conceivably be the basis of a common-law trial like Udall's.
The Udall case was certainly a menacing precedent of which
Cartwright was acutely conscious. It would not be surprising if,
under Fuller's advice, he and the others protested against the interrogatories because the Star Chamber sought self-incrimination
in a case that brought life and limb into jeopardy. Fuller himself
might have made that argument before the Star Chamber. This is
mere speculation, but Fuller, unlike his clients, was not likely to
rest their case on the laws of God.[22]

It is certain that the Star Chamber trial ended in the same way as the High Commission's proceedings: the prisoners stubbornly refused to confess or answer incriminating interrogatories, thereby blocking the entire inquiry. They had simply compounded their one irrefutable crime—contempt of court—for which they were already in prison. The Star Chamber, despite its august majesty and a procedure which was not vulnerable to attack, had failed as dismally as the High Commission to break the prisoners. There is no evidence that the Star Chamber or Privy Council considered the sternest course of all, torture. That was reserved, apparently, only for Catholics and lay criminals, not for Protestant ministers, surely not for a man of Cartwright's distinction. Indeed, the government turned in the other direction, treating the prisoners to the finest measure of English justice—benefit of reasonable doubt. Burghley, who had been ill during the Star Chamber hearings, was not satisfied that the elusive evidence, which had raised such suspicion against the prisoners, sufficiently proved their guilt of the crimes charged. Instead of the Star Chamber's rendering a decision, a most unusual course was adopted. Burghley, for the Privy Council, ordered Sir John Popham, the Attorney-General, to read all the documents relating to the trial and to give his judgment on the evidence. Hatton, the Lord Chancellor, ordered Whitgift to appoint a doctor of divinity and a doctor of civil law to assist Popham in his review of the case.[23]

The prisoners remained in jail while the government decided whether to bring them to trial before a common-law court for seditious conspiracy, or to punish them corporally, or banish them as Whitgift had suggested. Popham, near the close of 1591, reported that the evidence was inconclusive. He believed that the prisoners had resolved to establish their form of ecclesiastical discipline but only "so farre forth as the same might be done with the peace of the Church, and laws of the land." On the other hand Popham thought that the evidence proved the prisoners to be culpable, because some of their assemblies, believing that the consent of queen and Parliament was not forthcoming, intended to convert other ministers to their view and through them win over the people. Popham, in other words, placing as black a construction as possible on the evidence, found only criminal intent without criminal activity. The latter could not be punished, theoretically, without proof of the former, but the former was not punishable at all without some proof of the latter. As another member of the bar, Fuller probably, volunteered to Burghley, "there was no matter proved of any meetings or conventicles, seditiously made and executed by Cartwright and his fellows." Finally, Sir Christopher Wray, the Chief Justice of the Queen's Bench, the highest criminal court in England, persuaded the Lord Chancellor and other members of the Star Chamber that "they should not deal against Cartwright and his fellows, until they should have matter to prove some seditious act *de facto* to be committed by them." [24]

So the case stood, with the government not quite willing to believe them innocent, but unable to prove them guilty because they would not furnish evidence against themselves. As Sir Francis Knollys, one of the privy councilors sympathetic to the Puritans, said, if the bishops or any lord or Hatton could have proved *de facto* sedition, "then Cartwright and his fellows had been hanged before this time." Meanwhile the prisoners had been besieging the government with petitions for their release. In March of 1592, Whitgift sought to exact from them a complete submission as the price of freedom: they must subscribe to a document acknowledging that the established church was lawful and godly in every manner, and that any attempt to alter it was seditious. As Cartwright's biographer so strikingly said, their signatures would have meant a recantation "extorted by despotism from cowardice. . . . They preferred liberty of conscience to liberty of body and so refused to subscribe." But their deliverance was not long delayed, for in May they were released on a probationary basis after being admonished to behave themselves. They did. Whitgift, Bancroft, and the High Commission had failed to convict them, but succeeded in crushing the *classis* movement and intimidating the Presbyterian leaders. Cartwright and the other ministers lapsed into obscurity and silence after gaining their freedom.[25]

The High Commission turned next to the Separatists, whose numbers increased in spite of persecution. In 1593 Sir Walter Raleigh estimated that there were twenty thousand of them in England, a wild exaggeration; several hundred seem to have been enough to frighten the government into intensified repressions. By

1592 most of the London Separatists who had been captured with Greenwood and Barrow were at liberty, though their leaders and some others still lay in jail. Greenwood himself, after more than four years of imprisonment, seems to have enjoyed a brief period of freedom in 1592, but near the close of the year was taken into custody again, together with Francis Johnson. Johnson, another remarkable zealot, had taken the leadership of the movement when Barrow and Greenwood were locked up. He had a record of frequent troubles with the authorities even before he became a Separatist. In 1589 he and one Cuthbert Bainbrigg, both Fellows of Christ's College, Cambridge, had boldly preached against the bishops. At the inquisition against them, they adamantly refused the oath *ex officio*, claiming that it would constrain them to furnish proof against themselves. Their obstinate pleas and petitions against the oath led to a formal declaration of its lawfulness by the leading lawyers of the High Commission. The defendants were thrown out of the university, "deprived," and jailed for twenty weeks. Johnson, who was then a Puritan of the Presbyterian stripe, drifted away from the established church. The works of Barrow and Greenwood converted him to Separatism, and in September of 1592, he revived their congregation in London, becoming the new pastor. Within three months, pursuivants of the High Commission, raiding private homes in the middle of the night, made a batch of arrests. Johnson and Greenwood were apprehended together. In March of 1593, fresh raids resulted in fifty-six arrests, bringing to seventy-two the number of Separatists then in prison. Later in the same month the High Commission scored one of its greatest catches when it arrested several others including John Penry. A notorious Martinist wanted by the government since 1589, Penry was a recent convert to Separatism, at the time of his apprehension a member of the Johnson congregation.[26]

Archbishop Whitgift's cup was brim full, and he meant to slake a vengeful thirst. The Barrowists were a despised and friendless sect, wholly at the mercy of the High Commission. Unlike Cartwright, they had no powerful patrons to intercede on their behalf. From a "Lamentable Complaint and Supplication, of the persecuted," written a week after the capture of the fifty-six, we learn that men and women, including the aged, lay in irons in dungeons, so cold and hungry that they thought the prelates meant purposely "to emprison them unto death, as they have doon 17 or 18 others in the same noysome Gaoles within these .6. yeeres." They begged to be treated mercifully and to be turned over to the civil authorities for trial according to the laws of England. "But let not these bloody men both accuse, condemne & closely murther after this sort, contrarie to lawe, aequitie & Conscience, Where they alone are the plaintiffes, the accusers, the Judges, and the Executioners of theyr most fearefull & barbarous tyrannie. . . . For streames of innocent blood are likely to bee spilt in secret by these bloodthirstie men, except her Majestie and Your Honours doo take order with theyr most cruell & inhumane procedinges." [27]

Another petition piteously complained that the High Commission, by denying them knowledge of the charges against them and by subtle interrogation, sought to place them in criminal danger. Indeed, great as their mistreatment was, their situation could have become worse, for the High Commission was searching for evidence of something that would pass for overt acts of sedition and not merely proof of failure to attend established services. The Commission first rifled their homes and then their consciences in its examination of dozens of suspects. Some confessed to their Separatist beliefs and their attendance at secret conventicles; others were contumacious. Many, like George Johnson, a school teacher, and George Knifton, an apothecary, refused the oath *ex officio* and would answer no interrogatories. Others, like Daniel Bucke, a scrivener, and John Nicholas, a glover, refused the oath yet made damaging admissions in response to unsworn interrogatories. Some were made of a granite that nothing could erode. A haberdasher named George Collier, for example, had been in jail for five years without ever having been examined. In spite of the suffering he must have undergone in all that time, when finally brought before the Commission he refused to answer or to conform. Christopher Bowman, a goldsmith who served as deacon to Johnson's congregation, had already spent three years in prison; after two years of freedom, he was back in jail, prepared to stay indefinitely rather than swear the oath. Some who gave unsworn testimony, having refused the oath, answered cautiously. Christopher Simkins, a coppersmith, admitted that he had not been to the parish church for a year and a half and had frequently attended Barrowist assemblies, but he would provide no details and refused to say whether he owned or read books by Penry or Barrow. William Smyth, a minister of the established church, admitted, though not under oath, that he had attended a private conventicle of Johnson's church; yet he refused to say whether he was a member of it, nor would he answer any questions about seditious books. Thomas Settle, a minister whom Whitgift imprisoned in 1586, responded the same way.[28]

John Penry, the principal catch, foolishly allowed himself to be drawn into a disputation about his religious beliefs and practices, after a period of initial intransigeance. At his first examination, he refused to answer anything, demanding a public conference. At the next examination, he admitted that he had escaped to Scotland and published a book entitled *Reformation no Enemie*, but refused to answer other questions. Yet at his third examination, although the record shows nothing whatever about the oath *ex officio*, he replied candidly and in detail to a variety of incriminating questions, ending with the valiant assertion, "Imprisonments, inditements, yea, death itself, are no meet weapons to convince mens consciences." Francis Johnson, the most important catch next to Penry, was far cagier, standing off the High Commission's lawyers, the archbishop, and the Lord Chief Justices of England, in several examinations. He freely discussed his baptismal practices, but nothing else of consequence. He would not discuss meetings of his congregation nor anything relating to books by Penry, Barrow, or Greenwood. The record shows a refrain, "he refuseth to answer." [29]

The Separatists were religious fanatics whose spiritual courage and devotion matched the repellent narrowness of their beliefs. By 1593 the government regarded them as a greater danger to the peace of the realm than the Catholic recusants. The Barrowists were actually quite harmless, but the extremity of their views—their savage denunciation of the prelates, their rejection of the Church of England as the church of Anti-Christ, their refusal to acknowledge the queen as supreme ecclesiastical governor—thrust them, like the Anabaptists, beyond the pale of what then passed as civilized society. Even Burghley, a moderate man in the Tudor autocracy, on listening to Barrow expound his views, exclaimed that there should be "streighter lawes" made against him and his kind. Whitgift, whom Barrow called "a monster," was a sinister figure, yet compared to Barrow was neither dogmatic nor intolerant. Had the Barrowists ruled England there would not have been jailors and hangmen enough to enforce their version of Old Testament law; no one but those sharing their precise shade of belief in every respect would have been safe. But the Barrowists did not rule England. Its queen and her government, civil and ecclesiastical, were as a lion savagely bashing a tick rather than majestically ignoring its insignificant presence.[30]

Barrow and Greenwood were the founders of the sect. Although Francis Johnson was its new leader, and no less a contumacious one, he had not committed the one crime that would make him as menacing or as vulnerable as they. He wrote no books, while they, even in prison, somehow continued to be prolific authors. Barrow wrote a huge tome in 1590 excoriating the established church. His choicest invective was aimed at the prelacy. A section of some ten thousand words scathingly described the Court of High Commission and its oath procedure, comparing it unfavorably to the Holy Inquisition. Penry, too, was incorrigibly given to broadcasting his radical opinions in print. Such men exerted an influence far beyond the confines of their miserable little conventicles. They stirred sedition throughout the land. The upshot of the Barrowist adventure in England was the execution of the three.[31]

Like Udall, they were tried under a statute of 1581, passed originally to punish papist propaganda; the charge was seditiously libeling the queen whom they professed, quite literally to their dying moments, to love and obey. They all would have been pardoned, their lives spared, had they recanted and promised to attend established services. Barrow and Greenwood, who died together, were taken secretly to the place of execution at Tyburn where with ropes about their necks they were permitted to speak their last words—protests of innocency and loyalty. Not even the terror of the final moment induced them to change their minds. Nevertheless, they were reprieved and returned to prison, only to be suddenly executed a week later. A month and a half later,

Penry was tried. His legal defense in his own behalf was so good —an argument to the effect that his books did not come within the terms of the statute—that the government compounded the legal flummery by resting the prosecution mainly on his private papers and unpublished notebooks. Penry really paid with his life for complicity in the Martin Marprelate publications—crimes not charged against him. The young minister was hanged the same day in May 1593 that Archbishop Whitgift and Chief Justice Popham signed his death warrant. Barrow, Greenwood, and Penry were martyrs for the sake of conscience; each, but especially Barrow, by their objections to the oath *ex officio* and to inquisitorial procedures, contributed in a small way to the sentiment that the law should not force a man to incriminate himself.[32]

At this juncture James Morice, the Puritan lawyer, made his main contribution to the same end. In 1591 or 1592 he finished what he modestly described as a "brief treatise" against the High Commission and sent the manuscript to Burghley for approval. In a letter he explained that he had perceived abuses by the ecclesiastical courts "by reason of the daily practice of inquisition in causes criminal *ex officio mero*, that is, upon secret suggestions or insinuations, without legal accusation, by putting the party to take an oath to answer, before he knoweth whereunto, and by the unjust imprisonment of her Majesty's people, for the refusal of such oath." He therefore thought it to be his duty to write a "brief treatise" showing the iniquity of such proceedings as repugnant to the laws of God and of the realm. As indicated above, Morice's manuscript, like Beale's, traveled from Burghley to Whitgift, the official censor, to Dr. Richard Cosin. Cosin, who referred to Morice as "the Treatisour" and Beale as "the Note-Gatherer," generously quoted and paraphrased their opinions, which he held up to ridicule by the standards of High Commission law. Morice rewrote his treatise to incorporate criticism of Cosin's *Apologie*, showing more fully the injustice of compulsory self-incrimination. Fearing that offense might be taken, he did not circulate the manuscript, yet Whitgift learned of its existence and demanded a copy. Loathe to comply, Morice did so on the condition, to which Whitgift agreed, that he would not be brought into trouble for private writings. To Burghley, Morice complained bitterly that Cosin was free to publish a book in favor of unjust inquisitions, while he could not publish his book nor even "in such private and privy manner, maintain the right cause of justice," without suspicion being cast on his loyalty.[33]

Morice's book, *A briefe treatise of Oathes exacted by Ordinaries and Ecclesiasticall Judges*, was published abroad in 1598, a year after his death, and was reprinted in 1600. Its tone and theme may be gathered from his description of the High Commission as "a Court of Inquisition more then Spanish to sifte & ransacke by oath the most secret thoughtes and consciences of all men in generall, enforcing them either to accuse themselves . . . to the publique shame, reproach, and condemnation, or els for the avoyding of such mischiefe and inconvenience, to committe most wilfull and damnable perjurie." Morice's target was the oath *ex officio* which he distinguished from all other oaths, particularly the oath of purgation with which apologists for the High Commission were apt to confuse it. The sworn statement of innocency, he explained, conclusively cleared a suspect, ending all controversy, while the oath *ex officio* was but the point of departure for a controversy, which presumed the guilt of the suspect and sought from him proof of that guilt. Such an oath, he found, contradicted every principle of morality, justice, and the common law of England. Morice was particularly irked by a scornful comment of the Archbishop of Canterbury, made in 1585, when rejecting a petition of the Commons against the oath. Whitgift had compared opponents of the oath *ex officio* with Jesuits and seminary priests who, allegedly, first opposed it. In a long historical section, drawn heavily from Foxe's *Book of Martyrs*, Morice rehearsed the ancient opposition to the oath on the part of early Protestants to prove that it had been first opposed by good Christians for a just cause. Morice's own history was somewhat deficient when he concluded that the maxim *nemo tenetur seipsum prodere* expressed an old principle of English liberty, going back to Magna Carta. He claimed that learned doctors of the canon and civil law, who sought to restrict the maxim to secret or unknown crimes, placed on it a gloss that destroyed the principle. If a man must swear generally to answer truthfully to whatever might be asked of him, however incriminating, merely because he has been accused by fame or common report, the laws of God and of the realm were both abridged.[34]

Morice took great pains to prove that nothing like the oath existed in the common law, neither in civil nor criminal cases. By the common law, he claimed, there was neither oath nor torment to force a man to accuse himself. Like torture, the oath stood condemned as cruel and barbarous in any well-governed commonwealth. Parliament controlled the law of the land, Morice argued. If by implication it had authorized the oath by an act of 1401, it had made the oath illegal by its repealer in 1534. The crown, on its own authority, could not alter the law of the land by letters patent establishing commissions. Magna Carta, especially by chapter twenty-nine, so often confirmed, laid down the procedure to be followed in all criminal causes. "And how then shall that kind of proceedinge Ex officio by forced oathes and the urging of this generall oathe and straighte imprisoninge of such as refuse to sweare bee justifiable?" He concluded that the oath was "a wrong and injurie to the freedome and libertie of the subjects" of the realm.[35]

Morice could not publish his book, but on the floor of the Commons his remarks were presumably privileged. Parliament met in February of 1593. Morice dominated its first day of business. He did so at a risk, for the queen, more imperious than ever, at the outset cautioned the House that she granted "liberal but not licentious speech." Each member must restrict his speech within the bounds of loyalty and discretion, "as the contrary is punishable in all men." The "true" liberty of speech did not consist of a right to say whatever one pleased nor to frame a form of religion or a state of government. No monarch fit for his state would suffer such absurdities. So the crown informed the Commons. Despite this caution, Morice rose to defend the "lawes and publique Justice of this Kingdome, and the Liberties of us that are the Subjects thereof." His duty to God and love of country, he claimed, constrained him to discuss great injustices that had "lately crept in . . . under colour and pretence of lawfull Authority." The offenders were those exercising ecclesiastical jurisdiction. They were guilty of practicing an "ungodlye and intollerable Inquisition":

> Their Inquisition is in this manner, eyther upon complaint made of some Cryme or Offence, by seacret and for the most

part malitious Enformers, or uppon bare suspition conceyved of their owne Phantazies, they cause to be cyted and convented before them hir Ma(jes)ties subjects both laie and Clergye men: uppon Apparaunce, no Accuser, lawfull Presentment, or matter of accusation appearinge, the Party convented is commaunded and urged to take an Oathe to aunswer all such Questions and Interrogatories as by them shall be propounded, not declaringe unto him, whereof he shall be examined, althoughe he instantlie desier to knowe it. Yf through feare of further troble, he accept the Oathe, then by captious and searchinge Questions concerninge his actions words and thoughts they draw from him some matter, whereuppon to frame an accusation, which obteyned, they proceede to their solemne sentence of Deprivation, suspention, Degradation, Imprisonment, or peynes pecuniarie at their licentious pleasure. Yf the Party convented standinge uppon his lawfull libertie refuse to take this indefinite Oathe, then as for a heynous contempt ageinst God and hir Ma(jes)ties he is comytted to hard and miserable Imprisonment, there to remayne duringe pleasure without Bayle or Mayneprise. A Course not tollerable in anye well governed Estate or Commonwealthe.[36]

By wrested oaths which were contrary to all legal procedure, Morice continued, the queen's subjects were constrained to be "both Accusers and condemners of our selfs." One's secret deeds, words, and thoughts, in no way offensive to the public peace, became the means of depriving one of his precious liberty. "Wheare is nowe become the greate Charter of England, obtayned by many difficulties, confirmed by sondry Acts of Parliament," which protected the subject from punishment except by the law of the land? Quoting chapter twenty-nine of Magna Carta, Morice asked rhetorically what had happened to its guarantee that "utterlye forbiddeth the imposeinge of an Oathe uppon him that is accused of anye Crime or matter of disgrace?" What had happened to the confirmation which provided that no man should be put to answer without presentment or due process of law? These ancient guarantees, he alleged, had been "cast aside by our Ecclesiasticall Judges." Depicting them as the sappers of English liberty, Morice reminded the Commons that when its own committee had petitioned for forbearance in the use of the examinations *ex officio mero*, the lords spiritual had deflected blame from themselves by comparing their opponents to "Jesuite Seminaries and suche as would bringe the Churche to an Anarchie." He, for one, resented such distortions of the facts, and in an indiscreet distortion of his own asserted that unjust inquisitions had been "invented and brought in first for none other purpose, but to maintayne a Romishe Hierarchie . . . derogatorie to the lawes and liberties of England." [37]

After more of the same, borrowing from his unpublished treatise, Morice proceeded to his memorable and dangerous peroration:

Wee . . . the Subjects of this Kingdome are borne and brought upp in due obedience, butt farre from Servitude and bondage, subject to lawfull aucthoritye and commaundement, but freed from licentious will and tyrannie; enjoyinge by lymitts of lawe and Justice oure liefs, lands, goods, and liberties in greate peace and security, this our happy and blessed estate if wee maie continue the same dearlie pourchased in a greate part not manye years paste by our Auncestours, yea even with the effusion of their bloud, and losse of their liefes. And shall wee as a degenerate offspringe by negligence and Securitie suffer the losse of a pretious Patrimony, yeild our bodies to be burned, our consciences to be ransacked, and our Inheritaunce to be disposed at the pleasure of our Prelates, and not so much as once open our mouthes to the contrarie? forgettinge that the lawes, liberties, and Customs of this our Countrye are the sinnewes and bindinge Bands of our Body Politique. If the Sinnewes be weakened, shall not the whole Bodye be enfeabled? If these things move us not, at the least let the regard of our Posterity, whom wee suffer to fall into extreame thraldome.[38]

His speech ended, Morice introduced two bills, the first "An Act agenst unlawfull Oathes, Inquisitions, and Subscriptions." The elaborate preamble recapitulated his speech in eloquent, libertarian rhetoric that glorified Magna Carta and the procedure of the common law on the one hand, and on the other damned the ecclesiastical courts, especially the Court of High Commission. Its "Corporall oath" procedure was his particular target mainly because it was a repugnant and illegal device for coercing a suspect into revealing "matter of crime" against himself. At no point did

Morice confront the fact that the common law, both in the preliminary examination of a suspect and in the public trial of one
who was indicted, habitually sought to convict him by badgering
him into a confession. Morice saw only the differences between
the two legal systems—and they were many and vital—but he
never noticed their similarities. Without the rhetoric, his proposed
bill provided that any person exercising ecclesiastical jurisdiction
should incur the penalty of praemunire—forfeiture of property
and life imprisonment—for ministering the oath *ex officio*, practicing "any such manner kind or form of Inquisition" in any criminal cause, or imprisoning anyone or otherwise hurting him for his
refusal to take the oath.[39]

The second bill was aimed at the practice of the prelates in forcing ministers to subscribe to certain articles of belief and practice
"against scruple of conscience." The preamble of the bill, like a
section of his speech, made the intriguing if far-fetched argument
that to suspend or deprive a minister from his spiritual office was
equivalent to dispossessing him from his freehold and denying him
his liberty, contrary to Magna Carta's guarantee that no man
should be disseised of his freehold or denied his liberty without
common-law process. Morice proposed that if the archbishop or
any ecclesiastical judge should permit or enforce any subscription
or inflict any pain, fine, loss, or imprisonment for refusal to subscribe to any articles not commanded by the common law or some
act of Parliament, the offender should incur the penalty of praemunire.[40]

Morice's speech made supporters of the High Commission
wince and embarrassed the queen's defenders who did not relish
speaking for its procedures. The ground on which Morice chose
to make his stand was not Presbyterian reform of the church; it
was the hallowed ground of the liberty of the subject, ancient
common-law procedures, and the great charter of England. James
Dalton, a common lawyer who hated Puritanism, defended the
High Commission from Morice's charges by an irrelevant assault
on the Cartwright party; the House showed its disapproval by so
much "spittinge and coughinge" that he was forced to take his
seat. Dr. William Lewin, a member of the High Commission, was
more to the point as he justified its oath procedure from the stand-

point of both expediency and the standards of ecclesiastical law. Robert Beale and Henry Finch, another common lawyer who was close to the Puritan cause, backed up Morice. So, in fact, did Sir Francis Knollys, even though he was a privy councilor. Other privy councilors, Sir John Wooley and Sir Robert Cecil, who was Lord Burghley's son, avoided speaking to the merits of the controversy. They would neither endorse nor oppose Morice's views, but tactfully sought to persuade the House to table the bills by reminding the members of the queen's express injunction against their meddling with ecclesiastical matters. The House nevertheless called for a first reading of the bills, indicating that sentiment was with Morice even at the risk of royal displeasure. At this point the Speaker of the House, Sir Edward Coke who doubled as the Queen's Solicitor-General, engaged in delaying tactics. He hated the High Commission and its oath procedure as much as Morice or Beale, but as speaker, though he was the voice of the Commons, he was Elizabeth's appointee—and he was an ambitious man. Morice's bills, he said, were long and complicated, and the hour drawing late. Morice asked for immediate consideration of the second and shorter bill, but Coke, apparently eager to consult with Cecil, ruled the day's business to be at an end.[41]

Elizabeth, who had called Parliament to pass a new subsidy bill, angrily summoned Speaker Coke within two hours of the time the House rose. Only the day before she had given her royal warning against licentious speech. She did not need Whitgift's message denouncing Morice's bills nor his prediction that she would find that "those which now impugne the ecclesiastical Jurisdiction, indevor also to impare the temporall and to bringe even Kinges and princes under there Censure." The next morning Coke reported to the House on his audience with the queen. There was none "whom the presence of such a majesty would not appalle, and it did greatly feare me," he said. Elizabeth told him that only she could call or dissolve a Parliament, and "It is in my power to assent and disassent to any thing done in the Parliament." She had reminded him, he reported, of her purpose in calling a new Parliament and the fact that it "is not meant, that wee should meddle either in matters of State, or Causes Ecclesiasticall. . . ." She was "highly offended" at the Commons' disobedience and commanded them not to read bills touching such matters, on pain of their allegiance being questioned.[42]

Morice was not present in the Commons to hear Coke's report: he was a prisoner of the Privy Council. Puckering, the Lord Keeper—a title reserved by Elizabeth for one of low birth whom she appointed Lord Chancellor—told Morice that he had incurred the queen's "highe displeasure" for which he should be "sharplie chidden, yea and committed also." He would be committed in some councilor's house, Burghley interjected. Puckering continued, Morice recalled, "with some warmenesse ageinst me." Burghley, who was friendly, remarked that what he had heard of Morice's bills led him to think they contained "good matter . . . your fault is onlie in forme." He should have informed the queen privately of his opinion, rather than bringing his bills before Commons in violation of the queen's commandment.

Morice begged forgiveness for his unintended offense, but he did not alter his position. He had not realized, he said, that the queen's commandment applied to matters of state as well as religion; his speech and bills touched only the former. Defending his views on points of law raised by Puckering, Morice provoked Lord Buckhurst to caution that he would do well to show a little submission. Burghley again interceded on his behalf, insisting that the "fault or error was in forme," to which Popham retorted, "And somewhat in matter." The Privy Council finally told Morice to consider himself her Majesty's prisoner in the custody of Sir John Fortescue, a member of the Privy Council. Fortescue, a grandee who had some seventy servants, treated Morice more like a guest than a prisoner, but the intrepid lawyer was effectively silenced; he did not regain his freedom till Parliament ended over two months later. It was his last Parliament. He had failed, utterly, though it took the queen herself to defeat him. Yet he had held high the torch for another generation to grasp and keep alight the flame of just procedures and limited government. As Sir John E. Neale, the historian of Elizabeth's parliaments wrote, Morice's speech of February 27, 1593, earned him a "place on Liberty's long and honoured roll."[43]

A few weeks later Robert Beale was also chastened by the queen for being "a plotter of a new ecclesiastical government." It seems that he spoke so openly against the bishops, though knowing it would offend Elizabeth, that she commanded Burghley to instruct Beale to absent himself from both the Commons and her court. At home, under "restraint," expecting "daily and hourly" to be summoned by the Privy Council, Beale wrote an inordinately long letter to Burghley aggressively defending himself by arguing, once again, the illegality of the oath procedure. He recapitulated the entire argument: the inquisition that was worse than Spanish, the old writs, the reference to heresy cases in Foxe's *Book of Martyrs*, and the proposition that "these encroachments were against Magna Charta . . . the ancient and greatest part of the common law of England. That they were against the custom of the land, for any to be drawn or forced to accuse himself. . . ." Burghley must have known the whole argument by heart, so often had he read it in one manuscript or another by Beale or Morice. Both men were driven by devotion to a cause that blended religion and law, and both helplessly chafed under the muzzle that the queen and archbishop put on them. Cosin's *Apologie* was published at this time, so that it "concurred" with the sitting of Parliament, as Morice noted. Beale complained to Burghley that Cosin could answer unpublished manuscripts by him and Morice, yet they could not even reply in speech. How easy it was, Beale ruefully observed, to fight a man "whose hands were bound." Cosin, Lewin, and other High Commissioners might say what they wanted in print or speech when "others had not the like liberty." It was this sense of injustice that honed Beale's passion and his pugnacity. That his letter, by which he sought to justify himself, had any mitigating effect on his immediate fate may be doubted. Like Morice he may have been committed to some councilor's house for a while. In any case, neither man figured prominently thereafter in the battle against compulsory self-incrimination.[44]

In 1593 and for some years thereafter that battle seemed to be lost. The Parliament of 1593, which began with Morice's valiant speech and two bills, ended in some of the worst repressive legislation yet enacted. To be sure, Elizabethan legislation against recusants was not intended to be enforced except sporadically, on the theory that a few draconian examples sufficed to terrify and subdue potential offenders. Even so, the acts of 1593 vividly demonstrated that neither religious toleration nor a privilege against self-incrimination yet existed. The "Act against Popish Recusants" contained a provision, mentioned earlier, requiring compulsory self-incrimination. Any person who refused to answer truthfully whether he was a priest would be jailed, without bail, until he did answer. The main body of the act restricted to an area within five miles of his home any Catholic who was convicted for refusal to attend established services. "Popish recusants" who violated this immobilization requirement forfeited all goods and chattels and real property as well, or, if poor—not owning personal property to the value of twenty marks or real property worth forty pounds —would be banished.[45]

The companion act of 1593 was aimed at the Barrowists or, in the words of the statute, "wicked and dangerous practices of seditious sectaries and disloyal persons." Never before had England under Elizabeth passed criminal legislation against Protestants, yet it was all that fair-minded men could do to mitigate the severities of the original bill sponsored by the government. Harsh as the act against Catholic recusants was, that against the Barrowists was harsher, even the very much softened version that finally passed. Anyone not going to established services who either persuaded others, by written, spoken, or printed words, not to go or not to accept the queen's authority in ecclesiastical matters, or who attended, or persuaded others to attend, any unauthorized religious meetings, was subject to imprisonment without bail until he conformed. If, however, an offender did not conform within three months of his conviction by making a prescribed public confession and submission, he could be forced to abjure the realm. If he refused to abjure, or having abjured, refused to go, or having gone, returned without official permission, he would be hanged. Nicholas Fuller and Henry Finch who, in the absence of Morice and Beale, led the minority against this statute, vainly decried its dangers. They succeeded only in defeating its original provision which made the crime of Separatism treason. Whether they or any others spoke against the compulsory self-incrimination provision of the act against Catholic recusants is unknown. That someone might have is not impossible in view of the position taken earlier by some Puritan ministers, like Wigginton and Udall. They believed that all subjects were entitled to the equal benefits of the law, including a right not to furnish evidence of one's own guilt.[46]

Elizabeth remained on the throne for another decade, and Whitgift outlived her. They dominated and domineered, never during their declining years relaxing their grip or their principles. Neither toleration, which would have made protests against self-accusing unnecessary, nor reform in the system of criminal procedure was possible while either of them lived. Parliament submissively gave them the necessary legislation to keep the lid tightly clamped on the recusant problem, Catholic and Protestant, and no longer urged bills that would modify the status quo. In 1597, when Parliament again met, there were proposals that pecked at the ecclesiastical courts and their practice by which men "are forced to accuse themselves," but they came to nothing. During Elizabeth's last Parliament, in 1601, there was not even a murmur of protest. The Commons had been cowed, the Presbyterians silenced, and the Separatists banished. By 1597 the government had cleaned the Barrowists out of the jails, tried and convicted their leaders, and deported them, expunging that irksome problem for the time being.[47]

By the close of the reign, the High Commission had become a powerful branch of the English judicial system, a sort of Court of Star Chamber for Ecclesiastical Causes. It could be technically thwarted by anyone obdurately refusing the oath *ex officio*, thereby preventing his trial and conviction for the crime charged, but he would relish his legal triumph by languishing indefinitely in jail for the crime of contempt. In the Star Chamber itself, if a man refused to answer incriminating interrogatories after he had pleaded not guilty, they could convict him for the crime charged as if he had confessed. Although the High Commission did not enjoy that power, its power to punish for contempt achieved the same result: imprisonment. Whitgift, with the queen's unwavering support, had fastened on to the jurisprudence of England another dimension of the inquisitorial system. It flourished in the Star Chamber, the Chancery, and the Court of Requests, but in its purest or most noxious form prevailed throughout the system of ecclesiastical courts and nowhere more unremittingly than at the apex, in the High Commission. The opposition had practically petered out, or, rather, had gone underground, so triumphant was the Whitgiftian party. In the next reign, when the opposition surfaced again, the gauntlet passed from Catholics, Puritans, and Parliament to the common-law courts.[48]

CHAPTER VII

James I, Bancroft, and Prohibitions

The policies of James I on religion, politics, and law provoked a formidable opposition from the Puritans, the common-law courts, and the House of Commons. Each conscripted into its cause against the crown the claim that no man should be forced to incriminate himself before the ecclesiastical courts. The Puritans had convinced themselves that the oath *ex officio* was immoral and illegal, a vague contention at first supported by little more than scriptural inferences and blood-curdling stories from Foxe's *Book of Martyrs*. But common lawyers of the Puritan persuasion, led by Robert Beale, James Morice, and Nicholas Fuller, had originated the daring and novel argument that the oath, although sanctioned by the crown, was unconstitutional because it violated Magna Carta which limited even the royal prerogative. That argument, probably the earliest to exalt Magna Carta as the symbol and source of English constitutional liberty, found a sympathetic response in Parliament and in the common-law courts. The policies of the new king gave them strong occasion to foster the argument.

As a child James I suffered from a weak constitution. Stuart legs were spindly and needed support. When he was king of England, he sometimes leaned on the shoulders of his nobles and, figuratively, upon his church. His difficulties with the Commons and the common-law courts were partially caused by a congenital defect: he could not keep his mouth shut, and when he opened it, it

205

was as if to compensate for a weak constitution by asserting doctrinaire pretensions of divine right and an absolute prerogative. James was by no means power-mad. Rather he was unbelievably and foolishly conceited. Moreover, he was politically inept, though he fancied himself a master politician and a grand political theorist. To English ears the king from Scotland sounded more like a pompous, insulting foreigner who lacked understanding that the constitution of England was finding a substantial base in Parliament and the common law. James not only lacked understanding; he lacked the good sense to learn from experience, although he never repeated the horrifying mistake, which he made on his trip from Edinburgh to London to be crowned, of summarily ordering a pickpocket to be hanged without a trial or any semblance of legal process.[1]

James was not without his virtues. He was a highly learned man and an advocate of international peace, of union with Scotland, and of greater toleration for Catholics—priests excepted. Although allegedly opposed to persecution of anyone for religious reasons, he found Catholic priests to be intolerable because of their doctrine that the pope was the spiritual head of all Christians and had "an Imperial civil power over all Kings and Emperors." Moreover, James added, priests believed in the assassination of supposedly heretical kings. But for these views, which were more politically than religiously grounded, James affected to be more tolerant than Elizabeth had been. But she, though harsher, had earned the devotion of the nation. A wise judge of men who knew how to flatter as well as command, she had been able to manipulate individuals and Parliament to do her bidding. She had rarely indulged in verbal extravagances to expound her powers; she simply exercised them, quietly and effectively. James, by contrast, could inspire little affection in his subjects, was himself the victim of flatterers, and prated endlessly in an offensive manner about his authority.[2]

He thought necessary to assure his Privy Council, "I am neither a god nor an angel, but a man like any other," although he gave Parliament a contrary impression. He assaulted the privileges of the Commons, asserting that they existed by his grace rather than by right. He claimed an independent legislative power for the crown, including an authority to impose customs duties and to create new offenses by proclamation—a position foreshadowed in his book of 1598, when he wrote that the king might make statutes and ordinances without Parliament, possessed power of life and death over his subjects, and could suspend general laws of Parliament "upon causes only known to him." In the same book, *The Trew Law of Free Monarchies*, he ominously asserted that "the King is above the law." While he would govern according to law, "yet is hee not bound thereto. . . ." He told Parliament that kings were not only God's "lieutenants upon earth, and sit upon Gods throne, but even by God himselfe they are called Gods." He claimed the right to judge all and be judged by none, and as it was blasphemy to dispute what God might do, so it was sedition to dispute what the king might do. Seeking to intimidate the common-law judges, he warned them at their peril not to encroach upon the prerogatives of the crown—"no Subject for the tongue of a Lawyer." It was high contempt on their part, he affirmed, for them to dispute what he might do or say what he might not do; they should conclude their judgment on the basis of "that which is the King's revealed will in his law." [3]

James was sometimes inconsistent, for he infrequently practiced what he insistently preached, and he tried to be a constitutional monarch as he understood the term. The difficulty was, as J. W. Gough has put it, "that James laid more emphasis on the power of the king than on the liberties of his subjects, and fundamental law accordingly meant to him not so much the law which restricted as the law which amply supported the monarchy and kept subjects in their place." Yet James's exalted claims were by no means altogether groundless. The common law was scarcely supreme; Parliament or King in Parliament was still a long way off from being sovereign; and the concept of fundamental law to which the actions of the crown were subordinate was only beginning to be understood. The common law, that is, the non-statute law laid down by the common-law courts at Westminster, had pretensions to supremacy that were no better founded than the king's. [4]

Parliament, too, fondly advanced claims which were as much aspiration as reality. But the Commons, restive even in the later years of Elizabeth's reign, needed no longer to defer submissively to a great and beloved, aging queen. James gave provocation too much to endure. No one in the Commons contested his royal prerogative, that executive authority to summon and dissolve parliaments, to approve or veto legislation, to direct the nation's foreign affairs and conduct its wars, to prosecute any who violated the king's peace or to pardon the guilty, to control the coinage, to make appointments, and to exercise an undefined and undefinable discretionary power, especially in times of stress, to act in the best interests of the common welfare. The royal prerogative was the lawful authority of the crown, but not everything done by prerogative was lawful. Vast and impressive though the royal prerogative was, it was not at all an absolute or unlimited sovereign power, for it must always be exercised in accordance with certain formal procedures and never, but by common or statutory law, to the prejudice of the property or personal liberties of the subjects.[5]

The common-law courts, apprehensive about swelling encroachments from the ecclesiastical courts, and the Commons, swelled with their own sense of importance and resentful of the crown's arbitrary ways, were in no mood to be pushed about by James. He unequivocally backed his ecclesiastical courts and made laws or canons for the governance of the church by Convocation alone, without Parliament's assent. He denied that Parliament was a court of record, interfered with its right to settle disputed elections, encroached on members' rights to speak freely in Commons, legislated by proclamations, and generally used his prerogative to threaten "the utter overthrow of the very fundamental privileges of our House and therein of the rights and liberties of the whole Commons of your realm of England . . . and consequently to the rights of all your Majesty's said subjects and the whole body of this your kingdom"—so the Commons averred in 1604. At about the same time James told one of his ministers that he would rather live like a hermit in the forest "than be a King over such a People as the pack of Puritans are that overrules the lower-house." In this state of tension on both sides, any grievance touching the prerogative was especially divisive, ready to be seized as a constitutional issue that might vindicate the claims of one side or the other. The oath *ex officio* was such an issue.[6]

Parliament was not, of course, a "pack of Puritans," at least not in the sense that the Presbyterians dominated or could even claim the sympathies of most members. The trouble, rather, was that James, though born of Catholic parents and raised a Presbyterian, had embraced the English church and the episcopacy to such an extent that the mere suggestion of further reformation, however moderate, smacked of nonconformity to him. James's favorite aphorism, "No Bishops, no King," reflected his belief that the fortunes of crown and church were intimately entwined. At home in Edinburgh, where Cartwright's brethren ruled the kirk, James had called the Presbyterian establishment the purest in the world, while describing the Anglican service as "an evil-said mass in English" presided over by "papistical or anglicane bishops." In London, however, he found no courtiers more flattering, more agreeable, nor more obsequious than the prelates. A welcome change from the sternly critical Presbyterians of Scotland, the prelates of England swiftly endorsed the most strained interpretation of the royal prerogative. James took enormous satisfaction in the support that the divines of the establishment readily gave to his assertions of divine right. Little wonder, then, that the new king embraced Anglicanism and took its enemies to be his.[7]

The Puritans, however, originally expected that James would favorably consider their grievances. When he first arrived in London, the Puritan clergy, all members of the established church, presented him with the "Millenary Petition," so-called because it was supposed to represent the views of one thousand ministers. The petition did not speak for the Presbyterian minority. Rather, it spoke for all the clergy who preferred a broader reformation in ritual and discipline than Elizabeth had allowed. Accordingly it was quite moderate in every respect. It made no demands violative of the king's prerogative or of his position as the Supreme Governor of the church; it asked for no radical reforms of the Prayer Book and no recognition of a presbytery. It did not even attack the episcopacy. The petition covered four topics, the first of which was church service. Here the petitioners requested that the cross in baptism, the ring in marriage, and the term "priest" not be used; that the surplice not be urged; and that the length of the church service be shortened. The second topic requested that only able preachers be accepted in the ministry and that no minister should be forced to subscribe to any articles of religion not required by law. The third opposed the practice of many bishops in holding several ecclesiastical livings. The final topic, church discipline, requested an end to excommunication for trivial causes and speedy decision of ecclesiastical suits which sometimes took "five, six, or seven years," and pleaded "that the oath *ex officio,* whereby men are forced to accuse themselves, be more sparingly used. . . ." Other petitions similarly remonstrated against the oath. Thomas Cartwright, a voice from the past soon stilled by death, also added his objection to the oath.[8]

The Millenary Petition was a reasonable basis for a compromise that would have brought a substantial degree of peace and unity within the English church. The House of Commons was a "pack of Puritans" only in the sense that a majority supported reconciliation along lines proposed by the Millenary Petition. Its acceptance would have isolated the Presbyterians by robbing them of the widespread clerical and popular support for moderate reforms. A considerable latitude of doctrinal interpretation already existed within the church. Greater latitudinarianism in ceremonials and the correction of certain abuses, such as the oath *ex officio,* would have braced the Protestant cause and the royalist cause as well. The Millenary Petition had presented James with a splendid opportunity for a new religious settlement, and it seemed, at first, as if he would make the most of it.

To the consternation of Archbishop Whitgift and the bishops, the king called a conference at Hampton Court between the prelates and a deputation of four of the leading advocates of reform in the land. Next to hunting, drinking, and lecturing on his prerogative, James relished a theological controversy. Yet before the conference could meet, supporters of the establishment won him over to their side by depicting the reformers' request as the opening wedge of a seditious and antimonarchical Presbyterian conspiracy. As Whitgift's biographer put it, "the Archbishop gathered the good inclination of the king to the Church established." As a result, James issued a proclamation affirming his satisfaction with the state of the church and its "form and frame." He rebuked agitators, condemning as seditious any who opposed the episcopacy or criticized the "processes of their courts."[9]

In January 1604, the Hampton Court Conference met, with James himself personally presiding. Present were his Privy Council, Archbishop Whitgift, and eight or ten bishops, including Richard Bancroft who had been Bishop of London since 1597. For the Puritan moderates there were Dr. John Reynolds, President of Corpus Christi College, Oxford; Laurence Chaderton, Master of Emmanuel College, Cambridge; Dr. Thomas Sparke, an archdeacon; and John Knewstubs, a rector. On the second day of the conference, Dr. Reynolds, the chief spokesman for the reformers requested a resumption of the prophesyings that Archbishop Grindal had encouraged until Elizabeth suppressed them. Reynolds remarked that if the prophesyings raised questions that could not be resolved, the "Episcopal Synod" might settle them. At the mention of "synod," James flared out: "If you aim at a Scottish Presbytery, it agreeth as well with monarchy, as God and the devil. Then Jack, and Tom, and Will, and Dick, shall meet and censure me and my council." Turning to the assembled prelates, James added, "if once you were out, and they in, I know what would become of my Supremacy, for no Bishop, no King." James then demanded to know whether there was anything more to be said. Reynolds, overawed by this display of royal hostility, said no, whereupon the king concluded the day's conference with a threat: "If this be all your party hath to say, I will make them conform themselves, or else I will harrie them out of the land, or else do worse." [10]

On the next day many canonists and civil lawyers were present, because the subject for discussion was the High Commission. The oath *ex officio* proved to be an issue on which the king had fixed opinions. Some member of the Privy Council said: "The proceedings in that court are like the Spanish Inquisition, wherein men are urged to subscribe more than law requireth, and by the oath *ex officio*, forced to accuse themselves, being examined upon twenty, or twenty-four Articles on a sudden, without deliberation, and for the most part against themselves." The unnamed speaker might have been Lord Burghley's son, Robert Cecil, the king's Principal Secretary. He then read a copy of Burghley's letter of 1584 to Whitgift, denouncing the High Commission's proceedings as "savouring of the Romish Inquisition." The aged archbishop himself, apparently ill in mind as well as body, replied with a piece of information that Udall, Greenwood, Barrow, Penry, and a generation of the High Commission's prisoners would have been astonished to hear. "Your lordship is deceived in the manner of proceeding," declared Whitgift, "for, if the Article touch the party for life, liberty, or scandal, he may refuse to answer." Ellesmere, the Lord Chancellor, who presided over the courts of Chancery and the Star Chamber, both of which employed the oath *ex officio*, added that the oath was used in "divers courts." [11]

If anyone present intended to make relevant distinctions, the king's opinion, virtually a judgment concluding the issue, silenced him. In contrast to the practice of other courts which might punish only deeds, said James, the ecclesiastical courts had to examine "Fame and Scandals." For the detection of the offender, especially when the crime was grave and either suspicion or "public fame" existed, the oath was necessary. "And here," reported Bishop Barlow, who rendered an official account of the proceedings, the king "soundly described the oath *ex officio*, for the ground thereof, the wisdom of the law therein, the manner of proceeding thereby, and profitable effect from the same." Whitgift was so moved by the king's exposition that he declared, "Undoubtedly your majesty speaks by the special assistance of God's spirit." Not to be outdone, Bishop Bancroft added, "I protest my heart melteth with joy, that Almighty God, of his singular mercy, hath given us such a king, as, since Christ's time, the like hath not been." The conference ended shortly after with another warning from the king that he expected conformity "or they shall hear of it." [12]

Never realizing that he had bungled an opportunity to reconcile most Protestant dissidents to the established church, James reveled in his own cleverness in besting the learned Puritan spokesmen. He never understood that he had constrained them by intimidation and by championing the cause of the prelates. The Puritans, he reported exultantly, had fled from argument to argument without ever having answered him directly; therefore, he had been compelled to tell them that if he had been disputing a college student who answered as they did, he would have taken a rod and "plyed upon the poor boyes buttocks"—this to the President of Corpus Christi College, Oxford! The king was too blind to see that his easy victory had generated bitterness, discredited the lead-

ership of the moderate cause, and strengthened the hold of presbyterianism upon the discontented. Nor did James realize that his
shabby treatment of the Puritan leaders helped to alienate the
Commons, which soon met for its first session under the new
king.[13]

James's opening speech to Parliament referred disparagingly to
the Puritans. Their discontent and impatience, he declared,
"maketh their sect unable to be suffred in any wel governed Commonwealth." In line with this statement, which James preceded
with a proclamation demanding religious conformity, representatives of the church, meeting in Convocation at the same time as
Parliament met, framed one hundred forty-one canons for the
government of the church. The canons of 1604 systematically revised and codified a hodge-podge of old regulations, orders, injunctions, and articles, and added new ones. They were a constitution for the church, covering minutely everything from membership and polity to rites, doctrines, and discipline. Canon thirty-six,
one of the forty-seven that were aimed against the Puritans, revived Whitgift's three articles of 1583 and required subscription
to them by anyone exercising any ecclesiastical function. The
penalty for nonconformity or refusal to subscribe was suspension,
deprivation, and excommunication.[14]

Whitgift having died just before Parliament and Convocation
met, Richard Bancroft, the Bishop of London who became the
next Archbishop of Canterbury, supervised the preparation of the
canons of 1604. He would enforce them with a vengeance. Long
the most influential member of the High Commission, Bancroft
was a man of enormous and varied talents, but he was also a
narrow-minded zealot with a mean disposition, servile and syco-
phantic like a petty courtier before the king, domineering to
others. Whitgift had persecuted out of duty to office and political
expediency, Bancroft out of hatred for the Puritans and duty to
God. He enjoyed the role of grand inquisitor and was suited for
it. At the Hampton Court Conference he had objected to the
presence of the Puritan leaders on the ground that the king should
not tolerate heretics to speak. He saw to it that the canons on the
ecclesiastical courts did not alter the inquisitorial oath procedure.[15]

A majority of the House of Commons supported the Millenary

Petition, perhaps even greater reforms. When a conference was held between Commons and the bishops in May of 1604, the Commons program, according to Roland G. Usher, an unsympathetic historian, "embodied the full Puritan scheme for the indirect introduction of the Book of Discipline." The oath *ex officio*, of course, was one of the grievances for reform. "Whatever power was left in the ecclesiastical courts," Usher added, "and all the authority of the High Commission, would vanish with the possibility of refusing the oath." Inevitably the conference was unproductive. A committee of the Commons then petitioned the king against the impending deprivation of the Puritan ministry. A bill was also drawn under the title "An Act for the due observation of the Great Charter of England," declaring null and void more than a score of the principal canons as violative of Magna Carta. Even the House of Lords brought to its second reading, before being stopped, a bill enjoining the execution of any canons not confirmed by Parliament and fixing the penalty of praemunire for disobedience. The king, nevertheless, approved the canons of 1604 and issued another proclamation against nonconformity. The bishops, under Bancroft's leadership, proceeded to enforce the new laws of the church. Although the Puritans in and out of Parliament claimed that three hundred ministers were deprived, Bancroft denied that the number was more than sixty. Recent estimates indicate that the actual number was about ninety, but about one hundred more were suspended and silenced. There is no record of how many hundreds were examined by the ecclesiastical courts of the bishops or by the High Commission itself for nonconformity, that is, for violation or suspected violation of any of the canons.[16]

The oath *ex officio* continued, of course, to be the crux of the examinations and a focal point of Puritan opposition. In one case, seven ministers refused the oath before the High Commission and were suspended for their contempt. A Puritan tract of 1605 condemned the oath "whereby Popish and English Ecclesiastical Governors . . . go about to bind mens consciences to accuse themselves, and their friends of such crimes or imputations, as cannot by any direct court of law be proved against them . . . such an oath (on the urgers part) is most damnable and tyrannous, against the very Law of Nature, devised by Antichrist, through the inspiration of the devil. . . ." Because of the oath, the writer asserted, true Christians were forced to reveal religious acts which, though done for the advancement of the Gospel, brought sentences against themselves and their friends. If they took the oath, yet did not confess, they might be tempted "in their weakness, by perjurie, to damn their own souls." [17]

That the Puritan view of the oath *ex officio* had begun to take root among men who had no sympathy for Puritanism is evident from an essay of this time written by the great Francis Bacon. Philosopher, lawyer, and member of Parliament, Bacon's incredible range of interests led him to discourse, from the standpoint of an Erastian *politique*, on problems of church and state. Speaking of the ecclesiastical courts, he declared that one point of their procedure was

> contrary to the laws and customs of this land and state . . . and that is the oath 'ex officio': whereby men are enforced to accuse themselves, and, that what is more, are sworn unto blanks, and not unto accusations and charges declared. By the law of England, no man is bound to accuse himself. In the highest cases of treason, torture is used for discovery, and not for evidence. In capital matters, no delinquent's answer upon oath is required; no, not permitted. In criminal matters not capital, handled in the Star Chamber, and in causes of conscience, handled in the chancery, for the most part grounded upon trust and secrecy, the oath of the party is required. But how? Where there is an accusation and an accuser, which we call bills of complaint, from which the complainant cannot vary, and out of the compass of which the defendant may not be examined . . . But to examine a man upon oath, out of the insinuation of fame, or out of accusations secret and undeclared, though it have some countenance from the civil law, yet, it is so opposite 'ex diametro' to the sense and course of the common law, as it may well receive some limitation.[18]

The common law was by no means tender to an accused person, and while it neither required nor permitted the accused to swear against himself in cases involving life or limb, it sought to convict him, if possible, by his own confession, even if it was unsworn. If, as Bacon said, by the law of England no man was bound to accuse himself, it was because a grand jury accused him. He did not have to answer incriminating interrogatories at his trial, yet if he did not rebut the crown's prima facie case against him, his silence would convict him. On the other hand, he knew the charges, his accusers, and the evidence against him, and his guilt was judged by a jury. To the High Commission's Puritan victims, common-law procedure seemed infinitely fairer than ecclesiastical procedure.

Salvation, in this world as well as in the next, seemed to the Puritans to hinge upon access to common-law procedure and the crippling of the Commission's performance of its duties. Powerless to redefine the substantive law that made their activities criminal, the Puritans turned to the common-law courts and to legal obstructionism as a means of self-defense. They challenged the Commission's jurisdiction and procedures in the common-law courts, concentrating their attack on the oath *ex officio* the use of which in incriminatory examination made that court so terrible an instrument of oppression. They focused, too, on the Commission's punitive temporal powers to fine and imprison, hoping to leave it with merely the spiritual powers of excommunication and, in the case of ministers, of deprivation. Parliament continued to be the scene of abortive bills that would even end deprivation as well as inquisitional procedures and temporal punishments. But the common-law courts were more suitable instruments, in the absence of favorable legislation, for immediate, *ad hoc* obstruction of the Commission.

In the legal profession devoted to the common-law—the common lawyers and the common-law judges—the Puritans found allies in a common cause: hostility to the ecclesiastical law. The common law was intensely nationalistic. It was England's native law, and it was unique. Elsewhere in Europe the influence of Roman civil law and its ecclesiastical counterpart, the canon law, prevailed. During the Renaissance when the Roman law spread throughout the Continent and made itself felt in England, it was resisted, successfully, by the common law. The main reason for the common law's survival and supremacy was that the common lawyers perpetuated themselves and their system of law through a unique guild that superbly trained new generations of common lawyers. Maitland has said that what distinguished medieval England from the rest of the world was neither Parliament nor trial by jury; it was, rather, "schools of national law." These schools, the inns of court, preserved a tough and traditional body of native law to which its adherents owed their pride and loyalty as well as their livings. Common lawyers of bench and bar, having survived the long and rigorous training of the inns of court, were dedicated to a profession, a way of life, that resented rival legal systems.[19]

The hostility between the common law and ecclesiastical law went back to the twelfth century. The case of the "criminous clerks" that divided Henry II and Becket, and the Constitution of Clarendon in 1164, reflected that hostility. The common-law courts, which were the royal courts, offshoots of the king's Council, engaged in jurisdictional disputes with the ecclesiastical courts for centuries. As early as the twelfth century royal writs of prohibition were devised as a means of enabling the king's courts to make good their claims against rival courts, whether feudal or ecclesiastical. The writ of prohibition ultimately bore the same relationship to the right against compulsory self-incrimination that the writ of habeas corpus bore to the personal liberty of the subject. The writ of prohibition, which originated as a prerogative writ, enjoined the hearing and decision of a suit by a court of rival jurisdiction. The writ issued from the king's court to prohibit its rival from continuing with a suit allegedly within the cognizance of the king. Thus a writ of prohibition might issue to a sheriff holding a plea in a manorial court against a tenant who had put himself on the Grand Assize, or it might issue to an ecclesiastical judge hearing a case of lay fee. When used against ecclesiastical courts, the writs of prohibition, whether involving cases of crime, contract, or land, stayed proceedings which supposedly concerned temporal matters.[20]

Inquisitional tactics by the ecclesiastical courts employing the oath *ex officio* had been the targets of prohibitions as early as the thirteenth century. Henry III issued writs of prohibition against Bishop Grosseteste of Lincoln in 1246 and 1252 commanding that laymen not be examined under oath in ecclesiastical courts except in matrimonial and testamentary causes. The conflicts between the common-law courts and their ecclesiastical rivals grew so intense that both kings and parliaments intervened to draw their respective jurisdictional bounds. Parliament's *Prohibitio Formata de Statuto Articuli Cleri*, passed about 1316, specifying the exclusive jurisdiction of the common-law courts, prohibited the ecclesiastical courts from hearing matters that belonged to the common law. The same act revived the injunctions of Henry III against examining laymen under oath. In 1353 Parliament responded to complaints of papal usurpation and aggression against the common-law courts by passing the Statute of Praemunire, which fixed forfeiture and imprisonment as the punishment for those who sued in papal or ecclesiastical courts on matters cognizable in the king's courts. Until the Reformation and, from the standpoint of common lawyers and of Puritans, even after the Reformation, the ecclesiastical courts were "foreign" courts in the sense that they represented the pope's law.[21]

The enmity, then, between the common-law courts and the ecclesiastical was of long standing. The attack by the common lawyers on the High Commission and other ecclesiastical courts during the reigns of Elizabeth and James I was simply a continuation of an old struggle. In a still broader sense, that attack by the common lawyers was merely part of their general assault on courts of other jurisdictions and other legal systems. There was, for example, a concurrent attack in both Tudor and Stuart England on the courts of admiralty, requests, and chancery; none employed the common law, and all followed canonist procedure. As Holdsworth said, "When two separate and partially competing jurisdictions exist in one state, a conflict between them is sooner or later inevitable."[22]

The conflict between King's Bench and Common Pleas on the one hand and the High Commission on the other would have become serious by the close of the sixteenth century even if the oath *ex officio* had never existed. The goal of the common law seemed to be an omnicompetent jurisdiction. To suffer competition from a court whose substantive law and procedure were so different was bad enough; to suffer it from a new court whose business thrived was worse still; but to suffer it from a new court whose jurisdiction overlapped that of the common law was quite intolerable. Stealing in church, brawling in the churchyard, and letting sheep graze on church property were ecclesiastical crimes, but like other misdemeanors, assaults, and trespasses, they were, as logically, temporal matters for determination by the common law. Offenses against the king's peace were common-law crimes, yet the ecclesiastical jurisdiction extended to all cases involving clergymen and to any offense occurring on church lands. If a clergyman stole a chicken from one of his parishioners, or if the parishioner invaded church land to steal one of his minister's chickens, was the case temporal or ecclesiastical? The Commission, whose status as a court of law corresponded roughly with Whitgift's accession to the primacy, aggressively pressed its jurisdictional claims and defended those of the lesser ecclesiastical courts.[23]

The procedure of the High Commission, being inquisitorial and therefore so very different from the accusatorial procedure of the common-law courts, simply aggravated the tension. The procedural differences by no means worked to the advantage of the common law in all cases. Many suitors preferred to seek justice in the ecclesiastical courts rather than risk facing a jury or the exceptionally complex forms of action, the rigid and technical rules of pleading, and the higher costs of a common-law trial. *Ex officio mero* prosecutions by the High Commission, especially for offenses of nonconformity, constituted only one category of its cases. The bulk of its work involved suits between parties, and their frequent choice of the ecclesiastical rather than the temporal courts provoked the jealousy and diminished the fees of the latter. The High Commission, like the Star Chamber, was in many respects, a popular court. It may have been a dread abomination to a Cartwright or a Barrow, but to John Doe and Richard Roe it was not infrequently a fount of justice. That fact marked it as a target of the common lawyers.[24]

To lose business was galling enough, but to lose it to an upstart prerogative court which had the stamp of illegality upon it was not to be countenanced. Parliament, to be sure, had authorized the establishment of the High Commission by letters patent from the crown to persons who would exercise "all manner of jurisdictions . . . in any wise touching or concerning any spiritual or ecclesiastical jurisdiction" and who would reform and correct all "errors, heresies, schisms, abuses, offences, contempts, and enormities" which could be reformed and corrected by such jurisdiction. Loose as that grant was, it did not literally authorize a new court nor its particular procedures. Moreover, the common-law courts claimed authority to construe the meaning of acts of Parliament in particular cases, and might therefore decide whether those procedures and the exercise of jurisdiction in a given instance were lawful.[25]

The writ of prohibition was an apt instrumentality for asserting common-law rights against ecclesiastical invasion. That writ brought all ecclesiastical proceedings to a stop until a hearing could be had before the common-law judges on the question whether temporal or ecclesiastical jurisdiction was involved, or, more broadly, on the question whether any illegality on the part of the ecclesiastical court vitiated its action or infringed a common-law right. The common-law court might sustain its writ, making it a permanent injunction, or might sustain the action of the ecclesiastical court by issuing a "writ of consultation" which canceled the writ of prohibition. The writ of prohibition if sustained did not transfer the case to the common-law court. The matter at issue might not even constitute a cause of action at common law. That the ecclesiastical court had erred by encroaching in some temporal way sufficed to sustain the injunction.

Writs of prohibition proved to be the nexus between Puritanism and the common-law courts. Both had an interest in combatting the High Commission, and prohibitions were ideally suited for the task. But legal obstructionism was a dangerous, if fruitful, game played for high stakes. A case seemingly trivial might pit the amorphous principle of the supremacy of the law—that is, of the common law—against the royal prerogative. The Act of Supremacy notwithstanding, letters patent from the crown in the last analysis nourished the High Commission's jurisdiction and procedure. Without royal support the High Commission would be a house of straw that its enemies in the Commons and the common-law courts could demolish at will. James I, the prelates, and the Commission provided not only the provocation but the issues with which the common-law courts could color their efforts, quite legitimately, as a defense of constitutional liberties.

Old as the writ of prohibition was, it became a common device for crippling the ecclesiastical courts only when the High Commission rose to prominence as a court under Whitgift, challenging the common-law courts and extending its corrective powers from Catholic recusants to Puritan Nonconformists. Whitgift complained in 1598 that prohibitions had been granted with unusual frequency "of late years." In 1605 Bancroft alleged that there had been 488 prohibitions issued during Elizabeth's reign against just the Court of Arches, which was the provincial court of the Archbishop of Canterbury, the court of appeal from all diocesan courts. Little is known about these harassing prohibitions except that many were issued on almost any pretext only to be followed by writs of consultation. The judges do not seem to have laid down a consistent line of decisions, as is evident from two cases involving the oath *ex officio*.[26]

The first of these was a 1589 case, *Collier v. Collier*, which is of special interest because the attorney seeking the prohibition was Edward Coke, the greatest figure in English legal history. In the reign of James I, Chief Justice Coke would give authority and respectability to the arguments of Beale, Morice, and Fuller against the oath. In 1589, Coke, then a leading member of the bar, argued before the Court of Common Pleas that a husband, being sued by his wife for incontinency before an ecclesiastical court, could not be put to the oath *ex officio*: "But because *nemo tenetur prodere seipsum* in such cases of defamation, but only in causes testamentary and matrimonial, where no discredit can be to the party by his oath, Coke prayed a prohibition; and it was granted." A second report of the same case confirms the grant of the prohibition, but a third report leaves the outcome in doubt. The reporter stated that the ecclesiastical court would have Collier answer upon his oath whether he had carnal knowledge of a certain woman, "upon which he prayed a Prohibition: *Et nemo tenetur seipsum prodere:* But the Court would advise of it." That Coke argued the *nemo tenetur* doctrine, apparently out of the context of the canon-law rule of which it was a part, is unquestionable. In doing so he followed the precedent of Chief Justice Dyer in Leigh's case of 1568 and confirmed in Hynde's case in 1576. Whether the court followed these precedents of its own making is uncertain.[27]

Dr. Hunt's case, which did not involve a writ of prohibition, was decided on a different principle by the Queen's Bench in 1591. Hunt, an ecclesiastical judge of the archidiaconal court of Norwich, was indicted for compelling a man to take the oath *ex officio* to answer to a charge of incontinency. That a grand jury in Norwich indicted Hunt shows its belief that the oath was illegal in such a case. Yet the court thought otherwise and dismissed the indictment. The judges reasoned that incontinency, being a matter within the jurisdiction of the ecclesiastical courts, might be prosecuted in accordance with the rules of those courts. In such a case, if two witnesses presented the "fame," ruled the Queen's Bench, the oath was lawful. In the same year, the leading common-law judges of England, sitting with the Court of Star Chamber, told Cartwright and his associates that their refusal of the oath *ex officio* before the High Commission was unlawful, presumably because their case did not involve life or limb and because the rule against requiring the oath of laymen, except in certain instances, did not apply to ministers. A year earlier, in 1590, Judge Anderson, who sat in Dr. Hunt's case, had informed Udall, who was later tried for his life, that he ought to answer under oath because his case did not involve loss of life; but Anderson had also declared that the answer need not be given if the case were a capital one. The judges at this time had apparently not conclusively determined on the legality of the oath *ex officio*, though they tended to support the ecclesiastical courts.[28]

Cawdrey's case produced the leading decision of Elizabeth's reign on the legality of the High Commission. The decision of 1591 had no direct bearing on either the oath *ex officio* or the writ of prohibition, yet the Commission could not have hoped for a more favorable view of its authority by the common-law judges. Cawdrey, a Puritan minister, having taken the oath *ex officio* under protest, was examined by the High Commission for nonconformity and deprived because he left out the ring in marriage and the cross in baptism. Challenging his sentence, Cawdrey employed James Morice as his counsel and brought a suit for trespass against the clergyman who had been appointed in his place as rector of his parish in Rutland. Morice argued that Cawdrey's deprivation was illegal because of numerous irregularities in the Commission's proceedings. The jury returned a special verdict in favor of the defendant, Cawdrey's replacement, if in the opinion of the court the High Commission was lawfully empowered to deprive Cawdrey. On review of the legal questions, the Queen's Bench, ignoring all of Morice's technical objections to the deprivation, ruled that the suit for trespass could not be maintained because the High Commission possessed the lawful authority to deprive a minister for nonconformity.[29]

The Court's dicta made the case a significant victory for the Commission and the ecclesiastical powers of the crown. The judges declared that the Act of Supremacy had merely restored the ancient prerogative of the monarch to govern the ecclesiastical affairs of the nation. The statute being declaratory in nature rather than an introduction of new law, the crown possessed "plenary and entire power, prerogative, and jurisdiction" to establish an ecclesiastical commission and render justice in ecclesiastical causes—"the conusance whereof belongs not to the common lawes of England"—according to the ecclesiastical laws of the realm. Coke, reporting the case some years later, spelled out the ecclesiastical jurisdiction which "doth not belong to the common law." He concluded that the judges had decided in favor of the principle that the kingdom of England was an absolute monarchy, and that the King is the only supreme governor, as well over ecclesiastical persons, and in ecclesiastical causes, as temporal, within this realm. . . ." Thus Cawdrey's case elicited from the highest court of the land a recognition of the Court of High Commission as a lawful court, sustained by the prerogative and properly exercising royal jurisdiction in religious matters.[30]

Cawdrey's case did not prevent the common-law courts from issuing scores of prohibitions during the 1590's, many of them frivolous and inconsistent. Sometimes a writ of consultation annulling a prohibition issued by Queen's Bench was followed by another prohibition from Common Pleas in the same case. The same court would issue a consultation only to follow it with another prohibition in the same kind of case. Prohibitions were apparently issued on the mere allegation, unsupported, that a case before an ecclesiastical court involved some temporal matter. Often a lawyer would simply inform the common-law court that the case did not concern matrimony or testaments; prohibition was then issued even if, as later facts revealed, the case concerned some other matter of undoubted ecclesiastical jurisdiction, such as alimony, adultery, heresy, or tithes. The issuance of prohibitions in cases that did not concern matrimony or testaments is traceable to an old rule dating from Henry III's prohibition against Grosseteste and reported in both the "Register of Writs" and Fitzherbert's *New Natura Brevium*. That rule, of course, was that laymen should not be examined on oath by the ecclesiastical authorities except in matrimonial and testamentary cases.[31]

Harried and resentful because of the multitude of prohibitions, Whitgift, aided by Bancroft and Cosin, complained to the Privy Council. Their brief against prohibitions was written with remarkable reserve, in the form of queries for the Council's consideration. "Whether," for example, "by law a prohibition may be granted after sentence is given. . . . Whether to be granted upon the suggestion, that the ecclesiastical court may hear no cause, but matters testamentary and matrimonial. . . ." Other queries complained about inconsistencies on the part of the common-law courts, the unwarrantable delays, increased expenses, and other inconveniences that defeated ecclesiastical justice. One query asked whether prohibitions should not be issued by the Court of Chancery only, and another asked whether prohibitions could be justified in any case under the jurisdiction of the High Commission. The theory behind the latter point was that the Reformation united both temporal and ecclesiastical jurisdiction in the crown. Consequently the original purpose of the writ or prohibition, to preserve the jurisdiction of the crown against papal incursions, no longer existed. The law of the High Commission was therefore as much a part of the law of the realm as the law of the common-law courts.[32]

Whether the Privy Council took any action on these ecclesiastical complaints and recommendations is not known, but there was no abatement of prohibitions from the common-law courts. Although their contradictory and poorly based line of decisions continued, there were also cases in which they properly defended their jurisdiction against ecclesiastical aggressions, and, more importantly, there were cases in which they upheld the liberty of the subject. *Smith* v. *Smith*, decided in 1600, is an example of the latter.

The High Commission, having excommunicated a woman for adultery, sent a pursuivant with letters missive to apprehend her. The pursuivant, in the company of a constable, broke into her house at night. The Court of Common Pleas denounced this practice, holding that it was unlawful except in the case of a felony or treason for anyone to break into a house at night. Going further, the court declared that it was unlawful for the High Commission "to meddle with the person of any man, or to send any process to have the body before them." The Act of Supremacy, "which gave authority to the High Commissioners, doth not alter the law," for it specified that their proceedings must be according to spiritual law. *Smith* v. *Smith* was one of many cases which did not comport with the dicta in Cawdrey's case to the effect that the royal prerogative, as expressed in letters patent to the Commission, sustained its authority.[33]

Although the number or prohibitions increased after James became king, the common-law judges never endorsed Morice's radical argument that deprivation was the equivalent of dispossessing a subject from his freehold and denying him his liberty, contrary to Magna Carta's guarantee that no man should be disseised of his freehold or denied his liberty without common-law process, namely, indictment and trial by jury. On the contrary the common-law judges and law-officers of the crown did not question the right of the ecclesiastical authorities to deprive a minister for appropriate cause. Archbishop Bancroft informed his bishops in late 1604 that "the Lord Chief Justice, and Mr Attorney generall" —Popham of King's Bench and Coke—believed that the church could deprive obstinate ministers.[34]

When Bancroft enforced the canons of 1604, depriving those who refused to subscribe or who engaged in Nonconformist practices, two of his victims brought a test case, seeking a prohibition on ground that the ecclesiastical proceedings against them were illegal. Bancroft sought an advisory opinion from a special meeting of the Star Chamber attended by the leading common-law judges. Lord Chancellor Ellesmere, on behalf of the High Commission, put three questions to the judges. The first was on the lawfulness of depriving Puritan ministers who refused to conform; the second was on the lawfulness of the Commission's *ex officio mero* procedure in such cases; and the last was on the lawfulness of the Puritan practice of framing petitions "with an intimation to the King, That if he denyed theire sute, many thousands of his subjects would be discontented." [35]

To the first and second questions all the judges replied in favor of the High Commission. They reasoned that the Commission possessed the power of deprivation by canon law because the king had delegated to it his supreme ecclesiastical power. He possessed that power even in the absence of the Act of Supremacy; therefore "the King without Parliament might make orders and Constitutions for the Government of the Clergie, and might deprive them if they obeyed not. And so the Commissioners might deprive them." The king, greatly relieved, announced that there would be no more prohibitions. Thus, as in Cawdrey's case, the judges supported the authority of the High Commission as a prerogative court. On the third question, relating to the petitions, the judges declared, "That it was an offence fineable at discretion, and very near to treason and Felony in the punishment. For they tended to the raising of Sedition. . . ." Thus the Puritans could not even publicly complain without running afoul of the law which seemed to be spread out like a chicken wire of constraint against them.[36]

Yet, the prohibitions continued, hacking and whittling away at the ecclesiastical courts. In less than three years from the time James became king, the common-law judges admitted that they had issued 313 prohibitions, 251 from the King's Bench and 62 from Common Pleas, against the various ecclesiastical courts. Bancroft angrily framed a lengthy document of twenty-five objections against "this over lavish granting of prohibitions in every cause without respect." The document, which Bancroft presented to the Privy Council on behalf of the clergy, sought to discredit the common-law courts and win over the government to the side of the ecclesiastical courts. At the very least Bancroft hoped to curtail drastically the number of prohibitions.[37]

But he urged other policies which, if adopted, would have ended altogether the authority of the common-law courts to issue prohibitions. One recommendation looked hopefully to the Court of Chancery, a sister court of the civil law, as the only body that should be authorized to issue prohibitions. Another recommendation even more radically suggested that the writ of prohibition be abolished, because it was a relic of the time when the ecclesiastical jurisdiction was not united in the crown as part of the law of the realm, like the temporal jurisdiction. Bancroft also suggested that the king had sufficient authority, acting with his Privy Council, to decide all cases of jurisdictional disputes. Many of the complaints made in 1598 were now restated, not in the form of queries for consideration, but dogmatically as part of an indictment. One such point dealt with the practice of the common-law courts in issuing prohibitions when a case did not concern matters testamentary or matrimonial. One of the new objections was that the common-law courts had freed, by habeas corpus, persons imprisoned by the High Commission for contempt. Throughout the document, which Coke dubbed the *"Articuli Cleri,"* there ran the refrain that the common-law courts violated the royal prerogative as expressed, particularly, in the letters patent establishing the High Commission.[38]

The *Articuli Cleri* was presented to the Privy Council in October 1605. In the following spring, the judges of the King's Bench, Common Pleas, and Exchequer gave their unanimous reply. Parliament alone, they said, had authority to abolish the writ of prohibition or vest control over it in any but the common-law courts. The judges dismissed most of the specific objections of the clergy on ground that no specific cases had been mentioned to prove the charges of abuse by the common-law courts. Steadfastly defending their course in issuing prohibitions, the judges argued that it was their duty to prevent the ecclesiastical courts from hearing temporal causes or infringing temporal rights. They admitted having set at liberty persons who had been imprisoned by the High Commission, but only in cases where the cause of imprisonment was not "sufficient" or the matter was not of ecclesiastical cognizance. One of the strongest complaints of the clergy had been that prohibitions ought never to be issued in cases of acknowledged ecclesiastical jurisdiction, despite common-law objections against ecclesiastical procedure. The judges replied that the charges must be made known to the parties before their examination in *ex officio* proceedings, "otherwise they ought not to examine them upon oath." Following the formal reply of the judges, a conference was held between them and the prelates before the Privy Council. We know only that some sort of truce or compromise was arranged which pleased the king. It was short-lived.[39]

In 1606, as in 1604, and again in 1607 and 1610, Parliament sought to reconfirm chapter twenty-nine of Magna Carta. Nicholas Fuller, reviewing Puritan grievances against the High Commission in the sessions of 1606 and 1607, carried on in the spirit of Beale and Morice. More surprising is the qualified criticism of the Commission from Sir Henry Hobart, who as Attorney-General was shortly to become a voice of the royal prerogative and defender of the Commission. In 1606 Hobart, while recommending only the mildest of reforms, declared that the Commission exercised "absolute authority," that there was no appeal from its decisions, that it possessed power to fine and imprison "without limitacion of tyme or some," and that by its proceedings a man "may accuse himself." Accordingly he urged that the Commission sit always in a public place "and not in bishops chambers," that lawyers might advise and prevent errors, and that sentences be given by lay judges "& not the bishop with his chaplens." Sir Henry Montague, who became Chief Justice of King's Bench in 1616, contended that the ecclesiastical courts should be bound by the procedure of the common-law courts. He condemned the practice of the Commission in compelling defendants "to take an oath to accuse themselves, which is against all lawes in causes criminall." Like the High Commission's protests against prohibitions, the protests in the Commons against the High Commission were ineffective. The debate in 1606 was unproductive. In 1607, immediately following an argument by Fuller before the King's Bench on the unconstitutionality of the oath *ex officio*, he and others engaged in an assault on the Commission from the floor of the House, but a bill for proposed restrictions died after a second reading. Thus after several years of protests and prohibitions, the situation was substantially unchanged. Then Chief Justice Coke entered the scene.[40]

CHAPTER VIII

Fuller and Coke

In the summer of 1606 James I rewarded Sir Edward Coke for his services to the crown by appointing him Chief Justice of the Court of Common Pleas. No man more deserved that reward, and no man, the king least of all, could have predicted that the judicial robe would transform a formidable, though in some respects a despicable, advocate for the crown into a magnificent, independent stalwart of the rule of law. Coke was a man of exceptional abilities, all harnessed to the service of his mistress, the common law. He had a mighty intellect but it served his mistress only; few men of such learning were so narrow, yet none was remotely as erudite as he in matters of law. Eloquent, lucid, ever concerned with roots and reasons, he had a gift for expression that was attractive and instructive. In literary style or legal forensics he had a persuasive flair that was augmented in conversation or formal speech by a handsome appearance and a commanding manner. But he was always the advocate, the player of a part, the representative of a position with which he completely identified. It was an occupational characteristic that marked Coke more than other lawyers.[1]

In 1589 he had argued *nemo tenetur seipsum prodere* in Collier's case; had he been employed on the other side, he would have sounded more like Cosin than Morice. When Morice argued the same position in Parliament in 1593, on behalf of two bills that would have crushed the High Commission, Coke, then Speaker of the House, did the crown's bidding as was expected of him. As

Attorney-General from 1593 to 1606, he was an advocate of the royal prerogative and an overzealous champion of the state. Unfairness, even brutality, toward prisoners and interrogation under torture were common at that time on the part of the leading prosecutor for the realm in cases of sedition and treason; but Coke, as Holdsworth and Stephen observed, was uncommonly brutal. Yet the ideal of the law is an impartial and incorruptible judge who administers justice without fear or favor, whether the party is the king or a begger. Coke was such a judge. But he was by no means passionless. He devoted all of his prodigious talents to the service of the law, and from Coke such devotion was equivalent to the reverence of a religious fanatic for his god. The common law, supreme and fundamental, became Coke's god, and he was its oracle before whom all else, including the royal prerogative and rival jurisdictions, must yield in cases of conflict. The common law, as Maitland said, "took flesh in the person of Edward Coke." [2]

At the beginning of 1607 Coke, other common-law judges, and the serjeants-at-law debated the question whether the High Commission possessed the lawful authority to imprison anyone by virtue of letters patent from the crown. It was resolved by all, Coke recorded, that the Commission lacked that authority. Prior to the Act of Supremacy, the Commission could neither fine nor imprison without authority from Parliament. Parliament alone might empower the crown to prescribe by letters patent the "manner of proceedings or punishment concerning the lands, goods, or bodies of the subject. . . ." This resolution, challenging the legality of the letters patent that created the Commission, did not yet square with actual decisions. Even in their answers to the *Articuli Cleri* a year earlier, the judges had not taken so extreme a position. They contended on that occasion that they rightfully freed persons *unjustly* imprisoned.[3]

Parliament met soon after the judges and serjeants resolved that the Commission could not fine or imprison—a resolution which had no effect on the Commission's practice. But the Commons carried on the bench's attack, aiming at the oath *ex officio*. On a motion by the Commons, the Privy Council requested an advisory opinion from Coke and Sir John Popham, the Chief Justice of King's Bench, on the question whether the "ordinary" or ecclesiastical judge might examine any person on the oath *ex officio*. Popham, who once thought that Cartwright's refusal of the oath was illegal, had fallen under Coke's spell. The two chief justices presented the following opinion to the Privy Council:

> 1. That the Ordinary cannot constrain any man, ecclesiastical or temporal, to swear generally to answer to such interrogatories as shall be administered unto him; but ought to deliver to him the articles upon which he is to be examined, to the intent that he may know whether he ought by the law to answer to them: and so is the course of the Star-Chamber and Chancery; the defendant hath the copy of the bill delivered unto him, or otherwise he need not to answer to it.
>
> 2. No man ecclesiastical or temporal shall be examined upon secret thoughts of his heart, or of his secret opinion: but something ought to be objected against him what he hath spoken or done. No lay-man may be examined *ex officio*, except in two causes, and that was grounded upon great reason; for lay-men for the most part are not lettered, wherefore they may easily be inveigled and entrapped, and principally in heresy and errors of faith: and this appears by an ordinance made in the time of Edward I. tit. Prohibition, in Rastal.[4]

In his *Reports* Coke amplified this opinion, filling in the medieval precedents. The thirteenth-century prohibition to which he and Popham had referred specified that laymen should not be tried on oath except in matrimonial or testamentary causes. Such causes, Coke explained, did not concern "the shame and infamy of the party" as did adultery, usury, or heresy. The oath *ex officio* he described in Latin as "the invention of the devil to send the souls of sinners to hell." Jumping from the "Register of Writs," which agreed with the ordinance of Edward I, he cited the cases of Leigh and Hynde in 1568 and 1576 respectively, both of whom had been committed illegally for having refused the oath. Coke added the authority of a statute of 1534 condemning captious interrogatories on oath, and also the books by Crompton and Lambard on the office of the justice of the peace. He concluded, after this parade of authorities, that to compel anyone against his will to take the oath was "a great oppression." [5]

Deciding moot cases in the Serjeants' Inn and giving advisory opinions was one thing; carrying principles into practice by deciding real cases against royal orders was another. When the first test came it was the most important since Cartwright's case. The judges, Coke included, equivocated and backed down. The case involved Nicholas Fuller. He had been Cartwright's counsel, had served in the Commons with Beale and Morice, and had become the leader of the cause after their deaths. No man had made himself more obnoxious to James I and Bancroft than Fuller. When a Puritan courier was arrested with secret instructions on his person concerning the ways and means of combatting the canons of 1604 and the impending deprivations, Fuller was mentioned as the common lawyer whose counsel should be sought. When the king sought subsidies from Parliament, Fuller urged delay. When Bates's case was decided in favor of the royal prerogative, Fuller spoke against the crown in the Commons. When James proposed a union with Scotland and new subsidies for the crown, Fuller was in the forefront of the opposition. When bills were introduced to reconfirm Magna Carta, or to cripple the High Commission, or to aid the deprived ministers, Fuller sponsored them. When the High Commission prosecuted Puritans, Fuller more than likely was their attorney. In March of 1607, when representing twenty men who were jailed by the Commission for contempt, his vehement denunciations of the oath *ex officio* before the common-law courts earned him a warning from Bancroft and the High Commission: he would be fined five hundred pounds and would join his imprisoned clients if he repeated his performance. Within a month he accepted the cases of two Puritans whose causes he advocated with such candor and intemperance that he became victim rather than attorney.[6]

One of Fuller's new clients, Thomas Ladd, a merchant, was arrested for attending a conventicle. His contradictory responses before the local ecclesiastical court led to his being cited before the High Commission on a charge of perjury; but Ladd refused to take the oath again unless first shown the transcript of his earlier examination. The Commission imprisoned him. Richard Mansel, a Puritan minister, met the same fate. He had signed an offensive petition to the House of Commons and, when prosecuted, refused the oath. Fuller applied to the King's Bench for writs of habeas corpus on behalf of Ladd and Mansel. His argument to the effect that they had been unjustly imprisoned was so elaborate that it took two days, spaced a month apart, to deliver. When Fuller concluded, the judges of King's Bench, instead of reaching a decision, reserved the case for reargument before a joint session of the twelve leading common-law judges of England—the combined benches of King's Bench, Common Pleas, and Exchequer.[7]

Fuller's argument led to his commitment by the High Commission. Discreetly waiting until the king prorogued Parliament, but before the common-law judges could hear rearguments, the Commission jailed Fuller on a grab-bag of charges. They indicated the tenor and content of his remarkable defense of Ladd and Mansel. The articles against Fuller mentioned slander of the church, of the king, and of the Commission; malicious impeachment and contempt of the Commission; schism; heresy; and erroneous and pernicious opinions in religion. Fuller was alleged to have committed all these crimes by making the following remarks. He described the Commission's procedure as "Popish" mainly because of the practice of examining men against their wills on the oath *ex officio*. That oath, he said, brought souls to damnation, was illegal, and caused many miscarriages of justice. He also denied the validity of the Commission's power to punish temporally, adding that it imprisoned men without showing cause and kept them in prison indefinitely without permitting bail. Tracing the authority of the Commission to the Act of Supremacy, which did not empower it to use the oath or to inflict temporal punishments, Fuller contended that the royal letters patent, which did vest those powers, were "contrarie to the lawe." Moreover, he described the Commission's jurisdiction as "not of Christ, but of Anti-Christ." In the course of his argument, he seems also to have insinuated that members of the High Commission embezzled the fines which they illegally exacted.[8]

That Fuller's argument before the King's Bench was spiced with injudicious and even bigoted remarks, some of which were unquestionably defamatory, is beyond doubt. Every article against him began with the charge that his utterances were made "publiquely and in the hearing of many." He did not claim that he had been misquoted. Yet it passes belief that Fuller, who was a good lawyer, spewed bilge for two days, or that King's Bench would have listened to such stuff for so many hours. They considered the case to have raised issues important enough to warrant a re-argument before all of the common-law judges. Coke's report begins with the words, "In the great case of Nicholas Fuller. . . ." Epithets like "Popish" and "Anti-Christ" and the sensational, if irrelevant, charge of embezzlement must have been submerged in a powerful presentation.[9]

The High Commission's articles against Fuller mentioned among his other crimes that he attacked as illegal its oath procedure and its power to punish temporally. This attack constitutes the entirety of the published version of Fuller's argument, as the title of the pamphlet suggests: *The Argument of Master Nicholas Fuller, in the Case of Thomas Lad, and Richard Maunsell, his Clients. Wherein it is plainely proved, that the Ecclesiasticall Commissioners have no power, by vertue of their Commission, to Imprison, to put to the Oath* Ex Officio, *or to fine any of his Majesties Subjects*. The pamphlet, which was published by Fuller's friends some months after his argument before the King's Bench, purported to be the speech that led to his commitment; but Fuller denied that it was, saying that the pamphlet contained an argument that he had intended to make. He did not make it because he was jailed. It seems, therefore, to be the argument intended for the special session of all the common-law judges of England. Accordingly, it could not have differed very much in substance from the original argument before the King's Bench, except that it had none of the abusive remarks that marred the first presentation.[10]

A distinguished historian, Roland G. Usher, who usually took the side of the High Commission and of the established church against all of their critics, especially Puritan critics, described Fuller as a "forgotten exponent of English liberty" whose published argument was "among the very first enunciations, if not the first, of that great theory of English constitutional law and history which Hakewill was to use so effectively in the case of Impositions in 1610, and which St. John was to render ever memorable in the great case of Ship Money in 1637. Some of the best-known sentences attributed to Chief Justice Coke might be almost a quotation from this pamphlet. The brochure became so well known and was so much admired by the radical party that it was reprinted in 1641 as a manifesto of the Great Rebellion." This is but another way of saying that the struggle for the right against compulsory self-incrimination was intimately connected with, and in some respects triggered, the greater struggle for constitutional liberty by the Commons and the common-law courts against an unlimited royal prerogative. Coke owed much to Fuller who, in turn, was indebted to Beale and Morice. All four relied on Magna Carta to combat the inquisitorial procedures of the ecclesiastical courts. The Great Charter first emerged as a "liberty document" in their opposition to the oath *ex officio*.[11]

Fuller's first point in defense of Ladd and Mansel was that their imprisonment violated Magna Carta. Ecclesiastical jurisdiction, he contended, never included the power to fine and imprison or, prior to an act of 1401, the power to force men to accuse themselves. "For the lawes of England did so much regard and preserve the liberty of the subjects, as that none should be imprisoned, *nisi per legale judicium parium suorum aut legem terrae* [except by the lawful judgment of his peers or by the law of the land], as it is sayd in *Magna Charta cap. 29,* which Charter by divers other statutes after, is confirmed, with such strong inforcements in some of them, as to make voyd such statutes, as should be contrary to *Magna Charta.*" Fuller then developed a detailed argument against the constitutionality of the act of 1401, commonly called the Statute *Ex Officio,* which had authorized the oath until the repeal act of 1534.[12]

He used the act of 1401 as a foil for a learned discourse against the compulsion of self-accusing. Fuller invoked Aristotle on the principle of self-preservation to buttress his contention that the oath was against the law of nature because it tended to self-destruction; and he cited both Foxe's *Book of Martyrs* and Coke's assertion that swearing against one's self in a criminal cause was an invention of the devil. In addition to chapter twenty-nine of Magna Carta, which was his touchstone, Fuller cited chapter twenty-eight to the effect that no man should be put to oath without witnesses to accuse him. Beale had similarly misread this provision of the great charter. That gloss on chapter twenty-eight was historically insupportable, but common lawyers characteristically marched into the future facing backwards, in the illusion, however far-fetched, that they were conserving ancient liberties, not inventing new ones. Indeed Fuller's entire argument—and this may be said of Beale, Morice, and Coke, too—possessed a medieval cast, giving the impression that he spoke for traditional liberties. To this end he cited a great many old statutes, including several reconfirmations of the Great Charter. One of these, an act of 1368 providing that no man should be put to answer without presentment before justices or by due process of law, contained a clause, which Fuller used, saying that anything done to the contrary should be "voyd in law & holden for error." His use of a statute of 1375 was even more pointed. A juror, he noted, could be challenged for a number of reasons and must answer on oath, but if the challenge touched his credit or his loss, he could not be forced to answer on oath, although his answer might further the cause of justice, "*quia nemo tenetur prodere seipsum*, as is ruled *49 Edw. 3. fol. 2.*" Fuller's examination of the old statutes, climaxed by the act of 1534, led to his conclusion that the oath *ex officio*, because it forced self-incrimination, was against the old laws of England, the law of nature, justice, and equity.[13]

These general principles had little validity, however, if the letters patent issued by Elizabeth and James under the Act of Supremacy lawfully authorized the High Commission to inflict temporal penalties and to impose the oath. But Fuller argued that "the lawes of the kingdome of England, and the manner of proceeding in cases of law and justice, are settled in the Realme, as parte of the inheritance of the subjectes . . . by which both King and subjectes are guided; and that without lawes there would be nether King nor inheritance in England." His point was that the royal prerogative was bound by what he regarded as a fundamental law protecting the liberties of the subject. The "law admeasureth the Kings prerogative," he declared, "so as it shall not extend to hurt the inheritance of the subjectes. . . . And the law doth restrayne the liberall words of the Kings grant, for the benefit both of the King and the subjectes, and to the great happines of the Realme; especially when the Judges are men of courage, fearing God; as is to be proved by many Cases adjudged in these Courtes of *Kings Bench* and *Common Pleas;* which Courtes are the principall preservers of this high inheritance of the law." The king could neither dispense with nor alter the common law, nor could he deny his subjects their inheritance of the law "which was alwayes accompted one of the great blessings of this land, to have the law the *meat-yeard*, & the Judges the *measurers*." Fuller backed up this argument with citations to several cases in which the judges had ruled against the king.[14]

Fuller had laid the groundwork for contesting the validity of the letters patent which authorized the High Commission to use the oath, to fine, and to imprison. Quoting the provisions which he thought "to be against the lawes of England and liberties of the subjects," he asserted that while the Act of Supremacy had simply intended to restore to the crown its ancient ecclesiastical jurisdiction, the Commission, "being so indefinite without limitation or restraynt," had swelled enormously in functions and powers under the letters patent. Parliament had intended it to be merely an executory commission, not a "setled court for continuance for ever." Under the letters patent, the commissioners cited men from all parts of the realm on mere suspicion, held them without bail, and subjected them, by fines, to loss of lands and goods as well as loss of liberty. Such punishments, Fuller believed, should follow common-law proceedings only, "yet the party suspected may be forced by this Commission, to accuse himselfe upon his owne oath, upon such captious *Interrogatories*, as the witt of man can devise, when there is neyther accuser, nor libell of accusation. . . . Which kind of proceedinges how farr they doe differ from the common lawes of England. . . ."[15]

Turning to the Act of Supremacy, Fuller sought to prove that it not only did not warrant the powers in question, "but contrary-wise doth expresly abolish their Jurisdiction to imprison subjectes, fyne them, and force them to accuse themselves. . . ." He contended that the "auncient Jurisdiction" to which the act referred was the jurisdiction that existed prior to the act of 1401. That act and its revival under Queen Mary had been explicitly repealed by the Act of Supremacy which "doth abolish the oath Ex officio, by making voyd the statute . . . which first gave life to that kind of proceeding. . . ." The Act of Supremacy, he added, also contained a clause providing that no person should be indicted or arraigned for any offense within its purview without the testimony of two witnesses who must be brought "face to face before the party so arraigned." From this provision Fuller thought it plain that Parliament had not meant to empower any commission founded under the act to try offenses "by the parties owne forced oath, against his will, without any witnes or accuser" as was the practice of the High Commission; "and yet it is pretended to be grounded upon this statute." [16]

Fuller concluded with an invitation to the judges to strike down the letters patent as unconstitutional. The exposition and construction of the laws belonged to the judges: ". . . to uphold the right of the lawes of England, the Judges in ages past have advisedly construed some wordes of divers statutes contrary to the common sence of the words of the statute, to uphold the meaning of the common lawes of the Realme." If the Act of Supremacy were construed "according to the tenor of the sayd letters Patents, there might be erected, in this common wealth of England, a course of an arbitrarie governement at the discretion of the Commissioners, directly contrary to the happie long continued goverment and course of the common lawes of the Realme, and directly contrary to *Magna Charta:* which if the statute of *42 Edw. 3* [1368] did so highly regard, as to make voyd Acts of Parliament contrary to the same, it would, *a fortiori*, make voyd all construction of statuts contrary to *Magna Charta.* . . ." [17]

Fuller never delivered this great speech, though it received far greater publicity as a pamphlet than it would have received had he merely delivered it orally. The speech that he had delivered before the King's Bench earlier, in May and June of 1607, must have been similar, with the addition of certain defamatory remarks. Of course the Commission regarded the attack on its powers and on the letters patent as defamatory too. By imprisoning Fuller, the Commission converted the case of Ladd and Mansel into the case of Nicholas Fuller. He remained in jail but managed to secure from the King's Bench a writ of prohibition which stopped the Commission from proceeding to sentence against him until the court reconvened at the end of summer for a hearing on the question whether the prohibition should be made permanent or be cancelled by a writ of consultation.

James I and Robert Cecil, now Lord Salisbury, the king's Secretary of State and Lord Treasurer, agreed that Fuller's argument threatened the government. James instructed Salisbury to see to it that the prohibition was not sustained; calling Fuller a villain, the king prophecied that if the High Commission lost the case, his government would be held in contempt "and the monarchie shall fall to ruine. . . ." When the courts reopened in the fall after summer vacation, the judges of the King's Bench, realizing the gravity of the case, sought the advice of Chief Justice Coke, the judges of his court, and the barons of the Exchequer. The court was trapped in an awkward situation of its own making. To sustain the prohibition would invite the wrath of the king and Privy Council. To annul the prohibition by a writ of consultation would not only sacrifice Fuller to the High Commission; it would admit that the prohibition had been groundlessly issued in the first place. But Fuller was the least consideration: he deserved to be punished because of his intemperateness. What was at stake was the *amour propre* and claims of the common law against the ecclesiastical law. The judges decided to throw Fuller to the Commission by issuing a writ of consultation on the narrowest grounds possible; they authorized the Commission to proceed against Fuller for schism, heresy, impious error, and pernicious opinions. Quite explicitly the court refused to give any opinion on the authority and validity of the letters patent or on the exposition and interpretation of the Act of Supremacy. With equal explicitness the court observed that it was not passing on certain "scandals, contempts, and other matters which by the Common law and statutes of our Realm of England should be punished or determined." Thus the judges denied to the High Commission jurisdiction over its principal charges against Fuller, though acknowledging its authority to prosecute him for schism, heresy, and pernicious opinions. Not a word was said about the Commission's power to fine, imprison, or exact the oath.[18]

Coke, in his report of Fuller's case, gave a more favorable account of the judges than would appear from their writ of consultation. He declared that all the common-law judges of England had resolved the following points. They had exclusive jurisdiction to construe the Act of Supremacy and the letters patent under it;

although the Commission's jurisdiction and procedure was ecclesiastical, its authority and power derived from an act of Parliament as did the letters patent. The judges did not, however, actually construe the Act of Supremacy nor did they pass on the validity of the letters patent. Instead they asserted that "when there is any question concerning what power or jurisdiction belongs to Ecclesiastical Judges, in any particular case, the determination of this belongs to the Judges of the Common Law" who might therefore issue a prohibition to decide proper cognizance. The judges also resolved that if a lawyer in his argument should scandalize the king or his government, temporal or ecclesiastical, he had committed a misdemeanor and contempt to the court, for which he should be punished, though not by the ecclesiastical court. But, for heresy, schism, or erroneous opinions in religion, the ecclesiastical judges might punish him by ecclesiastical law, because such matters did not belong to the cognizance of the common law.[19]

These resolutions may have salved the consciences of the judges, but for all practical purposes Fuller had lost his case and the judges had capitulated because they issued the writ of consultation. The High Commission promptly convicted Fuller on technically correct charges, fined him two hundred pounds, and imprisoned him for an indefinite period. But Fuller, a wily lawyer, sought a writ of habeas corpus from the King's Bench. The judges granted it, thus requiring his jailors to defend their commitment of him against a claim of illegal imprisonment. The Commission's jurisdiction over Fuller's offense had been settled; therefore, the only issues that could now be raised on the return of the habeas corpus, were the Commission's authority to fine and imprison. These issues, like the oath *ex officio*, brought into question the validity of the letters patent and thus the prerogative authority of the crown. James, who had been very pleased when the prohibition had been canceled, now grew alarmed again. He instructed Salisbury to see to it that the royal honor and prerogative were not impugned. Salisbury directed Sir Henry Hobart, Coke's successor as Attorney-General, to argue the case against Fuller. We may surmise that the king's wishes were strongly represented to the judges, and, moreover, that Fuller himself was warned not to restate his argument against the High Commission's powers or against the validity of the letters patent. Although the case was before the King's Bench, rather than Common Pleas, Coke was persuaded to use his influence on behalf of a solution satisfactory to the crown. The hearing on the writ of habeas corpus turned out to be a petty wrangle on the technical sufficiency of the warrant for commitment. The great issues were not even mentioned. The King's Bench, finding no error in the warrant, remanded Fuller to the custody of the jail-keeper, bringing an end to the case. James, once again pleased, sent his thanks to Coke and the other judges, yet remarked, probably not for the first time, that if they had decided otherwise, he would have committed them. Fuller paid his fine and was released a few months later after framing an acceptable submission. The one thing he could not retract was the publication of his powerful argument in the tract that gave the case its enduring significance.[20]

When James declared that he would have imprisoned the judges had they maintained their writ of habeas corpus, he also spoke angrily about their prohibitions. There were, as Professor Usher said, a "flood" of them issued in 1607 and 1608. Although the judges might make a tactical retreat when challenged by the crown in a sensational case like Fuller's, their sympathies were unquestionably with Fuller's argument. Their prohibitions in 1607 and 1608 showed, said Usher, that they meant to "destroy" the High Commission and to this end they "educed new claims. They declared that the oath *ex officio*, as employed by the ecclesiastical courts and the High Commission, had been abrogated by the reformation statutes as repugnant to the common law. . . . If this contention were true, it . . . would in effect nullify a cardinal ecclesiastical procedure, without which a culprit could not be legally examined, tried, convicted, or sentenced. Whether it was or was not legal, and whether it was or was not unjustly and tyrannically used, the oath *ex officio* certainly was the keynote of ecclesiastical procedure and without it the ancient process, which had been in vogue for centuries, would simply be unworkable." In any case in which a confession was needed for a conviction, because two eyewitnesses to the crime did not exist, Usher's statement about the oath was certainly true. Yet the oath did not feature in many prohibitions, though their number was described by Bancroft as "infinite." He was not wrong in believing that the com-mon-law judges issued prohibitions out of malice, purely for the purpose of obstruction and harrassment, even in cases clearly ec-clesiastical. Moreover, there was scarcely any warrant, historical or legal, for prohibitions that concerned purely procedural, as dis-tinguished from jurisdictional, matters, such as the oath or the right of the Commission's pursuivants to make arrests or the right to summon defendants. In one case Coke issued a prohibition that freed a man who had been arrested on bare surmise. In his remark-able opinion Coke declared that if a person resisting arrest should kill the Commission's pursuivant, it would not be murder because the Commission had no authority under the Act of Supremacy to make arrests; ecclesiastical courts must proceed under ecclesiastical law by citations only.[21]

Constant complaints by the Commission about prohibitions led James to summon the common-law judges for an explanation of their behavior. James understood that more than aggravating juris-dictional disputes between his temporal and ecclesiastical courts was involved. Beneath the technical niceties was an assault on his prerogative: no High Commission, no bishops; no bishops, no king. Troubled enough by Parliament, James was not about to permit strained interpretations of Magna Carta to fence him in, surmount his letters patent, or cripple his ecclesiastical courts. Dis-tinguished authorities fortified his view of his legal powers. Fran-cis Bacon, his Solicitor-General, who could have been as great a lawyer as Coke had he not spent so much time in philosophical, scientific, and literary pursuits, backed James without reservation. Dr. John Cowell, Regius Professor of Civil Law at Cambridge, a member of the High Commission, and a co-author of the canons of 1604, published a law dictionary in 1607, *The Interpreter*, which said that the king was "above the Law by his absolute power" and could not be bound even by laws of Parliament. Above all, Lord Chancellor Ellesmere, who presided over the High Court of Parliament, the Court of Star Chamber, and the Court of Chancery, a man who had precedence over all the common-law judges, said, in 1606, that "before Magna Charta was, the prerogative was; for Magna Charta is but a declaration or manifestation thereof. . . ." In Calvin's case, in 1607, Ellesmere declared that God himself, having ordained kings, gave them the power to make laws; *"rex est lex loquens"* (the king is the law speaking), said Ellesmere. If a difficult question could not be solved by the judges, the "true and certen rule" by which it could be solved in accord with both the civil law and the common law would be by decision of "the most religious, learned, and judicious king that ever this kingdome or island had." [22]

James, taking his Lord Chancellor's welcome advice, convened before him and his Privy Council the two chief justices, the chief baron, and all their associates, together with Bancroft and other prelates. The subject was prohibitions. Coke made the occasion a memorable one in the history of constitutionalism. The debate began with some technical points about prohibitions but soon became a row between James and Coke. Someone, probably Bancroft or Ellesmere, suggested that on questions concerning the cognizance of ecclesiastical courts, or the exposition of the Act of Supremacy in relation to the High Commission, the king himself might make decisions. All judges, temporal and ecclesiastical, being but delegates of the king, he might repossess his jurisdiction in whatever cases he pleased. The archbishop, Coke reported, said "this was clear in divinity, that such authority belongs to the king. . . ." Coke answered that the king could not personally decide any case nor remove any from his courts of justice; they alone could decide. Magnifying the role of the common-law courts in providing justice to the lowliest and the highest, Coke quoted chapter twenty-nine of Magna Carta against the king.

James, becoming angry, answered that the judges were like papists who quoted Scriptures but insisted on their own interpretation of them. As king he was supreme judge, he declared, and under him were all the courts. If he chose to, he might sit on the bench himself and decide cases. The law was founded on reason which he possessed as well as the judges, and he would protect the law. Coke replied that though the king had reason, he lacked the legal knowledge necessary to decide cases; the judges would protect both the subjects and the king. James then burst out that Coke had made a "traiterous" speech; the king protected the law, not the law the king. Coke's view, he said excitedly, meant that he was under the law. Coke, in his own account of the case, reported that he replied with a quotation from Bracton, that "the king ought not to be below any man but under God and the law." James denounced Coke for "treason" and, rising from his seat, shook his fist in Coke's face. Frightened, the chief justice, it seems, fell on all fours, beseeching the king's pardon for having permitted his zeal to carry him beyond allegiance. Salisbury, Coke's kinsman by marriage, interceding on his behalf, finally persuaded the king to pardon the chief justice.[23]

What was really said during this altercation between Coke and James is by no means clear. Coke's own account, which cast him in the role of St. George against the dragon, imperishably fixed the record for posterity. When that account was published long after in the twelfth volume of his *Reports*, his courageous stand against the prerogative, capped by the noble maxim from Bracton, like his reinterpretations of Magna Carta, became an inspiration on both sides of the Atlantic to men who fought for the rule of law.

It is part of the folklore of modern scholarship, inadvertently planted by the error of Usher, one of Coke's most skeptical critics, to believe that on November 14, 1608, the very day after his dispute with James, Coke issued another prohibition against the High Commission, one "which easily exceeded in its 'enormity' all previous agressions." The chief justice had grit, but he also had sense enough not to play at knight-errantry the "morning after." The case that Usher described, in which Coke invoked chapter twenty-nine of Magna Carta to support a prohibition for a deprived minister, was a day and a year later. Yet Coke was prodigal in issuing prohibitions on quite extravagant grounds which challenged the king's prerogative. Many of these were in 1609, and they began soon enough after the scene with the king.[24]

In January 1609, in the case of Burneham and Stroude, Coke issued a prohibition that deserves Usher's play on the word "enormity." The Act of Supremacy vested in the High Commission jurisdiction over all "heresies, errors, schisms, abuses, offences, contempts and enormities whatsoever" which could be corrected by ecclesiastical power. Coke read the word "enormities" to qualify all the preceding words, as if the statute meant only enormous or exorbitant heresies, errors, and the like. The offense might be of undoubted ecclesiastical jurisdiction, but Coke always seemed to doubt that it was an enormous one. Burneham and Stroude, the defendants whom Coke freed, had been convicted for laying "violent hands" on their minister, pulling his surplice off, defaming him, and preventing him from performing divine service. Coke did not deem the offense to be an enormity, and the High Commission, he added, could not imprison for it, because no free man could be imprisoned but by the judgment of his peers or by the law of the land. In a manuscript summarizing seventeen of Coke's prohibitions between 1609 and 1611, every one of which quoted chapter twenty-nine of Magna Carta, the clerk rendered the Latin in progressively shorter phrasing from case to case until he ended with "*nullus liber homo etc.*" [25]

Several of these cases were also grounded on an objection to the oath *ex officio*. In the case of Rochester and Mascall who had been convicted by the Commission for notorious adultery, Coke stated, "*nemo tenetur in Causis criminalibus prodere seipsum.*" In the case of Giles and Symonds, who were also convicted for adultery, Coke declared that the defendants, being free subjects, were entitled to enjoy "the freedom of all Laws and privileges of the Kingdom, and that they are not bound to answer articles touching these premisses on their oathes." In the Pierces' case Coke said that "all cannons and constitutions, &c. made to compell any person (questioned in a court Ecclesiasticall) to take his oath against his will, except in causes Testimentariis or Matrimonialibus are void. . . ." On another occasion, the Commission convicted Edward and Anne Jenner for having disturbed church services, defended Brownists, published schismatical books, and called the minister's wife "a priests whore." Yet, Coke said, in Latin, "no free man should be compelled to answer for his secret thoughts and opinions." [26]

This statement in the Jenners' case was preceded by the advisory opinion that Coke and Popham had given in 1607 and by Coke's opinion in the case of Thomas Edwards in 1609. That 1609 case later appeared in Coke's *Reports* where it could be read by all who objected to compulsory self-incrimination. Charged with having libeled a bishop, Edwards refused the oath *ex officio* when required to swear to the meaning of certain shocking innuendoes about the bishop and his wife. Granting the application for a prohibition, Coke found that the cause belonged to temporal jurisdiction and that "the Ecclesiastical Judge cannot examine any man upon his oath, upon the intention and thought of his heart, for *cogitationis poenam nemo emeret* [no man may be punished for his thought]. And in cases where a man is to be examined upon his oath, he ought to be examined upon acts or words, and not of the intention or thought of his heart; and if any man should be examined upon any point of religion, he is not bound to answer the same; for in time of danger, *quis modo tutus erit* [how will he be safe] if everyone should be examined of his thoughts . . . for it hath been said in the proverb, *thought is free.*" Lambert had said it long before when he associated the proverb with the maxim, *nemo tenetur seipsum prodere.* Coke made the same nexus, always associating with his point the principle of chapter twenty-nine of Magna Carta.[27]

Coke's innumerable prohibitions, of which only a few involved the oath, overwhelmed the High Commission. The scene with the king was only one of the many extra-judicial debates in which he was forced to defend his decisions. He had become so committed to his course of action that he could no longer back down, even though he was ordered on various occasions either to issue no more prohibitions or to be more moderate. In 1609, Coke was called first before Ellesmere, the Lord Chancellor; then before the king in the presence of the Privy Council, at which time he debated Archbishop Bancroft; and then again before king and Council to debate Attorney-General Hobart and Solicitor-General Bacon. No one could budge him from his position. Defending it in debate with his accustomed vigor and learning, he then redefended it in five treatises which he presented to the king. One of these was devoted to the rule he embodied in so many of his prohibitions, namely, that the High Commission, except in a few rare instances, had no authority to fine or imprison. That his view, particularly of Magna Carta, was unorthodox is evident from Hobart's argument that the decision by the King's Bench "lately in Mr. Fullers Case . . . adjudged that his Imprisonment by the Highe Commission was Lawfull. And therefor to alledge now the Statute of Magna Charta cap. 29 Nullus liber homo capiatur vel imprisonetur nisi per legale Judicium parium suorum, vel per

Legem terrae against this Imprisonment by the Highe Commission is out of Season, because this latter Law abrogats the former and the Statutes are infinite that have given Imprisonment in sondry Cases synce that Statute of Magna Charta." Coke was never more spirited than when defending the Great Charter as a vital fundamental law.[28]

Puritan pamphleteers also cited Magna Carta in their argument against the legality of the oath and kept up their din against involuntary self-accusing. And Parliament, after a quarter of a century of abortive efforts, finally took a decisive stand in 1610. James inadvertently lit the Parliamentary fuse by delivering one of his arrogant speeches to the Lords and the Commons. After expatiating about the divine right of kings, his powers over his subjects "in all causes, and yet accomptable to none but God onely," he turned to the subject of the "swelling and overflowing of prohibitions." It was the occasion of only one of his several criticisms of the common law, some of which were obviously aimed at Coke who was becoming a hero to the Commons. After chastising the common-law courts for being "prodigall" with rash and unreasonable prohibitions, James touched on the subject of "Grievances." They too had multiplied, especially in the lower house. Warning the Commons to beware against presenting grievances that contained "Treason or scandal" against him, James advised that it was best that they should not "meddle with the maine points of Government." He also advised against the presentation of grievances which all knew in advance that he would turn down. He gave as an example the subject of the High Commission. He would listen to genuine complaints about its abuses, but he would neither abolish it nor abridge its powers.[29]

The Commons answered in July 1610 with a "Petition of Grievances." The petition praised the writ of prohibition and censured the High Commission. The words "inconvenient and dangerous" were used to describe the provision in the Act of Supremacy that authorized the making of a commission for ecclesiastical cases. The intention of the statute, said Commons, was simply to restore the crown's ecclesiastical jurisdiction and to permit that jurisdiction to be vested in commissioners. There was no intention to empower the commissioners to fine and imprison or to "exercise other authority not belonging to the ecclesiastical jurisdiction restored by that statute"; in other words, the commissioners could not arrest, search and seize, hold without bail, or cite a man out of his diocese—"very grievous" said the Commons. Moreover, the High Commission exercised both spiritual and temporal jurisdiction, inflicted both spiritual and temporal penalties, yet could "force the party by oath to accuse himself of any offense." There was no appeal from a decision of the High Commission, "though a judgment or sentence be given against him, amounting to the taking away of all his goods, and imprisoning of him during life." It was "very unreasonable" that a court should exercise such powers and "enforce a man upon his own oath to accuse and expose himself to those punishments. . . ." It was grievous, too, that the Commission's pursuivants, who were employed to apprehend suspects and to search for scandalous books, "break open mens houses, closets, and desks, rifling all corners and secret custodies, as in cases of high treason or suspicion thereof." The Commons therefore asked the king for his assent to a statute that would reduce the Commission "to reasonable and convenient limits." A bill to this effect, abolishing the oath *ex officio*, had already been passed, but it never became law.[30]

Prohibitions, declared the Commons, were among the most honorable writs of the realm, like the writs of habeas corpus and *de homine replegiando*, a "chief means of relief unto the poor, distressed and oppressed subjects." Lately there had been "some obstruction" to writs of prohibition from those who wished the support "of inferior courts against the principal courts of the common law." The king, concluded the Commons, should require his judges in the courts at Westminster to grant prohibitions when warranted, especially if the party might be imprisoned when the courts were on vacation. The Commons also remonstrated in its petition against royal proclamations, saying that the people had a right not to be subjected to any punishment extending to life, lands, body, or goods, except by punishment "ordained by the common laws of this land, or the statutes made by their common consent in Parliament."[31]

James promised a favorable consideration of the Petition of Grievances, but never fulfilled his word. He knew what Coke thought of prohibitions and of the oath *ex officio,* but did not know his opinion on proclamations. As was the custom, the king asked his chief justices for an advisory opinion on a disputed point of law. At a conference before the Privy Council, Coke reported, the judges unanimously agreed that the king could not by proclamation create any new offenses, because he could not "alter the law of the land." The law of England, the judges said, was divided into the common law, statute law, and custom, "but the King's proclamation is none of them. . . . Also it was resolved, that the King hath no prerogative but that which the law of the land allows him." After this resolution, Coke reported, "no proclamation imposing fine and punishment was afterwards made." Coke won his point, but the king's hostility was mounting.[32]

In 1611, two new prohibitions from Coke, one against the oath, provoked James to speak of the "perversenes" of the chief justice. "My spirit shalbe no longer vexed with this man," the king declared. We know only that he summoned Coke for an explanation in private and that, whatever was said, Coke's prohibitions, including writs based on the illegality of the oath, continued. As a result Coke and his associate judges were summoned by the Privy Council to answer to charges by the new Archbishop of Canterbury, George Abbot. The archbishop made an effective argument, quoting Coke's report of Cawdrey's case of 1591 and citing the fact that when Coke was Attorney-General, he himself had drawn the letters patent of 1605 which authorized the High Commission's procedures and powers. Speaking for his associates, Coke defended their independent findings as judges. The Lord Chancellor thought that he might succeed in a debate with the judges before the Privy Council if the prelates were not present; but Coke, always the judicial spokesman, was as obstinate as a heretic. The king himself, intervening at a third meeting between the Privy Council and the judges, unsuccessfully sought to divide them from Coke by reasoning with them separately. Finally, the king announced to the Council, in the presence of the judges, that he would reform the High Commission by issuing a new letters patent; once that was done, they must obey. It looked as if Coke had won. Salisbury, after the king's remarks, said that nothing would be left of the Commission "but stumps." [33]

James, however, had second thoughts. In all crucial respects the new letters patent proved to be a repetition of the old. The requirement of the oath, the power to fine and imprison, and other objectionable provisions remained. There was, however, an alteration in the provision on the oath. The letters patent of 1559 and 1583 contained the identical provision, one that simply authorized the commissioners to examine suspects and witnesses on their "corporall oathes." The letters patent of 1611 was comparatively elaborate. In one place, the commissioners were empowered to make inquiry by examination of the accused persons "upon their oath (where there shall first appear sufficient matter of charge by examination of witnesses or by presentments or by public and notorious fame or by information of the ordinary)." This passage began by restricting the use of the oath and ended, in effect, by vesting its use in the discretion of the commissioners, because they alone decided whether the prerequisite of "notorious fame" existed. In a different section the letters patent of 1611 provided further detail, authorizing the use of the "corporal oath" against persons accused or suspected by notorious fame "in case it do first appear that the parties unto which the said oath shall be so ministered are thereof detected either by examination of witnesses or by presentments or by public or notorious fame or by information of the ordinary where the offence was committed." Suspicion based on notorious fame had never been an obstacle to the High Commission, and once it exacted the oath, it could launch any sort of fishing expedition. Another provision made all witnesses liable to the oath.[34]

One provision in the letters patent of 1611 was an innovation that fortified the oath procedure. The Commission could imprison anyone refusing the oath or refusing to answer "fully and directly" after having taken it, and could keep such a person in prison until he purged himself of his contempt by taking oath and making answer. Or, alternatively, the Commission could "proceed" against anyone refusing to take the oath or to answer fully and directly. The first part of this provision endorsed the Commission's customary practice; the second part inferentially enabled it to convict an obstinate defendant as if he had confessed, which was the practice of the Star Chamber.[35]

The letters patent of 1611 named Coke a member of the High Commission. He had been made a member in 1601 and again in 1605 when he was Attorney-General. As Chief Justice of Common Pleas he had again been appointed in 1608. Yet Coke, though taking a leading role in the Court of Star Chamber, had always refused to sit on the High Commission. The new letters patent named him, Chief Justice Thomas Fleming of the King's Bench, and six other judges. Under Coke's leadership they boycotted the new Commission after its first meeting. They attended that meeting not to participate but to obstruct, embarrass, and contest. All members of the Commission, including prelates and great state magnates, took their seats except for the common-law judges. They, very conspicuously, remained standing. "And I was commanded to sit," Coke reported, "by force of the said commission, which I refused. . . ." He had not seen a copy of the new letters patent, he said, and therefore could not execute his commission for fear that it might be against the law. Archbishop Abbot and Lord Salisbury expostulated and pleaded with Coke, in private and before the other commissioners. With reluctance Abbot finally read a copy of the commission. It "contained divers points against the laws and statutes of England," Coke reported, ". . . and all the time that the long Commission was in reading, the oath [of allegiance and supremacy] in taking, and the [archbishop's] oration made, I stood, and would not sit, as I was requested by the Archbishop and the Lords, and so by my example did the rest of the justices." Coke and the judges never did sit on the High Commission. It simply carried on without them, leaving them free to carry on their war against it.[36]

And the prohibitions continued. Two of Coke's most extreme prohibitions, grounded on Magna Carta and the illegality of the oath *ex officio*, were issued in late 1611, after the new letters patent had gone into effect. The extrajudicial objections against the oath continued too. In 1612, for example, William Sayer, whose religious views were a compound of Anabaptism and Barrowism, claimed that it was unlawful to take the oath before any ecclesiastical officer, even "though it be to the detecting of a Jesuite, or an Heretick, or making knowne his brothers offence being a delinquent." Archbishop Abbot, in response to what seems to have been a recommendation from the Bishop of Norwich, John Jegon, that Sayer "should burne as an Hereticque," replied that the law would not "frie him at a Stake" unless he obstinately denied the divinity of Christ. That great crime had been committed earlier in the same year by Bartholomew Legate and Edward Wightman, the last Englishmen to suffer death by burning for the crime of heresy. Coke cast doubt on the legality of the writ *de haeretico comburendo*. When Abbot requested Ellesmere to appoint a commission of lay and ecclesiastical judges to decide Legate's case, he pointedly asked that Coke be excluded. At about this time, Randal Bate, who was some kind of Separatist, wrote a book while in prison in which he offered twenty-one reasons to prove that the oath *ex officio* was "not lawful against any, especially against Ministers." None of Bate's reasons were original, but his book kept before the public the idea that the oath was cruelly unfair, a snare of the Spanish Inquisition, because it tended to bring a man to his own self-destruction.[37]

In 1613 King James, following the crafty suggestion of his Solicitor-General, Francis Bacon, appointed Coke to the chief justiceship of King's Bench, the position known as "Chief Justice of England." As head of Common Pleas, Coke was damaging the royal prerogative and growing in popularity with the people and the Commons. "To deal rashly with such a man," may not, contrary to Holdsworth, have been "dangerous," but might unnecessarily have invited trouble. Bacon's solution was inspired: promote him to the place left vacant by the death of Sir Thomas Fleming. Coke would receive far fewer cases of jurisdictional disputes to resolve, and he could not be as effective in his obstructionism. The King's Bench was England's highest criminal court, whose judges sat to defend the king's peace. Coke, the advocate, the player of roles, would be a bulwark to the crown, as he had been when he was Attorney-General. Yet the new post, Bacon pointed out, was less profitable than that as head of Common Pleas, so it "will be thought abroad a kind of discipline to him for opposing himself in the King's causes, the example whereof will contain others in more awe." Bacon recommended Attorney-General Hobart, a pliable man, as Coke's successor on the bench of Common Pleas, and himself, a vigorous prerogative man, as Hobart's successor. He suggested, finally, that the prospect of a privy councilorship should be held out as a carrot to Coke to make him "turn obsequious." James accepted Bacon's plan, but sought to win Coke over by making him a member of the Privy Council at once. It was a brilliant move which misfired in one respect only: Coke's judicial experience had given him standards of incorruptibility and independence to which he was committed beyond all seduction. Not only had his views become fixed; he regarded the position of Chief Justice of England as one that obligated him to do justice between the king and accused subjects, not as one that necessarily placed him on the side of the prosecution. Coke remained the role-player, but his concept of his new role bore little relationship to Bacon's. The chief justice still issued prohibitions, applied the *nemo tenetur* maxim, and what was even worse, from the standpoint of the king, he assaulted Ellesmere and the Court of Chancery, thwarted the king himself in a treason case, and challenged the prerogative against the king's express wishes.[38]

In one of his earliest King's Bench prohibitions, in Boyer's case, Coke declared, "They would have examined him on oath; as touching this, the Rule of Law is, Nemo tenetur seipsum prodere; they may there examine upon oath if he be a Parson, or an Ecclesiastical man, but not a lay person." Every such opinion implicitly denied the legality of the king's letters patent. Each year Coke's offenses against the king seemed to increase in enormity. In 1615, for example, there was Peacham's case involving an old rector with Puritan sympathies who had frequently been in trouble with the High Commission. Pursuivants rifling his study had found some manuscript notes of a treasonable nature. Peacham, wrote Attorney-General Bacon, was examined "before torture, in torture, between torture, and after torture," but would not confess to treason. The king, whose death Peacham had hinted at, thought it advisable to seek the opinion of King's Bench on whether he could be convicted, but James took the precaution of sounding out the judges, via Bacon, individually, so they could not be influenced by Coke. He alone remonstrated against James's tactic, denouncing it as a violation of the custom of the realm. When finally he was persuaded to give his opinion on the merits of the case, Coke advised that Peacham was not guilty, thereby angering the king still further.[39]

Then came a case in 1616 involving the king's right to stay proceedings in the King's Bench on a matter in which James was interested. The common law, said Bacon, arguing for the king, was a servant of the crown, and the twelve common-law judges were like twelve lions under Solomon's throne. "They must be lions, but yet lions under the throne, being circumspect that they do not check or oppose any points of sovereignty." Coke did not agree; he believed that the king was under God and the law. The case ended in a compromise which sidestepped the main issue, but that issue arose again shortly after. The king ordered a stay in a certain matter before the judges, and Coke, who saw the royal interference as an attack upon the independence of his court, refused. Bacon, in the name of the king, then commanded the twelve common-law judges to obey the stay-order, yet the judges defiantly proceeded. In a letter drawn by Coke, signed by all, they pleaded that they had sworn an oath to discharge their judicial duties. Jumes, infuriated, summoned all the judges before him and the Privy Council, tore up their letter, and denounced them for disobedience. The twelve judges fell to their knees and craved his Majesty's pardon, while Ellesmere, at the king's instruction, lectured them on their dereliction of duty and allegiance. James then asked the judges whether they would, in the future, obey his stay orders. Still on their knees the judges answered: "They all (the Lord Chief Justice only except) yielded that they would, and acknowledged it to be their duty to do so; only the Lord Chief Justice of the King's Bench said for answer, That when the case should be, he would do that should be fit for a Judge to do." In November of 1616, James dismissed Coke from office.[40]

Earlier in 1616 Coke decided the most important case of his career on the oath *ex officio*, *Burrowes and Others* v. *The High Commission*. It dragged on so long and was reargued so many times that Coke called it "an old and beaten case," but he deliberately set out to make it the leading case on the subject. The Commission had imprisoned eight Puritan laymen who had been cited for holding private conventicles, refusing to kneel at communion, and sundry religious crimes. One or more of the eight were also suspected of stealing a surplice from a church. When their case came before the King's Bench on habeas corpus, the cause of their commitment was given as refusal to take the oath.

The case, said Coke at the first hearing, was "of very great consequence." It concerned the penal laws requiring religious uniformity and even a matter of felony. In such cases laymen were not to be examined on oath; it was lawful only in matrimonial and testamentary cases. Even if the High Commission had proper jurisdiction, Coke declared, they could not examine on oath because that would "make one thereby to subject himself to the danger of a penal law." He cited the *nemo tenetur* maxim and several Elizabethan precedents, chief among them Leigh's case. But the Court made no decision because the High Commission was not represented by counsel. Coke, moreover, wished to use the case to settle once and for all the question of the legality of the oath *ex officio*. He resolved to confer personally with the High Commission, declaring that he would "shew unto them what hath been done in like cases in former times. . . ." He would bring the evidence—the lawbooks and manuscripts of unreported decisions—"for it is very clear, they cannot proceed so, and I will satisfie them herein for the time to come," to prevent a repetition of similar cases.[41]

Whether Coke actually conferred with the High Commission is not known, but at the next hearing of the case, a Dr. Martin, the King's Advocate for the High Commission, was present to argue its position. Before letting him speak, Coke restated his argument against the oath, once again describing the case as one of great consequence. Dr. Martin agreed for different reasons: the Commission's prisoners, he pointed out, were guilty of great schism and had traduced the king himself by speaking against his laws of church government. "Crimes of this nature which concern the State," Martin declared, "do require diligent examination, and this by oath." As for Coke's contention that the accused were entitled to a copy of the charges against them, Martin noted that for some sixty years it had been against the policy of the state and the practice of the High Commission to show the accused "the particulars upon which they are to be examined." To hold either that the oath could not be required or that the accused must first have the particulars would mean that "this land will then overflow with blasphemous and wicked persons, and therefore they are to remain in prison until they do conform themselves." Coke, by way of reply, once again reviewed the precedents and declared that the prisoners should not be examined on oath to accuse themselves and must be given copies of the articles against them.[42]

Nine months later, the prisoners having remained in jail all this time, the Court gave its opinion. "I will not by any ways maintain sectaries," Coke announced. "But the subject ought to have justice from us in a Court of Justice." He then gave three reasons for sustaining the writ of habeas corpus and releasing the prisoners. "First, the statute of 1 Eliz. is a penal law, and so they are not to examine one upon oath upon this law; thereby to make him to accuse himself. . . ." A second and completely independent reason was that the prisoners were entitled to a copy of the articles. "A third reason may be drawn from the liberty of the subject, the which is very great as to the imprisonment of his body, and therefore before commitment, the party ought to be called to make his answer, and if he be committed, yet this ought not to be perpetually; if one shall have a remedy here for his land and goods, a multo fortiori, he shall have remedy here for his body, for delivery of him out of prison; being there detained without just cause." Coke recalled that Leigh, who was committed for refusal of the oath *ex officio* on a charge of hearing Mass, had been delivered by habeas corpus. Yet he inexplicably balked at issuing the writ after having given all the reasons why he should: ". . . but we here will not deliver them, as there the Judges did in 10 Eliz. Dyer. But we will here bail them. . . ." The court then released the prisoners on bail with the advice that they should submit themselves to the High Commission and conform. At the next session of the court, Burrowes and the others applied again for discharge on habeas corpus. Coke declared, however, that while the High Commission could not imprison them for refusal of the oath, it could do so for obstinate heresy and great schism; the court then remanded the prisoners to the custody of the High Commission.[43]

Although Burrowes and the others lost their case, Coke won his. He had clearly declared illegal both the oath *ex officio* and the denial of a copy of the articles. Yet the Star Chamber, of which Coke himself was a member, regularly required the same oath *after* presenting to the accused the charges against him. The Star Chamber oath-procedure was not objectionable to Coke, nor to other common lawyers, even though the accused's refusal to answer incriminating interrogatories was taken as a confession of guilt. There were two exceptions to this rule of compulsory self-incrimination by the Star Chamber. First, witnesses were protected. Second, the accused was privileged to withold his testimony if his answers might expose him to a penalty greater than that for misdemeanor, that is, if his answers might put him to trial for life or limb.

Thus Coke maintained several standards, one for the High Commission, another for the Star Chamber, and a third for the common-law courts. There was even a double standard in High Commission cases. Coke sought to illegalize once and for all the oath *ex officio* as to laymen, except in matrimonial and testamentary cases. But the rule was different if the accused was a minister. He had to take the oath, because he was especially subject to the jurisdiction of the church and its canon-law procedures, and because the old writs and statutes applied only to laymen. Nevertheless, Coke sought to mitigate the rigors of the oath by his rule that it could not be administered until after making available to the accused a copy of the articles. Moreover, a minister could not be compelled by the High Commission, according to Coke's rule, to accuse himself on oath if he might, as a result, expose himself to any temporal loss or punishment.[44]

After Coke's dismissal from the bench in 1616, the oath *ex officio* became for a time a less controversial issue than it had ever been since 1583. During the remaining period of Archbishop Abbot's primacy—he died in 1633—there were no more prohibitions in which the oath's illegality was a ground of decision, no more controversies between the common-law courts and the ecclesiastical courts, and no more cases reported in which the oath was an issue. Had Coke remained on the bench during this period, it might be argued that his continued opposition had an effect. That the oath should disappear as an issue after 1616, despite his removal from the bench, seems inexplicable, particularly in view of the very explicit provisions for the oath in the letters patent of 1611. At about the same time as the decision in Burrowes's case, in 1616, the Commission codified its rules of procedure, with Privy Council endorsement, and included a provision that defendants should be examined after taking the oath to make a full and true answer, but should not be shown the articles against them until after they had taken the oath.[45]

It passes belief, therefore, that the Commission might have yielded even briefly to Coke's rulings, yet it may have eased the requirement of the oath in lesser cases involving laymen. Roland Marchant's study of the church courts in the diocese of York reveals only twelve High Commission cases from 1617 to 1633 in which the oath is mentioned, and in every one of those cases the defendant was a Puritan minister. There are no cases in York involving laymen in which mention is made of the oath. Yet in London, the High Commission in 1632 captured about sixty-eight Separatists of whom some thirty-two were individually examined, and in every instance the Commission demanded the oath. In every instance it was denied. In most instances the prisoner gave a reason of conscience for his denial: he dared not forswear himself or thought an oath in God's name was too great a matter to be taken lightly. Some would take an oath if it was to end a controversy—the old oath of purgation—but would not take one that would begin controversy. Several prisoners rejected the oath on ground that they had not been properly accused or did not know the articles against them; one objected that the oath was condemned by the law of the land.[46]

Although it is true that the Commission in these Separatist cases refused to reveal the articles unless the oath was taken, the prisoners actually knew the reasons for their arrest and the nature of the questions that would be asked. The Commission, as a matter of fact, did not follow strict procedure. Until it lost patience, it examined the first batch of prisoners in an informal manner, asking and answering questions without the tender of the oath. The king's advocate, Sir Henry Martin, orally charged all of them before the Commission with having attended private conventicles, and he named the time and place. When John Lathrop, the minister of the congregation, demanded to know why he had been brought before the judgment seat of man, he was told that the accusation against him was schism. When Samuel Eaton was asked why he had attended a conventicle while others were at church, he answered evasively that the reason was not to hold the magistrate in contempt. The Bishop of London, William Laud, declared that the assembly was in contempt of the Church of England. Eaton claimed that the meeting was held "in conscience to God." Then followed questions about his activities and his reading. Only then did the king's advocate finally ask that Eaton take the oath. When he balked, they offered him a copy of the articles and plenty of time to consider his answers, if he would first take the oath and swear to tell the truth "so far as you are bound by law." When Eaton replied, "I dare not, I know not what I shall sweare to," the king's advocate answered, "It is to give a true answere to articles put into the Court against you, or that shalbe put in touching this conventicle of yours, and divers your hereticall tenentes and what wordes, and exercises you used, and things of this nature." Eaton still refused: "I dare not." He dared not answer incriminating interrogatories whose nature had been made as clear to him as if he had been presented with an indictment. It cannot be said the Commission was fishing on bare suspicion for something chargeable or that its procedure in this case was permeated by the inherent unfairness of an old heresy inquisition. Moreover, Eaton had been informed that the oath obliged him to answer only as far as the law required. The Commission finally imprisoned all the Separatists for an indefinite period, releasing many of them two years later when Lathrop petitioned for permission to depart with his congregation for New England.[47]

Although the Commission required the oath of laymen in the cases of the Separatists in 1632, the procedure was clearly not as harsh as in the time of Whitgift or Bancroft. Nor was the oath itself the beginning of the interrogation. The practice of the Commission had changed somewhat during Abbot's incumbency. Nothing shows the fact better than an incredible episode of 1624 when Coke's own daughter and her lover were tried before the High Commission for adultery. She refused the oath *ex officio*, claiming that no one was bound by law to accuse himself; the burden of proof, she added, was on her accusers. Sir Robert Howard, the father of her illegitimate child, also refused the oath. What is astonishing is the conclusion reached by Lord Keeper Williams, a member of the Commission. In a letter to the Duke of Buckingham, he wrote, "We found that Sir Edward Coke (far-seeing, out of a prophetical spirit how near it might concern a grand-child of his one day) hath expunged this clause [on the oath] . . . out of the Commission, and left us nothing but the rustie sword of the Church, Excommunication to vindicate the authority of this Court." The remark seems a bit addled yet suggests either that the Commission for a time was uncertain about the legality of the oath in lay cases, or no longer adamantly required it.[48]

The cases mentioned by Marchant in his study of the diocese of York show that the situation was quite different when the defendants were ministers. In the dozen cases between 1617 and 1633, each of which involved a Puritan clergyman, every one of them took the oath, an indication that the situation had certainly changed compared to that of Cartwright's time. The clergy had apparently resigned themselves to the inevitable, for even Coke had ruled that the oath was lawful in the case of a clergyman. Yet the small number of York cases—twelve from 1617 to 1633— suggests that the inquisitions into nonconformity considerably slackened during the years of Abbot's primacy. As archbishop, despite the burnings of Legate and Wightman, Abbot was both moderate and ineffectual, if not actually negligent, compared to his predecessors, Whitgift and Bancroft, and his successor, Laud.

The same might be said of the common-law judges, after Coke was no longer there to lead them. Never before had a judge been removed for purely political reasons, in Bacon's words for his "perpetual turbulent carriage, first towards the liberties of his [the king's] church and the state ecclesiastical; then towards his prerogative royal and branches thereof. . . ." If it could happen to the most fearless and independent of judges, it could happen to any. Sir Henry Montague, his colorless successor, was a prerogative man, though at his installation Ellesmere publicly admonished that he should remember "the removing and putting down of your late predecessor. . . ." James himself had warned all the judges that his prerogative was not to be disputed and that they should keep themselves narrowly to their own jurisdiction. When Chief Justice Randolph Crewe balked the king in 1626, he too was summarily removed. The crown influenced judicial decisions and was becoming more and more arbitrary. It is little wonder that the common-law courts abandoned the fight against the oath *ex officio* after 1616 and virtually ceased issuing prohibitions. In sum, the ecclesiastical courts, for reasons that are not clear, practiced moderation during Abbot's primacy and possibly examined laymen without oath in minor cases, while the common-law courts, packed with judges who were either compliant or intimidated, no longer scrutinized canon-law procedure.[49]

There are significant indications that the oath was no longer a pressing issue before William Laud became archbishop. No longer did the House of Commons complain about it, and, most revealing of all, neither did the Puritan pamphleteers. In 1621 there was a complaint to the Commons from the town of Northampton about the use of the oath by Sir John Lambe, chancellor to the Bishop of Peterborough. His fault seems to have been the summoning of men *ex officio mero* on his own suspicion and then tendering the oath. Coke, a member of the Commons, on that same day is supposed to have said, in what must be a garbled version of his remarks, "for the oth *ex officio* theay have power and not. Theay have power to examine all Ecclesiasticall men *ex officio*, because tis supposed theay are learned, And for somm cases Lay men; ther is an Act of Parliament for it." There are no other petitions to Parliament against the oath and no other Parliamentary statements about it during this period.[50]

Coke's principles did not alter when he was a member of the Commons. For opposing the king's policies in so outspoken a manner and demanding a protestation in defense of the parliamentary privileges of free speech and freedom from arrest, Coke was imprisoned in the Tower of London for seven months, after the Parliament of 1621 was dissolved. In the Parliament of 1628 he was the prime mover of the Petition of Right and the leading speaker against the crown—"It is a maxim, The common law hath admeasured the King's prerogative, that in no case it can prejudice the inheritance of the subjects. . . . Magna Charta is such a fellow that he will have no sovereign." That the Petition of Right did not speak against the oath *ex officio* suggests that it was no longer a pressing grievance whose redress was imperative.[51]

The Petition of Right did not, however, ignore the principle that inquisitional oaths breached the law of the realm. Parliament was aiming at the correction of specific abuses of the royal prerogative arising out of the imposition of a forced loan and the punishment of those who resisted it. The great Petition, accordingly, was not a comprehensive catalogue of various rights and liberties. The matters urgently demanding redress were taxes, loans, and charges without consent of Parliament; imprisonment without stated cause; denial of the writ of habeas corpus; and the quartering of troops in private homes. Parliament was also concerned with another matter, often unnoticed by historians: the compilation of a black-list of subjects who refused the forced loan, their interrogation under oath by a special commission, and their punishment. It was that incriminatory oath which the Petition of Right condemned.

To raise his forced loan, the king in 1626 instructed members of a special commission, which worked in groups of threes, to examine subjects privately in order to exact payment. Anyone refusing payment was to be put to an oath and interrogated to determine his reasons and his associations with others of like mind. Thus the oath operated to incriminate opponents of the loan and their confederates. Many subjects, protested Parliament in the Petition of Right, "have had an oath administered unto them, not warrantable by the laws or statutes of this realm. . . ." They were forced to appear before the Privy Council and many were "imprisoned, confined, and sundry other ways molested." The Petition prayed that there be an end to the inquisitional commission and "that none be called to make answer, or take such oath," or in any way be hurt for his refusal. The oath was not the oath *ex officio*, though it was very similar. Ten years later libertarians, like John Lilburne, assumed and claimed that the Petition of Right had outlawed the oath *ex officio*.[52]

The oath had not, of course, disappeared after the Petition of Right. It was still used in ecclesiastical procedure, but it had disappeared as an important issue from about 1616 to 1633. That the High Commission continued to exact it, and that there were occasionally persons who refused it or refused to answer incriminating interrogatories, is apparent from a ruling of 1632 which warned the obstinate defendant that he would be taken *pro confesso*. Nevertheless, it was not until Laud became Archbishop of Canterbury, in late 1633, and immediately revived intensive inquisitions against the Puritans that the oath once again became a prominent subject of controversy.[53]

We may conclude that the long campaign by the Puritans, by the Commons, and by the common-law courts against the oath *ex officio* had begun to some degree to take effect. By no means had a victory been won, yet the oath seems to have been used more sparingly for a while, in deference to the objections against it. Nor was it merely the oath *per se*, as used by the High Commission, which fair-minded men found objectionable. True enough, there were many grounds for opposing the oath *per se*, not the least of them that it sinfully infringed Biblical injunctions against swearing in the name of God, violated conscience, and supplanted proper accusation by witnesses or by grand jury. In addition, however, the oath had been condemned because it compelled a man to be his own accuser and thereby to convict himself involuntarily by his own testimony. There had been a time when the maxim that no man is bound to accuse himself meant merely that he was not obliged to disclose voluntarily his own guilt when he was not even suspected. But more and more people were beginning to think that to coerce a man to testify against himself, with or without oath, was simply unjust—an outrage on human dignity and a violation of the very instinct of self-preservation.

In 1620, for example, when the House of Lords was investigating the various crimes, frauds, and corruptions committed by Sir Giles Mompesson, many witnesses were examined, some of whom were Mompesson's victims, others his confederates, but none were forced to incriminate themselves. The Earl of Arundel reported that the "lords committees urged none to accuse himself, and admonished every man not to accuse another out of passion." In 1628 the judges unanimously agreed that it was against the common law for Felton, the murderer of the Duke of Buckingham, to be tortured to confess. In 1629 began one of the greatest cases of the period, the prosecution of Sir John Eliot and eight other members of Parliament for crimes of seditious conspiracy and treasonable utterance against the crown, committed by them in the course of speeches in the Commons. The prisoners took the position that they were not answerable out of Parliament for what was said in Parliament and therefore would not testify. On the question whether their refusal was a contempt, the two chief justices and the chief baron decided that each man was obliged to answer questions that "do not concern himself but another, nor draw him to danger of treason or contempt by his answer." The statement was somewhat oblique, but implicitly recognized that the prisoners were not required to incriminate themselves.[54]

In 1631 Lord Audley, who was tried for rape and sodomy, requested that he not be examined "of those things whereof he must accuse himself, and said, 'That condemnation should not come out of his mouth.' " The prosecution's case was securely grounded on the testimony of eye-witnesses; possibly for that reason the accused was not questioned at all. Fitz-Patrick, when a witness at Lord Audley's trial, confessed to a rape that he committed at Audley's instigation. When Fitz-Patrick was tried for his crime, his testimony was introduced against him, over his objection "that neither the laws of the kingdom required nor was he bound to be the destruction of himself." Chief Justice Hyde answered that "it was true, the law did not oblige any man to be his own accuser," yet he permitted the previous confession to be accepted in evidence. Coke himself had never condemned a confession voluntarily given, nor had he supported a right on the part of any defendant to refuse answer to incriminating interrogatories if he had been properly presented, if his case was within the jurisdiction of the trial court, and if his truthful answer would not expose him to a penalty higher than one which that court might impose, unless —and the exception is one of great importance, endorsed by judges since the late sixteenth century—the answer exposed the defendant to loss of life or limb.[55]

Even in such a case, however, the right against self-incrimination existed in a common-law court only in the sense that the defendant could not be required to answer involuntarily; nevertheless, his silence customarily spoke against him. It invited adverse comment from the prosecution and perhaps even from the trial judge, prejudicing the jury's deliberations. The indictment constituted a prima facie case of guilt against the defendant, for all practical purposes rebutting any supposed presumption of innocence. The prosecution had the burden of proving guilt beyond all reasonable doubt; but if the defendant, whose testimony was the focal point of the trial, did not satisfactorily contest the prosecution's case, if, that is, he remained silent, resting on a claim that the law did not oblige him to accuse himself, he could rely on a verdict of guilty. By 1633 the *nemo tenetur* maxim had made a noticeable impression, yet accused persons, whether in ecclesiastical or common-law courts, still had no meaningful right against compulsory self-incrimination.

CHAPTER IX

Lilburne and the Abolition of the Oath

Charles I was a patron of the arts and favored relieving Catholics of their disabilities; he had no other virtues. If supreme political stupidity in a king merits his execution, Charles richly deserved his fate. His father was an inept, arrogant braggart with just enough sense or not enough courage to practice what he preached. Charles kept his mouth shut but habitually lived by his father's principles, governing by divine right, *sans* Parliament, for eleven years, surrounded by second-rate sycophants in his Privy Council and packing his courts. He gave a free hand to the one man of towering ability in his government, William Laud, Archbishop of Canterbury, a severe disciplinarian of the Anglo-Catholic school. The Church of England under Charles enjoyed a greater influence over government policy than at any time since the Reformation. Laud even secured the appointment of the Bishop of London as Lord Treasurer.[1]

While Abbot had lived, Laud, then the Bishop of London, had been kept under restraints. When he succeeded Abbot in 1633, his repressive temper was unmuzzled, and the government embarked on an anti-Puritan policy which, combined with the personal and arbitrary rule of Charles, embittered great segments of the nation. Imposing Anglicanism on Presbyterian Scotland courted rebellion; suppressing even moderate Puritanism in England made Presbyterianism and a variety of sects thrive as never before. By his rigorous effort to coerce external conformity to high-church rituals and ceremonies, Laud simply drove appreciable numbers of his countrymen out of the national church, many of them to America, others to revolution. "Great praise to the Lord and little Laud to the devil" was but the mildest sentiment of his opponents.

Laud's persecutions were no greater than those of Whitgift or Bancroft; indeed, his predecessors probably matched him in every respect except a willingness to shed blood. Yet it is Laud whose name has been reviled as if none else could compare as England's Torquemada. His eventual imprisonment and execution required a justification which was found in an exaggeration of his "crimes." His ferocity, the seeming novelty of his inquisitions, and the confusion of the High Commission with the Star Chamber probably account for a good part of his execrable reputation. Laud certainly reinvigorated the Commission, armed with fresh letters patent from King Charles. The "Commission under Laud," wrote Usher, "was really, as contemporaries claimed, a much more powerful body than its Elizabethan and Jacobean predecessors." Yet there was nothing significantly new in its powers, its procedures, or its jurisdiction. What was new was Laud's governance and personality. After a long period of lassitude under Abbot, the Commission was suddenly very active, merciless, and formidable. It prosecuted Nonconformists as if to extirpate them, and it was everywhere.[2]

The Caroline Commission was the largest in history. Laud subdivided the huge membership into many more courts which sat in many more places more frequently than ever before. The jurisdiction of the Commission extended to Scotland and included the archbishopric of York which had formerly operated a quasi-independent commission of its own. The powers of the Commission for the first time were felt effectively in the local districts where formerly, in Usher's words, "only their shadow had been seen." Laud also revived the visitorial powers of his office, backed by the authority of the High Commission. He policed the dioceses by conducting inquisitions into the practices of local churches to determine whether they conformed to all canons and orders. He thereby spread the oath procedure even deeper into the localities. Visitations having been in disuse for about twenty years, Laud's revival of the practice, with an energy that had not been equaled since Whitgift's time, seemed, like his sharpening of the rusty High Commission itself, an illegal innovation. Opponents of the Commission, who had once argued that it was not a court and therefore could not prosecute them, now argued that because it was merely a court whose function was to try suits of an ecclesiastical nature between parties, it could not prosecute them. That a court of law should also operate *ex officio mero*, acting as accuser, prosecutor, judge, and jury, when at the same time it was a party to the case, seemed more outrageous and illegal than ever.[3]

Yet prohibitions were extremely rare. Lord Chief Justice John Finch, a close friend of the archbishop, told him in 1638 that a motion for a prohibition then pending before him was the first he had heard in his four years on the court. "I assure myself you are very confident," Finch wrote Laud, "that no man ever sat on a bench that was more tender how he invaded the jurisdiction of other courts especially those of ecclesiastical cognizance: and for the High Commission Court, I know (as I then openly said) that it is a court of a high and eminent nature, and it behoved us to be very wary of granting prohibitions to stop that court." One man sought to sue the High Commission for false imprisonment, and though he offered a huge fee, he could find no lawyer willing to incur royal displeasure by taking his brief. Laud was later charged with having "laid by the heels" anyone who tried to get a prohibition. The "Root and Branch" Petition of the City of London in 1640 condemned both the oath *ex officio* and the rejection of prohibitions "with threatening . . . the judges of the land are so awed with the power and greatness of the prelates . . . that neither prohibition, *Habeas Corpus*, nor any other lawful remedy can be had. . . ."[4]

As ever, the opposition to the Commission was based on the fact that nonconformity was a crime, and after half a century of struggle the possibility of changing that fact seemed more hopeless than ever. In the 1630's there were no parliaments that could be appealed to for reform of the substantive law. The common-law courts sat, but the judges had become jackals under the throne. Victims of the High Commission could only protest feebly that the oath *ex officio* was a device of the devil, a violation of the law of the land, an instrument of the Spanish Inquisition akin to torture. The real objection to the Commission was its purpose, the fact that it meant to punish the purest promptings of conscience, but its oath procedure remained the foremost target of its opponents. Victims still tried to block its proceedings chiefly by refusing the oath, and though they could no longer succeed even in the limited sense that Cartwright had once succeeded, they still refused to furnish the Commission with the evidence that would convict them. Refusal of the oath could no longer block the Commission, because of the *pro confesso* rule: anyone who would not swear or would not answer the Commission's interrogatories fully, plainly, and directly, would simply be taken as having confessed his own guilt. The theory of the Commission was simple enough. An innocent man had nothing to hide; the truth could not hurt him. Only the guilty had reason to refuse oath and answer, and a guilty man could scarcely claim injustice when convicted as if he had confessed. Yet the "guilty" continued to object to compulsory self-incrimination and to the *pro confesso* rule.[5]

Dr. Henry Burton, a Puritan preacher and pamphleteer, was one of Laud's leading victims. He had been in and out of Fleet prison several times, yet irrepressibly returned to his pulpit to scorch the prelates. In 1636 Laud hauled him before the Commission again for his sermons against turning communion tables into altars and setting up crucifixes. The charge was "sedition," a temporal crime, but sedition, schism, and heresy were convertible when an assault on the church was also an assault on the state. Burton refused the oath, landing back in the Fleet. Somehow he smuggled out a manuscript account of his troubles which was quickly turned into an illegal tract by one of the secret presses. He condemned the oath at considerable length, marshaling the usual arguments. The oath, he added, was more a "snare" than ever, because though the Commission pretended that one was bound to answer against himself no further than the law of the land required, once he took the oath "they presse it upon the mans conscience to answere in those things, which neither Law nor conscience bynds him unto. And in case he shall except against any Article, as not bound by Law to answer it, then they take it *pro confesso*, and so (although it be for accusing himselfe, or others, wherein he ought not, being a breach of charity and of that Maxime, *Nemo tenetur prodere seipsum:* and contrary to all Lawes of God and man) they illegally proceed to sentence without any just or further proofe of the things objected." Burton invoked an unexpected authority to back his claim that an oath to accuse himself in a matter of sedition was illegal: "Whitgift Archbishop of Canterbury in the Conference at Hampton Court, printed by authority, there publickly averred, that in matter of *life, liberty or scandall,* it is not the course of that Court to require any such Oath, or to inforce any man that hath taken the Oath, to answer to any such Articles." [6]

Another celebrated opponent of the oath at this time was Dr. John Bastwick, a Puritan physician who wrote abusive tracts against the bishops. He, too, was found *pro confesso*, was fined one thousand pounds for his "schismaticall & hereticall opinions," and was sentenced to an indefinite prison term. Continued opposition to the oath and the *pro confesso* rule led the archbishop to secure from the common-law judges, sitting in the Star Chamber, an opinion that Bastwick and others had been lawfully tried and sentenced. The king himself formally affirmed the legality of the *pro confesso* rule for anyone refusing the oath or having taken it, refusing to answer fully and plainly as directed.

For Laud to turn to the Star Chamber for an endorsement of what he had done in the High Commission was like buttering his bread on both sides. He was all-powerful in both courts, bringing the two together in a close partnership that made them seem like one in the public mind. The church had never before dominated the Star Chamber, although that tribunal had worked in conjunction with the High Commission for many years. From 1586, when a Star Chamber decree vested the power of censorship in the Archbishop of Canterbury, the High Commission carried out the Star Chamber's policy against "all heretical, schismatical and seditious books, libels, and writings" which were offensive to state or church or were printed without prior license. Subsequent letters patent confirmed the High Commission's role as the agency to enforce the censorship decrees of the Star Chamber. When the Star Chamber prosecuted a clergyman, it first turned him over to the High Commission for deprivation and deposition from the ministry; the Star Chamber, in turn, executed the temporal sentences of the Commission. In Laud's time the two courts became indistinguishable in many respects. Much of the odium that attached to his reputation, as well as to the courts themselves, derived from the fact that he turned High Commission victims over to the Star Chamber for trial so that they would suffer the peculiarly gory punishments which the ecclesiastical court could not inflict.[7]

The trial of Burton, Bastwick, and William Prynne on the same day in 1637 is the best illustration. Each had committed the same crime by publishing savage tracts against the prelates, Burton and Bastwick while in jail under sentence by the High Commission. The Star Chamber had punished Prynne, a violent Presbyterian bigot, in 1633 by disbarring him from the practice of law, fining him ten thousand pounds, and hacking off both ears, for his puritanical castigation of dancing, hunting, and play-acting. In 1637 the Star Chamber charged the three men with seditious libel. Although there was no semblance of fairness in their trial, their guilt was unquestionable. The conviction in each case was made *pro confesso*. Laud intended to revenge himself on his prisoners and to terrify others who might repeat their crimes. Thus, the sentence for each man was not only a fine of five thousand pounds and life imprisonment in separate, distant fortresses; in addition the hangman was to cut off their ears. That gruesome mutilation had already been executed on Prynne, but Chief Justice Finch discovered that there were stumps which could be severed—and they were. The hangman also branded Prynne's cheeks with the letters "S.L." for seditious libeler—"*stigmata Laudis*," the scars of Laud, Prynne said. When he had been mutilated a few years earlier, few cared. By 1637 Laud's policies had created droves of sympathizers for his victims. Their punishment was witnessed by hundreds who with tears and cries shared the religious ecstacy of their martyrdom.[8]

Late in 1637 pursuivants of the High Commission arrested a young Puritan named John Lilburne. He proved to be, by any standard, the most remarkable person connected with the history of the origins of the right against self-incrimination. Lilburne focused the attention of the whole of England on the injustice of forcing a man to be the means of his own undoing. His sensational case was the immediate reason for the abolition of the oath *ex officio* and of the courts which utilized it. In extraordinary abundance—everything about him was extraordinary—Lilburne had an incomparable ability to dramatize himself and his cause. He was a principled agitator with an incurably inflamed sense of injustice which he knew how to communicate vividly to an audience.

Had Lilburne been the creation of some novelist's imagination, one might scoff at so far-fetched a character. He was, or became, a radical in everything—in religion, in politics, in economics, in social reform, in criminal justice—and his ideas were far ahead of his time. From 1637 when he was but twenty-three years old, a mere clothier's apprentice whose formal education had ended when he was no more than fifteen, until his death twenty years later, he managed to keep his government in a hectic state. In successive order he defied king, parliament, and protectorate, challenging each with libertarian principles. While others supported civil liberties to gain their own freedom and denied it to their enemies, Lilburne grew more and more consistent in his devotion to the fundamentals of liberty, and he was an incandescent advocate. Standing trial for his life four times, he spent most of his adult years in prison and died in banishment. Yet he could easily have had positions of high preferment if he had thrown in his lot with Parliament or Cromwell. Instead, he sacrificed everything in order to be free to attack injustice from any source. He once accurately described himself as "an honest true-bred, freeborn Englishman that never in his life loved a tyrant nor feared an oppressor." In his own day he was known as Freeborn John because of his insistent references to the rights of every freeborn Englishman.

Such men as Lilburne who make civil disobedience a way of life are admirable but quite impossible. He was far too demanding and uncompromising, never yielding an inch of his ideals. He was obstreperous, fearless, indomitable, and cantankerous, one of the most flinty, contentious men who ever lived. As one of his contemporaries said, if John Lilburne were the last man in the world, John would fight with Lilburne and Lilburne with John. That trait helps explain his strength, but he was also a master of the arts of propaganda. He could convince and inspire his followers or confound his enemies with equal ease. No one in England could outtalk him, no one was a greater political pamphleteer. Lilburne, who was to become the leader of the Levellers, was the catalytic agent in the history of the right against self-incrimination. He appeared at the right moment in history.[9]

Lilburne's first offense was shipping seditious books into England from Holland, including several thousand copies of a pamphlet by Dr. Bastwick. On an order from the Privy Council, the case was turned over to Sir John Banks, the Attorney-General, for prosecution. Lilburne's guilt seemed certain, because two of his confederates had accused him in order to save themselves. One of them had made his accusation by sworn affidavit, naming Lilburne and John Wharton, an elderly book-dealer, as violators of the Star Chamber decree against importing unlicensed books. All that was needed were the confessions of Lilburne and Wharton. The Attorney-General's chief clerk examined Lilburne, who admitted only that he had been to Holland and had seen certain books and men there. Lilburne demanded to know the reason for questions which did not seem relevant to the cause of his imprisonment. "I am not imprisoned for knowing and talking with such and such men, but for sending over Books; and therefore I am not willing to answer you to any more of these questions, because I see you go about by this Examination to ensnare me: for seeing the things for which I am imprisoned cannot be proved against me, you will get other matter out of my examination." As for the charge against him, which the clerk clearly stated, he was innocent, he said, for he had sent no books from Holland to England (most likely a lie). Let his accusers be brought before him to accuse him face to face. Till then he would say nothing except that he would answer no "impertinent questions, for fear that with my answer I may do myself hurt." Lilburne at this stage had claimed a right "by the law of the land" to remain silent only to incriminating interrogatories that were not, in his opinion, germane to the charge. The charge itself he denied. The clerk revealed the specifics of the sworn affidavit against him, but he dismissed them as lies. The threat that he could be forced to answer left him unruffled. The clerk brought him to Attorney-General Banks who got no more from him.[10]

After holding him in jail for nearly two weeks, Banks sent Lilburne to the Court of Star Chamber, but failed to provide him with a bill of complaint setting forth the charges. The procedure followed in Lilburne's case was quite irregular; in "state" or "extraordinary" cases, the court was free to proceed at discretion. Ordinarily the crime was described in writing for the accused "with convenient certainty of the time, place, and person." He then took an oath truthfully to answer both the charges and any interrogatories that might subsequently be addressed to him. But he had ample time to answer in writing, initially with the advice of counsel. Or, if there was probable cause to think him guilty of a crime likely "to endanger the very fabric of the government," the court followed what William Hudson (*circa* 1636) called "an extraordinary kind of proceeding, more short and expeditious, which is called *ore tenus*"—an oral examination whose purpose was to elicit a quick confession. Some, said Hudson, censured that course of procedure "as seeming to oppose the Great Charter" because it bypassed all judicial proceeding, bill of complaint, and liberty to consult counsel. But there were supposed to be safeguards even in such a summary procedure. If the case involved a felony, "*nemo tenetur prodere seipsum*, but upon voluntary confession without oath." Neither oath "nor any compulsory means" was supposed to be used in an *ore tenus* proceeding on the theory that the confession must be strictly voluntary. If the accused denied the accusation, the court was supposed to proceed against him by bill of complaint and witnesses; should he confess but later repudiate the confession, even if he had signed it and members of the Privy Council testified to that fact, "so strictly held" was the rule of voluntariness that the court was supposed to proceed as if he had denied the accusation. The strange thing about Lilburne's case was the court's mixed procedure; there was no bill presented to him and no allowance of counsel, yet they demanded that he take the oath.[11]

The Star Chamber was following High Commission procedure, and Lilburne would have none of it. Several clerks examined him first. They tendered him a Bible and told him to swear.

"To what?"

"That you shall make true answer to all things that are asked of you."

"Must I so sir? but before I swear, I will know to what I must swear."

"As soon as you have sworn, you shall, but not before."

Lilburne persisted in his refusal to take the oath, fearing that they "went about to make me betray my own innocency, that so they might ground the bill upon my own words." Attorney-General Banks ordered Lilburne returned to prison.[12]

About two months after his capture, Lilburne was brought to trial before the Star Chamber, together with his accomplice, the book dealer John Wharton. Wharton, who was in his eighties, was a veteran of the Puritan wars against the High Commission; he had been imprisoned, according to his own testimony, no less than eight times for refusing the oath *ex officio*. He could quote both Sir Edward Coke and Archbishop Whitgift's Hampton Court statement against the oath. Lilburne, who was examined first, proved himself worthy of Wharton's company. Attorney-General Banks opened the proceeding against the prisoners with a verbal accusation that they had refused the oath, and then he read the affidavit of their confessed confederate who had turned state's evidence. On the principal charge, according to Lilburne's account, there was no discussion whatever beyond his simple allegation that the affidavit "is a most false lye and untrue." The Star Chamber appeared to be interested only in the fact that the prisoners would not swear the Star Chamber oath. Many men had refused the High Commission oath, but refusal of the Star Chamber oath was rare if not unique because the requirement of swearing normally followed, rather than preceded, presentment by bill of complaint. The affidavit in this case may have served as a substitute for a bill, but it didn't satisfy Lilburne who wrote that he had refused "that which had never been refused before." He stated his reasons once again before the Lords of the Star Chamber, and Wharton followed his example. The court, failing to persuade them to change their minds, returned them to prison in solitary confinement.[13]

A week later, the two were brought again before the court. Lilburne claimed that the oath was "one and the same with the High Commission oath, which Oath I know to be both against the law of God, and the law of the land. . . ." Yet he knew his accuser and the charges against him. On his second appearance before the Star Chamber, they read aloud a second affidavit from his accuser, filled with more detail than the first. Lilburne continued to deny the accusation, yet would not deny it under oath. Nor would Wharton. Both tried to lecture the court on the immorality and unlawfulness of the oath *ex officio*. The court answered not by finding them *pro confesso* on the charges, but by finding them guilty of contempt for refusal to answer interrogatories under oath. "I was condemned," wrote Lilburne, "because I would not accuse myself." The court sentenced them to a five-hundred pound fine, punishment in the pillory, and imprisonment until they conformed themselves by taking the oath. In addition, Lilburne was to be whipped through the streets on the way from Fleet prison to the pillory.[14]

On April 18, 1638, the sentence of corporal punishment was carried out on Lilburne. Although he was almost beaten to death, he put on such a spirited show of defiance that he became famous overnight. The torturous two-mile walk from the Fleet to the pillory was a religious pilgrimage for him and many onlookers. People lined the streets to watch the spectacle, moaning as they thrilled to his beating and spiritual exaltation. Tied to the back of a cart and stripped to the waist, he was lashed every few steps with a three-thonged whip tied full of knots. Lilburne later estimated that he had been whipped at least two hundred strokes; an eye witness who walked the route swore that the number was not less than five hundred. Lilburne's shoulders "were swelled almost as big as a penny-loaf" and the "wales in his back . . . were bigger than tobacco-pipes." A "multitude" of people thronged about the pillory, shouting words of encouragement. The hole for his neck was so low that he was forced to stand stooped over, unprotected from an "exceedingly hot" sun. Despite his pain, Lilburne addressed the sympathetic crowd, rejoicing in his role as a Christian martyr. "I own and embrace" the pillory, he said, "as the welcome Cross of Christ, and as a badge of my Christian Profession." He spoke for about half an hour, reportedly keeping his audience spell-bound. It is almost beyond belief that anyone could have had the strength to do that after such a terrible beating, or that the authorities should have permitted him to stir up the crowd. He told them in detail the story of his trial and the reason for his suffering. Paul had found more mercy from the heathen Roman governors, for they had not put him to an oath to accuse himself. Lilburne described the "inquisition Oath" which he had refused as sinful and illegal, "it being the High-Commission oath, with which the prelates ever have, and still do, so butcherly torment, afflict and undo, the dear saints and servants of God. It is an oath against the law of the land (as Mr. Nicholas Fuller in his Argument doth prove): And also it is expressly against the Petition of Right . . . Again, it is absolutely against the law of God; for that law requires no man to accuse himself. . . ." On and on he went, condemning the oath. And then he launched into a long tirade against the prelates, pulling from his pocket three copies of Dr. Bastwick's book and throwing them to his fascinated listeners. "There," he cried, "is part of the Books for which I suffer, take them among you, and read them, and see if you find anything in them against the law of God. . . ."[15]

Lilburne's speech was interrupted at last by the Warden of the Fleet who commanded his silence. The martyr could not be intimidated, answering that he would declare his cause though he were to be hanged for it. The warden then ordered him gagged to shut him up, and they did it so cruelly, reported an eye witness, that it seemed as if they "would have torn his jaws in pieces." He bled profusely from the mouth. After Lilburne had been in the pillory for another hour and a half, he was taken back to prison. That same day the Star Chamber, on the report of the Warden of the Fleet, issued a new order to punish Lilburne for his behavior in the pillory. He was to be "laid alone with irons on his hands and legs" in the part of the prison "where the basest and meanest sort" were kept and be denied visitors, books, and writing materials. His physician later testified that he was "again and again" denied access to him, and when finally admitted found him "in an extreme violent fever . . . to the extreme hazard of his life." They kept him in a dungeon, chained and without a bed, for five weeks, and for the first ten days starved him. But for food smuggled through floor boards by his fellow prisoners, Lilburne would have perished. He claimed that his religion had sustained him through his terrible ordeal. After about four months he was released from solitary confinement and his prison conditions improved.[16]

He managed to smuggle out accounts telling the world how he

had suffered for the sake of conscience because he would not accuse himself. The Star Chamber inexplicably seemed powerless to prevent him from writing his pamphlets or to locate the secret press that published them. Of the ninety-odd pamphlets that he published during his career, nine were written during his first imprisonment, which lasted almost three years. Aiming at the prelates, Anglo-Catholicism, the High Commission, and the Star Chamber, Lilburne helped bring a pustule of discontent to a head. Lord Clarendon, in his contemporary account, declared that Lilburne "afterwards confessed, in the melancholy of his imprisonment, and by reading the book of Martyrs, he raised in himself a marvellous inclination and appetite to suffer in the defence or for the vindication of any oppressed truth. . . ." [17]

In 1639, while he lay in prison, others followed his example of refusing the oath: Thomas Foxely, for example, a London minister who never knew the reason for his imprisonment, and John Trendall, a Dover stonecutter who preached the gospel in his home. Richard Ward, a learned preacher, wrote a tome of commentaries on the Book of Matthew from which Laud expurgated the exegesis of the lines, "But I say unto you, sweare not at all. . . ." Prynne published the censored passages in 1646 with their references to John Lambert and their explanation why a man might involuntarily incriminate himself in civil cases but "not in criminall offences." [18]

Meanwhile, the king's policies, fashioned by Laud and Strafford, were bringing England closer to civil war. Desperate for money, in the spring of 1640 Charles called his first parliament in eleven years. The Commons, under Pym's leadership, would vote no supplies without first discussing redress of grievances, with the result that Charles dissolved Parliament after about three weeks. But his government was breaking down. The Presbyterian Scots routed a royalist army at Newburn on the Tyne and occupied the north of England, demanding payment for their troops, while London crowds rioted and received the news of the Scottish victory as a national triumph. Leading peers called for a new parliament, and the king, having no choice because of the government's financial straits, yielded. He would have to accept radical reforms as the price for funds. Shortly before Parliament met, there were new riots in London. On October 22, 1640, a mob of some "2000 Brownists," according to Laud, broke into the Court of High Commission as it was preparing to sentence a Separatist and tore the room apart, throwing furniture out of the window and seizing books. They cried out, Laud reported, "that they would have no Bishops nor High Commission." The archbishop had lost his power over the Star Chamber, for that body turned down his proposal to punish the offenders. Prudence dictated a resort to common-law proceedings against the leaders of the riot, but the grand jury refused to return indictments. There was a fresh riot which led to the destruction of papers believed to be the records of the High Commission.[19]

The Long Parliament, dominated by Puritans and common lawyers, met a few days later, on November 3, determined to free victims of oppression, punish their oppressors, and institute reforms in church and state. Six days after the opening of Parliament, Oliver Cromwell, one of the new members from Cambridge, made his maiden speech on behalf of liberty for John Lilburne. A few days later he and other prisoners were set free; within three weeks Prynne, Burton, and Bastwick reached London from their distant prisons, escorted triumphantly by troops and joyous crowds. Laud and Strafford were quickly impeached and imprisoned, while other high government officers, including the Lord Chief Justice of England, fled to the Continent to escape their fate.[20]

Petitions from London, Kent, and elsewhere descended on the Commons, urging abolition of the oath *ex officio* "and other proceedings by way of inquisition, reaching even to men's thoughts." George Peard, a common lawyer and member from Barnstable, spoke eloquently in support of such petitions, though he thought it unnecessary to "light a candle to search out that which alreadie the Sunne hath made manifest." Even the supporters of the oath, he declared, admitted that it was unjustly tendered to any man unless "there bee a publique fame or particular Presentment or Articles testified against him." Examining the practice of the High Commission, he found that it violated its own legal principle that there must be adequate cause for suspicion before requiring an examination under oath. Such practice, said Peard, deserved severe censure, because "unjust proceedings upon unjust grounds, are double injustice." Yet, what was the best practice? "First fame (they say) is a just cause for them to take cognizance of a matter to procede against it. Fame wee knowe may arise uppon anie small and groundless suspitione, by secret whisperings creeping at first, but quickly it getts wings and as the poet saieith, *Crescit eundo* [it grows as it goes], this is the manner of all fame. If this bee fame theire Courte shall never want worke as long as a promoter hath an ill tongue or a knave can slander an honest man. Therefore I thinke fame noe good ground to procede uppon." [21]

It was a popular point, most relevant to the visitorial practices of the bishops under Laud, who conducted inquisitions in their districts by placing church-wardens under oath to inform against clergymen who violated any of the canons. The suspects named by the church-wardens were then put to the oath to testify against themselves. Yet the weight of such inquisitions fell mainly upon Puritan ministers. That is, there were usually adequate grounds for the oath procedure of the prelates: by their standards the Puritans were guilty, and so were the most celebrated victims of the High Commission and Star Chamber. Prynne, Burton, Bastwick, Lilburne, and Alexander Leighton, who suffered more than any of them, were as guilty as Udall, Cartwright, Barrow, and the authors of the Marprelate tracts. Men like John Cotton, John Davenport, Thomas Hooker, Thomas Sheppard, Charles Chauncey, and Richard Mather, who were troubled by the High Commission and fled to New England, were not innocent of the charges against them. That their beliefs and practices were censurable, even criminal, was the basic objection to the prerogative courts, yet the criminal procedure of those courts remained to the very end the focal point of attack by their opponents. It stretches credibility to dismiss a consistency of threescore years as nothing more than legalistic obstructionism.[22]

The sincerity of the opponents of the oath *ex officio* is beyond question. Puritans and common lawyers had convinced themselves that, as a matter of conscience and fairness, an oath that compelled self-incrimination was both evil and violative of common-law procedures, which by right every Englishman was entitled to when subjected to criminal jeopardy. "Let no accusation stand," said Peard in the Commons, "but under the mouth of two or three witnesses . . . but neither witnesses nor presentment can bee a just ground of the oath *ex officio:* for if the accused be examined noe further than is testified, then the oath *ex officio* is superfluous, if hee bee examined further or uppon other matter than is testified, then a man is made to betray himself which is unjust." He praised the virtues of the common law for not permitting any prisoners, not even murderers, to be examined under oath. By contrast a court that employed the oath of inquisition "uppon every occasion watches the conscience." Associating such procedure with the snares that caught the poor martyrs of Queen Mary's time, he concluded, "I desire the Lawe may punish not make offenders, I desire that our words and actions may bee subject to the Lawe, I would have thought free." [23]

Events moved swiftly. In February of 1641, Parliament propounded to the High Commission a series of hostile queries which seemed like a public indictment with question marks. What authority did the commissioners have to arrest? to search and seize? to issue warrants? to fine and imprison? to use the oath *ex officio?* to require it before making available to the accused a copy of the articles against him? In April a bill for regulating the abuses of ecclesiastical courts was introduced in the Commons, but sentiment was swelling for root-and-branch destruction. To head off such radical legislation, the more conservative House of Lords brought to its final reading its own version of a bill which might have gratified Morice or Fuller four decades earlier. The Lords proposed that a copy of the articles be delivered to the accused; that the *ex officio mero* proceeding be abolished; and that "none of the King's subjects hereafter be put to accuse themselves by or upon their own oaths in any criminal cause whatsoever in any of the said Courts Ecclesiastical," unless the oath were taken voluntarily as an oath of purgation. It was a reasonable bill, but the Commons insisted on its own version of what Laud once called a policy of "thorough." On July 5, 1641, the king reluctantly assented to bills wholly abolishing the Courts of High Commission and Star Chamber.[24]

The act against the Star Chamber began with a recitation of chapter twenty-nine of Magna Carta and four thirteenth-century reconfirmations that endorsed common-law procedure as the only

procedure when life, liberty, or property were at stake. Star
Chamber proceedings and censures, said the act, had been found
by long experience to be an intolerable burden on subjects and
"the means to introduce an arbitrary power and government."
Therefore it was enacted that that court be "absolutely dissolved," all trials to be determined "in the ordinary Courts of
Justice and by the ordinary course of the law." [25]

The act against the Court of High Commission announced that
the ecclesiastical judges, in accordance with royal letters patent,
had fined, imprisoned, and exercised other authority not warranted by the Act of Supremacy, to the great oppression of the
subjects—thus vindicating at last the theory of Coke and the common lawyers. Accordingly, Parliament abolished the High Commission. Moreover, the statute made it a criminal offense for any
person exercising ecclesiastical jurisdiction to fine or imprison, or
to force any person to take "any corporal oath, whereby he or she
shall or may be charged or obliged to make any presentment of
any crime or offence, or to confess or to accuse him or herself of
any crime, offence, delinquency or misdemeanour, or any neglect
or thing whereby, or by reason whereof, he or she shall or may be
liable or exposed to any censure, pain, penalty or punishment
whatsoever. . . ." [26]

Thus, finally, was abolished the oath *ex officio*, and the right
against compulsory self-incrimination was established—but only in
the ecclesiastical courts. A great victory had been won, but it in
no way touched criminal procedure in the common-law courts.
They employed no oath, of course, yet in the preliminary examination prior to indictment and arraignment, it was still ordinary
practice to press a suspect to confess his guilt; and in the prosecution of an accused person before a jury, his interrogation was
still the focal point of the trial, the objective to trap him into damaging admissions. Yet the common law was like a glass house
whose residents—judges, lawyers, parliamentarians, and Puritan
defendants alike—had been throwing a rock, the *nemo tenetur*
doctrine, at the enemy: there had to be an impact. The common
law had always regarded torture as illegal when its purpose was to
extort a confession; it had long accepted the abstract principle that
no man should be forced to incriminate himself. Chief Justice

Hyde's remark in Fitz-Patrick's case in 1631 was an indication of that fact. But the principle and the practice were at considerable variance. There was not yet any recognition of the fact that refusal to answer an incriminating question did not imply guilt. The presumption of innocence had no real operation. Until there was respect in the courtroom for the claim that one had a right, enforceable by the court, not to incriminate himself, that right could not be said to exist.[27]

Sir James Fitzjames Stephen observed that after 1640 "the whole spirit and temper of the criminal courts, even in their most irregular and revolutionary proceedings, appears to have been radically changed from what it had been in the preceding century to what it is in our own days." In every case, he said, the accused had the witnesses produced against him and was allowed not only to cross-examine them, but to call witnesses of his own. "In some cases the prisoner was questioned, but never to any greater extent than that which it is practically impossible to avoid when a man has to defend himself without counsel. When so questioned, the prisoners usually refused to answer." These great changes, Stephen added, took place "spontaneously," without legislative enactment, and prevailed even in the political trials of the Restoration period. Stephen's view was generous. Criminal procedure undoubtedly became fairer before the Restoration, but the habit of addressing incriminating interrogatories to the defendant persisted. Without counsel he had to conduct his own defense, responding in some way, if he valued his life, to the accusations against him. Although the defendant could cross-examine the prosecution's witnesses, he could call his own only with the court's permission, and he could not subpoena their attendance nor have them testify under oath.[28]

Only the crown had a right to subpoena witnesses and take their testimony under oath. Sworn testimony was a privilege, for it added immeasurably to the credibility of the witness. Indeed, because sworn testimony was so highly regarded the accused himself was not permitted to testify under oath even if he wanted to. That the common law did not put him to oath, therefore, reflected at least in part an unfairness toward him. It prevented him from virtually exonerating himself by taking what in effect was a purgative oath. Much of the seventeenth century's praise of the common law for not putting the defendant to oath was somewhat misleading, unless it is understood that the oath referred to was the oath *ex officio*, that is, an oath to tell the truth *before* knowing the charges and accusers. But an oath to tell the truth after common-law indictment, could have been an advantage to the defendant and, it was thought, a great temptation to perjury. To a religious person, for whom an oath was sacred, as it was intended to be, an oath to tell the truth, even after he knew the charges and the identity of his accusers, put him in a terrible dilemma if he had in fact done the thing charged. The deed might be purely meritorious in his mind yet criminal as a matter of law, making the temptation to sin all the greater—and perjury was originally a sin. In the seventeenth century men did not take oaths lightly. That is why Lilburne, for example, a devout believer, though knowing the charges and his accusers, refused to make his denial under oath. And that is why he and his precursors, from Lambert to Cartwright, claimed that they should not be forced to testify against themselves. They had no choice, for their beliefs and actions were deemed criminal. As long as religious and political freedom did not exist, as long, that is, as there were crimes like nonconformity and seditious libel, men would have to claim in self-defense a right not to incriminate themselves. That right was a product of religious and political persecution. Like all rights associated with fair criminal procedure, it had to be fought for unceasingly. It did not develop "spontaneously," nor did any of the other rights that cluster around the concept of due process in criminal justice. Lilburne's later trials made that fact abundantly clear.[29]

The first sign of respect accorded to the right against self-incrimination came in 1642 at the trial of the Twelve Bishops. The Long Parliament, controlled by Puritans, had excluded the bishops from certain sessions in 1641 and excluded them altogether from the House of Lords by a statute of early 1642. The bishops had always sat in the upper house by virtue of their office. Twelve of them petitioned the king in protest of their exclusion. In the course of their petition, they alleged that all laws, votes, and resolutions made in their absence were null and void. For this the Commons impeached them on a charge of high treason. That is, the House of Commons, acting as a grand jury for the nation, drew articles of accusation against the bishops and prosecuted them before the House of Lords, whose members, as in all cases of impeachment, sat as judge and jury. At the trial the prosecution demanded to know whether the bishops endorsed the petition and had in fact signed it, as they had. "To this question," says the report of the trial, "the Bishops refused to answer, because they alleged, 'That it was not charged in the impeachment; neither were they bound to accuse themselves'." The question was not pressed and no answer was demanded.[30]

It is ironic that twelve of the leading prelates of England asked a Puritan Parliament for the very right which they themselves had denied to their Puritan victims. Here were the former judges of the High Commission, no less, claiming that no man is bound to accuse himself. Nor was it the canon-law concept of *nemo tenetur* that they were advancing, because they knew the charges and the evidence against them. They were stating in effect that the law did not obligate them to say anything that might be a link in the chain of evidence against themselves. The old formula, no man is bound to accuse himself, now meant that he might remain silent without prejudice to a question whose answer might tend to incriminate him. It is remarkable that those whom the bishops had persecuted honored their claim. Yet Parliament was soon to prove that it honored the right against self-incrimination more in the breach than in the observance; it would have to contend with John Lilburne.

Lilburne had risen in the world after his release from prison. His pen and his persecution had brought him fame, and he was honored for both. The Commons voted his sentence to have been "illegal and against the liberty of the subject," and "bloody, wicked, cruel, barbarous and tyrannical" as well. Lilburne was filled with devotion to the parliamentary cause. When the civil war broke out between royalist and parliamentary forces, he enlisted as a captain. Captured in action, he was held a prisoner in chains, tried for treason, and sentenced to death. Parliament sent word that if Lilburne were executed, royalist prisoners would meet the same fate. He was reprieved and eventually freed in an exchange of prisoners; on his return to London, crowds greeted him, said Lord Clarendon, "with public joy, as a champion that had defied the King in his own court." He turned down a lucrative government post, saying that he would "rather fight for eightpence a day, till he saw the liberties and peace of England settled, than set him down in a rich place for his own advantage. . . ." He became a confidant of Cromwell, returned to the front, and rose to a lieutenant-colonelcy. As time passed, however, Lilburne became increasingly disillusioned with the parliamentary program, and in the spring of 1645 he resigned from the army, exchanging his sword for his pen.[31]

Puritanism, once a predominately moderate movement to reform the English church from within, had been pushed steadily toward radicalism by the pressure of persecution, war, and revolution. Presbyterianism of the sort once advocated by Cartwright and in control of Scotland had become ascendant in England, dominating the Commons. The Presbyterians favored the establishment of a new state religion, their own, in place of Anglicanism. Their impulse to coerce conformity was even more intense than that of the Laudian church; their bigotry extended not only to the Catholics and Anglicans but even to the hodge-podge of dissenting sects that had mushroomed within the Puritan movement. But the Presbyterians, though a majority in Parliament, were divided on the question whether the state church, which they all wanted, should be controlled by Parliament or by the ministers and elders. Parliament itself was Erastian as well as Presbyterian, refusing to yield its supremacy on matters of religion. Its secular leaders were not only jealous of their own prerogatives; they understood better than the Presbyterian ministry the dangers of a policy of extreme coercion, for the highly individualistic sects were the backbone of the army.

The Puritan opponents of the Presbyterians were all known at first as the Independents, but they gradually fragmented into a center group, commanded by Cromwell, and numerous petty factions or "sectaries." Cromwell's group was not hostile to a Presbyterian establishment on condition that a large degree of toleration existed for other religions, Catholicism excepted. The rank and file of the army, where the sectaries were strongest, was as intolerant of Catholicism but fearful of any state establishment. Substantially Calvinistic in theology, like the dominant Presbyterian party, the sectaries were united in their opposition to any coercion of conscience (Protestant) and in their belief in the self-governance of each separate congregation. Largely in self-defense they were moving rapidly toward espousal of the principles of religious liberty and separation of church and state.

John Lilburne, who was something of a religious mystic, was moving in the same direction. He was appalled at the intolerance of Presbyterianism. In 1643 the Commons pledged itself to a Presbyterian church on the Scottish model, and in the following year acted to suppress assemblies of Antinomians and Anabaptists. Steps to establish Presbyterianism were taken in 1644 and 1645. Enforcement was spotty, but the evidences of intolerance were frightening. Roger Williams's plea for religious liberty, *The Bloudy Tenent of Persecution*, was ordered to be burned by the hangman, while laymen, the ministry of the sectaries—cobblers, peddlars, and ordinary people of all sorts who were moved by the spirit to preach the gospel—were forbidden to preach. Simultaneously Parliament acted to suppress religious and political controversialists who were advocating their views in print without check of any sort. The system of censorship having collapsed after the abolition of the Star Chamber and High Commission, the press had become free to anyone with a passion for expression. There were four "newspapers" in 1641, 167 in 1642, and 722 in 1645. There were only twenty-four pamphlets published in 1640, close to a thousand in 1641, and about two thousand in 1642. Every viewpoint from royalism and Anglo-Catholicism to democracy and Anabaptism showed up in print, bidding for public support. Harassed and outraged by the stream of criticism, Parliament established a licensing system designed to suppress seditious literature and to control the agencies of printing. The system of censorship which had formerly existed under royal auspices was revived with a difference: Parliament rather than Star Chamber governed the licensing as well as the detection and imprisonment of offenders. Milton's immortal *Areopagitica* of 1644 was merely one of many protests against official censorship. "The outstanding defender of Liberty of the Press during the Puritan Revolution," according to Siebert, the foremost historian on the subject, "was John Lilburne." [32]

Lilburne was quickly rising to the leadership of those who would be contemptuously called the "Levellers." His close friends William Walwyn and Richard Overton were more sophisticated intellectually, more original, more subtle, more rational, and even more radical than he; they greatly influenced his development. Yet he had a dramatic flair and personal magnetism that fitted him for leadership. In 1645 Dr. Bastwick, his former friend who had become an outstanding spokesman of the narrowest Presbyterianism, observed derisively that the "crowds and multitudes that run after him . . . look upon him as their Champion, applauding all his actions." Prynne, who sided with Bastwick, declared that Lilburne kindled "great combustion and tumults . . . among the Ignorant Vulgar, who adore him as the onely Oracle of Truth," while Thomas Edwards, another Presbyterian stalwart, spoke of Lilburne as "an Arch-Sectary, the great darling of the Sectaries." Even before he quit the army to battle those who had "bitter designs against the poor people of God," Lilburne wrote a tract attacking Prynne and his party for religious persecution and censorship of the press. Commons' Committee on Investigation, a sort of House Committee for the Investigation of Un-English Activities, condemned Lilburne's "scurrilous, libellous, and seditious" pamphlet, and summoned him to answer for it. He defended his position vigorously before the Committee, in May 1645, denouncing Parliament for its intolerance, yet he was released. A month later the Committee re-examined him because of his authorship of another illegal, critical pamphlet, yet again overlooked both his offense and his offensiveness. But in July the Committee arrested him for libeling the Speaker of the House, William Lenthall.[33]

This time the Committee had a most unco-operative witness, for Lilburne obstinately refused to testify. He had decided to challenge the authority of Parliament to investigate his opinions or to subject him to incriminating interrogatories. Such behavior was unprecedented, but Lilburne saw in his case an issue that concerned the rights of every subject. Convinced that the Committee acted illegally, he flatly refused to answer questions against himself. Taking the offensive, he demanded to know the charges against him. His strategy was to demand common-law procedures from a legislative investigating committee, but the Committee scarcely felt itself bound by court-room requirements. It did not even agree that it was obliged to state the cause of Lilburne's commitment, although he claimed "a right to all the privileges that do belong to a free man as the greatest man in England . . . and the ground and foundation of my freedom I build upon the Great Charter of England." The Committee listened to him read chapter twenty-nine, his "birthright," satisfied itself that he would not testify, and sent him back to jail. Furious, he wrote a pamphlet depicting himself as the victim of tyrannical proceedings. Pridefully recounting his refusal to be a witness against himself, he explained to his readers that when a legislative investigating committee "sits upon criminal causes betwixt man and man concerning life, liberty, estate," it must honor the methods and rules of courts of justice. Its doors must be kept open to all the free people of England who wish to be present, and it must observe "that men should have the liberty of Magna Carta and the Petition of Right—for which I have fought all this while—and not to be examined upon interrogatories *concerning* themselves as we used to be in the Star Chamber, and for refusing to answer to be committed." [34]

Lilburne failed miserably in his novel effort to establish the right against compulsory self-incrimination in a proceeding before a House committee, but he would not abandon the principle for which he fought. In view of the fact that the Committee on Investigation had the authority to arrest, try, and convict him, his argument was not at all fantastic. There was no literal basis for it in the documents of fundamental law which he invoked, but it was reasonable to expect that a right which originated as a means of thwarting one species of inquisitorial examinations should apply to another. It was also reasonable to expect that a body having the authority of a court of law should follow the rules of such a court. The existence of the right itself in a court of law was something which Lilburne took completely for granted; his effort to extend the right was a case of necessity straining for an historical justification—chapter twenty-nine and the Petition of Right—that yielded new insights, however fictitious, on the meaning of fundamental law. If, as in Lilburne's thinking, the purpose of fundamental law was to protect the inviolability of the human personality and conscience, his argument, though inspired by revelation and intuition, made sense. But his much publicized claims worsened his situation. The Committee summoned him again to answer for his latest pamphlet; again he refused to testify. The Committee indignantly informed him that he had committed "the greatest affront and contempt that can be given to the authority of the House of Commons that when the House itself shall order that you shall be examined upon a business, you shall contemptuously say that you will answer to no interrogatories." [35]

Imprisoned in Newgate for what was technically the crime of breaching the privileges of Parliament, Lilburne wrote a new pamphlet, *Englands Birth-Right Justified Against all Arbitrary Usurpation, whether Regall or Parliamentary*. It showed the influence of Nicholas Fuller's *Argument* and of the commentaries on Magna Carta in the second volume of Coke's *Institutes*, both of which Lilburne had studied. He had become a jail-house lawyer. Indeed Prynne called him an "upstart monstrous lawyer" who "since he was called to the bar of Newgate, where he now practiseth, hath the Book of Statutes there lying open before him, which he reads and interprets to all the poor ignorant people that visit him. . . ." *Englands Birth-Right* argued that Parliament was limited by its own laws and could not justly punish any one who should "crosse some pretended Privilege of theirs." He claimed that the proceeding against him violated the act abolishing the Star Chamber, for its outlawed practices were not to be exercised by any other authority. In the Petition of Right which, he said, also bound Parliament, the true meaning of Magna Carta had been laid bare, because "amongst other things there expressed, it is declared to be contrary to law, to imprison a man without cause shewed or expressed, and also that it is contrary to *Law*, to force a man to answer to Questions concerning himself, or for refusall, to commit him to prison." By alleging a right not to be asked question *concerning* himself, he enlarged considerably the claim to a right which he did so much to establish.[36]

So obsessed had he become with the idea that no man should be forced to incriminate himself that Lilburne even believed that no one should be bound by law to answer to an indictment by pleading "guilty" or "not guilty." Questions to make him plead put him to "a criminall Interrogatory, concerning a mans selfe." It was a great snare to a conscientious man who could not lie, he argued. If he had committed the deed, he dared not plead "not guilty" for fear of lying, yet he destroyed himself contrary to the law of nature by pleading guilty to that which his adversaries might not be able to prove against him. From Fuller he got the notion that chapter twenty-eight of Magna Carta, like twenty-nine, buttressed the right for which he contended. The only course for a free man, he advised, was silence: let his adversaries state the charge against him and prove it to his face by witnesses. Christ himself by not answering had put off his enemies who sought to catch him by interrogatories. Hence, concluded Lilburne, justice demanded that Parliament not condemn a man for his refusal to reply to questions against himself. He acknowledged that it was "the usuall course of the COMMON-LAW" to put incriminating interrogatories to a defendant, but the question was, he asked—leaving no doubt of his answer—"whether that practise be just or no?" [37]

Englands Lamentable Slaverie, by Lilburne's friend William Walwyn, was published at about the same time. It was dedicated to Lilburne, the "Instrument of Englands Freedome." He lay in Newgate prison, said Walwyn "for refusing to answer upon Interrogatories to their Committee of Examinations, Contrarie to 1. The Great Charter of England, 2. The very words of the Petition of right. 3. The Act made . . . for the abolishing the Star-Chamber." Walwyn, who had already presented to the Commons a petition on Lilburne's behalf bearing over two thousand signatures, now extolled him in print for his valiant defense of the liberty of the subject. He had stood his ground when questioned by Parliament, alleging that it was against his liberty as a free-born Englishman to answer against himself, claiming Magna Carta as his justification: "you are the first indeed," applauded Walwyn, "that ever raised this new doctrine of MAGNA CHARTA, to prove the same unlawfull. Likewise, You are the first, that compareth this dealing to the crueltie of the Starre Chamber. . . ." Walwyn's pamphlet helped spread Lilburne's ideas, but it was Cromwell, the victorious general, who persuaded Parliament to liberate him. It would "discourage" the army, he said in a letter, "to censure an officer for his opinion in point of conscience; for the liberty whereof, and to free themselves from the shackles in which the bishops would enslave them, that the army had been principally raised." In October of 1645, after four months in jail, Lilburne was freed.[38]

The following March, the authorities arrested William Larner, whose illicit press had published Lilburne, Walwyn, and other sectaries. Larner "had learned so much of Lilburne's language," said the man who tracked him down, that he objected to questions tending to incriminate him. "I desire," said Larner, "the liberty of a Free-man of England not to answer to any interrogatories." He first made this claim before the court of the Lord Mayor and repeated it before the House of Lords. Two of his employees followed suit. Soon, the model of all this emulation joined Larner and his employees in prison. Lilburne had this time breached the privileges of Parliament by his criticism of a member of the House of Lords. Summoned for examination, he refused to testify and, as usual, compounded his affront by relating the whole story in a pamphlet. Magna Carta, he claimed, gave the Lords no jurisdiction to sit in judgment on a commoner in a criminal cause. Summoned again, he made a show of extravagent defiance, barricading himself in his cell; he had to be taken by force and dragged to the bar of the House. Once there he made a scene, refusing to kneel. The Lords retaliated by placing him in solitary confinement and—worst blow of all—denied him writing materials. A couple of weeks of such treatment simply aggravated his obstinacy. Summoned again to answer for his publications, he again refused to kneel and protested the proceedings. When the charges against him were read aloud, he stopped up his ears with his fingers. The Lords retaliated by sentencing him to a fine of two thousand pounds, and indefinite imprisonment in the Tower of London; they also disqualified him from holding any public office, civil or military, for the remainder of his life.[39]

Once more Walwyn rushed to Lilburne's defense with an eloquent review of his career entitled *A Pearl in a Dunghill*. Its purpose was to persuade readers that Lilburne's cause was their own, for he had done more than any man, Walwyn argued, to resist oppression and champion the liberties of England. Walwyn depicted the House of Lords as a new Star Chamber unjustly punishing free commoners by examining them as if the oath *ex officio* were still the law of the land. Richard Overton also spoke for Lilburne in 1646 in his influential *Remonstrance of Many Thousand Citizens*, "the most revolutionary tract that the Puritan Revolution had hitherto evoked." He too charged Parliament with behaving like the High Commission and Star Chamber: "Yee examine men upon *Interrogatories* and *Questions* against themselves, and Imprison them for refusing to answere." The pamphlet's frontispiece carried a portrait of Lilburne behind bars.[40]

Overton was soon behind bars, too. He wrote and smuggled out of prison an inflammatory pamphlet describing what had happened to him. Armed men, like pursuivants of the High Commission, broke into his house, "surprized me in my bed without any appearance or shew of any warrant," and brought him before a committee of the House of Lords. There, "being put High Commission like to answer to Interrogatories against my selfe," he refused to answer, not even to the question whether he was a printer, which was his trade. "But this is Lilburne-like," exclaimed one Lord. For his contempt the Lords sentenced Overton to indefinite imprisonment. Some months later their tyranny fell upon his family, too, because of their connection with the secret press which had not been silenced by the incarceration of Larner and Overton. Agents of the Lords' Committee on Examinations "rifled, plundered, and ransacked" his home in a search for evidence and arrested his wife and brother, all without warrant, he complained, or indictment, verdict of equals, lawful judgment, "or other due processe of Law proceeding contrary to the Fundamentall Laws of the Kingdom." His wife and brother, refusing to answer interrogatories concerning Overton, themselves, or "life, liberty, or goods," were also committed indefinitely. Overton, who did not usually share Lilburne's emphasis on legal rights and procedures, angrily detailed the various infringements of Magna Carta and the Petition of Right "which condemnes all High Commission like Interrogatory proceedings in a mans own cause. . . ." He accused Parliament of high treason, damned it as unrepresentative, and pleaded that conscience must be free of coercion. His *Appeal* was "one of his many classic statements of toleration." It was an appeal from the "degenerate" body of Parliament to the "free people in generall" and especially to members of the army. To the army alone he addressed his concluding recommendations, one of which was that no free commoner of England should be forced by the high court of Parliament, by any subordinate court of justice, or by any government authority, to take an oath "or to answer to any Interrogatories concerning himselfe in any criminall case, concerning his life, liberty, goods, or free-hold." [41]

The idea was certainly catching on. In 1646, according to the Presbyterian divine Thomas Edwards, who catalogued the "gangraena" in the realm, Andrew Wyke, a mechanic who became a Baptist minister, was brought before the local authorities in Suffolk because of his "Preaching and Dipping." Wyke "carried himself like Lilburne, Overton, and other fellow Sectaries, refusing to answer the Chair-man any questions . . . saying, I am a free man, and not bound to answer any Interrogatory, I will answer to no Interrogatory, either to accuse myself or any other." He was committed. His case is significant because like Larner, who first refused to incriminate himself before the common-law court of the Lord Mayor, Wyke's behavior before some "committee" of Suffolk County, shows that the right was being claimed before all sorts of tribunals of criminal jurisdiction. It was being claimed, too, in the absence of an inquisitional oath and whether or not due accusation was made prior to interrogation. [42]

Lilburne, still in prison, though supposedly denied writing materials, was irrepressible. By bribing his jailors and in ways unknown, he managed to keep producing tracts, and they grew increasingly democratic in character. Religious liberty, freedom of the press, and the rights of the criminally accused were only part of his concern. He advocated social, economic, and political reforms that provoked the epithet of "Leveller" to be hatefully applied to him and his ideas. He rarely lost an opportunity to make his own case the case of the people. The titles of his pamphlets during this period suggest their incendiary nature: *The Just Mans Justification, The Freemans Freedome vindicated, Liberty vindicated against Slavery, Londons Liberty in Chains, An Anatomy of the Lords Tyranny,* and *The Charters of London* were part of his output of 1646, while he was imprisoned in Newgate. Attempts to silence him inexplicably failed, while the severe treatment accorded to him and his wife made him more contumacious, more provocative, more radical. Early in 1647 his house was raided, three loads of seditious papers and tracts were confiscated, and Mrs. Lilburne was taken into custody. John and she were both summoned before the Committee of Examinations, and she followed his lead in protesting that they had no right to demand her answers to incriminating questions. Lilburne told the world about this latest oppression, resolving in the *Resolved Mans Resolution* to defend his civil liberties "with the last drop of his hearts blood." [43]

The government's attempt to silence him was as impolitic as it was illegal by his standards. As one historian has observed, "By its injudicious treatment of the most popular man in England, Parliament was arraying against itself a force which only awaited an opportunity to sweep it away." During the winter of 1646–47, in London and in the army, the two sources of Leveller strength, the common people frenetically debated politics and religion. Like the essays of Tom Paine at Valley Forge in a later era, the essays by the Leveller leaders were avidly read, circulated, and discussed by the soldiers around their campfires. Richard Baxter, a Presbyterian leader, visited the army after the victory at Naseby and found a disturbing revolutionary spirit. A "great part of the mischief," he reported, was caused by the distribution of pamphlets by Lilburne, Overton, and Walwyn, whose work "seduced" honest men of ignorance into a "disputing vein" which made them argue "for Church democracy or State democracy . . . against the King and the ministry and for liberty of conscience." By the spring of 1647 a newswriter reported that the army was "one Lilburne throughout" and that the soldiers quoted his work as if it were law. That "law," which became their credo, taught them that it was un-Christian, un-English, and against fundamental liberties to oblige men to answer interrogatories against or concerning themselves.[44]

The spring of 1647 saw the publication of a democratic manifesto, the work of Walwyn, called "The Humble Petition of Many Thousands," which was addressed to the House of Commons. It by no means represented all the Leveller proposals, but it contained a program, as M. A. Gibb, Lilburne's biographer stated, "not for one Parliament, but for three hundred years" of Parliaments. Among its many recommendations was that Commons should permit "no authority whatsoever, to compell any person or persons to answer to questions against themselves," and it called for the release of all who had been imprisoned for their refusal. The right against self-incrimination which had begun as a protest against the coercion of conscience was growing as part of what Margaret Judson has called "the first great outburst of democratic thought in history, with John Lilburne and Richard Overton leading the way." One major Leveller document after another repeated with almost monotonous regularity an insistent demand for the right. It appeared, most importantly, in a clause drafted by Lilburne in the magnificent "Second Agreement of the People" of 1648, which anticipated so many fundamentals of the United States Constitution and Bill of Rights, and again in the equally prescient and democratic "Third Agreement of the People" of 1649. In these documents the Levellers proposed a written constitution to define the government of England, abolish arbitrary power, set limits to authority, and remove grievances. They advocated a unicameral legislature whose members would be apportioned among localities on the basis of population and be elected annually by all men over twenty-one excepting paupers and servants. There was to be freedom of religion and of the press; equality of all persons before the law; no judgment touching life, liberty, or property but by jury trial; no military conscription of conscientious objectors; no monopolies, tithes, or excise taxes; taxation proportionate to real or personal property; election of ministers by the people of their parish and voluntary support of public worship; election of all army officers excepting members of the general staff; the grading of punishments to fit the crime and the abolition of capital punishment except for murder; and the abolition of imprisonment for debt. This was the context of the insistent Leveller demand for a right against self-incrimination.[45]

The reason for the demand was simple enough. Parliament, the army's courts-martial, and Cromwell's Council of State all suppressed critical remarks as seditious speech, subjecting suspects to inquisitorial examination. In the absence of freedom of political discourse, the surest defense was the claim that no authority had the lawful power to address incriminating interrogatories. Nor were the Levellers the only victims and the only ones to invoke the right. In 1648, preliminary to Pride's purge of the Presbyterian majority of Parliament, a special subcommittee of a Joint Committee of Examinations was appointed to investigate in secrecy the loyalty of members whose religious and political opinions were offensive to the army leaders. The subcommittee concealed the names of accusers and examined Presbyterian members under oath as if it were the Star Chamber. Several indignantly refused to undergo oath or examination. Edward Baynton, for example, declared that it was "illegal to squeeze examinations out of a mans owne mouth; neither was a man bound to answer, where his words may condemn, but not absolve him. . . ." Clement Walker protested that no man could defend himself when the subcommittee carried on its business in the dark. We are called, he said, "to answer for our lives, *ore tenus*; and our accusation beginneth with the examination of our persons, to make us state a charge against ourselves, to betray ourselves, and cut our owne throats with our tongues, contrary to Magna Charta, the Petition of Right. . . . And no Witnesses are produced, nor so much as named." Walker recorded the episode in an understandably vehement tract.[46]

Another victim was John Maynard, whom the subcommittee also suspended and imprisoned in the Tower for his contumacy. *The Lawes Subversion: or, Sir John Maynards Case truly stated* denounced the proceedings. The passion of the Presbyterian author, John Holden, was worthy of Lilburne. Could anyone believe, he asked, that Parliament would have deviated so far from the rules of law and justice

as to examine any man on interrogatories against himself in a criminal case? Would any have believed that this Parliament should have degenerated so far, as to indeavour to compell a man to destroy himself? Is it not a riddle surpassing all, that this monstrous age hath produced, that this Parliament, that hath deemed the Starre-Chamber and the Councell Tables names worthy to be a curse and a by-word to posterity, because of their cruelty in censuring men for refusing to answer interrogatories, that this Parl. I say, should urgently presse Sir Jo.

Maynard to answer interrogatories against himself in a criminall
case? [47]

Army control of Parliament benefited Lilburne and Overton
who were released in August 1648. They remained true to their
principles, denouncing tyranny whatever the source, even if from
erstwhile friends. They had expected "things of an other nature"
they declared sadly in a public petition to Parliament. They had
expected that "you would have freed all men from being examined against themselves. . . ." Lilburne wrote *A Defiance to Tyrants, The Peoples Prerogative, The Lawes Funerall, A Plea for
Common Right and Freedom*, and, early in 1649, *Englands New
Chains Discovered* and *The Hunting of Foxes*. His disillusionment
with Cromwell and the army leaders was bitter, his expression of
it savage. England was once ruled by a king, Lords, and Commons; it was now ruled by General Cromwell, military courts-
martial, and Commons—"and we pray you," he asked, "what is
the difference?" One kind of oppression had been exchanged for
another, the rule of an oligarchy based on military despotism. The
Courts of High Commission and Star Chamber "are all alive in
that Court, called the General Council of the Army," which had
court-martialed five soldiers who presented Leveller petitions.
Each, Lilburne related, had been asked whether he had had a hand
in the authorship of the petitions. One set a course which all
others had followed, when he replied that he thought the court
"had abominated the Spanish Inquisition, and Star-chamber practice, in examining him upon Interrogatories, contrary to their own
Declarations; and he would rather lose his life, then betray his
Libertie." A few days after this pamphlet appeared, Lilburne published a second installment of *Englands New Chains*, accusing
Cromwell of having betrayed the revolution and all its principles.
The general could stand no more. Parliament therefore declared
that the pamphlet was "false, scandalous . . . highly seditious,
and destructive to the present Government," its authors to be proceeded against as traitors.[48]

Several days later, on March 28, 1649, before five o'clock in the
morning—an hour discreetly chosen to avoid the possibility of
contending with a pro-Leveller mob—between one and two hundred armed men surrounded Lilburne's house, forced their way in,

and took him prisoner. That same morning Cromwell's troops also arrested William Walwyn, Richard Overton, and Thomas Prince. The four prisoners were brought before the Council of State. John Bradshaw, the presiding officer, had served as Lilburne's counsel in 1645 when he had petitioned the House of Lords to join the House of Commons in voting his Star Chamber sentence illegal and award him reparations. On that occasion Bradshaw had condemned the Star Chamber sentence because it had been grounded on Lilburne's refusal to take the oath *ex officio,* "it being contrary," Bradshaw had said, "to the laws of God, nature, and the kingdom, for any man to be his own accuser." But in 1649 Bradshaw was in effect Lilburne's prosecutor; he asked the prisoner whether he had written *Englands New Chains.*[49]

Lilburne, "wondering at the strangeness of the question," answered that he was "amazed" at Bradshaw's having asked it. It had been only eight years since Parliament had annihilated the Star Chamber and High Commission "for such proceedings as these," less since Bradshaw himself had argued that incriminating interrogatories were illegal. He would never, said Lilburne, commit so "un-Englishman-like" a deed as to answer. He would neither betray England's liberties nor himself. The Council should be "ashamed to demand so illegal and unworthy a thing of me as this." Bradshaw told Lilburne that they were not trying him, only seeking information for his trial. Lilburne would not even acknowledge their jurisdiction over him. Walwyn, Overton, and Prince in turn also invoked the right against self-incrimination. The four were herded into an ante-chamber while the Council debated their fate. Lilburne, listening at the keyhole, heard Cromwell bang his fist on the Council Table and shout, "I tel you Sir, you have no other Way to deale with these men, but to break them in pieces . . . if you do not break them, they will break you!" The four were committed to the Tower on suspicion of high treason. They promptly published a vivid account of their arrest and examination.[50]

In the succeeding months petitions flowed into Parliament demanding their release—some had as many as ten thousand signatures—and tracts written in the Tower flowed out. The four men were finally separated, kept in close confinement, and security regulations tightened to prevent their access to writing materials and the smuggling out of manuscripts. But their publications had already done a great deal of damage to the government, stirring resentments—so claimed the government—that led to mutinies in the army. In any case it seemed to be impossible to silence them even in the Tower. New pamphlets continued to appear. The "Third Agreement of the People," written by all four, was published on May 1, 1649, and by September Lilburne alone had written nine more tracts including *The Legall Fundamental Liberties* and the incendiary *Impeachment of High Treason against Oliver Cromwell and Henry Ireton.* The "Third Agreement of the People" had driven Cromwell to say that "the Kingdome could never be setled so long as Lilburne was alive." Cromwell blamed the army mutinies on Lilburne. *The Impeachment* provoked him to a fury; he vowed that either Lilburne or he must perish. In September 1649, a warrant issued from the Council of State for the trial of Lilburne by a special tribunal on the charge of high treason. In October a grand jury indicted him and he was put on trial for his life.[51]

CHAPTER X

The Right Secured

John Lilburne was tried by a jury before an Extraordinary Commission of Oyer and Terminer consisting of eight common-law judges, the Lord Mayor of London, the Recorder of London, four sergeants-at-law, and twenty-six other special judges, including city aldermen and members of Parliament. The panel of judges was indeed extraordinary, but so was everything about the trial. All London focused on the event. The scene was the great Guild Hall of London, jammed with spectators. The streets near the courtroom were lined with troopers to prevent public demonstrations against the government, and soldiers kept Lilburne himself under constant surveillance during the trial. His own friends and supporters overwhelmingly outnumbered the government's adherents in the courtroom. One of his critics alleged, with probable exaggeration, that he had placed "hundreds" of his "myrmidons" in the audience to intimidate the court.[1]

Throughout his two-day trial Lilburne complained that he was being unfairly tried, but the trial was uncommonly fair by the standards then prevailing. Time and again the judges reminded Lilburne that he was receiving more favor than any prisoner charged with treason ever had, though he repudiated the court's "favors," saying that he claimed only the rights to which he was entitled by law, justice, and equity. The court was unbelievably patient with him, indulging his demands whenever the practices of the time permitted, because in a figurative sense, the government, too, was on trial; it was eager to prove before the bar of public opinion that it was lawfully constituted and just. Lilburne aimed at proving the opposite. Though he had no formal training in law, he had Coke's *Institutes* and other law books at his side, and had mastered them well enough to conduct his own defense as well as any attorney could. As long as he was permitted to speak—and there was no keeping him quiet—he outmatched all the judges before him. His great achievement at the trial was holding at bay the judges and Attorney-General Prideaux, his prosecutor, while he expounded to them and to his fellow citizens in the jury box and in the audience the fundamentals of fair criminal procedure from the time of arrest through trial. He placed the right against self-incrimination in the context of what he called "fair play," "fair trial," "the due process of the law," and "the good old laws of England." [2]

Lilburne's strategy was to challenge every step of procedure, pick to pieces each bit of evidence against him, depict the court as his oppressors, and appeal to the jury over the heads of the judges. From the moment the trial began, he sought to sabotage its proceedings in order to demonstrate unfairness or illegality or his pretended ignorance of law. Asked to hold up his hand so that he could plead to the indictment, he launched into a speech that spreads through thirteen pages of the report of the trial. The first words were that he was a freeborn Englishman who claimed his liberties. He demanded liberty to make exceptions to errors in the indictment before pleading to it. He claimed not to know the "formalities, niceties, and punctilios" of the law, though he proved himself to be far more adept than the court in excruciating quibbles. He had noticed that the doors of the courtroom had been closed and demanded that they be opened—which was done. He spoke of his record of patriotism, military valor, and championship of England's liberties. Citing Magna Carta, the Petition of Right, and Coke to prove that the court had no authority to try him, he insisted that he was entitled to trial by an ordinary court, rather than by an extraordinary, packed, and overawing tribunal. He, not the court, was overawing.[3]

He constantly associated the court with the Star Chamber and illegality. He related the story of his illegal arrest by armed men,

Bradshaw's illegal interrogation when he was before the Council of State, and Bradshaw's earlier defense of his right not to be asked questions against himself. He even claimed a right not to be asked questions concerning himself. He had been denied, he protested, "the undeniable privileges of the due process of the law from first to last." For months he had been held prisoner without the least pretense of a charge against him, though he was entitled to a speedy trial. Now that he was being put to trial he could find nothing in the "good old fundamental laws of England" that provided the least basis for the proceedings against him. Finally he demanded to know why he must hold up his hand—the request that provoked his long speech.[4]

When the judges sought to answer him and defend the lawfulness of his trial, he invariably interrupted them, alleging that they were taking advantage of him with "punctilios and niceties." When they tried to hush him up in order to proceed with the trial, he complained bitterly that they were denying him liberty of speech to defend himself when his life was at stake. When he finally permitted the indictment to be read, he discovered that the charge of high treason was not based on any of the writings or activities which had led to his arrest; the indictment was founded only on the tracts he wrote while in the Tower. Moreover, the indictment was founded on *ex post facto* statutes; they had been enacted after he was in custody and were tailored to punish his political propaganda. The accusation against him was that he had committed high treason by publishing that the government was tyrannical, usurped, and unlawful; by his writings he had sought to subvert the government and stir the army to mutiny. The nine-page indictment quoted generously from Lilburne's writings and when read in court stirred a commotion among the spectators. While the reading progressed, Lilburne noticed Attorney-General Prideaux whispering with one of the judges. He cried out that such whispering was "contrary to the law of England, and extremely foule and dishonest play"—he would have no more of such injustice. The judge defensively explained—Lilburne was always on the offensive, the court defensive—that it was necessary occasionally for the court to confer with the prosecutor. Not unless it be "openly, audibly, and avowedly," answered Lilburne; he would have no "hugger-mugger, privately or whisperingly." [5]

When at last the indictment had been read, Lord Keble, the presiding judge, asked Lilburne to plead guilty or not guilty. Instead Lilburne requested permission to make another speech. The court insisted that he plead. By the laws of England, he replied, "I am not to answer to questions against or concerning myself." "You shall not be compelled," answered Lord Keble, acknowledging the right to remain silent to incriminating interrogatories. But Keble had not realized that Lilburne was actually alleging that to require him to plead to the indictment was violative of his right, a view he had advanced three years earlier in *Englands Birth-Right*. One of the judges explained that by pleading to the indictment he would not accuse himself. By the Petition of Right, Lilburne replied, he did not have to answer any questions concerning himself, a familiar but strained Leveller interpretation of that great document which none of the judges corrected. Lilburne did not persist, however, in his unique refusal to plead. He would plead, he said, if afforded the privileges of the laws of England: he then requested a copy of the indictment, counsel to defend him, and "reasonable" time to consult with counsel even if it be "but eight or nine days." The court refused to breach precedent by granting his requests. He argued that he did not wish to plead until he had the opportunity of making exceptions to the indictment which was long, complicated, and in French and Latin which he did not understand. In fact, however, an explanation in English had been provided. When the court demanded that he plead, he burst out that they were trying to "ensnare and entrap" him. He demanded "fair play according to the laws of England." After a long wrangle, he offered to plead if the court would either provide him with counsel or promise not to take advantage of his ignorance of the law. Keble then promised him "fair play, and no advantage taken against you. . . ." At long last he pleaded not guilty. Excluding the reading of the indictment, the report of his trial covered twenty-five pages before reaching his plea; it should have been settled in a few minutes.[6]

The next step, the court informed him, was choosing a jury, but that proved to be a distant event, for the fiery Lilburne engaged the court in a long debate on his rights. He again demanded a copy of the indictment, the right to counsel, time to consult him, and the right to subpoena witnesses in his favor. Keble explained that the court would act as his counsel in matters of fact and that he needed no other counsel except for such matters of law that might arise. If they arose, he might have counsel. Lilburne insisted that the indictment involved matters of law. He complained that he had been in prison for seven months, could not have come to court prepared to defend himself against charges he had just heard for the first time, and he wanted to make exceptions to the indictment—for which he needed the aid of counsel. If the court would not grant his request, he asserted, "then order me to be knocked on the head immediately in the place where I stand, without any further trial, for I must needs be destroyed, if you deny me all the means of my preservation." He made such a fuss and so interrupted the judges who sought to answer him that Keble said, "Hear me one word, and you shall have two." Lilburne replied that because he was on trial for his life, he must have freedom to speak, but if they would not let him have counsel, he would say no more and they might as well murder him. Though the court tried to reason with him, he decried the injustice of it all. The prosecution and the judges, he said, had had months to "beat their brains together" with the assistance of his enemies to destroy him, yet took advantage of him by denying him counsel and a copy of the indictment—rights still half a century away. "O Lord!" he exclaimed, "was there ever such a pack of unjust and unrighteous judges in the world?" His counsel, a Mr. Sprat, was in the courtroom and declared that it would be easy to prove that the indictment involved matters of law which warranted the assistance of counsel. The court shut Sprat up. Lilburne burst out that the judges had reneged on their promise to give him a "fair trial." They aimed to kill him, he declared, despite his innocence; in a passion he called on God to deliver him from such tyranny and injustice.[7]

Lilburne had been offensively belligerent, obstructive, and abusive. It was his nature to be so, but it was also a clever stratagem. He finally prodded the court beyond endurance, provoking the long-suffering Keble to reveal his prejudice. The time had come, Keble said, to get on with the trial so that Lilburne's "secret actions" could be exposed to public view as "heinous." "You have had times to complot your treasonable venomous books, which shall be proved upon you; and till this be done, there is no matter of law to be looked at." When a man had "done such treasonable things," he must plead. Keble's speech proved, Lilburne answered, just what he thought. He knew that the judges had met several times over a period of months with Attorney-General Prideaux to plan his conviction. He wanted counsel to defend him. Prideaux asked the court to get on with the trial so that Lilburne could be "proceeded against for his notorious Treasons." That provoked Lilburne to a speech about the presumption of innocence. Until proved guilty and convicted by the jury, he was as innocent, he claimed, as those who called him traitor.[8]

The interminable altercation about his rights continued. He wanted not only counsel and a copy of the indictment; he demanded time to call witnesses. Keble said he should have brought his witnesses to court with him. How could he, Lilburne retorted, when he had just heard the indictment against him? The court gave him till seven o'clock the next morning to produce his witnesses. Some of them, he protested, lived a hundred miles away; others were "parliament men" and army officers who would not come voluntarily but must be subpoenaed. The court refused his request. The whole day had passed; it was time for adjournment. The court observed that all present should notice that "the prisoner at the bar hath had more favour already, than ever any prisoner in England in the like case ever had . . . the doors are wide open that all may know it." Lilburne sarcastically thanked the court, and they adjourned.[9]

The next day there was repeated squabbling between the defendant and the court, but at last a jury was impaneled and the case got under way. The prosecution called witnesses to prove Lilburne's authorship of the treasonable pamphlets, and he cross-examined them closely. At one point Prideaux asked Lilburne whether the manuscript of a tract was in his handwriting. Scornfully he refused even to look at the document, declaring he would answer no questions concerning himself. The court urged him to answer whether the handwriting was his, but he retorted that the judges were ignorant of the law on his rights. "My lord," said

Prideaux, "you may see the valiantness of this champion for the people's liberties, that he will not own his own hand; although I must desire you gentlemen of the jury, to observe that Mr. Lilburne implicitly confesseth it." Stubbornly Lilburne declared again that the Petition of Right taught him to answer no questions "against or concerning" himself, and he had read "the same to be practised by Christ and his Apostles." A few minutes later, when a witness testified that he knew Lilburne's writing and identified as his the manuscript of *An Impeachment of High Treason against Oliver Cromwell,* Prideaux taunted Lilburne again for being "ashamed" to acknowledge his work. Again he invoked his right to remain silent, declaring that he was on Christ's terms and like Christ demanded that his accusers prove the accusation against him. Judge Jermin, interposing that Christ had said that he was the son of God, vainly urged Lilburne to confess also. The prosecution concluded its case by reading the statutes on which the indictment was based and some twenty pages of the most patently violative language from Lilburne's tracts.[10]

Lilburne's formal defense was that the prosecution had not proved his authorship. He neither denied nor affirmed his authorship; indeed, the most vehement tracts had his name on the title page. But he noted that whoever wrote them had done so after his imprisonment; moreover, that the treason statutes had been enacted after publication of some of the tracts charged against him. He insisted, too, that the tracts ascribed to him might be forgeries and that the treasonable passages might be part of the *errata!* Above all, he argued effectively that there was no proof that he was the author. In a few instances witnesses had testified to their knowledge of his authorship, but Lilburne claimed that in a legal sense they had proved nothing because two witnesses were required to each particular fact of treason. There was another long altercation between him and Prideaux on whether one witness to a pamphlet was enough. Although the court ruled in favor of the prosecution, Lilburne was interested in the opinion of the jury, not of the judges. He continually and deliberately wandered from the point to engage in a technically irrelevant argument which was his greatest strength—a passionate account of his illegal arrest and confinement, his war record, the unlawfulness of the court's authority to try him, his long struggle against injustice and tyranny, the refusal to give him a copy of the indictment or to allow him counsel, the persistent denial of due process and fair play, and the aim of the court to destroy him. Prideaux had done almost as much for Lilburne's cause by reading so extensively from his tracts against the government.[11]

It was a political trial, and Lilburne conducted himself as if public opinion on affairs of state and on matters of liberty and justice would be decisive. There was a reason why he repeated his remarks of the preceding day when he had spoken before the impaneling of the jury. On the second day of the trial he rehashed it all for the benefit of the jury. Against the authority of the judges, he openly appealed to the jury, telling them that they were the judges of law as well as of fact. The court, indignantly rejecting his aspersions on their authority, denied that the jury could decide matters of law. When Lilburne persisted in reading from Coke to teach the jury the law governing his case, the court tried to stop him, but it was impossible to shut him up. He would blare out against the "bloody judges" and call upon the jury to witness the fact that the court refused him freedom of speech to conduct his defense. He finally got his way and expounded law to the jury. During each altercation, when balked by the court he would accuse it of horrendous crimes against him, forcing Lord Keble apologetically to insist that he was getting "fair play." On one of these occasions, Keble assured Lilburne that no one previously had ever been tried before "so many grave judges of the law," thus allowing Lilburne again to denounce the irregularity of the court's commission to try him. He would rather, he said, be tried before one judge in an ordinary court, as was his right. If there had been "one judge, and no more," Keble foolishly answered, "and if you had not had this great presence of the court, you would have outtalked them; but you cannot do so here." Lilburne's retort proved that the "great presence" was no match for him. "Truly, Sir," he replied, "I am not daunted at the multitude of my judges, neither at the glittering of your scarlet robes, nor the majesty of your presence, and harsh austere deportment towards me, I bless my good God for it, who gives me courage and boldness." He had the boldness to complain whenever he was interrupted and even to claim that no one should talk when he was interrupting, because he was battling for his life.[12]

When Lilburne finally completed his defense with a long emotional appeal to the jury, the audience broke out in loud shouts of "Amen, Amen, and gave an extraordinary great hum," alarming the judges and the military commander who immediately sent for three more companies of foot-soldiers. Keble then gave a hanging charge to the jury—"your plot was the greatest that England ever saw, for it struck at no less than the subversion of this Commonwealth, of this state, to have laid and put us all in blood; your plot was such, that never such was seen in the world before to proceed from a private man. . . ." Lilburne interrupted to declare that there had never been such an unfair trial. Judge Jermin replied that never had judges been so badly abused before.[13]

The jury, after deliberating for an hour, returned a verdict of "Not Guilty." Pandemonium struck the courtroom. The reporter of the proceedings noted that "the whole multitude of people in the Hall, for joy of the Prisoner's acquittal, gave such a loud and unanimous shout, as is believed was never heard in Guildhall, which lasted for about half an hour without intermission." The acclamations for Lilburne's deliverance extended into the streets, where "the like hath not been seen in England . . . for joy the people caused that night abundance of bonfires to be made all up and down the streets." Two weeks later the Council of State, over the signature of President John Bradshaw, ordered Lilburne's release from the Tower. Overton, Prince, and Walwyn were freed with him.[14]

Notwithstanding Lilburne's triumph and popularity, or perhaps because of them, he was a man marked by the government for elimination one way or another. One of his pamphlets again provided the opportunity. Having intemperately assaulted the reputation of an influential member of Parliament, technically a breach of privilege, Lilburne was summoned before the bar of the Commons at the close of 1651. His enemies summarily convicted him without formal accusation, opportunity of defense, or semblance of trial. Retribution was swift and shockingly severe. By an attainder, they fined him seven thousand pounds, banished him for life, and sentenced him to death if he ever returned to England.

Lilburne had always been quick to smear the epithet of "Star Chamber" on any procedure that fell short of his standards. But he had never been exposed to such monstrous injustice, nakedly violating every basic precept of English liberty. Yet he was helpless; he fled to Holland to escape the death penalty that automatically attached if he remained in the realm beyond twenty days.[15]

In June of 1653, after Cromwell had dissolved the Rump Parliament which had convicted Lilburne, the exile returned, confident that a changed political situation meant his safety. But the dictator, whose position was uncertain, could not permit the freedom of the realm to anyone as politically dangerous and popular as Lilburne, who had already announced that he would be peaceable only if England's liberties were re-established. The Council of State imprisoned Lilburne and put him to trial for his life, giving him every benefit of common-law procedure. After all, the government had only to prove that he was the John Lilburne mentioned in the bill of attainder in order to convict and execute him. But even Cromwell had underestimated his antagonist's amazing popularity and his legal ingenuity. "It is not to be imagined," said a contemporary, "how much esteem he hath got, only for vindicating the laws and liberties against the usurpations of his time." London rallied around him with petitions, pamphlets, and demonstrations of affection. Cromwell policed the streets with three regiments at the time of the trial in Old Bailey.[16]

The trial itself was long drawn out, in other respects much like the trial of 1649, with Lilburne using all his old tricks and demanding rights never before granted. This time, however, he succeeded in wresting from the court a copy of his indictment and the assistance of counsel to challenge it. No one had ever before managed such a remarkable feat. Lilburne then attacked the indictment in such a way as to put the government on trial too, leaving the jury to choose between it and him. He reasoned that the indictment was based on his illegal conviction and bill of attainder of 1651; moreover, that the Parliament which had passed the bill had been an illegal body whose acts were not worthy of respect. Cromwell himself had dissolved that Parliament. If it had been a lawful and just body, then Cromwell's act was an unlawful usurpation, rendering illegal the very government that was prosecuting him. He backed up these bold "exceptions to the indictment" with a variety of formidable technicalities and shifty delaying tactics. When the court convened to hear the exceptions, after having capitulated to his demands for ample time to prepare them, he had already published a pamphlet, *The Exceptions of John Lilburne to a Bill of Indictment.*

Hundreds of his supporters were reported to be in and around the courtroom, armed and prepared for a rescue in the event of an adverse verdict. But Cromwell virtually had London under martial law. In Old Bailey the altercations between the prisoner and the court were stormy, filling the air with "furious hurley-burleys." Lilburne, as usual, would admit nothing, not even that he was the John Lilburne mentioned in the act of banishment. But he played his role as Freeborn John with gusto and drama, appealing once again to the jury to stand fast for English liberties. If he died on Monday, he told them, on Tuesday Parliament might pass sentence on every one of the twelve, on their families, eventually on the people of London and on all of England. The jury acquitted. The "joy and acclamation" of the spectators was so great that their shouts were heard "an English mile." The jubilation spread even to the troops who beat their drums and sounded their trumpets. Cromwell, "infinitely enraged," said Clarendon, regarded the verdict "as a greater defeat than the loss of a battle would have been." [17]

Parliament ordered the examination of the jury before the Council of State. The foreman would only say that he had acted in accordance with his conscience; he would answer no questions. Another juror, when asked to account for the verdict, replied, "What he can tell is one thing; but to accuse himself is another thing." He claimed that he did not think that the Lilburne before the court was the Lilburne mentioned in the attainder; when asked why, he replied that he was accountable only to God and would not answer. Another juror admitted that despite the ruling of the court, "He and the rest of the jury took themselves to be Judges of matter of law, as well as matter of fact"—proof that Lilburne had persuaded them to decide on the injustice and illegality of the 1651 bill of attainder, or of the prosecution of 1653, or both.

Most members of the jury would say only that they had decided according to conscience.[18]

Lilburne's courtroom triumph was his last. Cromwell had a tiger by the tail and simply could not let him go. The risk that he would spearhead intrigues against the government and promote discontent among the people was too great. In the dead of night, troops moved Lilburne from Newgate prison to the Tower—"for the peace of the nation." The government ordered the commander of the Tower to refuse obedience to any writ of habeas corpus in Lilburne's behalf. The prisoner was kept under such strict surveillance that he managed to produce only one more pamphlet, *An Hue and Cry after the Fundamental Lawes and Liberties of England*. He proved to be utterly intractable, rejecting overtures from the government to trade his silence for his liberation. Even in the Tower he was too much to endure. There were conspiracies against the government, even attempts on Cromwell's life, in which Lilburne's supporters were implicated. In the spring of 1654, therefore, Lilburne was transported out of London and out of the country, to a lonely exile in a prison fortress on the island of Jersey. Isolated from news, from intrigues, from visitors, from secret printing presses, he was, at last, a defeated man. He returned to religion, becoming a Quaker. The new faith suited him, for the Quakers were at that time a fighting sect of intense zealots, democratic in every respect and sensationally controversialist. The government imprisoned them by the hundreds. But Lilburne, cut off from the tumult, took refuge in the more spiritual aspects of Quakerism. Late in 1655 the government yielded to petitions and transferred him to Dover where the conditions of his imprisonment improved. But his health steadily deteriorated. In 1657, at the age of forty-three, he died. Two years later Parliament revoked his illegal sentence.[19]

The militant Christian democrat and libertarian had bequeathed to the English nation "his old buckler, Magna Carta," reconstrued to represent principles that free men would cherish and fight for. "I shall leave this Testimony behind me," he once predicted, "that I died for the Laws and Liberties of this nation." The outcome of his trial, he had predicted to the jury in 1653, would be a precedent for the good or evil of all the people of

England. His entire career was a precedent for freedom, for freedom of religion, speech, press, and association. By his writings and his trials he sought to educate a nation on the relation of liberty to "fair play" in criminal procedure. Twice he convinced juries to decide on the injustice of laws used to prosecute political or religious prisoners. Accordingly he helped to make the jury the celebrated "palladium of liberty" so rapturously extolled by later writers. And more than any other individual he was responsible for the acceptance of the principle that no person should be compelled to be a witness against himself in criminal cases.

Lilburne had made the difference. From his time on, the right against self-incrimination was an established, respected rule of the common law, or, more broadly, of English law generally. *Examen Legum Angliae: Or the Laws of England,* a book published in 1656, recalled that the oath *ex officio* had violated "the Law of Nature," claimed that the *nemo tenetur* maxim was "agreed by all men," discoursed on the soundness of the maxim, cited Nicholas Fuller's *Argument,* and observed that in neither criminal cases at common law nor in chancery cases involving fraud was a man obliged "to confess the truth against himself." The right against self-incrimination did not prohibit inquiry nor even incriminating interrogatories, but it did permit a refusal to answer without formal prejudice or penalty. As early as 1649, at the trial of King Charles, the right was extended to witnesses. The prosecution called Holder to give evidence against the defendant. When Holder objected, the court, finding him to be in custody as a prisoner "and perceiving that the Questions intended to be asked him, tended to accuse himself, thought fit to wave his Examination. . . ." That the right was securely entrenched for both witnesses and defendants is apparent from the fact that it was honored even in the turbulent political trials of the Restoration period. In 1660, for example, when the newly restored Stuart regime prosecuted the Puritan regicides for treason, Adrian Scroop, who had been one of the judges responsible for the execution of Charles I, interrupted the proceedings to admit that he had been a member of the tribunal that tried the king. Chief Justice Kelyng asked whether Scroop confessed to having sat on the tribunal on the day it handed down its sentence, adding: "You are not bound to answer me, but if you will not, we must prove it." Never before had a trial judge voluntarily apprised the defendant of his right to remain silent.[20]

There was no need to apprise Quaker defendants of their rights. They were demanding and aggressive. At the trial in 1662 of three Quakers who had not sworn allegiance to Charles II, the judge opened the proceedings by asking, "John Crook, when did you take the oath of Allegiance?" Crook did not offer conscientious objection to swearing as his defense. Rather, his first words were, "I have been about six weeks in prison, and am I now called to accuse myself? For the answering to this question in the negative is to accuse myself, which you ought not to put me upon; for, 'Nemo debet seipsum prodere?'" Sounding as if he had read Lilburne, Crook averred that he was an Englishman and, demanding his "birth-right," he quoted Magna Carta, several thirteenth-century reconfirmations, and the Petition of Right. The judge, nevertheless, insisted that he must take the oath of allegiance if he had not done so, and tendered it on the spot. Crook, calling for his accusers, refused to accuse himself, though taking the oath would have exonerated him, not incriminated him. They read the statute that required his oath and then read the indictment, but he was recalcitrant. He would not even plead to the indictment, insisting that the demand for him to plead was "a trepan to ensnare" him. He would answer no questions against himself, demanded a copy of the indictment and counsel. Isaac Grey and John Bolton, co-defendants with Crook, followed his example. The three finally pleaded "not guilty," but the jury convicted them.[21]

The trial of William Penn and William Mead in 1670 is worth noting for several reasons. Penn's subsequent fame gave his account of the case more than evanescent importance. Moreover, the case showed that even a viciously partisan bench respected the right against self-incrimination, though it had no regard whatever for the claims of liberty of conscience and free assembly. The indictment charged that Penn, abetted by Mead, had breached the peace by unlawfully preaching to a street crowd of some three hundred people. The trial of the two Quakers began when the court—the Lord Mayor, the Recorder, and several aldermen of London—summarily fined them for contempt because they had not removed their hats as a mark of respect. Several eye-witnesses testified that Penn had preached to the street meeting, and that Mead had been present, but one remarked that he had not seen Mead. Recorder Thomas Howell then asked Mead whether he had been present, to which Mead answered: "It is a maxim in your own law, 'Nemo tenetur accusare seipsum,' which if it be not true Latin, I am sure it is true English, 'That no man is bound to accuse himself.' And why dost thou offer to insnare me with such a question? Doth not this shew thy malice? Is this like unto a judge, that ought to be counsel for the prisoner at the bar?" Howell replied, "Sir, hold your tongue, I did not go about to in- snare you." Shortly after, Howell admitted that he looked upon Mead as "an enemy to the laws of England," not worthy of "such privileges as others have," and Mayor Samuel Starling later de- clared that Mead deserved to have his tongue cut out. Yet the same court instantly dropped the incriminating question.[22]

The remainder of the trial relates to Penn's stand on liberty of conscience, his assault on the indictment, and the celebrated fight over the jury's verdict. The jury acquitted Mead and found Penn guilty "of speaking," but not guilty of speaking to an unlawful as- sembly. The court's effort to browbeat the jury into changing its verdict made the case a landmark in English history. Adamantly refusing to convict, the jury finally defied the court altogether by changing its verdict to a clean acquittal. Penn himself contributed to their courageous stand by his stirring speeches in favor of the freedom of an English jury to decide according to their con- sciences without being menaced by the court. In the end, the court fined the members of the jury forty marks each and impris- oned them till they paid; they had followed their own "opinions, rather than the good and wholesome advice which was given" by the judges. Edward Bushell and three other jurors appealed their fines, and the Court of Common Pleas held that a jury could not be punished for its verdict. After Bushell's case in 1670 the courts no longer questioned nor molested a jury because of its verdict in a criminal case.[23]

In another great case, involving Francis Jenkes, celebrated be- cause it led to the Habeas Corpus Act of 1679, the Privy Council initially examined the prisoner to discover the circumstances surrounding his offensive political speech. No better example could be imagined to show the striking change from the Star Chamber days of the Council. At one point Lord Chancellor Finch instructed Jenkes to answer directly to a question requiring him to inform on confederates. He would not, declaring, "I desire to be excused all farther answer to such questions; since the law doth provide, that no man be put to answer to his own prejudice." King Charles himself replied, "We will take that for an answer," and the interrogation ended. Whether the Privy Council respected the right against self-incrimination or a right not to disgrace oneself by playing Judas is not clear.[24]

In the tragic trials of 1678–80 involving the hated Catholic conspirators of the so-called Popish Plot, the infamous Titus Oates gave his bigoted, perjured testimony for the prosecution. The equally infamous judges, George Jeffreys and William Scroggs, made their names synonyms for judicial tyranny. Nevertheless, the right against self-incrimination prevailed as an honored feature of English fair play. The Popish Plot was supposed to have been a conspiracy on the part of the Jesuit Order and influential English Catholics to murder the king, massacre leaders of English Protestantism, and establish the Church of Rome as the Church of England. The revelation of the conspiracy by perjured evidence led to twenty-two trials for treason, three for murder or attempted murder, and eleven for perjury and other misdemeanors. Fourteen innocent men were executed for treason. While the trials ran their course, England was seized by an hysteria which perverted the administration of criminal justice with a predisposition to believe any wild accusation by self-confessed accomplices. Yet defendants and witnesses alike benefited from the forms of due process which then included a right to be protected against anything remotely resembling an inquisitorial examination. The historian of the Popish Plot wrote:

> The inquisitorial nature of the old trial was gradually disappearing. Chief among the differences which may be noted as having arisen is the fact that the prisoner was no longer systematically questioned in court. When he was questioned, it was now, if he were innocent, in his favour. His examination was no longer what it had been in the days of Elizabeth and James I, the

very essence of the trial. Questions were still put to him, but now they were directed by the judges and not by the prosecution. The process was of no greater scope than was demanded by the necessities of the defence of a prisoner who has not the assistance of counsel. It was used as a natural means of arriving at the truth of statements made on one side or the other, and served to set in a clear light the strong and weak points of the defence. . . . The prisoner moreover could, if he wished, refuse to answer questions put to him.[25]

In 1679, for example, at the trial of Nathanael Reading, a lawyer, the defendant sought to ask Bedlow, a witness for the prosecution, whether he had planned to set fire to the city of Westminster. Lord Chief Justice Francis North interposed, "Mr. Reading, we must see justice done on all sides: if you offer to ask him any question upon his oath, to make him accuse himself, we must oppose it." Justice William Dolben added that because Bedlow had been pardoned for his crimes, the question ought not be put to him. Reading replied that the pardon remitted Bedlow's punishment but could not prevent an effort to invalidate his testimony. The pardon, North ruled, not only gave Bedlow immunity from prosecution; it saved him from being forced to "calumniate himself." The question was therefore illegal in any case: in the absence of the pardon, it exposed the witness to criminal jeopardy; despite the pardon, it exposed him to public reproach and calumny. The law was that "neither his life nor name must suffer, and therefore such questions must not be asked him." The significance of this ruling is that it marked the first time that a court construed the right against self-incrimination to protect some one against being compelled to disclose information that would merely infame or disgrace him.[26]

However harsh it may be to require a reply to a question whose answer must destroy a man's character or reputation by making him infamous publicly, there is a distinct difference between forcing him to give evidence that tends to convict him criminally and forcing him to reveal turpitude that heaps ignominy and ruin upon his head without touching him criminally. Nevertheless, objections against self-infamation and against self-incrimination originated and grew together, at least from the time of Tyndale in

1528. Cartwright, Beale, Morice, and Fuller were among those who followed Tyndale in protesting against the compulsion of self-infamation when arguing for a right against self-incrimination. That such a right extended against self-infamation may have judicially derived, without much foundation, from a proposition in the last volume of Coke's *Institutes* to the effect that a witness alleging his own infamy or turpitude is not to be heard. In a 1658 book on maxims of the common law, under the heading "nemo tenetur accusare seipsum," the first point, made on Coke's authority, was that a juror might be challenged and examined under oath only if the cause of the challenge did not touch his dishonor or discredit. By the end of the seventeenth century, the extended principle against self-infamation had become fully accepted. In 1696, for example, Lord Chief Justice George Treby declared: "Men have been asked whether they have been convicted and pardoned for felony, or whether they have been whipped for petty larceny: but they have not been obliged to answer; for though their answer in the affirmative will not make them criminal, or subject them to a punishment, yet they are matters of infamy; and if it be an infamous thing, that is enough to preserve a man from being bound to answer. A pardoned man is not guilty, his crime is purged; but merely for the reproach of it, it shall not be put upon him to answer a question whereon he will be forced to forswear or disgrace himself. . . . The like has been observed in other cases of odious and infamous matters which were not crimes indictable." The principle, as stated in Blackstone much later, was "no man is to be examined to prove his own infamy." Still later, however, judicial decisions contracted this principle to the point that the narrower right against self-incrimination remained. That the expanded principle first received judicial approval during the trials of the conspirators in the Popish Plot suggests how scrupulously the courts adhered to the right against self-incrimination at the time of its general reception by the common law. Indeed, another notable point about Reading's case in 1679 is that the court on its own initiative forbade both incriminating and infaming questions. What had been a right to decline answer, a right that had to be claimed, almost became a right to be protected against forbidden questions.[27]

The fact that the court's ruling in Reading's case protected a witness for the prosecution is irrelevant, though it might at first seem that the crown—and the court was a partisan instrument of the crown—might naturally be eager to secure the testimony of its star witness against impeachment by the defense. In the same year, at the treason trial of Father Thomas White, alias Whitebread, who was the head of the English Jesuits, Oates wanted to ask a *defense* witness whether he was a priest. Lord Chief Justice Scroggs, whose misbehavior on the bench during these trials was compared by Sir James Fitzjames Stephen "unfavourably even with the brutality of Jeffries," interposed to protect the witness: "That would be a hard question to put to him to make him accuse himself. It would bring him in danger of treason." The question was dropped. In Langhorn's trial for treason in the same year, the defendant tried to turn the tables on Oates by asking him whether he had been a Jesuit. The court chastised Langhorn because as "a man of the law" he was supposed to "know it is not fair to ask any person a question about a criminal matter that may bring himself in danger." Langhorn replied that he thought Oates's pardon put him out of danger. The court left it up to Oates to decide whether he would answer; he chose not to. In the following year, 1680, at the treason trial of Roger Palmer, Scroggs actually tried to prevent the defendant from asking his own witness a question that incriminated him, whether he had reconciled Oates to the Church of Rome.[28]

When Oates himself was put on trial for perjury in 1685, Lord Chief Justice Jeffreys kept a close watch on Oates's cross-examination of witnesses, insisting that he ask "fair" questions. The following exchange shows Jeffreys's extraordinary tenderness toward the witness's right not to be questioned against himself. The witness, Hilsley, was a Roman Catholic and probably had been or was a priest.

> OATES. My lord, I would know what was his employment there at St. Omers?
> JEFFREYS. But, Mr. Oates, you must not ask any such question; what know I, but by asking him the question, you may make him obnoxious to some penalty, but you must not ask any questions to ensnare him.

OATES. My lord, it tends very much to my defence to have that question truly answered.

JEFFREYS. But if it tends to your defence never so much, you must not subject him to a penalty by your questions.

OATES. The nature of my defence requires an answer to that question.

JEFFREYS. But shall you make a man liable to punishment, by ensnaring questions? If a man should ask you what religion you are of,—

OATES. My lord, I will tell you by and by my reason, and I hope a good one, why I ask it.

JEFFREYS. I do not believe you can have any reason; but to be sure we must not suffer any such entangling questions to be asked. . . .

OATES. I desire you would ask him, Whether they were not priests and jesuits that governed that house?

JEFFREYS. What a question is that! I tell you it is not fit to be asked. . . .

OATES. My lord, I desire to know, whether they are not set on by their superiors to do this?

JEFFREYS. That is not a fair question neither.[29]

The indulgent respect, even protective attitude, of the courts toward the right against self-incrimination reflected itself in new judicial glosses that widened the scope of the right. As indicated, it applied to questions that exposed one to disgrace or infamy. It also applied in civil cases with respect to questions that might require disclosure of information which could be used against a person in a criminal proceeding, and even with respect to questions that might expose one to the forfeiture of property by way of a penalty. A ruling of 1704 even foreshadowed the development of a new doctrine that the right against self-incrimination, which originated to protect against the compulsion of oral testimony, applied to papers and documents that might incriminate.[30]

But the right benefited most greatly from meliorations in criminal procedure that minimized the need to expose the accused to a situation in which he might incriminate himself involuntarily during his trial. The adversary system in criminal proceedings had always been a one-sided affair, with the crown enjoying advantages denied to the accused. Procedural reforms of the very late seventeenth century redressed the imbalance, giving to the accused a greater measure of parity. The right to make one's defense through the testimony of witnesses was a crucial step in this direction. In cases involving petty crimes or misdemeanors, as was the practice in civil cases, the accused could produce witnesses on his behalf, have their testimony taken under oath, and be represented by counsel. But in capital cases—and there were scores of felonies that were capital crimes—none of these benefits was available except to the crown.

Like the right against self-incrimination itself, some procedures indispensable to fair trial or due process of law imperceptibly crept into common-law practice as a result of judicial indulgence rather than statutory enactment. In 1591 the court had denied Udall permission to produce witnesses who were present in court to testify on his behalf, but in the 1630's there begin to be felony cases in which the defendant's witnesses were heard unsworn. Despite Coke's statement that there was no case, rule, or authority of any kind for the proposition that the accused's witnesses should not be sworn, the judges would not allow sworn testimony against the crown for several decades. The disadvantage to the accused was evident from the fact that unsworn testimony did not carry the same weight as testimony given under oath, a fact that judges as well as prosecutors pointed out to juries. Sir Matthew Hale, who was the Lord Chief Justice of England in the 1670's, wrote in his *Pleas of the Crown* that there was no reason for such a manifestly unfair practice. Even Scroggs, though enforcing that practice, advised a jury to "take great heed" of the unsworn testimony for the accused and "be governed according to the credibility of the person and the matter." A rule which the judges sometimes relaxed, beginning in the 1660's, was the one denying the accused felon compulsory process to call his witnesses, but there was no consistency in judicial practice. Finally, in 1696 an act of Parliament inaugurated vital reforms, applicable at first only in treason cases but extended in 1701 to all felony cases. Thereafter the defense could subpoena witnesses and offer their testimony under oath. The act of 1696 also guaranteed the accused a copy of the indictment and the right to make his "full defence by counsel learned in the law." [31]

The right to counsel was easily the most valuable to the accused's armory of defense. Justice Bulstrode Whitelock in 1649 had pointed to the anomaly in the law when he declared, "I confess, I cannot answer this objection, that for a trespass of 6d. value, a man may have a Counsellor at Law to plead for him, but where his life and posterity are concerned, he is not admitted this privilege, and help of lawyers. A law to reform this, I think would be just, and give right to people." Yet the theory of the law was that the court sat to advise the defendant in matters of law, as distinct from matters of fact, in capital cases. It was a theory that had no substance in practice; barely less fictitious was the conflicting theory that the court would permit counsel in the event that doubtful matters of law arose. In practice the defendant was left to make his own defense no matter how ignorant and helpless he was. Even Jeffreys, who rigorously enforced the rule against counsel, openly acknowledged that it worked a severe handicap: "I think it is a hard case, that a man should have counsel to defend himself for a two-penny-trespass, and his witnesses examined upon oath; but if he steal, commit murder or felony, nay, high-treason, where life, estate, honour, and all are concerned, he shall neither have counsel, nor his witnesses examined upon oath: But yet you know as well as I, that the practice of the law is so; and the practice is the law." While the statute of 1696 rectified this situation in cases of treason and "misprision" (or concealment) of treason, even requiring the court to appoint counsel "immediately upon . . . request," it was not until 1836 that there was a statute guaranteeing the right to be represented by counsel in all other felony cases. As Blackstone pointed out, the rule that counsel was not allowable in capital felonies unless some debatable point of law arose was "not at all of a piece with the rest of the humane treatment of prisoners by the English law." Politicians, who might themselves be tried for political crimes, had seen to it that every means by which an accused might make his defense had been guaranteed, but they had no stake in providing for the same degree of fairness in the trial of someone accused of robbery, murder, or other felonies.[32]

The actual practice of the courts in felony cases, nevertheless, was more humane than their abstract rule of law. At the trial of

Lord Oxford in 1717, who stood impeached for every degree of crime—misdemeanors, felonies, and high treason—the House of Lords permitted him to have the benefit of counsel on any point of law relating to the treason charge "and also to make that Lord's full Defence on the Articles of Impeachment of High Crimes and Misdemeanours, as well in matters of fact as matters of law." By the middle of the eighteenth century a practice had "sprung up," as Stephen put it, of permitting counsel to do everything for the defendant accused of felony except address the jury for him. Thus Blackstone, though aspersing the "defect" in the law, noted that the judges themselves were so sensible of it "that they never scruple to allow a prisoner counsel to instruct him what questions to ask, or even to ask questions for him, with respect to matters of fact: for as to matters of law, arising on the trial, they are *entitled* to the assistance of counsel." [33]

Accordingly, by the early eighteenth century both judicial and statutory alterations in procedure made it possible for a defendant to present his defense through witnesses and by counsel. As a result, though he always retained his right to address the court unsworn at the close of his trial, and to range freely over any matters of his choice, he was no longer obliged to speak out personally in order to get his story before the jury, to rebut incriminating evidence, or to answer accusations by the prosecution. Indeed, by the end of the seventeenth century a subtle change in both the tone and procedure of criminal trials was noticeable. Pressing, urging, and bullying the defendant began to die out. The prosecution made its case without interrogating him at all, while the court's practice of questioning him in a hostile manner died with Lord Holt in 1710. [34]

The security of the state after the Revolution of 1689 was doubtless the most important force working for greater and greater fairness in criminal trials. Political trials of any sort became fewer in number, while the incidence of treason trials dropped precipitously. What once passed for treason became regarded as seditious libel, a mere misdemeanor, for the trial of which the accused possessed all rights in making his defense. The typical criminal trial was no longer a "state" trial in the old sense that the government instituted the prosecution against a political enemy whose destruction it sought. After the Revolution, as Stephen said, the administration of criminal justice became "dignified . . . decorous and humane; and . . . it was mainly left in the hands of private persons [to prefer charges], between whom the judges were really and substantially indifferent. . . ." Therefore, the circumstances provoking a need to claim the right against self-incrimination substantially diminished.[35]

At the same time, another remarkable development in the law contributed to the same end. The principle of disqualification for interest, which emerged first in civil cases, gradually extended to criminal cases, rendering the accused incompetent to be a witness in his own cause. Anyone having a personal stake in the outcome of a trial was thought to be so irresistibly tempted to perjury that his testimony was regarded as untrustworthy. No one could have a greater stake in the outcome of a suit than the party criminally accused. While he could speak on his own behalf, unsworn, if he desired, he could not give testimony under oath. In point of fact, the defendant had never been sworn because his oath was a form of proof belonging to an older form of trial, antedating trial by jury. His sworn testimony would have been, if not decisive in his behalf, at least to his great advantage. Toward the end of the seventeenth century, the notion that his sworn testimony was an alien, advantageous form of proof was augmented and then supplanted by the belief that his interest so disqualified him as a witness that he must be totally excluded from the stand. The competency of the criminally accused to testify under oath was not finally established in England until 1898! His incompetency which was established at about the time when the right against self-incrimination became firmly secured, blended with the idea that he should be safe-guarded against cross-examination that might elicit his self-incrimination. The two principles, however diverse in origin and purpose, worked to the same end: the protection of the accused from exposure to questions whose answers might *tend* to put him in criminal jeopardy. It is difficult to say whether the interrogation of the accused at his trial ended altogether because of exaggerated indulgence of his right against self-incrimination or because his word was not trusted. The latter idea, in any event, buttressed the former.[36]

By the early eighteenth century, the right prevailed supreme in all proceedings with one vital exception, the preliminary examination of the suspect. In the initial pre-trial stages of a case, inquisitorial tactics were routine. Statutes of 1554 and 1555 had authorized justices of the peace to take the examination of persons suspected of felony. Examination on oath was not authorized, and if it ever existed was flatly condemned by the common law. Every *vade mecum* for petty magistrates, beginning with the manuals of Fitzherbert and Lambard in the 1580's, declared examination on oath to be a violation of the *nemo tenetur* maxim. But the proposition as phrased in Dalton's guidebook allowed the justices of the peace considerable leeway in the conduct of the examination of suspects: "The offender himself shall not be examined upon Oath: for by the Common Law, *Nullus tenetur seipsum prodere*. Neither was a mans fault to be wrung out of himself, (no not by Examination only) but to be proved by others, until the Stat. 2 & 3 P. & M. cap. 10 gave Authority to the Justices of the Peace to examine the Felon himself." Other manuals made the same point more tersely, saying that the suspect might be examined before being committed, "but not upon Oath, because *Nemo debet seipsum accusare.*" The principle, in other words, was restrictly narrowly to prohibition of the oath and to the right of the suspect to refuse answer. But the purpose of the examination was to wring out of him a confession of his guilt, unsworn, or enough damaging testimony to put him on trial for the crime. Secret examinations characterized by bullying and incriminating interrogatories were common practice. Justices of the peace were prosecutors and policemen as well as magistrates. Any admissions which they might extort from a suspect could be introduced against him as evidence at his trial. His signature to an actual confession was as good as his plea of guilty. If he refused to acknowledge his confession or repudiated it in court, the testimony of two justices of the peace or of any two witnesses, to the fact that he had confessed, would be enough to convict. For all practical purposes, therefore, the right against self-incrimination scarcely existed in the pre-trial stages of a criminal proceeding.[37]

On the other hand, there were in the pre-trial stages two significant developments that were directly related to the right. One was the end of the use of torture, the other the rule that confessions had to be voluntary. Stephen observed that the "general maxim, that confessions ought to be voluntary, is historically the old rule that torture for the purpose of obtaining confessions is, and long has been illegal in England." Torture, though never recognized as legal by the common law, had by no means been uncommon in matters that concerned the state's security. The royal prerogative was the sole basis for its existence, and it could be authorized only by a warrant from the Privy Council. England defined torture as the application of pain to the body for the purpose of extorting from the prisoner information or evidence against himself or supposed accomplices. If the objective was not incriminating admissions or a confession, physical torment or pain was not torture. Thus *peine forte et dure*, the purpose of which was to force an obstinately mute prisoner to plead to an indictment, was not torture and bore no relation to the right against self-incrimination. The "punishment strong and hard"—pressing to death—was never used to coerce a confession, only to compel a plea, and the objective was satisfied as much by a plea of not guilty as by one of guilty.[38]

Similarly, "cruel and unusual punishments," in the words of the Bill of Rights of 1689 were not torture either. The barbaric butchery, for example, that followed conviction for treason was regarded as a penalty inflicted on one who had been tried and found guilty by the ordinary processes of the law. Aggravated forms of the death penalty for murder, as well as treason, persisted long after the Bill of Rights, but in the eighteenth century gibbeting, mutilation, dissection, and the like were performed only after the doomed victim was hanged until dead. In any case, his punishment was in no legal sense regarded as a form of torture and had nothing to do with self-incrimination.[39]

Torture in the English usage of the term died out after 1640. Where there is a right against self-incrimination, there is necessarily a right against torture. The rise of the right against self-incrimination was not solely responsible for the disuse of torture to obtain confessions. But the same forces that brought about the right against self-incrimination brought about an end to the use of torture. The act abolishing the Star Chamber, for example, specified that neither the king nor his Privy Council should have any jurisdiction or authority "to examine or draw into question" anyone on matters touching life, limb, liberty, or property, which were henceforth to be tried in the ordinary common-law courts by the ordinary course of law. But the *threat* of torture did not cease until later. In a treason trial of 1662 the defendant declared in open court, "I confess I did confess it in the Tower, being threatened with the rack." Despite the coercion, the court accepted his confession as evidence against him. The act of 1696 governing treason trials introduced a change requiring that confessions must be made willingly, without violence, and in open court. Frightening a prisoner, by the threat of torture, into incriminating admissions appears to have disappeared before that time. But physical maltreatment short of torture or the threat of such maltreatment was undoubtedly employed in some felony cases to force confessions after the act of 1696.[40]

Informed commentators took notice of the connection between the *nemo tenetur* maxim and both the abolition of torture and the introduction of the rule that coerced confessions are illegal. In 1730 Sollom Emlyn, in the introduction to his edition of the collected state trials, proudly remarked, "In other countries, Racks and Instruments of Torture are applied to force from the Prisoner a Confession, sometimes of more than is true; but this is a practice which Englishmen are happily unacquainted with, enjoying the benefit of that just and reasonable Maxim, *Nemo tenetur accusare seipsum.*" Lord Chief Baron Geoffrey Gilbert, in his *Law of Evidence*, written before 1726 though not published until thirty years later, stated that though the best evidence of guilt was a confession, "this Confession must be voluntary and without Compulsion; for our Law in this differs from the Civil Law, that it will not force any Man to accuse himself; and in this we do certainly follow tht Law of Nature, which commands every Man to endeavour his own Preservation; and therefore Pain and Force may compel Men to confess what is not the truth of Facts, and consequently such extorted Confessions are not to be depended on." Gilbert's phrasing, "our Law . . . will not force any Man to accuse himself," expressed the traditional English formulation of the right against self-incrimination, or rather against *compulsory* self-incrimination. The element of compulsion or involuntariness was always an essential ingredient of the right and, before the right existed, of protests against incriminating interrogatories. Gilbert stated the principle in the most general terms and grounded it in the eighteenth century's most appealing rationale, the "Law of Nature." By that time, the principle was so self-evident that no further explanation was required.[41]

Gilbert's statement, however, introduced a significant point, namely that extorted confessions are not to be depended upon because under pain a man might confess anything. He might even be induced to confess by bribery or the promise of some reward. A rule therefore developed that a confession not freely given of one's own volition was suspect and, consequently, inadmissable as evidence. In 1741, for example, the court examiner asked a witness whether he had seen the accused freely sign his confession at the preliminary hearing. Only after an affirmative answer was given did the order issue for the statement to be read. In the same murder case, the counsel for another defendant objected to the reading of his client's confession unless the examining magistrate was first asked whether the confession was made voluntarily, "For if it was not voluntarily, it ought not to be read." The judge agreed that a confession "extorted by threats, or drawn from him by promises" could not be introduced. A generation later it had become an accepted rule that any confession not free and voluntary must be rejected because no credit could be given to it. Thus the rule against coerced confessions became grounded on a separate rationale unrelated to the right against self-incrimination. There remained, however, an indissoluble nexus between the two, because both involved the involuntary acknowledgment of guilt. Every coerced confession was a violation of the right against self-incrimination unless made under a grant of indemnity—the American usage is *immunity*—against prosecution for the confessed crime. In such a case the question would arise, independent of the right against self-incrimination, whether the inducement to confess—the grant of indemnity—rendered the testimony untrustworthy because of the witness's interest.[42]

This point, as well as the nexus between the right against self-incrimination and the rule against involuntary confessions, emerged in the Parliamentary debates in 1742. Following the refusal of Nicholas Paxton, the Solicitor of the Treasury, to answer incriminatory questions before an investigating committee, the Commons passed a bill of indemnity immunizing incriminatory testimony against prosecution, but the bill failed in the House of Lords. The Secretary of State, Lord Carteret, presented the victorious argument when he declared: "It is an established maxim, that no man can be obliged to accuse himself, or to answer any questions which may have any tendency to discover what the nature of his defence requires to be concealed. His guilt must appear either by a voluntary and unconstrained confession . . . or by the deposition of such witnesses as the jury shall think worthy of belief. . . . The first requisite qualification of a witness . . . is disinterestedness. . . . But this qualification, my Lords, the bill now before us manifestly takes away; for every man who shall appear against the person into whose conduct the Commons are enquiring, evidently promotes, in the highest degree, his own interest by his evidence . . . Nothing, my Lords, is more obvious than that this offer of indemnity may produce perjury and false accusation. . . ." Lord Chancellor Hardwicke, one of the great English lawyers of all time, agreed with Lord Carteret.[43]

The rule against involuntary confessions remained the principal bulwark of the right against self-incrimination in the pre-trial stages of a criminal proceeding. It was not until the mid-nineteenth century that the preliminary examination of the suspect became a judicial process in which the right was fully respected. An act of 1848 required that the suspect be present at the examination of the witnesses accusing him and have the liberty to cross-examine them. The act also required the examining magistrate to inform the suspect that though he might make a statement if he wished, he was not obliged to say anything; moreover, he must be warned that anything he said might be given in evidence against him at his trial.[44]

The *nemo tenetur* maxim had come a long way from its mysterious origins. Reputedly a canon-law maxim, it had never existed in any canon-law text. At best there was the general principle in Gratian, wiped out by Innocent III, Aquinas, and the Inquisition, that no man had to come forward voluntarily to confess a crime for which he was not even suspected. Gradually that came to mean that no one was bound to take an oath requiring him to answer truthfully to interrogatories concerning his guilt if he was merely suspected and had not been formally charged with crime. There was a natural repugnance to self-destruction, opposition to the oath as a form of spiritual torment, and conscientious objection to forswearing oneself. Conscience and an unwillingness to supply the evidence to convict oneself remained major forces against the oath; when it was abolished, they remained reasons for refusing to answer incriminating interrogatories.

The fact that the preliminaries of presentment according to common-law procedures had not first been fulfilled also accounted for much of the resistance to the oath. Anyone swearing it might be required to confess to a crime of which he had not been accused by the indictment of a grand jury; that the crime might not otherwise be proved against him aggravated detestation of the oath. The customary accusatorial system of criminal justice, consecrated by the symbolism of Magna Carta and then by the Petition of Right, fortified depiction of the oath as an instrumentality of the inquisitorial system, alien and contrary to the old liberties of the subject. Opposition to the oath came to focus on the fact that it compelled self-incrimination. There was nothing remarkable, therefore, in the perfectly natural step of claiming that it was unjust, unnatural, and immoral to demand that a man furnish the evidence against himself even when all formalities of common-law accusation had first been fulfilled. The prisoner demanded that the state prove its case against him without his aid, even though he knew in advance the charges against him and confronted the witnesses who testified against him. To furnish testimonial evidence against himself, with or without oath, was likened to drawing one's blood, running oneself upon the pikes, or cutting one's throat with one's tongue. Thus, the initially vague maxim that no man is bound to accuse himself had come to mean that he was not required to answer against himself in any criminal cause or to any interrogatories that might tend to expose him to prosecution. Glimmerings of this principle can be found even in sixteenth-century rulings of the Star Chamber, of the Court of Chancery, and of the common-law courts. The Levellers, led by Lilburne, even claimed a right not to answer any questions concerning themselves, if life, liberty, or property might be jeopardized, regardless of the tribunal or government agency directing the examination, be it judicial, legislative, or executive.

The claim to the right emerged in inquisitorial examinations, initially conducted by the Church, then by the State. It emerged also in the context of the great political struggle for constitutional limitations on arbitrary prerogative; during the late sixteenth century and early seventeenth, it was a focal point in that struggle to establish individual liberties and more representative government. It foreshadowed the basic constitutional issue of the Stuart period: was the monarchy or, for that matter, was the state supreme or, as Lilburne once put it, was England "Governed, Bounded, and Limitted by Laws and Liberties?" [45] Constitutional government developed out a struggle to fetter powers that had been sovereign unto themselves. The later and best-known stage of the struggle centered on the crown's power to tax and imprison at discretion; but the first and formative period of the struggle had focused on the power of a prerogative court, the High Commission, to exact an inquisitional oath which forced men to accuse themselves. Thus the claim to a right against self-incrimination raised the generic problem of the nature of sovereignty in England and spurred the transmutation of Magna Carta from a feudal relic of baronial reaction into a modern bulwark of the rule of law and regularized restraints upon government power.

The claim to this right also emerged in the context of a whole cluster of criminal procedures whose object was to ensure fair play to the criminally accused. It harmonized with the principles that the accused was innocent until proved guilty and that the burden of proof was on the prosecution. It was related to the idea that a man's home should not be promiscuously broken into and rifled for evidence of his reading and writing. It was intimately connected to the belief that torture or any cruelty in forcing a man to expose his guilt was unfair and illegal. It was indirectly associated with the right to counsel and to have witnesses on behalf of the defendant, so that his lips could be sealed against the government's questions or accusations. It was at first a privilege of the guilty, given the nature of the substantive law of religious and political crimes. It was also a protection of the innocent. But the right became neither a privilege of the guilty nor a protection of the innocent. It became merely one of the ways of fairly determining guilt or innocence, like trial by jury itself; it became part of the due process of the law, a fundamental principle of the accusatorial system. The right implied a humane or ethical standard in judging a person accused of crime, regardless how heinous the crime or strong the evidence of his guilt. It reflected consideration for the human personality in that respect, but it also reflected the view that society benefited by seeking his conviction without the aid of his involuntary admissions. Forcing self-incrimination was thought not only to brutalize the system of criminal justice but to produce weak and untrustworthy evidence.

Above all, the right was most closely linked to freedom of religion and speech. It was, in its origins, unquestionably the invention of those who were guilty of religious crimes, like heresy, schism, and nonconformity, and, later, of political crimes like treason, seditious libel, and breach of parliamentary privilege—more often than not, the offense was merely criticism of the government, its policies, or its officers. The right was associated then with guilt for crimes of conscience, of belief, and of association. In the broadest sense it was a protection not of the guilty, or of the innocent, but of freedom of expression, of political liberty, of the right to worship as one pleased. In sum, its subtle and slow emergence in English law was, in the words of Dean Erwin N. Griswold, "one of the great landmarks of man's struggle to make himself civilized," "an expression of the moral striving of the community," and "an ever-present reminder of our belief in the importance of the individual." The symbolic importance and practical function of the right was certainly a settled matter, taken for granted, in the eighteenth century. And before that it was part of the heritage of liberty which the common law bequeathed to the English settlers in America.[46]

CHAPTER XI

The American Colonies in the Seventeenth Century

The right against self-incrimination evolved in America as part of the reception of the common law's accusatorial system of criminal procedure. American constitutions enshrine the various rights that cluster around that system; indeed, our "bills of rights" deal for the most part with such procedural matters as indictment, trial by jury, confrontation, representation by counsel, freedom from unreasonable searches and seizures and from cruel and unusual punishments, bail, and habeas corpus. The right against self-incrimination had been, of course, a common-law right since the middle of the seventeenth century. As such it was part of the common-law inheritance.

That does not mean that the right was easily, ritualistically, or uniformly adopted in America. Virginia, the New England colonies, and Maryland were settled before the overthrow of the Star Chamber and the High Commission, before the Leveller agitation and the treason trials of John Lilburne, and before the right had become entrenched in the common law. Whether the right became known and respected in these early colonies, and, if so, when, how, and why it became known and respected are unanswered questions. Given the extraordinary diversity of the American colonial experience, there is reason to ask the same questions even about the colonies that were established after the right had achieved common-law status. Its reception cannot be taken for granted in any colony. Despite professed American commitments to principles of fair play in the administration of criminal justice, there were many grievous inconsistencies and lapses in practice, some of them inexplicable, just as there were inexplicable omissions from bills of rights. As late as 1787, for example, the right to the writ of habeas corpus, surely one of the most treasured of all rights, was constitutionally protected by only four states. Most rights, in fact, whether recognized by some great English statute such as the Petition of Right or the Habeas Corpus Act of 1679, or whether transmitted by common-law tradition like trial by jury, had to be fought for and won in America against England or local authorities or both. Before as well as after its acceptance in England, the right against self-incrimination had to win its way to recognition in every colony.

The story is obscure because the evidence is so thin. "Legal development," as Samuel Eliot Morison wrote, "is probably the least known aspect of American colonial history. Judicial opinions were not recorded in the colonies, no year books were issued, and the printed materials for legal and judicial history have been so scanty as to preclude the more cautious historians from dealing with this important side of colonial life; while less cautious historians have indulged in generalization for which slight support can be found in fact." This situation seems to be particularly relevant to the history of the right against self-incrimination in colonial America. In 1908 the Supreme Court of the United States resorted to "every historical test" to plumb the early meaning and importance of the right; the Court's purpose was to determine whether it was "a fundamental principle of liberty and justice which inheres in the very idea of free government," entitling it to be included within the concept of due process of law. The 1908 decision, which was adverse to the right, was founded upon "history," although the justices were unbelievably ignorant of the English backgrounds and admitted that they were forced to "pass by the meager records of the early colonial time, so far as they have come to our attention, as affording light too uncertain for guidance." The justices did observe, however, that the famous trial of Anne Hutchinson in 1637 proved that the Massachusetts authorities were "not aware of any privilege against self-incrimination or conscious of any duty to respect it." The Court's opinion—and its history—was all the more remarkable, because it found that the right had never been regarded as part of the law of the land of Magna Carta. Nevertheless, the justices asserted that the right had become embodied in the common law of all the states by 1787; they even declared that the existence of this particular right "distinguished" the common law "from all other systems of jurisprudence." [1]

Although colonial legal history is so little known, the published legal records for a few colonies are extraordinarily rich and detailed, yet are nearly unmined. The *Archives of Maryland*, for example, now extend through some seventy thick volumes, covering the records of the various branches of the government during the colonial period. Yet that mountain of information yields only a few scraps of data about the right against self-incrimination—and that is more than can be gleaned from the published records for some other colonies.[2]

Nor do unpublished records seem to hold more information about the right. The mammoth book, *Law Enforcement in Colonial New York: A Study in Criminal Procedure (1664-1776)*, by Julius Goebel and T. Raymond Naughton, was based on apparently exhaustive research in voluminous manuscript sources, yet the authors concluded: "We think that the existence before the Revolution of a privilege of defendants is an illusion. The fruit grown from the seed of the maxim *nemo tenetur prodere seipso* was an exotic of Westminster Hall, and of it neither the local justices in England nor in New York had eaten, or if they had, they took good care to keep their knowledge to themselves." [3]

Goebel and Naughton added that the fact that the "privilege against self-incrimination did not develop in a jurisdiction where the inhabitants were constantly rummaging in the storeroom of common-law liberties, was the fault of neither the judiciary nor the bar, but was the result of a prevailing indifference which is reflected in the general temper of colonial legislation." There had been a "great to-do" in the mother country during the early seventeenth century over the oath *ex officio* in ecclesiastical procedure; and, "some disgruntled subjects had protested in 1640" that the secular adoption of a similar procedure involved a similar infraction of fundamental right. Yet, "nothing had come of the

protest." There was, we are further informed—or misinformed—
"a failure to carry over notions about self-incrimination to temporal justice," as is supposedly evident from penal legislation that
permitted convictions on the sworn testimony of one or two witnesses or on the defendant's confession alone.[4]

Aside from this remarkably belittling and inaccurate portrayal
of the history of the right in England by distinguished legal historians, the fact is that convictions based on voluntary confessions
or on the evidence of witnesses do not disprove the existence of
the right. The question remains, however, whether the right did
exist in New York or in any of the other colonies.

There is no doubting that England intended her law, the common law included, to be transplanted to her colonies. The common law, administered by local justices of the peace, quarter sessions courts, and the central courts of Westminster, was but one
branch of English law. Among others, there were chancery law,
admiralty law, ecclesiastical law, and Star Chamber law; Coke described fifteen branches of English law, each administered by its
own judiciary. But the law that was supposed to govern most
criminal offenses, including all felonies, was the common law. The
first generations of colonists may have been most familiar with the
customary law of the local courts of the county, borough, or
manor in civil matters, but it was the common law, especially its
instrumentalities and procedures, that they knew best and emulated in criminal matters.[5]

The first charter issued to an American colony, that for Virginia in 1606, included a cherished provision that the colonists and
their descendants were to "have and enjoy all liberties, franchises,
and immunities . . . as if they had been abiding and born, within
this our Realm of England, or any other of our said dominions."
In time the colonists inferred from these words broad guarantees
of civil liberty and self-government, although in 1606 the words
imported considerably less. But they did signify trial by jury and
whatever related procedural rights the criminally accused then
possessed in England. Subsequent charters of Virginia, of New
England in 1620, of Massachusetts Bay in 1629, of Maryland in
1632, and of later colonies carried a similar guarantee. Royal in-

structions to the mother colony of Virginia as early as 1606 specified that all laws should be "as neer to the common lawes of England, and the equity thereof, as may be," and explicitly provided for trial by jury. An ordinance of 1621, known at the time as Virginia's Magna Carta, ordered her government "to imitate and follow the Policy of the Form of Government, Laws, Customs, and Manner of Trial, and other Administration of Justice, used in the Realm of England, as near as may be. . . ." To the north, in the colony of New Plymouth, the first law recorded, in 1623, established trial by jury, and the code of 1636 for that colony declared that all proceedings should be according to "the presidents of the law of England as neer as may be." When Massachusetts adopted a "Body of Liberties" in 1641, the first provision paraphrased chapter twenty-nine of Magna Carta. In effect, the Great Charter of England, the Petition of Right, and all that they symbolized made the ocean crossing with the colonists.[6]

An exact duplication of English common-law criminal procedure did not exist anywhere in the colonies in the seventeenth century, especially not in the earlier decades. Nor was the procedure the same in the various colonies. Significant variations existed among them, as well as between England and them, because of the differences among the colonies and between the new world and the old. The thirteen colonies were settled at different times—the first settlements in Virginia and Georgia were separated by a century and a quarter—under different circumstances by different groups for different purposes. Great distances, frontier conditions, political and religious dissimilarities, and a scarcity of lawyers and law books required improvisation that resulted in some indigenous legal developments from colony to colony, especially on the substantive side of the law. But the common law was so much a part of the colonial inheritance that not even the popular hostility to England during the Revolutionary era could alter that system as the basis of the emergent American law. Indeed, from a purely legal interpretation the American Revolution itself, as the Americans saw it, was largely the result of England's disregard of the common-law rights of the colonists. When the First Continental Congress of 1774 issued a Declaration of Rights and Grievances, the American position was founded in part on the assertion that "the respective colonies are entitled to the common law of England. . . ." [7]

After the Declaration of Independence, every state except Connecticut and Rhode Island provided by constitution or statute that the common law of England as previously practiced should remain in force until such time that it might be altered legislatively. What is significant is that the American devotion to the common law was based not on a respect for its crabbed technicalities nor on its many reactionary features, but on its emphasis upon fundamental law and the liberty of the subject. Americans abhorred Coke's disquisitions on feudal tenures; they venerated the Coke who sought to fix limits on the royal prerogative, who declared that the common law will void an act of Parliament that is against common right, who made the imperishable remark that Magna Carta "is such a Fellow, that he will have no Sovereign," and who resisted incriminatory oaths, arbitrary imprisonment, and taxation without legislative consent. In American thinking, the common law was a repository of constitutional principles that secured individual rights against government intrusion. [8]

The common law was no shelter, however, for the great substantive rights of the spirit and the mind; it was hostile to freedom of expression, whether religious or political. The courts of the common law punished a wide variety of offenses against religion and God. The trials of Campion, Udall, Barrow, and Penry are among the more sensational reminders. Lesser prosecutions for blasphemy, recusancy, impiety, and reviling the church, were more common. On the political side, laws against treason and sedition were enforced to muzzle criticism of the government. The right against self-incrimination, as we have seen, arose as a shield against inquisitions into crimes essentially political or religious in nature. It was an indispensable ally to Lambert's proverb that thoughts be free and need pay no toll, or, rather, was a device of desperation on the part of a Nonconformist to ward off the necessity of responding to incriminating interrogatories that sought to establish his guilt for a crime of opinion. The same conditions that gave rise to the invention of the right in England could reproduce it in America.

To say that the struggle to establish the right in America dupli-
cated or even paralleled the struggle in England would be a gross
exaggeration, because there was never in the colonies a Court of
High Commission or of Star Chamber. Yet, they had their rough
equivalents at certain times in certain colonies—under Berkeley,
for example, in Virginia, or under Andros in New England.
There were also established churches, laws against sedition and
heresy, and a system of censorship. There was, additionally, a considerable degree of persecution of obstreperous or overly conscientious Nonconformists. The banishment of Roger Williams
for disseminating "newe and dangerous opinions" against the authority of the magistrates was, for example, only the most celebrated case of its kind in Massachusetts. Anne Hutchinson, John
Wheelwright, eight of their Antinomian followers, Peter Hobart
and others involved in the Hingham Affair, Robert Child and his
six associates, and Samuel Gorton were all convicted for seditious
sermons, petitions, or remonstrances against the civil authority between 1637 and 1647. In 1652 William Pynchon, a magistrate, by
fleeing from the colony, avoided the distinction of being the first
person to be prosecuted in Massachusetts for opinions expressed in
print. The legislature condemned his tract, which had been licensed in England, as "erronyous and hereticale" and commanded
the public executioner to burn it. There had been several earlier
cases in which the legislature censored or burned unpublished
manuscripts. In 1654 the first president of Harvard, Henry Dunster, became the first person to be prosecuted under common-law
process for a religious speech; his crime was talking against infant
baptism. The persecution of the Baptists and Quakers which began in Massachusetts in the 1650's and lasted through the century,
though religiously inspired, was legally grounded on the victims'
censure of the government and their tendency to breach the peace
in seditious fashion. The example of suppression in Massachusetts
is typical as well as familiar. But for differences in names and
dates, the seventeenth-century experience of other colonies was
similar.[9]

Not surprisingly the first American echoes of the English experience with the right against self-incrimination were heard in Massachusetts where Puritan statecraft, religion, and intolerance could

be practiced in a way never possible in England and where the most widely read book, next to the Bible, was probably Foxe's *Book of Martyrs* with its dozens of instances in which Protestants claimed that no man was bound to accuse himself. Interestingly, the claim first cropped up in Massachusetts in 1637, the same year that John Lilburne, to whom, said Dean Erwin N. Griswold, "we owe the privilege," made his first refusal to respond to ensnaring questions "for fear," he pleaded, "that with my answer I may do myself hurt." The protagonist of the Massachusetts affair, which occurred about six months earlier, was the Reverend John Wheelwright, a new arrival in the colony. Wheelwright, who had been deposed from the ministry in England because of his religious heterodoxy, was the brother-in-law of Anne Hutchinson. He shared with her the Antinomian idea that faith alone, rather than good works, was necessary for salvation because everything depended upon God's grace. In Massachusetts, where orthodoxy was represented by the covenant of works, Antinomianism was a dangerous heresy.[10]

Wheelwright, in a Fast Day Sermon from the pulpit of John Cotton's church in Boston, offended the ministry and the magistracy by inviting his listeners to reject the prevailing orthodoxy. He "inveighed against all that walked in a covenant of works," John Winthrop recorded in his *Journal*, ". . . and called them antichrists, and stirred up the people against them with much bitterness and vehemency." Wheelwright's sermon, according to Charles Francis Adams, threw the community "into a state of commotion without a parallel in its history. It was, perhaps, the most momentous single sermon ever preached from the American pulpit." It was, at any rate, politically as well as religiously explosive, for Wheelwright and Hutchinson were allied with Governor Henry Vane against Deputy-Governor John Winthrop and most of the ministry of the colony. Modern readers may find the distinctions that seventeenth-century Calvinists made between a covenant of grace and a covenant of works to be theologically incomprehensible and arid; but those distinctions then divided men, said Winthrop, as bitterly as they were elsewhere divided by the differences between "Protestants and Papists." Consequently, Wheelwright's outspoken remarks could be taken as painfully offensive to the Winthrop faction, which dominated state and church. "Priest and inquisition," as Adams wrote, "had given way to bishop and high-commission, and they in their turn to minister and magistrate." Most ministers and magistrates regarded Wheelwright's sermon as tending to sedition and disturbance of the peace. As a result, the General Court, or provincial legislature, which also exercised supreme judicial authority, summoned Wheelwright for an examination.[11]

Wheelwright's friends were determined that he should receive a fair hearing. They had apprised him in advance of the reason for the examination, and on his appearance the General Court immediately informed him that he had been summoned to account for certain controversial passages in his sermon. The examiners produced a copy of that sermon and asked whether he acknowledged it as his own. Wheelwright, who had come prepared, turned over to them his own copy. The General Court then dismissed him "gently" while it studied the evidence. When Wheelwright was summoned the next day, his supporters were ready with a petition signed by some forty persons, mostly members of John Cotton's church. They demanded a right to be present, and they questioned the authority of the legislature to "proceed in cases of conscience," which allegedly belonged only within the jurisdiction of their church. The General Court curtly answered that they would advise what was "fit to be done" in matters of conscience; moreover, that while privacy was never used in judicial proceedings, "in preparation thereto by way of examination of the party," privacy was proper. The doors were therefore closed to the public, and the preliminary examination began.[12]

Wheelwright, on being advised that he was to be asked questions that might tend to clarify the meaning of certain seemingly offensive passages, demanded to know whether he had been sent for as an innocent or guilty person. Neither, was the answer; he was only suspected. When he demanded to know who were his accusers, they told him that his own sermon, which he had voluntarily acknowledged, accused him and, therefore, the court might proceed "*ex officio.*" Winthrop, in his account of the trial, stated that at the mention of an *ex officio* proceeding, "great exception was taken, as if the Court intended the course of the High Commission, &c." Reference to that hated body having thrown the court on the defensive, they apologetically explained that *ex officio* meant merely by the court's own authority and was therefore "no cause of offence, seeing the Court did not examine him by any compulsory means, as by oath, imprisonment, or the like. . . ." All that was wanted, they explained, was for Wheelwright to answer some questions, but he still refused.[13]

His friends among the deputies finally persuaded him that he had misunderstood the court's reference to *ex officio*. Nevertheless, he would not answer the first question, whether he knew that most of the ministers taught the doctrine called a covenant of works. The record merely shows that "he did not desire to answer," but his stand provoked one of his friends to object that "the Court went about to ensnare him, and to make him to accuse himselfe." Wheelwright then refused to answer any further questions. Winthrop defensively explained that the reason for the controversial question "was not to draw matter from himselfe whereupon to proceed against him"—a tacit recognition of his right not to answer an incriminating question, or, at least, a denial that the court sought to convict him on his involuntary confession. Winthrop was certainly right in pointing out that the testimony of witnesses was easily obtainable, and the court already had Wheelwright's sermon. Because there was sufficient evidence to proceed against him, "neither was there any need" to draw matter from him to convict him.[14]

The rest was anticlimactic. Faced with Wheelwright's recalcitrancy, the court reconvened in public session, after summoning all the ministers "to beare witnesse" and to give advice as needed. Witnesses did, in fact, testify concerning their opinion of the sermon; every minister except Cotton pointed to "the great dangers that the Churches and Civill State were falne into" because of religious differences engendered by the views of the defendant. They acknowledged that their doctrine of salvation was identical to what he had condemned as the covenant of works. He himself acknowledged his sermon and sought to justify it. The court then voted that he had "run into sedition and contempt of the Civill authority." Later that year they sentenced him to banishment.[15]

At about the same time, they tried and convicted Anne Hutchinson, although her "so-called trial," in Adams's words, "was, in fact, no trial at all, but a mockery of justice rather—a bare-faced inquisitorial proceeding." If so, it was because she chose to debate her judges. They asked her questions about her beliefs and she answered voluntarily and candidly, never once objecting to incriminating interrogatories. Nor had Wheelwright objected either, once the preliminary examination was over and he was tried publicly. Nor had those who supported him, after his conviction, by signing a petition that censured the General Court for having condemned the truth of Christ. The leading petitioners, including two deputies, William Aspinwall and John Coggeshall, were called to account for their "scandalous and seditious" remarks. Like Wheelwright and Hutchinson, they sought to justify their sentiments; they also stood vainly on the right to petition, rather than on a right not to accuse themselves. All were convicted and punished.[16]

In these Antinomian prosecutions, the facts in each case were really incontestable. Anne Hutchinson's teachings were a matter of public knowledge. Aspinwall's signature was on the petition. Wheelwright gave the court the manuscript of his sermon. None of these persons would or could deny their religious convictions; rather, they flaunted them, openly justifying themselves, seeking converts, and abusively castigating all, including those in authority, who denied the truth as they saw it. When asked to explain their religious opinions in a public trial, they saw not an incriminating interrogatory but an opportunity to reveal God's word. Under such circumstances it is not to be expected that any one would have claimed a right against self-incrimination. It was only when Wheelwright was preliminarily examined behind doors that barred the public and when the court referred to its *ex officio* authority, bringing to mind the dread oath *ex officio*, that there were objections to the procedure on ground that it sought self-accusation. When that occurred, the court promptly denied that its purpose was to provoke or elicit damaging admissions from the lips of the accused by "any compulsory meanes." If the defendants incriminated themselves, they did so freely, even aggressively.

The proof of their "guilt," judged by the standards then prevailing, was abundant and incontestable. Had Wheelwright acted out of character by claiming a right against self-incrimination in open court, when confronted by witnesses who could testify to what he had said, there is no reason to believe that the court would have pressed him to answer against himself. What Winthrop said of the preliminary hearing, which was roughly the equivalent of a grand jury proceeding or an investigation by justices of the peace, was equally applicable to the public trial: there was no need to draw matter from Wheelwright against himself. Had the Antinomians kept their beliefs to themselves, they probably would not have been molested; despite the intolerance of the Winthrop faction, they did not conduct inquisitions to ferret out religious deviants or secret conventicles. On the other hand, intolerance or, as the Bay authorities saw the matter, the imperative of preserving the state and church against internal subversion, was far stronger than respect for procedural niceties. If there was a limited recognition of the right against self-incrimination in the Wheelwright case, it worked no miracles: the right was no more established in New England because of Wheelwright than in England, in 1637, because of Lilburne. State and church in Massachusetts Bay were too insecure, the opposition too weak.

The Body of Liberties of 1641 and its subsequent explication show more clearly the state of the right in early Massachusetts. That remarkable document, one of the earliest codifications of the law, was intended, at least in part, as a bill of rights or, rather, a bill of restraints on the discretionary power of the magistrates. In 1635 the deputies, Winthrop recorded, "conceived great danger to our state" because the magistrates, "for want of positive laws, in many cases, might proceed according to their discretions. . . ." It was therefore agreed that the colony should have a "body of grounds of laws, in resemblance to a Magna Charta, which . . . should be received for fundamental laws." After several committees had deliberated over a period of six years, the General Court adopted the revised Magna Carta, or Body of Liberties. Although it was no flaming libertarian document—blasphemy and the worship of false gods were among the capital crimes—there were a number of significant guarantees that matched the best of English fundamental law. Beginning with a paraphrase of chapter twenty-nine of Magna Carta, the Body of Liberties provided for equal protection of the laws, compensation for the public taking of property, the abolition of monopolies, open access to all courts and town meetings with the right to speak and write respectfully, trial by jury, the right to bail, freedom from double jeopardy, freedom from cruel physical punishments, the right of all freemen to vote, a limited freedom from imprisonment for debt, and the right to travel.[17]

In this context Liberty 45 provided in somewhat equivocal terms for the right against self-incrimination: "No man shall be forced by Torture to confesse any Crime against himselfe nor any other unlesse it be in some Capitall case where he is first fullie convicted by cleare and suffitient evidence to be guilty, After which if the cause be of that nature, That it is very apparent there be other conspiratours, or confederates with him, Then he may be tortured, yet not with such Tortures as be Barbarous and inhumane." Clearly Liberty 45 was intended to restrict the use of torture, but just as clearly the purpose of the restriction was to establish, at least partially, a right against self-incrimination, for it completely abolished torture to force a confession of one's own guilt. It permitted torture only for the purpose of incriminating others, and then only after the victim had been convicted in a case where it was obvious that he had had confederates. However chilling Liberty 45 seems to the modern reader, it was comparatively humane in 1641. Yet it most certainly did not recognize a right to remain silent before an incriminating question in a public trial, when the defendant had been duly accused. Liberty 45 even left unanswered the question how far a magistrate might go in exacting a confession from an accused person in a capital case. Indeed, neither Liberty 45 nor any other provision of the Body of Liberties explicitly outlawed the use of the oath *ex officio*. Liberty 3 provided that no man should be obliged to take any oaths except "such as the Generall Court hath considered, allowed, and required," and while it may seem inconceivable that any Puritan body should have required the oath *ex officio*, the Body of Liberties did not prevent that possibility.[18]

The ambiguities in the Body of Liberties perplexed even its authors. The need for clarification arose almost immediately when the General Court was confronted by an alarming increase in sexual offenses for which proof of guilt was difficult to obtain. On behalf of the General Court, Governor Richard Bellingham, early in 1642, sought the counsel of the magistrates and elders of the Bay colony and of kindred settlements in Plymouth and Connecticut. The most perplexing problem concerned the procedures to be followed in the gathering of evidence. Was the testimony of one witness, together with "other circumstances," sufficient to convict in certain capital cases, or was no conviction possible without two witnesses? More to the point, "How farr a magistrate may extracte a confession from a delinquente, to acuse himselfe of a capitall crime, seeing Nemo tenetur prodere seipsum"? [19]

Regrettably, only the answers of the three Plymouth elders have survived. One of them, Charles Chauncy, who was to become the second President of Harvard College, had twice been before the High Commission and once was imprisoned, but on both occasions eventually submitted. He took a hard view on the question of coercing confessions, though he opposed the oath *ex officio* as a snare to conscience that was not warranted by God's word. "But now," Chauncy replied, "if the question be mente of inflicting bodly torments to extracte a confession from a mallefactor, I conceive that in maters of higest consequence, such as doe conceirne the saftie or ruine of stats or countries, magistrats may proceede so farr to bodily torments, as racks, hote-irons, &c., to extracte a conffession, espetially wher presumptions are strounge; but otherwise by no means." Thus Chauncy would not force self-incrimination by the oath, but he would employ torture in matters such as sedition or treason. Unless a man confessed his guilt, Chauncy would not support his conviction on the evidence of one witness only, "espetially not in capitall cases." [20]

The views of the Reverends John Reynor and Ralph Partrich were more in accord with Liberty 45. Reynor would accept an "unforced confession when there was no fear or danger of suffering for the fact," thus, inferentially, recognizing a right against self-incrimination. He would not inflict any punishment, least of all torture, in order to extract a confession, not even in a capital case. "That an oath (ex officio)," he added, "for such a purpose is no due means, hath been abundantly proved by the godly learned, & and is well known." However, even Reynor believed that in a capital case, if the suspect's guilt was indicated by "commone reporte, or probabilitie," it was the duty of the examining magistrate to use all "due means"—oath and torture excluded—to procure a confession, "for though nemo tenetur prodere seipsum, yet by that which may be known to the magistrat by the forenamed means, he is bound thus to doe, or els he may betray his countrie and people to the heavie displeasure of God. . . ." In sum, Reynor would have permitted the sharpest questioning to snare a confession in such a case; he said nothing of the rights of the suspect except that he should not be forced to confess by oath, torture, or fear.[21]

Partrich's opinion was similar, but more humane in tone. He thought that the magistrate was bound to "sift" the accused and by force of argument to draw from him "an acknowledgement of the truth," but he condemned the use of any "violent means" to extract a confession even in a capital case. Neither oath, torture, nor the threat of any punishment was proper, because by such means of examination, "a fearfull innocente" might be induced to confess; "if guilty, he shall be compelled to be his owne accuser, when no other can, which is against the rule of justice." [22]

Winthrop, who received the opinions of the elders and magistrates of Massachusetts Bay, New Haven, and Connecticut, as well as of Plymouth, recorded that "most" answered that in a capital case if one witness or "strong presumptions" pointed to the offender, the judge could examine him "strictly, and he is bound to answer directly, though to the peril of his life." If, however, there was merely "light suspicion," the judge should not press him to answer, "nor is he to be denied the benefit of the law, but he may be silent, and call for his accusers. But for examination by oath or torture in criminal cases, it was generally denied to be lawful." Nothing in the answers of the Plymouth elders, not even in Chauncy's, supported Winthrop's statement that the accused was obligated by law to answer "to the peril of his life" if his guilt seemed strong. According to Winthrop, however, the right against self-incrimination—"he may be silent"—existed in a capital case only if there was slight suspicion. Whether the distinction between strong and light suspicion obtained in noncapital cases is uncertain; perhaps a person accused of a minor crime did not have to answer against himself at all. The tone of the answers of the

Plymouth elders suggests that the seriousness of the crime warranted procedural exceptions, though no one recommended exceptions to the Biblical rule requiring two witnesses in capital cases.[23]

The state of the law in early Massachusetts and Connecticut, with respect to the right against self-incrimination, seemed at best to be similar to that of England in 1641, before the Leveller agitation. At worst, Winthrop's restrictive summary of the matter, if reliable, indicates that only a stunted version of the right existed in New England. In old England, even before the close of the sixteenth century, the courts, including the Star Chamber and High Commission as well as King's Bench, recognized in principle that the *nemo tenetur* doctrine meant, at the least, that no man was bound to answer "to the peril of his life," regardless of the presumptions, suspicions, or evidence against him. In view of Winthrop's summary, which admittedly lacks corroboration, it is misleading to allege that the law of Massachusetts at about the time of the Body of Liberties "roughly paralleled" England's, or that the Body of Liberties included a meaningful right against self-incrimination, or that the prohibition of torture for the purpose of compelling a man to confess any crime against himself was an advance beyond English practice, torture having ended in England in 1641. Winthrop's statement meant that Massachusetts lagged behind England in the development of the right against self-incrimination.[24]

Legal practice, or the law in action, tells at least as much as legal ideals. The cases of Samuel Gorton and of the Robert Child remonstrants suggest that the right against self-incrimination held no honored place in Massachusetts legal practice, despite Puritan familiarity with the *nemo tenetur* doctrine. Those cases also suggest that when confronted by obstreperous religious enemies, the Puritan authorities would surrender *any* standard of criminal procedure in order to insure the triumph of their suppressive objectives.

Samuel Gorton had a marvelous capacity to provoke the authorities to silence him at any cost. They first convicted him in 1637, shortly after his arrival in Massachusetts from England, for loudly advocating the Antinomian heresy. The sentence called for fines, imprisonment, and banishment. Even the Pilgrim fathers in

Plymouth found his "seditious carriage" so unsettling that they banished him. In 1642, Gorton took refuge near Newport in tolerant Rhode Island. This time his rasping abusiveness, rather than his eccentric religious beliefs, got him in trouble. When one of his servants was tried before Governor William Coddington, who had been banished from Massachusetts for supporting Wheelwright, Gorton gave evidence for the defense. He denied Coddington's authority, reviled him, and accused him of improper practices in the conduct of the trial. For his contempt of court, Gorton was indicted on fourteen counts, one of which, significantly, was his claim that the governor had tried to make him accuse himself. According to the indictment, Gorton had said, "Ye intrude oathes, and goe about to catch me." That this should have been regarded as a criminal utterance indicated that the right against self-incrimination, even if only in rudimentary form, was respected in Newport. Convicted, whipped, and once again banished, Gorton and the followers of his sect settled in what is now Warwick, Rhode Island. There, the long arm of Massachusetts reached out to expose him to Star Chamber treatment.[25]

Gorton had purchased his land in Warwick from Indians whose title was questioned by a rival tribe that had put itself under the protection of Massachusetts. In 1634 the General Court summoned Gorton and his followers to answer Indian complaints, but he replied in a contemptuous letter that, according to the authorities in Massachusetts, was full of "horrible and detestable blasphemies, against God, and all Magistracie." When Gorton defied further warnings and repeated his flagrantly offensive charges, Governor Winthrop dispatched a military expedition of over forty men to capture him and those who had subscribed to his letters. After a battle, the soldiers seized Gorton and eight of his followers as prisoners and marched them back to a Boston jail to await trial before the General Court. Compelled to attend Sunday services, Gorton requested and received permission to speak after the sermon. Before a horrified congregation he openly declared his religious views, denying the Trinity, abominating baptism and several other sacraments, rejecting the existence of heaven or hell, and reviling the magistrates as idols.[26]

The General Court, advised by the elders, found twenty-six

counts of blasphemy against the Gortonites. The trial was devoid of any semblance of a common-law proceeding. It was an old-fashioned inquisition which inevitably ended in a conviction. Only the nature of the sentence troubled the court. All the magistrates except three voted for the death penalty, but a majority of the deputies dissented. The court finally sentenced the prisoners for an indefinite period to hard labor in leg-irons, under threat of death for a repetition of any of their blasphemous opinions. After six months, the authorities banished Gorton and his followers in order to rid the colony of their dangerous presence.[27]

When Gorton later published a tract telling the world the story of his persecution, he bitterly protested his examination by "Inturgatories." The court, consisting of about a dozen magistrates and forty deputies, assisted by many ministers, had "questioned and examined us apart, to the uttermost they could, to get some matter against us from our owne mouths," and had sent elders "unto us in prison, frequently putting questions unto us to get occasion against us. . . ." The close interrogation had continued for "two or three weeks." The impression given by Gorton is that the court had violated sacred English liberties including freedom from coerced self-accusation. That the court showed no respect for that freedom or for fair procedures is undeniable, but there had been no breach of the letter of the Body of Liberties. Liberty 45 had simply prevented torture for the purpose of extorting confessions, while Liberty 94, which spelled out the capital laws, had explicitly decreed that blasphemy, the crime charged against the Gortonites, was to be punished by death. Moreover, Gorton's letters, aggravated both by his speech in church, which had been heard by many witnesses, and by what Winthrop had called "strong presumptions," warranted a strict examination, according to the elders' interpretation of the *nemo tenetur* doctrine the year before. Gorton, in self-defense, had indirectly claimed a right not to answer incriminating interrogatories. The authorities, confronted by those whose guilt was proved by their own religious professions, could fall back on the alleged obligation of the guilty to answer directly even to the peril of life, although the law in England by this time clearly protected a defendant against that very obligation.[28]

The Gorton case fits the pattern of its precursors, showing that religious persecution and inquisitorial tactics produced the claim by the outraged victim that he should not be the unwilling instrument of his own harm. In view of the fact that the "third degree" has not disappeared more than three centuries later, notwithstanding constitutional and judicial injunctions of long standing, it is hardly shocking to find Governor Winthrop behaving rather like Archbishop Laud when confronting religious subversives who, in that age, were invariably also political subversives. The official who is completely convinced that he has in custody a dangerous criminal whose guilt must be exposed can be irresistibly tempted to ignore what Lilburne once called "formalities, niceties, and punctilios." It is, nevertheless, unexpected to discover that the Puritan authorities in Massachusetts could employ something like the oath *ex officio* and do so as late as 1647.

That is what happened in the case of the Child Remonstrance which capped a series of assaults on church and state during the critical years of English Civil War. In Massachusetts, where the Congregational polity prevailed, only church members possessed the political rights of freemen and the free exercise of religion. In England, where the Presbyterians controlled Parliament and the Independents the army, "such a vast liberty was allowed," wrote Winthrop in 1646, doubtless with a shudder at the very thought of sects or liberty, that even "the anabaptists, antinomians, familists, seekers," and their like enjoyed "their liberty of conscience." Appalled by the specter of either a Presbyterian establishment or the anarchy of sectarianism, Massachusetts remained resolutely neutral in the war, hoping to avoid making enemies in England so that the New England way in church and state might be maintained. But the repercussions of the struggle for power in England inevitably struck New England, threatening its own brand of independency.[29]

In 1645, Peter Hobart, the pastor in Hingham, "being of a Presbyterial spirit," said Winthrop, and "the principal in this sedition," provoked a sensational quarrel over the powers of the magistrates and the liberties of his church. He even accused the government of having violated the colonial charter. The Hingham affair led to an unsuccessful attempt to impeach Winthrop. It was hardly over when William Vassall of Scituate, a man of "factious spirit, and always opposite to the civil governments of this country and the way of our churches," organized a petition on behalf of those who were not members of the established church. The petitioners, demanding religious freedom, urged that both Massachusetts and Plymouth should be "wholly governed by the laws of England," and they requested Parliament, no less, to redress provincial denials of the liberty of subjects "both in church and commonwealth." Intervention by Parliament was what the authorities feared most; moreover, they had made it a capital crime should anyone "treachorously or perfediouslie attempt the alteration and subversion of our frame of politie or Government fundamentallie." Vassall's petition invited severe retaliation, but before appropriate measures could be decided upon, the Child Remonstrance worsened the crisis by spreading the seditious opposition to the government.[30]

Dr. Robert Child, a truculent Presbyterian physician who had just returned from England, joined with Samuel Maverick, a well-known Anglican merchant, and five others, none of whom were freemen, in a movement for expansion of religious and political liberties. Their public remonstrance daringly affronted the General Court. The remonstrants depicted a colony groaning under arbitrary rule, mismanaged and sunk into depression, immorality, and tyranny. There was no "settled forme of government according to the lawes of England," no adequate body of laws or liberties, no respect for the "natural rights" of "freeborne subjects of the English nation." Illegal imprisonments and unjust taxation jeopardized the enjoyment of life, liberty, and property, while thousands of law-abiding taxpayers were denied the privilege of voting. The rulers regarded English laws as foreign and Massachusetts as an autonomous state rather than a mere colony or corporation of the mother country. Justice demanded that "civill liberty and freedom be forthwith granted to all truely English," regardless of church membership, "as all freeborne enjoy in our native country," and toleration for all godly men "not dissenting from the latest and best reformation" in England. If these reforms were not introduced, the remonstrants threatened, they would go to England and petition directly to Parliament.[31]

The General Court, after consulting with the elders, issued a public declaration repudiating the contemptuous charges of the remonstrants, some of whom then prepared to sail for England to carry out their threat of appealing to Parliament. The General Court summoned the culprits who aggravated their crimes by refusing to answer questions, denying the jurisdiction of their prosecutors, and demanding to know the charges. According to Governor Winthrop and the official records, the public proceedings were both formal and proper. Although Winthrop denied the defendants the right of making an appeal to England, due process was provided as in any case tried by the General Court itself. That meant, as Roger Williams, John Wheelwright, Anne Hutchinson, and Samuel Gorton had learned, that the aggrieved party, the legislature, was accuser, prosecutor, judge, and jury. There was a indictment against the Child remonstrants, consisting of twelve counts, one of which specified that when they had first been called to account for their "evil expressions . . . they refused to answer." The records do not make clear whether their refusal was grounded in part on an unwillingness to incriminate themselves or whether they merely denied the jurisdiction of the General Court.[32]

Unfortunately, none of the remonstrants published a report of the proceedings giving their side of the story. But Samuel Maverick, who was convicted with the others, when petitioning the General Court in 1649 for a remission of the fines imposed upon him, enumerated "errors" in the proceedings. His first was that "your whole proceeding against us seemes to depend on our refusall to answer Interrogatories upon oath," a committee of magistrates and deputies having examined the defendants, presumably in private, before the public trial.[33]

There is no doubting the fact that Governor Winthrop sought to exact self-incriminatory statements from the defendants. Indeed, the second trial came about when he set a trap by which they incriminated themselves through their private papers, which the government seized. Although the first trial had ended in a conviction and heavy fines, the court made no attempt to collect them or to restrict the liberty of the remonstrants. They took the bait as expected. Dr. Child immediately prepared to sail for England to prosecute his charges against Massachusetts, but on the very eve of his departure, Winthrop sent officers to seize Dr. Child's sea-trunk and to search the study of his fellow conspirator, John Dand. The search yielded three documents, addressed to the English authorities, confirming the government's worst suspicions: the purpose of the conspiracy was to destroy both state and church in Massachusetts.[34]

The first document appealed the unjust convictions of the remonstrants, renewed their original demands, and, from the standpoint of Massachusetts, treasonously asked for the appointment of a royal governor. The second was a petition from twenty-five nonfreemen of the colony endorsing all the subversive requests of the remonstrants. The third, as George Lyman Kittredge has observed, was "openly revolutionary." It was a series of queries by the remonstrants, inviting England to abrogate the charter of the colony, and to investigate whether ministers and magistrates of the establishment had committed high treason by a variety of deeds and words. Although the incriminating documents proved, in Winthrop's opinion, a capital offense, the prisoners were freed, after conviction, on payment of crushing fines. Severer sentences might have invited English intervention and, at home, some sort of populistic uprising. The Child remonstrants paid heavily for their opinions and daring, but they helped mightily to force the government to accept certain reforms. A law of 1647 extended to nonfreemen the right to vote on local matters, the right to hold local office, and the right to serve on juries. A year later, the legislature superseded the Body of Liberties of 1641 by adopting a far more comprehensive and detailed code, the General Laws and Liberties of 1648. The code of 1648 re-enacted Liberty 45 of the Body of Liberties, outlawing the use of torture to coerce self-incrimination, though permitting torture after conviction to force the revelation of fellow conspirators. Liberty 3 was also re-enacted, forbidding all oaths except as the General Court might require. As the Maverick petition of 1649 proved, there was at least one case in which a Puritan legislature had sought to require answers under oath to incriminating interrogatories.[35]

In Connecticut, where the legal code was influenced by that of Massachusetts, the legislature adopted a liberalized version of Liberty 45 in 1673, omitting the exception to the rule against torture. Although no one could be physically forced to testify against himself, nor by tacit understanding be put to any equivalent of the oath *ex officio*, Connecticut did not prohibit incriminating questions nor bullying the prisoner. But even in England at that time, the right against self-incrimination merely vested a lawful option to remain silent; it did not immunize either the suspect or the accused against sharp and intimidating interrogation that aimed at drawing his confession. There is nothing showing a tender regard for the rights of criminal defendants in Connecticut or elsewhere in the mid-seventeenth century. At the preliminary examination the justice of the peace very likely badgered suspects to confess; that examination retained the character of the old inquisitorial proceeding. Even at the trial the magistrate probably urged the accused to admit his guilt, and the prosecutor, who in lesser cases was probably the examining magistrate himself, surely conceived his duty to be the wresting of an incriminating admission. Yet the suspect or defendant was always free, as in the case of John Tharpe of New Haven, in 1666, to refuse the court's importunities. When Tharpe was instructed to reply to the charges against him, he simply responded that "he could not accuse himselfe," and he denied the charges, thereby throwing the burden of proof upon the prosecution. Massachusetts in 1657 gave statutory recognition to the principle that the defendant should be presumed innocent until proved guilty, yet in Massachusetts, as in Connecticut and Plymouth, men were convicted in some cases not because their guilt was proved but because they refused to take an oath of purgation. Such an oath, by which the criminally accused swore his innocence, was routinely used in prosecutions for selling liquor to Indians.[36]

To the innocent who had no conscientious objections against swearing, or to the guilty who were willing to commit perjury, the oath of purgation was a boon. But to the guilty who dared not commit the mortal sin of falsely swearing and to the innocent who did conscientiously object to oaths, the oath of purgation was a trap. Failure to take it had the same incriminating effect as a confession, and in such cases the oath of purgation operated like the oath *ex officio*. In Maryland, however, the testimony of the accused was not taken on oath. In an inquiry of 1647, involving illicit trade, the governor directed his commission to obtain the truth by testimony given under oath, if necessary, by all persons "other than the parties themselves." By the ordinary practice of the common law, the accused was never examined under oath.[37]

Rhode Island, the most enlightened of all the colonies, boldly declared in 1647 that its form of government was "democraticall." Since the founding of Providence in 1636 by Roger Williams, religious belief and practice had enjoyed exemption from the power of the civil government. There was a greater scope for the expression of opinion, political as well as religious, than in any other colony. Nothing like purgative oaths or the oath *ex officio* was known in Rhode Island. The great code of 1647 that embodied the laws of the colony, recognizing that "the consciences of sundry men . . . may truly scruple the giving or taking of an oath," made "solemn" testimony equivalent to testimony given under oath. The provisions of the code on criminal procedure borrowed heavily from English statute and common law, especially from Dalton's *Countrey Justice*. There was an express prohibition against taking the examination of a suspect on oath, yet nothing in the elaborate provisions of the code recognized the right of the accused to be immune from compulsory self-incrimination. One might expect that the laws of Rhode Island, of all the colonies, would most likely have included some application of the *nemo tenetur* maxim to the proceedings following the preliminary examination, but the maxim was unrecognized. On the other hand, Rhode Island has the distinction of having been the first government in the Anglo-American world to have protected the right to counsel. In 1669 the colony provided that "it shall be the lawful privilege of any person that is indicted, to procure an attornye to plead any poynt of law that may make for the clearing of his innocencye." England did not permit counsel in treason cases until 1696, in some felony cases until 1836. With counsel as his spokesman, an accused person could avoid the necessity of answering personally to incriminating questions. Thus, the respect accorded by Rhode Island to common-law procedures and her guarantee of the right of counsel at an early date suggests, in the absence of evidence to the contrary, that progressive Rhode Island may have given to the right against self-incrimination the same recognition as England did in the seventeenth century. But that conclusion is speculative.[38]

The passage of time, greater familiarity with English decisions and law books, and the resentment against the inquisitorial tactics of prerogative courts had the combined effect of making the right better known. In New York under Dutch rule it was not a right at all, but the concept behind the right was not unknown. In Massachusetts a quarter of a century after the Child Remonstrance the judiciary may have routinely respected invocation of the right. In Virginia, shortly after, there is definite evidence of its acceptance.

The claim, futilely made, that the criminally accused should not be obligated to furnish evidence of their own guilt, was first advanced in New York by English victims of religious persecution. The government of New Netherland in 1661 arrested Henry Townsend and Sam Spicer because they had given lodging to a Quaker and had listened to him preach. Governor Peter Stuyvesant and his councilors summoned the prisoners and demanded that they confess. The record says that "they would not criminate themselves" and insisted that their guilt be proved. It was, and they were convicted, but not until they were fined and imprisoned for their contempt in not answering to the charges. Townsend finally confessed, though he insisted that regardless of what they might do to his person or his property, his opinions belonged to him and his soul to God. A year later Stuyvesant arrested John Browne, who was also a Quaker, on a charge of having maintained illegal conventicles in his home. Browne also refused to incriminate himself and announced that he would accept any consequences which God would permit his persecutors to inflict on him. They kept him in a dungeon, in solitary confinement, on bread and water, but were not able to break his spirit. In the end, he, like Spicer, was banished from New Netherland. But they left behind a band of English Quakers who were obviously familiar with the principle that no man should be required to accuse himself. When the English occupied New Netherland in 1664, making it New York, they brought with them common-law procedures and a policy of religious toleration that were welcome to the English settlers.[39]

That changes were occurring in Massachusetts was apparent from the obscure case of John Stewart in 1671. The crime was a stabbing, not heresy or sedition; the court was a mere county court on the colony's western frontier, not the General Court in Boston; and there was not enough evidence against the defendant to convict him. He "refused to confess against himself," with the result that the court dismissed him with only a "serious admonition." Whether the court honored the defendant's refusal to incriminate himself because the right had become accepted as part of the common law is uncertain. It is not even certain that the defendant invoked the right when refusing to confess. In any case, the treatment of Stewart sharply contrasts with that meted out to Wheelwright, Gorton, or Maverick a generation earlier.[40]

Virginia is one of several colonies in which the origin of the right is shrouded in mystery. The only reference to the right in Virginia's long colonial history crops up, perhaps significantly, in 1677, in the aftermath of Bacon's Rebellion. The first General Assembly that met after Sir William Berkeley left the governorship enacted a statute whose phrasing suggests that the right, for witnesses as well as for the criminally accused, had already existed in Virginia, had been recently deprived, and required reaffirmation. The Grand Assembly, then the supreme judicial body as well as provincial legislature, "declared that the law has provided that a witness summoned against another ought to answer upon oath, but noe law can compell a man to sweare against himself in any matter wherein he is lyable to corporal punishment." This declaratory statement of the law followed a rule of the common law of England which since 1649 had extended the right against self-incrimination to witnesses. Not a scrap of information exists to show the reason for the enactment of the Virginia statute of 1677. It followed Governor Berkeley's bloody suppression by summary trials and executions of Bacon's supporters, in the wake of the rebellion. One surmises cause and effect: the statute was a reaction to Berkeley's inquisitional methods to detect and punish the rebels. But there is no evidence, only surmise. About a century later, Virginia became the first state to elevate what had merely been a common-law right to constitutional status.[41]

In Pennsylvania, which followed Virginia's example in 1776, the history of the right against self-incrimination is clearer. The trial of Penn and Mead at Old Bailey in 1670 proves that William Penn was familiar with the right against self-incrimination. The author of *The People's Ancient and Just Liberties Asserted* and of *The Great Case of Liberty of Conscience* founded a colony in which one might expect, as in the instance of Rhode Island, that the right would be respected. The "fundamental" laws of 1682 provided rules for the courts and the conduct of trials; these laws specified the rights of accused persons, yet did not guarantee the right against self-incrimination. Nevertheless, an incident of 1685 is revealing. In that year the Pennsylvania Assembly impeached a judge, Nicholas More, who was also a member of the Assembly, for his various misdemeanors on the bench. More's troubles began when he browbeat a witness and trapped him into damaging admissions after the witness had denied knowing anything about a stolen pig; that is, More forced him to incriminate himself and then ordered the jury to find him guilty of perjury. In its investigation of More's judicial conduct, the Assembly required Patrick Robinson, the clerk of More's court, to produce certain court records. Robinson refused, provoking the Assembly to order his arrest and summon him for an examination. Confronted by his recalcitrance and possible complicity in More's misconduct, the Assembly assured Robinson that "they did not in the least seek any Occasion against him." He replied "evasively" and, despite the Assembly's assurance, "refused to make Answer to the Point," alleging that his interrogators acted arbitrarily and lacked authority over him. Because the Assembly had virtually offered Robinson immunity against prosecution in return for his testimony and records, they protected his right against self-incrimination. Therefore, his obdurate behavior, which was compounded by his affront to the Assembly, provoked the members to declare him to be a "publick Enemy" undeserving to hold public office. They also expelled Judge More from membership in the house. The episode is significant as the first recognition in America that the right against self-incrimination could extend to a legislative investigation.[42]

Four years later, in 1689, the government of Pennsylvania was split by a struggle for power between Penn's deputy governor,

John Blackwell, a Puritan, and his Quaker councilors. The quarrel occasioned an investigation by the governor in which he was forced to acknowledge the right against self-incrimination. Blackwell, having been thwarted at every turn by his jealous and resentful councilors, sought to impeach their leader, Thomas Lloyd. To support his action, Blackwell was driven to an autocratic interpretation of the provincial Charter of Liberties which he claimed vested all power in the Lord Proprietor; in Penn's absence, his deputy, Blackwell himself, possessed that power. But Penn's "Frame of Government" of 1682 had also vested great powers in the council. Joseph Growdon, a member of the council, paid William Bradford, the local printer, to publish 160 copies of the charter and Frame of Government with anonymous comments by Growdon, for use in the struggle against Blackwell. Infuriated by this "high presumption," Blackwell, believing that nothing could be printed without his prior license, brought the matter before the council where he traced the responsibility to Growdon. On interrogation, Growdon refused to answer any questions concerning the unlicensed publication of a pamphlet described by the governor as of "a dangerous nature." Even on threat of censure, Growdon answered, "He was not bound to accuse himself." A year later, incidentally, Growdon became a provincial judge and in 1693 became speaker of the house.[43]

Unable to satisfy his wrath against Growdon, the governor summoned William Bradford before the council. Bradford, who was the only printer in the province, indeed the only printer south of Boston, was no more co-operative than Growdon. According to his manuscript account of the examination, Bradford would not even admit to printing the pamphlet.

GOVERNOUR: I desire to know from you, whether you did print the Charter or not, and who set you to work.
BRADFORD: Governour, it surely is an impracticable thing for any man to accuse himself, thou knows it very well.
GOVERNOUR: Well, I shall not much press you to it, but if you were so ingenuous as to confess, it should go the better with you.
BRADFORD: Governour, I desire to know my accusers, I think it very hard to be put upon accusing myself.

GOVERNOUR: Can you deny that you printed it: I know you did print it and by whose direction, and will prove it, and make you smart for it too since you are so stubborn.

Despite alternating threats and cajolery, Bradford stood fast. He had been invited to Pennsylvania four years earlier by Penn himself to be the Printer, and believed that he might earn his living by printing whatever came to hand. He meant no offense, he said, but believed that no imprimatur had been appointed over him. "Sir," Blackwell replied, "I am Imprimatur and that you shall know." He threatened to bind Bradford to a bond of five hundred pounds to print nothing that he had not licensed "or I will lay you fast." On the other hand, if Bradford confessed, he might expect favor. The examination turned to the risks of unlicensed printing, the governor taking the position that printing, if not "rightly managed" could be a great mischief. Printing the Charter of Liberties at that critical time was proof of such mischief. Bradford, by contrast, thought that because the charter was the foundation of the laws, the people had a right to know its provisions.

GOVERNOUR: There is that in this Charter that overthrows all your Laws and priviledges: Governour Penn has granted more priviledges or power than he hath himself.
BRADFORD: That is not my business to judge of or determine. But if anything be laid to my charge let me know my accusers. I am not bound to accuse myself.
GOVERNOUR: I do not bid you accuse yourself; if you are so stubborn and will not submit, I will take another Course.

Thwarted by both the right against self-incrimination and Quaker intransigence, Blackwell soon resigned.[44]

A few weeks after the Growdon-Bradford examination in Philadelphia, there was a rebellion in Boston that overthrew Governor Edmund Andros and his Dominion of New England. Andros had enjoyed power that Blackwell never knew. His commission as governor of a territory that extended from Maine to the Jerseys, vested in him supreme legislative, executive, judicial, and military authority, subject to the concurrence of a council whose members he could suspend at pleasure. His administration levied taxes without the consent of a representative legislature, harshly enforced his laws, and offended the religious sensibilities of the Puritans. News of the Glorious Revolution in England touched off the overthrow of Andros in Boston, followed by a rash of justifications for the event. Among the grievances alleged against Andros's oppressive rule was the charge that persons were summoned from remote counties before the governor and council for examinations which were "unreasonably strict, and rigorous and very unduely ensnaring to plain unexperienced men." Andros had apparently turned the tables on Winthrop's descendants by forcing them to incriminate themselves. The experience inspired a fresh respect for a common-law rule that had become firmly established in England. In 1692, a year after Massachusetts received a new charter restoring a large measure of self-government, an act of the legislature controlling the sale of liquor obligated all persons to give evidence under oath respecting breach of the laws, excepting the accused party, his family, and servants. The act, in other words, exempted him from having to testify against himself and even exempted his dependents.[45]

That this statute was enacted in 1692 is ironic, for it was the year of the Salem witchcraft trials. Surprisingly, the records of those trials, which in some cases are quite complete, show that very few of the accused claimed the right against self-incrimination. The courts that tried these cases engaged in a parody of common-law procedures, though many of the forms of procedure were present; when suited to the objective of the prosecution, which was to secure confessions, they were rigorously followed. Giles Cory, for example, would not plead to his indictment. By standing "mute," he refused to consent to trial by jury, without which he could not be convicted. He thereby saved his property from the forfeiture which would have followed conviction. But, because of his refusal to plead either guilty or not guilty, the court subjected him to *peine forte et dure*. Obstinately remaining mute under the crushing weight of the rocks, he finally died. Cory was the only martyr to that peculiar form of torture in our history. Yet *peine forte et dure* was not calculated to coerce a confession.[46]

Torture for that purpose had been outlawed in Massachusetts since 1641. Nevertheless, the judges in the witchcraft trials not only showed no familiarity with the right against self-incrimination; they repudiated its invocation, coerced confessions and used both psychological and physical torture. Although Cotton Mather advised against the "Un-English" method of torture, he urged "Crosse & Swift Questions" to bring the witches to a confession. Some women maintained their declarations of innocency for eighteen hours, "after most violent, distracting, and draggoning methods had been used with them, to make them confesse," according to Thomas Brattle who protested the prosecutions. Many, he reported, with tears in their eyes, said that they thought "their very lives would have gone out of their bodyes; and wished that they might have been cast into the lowest dungeon, rather than be tortured with such repeated buzzings and chuckings and unreasonable urgings as they were treated withal." Others were persuaded to confess by the denial of sleep or threats of horrible punishment. Several men who would not confess were tied "Neck and Heels" until the blood gushed from their noses. The greatest inducement to confession was the promise of pardon coupled with the prediction of conviction and death for refusal. Of the nineteen who were hanged, all on the basis of spectral evidence, none confessed; not one of the fifty or so who confessed to being witches were executed. Although the witchcraft trials seem to disprove the existence of the right against self-incrimination in Massachusetts, they were an exception. They were certainly the product of a frenzy or craze that was extraordinary in procedural as well as in other respects.[47]

The case of Thomas Maule, an irascible Quaker merchant of Salem, is more typical. In 1695 he published a book that was licensed and printed in New York after the Boston authorities denied a license. Maule assaulted the witchcraft trials and characterized them as a plague inflicted by the wrath of God upon New England for the persecution of the Quakers and other sins. His language was so vehement that the authorities arrested him for "wicked Lyes and Slanders, not only upon private Persons, but also upon Government, and likewise divers corrupt and pernicious Doctrines utterly subversive of the true Christian religion and professed faith." The sheriff searched his house, seized all available copies of the book, and brought Maule before the lieutenant-governor and council in

Boston for examination. But Maule was an aggressive witness who knew his rights. He absolutely refused to answer any of the "divers Insnaring Questions" and demanded a trial by a jury of his peers in his own county. His report of the examination does not reveal the response of the council, but Maule won his point although he paid dearly for it. Bail was set at a prohibitive price, thereby keeping him in jail for a year until the time of his trial, but he did win that trial by a jury of the vicinage. He conducted his own defense quite adroitly, openly maintaining the opinions in his book, and he won from the jury an acquittal. He then wrote a pamphlet describing his persecution, his refusal to incriminate himself before the council, and his victory at the trial.[48]

In Maryland a couple of years earlier it was not a dissenter like Maule but a man of great standing who invoked the right against self-incrimination. Sir Thomas Lawrence, Secretary of Maryland, a judge of the provincial court, and a member of the governor's council, broke politically with the government. Lawrence was a patronage mongerer who got into trouble by flagrantly selling offices for fees. He replied to criticism by denouncing the government, thereby lending credence to the suspicion that he was a Jacobite like his fellow conspirator, Edward Randolph. The council suspended him from his various offices and summoned him for examination. Charged with having received an incriminating letter from Randolph, Lawrence was ordered to give it to the council for determination whether it contained "treasonable treacherous matter." Lawrence refused "for that he Conceives he is in no wise bound to accuse himself or Ridicule Mr. Randolph." [49]

The council showed as little respect for Lawrence's right not to incriminate himself as for his other rights. The sheriff searched his pockets and discovered the letter which was read before the council. They summarily found him guilty of unspecified "high Crimes and Misdemeanours" and ordered him jailed without bail. Lawrence later claimed that they found him guilty first and then discovered the letter by an illegal search. He appealed his conviction to the Assembly, which had its own grievances against the council, and presented a perfect case against the legality of his commitment. He had been convicted without a jury trial and without knowledge of the charges against him or the names of his accusers;

had been arrested and searched without a warrant; and had been denied bail and habeas corpus, "which is the great security of the lives & Libertyes of every English Subject." The House vindicated English liberties by supporting Lawrence on every point and finding that all the proceedings against him were arbitrary and illegal. Set free, he recovered all his privileges.[50]

Compared to the issues involving Magna Carta, jury trial, and habeas corpus, the right against self-incrimination was of decidedly secondary importance in the Lawrence case. That case, therefore, wrought no miracles in securing the right against the practices of the governor and council, yet it was not without its effect. In a later case the council examined a seditious libeler who would not acknowledge certain letters used in evidence against him unless they were proved to be in his own hand; yet, when the proof was produced, he remained silent. Rather than bully or punish him, the council simply bound him over for trial. In another case, however, the outcome was different. A lawyer who had received prepayment for representing a client refused to return the money when he was disbarred before being able to discharge his duties as counsel. When the governor asked him whether he had in fact taken payment, he invoked his right against self-incrimination, saying that he would reserve answer until he learned whether a crime was involved. The governor ordered him to the stocks, but whether because of his answer or his guilt is not clear. In any event there is no doubting that the right was gaining some recognition in Maryland, and the same trend was apparent elsewhere.[51]

In New Jersey, for example, a witness in a civil action for damages in 1693, who was apparently implicated in the trespass that provoked the suit, refused to swear the truth "unlesse hee may be borne harmlesse." Rather than give him immunity or force his testimony, the court excused him as a witness, thereby protecting him from self-incrimination. In 1698 Connecticut regulated the testimony of witnesses in criminal cases by requiring that witnesses must give sworn evidence under an oath to tell the whole truth, on pain of being imprisoned for refusal, "always provided that no person required to give testimonie as aforesaid shall be punished for what he doth confesse against himself when under oath." Thus, he could be forced to give self-incriminating evidence, but it could not be used against him. In effect the statute extended the right to witnesses, implying its prior existence for criminal defendants. By an act of 1703 the policy of giving immunity was supplanted by vesting in the witness a right to remain silent about matters that might incriminate him personally. He must take the oath and tell all "so farre as it concernes any other person besides himselfe. . . ." The Pennsylvania Charter of Privileges of 1701 had achieved the same result by specifying, "That all Criminals shall have the same Privileges of Witnesses and Council as their Prosecutors." [52]

In Virginia Governor Francis Nicholson's arbitrary conduct led six magnates of his council in 1703 to petition the queen for his recall. Apparently he did not attempt to violate the right against self-incrimination, but the councilors complained that he compelled witnesses to give sworn testimony incriminating others. They thought that practice was an outrage on English liberty. Robert Beverley noted that Nicholson had said that Virginians had no right to the liberties of English subjects and had even threatened that those who opposed him would be hanged "with Magna Charta *about their necks.* Nicholson's "most extraordinary" practice, observed Beverley, "was a kind of inquisition." He would call a court to inquire into the lives and conversation of those whom he disliked to get evidence against him, though they had not been accused of any crime. "To these Courts he summon'd all the Neighbours of the Party he intended to expose, especially those that he knew were most intimate with him. Upon their Appearance, he administer'd an Oath to them, to answer truly, to all such Interrogatories, as he should propose. Then he would ask them endless Questions, concerning the particular Discourse and Behaviour of the Party, in order to find out something that might be the Ground of an Accusation." In their petition to the queen, the councilors charged that Nicholson "forced men upon oath to turn informers" and "tampered" with witnesses who did not co-operate, all the while denying the suspect the opportunity to defend himself. In one case a councilor censured Nicholson for his use of the inquisitional oath-procedure against a suspect himself.[53]

As the seventeenth century closed, the right against self-incrimination was uncertainly founded in America. There were several colonies, the Carolinas, for example, in which it appears to have been unknown or, to be more accurate, nothing about its existence can be determined from legislative or judicial records. In other colonies, as in Maryland, the right was known by some defendants but received unequal respect from the authorities, especially from the prerogative court of governor and council if not from the judicial courts of the common law. Elsewhere the laws or courts recognized the right, as in Jersey or Connecticut, but it was inconsistently observed, sometimes grossly breached, as in Massachusetts or Virginia; the breaches, significantly, occurred mainly in the prerogative rather than the common-law courts. On the whole, however, despite the silence of the sources, the breaches, the lapses, and the inconsistencies, there had been considerable progress over the course of the century toward the establishment of the right.

CHAPTER XII

Establishment of the Right in America

The right against self-incrimination was but shakily or unevenly established in America by the close of the seventeenth century. But a perceptible change was occurring in the legal development of all the colonies: the English common law was increasingly becoming American law. The degree to which that was true varied from colony to colony, and the pace was not the same in each. But in all, as their political and economic systems matured, their legal systems, most strikingly in the field of criminal procedure, began more and more to resemble that of England. The consequence was a greater familiarity with and respect for the right against self-incrimination.

In the eighteenth century the legal profession, which in the early years of every colony was virtually nonexistent and distrusted, rapidly grew in size, competence, social status, and political power. The rise of a substantial propertied class and the growing complexity and prosperity of colonial business required the services of a trained legal profession; the colonial governments also found an increasing need for the special skills of lawyers, both on and off the bench. Although lay judges still dominated the colonial bench at the time of the American Revolution, they increasingly included men who, though self-educated in the law, were highly knowledgeable and respectful of professional standards. Bench and bar resorted more and more to English law and English procedure as their guide. The complex, highly technical common-law system required well-trained lawyers to administer it, and they looked to Westminster, to the English law reports and legal treatises, for their rules and even for their training. There were more and more Americans educated at the Inns of Court with each passing decade, about sixty before 1760, triple that number by 1776. They became the leaders and teachers of the American bar and had a prodigious effect in making American law imitative of the English, by making English cases and English legal treatises the measure of competence, the fount of inspiration, and the precedent for emulation. Although law books, especially in the seventeenth century, had been in short supply in the colonies, there were always enough to provide instruction, especially in matters of criminal law and procedure. Michael Dalton's *Countrey Justice* was the universal handbook. It was one of the books, along with Coke's works, ordered by the General Court of Massachusetts in 1647 "to the end that we may have better light for making & proceeding about laws." Rhode Island relied heavily on Dalton in framing her criminal code in 1647; Maryland in 1678 required that all her judges keep copies of Dalton at hand, and in 1723 added Hawkins's *Pleas of the Crown* and Nelson's *Justice of the Peace* to the required list. In Virginia, where the assembly also prescribed Dalton for the courts, gentlemen increasingly read law books as part of their general education. A seventeenth-century Virginia lawyer named Arthur Spicer had a private library of fifty-two law books. In the eighteenth century the supply of law books became more and more plentiful as their importation increased and as American printers took to issuing local editions.[1]

The experience of New York is a good indication of the trend of the time. Beginning in 1683 the criminal law of New York became an extremely sophisticated duplication of the "practices and forms of the English central courts." From the beginning of the eighteenth century, according to Goebel and Naughton, New York's criminal courts were peopled by men with excellent legal training who conducted their work as skillfully as their counterparts in England. Because their "intellectual home . . . centered in the dingy streets about the Inns of Court, they read and cited what lawyers did at home." They prized English law books, "because it was from English precedent that provincial law was built." The standard of practice in the highest court of the colony became "really comparable" with that in King's Bench, while the inferior criminal jurisdiction was "administered in much the same way as . . . in English Quarter Sessions." Goebel and Naughton also said, with reference to the "malignant ferocity" of the judges, "If the case of Penn and Mead at Old Bailey was typical the proceedings were exactly similar," and presumably, therefore, they illustrate the sessions trials in colonial New York. It is to the point, then, to repeat that at that trial, Mead, on being asked an incriminating question, replied: "It is a maxim in your own law, 'Nemo tenetur accusare seipsum,' which if it be not true Latin, I am sure it is true English, 'That no man is bound to accuse himself.' And why dost thou offer to insnare me with such a question?" "Sir, hold your tongue," replied the judge, "I did not go about to insnare you," and he dropped the question.[2]

Goebel and Naughton heavily stressed the influence of English law books on the development of New York law generally and that colony's criminal procedure in particular. They pointed out that James Alexander, William Smith, Joseph Murray, John Tabor Kempe, and other New York attorneys "collected every [law] book they could lay their hands on" and subscribed to new ones as they were published. Alexander's collection of 152 law books as of 1721 was probably the largest in the colonies at the time, and he generously loaned them, making his, in effect, the first circulating library in New York. William Smith's library in 1770 contained three times as many law titles as Alexander had had. "No one," says Goebel and Naughton, "who has examined the memoranda and citations of any first-rate New York lawyer of the 1730's can doubt the general availability or spread of these sources or the competency to use them." For nearly everything done in the New York Supreme Court, precedent could be found in Hawkins's *Pleas of the Crown*, while the New York City Sessions Court trod "as closely as it may the path of the superior court," and the local justices of the peace found some manual like Dalton or Nelson to be the magistrate's vade mecum. Because the "patterns of practice were cut after the designs of Hawkins, Hale, and the *Crown Circuit Companion*," defiance of these tutelary geniuses was "exceptional." "The course of the typical criminal trial in New York during the eighteenth century," Goebel and Naughton concluded, "can be plotted with the Office of the Clerk of Assize or the *Crown Circuit Companion* in one hand and with Hawkins' *Pleas of the Crown* in the other. . . ." [3]

In view of the fact that the right against self-incrimination had by then become entrenched and respected in England, its existence in New York and in the other colonies should be expected, its absence would be an astonishing departure from the general reception of the common law's accusatorial system of criminal procedure. Because England provided the model, English history, English law books, and English criminal practice are at the source of any understanding of the right in New York and the other colonies. And since the colonial bar so avidly followed the English treatises and precedents, Goebel and Naughton would be justified in concluding that a strong prima facie case against the existence of the right could be constructed *if* it were passed over in those books and cases. As noted earlier, Goebel and Naughton unequivocally stated that the right was unknown in colonial New York. And they added that, "It is obviously idle to imagine that a 'principle' which even Baron Gilbert forbears to mention, should have been cosseted in our own courts." [4]

The existence of the right against self-incrimination in English case law, especially that of the central courts at Westminster, has already been established in earlier chapters. That the right was scarcely unnoticed by English law writers might be taken for granted had not a distinctly contrary impression been spread by such impressive authority as the authors of *Law Enforcement in Colonial New York*. Baron Gilbert, as a matter of fact, by no means forbore to mention the "principle," nor was it ignored by other writers or in the law books that were relied upon by the colonial lawyers of New York or of the other colonies. [5]

Geoffrey Gilbert's *Law of Evidence*, published in 1756, was, as Goebel and Naughton say, the first work on the subject with any analytic merit. Gilbert, whose words have been fully quoted earlier, observed that while a confession was the best evidence of guilt, it must be voluntarily made because "our Law . . . will not force any Man to accuse himself; and in this we do certainly follow the Law of Nature. . . ." Gilbert's statement of the right against compulsory self-incrimination reflected the age-old English phrasing which, by his time, required no explanation. His *Law of Evidence* was used in New York even before it was published in England. On February 5, 1753, William Smith, Jr., one of the luminaries of the New York bar, received from John McEvers, a fellow attorney, a manuscript volume "supposed to be done by Baron Gilbert." Smith copied 173 pages of the manuscript, including the passage against self-accusing, and in the margin later wrote, "Note this book is now printed under title Law of Evidence in 8 vo. 1 June 1756." Smith, by the way, not only knew of the right from many sources, in addition to Gilbert, but as an historian, councilor, and lawyer, he respected the right.[6]

Gilbert's book has been singled out for special consideration only because its alleged silence on the subject has been offered by Goebel and Naughton as proof that the right was not even known in New York's English-minded courts. Yet almost any law book that touched criminal law might be used to prove that information about the right was available to the colonists. In the most widely used English law dictionary of the eighteenth century, written by Giles Jacob, the broad proposition is stated under "Evidence" that "the witness shall not be asked any Question to accuse himself." Jacob cited Coke's *Institutes*, Hobbes's *Leviathan*, and the *State Trials* as his authorities. He restated the proposition in his popular guidebook, *Every Man His Own Lawyer*, the seventh edition of which was published in New York in 1768. In a political tract described by Clinton Rossiter as "the most popular statement of English rights during the second half of the colonial period," Henry Care condemned Star Chamber practice as contrary to all law and reason, "For No Man is bound to accuse himself." In *The Security of Englishmen's Lives*, a popular treatise on grand juries, John Somers, the Lord Chancellor of England, declared that it was lawful for witnesses before grand juries "to refuse to give Answer to some Demands which the Jury make; as where it would be to accuse themselves of Crimes." These seventeenth-century books by Care and Somers were reprinted in eighteenth-century America, each for the second time on the eve of the American Revolution.[7]

In Dalton's celebrated *Countrey Justice* the reason given to explain why the offender should not be examined under oath is that "by the Common Law, Nullus tenetur seipsum prodere." In a book on the same subject by William Nelson, also described by Goebel and Naughton as the magistrate's vade mecum, the same maxim was expressed in slightly different Latin, "*Nemo debet seipsum accusare.*" The identical phrase appeared in what was probably the most widely used American manual for justices of the peace, *Conductor Generalis*, attributed to James Parker, a New Jersey justice of the peace. His book went through sixteen American editions in the eighteenth century, including eight in New York, in most of which he also stated "a general rule, that a witness shall not be asked any question, the answering of which might oblige him to accuse himself of a crime. . . ." Other manuals repeated the same words. They were identical to those used in the classic *Pleas of the Crown* by Sergeant William Hawkins, first published in 1716. William Nelson's volume on *The Law of Evidence*, published in 1735, included the rule that "a witness ought not to be examined where his evidence tends either to clear or accuse himself of a crime."

Even the works of the libertarian Continental jurists, Jean Jacques Burlamaqui and Samuel von Pufendorf, who were read in America not only by lawyers but by political theorists from John Wise to John Adams, contained the principle that a criminally accused person is under no obligation to expose himself to punishment by answering incriminating interrogatories. Pufendorf even concluded that "no Man is bound to accuse himself" in civil as well as criminal cases. While he approved of putting a defendant to his oath, a practice condemned in English law, he observed that oaths should not be administered if the consequences of confessing the truth entailed capital punishment, "any grievous inconvenience," an offense to conscience, or "very considerable Damage." [8]

Edmond Wingate's *Maxims of Reason* of 1658, which included the earliest discussion under the heading "Nemo tenetur accusare seipsum," was in the libraries of such eminent New York lawyers as James Alexander, Joseph Murray, and William Smith, who also read Pufendorf and Burlamaqui. From Wingate to William Blackstone's *Commentaries*, the principle of the right against self-incrimination was recognized by the English law writers as well as by the English courts. The logic of Goebel and Naughton leads us, therefore, to expect its recognition by the bench and bar of the colonies, especially in New York. The right was in fact so recognized, if not "cosseted" or pampered.[9]

The evidence for its recognition in the colonies is not abundant, for the trial records, unfortunately, prove little. As Goebel and Naughton state, only a few trials were reported and those "execrably" so; the judgment rolls and *posteas* "are nearly always silent on what was said or proffered at trial, and the judicial minutes at best ordinarily furnish only a list of documents or the names of those who testified." Because "statements respecting testimony are rarely to be found in minutes of the provincial courts or the records of trials," a generalization based on trial records about the nonexistence of the right against self-incrimination in New York or elsewhere in the colonies, should be regarded as suspect. Historians who "cleave to a scintilla of evidence theory" are properly reprimanded by Goebel and Naughton: they disapprove of those who take a proposition as proven with the minimum of citation, who base a rule on a single case, or refer to statutes only when stating a judicial practice. "This is the way of advocacy, not of scholarship. . . . The ends of legal history are not served by the mere establishment of a prima facie case." [10]

The injunction, a sound one, has not been observed by Goebel and Naughton in their discussion of the right against self-incrimination. By way of proving the nonexistence of that right, they cite the case of a man who was incriminatingly questioned at his trial about the contradictory confessions he had made in his preliminary examination. "This case of course concerned a slave [one of the defendants in the Negro Plot to burn the city in 1742], but we have not noticed any special tenderness of white persons charged with felony, and it is not unlikely that similar tactics were used against them. There are numerous cases where the minutes reveal the reading at trial of a prisoner's confession." The passage illustrates the "scintilla of evidence theory" in practice and a badly mistaken assumption that the right against self-incrimination is nonexistent in a jurisdiction that accepts in evidence the confession of the accused. Never in history has the existence of the right placed the state under an obligation to prevent a person from incriminating himself.[11]

The fact must be emphasized that the right in question was a right against *compulsory* self-incrimination, and, excepting rare occasions when judges intervened to protect a witness against incriminating interrogatories, the right had to be claimed by the defendant. Historically it has been a fighting right: unless invoked, it offered no protection. It vested an option to refuse answer but did not bar interrogation nor taint a voluntary confession as improper evidence. Incriminating statements made by a suspect at the preliminary examination or even at arraignment could always be used with devastating effect at his trial. That a man might unwittingly incriminate himself when questioned in no way impaired his legal right to refuse answer. He lacked the right to be warned that he need not answer, for the authorities were under no legal obligation to apprise him of his right. That reform did not come in England until Sir John Jervis's Act in 1848, and in the United States more than a century later the matter was still a subject of acute constitutional controversy. Yet if the authorities in eighteenth-century Britain and in her colonies were not obliged to caution the prisoner, he in turn was not legally obliged to reply. His answers, although given in ignorance of his right, might secure his conviction, but by the mid-eighteenth century the courts, at least at Westminster, were willing to consider the exclusion of confessions that had been made involuntarily or under duress. The lawyers of the colonies, familiar with Gilbert's *Law of Evidence*, knew that a coerced confession was not to be trusted.[12]

After the first quarter of the eighteenth century, the history of the right in formal common-law proceedings centered upon the preliminary examination of the suspect, the legality of placing in evidence various types of forced confessions, the rights of witnesses, and the disadvantaged position of the felony defendant. He was, to be sure, excluded from the stand in the sense that he was not permitted to give testimony even if he wanted to. His interest in the case disqualified him on the theory that his evidence was unreliable. He was, nevertheless, permitted to tell his story unsworn at least in a final statement to the court. Deprived of counsel in many of the colonies, he was forced to conduct his own defense and, as a result, was vulnerable to comments and questions from the prosecution and the bench. This, at least, was the situation of the felony defendant in New York and several of the other colonies that followed English practice closely. Eighteenth-century England permitted counsel to the felony defendant only at the discretion of the trial judge and usually on points of law only. The accused could make his case through witnesses whom he could subpoena and put under oath, although there is some evidence that even in usually imitative New York, witnesses for the defense were not always sworn. Deprived of counsel, however, the felony defendant was left exposed to insinuations or charges that he had to rebut or else he risked the suspicion of the jury. Yet even the right against self-incrimination has always been exercised at the same risk.[13]

In some colonies—Rhode Island after 1664, New Hampshire after 1696, Pennsylvania, Massachusetts, and Delaware after 1701, South Carolina after 1731, and Virginia after 1734—practice was well in advance of England's, because counsel was permitted even in felony cases; in misdemeanor and treason cases the right to counsel was universal in England and America. The defendant who could afford counsel to conduct his defense, who had witnesses to testify for him, and who was not himself permitted to testify, was well insulated against the possibility of incriminating himself after the preliminary hearing. In the seven colonies where the right to counsel was provided even in felony cases, the right against self-incrimination was well secured in common-law trials. It bears re-iteration, however, that in all the colonies, New York included, the mere fact that neither the examining magistrate nor the trial judge were required to inform the prisoner that he could lawfully remain silent in the face of incriminating questions does not prove the nonexistence of the right against self-incrimination. Nor does the fact that there were in New York "occasional" instances, as late as the Revolution, of the ancient practice of questioning the defendant upon his arraignment in order to secure his submission. The "scintilla of evidence theory," abhorred by Goebel and Naughton, is clearly adopted by them in the proposition that the general indifference "to any privilege of self-incrimination probably embraced witnesses generally although we have found but one case." That case may be but the exception to the rule expressed in the English law books and precedents so dear to the hearts of New York's lawyers and judges.[14]

Given the facts—that so few trials were reported, that they were reported very incompletely and rarely included testimony, and that the accused was not permitted to give formal testimony —it is not at all surprising that a scrutiny of the records of the courts that employed common-law procedures yields so little data about the emergence or existence of the right against self-incrimination. The right had arisen in England as a shield against inquisitions by prerogative courts into crimes that were essentially political and religious in nature. The investigations of the governor and council, even of the legislature—bodies that tended to employ inquisitorial procedures—might be expected to produce protests that would reveal, at the very least, knowledge of the right against self-incrimination and refusals to answer based on that right. There is something symbolic in the fact that the first glimmer of the right in America is seen in Wheelwright's case, tried in 1637 by the legislature of Massachusetts sitting in its judicial capacity, but not using common-law procedures. Even in New York itself under the Dutch, in 1661, when Townshend and Spicer refused to incriminate themselves, their judges were the governor and council. So too in the Bradford-Growden case in Pennsylvania, in the Maule case in Massachusetts, and in the Lawrence case in Maryland, all in the closing years of the seventeenth century, the accused parties invoked the right in proceedings before the governor and council. That the right first became an issue in New York under English rule as a result of the inquisitorial tactics of the same prerogative court, in a case of 1698 heavy with political implications, fits a revealing pattern.

The issue arose as a result of the Earl of Bellomont's investigation into the administration of his predecessor, Governor Benjamin Fletcher. Assemblyman Henry Beekman (or Beckman) was a victim of Bellomont's effort to discredit Fletcher. Beekman, who had been close to Fletcher, was instrumental in having secured the passage of the Bolting Act of 1694 by which New York City lost its monopoly of the bolting and packing of flour. In 1698 governor and council summoned Beekman to be examined on his connection with the charge that the approval of the act by **Fletcher** and certain councilors had been purchased. Instructed to answer questions under oath, Beekman refused. Threatening to imprison him "without baile or mainprize" should he persist in his contemptuous refusal to take his oath without giving a "lawful" reason, the council finally "persuaded" Beekman to swear and answer the questions. That Beekman's case was not exceptional is evident from the accusations filed with the Board of Trade in London by John Key, the London correspondent of the New York merchants. Key complained that Bellomont "has tendred extrajudicial oaths to severall of His Majtys Subjects requiring them to make answer to such questions he should ask them, and upon their refusall to swear has threatned to committ them into custody." In one case he imprisoned two merchants, accused of having "farmed the excise," for refusing to "discover upon oath what profits they had made by that farme. . . ." Counsel for these merchants denounced the oath as "illegal and arbitrary . . . a great Instance of Infringement of English liberties." Bellomont's treatment of Beekman did not go unnoticed either.[15]

The merchants of New York understandably objected to testifying against themselves, particularly when they suspected that political motives were behind the governor's inquisition. Nicholas Bayard, one of Fletcher's most intimate associates who had been ousted from the council by Bellomont, complained in London to the Board of Trade about the governor's administration. He cited Bellomont's "undue method of forcing witnesses to swear, and instanced in his requiring Colonel Beckman . . . to make oath to answer whatever should be asked him (tho' he were himself concerned in the business of that Enquiry) with threats to send him to Gaol in case he refus'd." Bayard's protest, in other words, was that Beekman had been forced to incriminate himself.[16]

Thomas Weaver, a barrister-at-law of Inner Temple who was the governor's agent in London, defended Bellomont before the Board of Trade. In rebutting Bayard's accusation, Weaver made the significant point that both he and the attorney-general of the province agreed that "Beckman was obliged (as many man might be, especially in matters of state or other high concernment) to give evidence *in what did not concerne himself criminally* (which

was all required of him)." Thus Weaver, who later became
attorney-general, and James Graham, Bellomont's attorney-
general, explicitly acknowledged that a man might not be forced
to testify against himself in a criminal matter, not even by the
governor and council.[17]

In 1702 William Atwood, the Chief Justice of New York, and
Samuel Shelton Broughton, the new attorney-general, also acknowledged the right in connection with the sensational treason
trial of Bayard and Hutchins. The death of Bellomont had kindled
Bayard's hope of returning to power against the Leislerians who
controlled the government. To ingratiate himself with the new
governor, Lord Cornbury, Bayard drew up addresses accusing
Lieutenant-Governor John Nanfan, Chief Justice Atwood, and
members of the council, of nefarious actions ranging from bribery
to oppression. Nanfan retaliated by arresting Bayard on a charge
of treason under a statute of 1691 loosely drawn by Bayard himself against Leisler's followers. It provided that anyone who by
arms "or otherwise" endeavored to "disturb the peace" should be
deemed a traitor. For a crime which at worst was a mere misdemeanor, a seditious libel, Bayard in 1702 found himself on trial for
his life, along with his confederate Alderman John Hutchins.
From indictment to conviction the case was a travesty of common-
law procedure, a fact which saved the prisoners' heads, for their
conviction was condemned as illegal on appeal to the Privy Council.[18]

In the initial stage of the case, Nanfan and the council employed inquisitorial tactics to gather evidence about the addresses.
Several suspects refused to produce copies on demand. The council, after receiving a legal opinion from Attorney-General Broughton, decided to prosecute them for contempt. Broughton believed
that because the addresses "were not criminal or illegal," the suspects could be forced to produce copies without incriminating
themselves. Although the council thought the addresses criminal,
it sought to incriminate only the authors, not those examined to
betray them. Bayard, his son, and Hutchins were shortly arrested.
Bayard, complaining to friends in England, noted that Hutchins
had been jailed for treason, without bail, until he produced copies
of the addresses which the council "were pleased to call Libells."

After the conviction of the defendants, Bayard's friends petitioned the Board of Trade and charged that an attempt had been made to force Hutchins to incriminate himself in a criminal matter. Sir Edward Northey, Attorney-General of England, informed the Board of Trade that "it appears by the warrant for committing Hutchins that the Council required him to produce a libell he is charged to be author of *which was to accuse himself* and his refusal to produce it is alleged as part of his Crime." The Privy Council ruled that the convictions were illegal and ordered the annulment of the sentences.[19]

Chief Justice Atwood in an attempt to defend his conduct in the case, sought to justify the requirement of the provincial council that Hutchins produce the addresses. Although Atwood's statement of the facts differs from Bayard's, the significant point of his apologia is his denial that Hutchins had been forced to incriminate himself: "But since he was not committed for High Treason, as he might have been, and there wanted no Evidence against him; this, surely, may answer the Objection against requiring him to produce Papers which might tend to accuse himself." The right against self-incrimination may have been honored in New York in name only, but the highest officials of the colony vied with each other in denying that they had abridged it.[20]

In 1707, at the trial of Francis Makemie, a Presbyterian minister charged with preaching without a license, the defendant voluntarily, indeed, eagerly, answered all questions, however technically incriminating. His successful defense was based on the rights of conscience as protected by the Act of Toleration. In the contemporary account of his trial, which Makemie himself probably wrote, there is a heated passage against Governor Cornbury's attempt to induce Makemie's friends to incriminate each other, though not themselves. Several men were examined under oath "to discover what Discourse they had with sundry of their friends." The author of the account rages that "the practice is not to be outdone, yea, scarce parallelled by *Spanish Inquisition;* for no men are safe in their most private Conversations, if most intimate Friends can be compelled upon Oath, to betray one anothers Secrets. If this is agreeable to English Constitution and Priviledges, I confess, we have been hitherto in the Dark." It is not likely that the author would have regarded involuntary self-accusing in a better light.[21]

The right against self-incrimination next became an issue in New York politics as a result of merchant protest against Governor William Burnet's efforts to outlaw the fur trade between Albany and Quebec. When a prohibitory act of 1720 proved unenforceable because of the sheriff's inability to supervise the frontier, the legislature adopted an amendment in 1722 authorizing civil and military officers to exact from any suspected persons an oath of purgation that they had not in any way traded with the French. Refusal to take the oath automatically convicted one of the crime of illicitly trading, the penalty for which was a one hundred pound fine. The statute certainly compelled the guilty to incriminate themselves, a fact that its opponents used as the basis of their objections to the Board of Trade.[22]

Stephen DeLancey, Adolph Philipse, and Peter Schuyler cared little about abstract principle, but they recognized a good issue with which to mask their interest in the fur trade. John Sharpe, their London agent, argued that the statute of 1722 was illegal because the party suspected "was by a very extraordinary Oath, made liable either to accuse himself or to suffer very great penalties." A fur trader, John Peloquin, giving evidence at the hearing, mentioned that he had bought skins from the French and was asked when he had done so. Sharpe interposed to say that Peloquin's "answering that Question might be of ill consequences to himself, if it were since the passing of the said acts; & said he believ'd their Lordships did not expect Mr. Peloquin should accuse himself." Their Lordships changed the subject. Subsequently they recommended to the Privy Council that Governor Burnet be urged to halt the undesirable trade by other methods. The Board specified its objections: "There is an Oath impos'd upon all Traders whereby they are obliged to accuse themselves or else to be under the greatest temptation to perjury." New York enacted a new statute regulating the fur trade by a tax device. The oath was conspicuously absent from its provisions.[23]

On the other hand, the purgative oath that in effect compelled self-incrimination was a frequent feature of New York legislation during the colonial period. The right against self-incrimination was indeed an illusion, as Goebel and Naughton declared, under the acts of the Assembly from 1701 to 1759. The first act employing the oath of purgation, with a proviso that those refusing to take it should be subject to double the normal penalties imposed on the guilty, was intended to detect and deter evasion of the militia laws. Legislation of this kind was used against those suspected of selling liquor to the Indians, exporting specie, taking seamen's notes for liquor or food, entertaining slaves, stealing furs from Indians, selling liquor to servants, failing to report imported copper money, trading with the Iroquois for certain articles, and giving credit to servants. In all these cases, the statutes fixed criminal penalties for the refusal of a suspect to take the oath of purgation. Some declared that such a refusal automatically established guilt for the crime suspected; others provided for special fines and/or imprisonment. The purgative oath, like the oath *ex officio* of an earlier time, was a noose for the guilty: the mere requirement of it insured conviction for perjury, or contempt, or the crime suspected. Even the innocent could suffer, particularly conscientious objectors. However, the purgative oath was authorized by the legislature only once after 1759 and passed into disuse before the outbreak of the Revolution. The ever-increasing professionalization of the bar, the growing familiarity with "the liberty of the subject" and English rights, and the protests against self-accusing all contributed to the respectability of the right against incriminating oneself. William Smith, Jr., who had copied the passage against self-incrimination from the manuscript of Baron Gilbert's book on evidence, reflected the new spirit. A book of his own, published in 1757, contained a scathing passage against oaths of purgation. Recalling that the assembly had tendered such an oath to Robert Livingston in 1701, Smith wrote, "Mr. Livingston, who was better acquainted with English law and liberty than to countenance a practice so odious, rejected the insolent demand with disdain. . . ." [24]

The developing recognition of the right against self-incrimination in New York had its parallels elsewhere. In 1735 there was a sensational case in Pennsylvania that was unusual for that late date and place. The case involved an ecclesiastical inquiry into heresy, bringing Benjamin Franklin to the defense of the right. A special commission of the Presbyterian synod of Philadelphia examined the unorthodox beliefs of Samuel Hemphill, a Presbyterian minister with deistic notions. Franklin enjoyed his sermons largely because he preached good citizenship rather than good Presbyterianism. The commission of inquiry, however, unanimously censuring Hemphill's doctrines as "Unsound and Dangerous," suspended him from his ministry. Franklin, in an angry pamphlet which quickly sold out, reported that Hemphill had refused to submit his sermons to the commission, because "It was contrary to the common Rights of Mankind, no Man being obliged to furnish Matter of Accusation against himself." The commission, though acknowledging that it had no right to compel delivery of the sermons, had taken Hemphill's refusal as a virtual confession of guilt, provoking Franklin to denounce the commission still further. Hemphill finally decided to read his sermons to the commission, yet succeeded only in proving to its members that their worst suspicions were well founded. Bitingly, Franklin observed: "And here I am sorry, that I am obliged to say, that they have no Pattern for their Proceedings, but that hellish Tribunal the *Inquisition*, who rake up all the vile Evidences, and extort all the Confessions they can from the wretched Object of their Rage . . . and proceed to Judgment."

A defender of the synod's commission, responding to Franklin, vindicated its position that Hemphill's claim of a right not to accuse himself was "but a tacit Acknowledgement of his Guilt." Franklin, in what had become a pamphlet war—he wrote three popular tracts on the controversy—replied on the theme that Hemphill "was in the right to do so [that is, to claim the right against self-incrimination], since the . . . Commission was determin'd to find Heresy enough . . . to condemn him. . . ." Although Hemphill finally lost his case, it had provoked a public debate that educated the province on both the right against self-incrimination and freedom of religion, with which it was so closely allied in its origins.[25]

The best evidence that the right was honored in Pennsylvania derives from the conduct of the provincial Assembly. In 1756, for example, in an election-frauds case investigated by that body, counsel asked several questions of a witness who was being examined under oath. The questions, say the Assembly records, "were thought to have a Tendency to make him criminate himself. . . ." On an objection that he ought not be obliged to answer such questions, the Assembly, after debate, resolved: "That no Questions be asked the Witnesses of either Side, which may tend to make them criminate themselves; and that therfore all Questions shall be first proposed to Mr. Speaker, who is to put such of them as he judges not to have that Tendency." [26]

Two years later the same legislature conducted a drumhead trial of two leading Anglicans, William Moore, the chief judge of the Court of Common Pleas for Chester County, and William Smith, the president of the provincial college. Both men had publicly criticized the phlegmatic prosecution of the war against the French and Indians. The Quaker-dominated Assembly retaliated by publishing an address to the governor demanding Moore's removal from office on ground that he was corrupt and oppressive. Moore replied in print and with Smith's help published his self-defense in a German-language newspaper. The Assembly, deeming the publication to be a seditious reflection upon its honor, arrested and convicted both men in a proceeding that was about as fair as the trial of the Knave of Hearts for stealing the tarts in Wonderland. Moore, on being shown the manuscript of the libelous publication, written in his own hand and signed by him, incriminated himself by confessing his authorship, but refused to answer other questions on ground that the legislature had no competence to try him. Smith also faced incriminating questions, yet they were but trivial matters in his ordeal; for the House virtually convicted him before trial by adopting special rules that stripped him of every defense he might make to the charge of abetting a libel. Neither Smith nor Moore invoked the right against self-incrimination, making idle any speculation whether the House, which acted as if unaware of British justice, would have sought to compel their answers or honor the right.[27]

Hostile witnesses nevertheless received fair, if not considerate, treatment. Dr. Phineas Bond, a close friend of Judge Moore, on being asked to give whatever information he possessed about the seditious libel, evaded direct answer. The Assembly, surmising that he might be implicated, assured him that they would provide "the utmost Lenity in their Manner of taking his Evidence, and should ask him no Questions which had any Tendency to criminate that Gentleman [Moore], or himself, but only a third Person [Smith], to whom he was not publicly known to be under any Obligations." Asked whether Smith had assisted in the composition of Moore's address, Bond persisted in his refusal to answer. The Assembly then arrested him, but before acting further, formally resolved to grant him complete immunity against prosecution for any testimony that he might offer. Bond, nevertheless, continued his obstinate refusal to give evidence, though he could not incriminate himself. The Assembly therefore judged his refusal to be "an high Contempt" and imprisoned him until he relented. After a few hours behind bars, Bond's courage evaporated and he consented to giving damaging testimony in violation of "the Ties of Honour and Friendship." In a similar manner the Assembly exacted the testimony of Anthony Armbruster, the printer of the German-language newspaper.[28]

Whatever one thinks of the House's ethics, it went out of its way to protect hostile witnesses from the penalties of self-incriminatory statements, although not, of course, out of concern for them, but, rather, as a price worth paying to compel their testimony. The involuntary witness, when forced into the role of informer, does not, however, incriminate *himself*. Anglo-American law protected only against compulsory *self*-incrimination, not against the incrimination of others. What is striking about the proceedings in the Smith-Moore case is the Assembly's respect for that protection even as it arbitrarily suspended the writ of habeas corpus, made a mockery of fair trial and due process of law, and grossly abridged the freedom of political expression.

By the mid-eighteenth century the right against self-incrimination was also firmly fixed in Massachusetts law. The *Boston Post-Boy* found newsworthy a story from Halifax concerning the investigation by governor and council into the conduct of certain trial judges who had allegedly deprived defendants of their rights to examine and cross-examine witnesses against them. The public learned that the judges had been vindicated by proving that they had merely protected witnesses against questions that might tend to make them accuse themselves. A year later, in 1754, the legislature, whose devotion to the principle against compulsory self-incrimination was less than consistent, passed a liquor excise requiring consumers to give an account to tax collectors, on oath if necessary, concerning the amount spent by them for liquor. The bill was understandably unpopular and, because of its incriminating oath, thought to be a menace to freedom. Pamphleteers quickly condemned the bill. John Lovell, a Boston schoolmaster whose pupils included John Hancock and Sam Adams, courted the wrath of the legislature by overstepping the bounds of reasonable criticism. Lovell, calling the bill "the most pernicious Attack upon *English Liberty* that was ever attempted," alleged that its methods would enslave the country. Samuel Cooper, the minister of the Brattle Church, shared Lovell's use of hyperbole but focused more precisely on the oath. If an accounting of any part of one's innocent conduct could be so "extorted," he contended, "every other Part may with equal Reason be required, and a *Political Inquisition* severe as that in Catholick Countries may inspect and controul every Step of his private Conduct." Cooper exalted the British Constitution, lamenting that the oath was a step toward its overthrow and the establishment of "Arbitrary Power." Some thought the bill not to be such a menace, he wrote, "But will any one presume to say, that *this* will be no Diminution of our Liberties, if it be an essential Part of our Constitution, that no Man is held to convict himself in any Affair whereof he is accus'd? And whoever will undertake to prove, that a Man can consistent with the Constitution, be obliged to clear himself of an innocent Action by Oath, or forfeit an heavy Penalty, may *a fortiori* prove, that this Practice is defensible in Criminal Cases. If the argument for purging by Oath in one Case, is founded upon the Advantage the Publick will receive by *knowing the Truth*, the very same Argument will hold stronger in Criminal Cases." Finally Governor William Shirley refused to sign the bill, declaring it to be an unprecedented violation of "natural Rights." [29]

That same year, in 1754, an anonymous author had published a pamphlet with the intriguing title, *The Monster of Monsters*, also satirizing the legislative debate on the recent excise bill—the allegorical monster. The House, having taken more than it could bear, promptly condemned the pamphlet as a seditious libel, ordered the hangman to burn copies, and arrested Daniel Fowle, a bookseller. At his examination before the bar of the House, Fowle asked whether he was obligated to answer an incriminating question concerning his complicity. Speaker Thomas Hubbard, evading the question, pressed him to answer, and Fowle foolishly confessed his guilt. He also named Royal Tyler, a respected merchant and future councilor, as the man who had given him his stock of copies for sale to the public. The legislature illogically concluded that Fowle, rather than Tyler, was the author and locked him up, brutally keeping him incommunicado in a stinking, bedless cell exposed to bad weather.[30]

Tyler was more knowledgable about his rights and not the sort to be intimidated. When the speaker demanded his confession, Tyler requested counsel, which the House refused. He parried all questions by invoking his right against self-incrimination: "and the only Answer he would make," the record states, "was, *Nemo tenetur seipsum Accusare;* or, A Right of Silence was the Priviledge of every Englishman"—a magnificent free translation. The legislature jailed him anyway, not for a contempt resulting from his invocation of the right but because of Fowle's testimony incriminating him. Yet Tyler was free on bail in only two days. By contrast, Fowle, who had not known the magic formula, was severely reprimanded by the speaker, ordered to pay costs, and was jailed indefinitely under the worst of conditions. In an act of mercy, the legislature released him in a week because he was needed at home to nurse his sick wife. His new pamphlet, *The Eclipse of Liberty*, vividly expressed his outrage at the House's violations of Magna Carta's guarantees of due process and personal liberty. With public sympathy on Fowle's side, the House discreetly dropped further proceedings in the case. Like its counterpart in Pennsylvania, the Massachusetts legislature had behaved in a high-handed, even tyrannical manner, seeking to suppress criticism by arbitrary proceedings, but had yielded, if begrudgingly, to a direct invocation of the right against self-incrimination.[31]

In New York, meanwhile, the course of events signalized an ever broadening respect for the right. William Smith, Jr., in 1757, had lent his influence against incriminatory oaths of purgation. In 1760 William Smith, his father, also defended the right against self-incrimination. The elder Smith, who had learned his law at the Inns of Court, was one of New York's most distinguished attorneys, had served as provincial attorney-general, and had declined the chief justiceship, although he accepted a seat on the high court in 1763. In 1760, as a member of the governor's council, he presented a report on illicit trading with the enemy by some of the colony's leading merchants. The manuscript record, though damaged by fire, shows that Smith had received his information from one of the masters of the vessels trading with the French West Indies. Smith accepted his evidence against others but did not require him to inform against himself. The master himself, "being Particeps Crimin[is] [a party to the crime] can not be compelled to answer." Offenders, said Smith, should be prosecuted only if sufficient proof of guilt could be obtained. In a case of 1702, Chief Justice Atwood had prevented David Jamison from testifying on behalf of Bayard because Jamison "is *particeps criminis* for which reason he cannot be allowed as evidence." But the case of the master in 1760 involved one who could not be *compelled*. Jamison, as an alleged party to the crime, could not be *allowed* to testify because his interest in the case had disqualified him. The master, by contrast, was not disqualified for interest; he was protected against self-incrimination.[32]

John Taber Kempe, the attorney-general, did not wholly agree with Smith's opinion, which might deprive the prosecution of testimony needed for a conviction. In 1762, on the basis of information received from informers, Kempe obtained indictments against sixteen prominent men for trading with the enemy. In preparation for the trial of two of the merchants, he drafted a long brief in which he indicated his intention to call a number of witnesses who might be disqualified from testifying because of interest or excused because they were parties to the crime. Kempe carefully wrote out the arguments by which he intended to show that such persons were not necessarily incompetent to testify and, indeed, might even be compelled to. These witnesses, he declared, even parties to the crime, would be obliged to give evidence against others, "for the convictions of the persons on tryal will be attended with no punishment corporal or pecuniary to the witness—and he is not obliged to accuse himself." To the objection that no person should be compelled to swear against his own interest, Kempe noted: "He may—The Court of Chancery every day compels the party on oath to discover his own frauds. The rule that a witness shall not be compelled to swear to his own detriment goes not farther, than that he shall not be compelled to accuse himself of a crime." In conclusion, he wrote, "Every person being a *participis criminis*, may be a witness either for or against his accomplices, if he has not been indicted for the offence (2 Hawk. P. C. 432)." Thus, at three points in his brief, the attorney-general acknowledged the principle of the right against self-incrimination.[33]

Some of the ship captains whom Kempe had sworn as witnesses were unwilling to testify against the owners of their sloops. Captain William Dobbs, for example, simply refused to answer questions and was committed for contempt. Captain William Paulding at first was unwilling to be sworn, saying, "he understood he was not to declare anything that might affect himself." Informed that he had the king's pardon, he refused to accept it. Although he finally permitted himself to be sworn, he would not answer incriminating questions, and the court committed him also. The jury incidentally, without leaving the jury box, found the owner-defendants not guilty. The same verdict occurred in a companion case when Captain Theunis Thew refused to testify. He, too, was pardoned in order to protect him from the perils of the criminal law, but he remained silent to the questions and was committed. The court fined Dobbs, Paulding, and Thew for their respective contempts. Paulding had expressly invoked his right against self-incrimination, and the crown, eager for his testimony, immunized him against prosecution. Thew's pardon was similarly intended to safeguard him against self-incrimination. The cases scarcely bear out the allegation that the right was an illusion in New York. In Maryland at about this time the provincial court, in an action of trespass, upheld the right of a sheriff and his deputies not to be sworn as witnesses, against their will, to prove the defendant's claim that they had not given him notice of a resurvey as the duties of their office required. For the officers to have admitted their negligence would have exposed them to punishment. The court's matter-of-fact decision indicated that the law was settled in Maryland on the point that a witness in a *civil* case could not be required to answer questions that might reveal criminal liability.[34]

In the 1760's the opposition to general search warrants gave the right against self-incrimination a tremendous boost, first in England, then in America. The right was originally a "right of silence," in Royal Tyler's words, only in the sense that legal process could not force incriminating statements from the defendant's own lips. Beginning in the early eighteenth century the English courts widened that right to include protection against the necessity of producing books and documents that might tend to incriminate the accused. Thus, in a 1744 case the court refused the prosecution's request that the defendant be required to turn over the records of his corporation; that, said the court, would be forcing him to "furnish evidence against himself." Lord Mansfield summed up the law by declaring that the defendant, in a criminal case, could not be compelled to produce any incriminating documentary evidence "though he should hold it in his hands in Court." Yet it was an open question whether the government, though unable to subpoena such evidence, might lawfully seize it by a search warrant and introduce it at the trial against the accused. In the 1760's the English courts extended the right of silence to prevent the use of general warrants to seize private papers in seditious libel cases. Thus the right against self-incrimination and freedom of the press, with which it was so closely allied in its origins, were linked to a right to be free from unreasonable searches and seizures.[35]

The new departure originated in the Wilkes prosecution. John Wilkes's studied insult of the king's speech of 1763, in the forty-fifth issue of his journal, the *North Briton*, triggered the government's retaliatory instincts. Upon an information for libel filed by the attorney-general, one of the secretaries of state issued general search warrants leading to the arrest of forty-nine persons, including Wilkes, his printer, and his publisher. Within a short time about two hundred informations were filed, resulting in mass arrests, searches, and harassment of the press. In the treatment and prosecution of Wilkes the government found that it had mounted a tiger. No one since the days of John Lilburne, more than a century earlier, proved to be such a resourceful and pugnacious antagonist against the combined forces of all branches of the government. His private study had been ransacked on a general warrant and all his papers seized for incriminating evidence. The Commons voted that his *North Briton* Number 45 was a seditious libel, and Wilkes himself was expelled from the House, convicted in absentia for his criminal publications, outlawed, and, later, jailed and fined. Libertarian England rallied to his defense, spurred by Wilkes's own brilliant writings. He emerged from his persecution a popular idol, the personification of constitutional liberty in England and also in America, whose cause he championed. Although he himself held rather orthodox opinions on the subject of freedom of the press, his case touched off an intense public debate on the values and scope of that freedom and of others that were entwined. Though Wilkes focused mainly on the dangers of general warrants and the seizure of private papers, some of his supporters made notable contributions to libertarian theory, enlarging its concepts of freedom of the press and the right against self-incrimination.[36]

One pseudonymous author, a Gray's Inn lawyer calling himself "Candor," though defending the prosecution of seditious libels, blazed a fresh trail on the question of general search warrants. He described the seizure of private papers for the purpose of securing evidence of libel as an odious act comparable to "the worst sort of inquisitions . . . It is, in short, putting a man to the torture, and forcing him to give evidence against himself." Another lawyer, calling himself "Father of Candor," replied in a small book that went through three editions within as many months, seven altogether by 1771. It deserves to be ranked with Milton's *Areopagitica*, Andrew Hamilton's speech in the Zenger case, and the *Cato's Letters* of John Trenchard and Thomas Gordon, as one of the foremost expressions of English libertarian theory. "Father of Candor," who may have been either Lord Camden, the Chief Justice of the Court of Common Pleas, or Lord Ashburton, then John Dunning, one of the leading defenders of a free press, amplified what had been a passing point in "Candor's" pamphlet. Condemning the use of general search warrants as an "excruciating torture" that was inconsistent with every idea of liberty, he declared:

The laws of England, are so tender to every man accused, even of capital crimes, that they do not permit him to be put to torture to extort a confession, nor oblige him to answer a question that will tend to accuse himself. How then can it be supposed, that the law will intrust any officer of the crown, with the power of charging any man in the kingdom (or, indeed, every man by possibility and nobody in particular) at his will and pleasure, with being the author, printer or publisher of such a paper, being a libel, (however, which till a jury has determined to be so, is nothing) and that upon this charge, any common fellows under a general warrant, upon their own imaginations, or the surmises of their acquantance, or upon other worse and more dangerous intimations, may, with a strong hand, seize and carry off all his papers; and then at his trial produce these papers, thus taken by force from him, in evidence against himself; and all this on the charge of a mere misdemeanor, in a country of liberty and property. This would be making a man give evidence against and accuse himself, with a vengeance.[37]

The principle advocated by "Candor" and "Father of Candor" was destined for acceptance by the highest judicial authority on both sides of the Atlantic. Wilkes and others had urged editors, printers, and publishers whose papers had been seized to initiate suits for false arrest and trespass against the king's agents if their searches had been conducted on the authority of general warrants. *Entick* v. *Carrington,* one such suit, resulted in an opinion by Lord Camden that was later described by the Supreme Court of the United States as "one of the landmarks of English liberty." [38]

John Entick, an editor who sued for trespass, was represented by Serjeant Leigh who took his law from "Father of Candor," quite possibly the Lord Chief Justice sitting on the case. The crime, Leigh argued, was the publication, not the possession, of the libel. But even if its possession was criminal, "no power can lawfully break into a man's house and study to search for evidence against him. This would be worse than the Spanish inquisition; for ransacking a man's secret drawers and boxes, to come at evidence against him, is like racking his body to come at his secret thoughts." When opposition counsel replied that the secretary of state, having power to commit, must therefore have power to search and seize, Leigh replied tartly if illogically, "it might as

well be said he has a power of torture." On the question whether
the secretary of state or any crown officer had the power to
search and seize under a general warrant, without parliamentary
authorization, the court followed Leigh's path of reasoning. The
existence of that power of search, Lord Camden declared, would
open the "secret cabinets and bureaus of every subject in this
kingdom" to search and seizure, whenever the government suspected a person of seditious libel. "It is very certain," he continued, "that the law obligeth no man to accuse himself; because
the necessary means of compelling self-accusation, falling upon
the innocent as well as the guilty, would be both cruel and unjust;
and it should seem, that search for evidence is disallowed upon the
same principle." [39]

Camden held that neither arrests nor general warrants could issue on executive discretion, and implied that evidence seized on
the authority of a general warrant could not be used in court
without violating the right against self-incrimination. Camden did
not explain why, in accordance with the same principle, that same
right did not also illegalize the evidence obtained by special warrants as well as general warrants, even if issued by judicial or parliamentary authority rather than executive authority; nor did
Camden explain why the principle did not also apply in all cases
rather than merely in seditious libel cases. Clearly, he laid the
foundation of the right against unreasonable searches and seizures
in order to fortify the already strained principle of the old *nemo
tenetur* maxim. Never before had it extended to illegally seized
evidence. The Supreme Court of the United States in 1886, relying heavily on Camden, took notice of the "intimate relation" between the Fourth and Fifth Amendments:

> They throw great light on each other. For the "unreasonable
> searches and seizures" condemned in the Fourth Amendment are
> almost always made for the purpose of compelling a man to give
> evidence against himself, which in criminal cases is condemned
> in the Fifth Amendment; and compelling a man "in a criminal
> case to be a witness against himself," which is condemned in the
> Fifth Amendment, throws light on the question as to what is an
> "unreasonable search and seizure" within the meaning of the
> Fourth Amendment. And we have been unable to perceive that

the seizure of a man's private books and papers to be used in evidence against him is substantially different from compelling him to be a witness against himself.

Two centuries after *Entick* v. *Carrington*, the Supreme Court reaffirmed that the two freedoms—against unreasonable search and seizure and against compulsory self-incrimination—are complementary to, though not dependent upon, each other. At the very least, the two amendments when taken together assure that no man be convicted on unconstitutional evidence.[40]

In America, where libertarian thought, excepting on questions of religious liberty, usually lagged behind English models, the legality of general search warrants had been an earlier target of attack. Yet the American lawyers failed to make as imaginative a use of the right against self-incrimination, even though the warrants they vehemently opposed were more dangerous, that is, more general, than those associated with the prosecutions of Wilkes and Entick. The English warrants were general with respect to the objects of the search, but specific as to person, place, and time. In the colonies, the writs of assistance, as the warrants issued to customs officials were called, were general in every respect; on the other hand, they were issued by the courts on the authority of acts of Parliament. James Otis, in his famous argument against writs of assistance in 1761, described them as remnants of Star Chamber tyranny, yet he never connected them with a violation of the *nemo tenetur* principle. He might have done so had he been contesting the legality of evidence secured by an illegal search; instead, he was arguing against the re-authorization of the writs that had expired six months after the death of George II. Nevertheless, British lawyers when arguing against the principle of general search warrant, whether out of court, as in the case of "Father of Candor," or in court, even in a case of trespass, as in Serjeant Leigh's advocacy of Entick's cause, capitalized on the abhorrence of forcing a man to accuse himself. Not even in the American cases following *Entick* v. *Carrington* did the colonial lawyers copy that precedent. Their argument was that while specific search warrants might be legal if issued on probable cause, a general warrant was illegal because it threatened personal liberty by vesting arbitrary power in the officer conducting the search.[41]

The American argument brought the right against self-incrimination into play in connection with a procedure related to and following the use of writs of assistance. The writ was a device used by customs officials to search for contraband, goods that had been loaded from or smuggled into a colonial port in violation of the revenue acts or the acts regulating colonial trade. At the discretion of the customs officials, suits for penalties and forfeitures in such cases could be brought in the courts of vice admiralty. Those courts followed civil-law, rather than common-law, procedures. "The swarms of searchers, tide waiters, spies, and other underlings, with which every port in America now abounds," said a Philadelphia newspaper, "are not it seems, quite sufficient to ruin our trade, but infamous informers, like dogs of prey thirsting after the fortunes of worthy and wealthy men, are let loose and encouraged to seize and libel in the courts of admiralty the vessels of such as are advocates of the rights of America." Armed with the testimony of informers who might gain one-third of the value of ship and cargo in the event of a conviction, prosecutors initiated cases by merely bringing an accusation or "information." No grand jury indictment was necessary. The trial was without a jury. The judge held irregular sessions, used secret examinations and interrogatories, both written and oral, and then issued his decree.[42]

Admiralty procedures, Otis said in 1764, "savour more of . . . Rome and the Inquisition, than of the common law of England and the constitution of Great-Britain." Another American propagandist compared the vice-admiralty courts to the "high commission and star chamber courts." These exaggerations seemed true to anyone devoted to the common law, as were all Americans who opposed the revenue measures of the 1760's. When they damned the civil-law procedures of the vice-admiralty courts as violative of the rights of Englishmen, they knew that no jury would return a verdict of guilty against anyone accused of breaking one of Parliament's detested and allegedly unconstitutional revenue acts. In England, moreover, such cases could be tried only by the common-law Court of Exchequer.[43]

Henry Laurens, a wealthy, influential, and very conservative merchant-planter of South Carolina, fell prey to the rapacity of the customs officers and the vice-admiralty judge in Charleston. Within three months, in 1767, three of his ships were seized on insubstantial charges. In two of the cases, Judge Egerton Leigh released the vessels on ground that there was no evidence indicating intent to defraud the revenues or breach the acts of trade; yet Laurens was forced to pay court costs, including the judge's fees, in amounts exceeding the value of the ships. In the third case, for noncompliance with a technical formality of the law, Leigh condemned the ship in addition to assessing exorbitant costs. In one of these cases, he ruled that the searcher of the port, George Roupell, deputy to the collector, had acted without probable cause, leaving him open to a damage suit by Laurens. In 1768, Roupell retaliated by seizing the *Ann*, one of Lauren's most valuable ships, again on a highly technical charge. Leigh decreed an acquittal, though he again charged two-thirds of his fees and costs against Laurens; this time, however, the judge protected Roupell against a counter-suit by ruling that there had been probable cause for the seizure. He further protected Roupell by requiring him to swear an oath of calumny to prove that his actions were not motivated by malice. The oath of calumny brought the right against self-incrimination into play.[44]

Laurens, outraged by the injustice of oppressive suits and expensive fees, decided to expose customs racketeering and the venial admiralty judge. After publishing an article in the local press—newspapers as far away as Boston reprinted it—Laurens wrote an angry tract in 1768 detailing the history of his victimization. He denounced the vice-admiralty courts and extolled the protections of the common law. Of the various admiralty procedures that he found repugnant, none was worse than denial of trial by jury, but another, only slightly less obnoxious, was the willingness of the admiralty judge to abridge the right against self-incrimination. Laurens did not allege that Leigh had sought to force him to testify against himself. Rather, in an effort to support his argument against admiralty or civil-law procedure, he condemned Leigh for having exacted the oath of calumny from Roupell. Confusing the oath of calumny with the oath *ex officio*, Laurens warned against the dangers to liberty from that dread oath. He very effectively quoted Lord Bacon against the practice "whereby Men are inforced to accuse themselves," and in the next sentence alluded to torture. Laurens also quoted "the Learned Puffendorff" on the dangers of oaths when punishment or even "grievous Inconveniences" might be the consequence of confessing the truth. For his own part, Laurens added, he would rather have lost the case than have such an oath imposed on Roupell.[45]

Judge Leigh, replying to Laurens's many charges, exposed his accuser's confounding the oath of calumny and the oath *ex officio*. Leigh also denied that he had violated the right in question: "the benignity of our law will not suffer any man to accuse himself *criminally*. . . ." The case of the *Ann*, however, had not been a criminal one. Admiralty procedure, the admiralty judge observed, permitted the oath of calumny in order to protect the party against either the costs of the suit or a counter-action for damages in the event that probable cause for seizure were not established.[46]

The news of Laurens's ordeal reached Boston in the midst of a prosecution in the vice-admiralty court against another future president of the Continental Congress, John Hancock. In 1768 on the evidence of a confessed perjurer, the customs office in Boston libeled one of Hancock's ships for smuggling. The *Liberty*, as the ship was fatefully called, was seized, condemned, and forfeited. Then Hancock himself was sued for triple damages in a proceeding that in some respects really did savor of the inquisitorial. He was jailed and then released on bail of three thousand pounds sterling, an amount that would have been inordinately excessive in a common-law action, though in this case it was only one-third of the amount of the damages sought. Hancock's relatives, friends, employees, and business associates were privately examined and re-examined on interrogatories over a period of several months. Enemies and strangers, including pimps and informers, were paid to testify against him. His office was searched, his desk rifled, his papers seized. The patriot party launched a newspaper war against the admiralty court and in favor of common-law procedures. A special publication, *A Journal of the Times*, was issued almost daily in Boston as a news service detailing the prosecution, and newspapers in almost every colony copied or summarized its coverage of the case. *A Journal of the Times* obliquely assumed that the court violated the right against self-incrimination, as is evident from the unremitting and extravagant denunciations of "Star Chamber proceedings" by the "inquisitorial" tactics of examining men secretly and by "odious" interrogatories. In the hope that evidence could be "fished up" to sustain the prosecution, the court would stop at nothing, according to the patriot view. There were frequent references to the Laurens case, and the press asked whether the admiralty judge, being able to use interrogatories and the oath of calumny, might not next "put parties or witnesses to the torture, and extend them on the rack?"[47]

John Adams, who was Hancock's counsel, probably provided *A Journal of the Times* with its up-to-date accounts of the case, which dragged on for five months. Yet in his argument before the court, Adams was restrained both in tone and substance. He referred neither to the right against self-incrimination nor to the illegality of writs of assistance, though he did rely heavily on Magna Carta to prove that the statute authorizing trial by admiralty-court procedure in cases involving penalties and forfeiture violated the English constitution. He also argued that the case should be tried at common law, by a jury, with witnesses in open court, in the presence of the parties, face to face. "Examinations of witnesses upon Interrogatories," he added, "are only by the Civil Law. Interrogatories are unknown at common Law, and Englishmen and common Lawyers have an aversion to them if not an Abhorrence of them." Nevertheless, there is no reference to Hancock's having been examined under interrogatories, nor any real proof that they were used to incriminate the witnesses.[48]

The claim by an eminent historian that Hancock was "compelled to give evidence against himself" rests on the alleged use of his papers against him, though even that is not an established fact. Surely it is a gross exaggeration to claim, even as a probability, "that the constitutional provisions for indictment by a grand jury, trial by jury, forced self-incrimination, confronting witnesses face to face, excessive bail, depriving persons of property without due process of law, and excessive fines found in the earliest state constitutions and embodied in the fifth, sixth, seventh, and eighth amendments to the Federal Constitution are there because of the procedures of this case." On the other hand, these constitutional provisions, including the one in the Fifth Amendment, were stimulated, at least in part, by the kind of frenzied sense of injustice, real or feigned, that the Laurens and Hancock cases provoked in the patriot party. They exalted common-law procedures of criminal justice as expressions of fundamental law, and when the opportunity was theirs, they ritualistically gave constitutional embodiment to those procedures as if symbolically emancipating themselves from a tyranny, although it scarcely had existed.[49]

Despite the publicity of the Laurens and Hancock cases, in 1770 there was a move by the Customs Office in Philadelphia to question under oath every officer and seaman of a vessel that was supposed to have engaged in the smuggling of tea. But Attorney-General Andrew Allen informed the collector of the port: "I am very clear in opinion that the Court of Admiralty cannot with propriety oblige any persons to answer interrogatories which may have a tendency to criminate themselves, or subject them to a penalty, it being contrary to any principle of Reason and the Laws of England." [50]

That the right against self-incrimination was an illusion in New York is disproved by the sensational McDougall case, which occurred at this time. In December of 1769 a handbill addressed "To the Betrayed Inhabitants of New York," signed by a "Son of Liberty," was broadcast throughout the city. The author, criticizing the legislature for having voted to supply provisions for the king's troops, called upon the public to rise against unjust measures that subverted American liberties. The legislature condemned the handbill as a seditious libel and offered a reward for information leading to discovery of "Son of Liberty's" identity. A journeyman printer in the shop of James Parker, publisher of the *New York Gazette: or, the Weekly Post-Boy*, betrayed his employer as the printer of the broadside.[51]

On February 7, 1770, the governor and council summoned Parker and his employees. Having once before been jailed by the Assembly for publishing a reflection on its members, Parker was a reluctant witness. Claiming that he would be "wrecked" if he answered the council's questions, he asked for immunity in exchange for his co-operation. He remained reluctant even after being informed that he was not being asked to incriminate *himself*. The council then threatened him with the loss of his position in the post office and warned of his "danger"—punishment for contempt. Yet they did not threaten him criminally for a refusal to incriminate himself; they were after the author of the handbill. Giving Parker an opportunity to reconsider, the council brought in Anthony Carr, one of his journeymen. Carr, testifying under oath, denied knowledge of the identity of the author; however, he admitted that the offensive piece had been printed at Parker's. Councilman William Smith recorded in his diary that Carr was then told "at my Instance as Parker had been before, that he need not answer so as to accuse himself." Nevertheless, when Carr persisted in feigning ignorance, they bullied him with threats of imprisonment. Intimidated, he finally broke down, naming as author Captain Alexander McDougall. Carr's brother, John, also a journeyman printer in Parker's office, was next sworn and "told that he was not bound to accuse himself." John Carr willingly corroborated Anthony's testimony. The Council then recalled Parker. Upon being told that they knew everything about the writing and printing of the libel, he accepted the offer of a pardon and confessed both his role and McDougall's authorship. He was then sworn and his examination taken down.[52]

McDougall, a popular leader of the patriot party during these years of controversy with Britain—subsequently he was a delegate to both Continental Congresses and then a major-general during the Revolution—was arrested for seditious libel and jailed when he refused to pay bail. He turned his arrest into a theatrical triumph, consciously posing as America's Wilkes while the Sons of Liberty converted his prosecution into a weapon for the patriot cause. William Smith anonymously supported McDougall. Smith refused Governor Cadwallader Colden's request that he assist Attorney-General Kempe in the prosecution of "an unpopular suit." Then he published in Parker's paper a defense of McDougall, based chiefly upon liberty of the press, in which he censured the Star Chamber practice of examining "even the accused." The manuscript version of the article, which Smith considerably shortened for publication, also declared that "to the eternal scandal of this inquisition they examined sometimes the Party himself & even accepted against himself." [53]

When Parker, the principal witness for the crown, died, the

trial of McDougall was postponed a number of times. Finally the legislature, impatient for revenge, resolved to punish him on its own authority, and summoned McDougall before the bar of the House on December 13, 1770. Charged with having written "To the Betrayed," he was asked whether he was in fact the author. McDougall refused to answer, claiming his rights both against self-incrimination and against double jeopardy. The minutes of the Assembly's proceedings show his reply, in part, to be: "That as the Grand Jury & House of Assembly had declared the Paper in Question to be a Libel, he could not answer to the Question." [54]

In a letter to the press written from prison, McDougall more fully reported his statement as follows: "First, that the Paper just read to me, had been declared by the Honourable House to be a Libel; that the Grand Jury for . . . New York, had also declared it to be a Libel, and found a Bill of Indictment against me as the Author of it; therefore that I could not Answer a Question that would tend to impeach myself, or might otherwise be improper for me to answer." Because of McDougall's insistence that the Assembly could not try him on a criminal charge still being prosecuted in the courts, they voted him guilty of contempt and remanded him to prison for the remainder of their session, which continued for nearly three months. About a week after his release, the Sons of Liberty met to celebrate the anniversary of the repeal of the Stamp Act. One of the many toasts on that festive occasion was to Alexander McDougall; another was, "No Answer to Interrogatories, when tending to accuse the Person interrogated." McDougall's case not only popularized but made respectable the right against self-incrimination.[55]

The impact of McDougall's case is evident from the history of the use of oaths against suspects after 1770. Goebel and Naughton asserted that the legislature authorized oaths of purgation "until the very eve of the Revolution." Their proof is not only inaccurate; it omitted evidence to the contrary. The last statute employing the oath of purgation had been enacted in 1759. It prescribed, characteristically, an express disclaimer to be sworn by suspects: "I, A.B., do swear that I have not directly or Indirectly by myself or any other for me . . . [after publication of the statute] Bought Exchanged or taken in Pawn any Arms Ammunition or Cloathing of or from any Indian or Indians Whatsoever within any of the said Counties So help me God." Goebel and Naughton cited enactments of 1770 and 1774 as evidence of the continued use of "this purgation procedure," but neither contained an oath of purgation.[56]

The 1770 act authorized the examination "on oath" of any person suspected of concealing the assets of the estate of an insolvent debtor, but the oath was simply the usual one to tell the truth. The 1774 act is supposed to illustrate strikingly the "parallel between this purgation procedure and the ecclesiastical forms against which the English Puritans had so bitterly inveighed. . . ." But this act, which was directed against "excessive and deceitful gambling," simply made winners liable to suits for the recovery of their spoils; it also obliged suspects "to answer under Oath such Bill or Bills as shall be preferred against them for discovering the Sum and Sums of Money or other Thing so won at Play as aforesaid." Goebel and Naughton, having rather freely quoted this section of the statute, moved on to the "inescapable" conclusion that in New York Province there was "no attempt made to privilege a defendant . . . but on the contrary a great deal was done to make sure that in one form or other his testimony would be secured and that it would count against him. The shadowy protection offered by the rule that a confession could not be under oath, was quite offset in the cases where he could be convicted on a confession alone and by those where he was required to trap himself by a purging oath." But the oath authorized in the 1774 act against gambling was not an oath of purgation, and the act itself was more a manifestation of Puritan morality than of the ecclesiastical forms against which the English Puritans had inveighed. More important, Goebel and Naughton neglected to inform their readers that the next paragraph of the very same act against gambling provided that a person who confessed his winnings and repaid them "shall be acquitted, indemnified and discharged from any further or other Punishment, Forfeiture, or Penalty which he or they may have incurred by the playing for or winning such Money. . . ." Confession, in other words, "purged" him of his offense; it did not trap or incriminate him, for the statute—in the section omitted by Goebel and Naughton—provided for complete immunity. Then, as now, self-incrimination meant to expose oneself to "Punishment, Forfeiture, or Penalty," in the absence of which one cannot incriminate himself.[57]

The practice of providing immunity, which protects against self-incrimination, was begun by the legislature, significantly enough, in the first statute requiring an oath—but not an oath of purgation—that was passed after the McDougall case. This act of 1772 against private lotteries authorized justices of the peace to examine suspects under oath. Those who answered truthfully were "exempted from . . . Penalty, and from all Prosecutions in virtue of this Act. . . ." In the following year there was a re-enactment of an old statute against selling liquor to servants or extending them "large" credit. The original statute of 1750 had contained an oath of purgation; the re-enactment of 1773 made no mention of any kind of oath.[58]

In 1773, however, a new statute, overlooked by Goebel and Naughton, virtually authorized a purgative oath, though none was literally prescribed. To catch petty vandals, the legislature provided that a person caught in the vicinity, when a trespass such as the breaking of windows was committed, "shall be deemed guilty thereof" even if not an abettor. To absolve himself he must give evidence for the conviction of the parties "really guilty" or declare under oath that he was at the scene accidentally and did not know the identity of the real offenders. The obnoxious procedures authorized by this statute, the first and last of its kind since 1759, were the subject of a complaint to the Board of Trade, which recommended disallowance by the Privy Council. Mr. Jackson, the attorney for the crown, specifically censured the act as being "improper in that it provides for a Purgation by Oath in a criminal Matter, which is . . . contrary to the Genius of the Laws of this Country. . . ." The Privy Council, noting that Jackson's argument possessed "Weight," voted on July 6, 1774, to disallow the act despite its "useful" objective. However, the New York Assembly, on its own initiative and prior to the disallowance, re-enacted the statute against private lotteries, once again insuring immunity against prosecution to persons who confessed their guilt under a simple oath to tell the truth. In 1775 a new act on trespasses was passed without the objectionable procedures of the act of 1773 that had been disallowed—and without reference to oaths of any kind by the suspect. New York had surely come abreast the English common law. When the Revolution began, colonies and mother country differed little, if at all, on the right against self-incrimination.[59]

CHAPTER XIII

The Fifth Amendment

In 1776 several states elevated the common-law right against self-incrimination to the status of a constitutional right. The tie with Britain having been severed by war and the Declaration of Independence, the colonies professed the quaint belief that they had been thrown back into a state of nature. Consciously acting out the social compact theory, they adopted written constitutions to provide for permanent state governments and a paramount law which, as Virginia declared, would secure the inherent rights of the people as the basis of government. Virginia blazed the trail with her celebrated Declaration of Rights as a preface to her constitution. Its author, George Mason, gratifyingly recalled, "This was the first thing of the kind upon the continent, and has been closely imitated by all the States." To Mason belongs the credit for initiating the constitutionalization of the old rule of evidence that a man cannot "be compelled to give evidence against himself." Mason not only enshrined the rule in the fundamental law; at the same time he expressed it in an ambiguous way.[1]

Out of context, the phrase had a Lilburnian resonance, proclaiming the broad principle of the *nemo tenetur* maxim. In context, it guaranteed far less than the ordinary practice of the common law. Section 8 of the Virginia Declaration of Rights stated:

That in all capital or criminal prosecutions a man hath a right to demand the cause and nature of his accusation, to be confronted with the accusers and witnesses, to call for evidence in his favor,

and to a speedy trial by an impartial jury of twelve men of his
vicinage, without whose unanimous consent he cannot be found
guilty; *nor can he be compelled to give evidence against himself;*
that no man be deprived of his liberty, except by the law of the
land or the judgment of his peers.

The italicized words appear in the midst of an enumeration of the
rights of the criminally accused. Therefore the constitutional right
against self-incrimination was not extended to anyone but the accused, nor to any proceedings other than a criminal prosecution.
Since 1677, however, the law of Virginia had required that witnesses for the prosecution must give testimony under oath, "but
noe law can compell a man to sweare against himself in any matter
wherein he is lyable to corporal punishment." That language protected witnesses and parties in civil, as well as criminal, proceedings against the necessity of giving testimony that might expose
them to criminal penalties. Moreover, eighteenth-century manuals
of trial practice showed that criminal defendants were entitled to
have the sheriff subpoena witnesses to testify in their behalf under
oath, subject to the exception that the witnesses need not reply to
questions tending to self-incrimination.[2]

The right applied to all stages of all equity and common-law
proceedings and to all witnesses as well as to the parties. It could
be invoked by a criminal suspect at his preliminary examination
before a justice of the peace; by a person testifying at a grand
jury investigation into crime; by anyone giving evidence in a suit
between private parties; and, above all perhaps, by the subject of
an inquisitorial proceeding before any governmental or nonjudicial tribunal, such as a legislative committee or the governor and
council, seeking to discover criminal culpability. If one's disclosures could make him vulnerable to legal peril, he could invoke his
right to silence. He might even do so if his answers revealed infamy or disgrace yet could not be used against him in a subsequent prosecution. The law of Virginia at this time, as in England,
shielded witnesses against mere exposure to public obloquy. The
right against self-incrimination incorporated a protection against
self-infamy and was as broad as the jeopardy against which it
sought to guard. Yet the Virginia Declaration of Rights, though
vesting a testimonial rule with the impregnability of a constitu-

tional guarantee, provided only a stunted version of the common law.[3]

Read literally and in context, it seemed to apply only to a criminal defendant at his trial. If that was its meaning it was a superfluous guarantee, because the defendant at his trial was not even permitted to testify. If he had not confessed, the prosecution had to prove its case against him by the testimony of witnesses and other evidence; the prisoner, in turn, made his defense by witnesses, if he had them, by cross-examining the prosecution's witnesses, and by commenting on the evidence against him. If he could afford counsel, he need never open his mouth during the trial. With or without counsel, he could neither be placed on the stand by the prosecution nor taken the stand if he wished. Consequently, neither George Mason nor his colleagues in the legislature, who were acting as a constitutional convention, could have meant what they said. More likely, they failed to say what they meant.[4]

The provision against self-incrimination was the result of bad draftsmanship, which is not easily explained. Mason himself, though a planter, not a lawyer, indeed not even a college graduate, was probably more learned in the law than most lawyers; what is more, he had long been a justice of the peace for Fairfax County. Section 8 of the Declaration of Rights bespoke his familiarity with criminal procedure. The Declaration, taken as a whole, reflected stylistic elegance, a philosophic cast of mind, and a knowledge of English constitutional law and American experience. Mason's draft of the Declaration, done entirely alone, was far more comprehensive than the British precedents, such as the Petition of Right and the Bill of Rights. That draft was genuinely creative, embracing as it did, rights not recognized by English law. Nevertheless, Mason's handiwork has been more praised, and justly praised, than critically analyzed. There was a certain carelessness in his work, possibly the result of haste, which the convention remedied only in part. In Section 8, for example, Mason omitted the word "impartial" before "jury," and wrote that the accused should have a right to be confronted with the accusers "or"—instead of "and"—witnesses. The final draft retained the original's reference to "capital" prosecutions, a superfluousness in view of the reference to "all . . . criminal prosecutions." The convention also retained the inadequate statement that the accused had a right to "demand" rather than to "know" the cause and nature of the accusation; indeed, he should have been guaranteed the right to have a copy of the accusation. Similarly, his right to "call" for evidence in his favor was like the right to summon spirits from the deep: there was no knowing whether they would come. Compulsory process should have been guaranteed. More importantly, the convention, thanks to James Madison, altered Mason's guarantee of "the fullest toleration in the exercise of religion" to "the free exercise of religion." Among the omissions from Mason's draft, remedied by the committee, were a provision against general search warrants, which the convention accepted, and a ban on ex post facto laws and bills of attainder, which the convention, under the influence of Patrick Henry, deleted.[5]

The impressive catalogue of rights, both as drafted and adopted, inexplicably omitted the freedoms of speech, assembly, and petition; the right to the writ of habeas corpus; grand jury proceedings; the right to counsel; and freedom from double jeopardy as well as from attainders and ex post facto laws. The rights omitted were as important and nearly as numerous as those included, making the great Virginia Declaration of Rights appear to be an erratic document compiled in slipshod fashion. Under the circumstances the constrictive guarantee of the right against self-incrimination cannot be taken as a deliberate attempt to supersede the common law's more generous practice. Thoughtlessness, rather than indifference or a purposeful narrowing, seems to be the best explanation for the self-incrimination clause.

Jefferson was unbelievably more thoughtless, omitting all the rights omitted by Mason and far more. Even in his third draft of a proposed constitution—which arrived too late in Williamsburg to be of much influence—Jefferson forgot guarantees against exclusive privileges and excessive bail, and all the positive, specific rights of the criminally accused, except trial by jury, which Mason enumerated. Jefferson would have included a ban on legislative prescription of torture, but he neglected a ban against compulsory self-incrimination. By comparison Mason's work was a model of completeness. What is so surprising is not that he was careless or thoughtless, but that the committee or the convention did not remedy his omissions or deficiencies.[6]

As for the self-incrimination clause in Section 8, there is no evidence that it was taken literally or regarded as anything but a sonorous declamation of the common-law right of long standing. Other common-law rights that had been entirely overlooked by Virginia's constitution-makers, including such vital rights as habeas corpus, grand jury indictment, and representation by counsel, continued to be observed in daily practice. Thus the great Declaration of Rights did not alter Virginia's system of criminal procedure nor express the totality of rights which actually flourished. The practice of the courts was simply unaffected by the restrictions inadvertently or unknowingly inserted in Section 8.

Section 8, nevertheless, became a model for other states and for the United States Bill of Rights. Indeed the Virginia Declaration of Rights became one of the most influential constitutional documents in our history. The committee draft was reprinted in the Philadelphia newspapers even before Independence, making it available to the delegates from all the states assembled in the Second Continental Congress. That committee draft was republished all over America, and even in England and on the Continent, in time to be a shaping force in the framing of other state constitutions. Excepting the corporate colonies of Rhode Island and Connecticut which stood pat with their old colonial charters, the other states followed Virginia's example of framing a state constitution. Eight of them, including Vermont which was technically an independent republic from 1776 until her admission to the Union in 1791, annexed separate bills of rights to their constitutions.[7]

Every one of the eight protected the right against self-incrimination, and every one in essentially the language of Virginia's Section 8, because each followed the basic formulation that no man can be "compelled to give evidence against himself." Pennsylvania in 1776 adopted Section 8 in entirety, adding only the right to be represented by counsel and retaining the self-incrimination clause verbatim. Delaware in 1776 introduced a subtle but crucial change by making that clause an independent section instead of inserting it among the enumerated rights of the criminally accused. Moreover, Delaware's guarantee, "That no Man in the Courts of common Law ought to be compelled to give Evidence against himself," extended the right against self-incrimination to witnesses, as well as parties, in civil as well as criminal cases. Maryland in the same year also placed the self-incrimination clause in a section by itself and broadened it as did Delaware, extending it not only to "a common court of law" but also to "any other court," meaning courts of equity. But Maryland simultaneously qualified the right by providing for exceptions to it "in such cases as have been usually practised in this State, or may hereafter be directed by the Legislature." That qualification, in effect, required a man to give evidence against himself if a pardon or a grant of immunity against prosecution exempted him from the penal consequences of his disclosures. North Carolina in 1776 followed Virginia's Section 8, as did Vermont in 1777. In 1780 Massachusetts slightly modified the Virginia phraseology. Referring to a criminal defendant, Massachusetts provided that he should not be compelled "to accuse, or furnish"—instead of "give"—evidence against himself. In 1784 New Hampshire followed suit. George Mason's observation that his Declaration of Rights was "closely imitated" was certainly accurate with respect to the self-incrimination clause.[8]

Of the four states—New Jersey, New York, Georgia, and South Carolina—that did not preface their constitutions with a separate bill of rights, none secured the right against self-incrimination. All, however, guaranteed some rights, even if only a few, at various points in their constitutions. New Jersey, for example, had an omnibus clause that kept the common law of England in force, yet it specifically protected the right to counsel and trial by jury; New Jersey also protected freedom of religion, which the common law did not recognize. New York, too, provided that the common law, and English statutory law as well, should continue to be the law of the state, excepting the part that concerned English authority over New York or the establishment of religion. This omnibus clause has been termed a "terse bill of rights" because so many constitutional rights were embedded in the common law. Yet the right to indictment and trial by jury, which were expressly mentioned in New York's constitution, were surely secured by the common law. Why they were singled out above all other common-law rights is inexplicable, especially because the courts were enjoined to "proceed according to the course of the common law," and citizens were additionally protected by the standard "law of the land" or due process of law clause. The constitution also protected the right to vote, the free exercise of religion, representation by counsel, and a qualified freedom from bills of attainder. Perhaps these rights were singled out because they were either unprotected or, at best, inadequately protected by the common law. Yet, other rights in the same category were ignored, while trial by jury was superfluously secured. The whole process of selection in New York was baffling. No reasoned explanation nor any drawn from the evidence is available.[9]

Although the right against self-incrimination was not mentioned in New York's constitution, neither were the rights to freedom of speech and press—shade of Zenger!—nor the writ of habeas corpus. Additionally, New York ignored protections against unreasonable searches and seizures, ex post facto laws, and double jeopardy. The absence of express guarantees simply cannot be construed to indicate that these rights were not present in practice. One could no more reasonably argue that the omission of a ban against compulsory self-incrimination proved that it did not exist or was regarded without respect than he could argue that the right to the writ of habeas corpus was illusionary because it, too, was not constitutionally protected. In its enumeration of rights, New York's constitution was framed in an incredibly haphazard fashion, like New Jersey's, with no discernible principle of selection. The same observation applied to the constitutions of South Carolina and Georgia, neither of which protected the right against self-incrimination.[10]

The history of the writing of the first American bills of rights and constitutions simply does not bear out the presupposition that the process was a diligent or systematic one. Those documents, which we uncritically exalt, were imitative, deficient, and irrationally selective. In the glorious act of framing a social compact expressive of the supreme law, Americans tended simply to draw up a random catalogue of rights that seemed to satisfy their urge for a statement of first principles—or for some of them. That task was executed in a disordered fashion that verged on ineptness. The inclusion or exclusion of any particular right neither proved nor disproved its existence in a state's colonial history.

Twelve states, including Vermont but excluding Rhode Island

and Connecticut, framed constitutions before the framing of the United States Bill of Rights. The only right universally secured was trial by jury in criminal cases, unless freedom of religion be added to the list even though some states guaranteed only religious toleration and others, no less than five, constitutionally permitted or provided for an establishment of religion in the form of tax supports for churches. Two states passed over a free press guarantee. Four neglected to ban excessive fines, excessive bail, compulsory self-incrimination, and general search warrants. Five ignored protections for the rights of assembly, petition, counsel, and trial by jury in civil cases. Seven omitted a prohibition on ex post facto laws, and eight skipped over the vital writ of habeas corpus. Nine failed to provide for grand jury proceedings and to condemn bills of attainder. Ten said nothing about freedom of speech, while eleven—all but New Hampshire—were silent on the matter of double jeopardy. In view of this record, the fact that every state having a separate bill of rights protected the right against self-incrimination is rather impressive. And for all their faults, the state bills of rights adopted before the federal Bill of Rights were achievements of the first magnitude compared to anything in the past, on either side of the Atlantic. The remarkable thing perhaps is that in time of war, the constructive and unprecedented task of constitution-making was successfully carried out. The enduring heroics of the Revolution were to be found in George Mason's study and in the legislative halls as well as at Valley Forge and Saratoga.[11]

Revolution and war may engender handsome statements of libertarian principle but are scarcely propitious circumstances for the nurture of personal liberties or closing the breach between profession and practice. Everywhere there was unlimited freedom to praise the American cause, but criticism of it invited a tarring and feathering by the zealots of patriotism. A Tory, after all, as Jefferson himself said, had been "properly defined to be a traitor in thought, but not in deed." Throughout the years of controversy that led to the war, and during the war itself, the patriots denied to those suspected of Tory thoughts and sympathies the rights they claimed for themselves. The maxim congenial to the spirit of liberty, let justice be done though heaven fall (*fiat justitia ruat coelum*), yielded to the maxim that in time of war the laws are silent (*inter arma silent leges*).[12]

The case of George Rome in 1773 probably foreshadowed the eclipse of the right against self-incrimination during the war. Rome was a Rhode Island Tory who wrote a private letter scathingly criticizing the Assembly and judiciary. The letter fell into the hands of the patriot party and appeared in the *Providence Gazette*. The Assembly arrested him for "vile abuse" of the government. Summoned before the bar of the house, he refused answer to the question whether the opinions expressed in the letter were his own. "I do not think," he replied, "on the privilege of an Englishman, that the question is fairly stated, because I do not consider I am to be called here to accuse myself." Rome persisted on this ground, and the Assembly, showing no respect whatever for the right against self-incrimination, voted him guilty of contempt and imprisoned him for the remainder of its session. Earlier in the same year Governor Dunmore of Virginia and his council inquisitorially examined a group of men suspected of counterfeiting. The House of Burgesses, though protesting the breach of normal criminal procedure, mentioned only the governor's failure to bring the suspects before the local court for examination. Criminals with safe political opinions fared better than law-abiding Tories. During the war Virginia imprisoned persons on mere suspicion that they might aid the enemy during some future military emergency, kept them in jail without charges or a hearing, passed a bill of attainder and outlawry, and punished traitorous opinions as well as deeds. Respect for the right against self-incrimination or for other rights would have meant to the revolutionists that their Declaration of Rights was an instrument of their destruction.[13]

In New York, where the Tories were numerically strongest, a committee "for detecting and defeating conspiracies," organized at the suggestion of Congress, used short-cut procedures in the mass trial of suspects. The function of the committee was to examine persons, and their papers, who appeared dangerous to the safety of the state, to administer loyalty oaths, and to convict the guilty. About one thousand persons were tried and sentenced and another six hundred released on bail. The legislature ignored petitions of grievance like the one stating that "the *Star Chamber Court* of commissioners for detecting & defeating conspiracies ought to be abolished." On occasion, revolutionary authorities could afford to be more respectful of procedure. The military tribunal that tried Major John André, a British spy but an officer and a gentleman, afforded him the courtesy of being at liberty to answer or deny answer to interrogatories as he chose. A more intriguing and very important case was that of Silas Deane, the American envoy whose corrupt schemes abroad, mixing profits with patriotism, set off a Congressional investigation. Deane exercised his right "not to answer questions which might tend to criminate himself," and one of his chief opponents, Henry Laurens, President of the Continental Congress, supported his right of silence, describing the inquiry as "an ex-parte Inquisition." The Deane case remained controversial for several years. In 1781 "A Citizen," attacking Congressman Gouverneur Morris for having supported Deane, sought to embarrass him by asking in a newspaper letter whether he had been among those who had urged in Congress that Deane should be excused from answering questions that sought his incrimination. Exempting Deane from answer, wrote "A Citizen," by permitting him to plead the right revealed "a purpose which implies a conviction in the author and abettors of it, that abuses had been committed, and could have no other end than to screen the party from detection." Morris, repudiating the implication of guilt drawn from an invocation of the right, replied in the same newspaper: ". . . and when he (Deane) prayed that he might not be bound to answer questions tending to accuse himself, I voted for granting his request. If it were to be done over I would do the same thing even if I believed him to be a villain, which I certainly did not." Morris's statement implies that Congress actually voted in favor of the lawfulness of an invocation of the right by a witness in a Congressional investigation.[14]

Four years after the Treaty of Peace that ended the war, the Constitutional Convention met in Philadelphia to form a stronger national government. No bill of rights introduced the finished work of the delegates. Only a few days before adjournment, Mason of Virginia almost perfunctorily wished "the plan had been prefaced with a Bill of Rights," because it would "give great quiet to the people," and he offered to second a motion "if made for the purpose." His belated speech persuaded Elbridge Gerry of Massachusetts to make the motion, which Mason seconded. But the delegates, voting in state units, defeated it ten to zero. Not a man present opposed a bill of rights, but having been in session for four months, the delegates were weary and eager to return home. Morover, they had planned a government of limited, enumerated powers, making unnecessary, they reasoned, a list of restraints on powers that did not exist. When, for example, there was another motion to insert a clause declaring that "the liberty of the Press should be inviolably observed," Roger Sherman of Connecticut tersely objected, "It is unnecessary. The power of Congress does not extend to the Press." The framers were also skeptical of the value of "Parchment barriers" against "overbearing majorities," as Madison put it, knowing that even an absolute constitutional prohibition, as experience had proved, dissolved in the case of an emergency or public alarm.[15]

The usually masterful politicians who dominated the Convention had seriously erred. Their arguments were plausible but neither convincing nor politic. A bill of rights could do no harm, and as Jefferson said, might do some good. The contention that declaring some rights might jeopardize others not mentioned was specious, inconsistent, and easily answerable as the Ninth Amendment showed. But there was no answer to Mason's point that a bill of rights would quiet the fears of the people. Neither was it good politics to alienate Mason and his followers or to hand them a stirring cause around which to muster opposition to ratification. Supporters of the Constitution were trapped by the fact that their principal point, "why declare that things shall not be done which there is no power to do?," might arguably apply to freedom of religion or freedom of speech, but could have no bearing on the rights of the criminally accused or personal liberties of a procedural nature. The new and, to many, very frightening national government would operate directly on individuals and be buttressed by an undefined executive power and a national judiciary to enforce the laws made by Congress, and Congress had the authority to define crimes and prescribe penalties. Finally, the alleged needlessness of a bill of rights could not be squared with the fact that the proposed Constitution did explicitly protect certain rights. It tightly defined treason, provided for jury trials in criminal cases and for the writ of habeas corpus in the national courts, and banned both ex post facto laws and bills of attainder. No rational argument—and the lack of a bill of rights created a hyper-emotional issue that was not amenable to rational argument—could possibly ease the fear that guaranteeing a few rights left in jeopardy others that were equally familiar and cherished but ignored. Criminal defendants might be assured of trial by jury, but what prevented the national government from seizing evidence against them by the use of general search warrants, and would they have the benefit of indictment by grand jury, a trial by a jury of the vicinage, representation by counsel, or freedom from compulsory self-incrimination, excessive bail, and cruel punishments? Security lay in the certainty of express protections, rather than the bona fides of the defenders of the Constitutions.[16]

In Pennsylvania, the second state to ratify, the Anti-Federalist minority in the state's ratifying convention indicated a willingness to accept the Constitution on condition that a number of amendments be approved. But the Federalist-dominated convention, by a vote of 46 to 23, rejected the minority propositions and even refused to enter them in the journal of the convention or in the reporter's account of the debates. Immediately after the convention adjourned, the minority published their "Address and Reasons of Dissent," which was reprinted from Richmond to Boston. Among the proposed amendment was a verbatim duplication of Virginia's Section 8, including the self-incrimination clause, made applicable "as well in the federal courts as in those of the several States." Nothing in the statement of the Pennsylvania minority, nor anything in the debates, revealed the contemporary understanding of the clause.[17]

Massachusetts, the sixth state to ratify, was the first to do so with recommended amendments. The Anti-Federalists had entered the state ratifying convention with a very substantial majority of votes. One of their spokesmen, Abraham Holmes, focused on the alleged dangers surrounding the national judicial power. Trial by jury in criminal cases had been provided for, he admitted, but the mode of trial had not been determined, nor that it be a trial in the vicinage. There was no assurance of the benefit of counsel, confrontation of accusers and witnesses, or the advantage of cross-examination. Worse still, there was nothing to prevent Congress from establishing "that diabolical institution, the Inquisition." His frenetic forebodings unleashed, Holmes declared that in the absence of constitutional checks, Congress might invent "the most cruel and unheard of punishments . . . racks and gibbets may be amongst the most mild instruments of their discipline." What was needed, Holmes advised, was something to prevent Congress from passing laws that might compel a person, accused or suspected of a crime, from furnishing evidence against himself. Without such a check, if the worst did not come to pass, "it would be owing *entirely* . . . to the goodness of the men, and not in the *least degree* owing to the goodness of the Constitution." By overstating his case, Holmes lost it. Clearly, however, he spoke of the right against self-incrimination only in connection with the criminally accused.[18]

The Reverend Samuel Stillman, in defense of the Constitution, reminded the convention that Congress was a representative body, elected by the people of the states. "Who are Congress, then? They are ourselves; the men of our own choice, in whom we can confide . . . Why is it then that gentlemen speak of Congress as some foreign body, as a set of men who will seek every opportunity to enslave us?" Stillman observed that not even a perfect Constitution could secure the liberties of the people "unless they watch their own liberties. Nothing written on paper will do this." Knowledge and freedom were inseparable. If education were widespread and Americans remained an enlightened people attached to liberty, the cause of tyranny had no hope. When John Hancock and Samuel Adams, the most influential men in the convention, threw their support to Stillman's voice of reason rather than to Holmes's hysteria, there was no chance for amendments that would do battle against the revival of the Inquisition with its racks and gibbets.

The brief list of amendments recommended by Massachusetts mentioned only two matters that belonged with a traditional bill of rights, jury trial in civil suits between citizens of different states and indictment by grand jury. Ironically, the grand-jury system, which was as strong in Massachusetts as in any common-law jurisdiction, had no place in the state constitution. No principle of selection may be discerned for the choice of the civil jury and indictment among all the rights that could have been chosen for protection. To have marked them for enumeration rather than freedom of religion, speech, or press, or bans on general warrants and compulsory self-incrimination was capricious. Yet Massachusetts led the way toward recommended amendments.[19]

Every state convention thereafter urged amendments to the Constitution, but, inexplicably, only the last four to ratify recommended comprehensive bills of rights. As a result many crucial rights received the support of only these states. All four of them urged a self-incrimination clause. The first of these four to ratify was Virginia, where Patrick Henry, the demagogic idol of the people, zealously opposed ratification as if once again combating British tyranny. The Constitution seemed to him to be a conspiracy against the liberties of the people, proof that he was right in having turned down a seat in the Constitutional Convention because he had "smelt a rat." His credentials as the champion of individual freedoms had been besmirched by his responsibility for Virginia's having enacted a bill of attainder and by his leadership of the opposition to Jefferson's Statute for Religious Freedom. But he was the master of the rhetorical thunderbolt and creator of an emotional climate of fear that alarmed rather than informed. Denouncing the omission of a bill of rights and prophesying imaginary horrors masked more practical, even ignoble, objections to the Constitution. Objections to the powers of commerce and taxation were not as easily popularized in dramatic terms. Congress, Henry warned, might replace the common law with the civil law of Europe and "introduce the practice of France, Spain, and Germany—of torturing, to extort a confession of crime." On such reasoning he recommended that the states adopt amendments to the Constitution prior to its ratification, including a bill of rights modeled on Virginia's of 1776. Neither Henry nor anyone else explained the meaning of the self-incrimination clause of Section 8, nor, for the matter, of any of the other rights that they recommended. The only reply to him by an advocate of the Constitution, on the self-incrimination issue, came from George Nicholas who cynically observed that if a bill of rights was the only protection against torture, "we might be tortured tomorrow; for it has been repeatedly infringed and disregarded." Mason, misunderstanding him to have said that there was no guarantee against torture in Virginia's Declaration of Rights, pointed out that one clause provided that no man could give evidence against himself, "and the worthy gentlemen must know that, in those countries where torture is used, evidence was extorted from the criminal himself." Another clause, Mason added, prohibited cruel and unusual punishments. The convention adopted Henry's proposals, but only in the form of recommended amendments. Nothing in the proceedings provided any illumination of the meaning of the self-incrimination clause in Virginia, except perhaps that it applied to the criminally accused and barred torture.[20]

Among the proposed amendments offered by the New York ratifying convention was one insuring "that in all criminal prosecutions, the accused . . . should not be compelled to give evidence against himself." Unfortunately the record of the state convention's debates does not illuminate the reasons for this or for any other proposal included in the suggested national bill of rights. The debates are fully reported through July 2, 1788, when a bill of rights was mentioned for the first time in a speech by Thomas Tredwell, an Anti-Federalist delegate who expressed apprehension about the danger of tyranny on the part of the new United States courts. None could say, he declared, whether their proceedings would be according to the common law or the "civil, the Jewish, or Turkish law," and he warned darkly about the history of inquisitions in the Star Chamber Court of England. Tredwell's is the last reported speech on any subject. The proceedings of the convention are thereafter reported in brief minutes. We know little more than that on July 7, John Lansing, one of the Anti-Federalist leaders, reported a proposed bill of rights, that it was debated on the nineteenth, and was passed on the twenty-sixth.[21]

New York's recommended bill of rights, which included a provision on the right against self-incrimination, was the product of an interstate Anti-Federalist committee of correspondence. As early as June 9, a letter to John Lamb, as head of "the federal Republican Committee of New York," from George Mason, chairman of the Republican Society of Virginia, concurred in Lamb's suggestion of a "free correspondence on the Subject of amendments." George Mason, Patrick Henry, and William Grayson kept Lamb informed of the nature and progress of proposed amendments in the Virginia convention, while Lamb kept in touch with Eleazer Oswald of Pennsylvania, Rawlins Lowndes of South Carolina, Joshua Atherton of New Hampshire, and Timothy Bloodworth of North Carolina, all leading Anti-Federalists. The Pennsylvania minority, whose dissenting report was circulated in New York, had proposed an amendment securing the right against self-incrimination, taken from the Virginia Declaration of Rights of 1776. Copies of Virginia's declaration were forwarded to Lamb by Patrick Henry and to Robert Yates by George Mason.[22]

The initial proposal for a bill of rights, by Lansing, consisted of three sections: one securing the rights of life and liberty in general, another vesting sovereignty in the people, and the third a verbatim statement of Section 8 of the Virginia Declaration of Rights. On July 19, Melancthon Smith proposed amendments constituting a bill of rights. Excepting a comment by John Jay to the effect that no bill of rights was needed, there appears to have been no debate on the motion. On its passage, Smith moved adoption of "the Virginia amendments," the entire package proposed by the Virginia convention which on June 25 had voted for ratification with recommended amendments, including a provision copied from Section 8. The only debate in New York occurred on the question whether the amendments were to be recommended or made conditional. Thus, under the influence of Virginia, the right against self-incrimination was recommended by the New York convention, notwithstanding its absence in the state's own constitution. Other states also recommended rights not secured by their own constitutions. Virginia, for example, urged the right to counsel and the freedoms of speech, assembly, and petition, none of which were mentioned in her celebrated Declaration of Rights. In New York, both Anti-Federalists and Federalists unquestioningly accepted the right against self-incrimination as a desideratum in the procedures to be followed in federal criminal prosecutions. There is nothing in the circumstances surrounding the New York proposal to doubt that the right was a traditional and respected part of the state's common-law system of criminal procedure. One may suspect the political motives of the anti-Federalists in demanding that a bill of rights be affixed to the new national constitution, but not the sincerity of their belief in the value of their proposals.[23]

The other two states recommending amendments that included a self-incrimination clause were North Carolina and Rhode Island. Ratification by the latter, coming after the First Congress had already drafted the Bill of Rights, was too late to be of any influence. Both states used the Virginia formula, broadly stating the principle that no man should be compelled to give evidence against himself, but placing the clause in a context that unmistakably referred only to the criminally accused. New York alone had made that reference explicit. The Fifth Amendment's clause would be closer to the Virginia formula and yet be unique.[24]

In the First Congress, Representative James Madison redeemed a campaign pledge to fight for a bill of rights as soon as the new national government went into operation. Although he had originally opposed a bill of rights for the usual Federalist reasons, Madison, even if still somewhat skeptical of the efficacy of such a bill, had become a convert to the cause. He deserves to be remembered as "father of the Bill of Rights" even more than as "father of the Constitution," his usual appellation. Jefferson, his friend and mentor, in a brilliant exchange of letters had persuaded him to surrender his initial opposition, but political expediency was not without its influence, too. In addition to the promise Madison had made to his constituents, he realized that amendments would allay the apprehensions—misapprehensions he thought them—of a large part of the American public. He meant to prove that the new national government was a friend of liberty. He even included a proposed amendment to prevent the *states*, which opponents of the Constitution had represented as guarantors of personal freedom, from infringing the equal rights of conscience, freedom of the press, and trial by jury. This, he declared, was "the most valuable" of all his proposals. Madison also understood that the adoption of his amendments would do more than reconcile the people who had been frightened by the anti-Federalist cry that "they're taking away your liberties!" His amendments, if adopted, would make extremely difficult the subsequent passage of proposals, so close to the hearts of the opposition party, that were intended to hamstring the substantive powers of the national government. He argued that his amendments would raise a standard of conduct for government to follow and provide a basis for judicial review on behalf of civil liberties: "If they are incorporated into the Constitution, independent tribunals of justice will consider themselves in a peculiar manner the guardians of those rights; they will be an impenetrable bulwark against every assumption of power in the Legislative or Executive; they will be naturally led to resist every encroachment upon rights expressly stipulated for in the Constitution by the declaration of rights." [25]

Madison's proposals, introduced on June 8, 1789, were, in the words of Fisher Ames of Massachusetts, "the fruit of much labor and research." He had "hunted up," said Ames, all the grievances expressed in the newspapers, the state debates, and the recommendations of state ratifying conventions. His long, masterful speech on behalf of his proposals forced an apathetic House to take action, though men of both parties were reluctant; they were more interested in attending to tonnage duties and a judiciary bill. Many Federalists still thought that a bill of rights was unnecessary, while Anti-Federalists, who so recently had urged a bill of rights with all the rhetorical powers that they could muster, sought to scuttle Madison's proposals. They began by stalling, then tried to annex amendments aggrandizing state powers, and finally depreciated the importance of the very protections of individual liberty that they had formerly demanded. Madison would not be put off. He was insistent, compelling, unyielding, and, finally, triumphant.[26]

As originally proposed by Madison, the Fifth Amendment's self-incrimination clause was part of a miscellaneous article that read: "No person shall be subject, except in cases of impeachment, to more than one punishment or trial for the same offence; nor shall be compelled to be a witness against himself; nor be deprived of life, liberty, or property, without due process of law; nor be obliged to relinquish his property, where it may be necessary for public use, without a just compensation." This proposal reflects the research and novelty that characterized Madison's work. Not a single state, for example, had a constitutional guarantee that life, liberty, or property should not be deprived but by due process of law, although New York, but only New York, had recommended such a clause. No state had recommended a just-compensation clause, though both Massachusetts and Vermont had such provisions in their constitutions. New Hampshire was the only state with a provision against double jeopardy. But no state, either in its own constitution or in its recommended amendments, had a self-incrimination clause phrased like that introduced by Madison: "no person . . . shall be compelled to be a witness against himself." [27]

Not only was Madison's phrasing original; his placement of the clause was also unusual. In the widely imitated model of his own state, the clause appeared in the midst of an enumeration of the procedural rights of the criminally accused at his trial. Only Delaware and Maryland had departed from this precedent by giving the clause independent status and applicability in all courts, thereby extending it to witnesses as well as parties and to civil as well as criminal proceedings. In presenting his amendments, Madison said nothing whatever that explained his intentions concerning the self-incrimination clause. Nor do his papers or correspondence illuminate his meaning. We have only the language of his proposal, and that revealed an intent to incorporate into the Constitution the whole scope of the common-law right. From the very meaning of its terms, Madison's proposal seemed as broad as the old *nemo tenetur* maxim in which it had its origins, while at the same time it virtually amalgamated that maxim with another that was different in origin and purpose: *nemo debet esse testis in propria causa* (no man should be a witness in his own case).

Madison's proposal certainly applied to civil as well as criminal proceedings and in principle to any stage of a legal inquiry, from the moment of arrest in a criminal case, to the swearing of a deposition in a civil one. And not being restricted to judicial proceedings, it extended to any other kind of governmental inquiry such as a legislative investigation. Moreover, the unique phrasing, that none could be compelled to be a witness against himself, was far more comprehensive than a prohibition against self-incrimination. By its terms the clause could also apply to any testimony that fell short of making one vulnerable to criminal jeopardy or civil penalty or forfeiture, but that nevertheless exposed him to public disgrace or obloquy, or other injury to name and reputation. Finally, Madison's phrasing protected third parties, those who were merely witnesses called to give testimony for one side or the other, whether in civil, criminal, or equity proceedings. According to customary procedure, witnesses, unlike parties, could in fact be compelled to give evidence, under oath, although they were safeguarded against the necessity of testifying against themselves in any manner that might open them to prosecution for a criminal offense or subject them to a forfeiture or civil penalties. By contrast, neither the criminal defendant nor the parties to a civil suit could be compelled to give testimony at all. They could furnish evidence neither for nor against themselves. The law did require mere witnesses to give evidence for or against the parties, but not against themselves. Madison, going beyond the recommendations of the states and the constitution of his own state, phrased his own proposal to make it coextensive with the broadest practice. He might have achieved the same end by retaining the language of the Virginia recommendation, that no man can be compelled to give evidence against himself, but fixing it outside of the context of criminal prosecutions.[28]

Madison's proposed amendments were sent to a select committee of which he was a member. The committee, when reporting to the House, made no change in the positioning or language of the clause protecting persons from being witnesses against themselves. The report was taken up by the Committee of the Whole after Madison fought off further delaying tactics, and debate followed seriatim on each proposed amendment. There was no debate, however, on the clause in question. Only one speaker, John Laurence, a Federalist lawyer of New York, addressed himself to what he called the proposal that "a person shall not be compelled to give evidence against himself." Interestingly, he restated Madison's phrasing in the language of the more familiar clause deriving from Section 8 of the Virginia Declaration of Rights, as if they were the same. Calling it "a general declaration in some degree contrary to laws passed," Laurence thought that it should "be confined to criminal cases," and he moved an amendment for that purpose. The amendment was adopted, apparently without discussion, not even by Madison, and then the clause as amended was adopted unanimously. We do not know whether the House debated Laurence's motion or what the vote on it was. The speed with which the House seems to have acted, without the record showing any controversy over the significant restriction of the scope of the clause, is bewildering. Simple respect for the House's own distinguished select committee, a nonpartisan group that included one member from each state, five of whom had been delegates to the Philadelphia Constitutional Convention of 1787, ought to have required some explanation. The select committee, following Madison, had intended what Laurence rightly called "a general declaration." Taken literally, the amended clause, "No person shall . . . be compelled in any criminal case, to be a witness against himself," excluded from its protection parties and witnesses in civil and equity suits as well as witnesses before nonjudicial governmental proceedings such as legislative investigations. It now applied only to parties and witnesses in criminal cases, presumably to all stages of proceedings from arrest and examination to indictment and trial.[29]

Laurence's passing remark that the committee proposal was "in some degree contrary to laws passed" was inaccurate, yet illuminated the purpose of his motion to amend. Exactly a month earlier, on July 17, the Senate had passed and sent to the House the bill that became the Judiciary Act of 1789. Thanks to Madison's efforts, the House merely read the judiciary bill for a first and second time on July 20, then tabled it indefinitely while it attended to the matter of amending the Constitution. Not until the House approved of the proposed amendments and sent them to the Senate on August 24 did the Committee of the Whole take up the judiciary bill. Its provisions, which had been fiercely contested in the Senate, contained a section to which Laurence may have alluded when referring to "laws passed." Section 15 in the original Senate draft empowered the federal courts to compel civil parties to produce their books or papers containing relevant evidence. It also provided that a plaintiff might require a defendant, on proving to the satisfaction of a court that the defendant had deprived him of evidence to support his cause, "to disclose on oath his or her knowledge in the cause in cases and under circumstances where a respondent might be compelled to make such a disclosure on oath by the aforesaid rules of chancery." Opponents of that final clause described it as an authorization for "inquisitorial powers." Senator William Maclay of Pennsylvania argued that "extorting evidence from any person was a species of torture. . . . [H]ere was an attempt to exercise a tyranny of the same kind over the mind. The conscience was to be put on the rack; that forcing oaths or evidence from men, I consider equally tyrannical as extorting evidence by torture." The clause, he concluded, would offend his constitutents, whose state bill of rights provided that no person could be compelled to give evidence against himself. As a result of such opposition the oath provision was stricken from the bill as adopted by the Senate. Nevertheless, it retained the clause forcing the production of books or papers that contained pertinent evidence in civil cases "under circumstances where they might be compelled to produce the same by the ordinary rules of proceeding in Chancery," that is, in courts of equity.[30]

According to an early federal court ruling, this provision was intended to prevent the necessity of instituting equity suits to obtain from an adverse party the production of documents related to a litigated issue. The provision did not suspend or supersede the right against self-incrimination, but it did limit the reach of the general principle that no one could be compelled to be a witness against himself. The documents in question could be *against* the party without incriminating him. He might, for example, be forced to produce a deed proving plaintiff's ownership, thereby exposing himself to a civil, but not a criminal, liability. Thus Laurence, with this pending legislation in mind, may have moved the insertion of the words "in any criminal case" in order to retain the customary equity rule that compelled evidence of civil liability. To compel a civil defendant to produce records or papers "against himself," harming his case, in no way infringed his traditional right not to produce them if they could harm him criminally. The House, incidentally, passed the judiciary bill with Section 15 unchanged.[31]

In the Senate, the House's proposed amendments to the Constitution underwent further change. However, the Senate accepted the self-incrimination clause without change. The double jeopardy

clause in the same article was rephrased and a clause on the grand
jury, which the House had coupled with guarantees relating to
the trial of crimes, was transferred to the beginning of what became the Fifth Amendment. In what was to be the Sixth Amendment the Senate clustered together the procedural rights of the
criminally accused after indictment. That the self-incrimination
clause did not fall into the Sixth Amendment indicated that the
Senate, like the House, did not intend to follow the implication of
Virginia's Section 8, the original model, that the right not to give
evidence against oneself applied merely to the defendant on trial.
The Sixth Amendment, referring explicitly to the accused, protected him alone. Indeed the Sixth Amendment, with the right of
counsel added, was the equivalent of Virginia's Section 8 and included all of its rights except that against self-incrimination. Thus,
the location of the self-incrimination clause in the Fifth Amendment rather than the Sixth proves that the Senate, like the House,
did not intend to restrict that clause to the criminal defendant only nor only to his trial. The Fifth Amendment, even with the self-
incrimination clause restricted to criminal cases, still put its principle broadly enough to apply to witnesses and to any phase of
the proceedings.[32]

The clause by its terms also protected against more than just
"self-incrimination," a phrase that had never been used in the long
history of its origins and development. The "right against self-
incrimination" is a short-hand gloss of modern origin that implies
a restriction not in the constitutional clause. The right not to be a
witness against oneself imports a principle of wider reach, applicable, at least in criminal cases, to the self-production of any adverse evidence, including evidence that made one the herald of his
own infamy, thereby publicly disgracing him. The clause extended, in other words, to all the injurious as well as incriminating
consequences of disclosure by witness or party. But this inference
drawn from the wording of the clause enjoys the support of no
proof based on American experience, as distinguished from English, before the nineteenth century. Clearly, however, to speak
merely of a right against self-incrimination stunts the wider right
not to give evidence against oneself, as the Virginia model put it,
or not to be a witness against oneself, as the Fifth Amendment

stated. The previous history of the right, both in England and America, proves that it was not bound by rigid definition. After the adoption of the Fifth Amendment, the earliest state and federal cases were in accord with that previous history, which suggests that whatever the wording of the constitutional formulation, it did not supersede or even limit the common-law right.[33]

Pennsylvania's experience is to the point. The state constitution of 1776 had followed the Virginia model by placing in the context of criminal prosecutions the principle that "no man" should be compelled to give evidence against himself. In 1790 Pennsylvania, in a new constitution, replaced the "no man" formulation with a specific reference to "the accused." Nevertheless, in the first Pennsylvania case involving this clause, the state supreme court ignored the restriction introduced in 1790 or, rather, interpreted it as expressing in the most extraordinary latitude the *nemo tenetur* maxim. The case involved a prosecution for violating an election-law that required answers on oath to questions concerning loyalty during the American Revolution. Counsel for defense argued that the constitutional clause of 1790 protected against questions the answers to which might tend to result in a prosecution or bring the party into disgrace or infamy. Chief Justice Edward Shippen, who had studied at Middle Temple and began his legal practice in Pennsylvania way back in 1750, delivered the following opinion:

> It has been objected that the questions propounded to the electors contravene an established principle of law. The maxim is, 'Nemo tenetur seipsum accusare (sen prodere).' It is founded on the best policy, and runs throughout our whole system of jurisprudence. It is the uniform practice of courts of justice as to witnesses and jurors. It is considered cruel and unjust to propose questions which may tend to criminate the party. And so jealous have the legislatures of this commonwealth been of this mode of discovery of facts that they have refused their assent to a bill brought in to compel persons to disclose on oath papers as well as facts relating to questions of mere property. And may we not justly suppose, that they would not be less jealous of securing our citizens against this mode of self-accusation? The words 'accusare' and 'prodere' are general terms, and their sense is not confined to cases where the answers to the questions proposed would induce to the punishment of the party. If they would in-

volve him in shame or reproach, he is under no obligation to answer them.

The same court applied a similar rule in a purely civil case, holding that no one could be forced to take the oath of a witness if his testimony "tends to accuse himself of an immoral act." [34]

The state courts of the framers' generation followed the extension of the right to cover self-infamy as well as self-incrimination, although the self-infamy rule eventually fell into disuse. Both federal and state courts followed in all other respects Shippen's far-reaching interpretation of what on its face and in context was a narrow clause. In the earliest federal case on the right against self-incrimination, Justice James Iredell of the Supreme Court, on circuit duty, ruled that a *witness* was not bound to answer a question that might tend to "implicate" or criminate himself. In one of the most famous cases in our constitutional history, *Marbury* v. *Madison*, Attorney-General Levi Lincoln balked at a question relating to his conduct of his office as Acting Secretary of State when Jefferson first became President. Marbury's commission as a justice of the peace for the District of Columbia had been signed by the outgoing President and affixed with the seal of the United States by the then Secretary of State, John Marshall, who had had no time to deliver it. What, asked Chief Justice Marshall, had Lincoln done with that commission? Lincoln, who probably had burned it, replied that he did not think that he was bound to disclose his official transactions while acting as Secretary of State, nor should he "be compelled to answer any thing which might tend to criminate himself." Marbury's counsel, Charles Lee, who was himself a former Attorney-General of the United States, and Chief Justice Marshall were in agreement: Lincoln, who was in the peculiar position of being both a witness and counsel for the government in a civil suit, was not obliged to disclose anything that might incriminate him. In Burr's trial, Chief Justice Marshall, without referring to the constitutional clause, again sustained the right of a witness to refuse answer to an incriminating question. The courts have always assumed that the meaning of the constitutional clause is determined by the common law.[35]

Whether the framers of the Fifth Amendment intended it to be fully co-extensive with the common law cannot be proved—or disproved. The language of the clause and its framer's understanding of it may not have been synonymous. The difficulty is that its framers, from Mason to Madison and Laurence, left too few clues. Nothing but passing explication emerged during the process of state ratification of the Bill of Rights from 1789 through 1791. Indeed, in legislative and convention proceedings, in letters, newspapers, and tracts, in judicial opinions and law books, the whole period from 1776 to 1791 reveals neither sufficient explanation of the scope of such a clause nor the reasons for it. That it was a ban on torture and a security for the criminally accused were the most important of its functions, as had been the case historically, but these were not the whole of its functions. Still, nothing can be found of a theoretical nature expressing a rationale or underlying policy for the right in question or its reach.

By 1776 the principle of the *nemo tenetur* maxim was simply taken for granted and so deeply accepted that its constitutional expression had the mechanical quality of a ritualistic gesture in favor of a self-evident truth needing no explanation. The clause itself, whether in Virginia's Section 8 or the Fifth Amendment, might have been so imprecisely stated, or misstated, as to raise vital questions of intent, meaning, and purpose. But constitution-makers, in that day at least, did not regard themselves as framers of detailed codes. To them the statement of a bare principle was sufficient, and they were content to put it spaciously, if somewhat ambiguously, in order to allow for its expansion as the need might arise.

By stating the principle in the Bill of Rights, which was also a bill of restraints upon government, they were once again sounding the tocsin against the dangers of government oppression of the individual; and they were voicing their conviction that the right against self-incrimination was a legitimate defense possessed by every individual against government. Tough-minded revolutionists, the equal of any in history in the art of self-government, they were willing to risk lives and fortunes in support of their belief that government is but an instrument of man, its sovereignty held in subordination to his rights. None in history can be less justly accused than they of being soft, naïve, or disregardful of the claims of law and order. They were mindful, nevertheless, that the enduring interests of the community required justice to be done as fairly as possible. The Constitution with its amendments was an embodiment of their political morality, an ever-present reminder of their view that the citizen is the master of his government, not its subject. As Abe Fortas observed, "The principle that a man is not obliged to furnish the state with ammunition to use against him is basic to this conception." The state, he acknowledged, must defend itself and, "within the limits of accepted procedure," punish lawbreakers. "But it has no right to compel the sovereign individual to surrender or impair his right of self-defense." The fundamental value reflected by the Fifth Amendment "is intangible, it is true; but so is liberty, and so is man's immortal soul. A man may be punished, even put to death, by the state; but . . . he should not be made to prostrate himself before its majesty. *Mea culpa* belongs to a man and his God. It is a plea that cannot be exacted from free men by human authority. To require it is to insist that the state is the superior of the individuals who compose it, instead of their instrument." [36]

The same point underlay the statement of another distinguished federal judge, who observed, "Our forefathers, when they wrote this provision into the Fifth Amendment of the Constitution, had in mind a lot of history which has been largely forgotten to-day." The remark applies with equal force, of course, to the right of representation by counsel, trial by jury, or any of the other, related procedural rights that are constitutionally sanctified. With good reason the Bill of Rights showed a preoccupation with the subject of criminal justice. The framers understood that without fair and regularized procedures to protect the criminally accused, there could be no liberty. They knew that from time immemorial, the tyrant's first step was to use the criminal law to crush his opposition. Vicious and ad hoc procedures had always been used to victimize nonconformists and minorities of differing religious, racial, or political persuasion. The Fifth Amendment was part and parcel of the procedures that were so crucial, in the minds of the framers, to the survival of the most treasured rights. One's home could not be his "castle," his property be his own, his right to express his opinions or to worship his God be secure, if he could be searched, arrested, tried, or imprisoned in some arbitrary or ignoble manner. As Justice Frankfurter declared, "The privilege against self-incrimination is a specific provision of which it is peculiarly true that 'a page of history is worth a volume of logic.' " [37]

The framers of the Bill of Rights saw their injunction, that no man should be a witness against himself in a criminal case, as a central feature of the accusatory system of criminal justice. While deeply committed to perpetuating a system that minimized the possibilities of convicting the innocent, they were not less concerned about the humanity that the fundamental law should show even to the offender. Above all, the Fifth Amendment reflected their judgment that in a free society, based on respect for the individual, the determination of guilt or innocence by just procedures, in which the accused made no unwilling contribution to his conviction, was more important than punishing the guilty.

Talmudic Law

No description of the origins of the right against self-incrimination would be complete without acknowledging the existence of the right in ancient Jewish law. The phrase "from time immemorial," so often used in English common-law sources to describe a rule hundreds of years old, most fittingly dates the origins of the right in the Israel of Biblical times. Whether the right came into existence a thousand years prior to a common law of England, or two thousand years, or longer still, is unknown. Nor do we clearly understand the reasons for its existence. Nowhere in the sources for ancient Jewish law is there an extended discussion of the right. On the contrary, there are only fleeting references to it at various points in the Talmud and in post-Talmudic commentaries.

The Talmud is an encyclopedic compilation of the "Tradition," the ancient oral teachings based on the five books of Moses. Its composition was begun before the Christian era and ended in the sixth century A.D. Divided into six general subjects or "orders" consisting of sixty-three books or "tractates," its English translation spreads over fifty volumes. They include canonically authoritative discussions of virtually every subject, among which is the law. Talmudic criminal procedure was strictly accusatorial in character, reflecting a humane concern for life and liberty. If there was anything inquisitorial in the procedure, it was the severe examination by the court of the witnesses for the prosecution, matched by excessively harsh penalties for false or refuted testi-

433

mony. The sworn evidence of two eye-witnesses to the crime was required for conviction. The rabbis who served as the judges on the Sanhedrin, the criminal court, examined and cross-examined the accusers before charging the defendant. Stringent rules of evidence prevailed; the courts refused to accept either hearsay or circumstantial evidence. As an example of the latter, the Talmud gave this judicial admonition to a witness: "Perhaps ye saw him running after his fellow into a ruin, ye pursued him, and found him sword in hand with blood dripping from it, whilst the murdered man was writhing [in agony]: If this is what ye saw, ye saw nothing." The court would even reject the evidence of eye witnesses to the act of murder if their testimony differed on an essential point. If, for example, one said the weapon was a sword and the other a dagger, the discrepancy invalidated their evidence. The accused was presumed innocent until the proof of his guilt was demonstrated as a certainty by evidence that was exact, consistent in all important respects, and beyond any doubt.[1]

Woven into the texture of this criminal procedure of the old Rabbinic courts was the maxim *ein adam meissim atsmo rasha,* the Hebrew equivalent of *nemo tenetur seipsum tenetur.* Literally translated it means, a man cannot represent himself as guilty, or as a transgressor. At several points in the Soncino edition of the Talmud, the English translation is given as "no one can incriminate himself." That rule was an absolute and could not be waived or relinquished. In Anglo-American jurisprudence the right exists only with respect to compulsory self-incrimination. A voluntary confession of guilt is regarded as the best evidence, and a plea of guilty results in a sentence. The defendant goes to trial only if he should plead not guilty. He cannot be placed on the stand to give testimony, but may volunteer. If he fails to do so, neither the prosecution nor the court may comment adversely on that fact. However, if he takes the stand to testify in his own behalf, he relinquishes his right to remain silent to incriminating questions and may be cross-examined. In the United States a witness, other than the defendant, may refuse answer to any question that might tend to incriminate him, but once he freely discloses an incriminating fact, he has, knowingly or not, waived his right to refuse answers to all related facts. The rule of the Talmud was quite different.[2]

In Talmudic law there was no such thing as a plea of guilty, no distinction between voluntary and compulsory self-incrimination, and no waiver rule. Anglo-American law vests the individual with the option of claiming a right against self-incrimination if he chooses, at his discretion, to do so; Talmudic law, by contrast, prohibited the admission in evidence of any self-incriminatory testimony even if voluntarily given. The rule was, no one could be permitted to confess or be a witness against himself criminally. The opposite rule prevailed with respect to civil liabilities. If a man acknowledged in court that he owed a debt or confessed to an act of negligence that exposed him to civil damages, his testimony, according to a Talmudic maxim, was the equivalent of the evidence of a hundred witnesses. But if his words revealed his culpability for a crime, he was not liable to punishment under the criminal law. The court simply excluded his incriminating statements. There was no way he could convict himself of a crime by testimony from his own mouth. Indeed, in a criminal case, the accused was permitted to speak only in his own behalf. The court examined him not to secure his conviction but to find reasons for acquittal; once acquitted, he was protected by the law against double jeopardy: "The verdict may be reversed for acquittal only but not for condemnation." [3]

All Talmudic law was a gloss on the Scriptures. Although the laws of Moses do not state the right against self-incrimination, the rabbinical judges inferred it from the directive requiring two witnesses in capital cases (Deut. XVII: 6). The Talmud does not explain why the two-witnesses requirement was extended to noncapital cases of crime, nor why a self-confessed criminal should not be counted as one of the two witnesses. There were, in fact, certain cases in which the *civil* liability of a thief was established by counting his confession of guilt as if it were the testimony of one of the two required witnesses. Yet the criminal's confession was otherwise excluded or annulled to prevent its use for the purpose of making him criminally liable. For reasons that are obscure, though possibly humanitarian, in criminal cases the judges simply construed "witnesses" to mean persons other than the accused himself. At one point the Talmud asks the reason for maintaining that a defendant "admitting an offence for which the penalty is a fine would [even] where witnesses subsequently appeared still be exempt?" The answer turned on the scriptural phrase, "If to be found it be found" (Ex. XXII: 3), which was construed to mean that if guilt be proved or "found" by witnesses, it "will 'be found' in the consideration of the Judges, excepting thus a case where it was the defendant who incriminated himself." Where, in the Scriptures, asked the rabbis, "do we derive the rule regarding a defendant incriminating himself? From the text, 'Whom the judges shall condemn [which implies] but not him who condemns himself.' " The logic here seems to be that if the defendant could condemn himself by his incriminating admissions, there was no way to obey the injunction that the judges should condemn him on the basis of the testimony of other witnesses.⁴

Later, another rationale developed for the rule *ein adam meissim atsmo rasha*. It became a means of compelling reluctant persons to testify as witnesses. Serving as a witness, then as now, could be very inconvenient. Moreover, the judges, acting as counsel for both sides, cross-examined witnesses with a thoroughness that could be unmerciful, especially in criminal cases, above all in capital cases. The penalty for bearing false witness was severe. A proved perjurer was liable to *lex talionis*, the law of retaliation: the judges might exact from him fines equal to the amount to which the party would have been liable or, in a criminal case, sentence the perjurer to the punishment prescribed for the particular crime which he had accused the defendant of committing. In a capital case the truthful witnesses bore a different but unenviable burden: they became the executioners, required to throw the first stones. Thus, there are many reasons why a man might wish to evade the onus of testifying. In Talmudic law among the persons generally regarded as incompetent to testify were relatives, whose bias might render their evidence untrustworthy and even tempt them to perjury, and the sinful or criminal. Confessing to some transgression, hopefully, would disqualify a man as a witness by rendering him incompetent, for the injunction "put not thy hand with the wicked to be an unrighteous witness" (Ex. XXIII: 3) was construed to exclude the testimony of an evil-doer. The courts thwarted his attempt to evade the duty of serving as a witness by voluntarily incriminating himself. They simply applied to witnesses the rule previously used for the accused, reasoning, "Every man is considered a relative to himself, and no one can incriminate himself." This was not quite the same reasoning as applied to the accused.[5]

The accused could not convict himself by his own testimony because only the judges, basing their decision on the evidence of witnesses, could convict him. But the theory underlying the rejection of a confession by a witness other than the accused was more complex. He was not merely protected against incriminating himself; he was also regarded as incompetent to be a witness against himself, because he was "a relative to himself." That is, one's relatives could not testify against him—nor for him; he was his own relative or closest to himself; therefore, he could not testify against himself. In a sense, his confession, though self-incriminatory, was intended as a statement in his own interest, to relieve him of the burden of giving testimony. Consequently he was not believed. As a result, his confession could not be used against him criminally, and because he could not be condemned as a transgressor on his own word, he was eligible to testify as a witness for or against another.

The individual who incriminated himself, whether an accused or a witness, did not escape all the consequences of his guilt. If his confession made him civilly liable, it could be used against him on the theory that a man is believed if his testimony damages him financially. Thus if he confessed to arson, or robbery, or lending money at interest, although he could not on the basis of his confession be punished for his crime, he was liable for damages or restitution. Nevertheless, his capacity to obligate himself financially did not extend to the payment of penal fines. As the Talmud put it, his testimony against himself was divided in half, the court using only that half by which he incurred a civil liability. Although the criminal law acknowledged no exceptions to the principle that *ein adam meissim atsmo rasha*, there were exceptional cases. If a man repented and confessed to some crime or a religious transgression for the express purpose of avoiding a forbidden act, he would be believed. If, for example, a man did not wish to defile the Temple by performing a religious duty for which he had been disqualified by his sin, he was excused; or a rabbi who had committed a crime might confess to avoid the obligation of making a blessing. In such a case the confession, even though accepted, carried impunity at criminal law.[6]

Neither the two-witnesses rule nor the rule rendering a man incompetent to testify in his own case provided a satisfactory rationale for the right against self-incrimination in Talmudic law. The two-witnesses rule did not explain why the accused's word, if voluntarily given, should not count as that of one of the two witnesses, while the incompetency rule made little sense in the case of a confession. If a man testified in his own interest, disqualifying him might be justified on ground that he was biased, though no such reasoning applied when an accused spoke in behalf of establishing his innocence. But if he incriminated himself voluntarily, the rules for annulling his testimony seemed illogical.

Post-Talmudic commentators provided a more convincing rationale for excluding even a confession that was freely made. The great Maimonides, who codified the Talmud in the late twelfth century, made the following explanation: "It is a scriptural decree that the court shall not put a man to death or flog him on his own admission [of guilt]. This is done only on the evidence of two witnesses. . . . The Sanhedrin, however, is not empowered to inflict the penalty of death or of flagellation on the admission of the accused. For it is possible that he was confused in mind when he made the confession. Perhaps he was one of those who are in misery, bitter in soul, who long for death, thrust the sword into their bellies or cast themselves down from the roofs. Perhaps this was the reason that prompted him to confess to a crime he had not committed, in order that he might be put to death. To sum up the matter, the principle that no man is to be declared guilty on his own admission is a divine decree." By concluding that the principle was a divine decree, Maimonides in effect was saying that there was no satisfactory rationale for it. Yet he provided one, namely, that a confession of guilt, even if voluntarily given, was untrustworthy evidence. Taken alone it should not be believed and therefore should not be the basis of a conviction. The insight of the Talmud that a man is closest to himself, his own relative, recognized by implication that the instinct for self-preservation governs the actions of any normal person. Consequently, only a mentally deranged individual, heedless of his own life, would admit to a capital crime. His confession was a form of suicide, which was sinful and violative of the instinct of self-preservation.[7]

Rosh (1250–1328) carried this reasoning further by arguing that "a person really never intends to testify against himself voluntarily." David Ibn Zimra, a sixteenth-century commentator on the code of Maimonides and a chief judge of the rabbinic court, offered the most interesting and plausible explanation for the Talmudic rule against self-incrimination in capital cases. He reasoned that because a man's life belongs not to himself but to God, his admission of guilt was without legal effect. He could not "give away what is not his. His money, however, does belong to him. Wherefore we say: 'The admission of a party is worth a hundred witnesses.' Here just as a person has no right to kill himself so he has no right to confess that he committed an offense for which he may be liable to the death penalty for his life is not his private property." Realizing, perhaps, that this explanation neither existed in the Talmud nor accounted for the exclusion of incriminating statements in cases of non-capital crimes, David Ibn Zimra, like Maimonides, added, "Notwithstanding all this, I admit that this matter is a decree of the King of the Universe and we may not question it." Yet God's decrees, as given in the Scriptures, did not command the exclusion of self-incriminatory testimony, except very inferentially in the requirement of two witnesses.[8]

Whatever the explanation of the Talmudic rule, its existence invalidates the declaration made by the Supreme Court of the United States in 1908 that the right against self-incrimination "distinguished the common law from all other systems of jurisprudence." Similarly inaccurate was the comparable remark by John H. Wigmore, our greatest expert on evidence, who alleged of the right that "in other systems of the world it had had no place." In 1966 the Supreme Court, in the most important decision that it ever made on the right against self-incrimination, observed that its roots "go back into ancient times." In a footnote the Court added that Maimonides "found an analogue to the privilege grounded in the Bible." Such information has been available in English since 1901, when *The Jewish Encyclopaedia* was first published.[9]

Whether the existence of the right against self-incrimination in

Talmudic law in any way influenced the rise of the right in Anglo-American law is an intriguing question. But the answer, if based on evidence rather than speculation, must be negative. The Puritans were the only possible link between the Talmud and the common law. That they were religiously and intellectually attached to things Hebrew is a celebrated fact. The influence of the Old Testament on Massachusetts Bay Colony in matters of church and state, and particularly in the area of criminal law, is a more than twice-told tale and an exaggerated one. Every historian of our colonial period knows about John Cotton's proposed code of laws, "Moses His Judicials," and knows also that a few years later the Body of Liberties drew heavily upon the Mosaic code of the Old Testament. Four years of Hebrew study was at that time a requirement for all students at Harvard College, and the college library, wrote Samuel Eliot Morison, possessed an excellent collection of Talmuds and works of rabbinical exegesis. "The most distinctive feature of the Harvard curriculum," said Morison, "was the emphasis on Hebrew and kindred languages." Presumably many Puritan scholars, ministers, and even students read the various scattered passages stating the right against self-incrimination. Yet, no person connected with the development of that right in English or American history ever referred to the Talmudic precedent.[10]

Many of the English Puritans, from John Udall and Thomas Cartwright to John Lilburne relied, like the ancient rabbis, on the scriptural requirement of two witnesses as a justification for the principle that no man is bound to accuse himself. But the Old Testament contains only the two-witness requirement, not the inference drawn from it. That inference was found later, in the Talmud and in post-Talmudic commentators like Maimonides. "The English divines who gave us the King James Bible were excellent Hebraists, well versed in the whole field of rabbinic literature," said Morison. Hebrew had been prescribed for the Master of Arts degree at Cambridge since 1549. In the middle of the seventeenth century there were a group of English Hebraists, Puritans in the main, who were experts in the Talmudic sources. John Milton was one of them. Another was Edward Pococke (1604–91) of Oxford, who published a Hebrew text with the

Latin translation of some of Maimonides' commentaries. John Lightfoot (1602–75) of Cambridge was the author of *Horae Hebraicae et Talmudicae*, and his colleague, John Spencer (1630–95) wrote a treatise on Hebrew law, *De Legibus Hebraeorum Ritualibus et Earum Rationibus*. But all these scholars wrote in Latin and much too late to be of influence in providing a Talmudic basis for the claim that no man is bound to accuse himself. Moreover, of all the English Hebraists, only John Selden (1584–1654) is known to have explicitly described the right against self-incrimination in Talmudic law. The fact is especially significant in the case of Selden because he was a great lawyer and parliamentarian, an associate of Sir Edward Coke, jointly instrumental with him in securing the Petition of Right of 1628. In his *De Synedriis*, Selden translated—into Latin—the passage quoted above from Maimonides.[11]

Recently a scholar noted for his book on *The Spirit of Jewish Law* claimed that in this passage Selden "brought to the knowledge and attention of Englishmen the Jewish doctrine against self-incrimination." Though the statement is true with respect to Selden's Latin-reading contemporaries, it does not prove the influence of the Talmud on the development of the common-law right against self-incrimination. *De Synedriis* was published in 1653 and, like the works by Pococke, Lightfoot, Spencer, and others, appeared after John Lilburne's first treason trial. The self-incriminatory oath *ex officio* had already been abolished and the right against self-incrimination had already been established in the common law. The Talmudic source of the right merely provided an ancient lineage and a high moral authority for a principle that its Christian advocates already believed justified as having been supported by Jesus and Magna Carta.[12]

N O T E S

Chapter 1
Rival Systems of Criminal Procedure

1. "The Answers of John Lambert to the Forty-five Articles," in John Foxe, *The Acts and Monuments of John Foxe: A New and Complete Edition*, ed. by Rev. Stephen Reed Cattley (London, 1837–41, 8 vols.), V, 184. The principal documents on the Lambert case cover pp. 181–250.

2. *Ibid.*, V, 221.

3. William Stubbs, *The Constitutional History of England in Its Origin and Development* (Oxford, 1875, 2nd ed., 3 vols.), I, 90, 96, 101–3; James Bradley Thayer, *A Preliminary Treatise on Evidence at the Common Law* (Boston, 1898), 8–9; Sir Frederick Pollock and Frederic William Maitland, *The History of English Law before the Time of Edward I* (Cambridge, Eng., 1899, 2nd ed., 2 vols.), II, 598–603; and R. C. Van Caenegem, *Royal Writs in England from the Conquest to Glanvill* (London, 1959), Publications of the Selden Society, LXXVII, 16–17.

4. Thayer, 24–34. For a history of proof by oath and compurgation, also called "wager of law," see Homer C. Lea, *Superstition and Force* (Philadelphia, 1878, 3rd ed.), 22–99; see also Eugene James Moriarty, *Oaths in Ecclesiastical Courts* (Washington, 1937), Catholic University of America Canon Law Studies, CX, 12–22.

5. On ordeals, see Lea, 249–428, and Thayer, 34–9. For Anglo-Saxon documents on oaths, ordeals, and criminal procedure, see Carl Stephenson and Frederick G. Marcham, eds., *Sources of English Constitutional History. A Selection of Documents from A.D. 600 to the Present* (New York, 1937), 2–25.

6. On trial by battle, see Lea, 101–247; Sir James Fitzjames Stephen, *A History of the Criminal Law of England* (London, 1883, 3 vols.), I, 245–6; and Sir William Holdsworth, *A History of English Law* (London and Boston, 1903–66, 16 vols., vols. individually rev.), I (6th ed., rev.), 320; II (4th ed.), 197–8 and 360–4; III (6th ed., rev.), 609.

7. Thayer, 41–60; Pollock and Maitland, I, 137–42; Holdsworth, I, 312–13; and Charles Homer Haskins, *Norman Institutions* (Cambridge, Mass., 1925), 196–238. Some historians, returning to a view once popular in the nineteenth century, hold that the origins of the jury are to be found in Anglo-Saxon institutions. See Naomi D. Hurnard, "The Jury of Presentment and the Assize of Clarendon," *English Historical Review*, LVI (July 1941), 377–410; Van Caenegem, *op. cit.*, ch. 4, "The Recognitions," 51–103; H. G. Richardson and G. O. Sayles, *The Governance of Medieval England from the Conquest to Magna Carta* (Edinburgh, 1963), 205–8;

Doris M. Stenton, *English Justice between the Norman Conquest and the Great Charter, 1066–1215* (Philadelphia, 1964), 15–17. Van Caenegem, whose work is pre-eminent, distinguished between the inquest, which he associated with royal rights, chiefly fiscal, and recognitions, which he associated with judicial procedures of a "popular" origin before the Conquest. He concluded that "the older English historians were right. The jury was not some alien importation . . ." (p. 103). The evidence for this thesis seems slim and supposititious. Van Caenegem does not, however, reject the view that the jury owed much to the Norman inquest: "We maintain that the common law recognitions were the outcome of two traditions . . ." (p. 60). Some historians evasively straddle the issue. See, *e.g.*, Sir Frank Stenton, *Anglo-Saxon England* (Oxford, 1947, 2nd ed.), 643. The single outstanding fact is that until Henry II's time, the dominating modes of proof were compurgation, ordeal, and battle; that is, even a century after the Conquest, recognition and inquest were very weak and irregular institutions. Trial by jury developed because of the reforms of Henry II. V. H. Galbraith, *The Making of Domesday Book* (Oxford, 1961), disputes the old thesis that the main object of the Domesday census was to reassess taxes. He asserts, moreover, that the testimony of tenants as well as returns from the hundred provided the data for the making of the book. Although the Norman kings used the inquest mainly for administrative and financial inquiries until Henry II's time, they used it also, and very early, in land disputes. See the documents on inquests at Ely in 1080 and 1082, in Stephenson and Marcham, 39–40.

8. Van Caenegem, 61–8; F. W. Maitland, *Domesday Book and Beyond* (Cambridge, Eng., 1897); Holdsworth, I, 49–51, 264–73, 316, and II, 155–65; Pollock and Maitland, I, 150–52, 154–6; and Stephen, I, 101–2, 253. The quotation from Stephen is at p. 102.

9. Lea, 67–72, 84–7, and 179–98.

10. For an English translation of the Constitutions of Clarendon, see Stephenson and Marcham, 73–6, or George Burton Adams and H. Morse Stephens, eds., *Select Documents of English Constitutional History* (New York, 1929), 11–14. Articles 6 and 9 are relevant. See also Pollock and Maitland, I, 145; Holdsworth, I, 329, and III, 25; and Van Caenegem, 86–7.

11. The Assizes of Clarendon and Northampton are in Stephenson and Marcham, 76–82, and Adams and Stephens, 14–18, 20–23. See also Pollock and Maitland, I, 152, and II, 641; Holdsworth, I, 77; and Van Caenegem, 28–30. Cf. Richardson and Sayles on the rise of the eyre and for criticism of the stress conventionally placed on the Assize of Clarendon, which they regard as apocryphal, at pp. 173–215, 438–49. The Assizes in time filled the forests with outlaws—those who refused to show up for the ordeal or who failed it and fled to the forest rather than go into banishment. See Morris Keane, *The Outlaws of England* (Toronto, 1961).

12. Max Radin, *Handbook of Anglo-American Legal History* (St. Paul, 1936), 209–11; William Sharp McKechnie, *Magna Carta, A Commentary on the Great Charter of King John* (Glasgow, 1914, 2nd ed.), 359–67; Thayer, 68; Holdsworth, I, 57; and Pollock and Maitland, II, 587–8.

13. Van Caenegem, 55–6, 82–96, 260–335; Pollock and Maitland, I, 145–9.

14. Pollock and Maitland, I, 146–7, 149, and II, 621; Holdsworth, I, 327–8; Thayer, 61–3; Van Caenegem, 87–91; and, for the quotation from Glanville, circa 1187, Stephen, I, 256.

15. McKechnie, 369–93; Pollock and Maitland, I, 173; Thayer, 65.

16. Henry Charles Lea, *A History of the Inquisition of the Middle Ages* (New York, 1955, 3 vols.), I, 306, 320; Lea, *Superstition and Force*, 418–20; Pollock and Maitland, II, 599.

17. Stephen, I, 254, and for the quotation from Glanville, *ibid.*, I, 256; Pollock and Maitland, II, 599.

18. Quoted in Theodore F. T. Plucknett, *A Concise History of the Common Law* (Boston, 1956, 5th ed.), 119.

19. Pollock and Maitand, II, 644–9; Holdsworth, I, 324–5; and Thayer, 81–6.

20. Holdsworth, I, 326–7; Thayer, 71; and Pollock and Maitland, II, 650.

21. Pollock and Maitland, II, 619; Thayer, 74; and Plucknett, 126, for the quotation from the Statute of Westminster, I, ch. 12 (1275).

22. Thayer, 75–80; and Stephen, I, 298–300.

23. Stephen, I, 257–9 and 297–8; Holdsworth, I, 276, 318, 322, and 325; Plucknett, 126–7; Pollock and Maitland, II, 648–9; and Thayer, 81–3.

24. Sir John Fortescue, *De Laudibus Legum Angliae*, trans. by A. Amos (Cambridge, Eng., 1825), 92–3, 100–101; Stephen, I, 263–4; Holdsworth, I, 332–5; Pollock and Maitland, II, 627–9.

25. For the quotation on Innocent III, John H. Wigmore, *A Panorama of the World's Legal Systems* (Washington, 1936), 953. See also Wigmore, *A Treatise on the Anglo-American System of Evidence in Trials at Common Law* (Boston, 1940, 3rd ed., 10 vols.), VIII (rev. 1961 by John T. McNaughton), ch. 80, "Privilege Against Self-Incrimination," sect. 2250, pp. 273–4; Lea, *Inquisition*, I, 320. On Innocent III and Magna Carta, see J. C. Holt, *Magna Carta* (Cambridge, Eng., 1965), 101, 139–48, 170. For the canon-law code of criminal procedure and for Innocent III's contributions, see Aemilius Friedberg, ed., *Corpus Juris Canonici* (Leipzig, 1879–81, 2 vols.), vol. II, book II, title VII, *de juramento calumniae*, ch. 6, pp. 267–9; book V, title I, *de accusationibus, inquisitionibus, et denunciationibus*, chs. 1–27, pp. 735–48; book V, title XXXIV, *de purgationen*, ch. X, pp. 872–3.

26. Wigmore, *Evidence*, VIII, 275, note 28; A. Esmein, *A History of Continental Criminal Procedure, with Special Reference to France* (London, 1914), trans. by John Simpson, 80 and 91; A. Esmein, *Le Serment des Inculpés en Droit Canonique* (Paris, 1896), 234–5, a pamphlet offprint of the essay of the same title published in *Bibliothèque de L'Ecole des Hautes Etudes—Sciences Religieuses*, VII (1896), 231–48; Lea, *Inquisition*, I, 214; Lea, *Superstition*, 513. See also St. Augustine, *The City of God* (New York, 1950, 2 vols.), II, Book XIX, ch. VI, p. 242. The quotation from Chrysostom is from *The Homilies of S. John Chrysostom, Archbishop of Constantinople, on the Epistle of S. Paul the Apostle to the Hebrews*, ed. P. E. Pusey (London, 1883), 362–3. The translation of the same passage, originally in Greek, by the Fathers of the English Dominican Province, is, "I do not say that you should lay bare your guilt publicly, nor accuse yourself before others." See The *"Summa Theologica"* of St.

Thomas Aquinas (London, 1912–29, 22 vols.), X, 255 (Question LXIX, 1st Art., Obj. 1). See also Gratian, *Decreti*, part II, causa XXXIII, question III, ch. 87, in Friedberg, ed., *Corpus Juris Canonici*, I, 1184–5.

27. Lea, *Inquisition*, I, 228, 229, 338, 372–3, 421, and 502. For a different view, see Albert C. Shannon, *The Popes and Heresy in the Thirteenth Century* (Villanova, Pa., 1949), and Norman F. Cantor, *Medieval History* (New York, 1963), 491–2. Aquinas stated and rejected the dictum from Chrysostom. "Whatever is opposed to the glory of God is a mortal sin. . . . Now it is to the glory of God that the accused confess that which is alleged against him. . . . Therefore it is a mortal sin to lie in order to cover one's guilt." Aquinas also argued that a man must obey his superiors, including his judges. "Therefore the accused is in duty bound to tell the judge the truth which the latter exacts from him according to the form of law. . . . When a man is examined by the judge according to the order of justice, he does not lay bare his own guilt, but his guilt is unmasked by another, since the obligation of answering is imposed on him by one whom he is bound to obey." In effect, what emerged from Aquinas is a rule that no man is bound to come forward and reveal his own guilt if it is unknown, or unsuspected, but once suspected he must answer an incriminating question; the judge decides whether the question is legitimate, under the circumstances, and whether answer is required. *Summa Theologica*, X, 255–8 (Quest. LXIX, 1st Art. and 2nd Art., replies to objections). Later canonists such as Durantis, Gandinus, and Panormitanus followed Aquinas. See Esmein, *Le Serment des Inculpés*, 233–40. Certain speculative moral theologians of the sixteenth and seventeenth centuries "allowed a defendant in a criminal case where there was liability to a very severe penalty to evade a direct question regarding guilt." John R. Connery, S. J., "The Right to Silence," *Marquette Law Review*, XXXIX (Winter 1955–56), 180, at 184. Father Connery wrote, "Should one be tempted to pass a rather harsh judgment on the theologians and jurists of the scholastic age who imposed on a criminal the obligation to confess his crime when legitimately questioned, it might be well to mention a few mitigating circumstances," chief among which was the theory of legal proofs. *Ibid.*, at 182. On legal proofs, see below, note 35.

28. Esmein, *Criminal Procedure*, 66–7, for the quotation. See also *ibid.*, 79–84, and Lea, *Inquisition*, I, 310–12. Van Caenegem observed that in the old trial by witnesses, where the parties brought witnesses, who supposedly knew the facts, to testify in their behalf, the ecclesiastical judge gathered the materials for his decision from their testimony; interrogating the witnesses was an obvious and easy step in this procedure. By contrast, under the English system the jurors were a neutral body from the neighborhood who knew or could find the facts and found their own verdict, binding on the judge. Van Caenegem, 54. See also on this point, Pollock and Maitland, II, 658.

29. Lea, *Inquisition*, I, 310; Esmein, *Criminal Procedure*, 84–9; Friedberg, ed., *Corpus Juris Canonici*, vol. II, book V, title I, *de accusat.*, ch. 24, 745–7.

30. Esmein, *Criminal Procedure*, 82; Esmein, *Serment*, 231, 243; Helen Silving, "The Oath: I," *Yale Law Journal*, LXVIII (June 1959), 1329, at 1345.

31. Silving, "The Oath," 1346–7; Moriarty, 33.

32. Wigmore, *Evidence*, 274; Esmein, *Criminal Procedure*, 87–9; and Lea, *Inquisition*, I, 401.

33. Esmein, *Criminal Procedure*, 92; Lea, *Inquisition*, I, 437–47.

34. Lea, *Inquisition*, I, 400–401.

35. A. Lawrence Lowell, "The Judicial Use of Torture," Part I, *Harvard Law Review*, XI (1897–98), 220, at 224–5; Lea, *Inquisition*, I, 416, 433–4; and especially Esmein, *Criminal Procedure*, 133, 251–75, and 622–6.

36. Lea, *Inquisition*, I, 337–8 and 421–22; the quotation from Gui is in *ibid.*, 431.

37. Lea, *Inquisition*, I, 421–8.

38. *Ibid.*, 407–21, 431, 434, and 440; Esmein, *Criminal Procedure*, 104–79, 288–321.

39. Holdsworth, I, 294, and III, 600–601; Stephen, I, 493; the quotation from Smith appears in Holdsworth, IX, 225, and Stephen, I, 347. For the original see Sir Thomas Smith, *De Republica Anglorum*, ed. by L. Alston (Cambridge, Eng., 1906), 99.

40. Holdsworth, I, 319–20, and III, 609, 615–20; Stephen, I, 245–6; Pollock and Maitland, II, 658–9; and R. F. Hunnisett, *The Medieval Coroner* (Cambridge, Eng., 1961), 55.

41. Stephen, I, 355; Lea, *Inquisition*, I, 401; Thayer, 157; Fortescue, 93; Holdsworth, V (2nd ed.), 196, citing John Hawarde, ed., *Les Reportes del Cases in Camera Stellata, 1593–1609*, ed. by W. P. Baildon (London, 1894), 320.

42. Fortescue, 70–71.

43. Charles Austin Beard, *The Office of Justice of the Peace in England* (New York, 1904), 72–4; Holdsworth, V, 165, 185–6, 191; James Fosdick Baldwin, *The King's Council in England during the Middle Ages* (Oxford, 1913), 298; Lea, *Superstition*, 563–71; Lowell, "The Judicial Use of Torture," Part II, 290–97; and especially David Jardine, *A Reading on the Use of Torture in the Criminal Law of England* (London, 1837), 7–25, 59–63. The quotation from Smith, *De Republica*, is in the Alston ed., 105.

44. Beard, 72; Holdsworth, IV (2nd ed.), 528–30; Stephen, I, 219–20, 237–8.

45. Holdsworth, I, 294–7, III, 600–601, 622–3, V, 156, 191, 195, and IX, 224–5, 229; Stephen, I, 225.

46. Thayer, 158–9. See Jay A. Sigler, "A History of Double Jeopardy," *The American Journal of Legal History*, VII (October 1963), 283–309.

47. *Ibid.*, 86–8; Holdsworth, I, 318; Stephen, I, 304; and Pollock and Maitland, II, 626–7.

48. Thayer, 137–55; Holdsworth, I, 337–42; and for Throckmorton's trial, see T. B. Howell, comp., *A Complete Collection of State Trials and Proceedings for High Treason and Other Crimes and Misdemeanors from the Earliest Period to the Year 1783* (London, 1816, 21 vols.), I, 869. Henceforth, this source will be cited as *State Trials*.

49. Holdsworth, IX, 228, 233, 235; Stephen, I, 350, 416; and Throckmorton's trial in *State Trials*, I, 869, at 884–5, 886, 897, and 898.

50. *State Trials*, I, 901–2; and for Bushell's case, *ibid.*, VI, 999. The quotation from Smith, *De Republica*, appears in Thayer, 163, and Stephen, I, 306.

51. Pollock and Maitland, II, 658, and I, 138; Holdsworth, I, 318.

52. Maitland, "A Prologue to a History of English Law," in *Select Essays in Anglo-American Legal History*, comp. and ed. by a Committee of the Association of American Law Schools (Boston, 1907, 3 vols.), I, 7.

Chapter II
The Oath *Ex Officio*

1. William Stubbs, *The Constitutional History of England in Its Origin and Development* (Oxford, 1875, 2nd ed., 3 vols.), I, 276–7, for the quotation, and 283–4; W. R. W. Stephens, *The English Church from the Norman Conquest to the Accession of Edward I* (London, 1904), 49; Felix Makower, *The Constitutional History and Constitution of the Church of England* (London, 1895), 384–94; and "The Conqueror's Mandate for Dividing the Civil and Church Courts," in Henry Gee and William John Hardy, eds., *Documents Illustrative of English Church History* (London, 1921), 57–8.

2. Makower, 399–444; Sir William Holdsworth, *A History of English Law* (London and Boston, 1903–66, 16 vols.), I, 614–32; Sir Frederick Pollock and Frederic William Maitland, *The History of English Law before the Time of Edward I* (Cambridge, Eng., 1899, 2nd ed., 2 vols.), I, 124–32; Sir James Fitzjames Stephen, *A History of the Criminal Law of England* (London, 1883, 3 vols.), II, 404–13. William Hale said that Chaucer's *Friar's Tale* gives "a most accurate account of the offenses for which persons were brought before the Archdeacon's Court, at the same time that he exposes the corrupt and inquisitional practices of the somners or apparitors who travelled about the country in search of suspected persons, and reaped a plentiful harvest by threatening them with citations, and accepting money to forbear the execution of their threats." Hale, *A Series of Precedents and Proceedings in Criminal Causes, Extending from the Year 1475 to 1640; Extracted from Act-Books of Ecclesiastical Courts in the Diocese of London* (London, 1894), lvi.

3. Hale, lvii–lviii. Hale's collection of cases are all proceedings *ex officio* and "are, in one fundamental point, exemplifications of a principle of criminal jurisprudence, wholly opposed to that which prevails in our Common Law; for whereas in the Temporal Courts, the principle that no man is bound to accuse himself, is that which universally prevails, even in many cases to the hindrance of justice and the security of crime, in the Spiritual Courts the whole energy of the discipline, which continued in the Church until the year 1640, was derived from the power of the Ecclesiastical Judge possessed of proposing the articles of charge to the accused in person and of requiring him upon oath to admit or deny the accusation. . . . The oath so administered was termed the oath *ex officio.*" See also Stephen, II, 402.

4. Constitutions of Clarendon, in George Burton Adams and H. Morse Stephens, eds., *Select Documents of English Constitutional History* (New York, 1929), 12; Pollock and Maitland, I, 151.

5. Pollock and Maitland, I, 131.

6. W. R. W. Stephens, 232. The Latin for the oath *de veritate dicenda*

is in John H. Wigmore, *A Treatise on the Anglo-American System of Evidence in Trials at Common Law* (Boston, 1940, 3rd ed., 10 vols.), VIII, 270, together with an unreliable English translation which omits the very phrase "*de veritate dicenda.*" The oath of calumny was originally a sworn statement required of a private accuser to the effect that he would not deny the truth, nor give false proof, nor protract the suit. See Eugene James Moriarty, *Oaths in Ecclesiastical Courts* (Washington, 1937), Catholic University of America Canon Law Studies, CX, 3–4, 9–10, 28.

7. Henry III's writs are in Matthew Paris, *Chronica Majora*, ed. by Henry Richards Luard (London, 1876, 7 vols. in *Chronicles and Memorial of Great Britain and Ireland during the Middle Ages*), IV, 579–80, and *Close Rolls of the Reign of Henry III, 1247–51*, ed. by E. G. Atkinson (London, 1922), 221–2, 554, and *Close Rolls of the Reign of Henry III, 1251–53*, ed. by A. E. Stamp (London, 1927), 224–5. The quotation from Matthew Paris is in Henry Richards Luard, ed., *Roberti Grosseteste. Episcopi Quondam Lincolniensis. Epistolae* (London, 1861), lxx. Other quotations are from William Prynne, *The Second Tome of an Exact Chronological Vindication and Historical Demonstration of our British, Roman, Saxon, Danish, Norman, English Kings Supream Ecclesiastical Jurisdiction* (London, 1665, 2 vols.), II, 698–9, 704.

8. Wigmore, VIII, 270, giving both the Latin and the English translation of Boniface's constitution; see also Sir Edward Coke on the oath *ex officio* in 12 *Coke's Reports* 26, at 29, 77 *English Reports* 1308. The acts of 1285 and 1316 are reproduced in Gee and Hardy, 83–5, 96–102. For the Prohibitio . . . Articuli Cleri, see *Statutes of the Realm*, ed. by A. Luders *et. al.* (London, 1811–28, II vols.), I, 209. See also Holdsworth, I, 584–5.

9. James F. Baldwin, *The King's Council in England during the Middle Ages* (Oxford, 1913), 38–68, 265–78, 280; I. S. Leadam and J. F. Baldwin, *Select Cases before the King's Council, 1243–1482* (Cambridge, Mass., 1918), Publications of the Selden Society, XXXV, xxvi–xxxv; Holdsworth, I, 32–54, 194–6, 204–11, 479–92.

10. Holdsworth, IX, 236–44; Baldwin, 286; and, for the quotations, Leadam and Baldwin, xxvi, xxvii.

11. Quotations from Baldwin, 296, 297, 298; see also Leadam and Baldwin, xliii, and for examples of the use of the inquisitional oath by the Council, see the cases in *ibid.*, 33, 40, 74, 79–80, 94, 103, 105–6.

12. On Magna Carta in the 14th century, see Faith Thompson, *Magna Carta, Its Role in the Making of the English Constitution, 1300–1629* (Minneapolis, 1948), ch. 3, especially 86–97; and Max Radin, "The Myth of Magna Carta," *Harvard Law Review*, LXX (Sept. 1947), 1060–91. The quotation is from Robert Beale, *A Collection Shewinge what Jurisdiction the Clergie Hathe Heretofore Lawfully Used*, (1590), Brit. Mus., Cotton MSS, Cleopatra F. I., No. 1, f. 18 *recto*.

13. 5 Edw. III ch. 9, *Statutes of the Realm*, I, 267, (1331); 15 Edw. III ch. 3, *Statutes R.*, I, 296 (1341); *Rotuli Parlimentorum; ut et petitiones, et placita in Parlimento tempore Edwardi R. I* [ad finem Henrici VII.], (London, 1767–77, 6 vols.), II, 168, No. 28, 21 Edw. III (1347); *ibid.*, II, 228, No. 16, 25 Edw. III (1351); *ibid.*, II, 239, No. 19, 25 Edw. III (1352); 25 Edw. III st. 5, ch. 4, *Statutes R.*, I, 321 (1352); 28 Edw. III ch. 3, *Statutes*

R., I, 345 (1354). For the statement by Mary Hume Maguire, see her essay, "Attack of the Common Lawyers on the Oath *Ex Officio* As Administered in the Ecclesiastical Courts in England," in *Essays in Honor of Charles H. McIlwain* (Cambridge, Mass., 1936), 207–8. The same statement appeared in her unpublished doctoral dissertation, Mary Ballantine Hume, "The History of the Oath *Ex Officio* in England," (Radcliffe College Library, 1923), 17–18, where the sources are given without the typographical errors of the published essay; she cited the petitions in *Rot. Parl.* for 1347 and 1352, referred to in this footnote. Those petitions refer to the Council, not the ecclesiastical courts, and no passage in the original French will bear the translation "fishing interrogatories *viva voce,*" although one may infer such a meaning from the objection in the petition.

14. *Rot. Parl.* II, 280, No. 37, 36 Edw. III (1363); 37 Edw. III ch. XVIII, *Statutes R.,* I, 382 (1363); 42 Edw. III ch. 3, *Statutes R.,* I, 388 (1368).

15. Pollock and Maitland, II, 544–51; Maitland, "The Deacon and the Jewess," *Roman Canon Law in the Church of England* (London, 1898), 158–79; and Makower, 183–5.

16. "Letter of Pope Gregory XI to Archbishop Sudbury . . . against Wycliffe, 1377," in Gee and Hardy, 105–8; "Wycliffe Propositions Condemned at London, 1382," in *ibid.,* 108–10; John Foxe, *The Acts and Monuments of John Foxe: A New and Complete Edition,* ed. by Rev. Stephen Reed Cattley (London, 1837–41, 8 vols.), III, 94–6, 814. Wycliffe's case is also reported in *State Trials,* I, 67–90.

17. "Letters Patent against the Lollards, 1384," in Gee and Hardy, 110–12; James Gairdner, *Lollardry and the Reformation in England* (London, 1908, 3 vols.), I, 3–21; W. W. Capes, *The English Church in the Fourteenth and Fifteenth Centuries* (London, 1903), 102–41; May McKisack, *The Fourteenth Century, 1307–1399* (Oxford, 1959), 510–17.

18. Foxe, III, 31, 36, 40, 107–31; Gairdner, I, 24–36; McKisack, 517–19.

19. The Biblical passage is in Matthew 5:33–37; see also Silving, "The Oath," *Yale Law Journal,* LXVIII, 1343–4. Brute's trial is reported in Foxe, III, 131–87; his protests against oaths is at p. 186. Another account of the trial is in W. W. Capes, ed., *Register of John Trefnant, Bishop of Hereford, A.D. 1389–1404* (Hereford, Eng., 1914), 278–360

20. Stephen, II, 443; "bastard statute" is from Foxe, III, 39, and see also 37–9, 808; McKisack, 521–2; H. G. Richardson, "Heresy and the Lay Power under Richard II," *English Historical Review,* LI (1936), 1–28, especially at 22.

21. Maitland, *Roman Canon Law,* 174; "The Royal Writ for the Burning of Sawtre," Gee and Hardy, 139; Sawtre's case is reported both in Foxe, III, 221–9, and in *State Trials,* I, 163–75, where the spelling is given as Sautre and a slightly different translation is given of the king's writ.

22. Maitland, *Roman Canon Law,* 176–7; Capes, *English Church,* 180; Stephen, II, 496–8; Gairdner, I, 51, said the writ was an innovation.

23. "The Act De Haeretico Comburendo, 1401," in Gee and Hardy, 133–7 (2 Hen. IV ch. 15); Maguire, 209; Foxe, III, 293, and Gairdner, I, 49, for the name Statute *Ex Officio;* Hume (Maguire), Radcliffe dissertation, 25–6 for Arundel's decree, citing Edmund Gibson, *Codex Juris Ecclesiastici Anglicani* (Oxford, 1761), 1053.

24. Foxe, III, 255; the examination of Thorpe is also reported in *State Trials*, I, 175–220, and in *Select Works of John Bale*, ed. by Rev. Henry Christmas (Cambridge, Eng., 1849, 2 vols.), I, 61–136, especially pp. 111–13.

25. Foxe, III, 274, 280.

26. *Ibid.*, III, 587–605, for the period 1428–32. For the number of burnings, I have relied on the incidents related in Foxe for the period 1401–1534, in vols. 3–5, discounting those that seemed uncertain. See III, 229, 239, 320, 584, 587, 591, 599, 600, 601, 704; IV, 7, 8, 124, 181, 182, 185, 207, 208, 213, 214, 217, 557, 558, 578, 579, 580, 619, 688, 705, 706; V, 16, 17. John A. F. Thomson *The Later Lollards, 1414–1520* (New York, 1965), was also useful.

27. Foxe, IV, 217–46. Philip Hughes, *The Reformation in England*, (London, 1950–54, 3 vols.), I, 128–9, gives the figure of 342; Hughes stated that five were burned.

28. Hughes stated that between 1527 and 1532, 218 persons were compelled to abjure in the London diocese, I, 131; Fox, IV, 560–70. For a discussion on some of these cases, see also Francis W. X. Fincham, "Notes from the Ecclesiastical Court Records at Somerset House," *Transactions*, Royal Historical Society, 4th ser., IV (1921), 103–39; at 114–15 is the case of John Woodward, 1528, an example of the oath's being initially refused and then taken. Hume, 30–31, mentions similar cases. Philip's case is in Foxe, V, 29–30, 862–5. See also Arthur Geoffrey Dickens, *Lollards and Protestants in the Diocese of York, 1509–1558* (London, 1959).

29. On Tyndale, see J. F. Mozley, *William Tyndale* (London, 1937). See also Richard Lovett, *A Collection of Early English New Testaments, Bibles and Other Books Illustrative Chiefly of William Tyndale and His Life-work* (Oxford, 1900); and the introduction by Edward Arber to his edition of *The First Printed English New Testament. Translated by William Tyndale* (Facsimile Text of the 1525 edition, London, 1871); and N. Hardy Wallis, ed., *The New Testament Translated by William Tyndale, 1534. A Reprint of the Edition of 1534 with the Translator's Prefaces and Notes and the Variants of the Edition of 1525* (Cambridge, Eng., 1938). The 1573 edition by John Foxe, *The whole workes of William Tyndale*, is now available on microfilm, *Short Title Catalogue* #24436, Reel 340.

30. Arber, *First Printed English New Testament* (Facsimile Text), 25; *An Exposition Uppon the V. VI, VII. Chapters of Mathew*, reprinted in *Expositions and Notes on Sundry Portions of the Holy Scriptures. By William Tyndale*, ed. by Henry Walter (Cambridge, Eng., 1849), 56. *An Exposition* was probably published in 1530.

31. Tyndale, *The Obedience of a Christen Man, and how Christen rulers ought to govern* (1528), reprinted in *Doctrinal Treatises and Introductions to Different Portions of the Holy Scriptures. By William Tyndale*, ed. by Henry Walter (Cambridge, Eng., 1848), 187, 203, and 335. See also "The truthe of that wch the Ministers in prison hold touchinge the othe of office ministred by her Maties high Commissioners" (1591), Yelverton MSS, lxx, 180 recto–181 recto, printed in Albert Peel and Leland H. Carlson, eds., *Cartwrightiana* (London, 1951), 28–45; the references to Tyndale are at pp. 44–5.

32. Gairdner, *History of the English Church in the Sixteenth Century, from the Accession of Henry VIII to the Death of Mary* (London, 1904), 129, says that Thomas Hitton refused to be sworn, in 1530, but does not mention his grounds; Gairdner's source, Foxe, IV, 619, makes no mention of Hitton's having refused the oath.

33. *A Treatise concernynge the Division betwene the Spiritualitie and Temporalitie* (1532), 16b–17b, S.T.C. #21587, Reel 145. On St. Germain, see Franklin Le Van Baumer, "Christopher St. German: the Political Philosophy of a Tudor Lawyer," *American Historical Review*, XLII (July 1937), 631–51. See Baumer, 634, and Gairdner, *Lollardry*, I, 308, on the royal influence on St. Germain. The name may also be spelled "St. German."

34. W. K. Jordan, *The Development of Religious Toleration in England* (Cambridge, Mass., 1932–40, 3 vols.), I, 41, and on More generally, 41–9; More, *The Apologye of Syr Thomas More* (1533), 219a–227b, *passim*, S.T.C. #18078, Reel 137. The standard biography is R. W. Chambers, *Thomas More* (London, 1935).

35. St. Germain, *Dialogue betwixte two englyshemen, whereof one was called Salem, and the other Bizance* (1533), 48b–50b, 83b–84a, S.T.C. #21584, Reel 145. More, *The Debyllacyon of Salem and Bizance* (1533), 1a, 2b, 72a, S.T.C. #18081, Reel 125.

36. (*Edward*) *Hall's Chronicle; containing the History of England during the Reign of Henry the Fourth, and the Succeeding Monarchs, to the End of the Reign of Henry the Eighth* (London, 1809), 784; "The Petition of Commons, 1532," in Gee and Hardy, 145–53, and for another version of the same document, Roger B. Merriman, *The Life and Letters of Thomas Cromwell* (Oxford, 1902, 2 vols.), I, 104–11. Hume, 40, who is my authority for the last point in the paragraph, relating to the oath *ex officio*, cited Theological Tracts 5, f. 217–21 (Public Records Office); she did not quote directly from the document, but seems not to have strained her evidence, G. R. Elton, "The Commons' Supplication of 1532," *English Historical Review*, LVI (Oct. 1951), 507–34, at 521, also refers to a draft that explicitly objected to the oath *ex officio*, in addition to objections to *ex officio* proceedings generally. The documents in Gee and Hardy and in Merriman do not mention the oath. I assume that Hume used a different draft; she cited four. Elton's article should be read in conjunction with the persuasive rejoinder by J. P. Cooper, "The Supplication against the Ordinaries Reconsidered," *English Historical Review*, LXXII (Oct. 1957), 616–41, and also Arthur Ogle, *The Tragedy of the Lollards' Tower* (Oxford, 1949), 307–23.

37. "The Answer of the Ordinaries, 1532," in Gee and Hardy, 154–76. For another version, see Ogle, 323–30.

38. Sir Maurice Powicke, *The Reformation in England* (London, 1961), 43; Gairdner, *Lollardry*, I, 448–9; 24 Henry VIII ch. 4, *Statutes R.*, III, 454 (1534); and the articles by Elton and Cooper cited above in note 36.

39. Jordan, II, 43; Hughes, II, 12, for the same period, reported only twenty-seven burnings, relying on Foxe as his source, but Foxe did not report burnings of Anabaptists.

40. Elizabeth Frances Rogers, *The Correspondence of Sir Thomas More* (Princeton, 1947), More to Margaret Roper, June 3, 1535, 557–8. More's

trial is reported in *State Trials*, I, 385–96. See also William J. Kenealy, S. J., "Fifth Amendment Morals," *The Catholic Lawyer*, III (Autumn 1957), 340, at 341. Father Kenealy assumed the existence of that "old Canon Law maxim."

41. Roland G. Usher, *The Rise and Fall of the High Commission* (Oxford, 1913), 15, 19–20; Foxe, V, 229, 251–2.

42. "The Six Articles Act, 1539," in Gee and Hardy, 303–19.

43. Foxe, V, 414–40, especially at 439, 440–43, 482, 485, 490–91, 496–8.

44. *Ibid.*, V, 527–50, at 546 for the quote from Anne Askew; see also Hughes, II, 68. Askew's case is also reported in *Select Works of Bale*, I, 137–248.

45. Hughes, II, 141, 173.

46. Usher, 21–22; Hughes, II, 105, 114, 128–9, 141, 150–59, 262.

47. Hughes, II, 300; see also II, 288. Hughes argues that Bonner's reputation has been unfairly maligned. Bonner's trial is in Foxe, V, 762–95; see especially 769, 775, 776, 782, 787. The trial is also reported in *State Trials*, I, 631–714.

48. Hughes, II, 255; see his discussion of "The Fate of Heretics," 254–304. Lord Acton to Lady Blennerhassett, Feb. 1879, in J. N. Figgis and R. V. Lawrence, eds., *Selections from the Correspondence of the First Lord Acton* (London, 1917), 55. See also John Emerich Dalberg, Lord Acton, "The Protestant Theory of Persecution," in Acton, *Essays on Freedom and Power*, ed. by Gertrude Himmelfarb (New York, 1955), 113–40.

49. Usher, 23–5; Usher printed extracts of the documents in Appendix I.

50. Foxe, VI, 626; VII, 292, 309, 312.

51. For the spitting incident, see Hughes, II, 191–2, 261; for Philpot's examination, Foxe, VII, 612, 614, 615.

52. Foxe, VII, 645–7.

53. *Ibid.*, VIII, 316, 329, 347, 368, 406, 417, 437, 471, 537.

54. William Haller, *The Elect Nation, The Meaning and Relevance of Foxe's* Book of Martyrs (New York, 1963), 118; Hughes, II, 259 and 257; Gairdner, *Lollardry*, I, 364. See also, J. F. Mozley, *John Foxe and His Book* (London, 1940).

55. Haller, 14, 221, 224; Gairdner, *Lollardry*, I, 335; and for the quotation, the article on John Foxe in the *Dictionary of National Biography*, VII, 588.

56. Haller, 182–3.

Chapter III
The Elizabethan Persecution of Catholics

1. On the number of heretics burned, see Philip Hughes, *The Reformation in England*, (London, 1950–54, 3 vols.) III, 31, 411. W. K. Jordan, *The Development of Religious Toleration in England* (Cambridge, Mass., 1932–40, 3 vols.), I, 151, 181–3, gave the number who were put to death for heresy as five, but he counted two who were hanged for treason.

2. In addition to the works by Hughes and Jordan, the books that I found most useful for the early years of the Elizabethan Reformation were, A. G. Dickens, *The English Reformation* (New York, 1964); W. H.

Frere, *The English Church in the Reigns of Elizabeth and James I* (London, 1904); J. E. Neale, *Elizabeth I and Her Parliaments, 1559–1581* (New York, 1958, vol. I of 2 vols.); J. B. Black, *The Reign of Elizabeth, 1558–1603* (Oxford, 1959, 2nd ed.); M. M. Knappen, *Tudor Puritanism, A Chapter in the History of Idealism* (Chicago, 1939); Powel Mills Dawley, *John Whitgift and the English Reformation* (New York, 1954); and Arnold Oscar Meyer, *England and the Catholic Church under Queen Elizabeth*, trans. by J. R. McKee (London, 1916), which is easily the best book on its subject.

3. For the legislation of 1559 (1 Eliz. ch. 1–2) and 1563 (5 Eliz. ch. 1), see G. W. Prothero, *Select Statutes and other Constitutional Documents Illustrative of the Reigns of Elizabeth and James I* (Oxford, 1894), 1–13, 13–20, and 39–41. For the remarks attributed to Elizabeth, see Neale, I, 391; Jordan, I, 99; and Conyers Read, *Mr. Secretary Cecil and Queen Elizabeth* (New York, 1955), 466.

4. On Mayne's case, see Frere, 210–13. The sentence for treason, which was rather standardized, is quoted from the case of the Jesuit priest Campion, in Richard Simpson, *Edmund Campion, A Biography* (Edinburgh, 1867), 308–9. For another example, see *State Trials*, I, 1112, and for a discussion, see Meyer, 185–7. The best study of the question whether the priests were guilty of treason is also in Meyer, 145–63; *cf.* Hughes, III, 344–53. The fullest statistics on the number of Catholics convicted for treason may be found in Hughes, III, 338–42; the quotation from Hughes is at p. 351.

5. Simpson, 144; Black, 134–44; Conyers Read, *Lord Burghley and Queen Elizabeth* (London, 1960), 24, 252; Read, *Mr. Secretary Cecil*, 455–65; Frere, 149–50; Meyer, 73–9 and, for the quotation, 85; for an English translation of the bull of 1570, see Hughes, III, Appendix V, 418–21, or J. R. Tanner, *Tudor Constitutional Documents, A.D. 1485–1603* (Cambridge, Eng., 1951), 144–6. The political section of the bull read as follows: "And moreover We do declare her to be deprived of her pretended title to the kingdom aforesaid, and of all dominion, dignity, and privilege whatsoever; and also the nobility, subjects, and people of the said kingdom, and all others who have in any sort sworn unto her, to be for ever absolved from any such oath, and all manner of duty of dominion, allegiance, and obedience; and . . . We do command and charge all and every the noblemen, subjects, people, and others aforesaid that they presume not to obey her or her orders, mandates, and laws; and those which shall do the contrary. We do include them in the like sentence of anathema. . . ." *Ibid.*, 146.

6. Meyer, 79, 85, 89–91, 135–6, 266–74; Hughes, III, 277–80; Black, 148–51, 158, 175, 178, 478; Lord Acton, "The Huguenots and the League," in Acton's *Lectures on Modern History*, ed. by Hugh Trevor-Roper (New York, Meridian Books, 1961), 160.

7. Black, 171–4; Hughes, III, 282–95; Meyer, 92–135, 169–75; Frere, 141, 207.

8. For the legislation of 1571, 13 Eliz. chs. 1–2, see Prothero, 57–63, or Tanner, 146–50, 413, 417; for discussion, see Neale, I, 192–6, 225–34. The quotation from Tanner is at p. 142. The Treason Act of 1559 is in Prothero, 23–5.

9. John Baptista Castagna to the Cardinal of Como, June 1571, quoted in Jordan, I, 131–2; the Star Chamber order, dated 15 June 1570, is State Papers Domestic, Eliz., vol. 12/71, no. 16, P.R.O. 907; Neale, 192–3, 212–16.

10. For the Jesuit mission, Simpson, 149–229; Meyer, 189–210; on Walsingham, see Conyers Read, *Mr. Secretary Walsingham and the Policy of Queen Elizabeth* (Cambridge, Mass., 1925, 3 vols.), II, 267 and, for the quotation, 284; Black, 181; for the act of 1581, 23 Eliz. ch. 1, Tanner, 150–54; Neale, I, 386–92; Hughes, III, 343.

11. For the act of 1585, 27 Eliz. ch. 2, Tanner, 154–9; Hughes, III, 344–5; J. E. Neale, *Elizabeth I and Her Parliaments, 1584–1601* (New York, 1958, vol. II), 31, 37–54; on Burghley, Read, *Burghley*, 251–4, and Jordan, I, 169–72; Read, *Walsingham*, II, 291, 299; for the quotation from Meyer, 92; for the quotation from Black, 186.

12. The quotation is from Edward Bennett Williams, *One Man's Freedom* (New York, Popular Library, 1964), 101; Campion's difficulty in raising his hand occurred at his arraignment, Simpson, 282; on the indictment, compare *State Trials*, I, 1049, with the report in Simpson, 279–81; on the confession, Simpson, 243–50; on Campion's torture, Simpson, 277–8, David Jardine, *A Reading on the Use of Torture in the Criminal Law of England* (London, 1837), 32–3, and Godfrey Anstruther, *Vaux of Harrowden, A Recusant Family* (Newport, Eng., 1953), 116, 135.

13. *State Trials*, I, 1049, at 1055 and 1062–63; Simpson, 297.

14. Letter of the Bishops of London and Ely to the Council, Sept. 13, 1562, in Samuel Haynes, ed., *A Collection of State Papers relating to Affairs in the Reigns of King Henry VIII, King Edward VI, Queen Mary, and Queen Elizabeth. From the Year 1542 to 1570. Transcribed from Letters and other Authentick Materials Never before Published, Left by William Cecill Lord Burghley* (London, 1740, 2 vols.), II, 359. Whitgift is quoted in Neale, II, 66.

15. For the quotation from the Act of Supremacy, 1 Eliz. ch. 1, 1559, Prothero, 6; *ibid.*, 227–32, for the full text of the commission of 1559 of the Court of High Commission. For the case of Leigh, whose name is also spelled Lee and Ley in the documents, sometimes varying on the same page of the same document, see Burrowes, Cox, Dyton, *et al.* v. High Commission, 3 *Bulstrode* 48, at 49–50 (1616), in 81 *English Reports* 42–50; 12 *Coke's Reports* 26, at 27, in 77 *Eng. Rep.* 1308, at 1309; 2 *Brownlow and Goldesborough* 271–2 (1609), in 123 *Eng. Rep.* 937; and Sir Edward Coke, *The Fourth Part of the Institutes of the Laws of England* (London, 1817), ch. 74, 333. Chief Justice James Dyer, who gave the opinion in Leigh's case in 1568, did not publish it in his *Reports*. Coke, in 3 *Bulstrode* 49–50, said that the opinion was in Dyer's "other book, a manuscript written with his own hand, which book I have, in which there are many cases, not in the printed book. . . ."

16. For Aquinas, see note 27 of ch. 1, this book; for the meaning of the canon law rule, *nemo tenetur seipsum prodere*, in Elizabethan England, see "Reasons why it is convenient, that those which are culpable in the articles . . . should be examined of the same articles upon their oathes," 1584, in John Strype, *The Life and Acts of John Whitgift* (Oxford, 1822, 3 vols.), I, 319, para. 8. See also the document entitled "The High Commission Court," in Thomas Fuller, *The Church History of Britain* (Oxford, 1845, 6

vols.), III, 87; Fuller dated the document 1587. Finally, see "Of Oathes in Ecclesiasticall Courtes," Cotton MSS, Cleopatra F. I., 70–75; another copy of this manuscript is in State Papers Domestic, Eliz., P.R.O. 907, 12/238, no. 47, where the date is given as 16 Feb. 1590 (old style); the document is printed in Strype, III, Appendix, 232–5, under the title, "A short discourse, being the judgment of several of the most learned Doctors of the Civil Law, concerning the practice of their courts, and of the oath *ex officio*."

17. 2 *Brownl. & Gold.* 271–2; 12 *Coke's Rep.* 26, at 27; and, for the quotation from Dyer on the *nemo* maxim, 3 *Buls.* 48, at 50. In Coke's *Institutes*, IV, ch. 74, 333, Coke reported another ground for the decision, namely that the High Commission had no lawful authority to imprison anyone.

18. The canon-law rule is quoted from the most conveniently available source, Strype, III, 234–5. The statute of 1368 was 42 Edw. III ch. 3; see this book, ch. 2, p. 53. John H. Wigmore, *A Treatise on the Anglo-American System of Evidence in Trials at Common Law* (Boston, 1940, 3rd ed., 10 vols.), VIII (rev. 1961 by J. T. McNaughton), sect. 2250, 287, note 90, clearly erred when stating that Leigh's case merely showed "an application of the ordinary ecclesiastical rule." Maguire probably erred in stating that the "first instance" of a prohibition being issued during Elizabeth's reign, by a common-law court against an ecclesiastical court, on ground of the illegality of requiring an oath in criminal matters, was in Skroggs v. Coleshill, 1559. The case is reported in 2 *Dyer* 175b, in 73 *Eng. Rep.* 386–7. It involved a dispute between the parties to the title of Exigenter of London. The queen directed her ecclesiastical commissioners to decide the dispute after the Court of Common Pleas had already awarded the office to Skroggs. The commissioners were directed to imprison Skroggs if he refused answer. Coleshill brought suit before the commissioners, and Skroggs, demurring to the jurisdiction of the commissioners, refused answer. For his contempt he was imprisoned. The Common Pleas freed him on habeas corpus, because "he was a person of the court." No other reason was reported; nothing was said about the *nemo tenetur* maxim nor about the illegality of self-accusing. In his discussion of "Oaths before an Ecclesiastical Judge ex Officio," 12 *Coke's Rep.* and 3 *Bulstrode*, 49, Serjeant Finch, of counsel, cited "Scrogs case" as a precedent for his argument that "a man needs not to answer . . . because that no man ought to accuse himself." It is noteworthy, however, that Coke, in his opinion for the court, did not cite Skroggs v. Coleshill, though he made a good deal out of Leigh's case. He also mentioned Hynde's case, which Wigmore completely confused with Skroggs v. Coleshill; Wigmore's summary in VIII, 287, note 90, purportedly of Hynde's case, is of Skroggs's. Hynde's case was first mentioned in the margin of *Dyer's Report* of Skroggs; the reference was obviously added years later because the date of Hynde's case is given as 18 Eliz. (1576) and the same marginal notation refers to a book which was not published till 1593. The notes may have been added when the first English translation was published, from the original French, in 1688; see Percy H. Winfield, *The Chief Sources of English Legal History* (Cambridge, Mass., 1925), 187. Hynde, accused of usury by the ecclesiastical commissioners, refused to answer questions under oath. From

Coke's opinion in Burrowes *et al.*, 3 *Bulstrode* 49, at 50, we learn that Hynde was imprisoned and released on habeas corpus by the Court of Common Pleas for the same reason given in Leigh's case; in 12 *Coke's Rep.* 26, at 27, we learn that he was delivered also because the commissioners had no power to imprison. Thus, Skroggs's case is of doubtful relevance to the history of the maxim *nemo tenetur* in the common-law courts, while Leigh's case and Hynde's are to the point, although the sources in all three cases are well removed from the original dates of the respective cases. Wigmore is wrong in saying that the question of the legality of the use of the oath *ex officio* was first raised in the Common Pleas in Collier v. Collier in 1589, Wigmore, VIII, 279.

19. "An Abstract of the exaicon. of such gentlemn of the Innes of Court wych have byn lately conventyd before the quenes mate. commissions appoynted for causes ecclesiasticall together with the Interrogations wheruppon every of them have ben severally exaimynyde," P.R.O. 907, S.P.D. Eliz. 12, vol. 60, no. 70. See cases of Waserer, Grenewood, Corham, Lother, Norton, and Godfrey.

20. Jardine, 26; see also Simpson, 202, 239.

21. Campion is quoted in Simpson, 161; Meyer, 110. See also the description of the attitude of Father Holforde, in the letter from the Bishop of Chester to the Earl of Derby, 23 May 1585, printed in John Hungerford Pollen, ed., *Unpublished Documents relating to the English Martyrs* (London, 1908, 2 vols.), I, 110.

22. For the inquisition of 1580 in York, see the record printed in Hughes, III, Appendix, 427–40; the minute on Baynes is at pp. 437–8. See also *ibid.*, III, 346 and 359. Briant and Sherwin are quoted in *State Trials*, I, 1078. For other examples, see John Strype, *Historical Collections of the Life and Acts of the Right Reverend Father in God, John Aylmer, Lord Bishop of London* (Oxford, 1821), 23 and 30, for the cases of Meredith, a priest, 1577, and Collins, a printer, 1580; the case of John Edwards, 1578, in Strype, *Whitgift*, I, 167; the case of Holforde, cited in the preceding note; and the case of the Jesuit, Martin Ara, 1586, in Strype, *Annals of the Reformation and Establishment of Religion* (Oxford, 1824, 4 vols.), III, 422. John A. Kemp, "The Background of the Fifth Amendment in English Law," *William and Mary Law Review* (1958), I, 247, at 268, said that in "many" of their letters of the period, Catholics objected to the use of the oath *ex officio*. Kemp's source is Pollen, I, 325, which does not support the point, nor is the proof available elsewhere in Pollen. The trial in 1606 of Father Henry Garnet, the head of the Jesuit mission in England, showed no development in Catholic thought. Tried for treason as a conspirator in the gunpowder plot to blow up Parliament, Garnet declared, "That when one is asked a question before a magistrate, he was not bound to answer *before some witnesses be produced* against him, 'Quia nemo tenetur prodere seipsum.' " *State Trials*, II, 217, at 244 (1606), italics added.

23. Black, 174; Meyer, 135–44, 157–8; Frere, 212; Read, *Burghley*, 253, who borrowed the phraseology from Meyer, 138.

24. For the Court of Star Chamber, see introduction by C. G. Bayne in Bayne and William H. Dunham, eds., *Select Cases in the Council of Henry VII* (London, 1958), Selden Society Publications, LXXV, xlix-lxxii, xciii-xcvii, clxx-clxxii; Edward P. Cheney, "The Court of Star Cham-

ber," *American Historical Review*, XVIII (July 1913), 727–50; and Sir William Holdsworth, *A History of English Law* (London and Boston, 1903–66, 16 vols.), I, 492–516, and V, 155–67, 178–88. The best account of the Star Chamber, written by a lawyer who practiced before it when its procedure was fully developed and formalized, is William Hudson, *A Treatise of the Court of Star Chamber* (*ante* 1635), printed in Francis Hargrave, ed., *Collectanea Juridica. Consisting of Tracts Relative to the Law and Constitution of England* (London, 1791–92, 2 vols.), II, 1–240. Hudson covers procedure in Part the Third, mainly at pp. 125–72, 181–231. The source for the trial of Vaux is Harleian MSS, no. 859, item 4, vols. 44–51; I labored a week transcribing a microfilm copy, from the British Museum, before discovering that there was a printed version, incomparably superior to mine, edited by John Bruce. See "Narrative of Proceedings in the Star-chamber against lord Vaux, sir Thomas Tresham, sir William Catesby, and others, for a contempt in refusing to swear that they had not harboured Campion the Jesuit," in *Archaeologia: or, Miscellaneous Tracts Relating to Antiquity. Published by the Society of Antiquaries of London* (London, 1844), XXX, 80–110. Bruce preceded his transcription of the manuscript report of the trial with a useful but anti-Catholic introduction. The author of the report is unknown; he was obviously present in the courtroom and was probably a Catholic lawyer. The report could not have been written by any of the defendants or judges. Citations are to the published report except when the oath *ex officio* or the *nemo tenetur* maxim is involved.

25. "Narrative," *Archaeologia*, XXX, 103, 104. For Campion's confession, see Simpson, 243–50, and Anstruther, 134–8. On *ore tenus* procedure, see Hudson, in Hargrave, II, 126–8.

26. "Narrative," 93, 98.

27. *Ibid.*, 92 and, for the maxim, 87; in the manuscript, the maxim is at fol. 45b.

28. *Ibid.*, 87.

29. *Ibid.*, 89–92.

30. *Ibid.*, 93–5.

31. *Ibid.*, 102–3 for Manwood; 104 for Dyer; 104–5 for Wray; and 103 for Mildmay. In the manuscript, the opinions of the common-law judges are at fols. 49d–50. For the sentence and length of imprisonment, see Anstruther, 127, 147.

32. Hudson, *Treatise of the Court of Star Chamber*, in Hargrave, ed., II, 64, 164, 169, 208–9.

33. On the statutes of 1554–55, see this book, ch. 1, p. 35; Fitzherbert's *L'Office et Auctoritie de Justices de Peace*, ed. by Richard Crompton (London, 1583), 128; Lambard, *Eirenarcha* (London, 1588), 213.

34. Act against Popish Recusants, 35 Eliz. ch. 2 (1593), in Tanner, 162–3.

Chapter IV
Whitgift and the High Commission

1. Parker to Sir William Cecil, April 12, 1566, in John Bruce and Thomas T. Perowne, eds., *Correspondence of Matthew Parker* (Cambridge, Eng., 1853), 278.

2. William Cecil, Lord Burghley, *The Execution of Justice in England, for Maintenaunce of publicque and Christian Peace, against certeine Stirrers of Sedition, and Adherents to the Traytours and Enemies of the Realme, without any Persecution of them for Questions of Religion* (London, 1583), reprinted in *The Harleian Miscellany: or, a collection of scarce, curious, and entertaining Pamphlets and Tracts* (London, 1744–46, 8 vols.), II, 126.

3. On the number of Puritan ministers, compare J. B. Black, *The Reign of Elizabeth, 1558–1603* (Oxford, 1959, 2nd ed.), 457, with M. M. Knappen, *Tudor Puritanism, A Chapter in the History of Idealism* (Chicago, 1939), 292. In London, in 1566, 38 per cent of the ministers were Puritans; see John Strype, *The Life and Acts of Matthew Parker, the First Archbishop of Canterbury, in the Reign of Queen Elizabeth* (Oxford, 1821, 3 vols.), I, 429. For the figures of 1584, see John Strype, *The Life and Acts of John Whitgift* (Oxford, 1822, 3 vols.), I, 307–8 and III, 99–103. Whitgift showed 786 ministers as conforming and 49 who were deprived; he did not count 233 others who were suspended. See Daniel Neal, *The History of the Puritans, or Protestant Non-Conformists from the Reformation to the Death of Queen Elizabeth*, revised and corrected by Joshua Toulmin (Portsmouth, N.H., 1816, 5 vols.), I, 399–400. A. G. Dickens, *The English Reformation* (New York, 1964), 313.

4. Bishops Grindal and Horn to Henry Bullinger, Feb. 6, 1567, in Hastings Robinson, ed., *The Zurich Letters, comprising the Correspondence of Several English Bishops and Others with some of the Helvetian Reformers, during the Early Part of the Reign of Queen Elizabeth* (Cambridge, Eng., 1842), 175–81. The statement on conscience was made by William White; for a transcript of his trial, see Neal, I, 328–30.

5. The best book on the Cartwright-Whitgift controversy is Donald Joseph McGinn, *The Admonition Controversy* (New Bruswick, N.J., 1949), which is hostile to the Puritan view. Pages 143–539 reprint selections from the original tracts, conveniently arranging the material under topical headings. The inclusion of material from Cartwright's rare works of 1575 and 1577, otherwise available only in the original edition, makes McGinn's book additionally valuable. The earliest and basic tracts in the controversy, by both Whitgift and Cartwright, are reprinted in John Ayre, ed., *The Works of John Whitgift* (Cambridge, Eng., 1851–53, 3 vols.). Good, short summaries of the controversy by modern scholars may be found in A. Scott Pearson, *Thomas Cartwright and Elizabethan Puritanism, 1535–1603* (Cambridge, Eng., 1925), 86–104, 145–53—an excellent, sympathetic biography; W. K. Jordan, *The Development of Religious Toleration in England* (Cambridge, Mass., 1932–40, 3 vols.), I, 137–51; and Powel Mills Dawley, *John Whitgift and the English Reformation* (New York, 1954), 133–45.

6. Pearson, 118, 270, 417.

7. *Works of Whitgift*, I, 173–4; II, 181–7, 446–7; III, 90, 183, 320.

8. *Ibid.*, I, 200–201, 270, 272–8, 329, 330–32; McGinn, 117–20, 512–22; Jordan, I, 142–7; Pearson, 91.

9. A. Scott Pearson, *Church and State; Political Aspects of Sixteenth Century Puritanism* (Cambridge, Eng., 1928), 113; on the subject generally, see Arthur Jay Klein, *Intolerance in the Reign of Elizabeth* (Boston, 1927). Pearson, in an effort to understand Cartwright in his set-

ting, saw him not as a bloodthirsty man but as a servant of God doing his will for his greater glory: "Cartwright is but an example of the godly man in the sixteenth century whose lack of toleration sprang from conviction, whose readiness to persecute and inflict the death penalty was inspired by the loftiest motives and by a deep sense of duty," *Cartwright*, 92. The Holy Inquisition may be similarly justified or explained, and, of course, the actions of Whitgift, Laud, and the High Commission.

10. Elizabeth to James VI, July 6, 1590, quoted in John Bruce, ed., *Letters of Queen Elizabeth and King James VI of Scotland* (London, 1849), Camden Society Publications, XLVI, 63.

11. Whitgift to Cecil, Aug. 19, 1570, in Strype, *Whitgift*, III, 16–17; Dawley, 82–3; Pearson, *Cartwright*, 28; Sandys to Henry Bullinger, Aug. 15, 1573, in *Zurich Letters*, 295.

12. *Works of Whitgift*, I, 27, and III, 189–91, 295–6, 554; Pearson, *Cartwright*, 95; Pearson, *Church and State*, 37–8, 61–3; Knappen, 229; J. E. Neale, *Elizabeth I and Her Parliaments* (New York, 1958), I, 202.

13. *Works of Whitgift*, I, 27, 261, and III, 299, 301; Parker to Burghley, July 18, 1573, in *Correspondence of Parker*, 437; Strype, *Whitgift*, III, 193–4.

14. Neal, *History of Puritans*, I, 295–300, 320–27; Strype, *Parker*, II, 320–22, 345–55; Pearson, *Cartwright*, 104–21; Knappen, 255–8; Parker to Sandys, Nov. 24, 1573, in *Correspondence of Parker*, 451.

15. Parker to a Member of the Ecclesiastical Commission, July 6, 1573, in *Correspondence of Parker*, 434; John Strype, *The History of the Life and Acts of Edmund Grindal* (Oxford, 1821), 327–32, 341–56, and, for Grindal to Elizabeth, Dec. 20, 1576, *ibid.*, 558–74; the quotations are from pp. 569–72.

16. Knappen, 262; Burghley to Aylmer, Dec. 1581, in John Strype, *Historical Collections of the Life and Acts of the Right Reverend Father in God, John Aylmer, Lord Bishop of London* (Oxford, 1821), 61–2.

17. W. H. Frere, *The English Church in the Reigns of Elizabeth and James I* (London, 1904), 307; "Mr. Barrowe His Examination at the Courte by the Counsayle," 1589, in Leland H. Carlson, ed., *The Writings of Henry Barrow, 1587–1590* (London, 1962), 188; Strype, *Whitgift*, I, 553, 571, and III, 218–20. The Whig historians are, respectively, E. S. Beesly, *Queen Elizabeth* (London, 1892), 228; Samuel Rawson Gardiner, *History of England from the Accession of James I. to the Disgrace of Chief-Justice Coke, 1603–1616* (London, 1863, 2 vols.), I, 152; Thomas B. Macaulay, *Critical and Historical Essays*, ed. by F. C. Montague (London, 1903, 3 vols.), II, 135. See also Dawley, 166, 186.

18. The injunctions of 1583, including the three articles, and the letter from Whitgift to the bishops are reprinted in Strype, *Whitgift*, I, 228–34. Whitgift's sermon is in *ibid.*, I, 264–5 and III, 70–81.

19. Roland G. Usher, *The Rise and Fall of the High Commission* (Oxford, 1913), 46–52.

20. *Ibid.*, 56, 64–71, 82.

21. *Ibid.*, 35–8, 61, 71–6; Knappen, 61.

22. "Reasons for the necessity of the Commission for Causes Ecclesiastical," Whitgift to Burghley, Nov. 1, 1583, in Strype, *Whitgift*, I, 266–7.

23. Usher, 71, 82–7; inexplicably, Usher barely mentioned the letters

patent of 1583 and omitted the commission of that year from the documentary section in his appendix. Standard documentary collections for this period, by Tanner and Elton, similarly omit the 1583 letters patent. Neal, *History of Puritans*, I, 408–10, first reprinted a copy, offering it as an "abstract" of a notarized document dated Jan. 7, 1584, but the only omission appears to be the names of the various commissioners. Strype, *Annals of the Reformation and Establishment of Religion* (Oxford, 1824, 4 vols.), III, 260, stated that the letters patent were dated Dec. 9, 1583. G. W. Prothero, *Select Statutes and other Constitutional Documents Illustrative of the Reigns of Elizabeth and James I* (Oxford, 1913, 4th ed.), included the 1583 document for the first time, Appendix 472a–472k.

24. The jurisdiction of the High Commission is stated in its letters patent. Neal, I, 408–10. My explanation of the overlapping jurisdiction of the High Commission and other ecclesiastical courts is based on Richard Cosin, *An Apologie for Sundrie Proceedings Ecclesiasticall* (London, 1593, 2nd ed.), S.T.C. #5821 Reel 210, Part II, 48–9. Cosin's book is the foremost primary source on the High Commission. The author was Dean of Arches and an outstanding authority on canon and civil law, long an influential member of the Commission, and close to Whitgift. His book is divided into three "Parts," each separately paginated; the whole is about 550 pp. The first edition was published in 1591.

25. The provision on the oath procedure is in Neal, I, 409. At p. 411 Neal incorrectly stated that there had been no such provision in the letters patent establishing earlier Elizabethan commissions. His error has been widely copied; *e.g.*, see note 28 below.

26. Neal, I, 399–406; Strype, *Whitgift*, I, 245–50.

27. Whitgift to Burghley, Feb. 4, 1584, in Strype, *Whitgift*, I, 250–55.

28. Cosin, Part II, 49–51. Mary Hume Maguire stated, "The oath *ex officio* was first specifically authorized in the Letters Patent of 1583," in "Attack of the Common Lawyers," *Essays in History and Political Theory*, 214. This inaccurate statement was copied from her "The History of the Oath *Ex Officio* in England" (unpub. Ph.D. diss., Radcliffe, 1923), 61–2, where the source is given as Neal's *History of Puritans*. The letters patent of 1583, as printed in Neal, I, 409, refer to the corporal oath, not to the oath *ex officio*. In this context and in accordance with the procedure of the High Commission, the two oaths were identical. A corporal oath can be any oath—an oath of allegiance, of supremacy, of purgation, etc.— sworn with the hand touching a sacred object or the Bible. The corporal oath of the High Commission was the oath *de veritate dicenda*—the oath to tell the truth. See Cosin's discussion of corporal oaths, Part III, 29–37, 39, 43, and 45–65 *passim*.

29. Cosin, Part II, 51. A good account of the High Commission's procedure, stressing the *ex officio promoto* rather than the *ex officio mero*, may be found in Usher, 106–20.

30. Cosin, Part II, 51–2, 57–8.

31. *Ibid.*, Part III, 113–16.

32. Usher, 56–7, 77. The best report of the cases of 1567 and 1574 to which Usher referred is in Neal, *History of Puritans*, I, 263–9 and 328–9; see also I, 276–9 for the Axton case of 1570.

33. Cosin, Part III, 43, 116.

34. *Ibid.,* Part II, 104; Part III, 43.

35. *"Apud Lamhith.* May. 1584. *Articuli sive interrogatoria objecta et ministrat. ex officio mero . . ."* reprinted in Strype, *Whitgift,* III, 81–7. The quoted provision is from Article 19 at p. 85.

Chapter V
Puritanism versus the High Commission

1. Knollys to Whitgift, June 8, 1584, in John Strype, *The Life and Acts of John Whitgift* (Oxford, 1822, 3 vols.), III, 103–4; Burghley to Whitgift, July 1, 1584, in *ibid.,* III, 105–6; and Brayne to Burghley, July 6, 1584, in *ibid.,* I, 323. Strype must have given the incorrect date for the last document, because Brayne's letter must have preceded the one from Burghley to Whitgift on July 1.

2. Burghley to Whitgift, July 1, 1584, in *ibid.,* III, 105–6.

3. Whitgift to Burghley, July 3, 1584, in *ibid.,* III, 107–15.

4. Burghley to Whitgift, undated letter, in *ibid.,* I, 316–17, and Thomas Fuller, *Church History of Britain* (Oxford, 1845, 6 vols.), V, 49.

5. Whitgift to Burghley, July 15, 1584, in Strype, *Whitgift,* III, 113; "Reasons why it is convenient that those which are culpable in the articles, ministred generally by the Archbishop of Canterbury, and others her Majesty's Commissioners for causes ecclesiasticall, should be examined of the same articles upon their oathes," reprinted in *ibid.,* I, 318–21.

6. *Ibid.,* and "Inconveniences of not proceeding *ex officio mero,* unto examination upon articles, *super fama aut denuntiatione alterius,* but only upon presentment and conviction by witnesses," in *ibid.,* I, 321–2.

7. The characterization of Beale is by Strype, *Whitgift,* I, 283; the reference to the "book against oaths" is from a statement of charges against Beale, drawn up by Whitgift in June or July, 1585, for the attention of the Privy Council, reprinted in *ibid.,* I, 401. In the sketch of Beale in the *Dictionary of National Biography,* Whitgift's reference to that book becomes italicized and passed off as an exact title, and the date of publication is incorrectly given as 1583. Whitgift's new High Commission did not begin operation until January 1584; the book could not have preceded that date.

8. For Whitgift's abridgment and quotations from Beale's book, see Strype, *Whitgift,* I, 284–7, and for Whitgift's reply, *ibid.,* III, 87–90. The manuscript, which the *Dictionary of National Biography* calls, "A Book respecting Ceremonies, the Habits, the Book of Common Prayer, and the power of Ecclesiastical Courts, 1584" is in the British Museum, Additional Manuscripts 48116, fols. 1–41. For the 1585 speech by Beale, see "A Treatise made by a Burgess of the house to use in Parliament, manifestly proving that the proceedings of the L. Archbishop of Canterbury against poore ministers is unlawful," British Museum, Additional Manuscripts 48116, fols. 154, 162–6, 199.

9. Beale to Whitgift, May 7, 1584, printed in Strype, *Whitgift,* III, 91–8; and see also in *ibid.,* I, 288–99. Letter from privy councilors to Whitgift and Aylmer, Sept. 20, 1584, in *ibid.,* I, 329–30. For the Benison case, see Daniel Neal, *The History of the Puritans . . . ,* revised and corrected by Joshua Toulmin (Portsmouth, N.H., 1816, 5 vols.), I, 430–31; John Strype,

Historical Collections of the Life and Acts of the Right Reverend Father in God, John Aylmer, Lord Bishop of London (Oxford, 1821), 137–8; Benjamin Brook, *The Lives of the Puritans* (London, 1813, 3 vols.), I, 292–3; Albert Peel, ed., *The Seconde Parte of a Register: Being a calendar of manuscript under that title intended for publication by the Puritans about 1593, and now in Dr. William's Library, London* (Cambridge, Eng., 1915, 2 vols.), I, 246–8.

10. The quotation from Fenn is in the Morrice MSS, vol. C., Transcript, 592, Dr. Williams Library, London; the next quotation is from Document 120 in Peel, ed., *Seconde Parte of a Register*, I, 179. For the report of the judgment of legal counsel, see Roland G. Usher, ed., *The Presbyterian Movement in the Reign of Queen Elizabeth as Illustrated by the Minute Book of the Dedham Classis, 1582–89* (London, 1905), Camden Society, Third Ser., VIII, 35. For the Puritan strategy on the oath, see Roland G. Usher, *The Rise and Fall of the High Commission* (Oxford, 1913), 127–8, quoting "Formes for Answering Interrogatories," Queens College MSS (Oxford), 121, fol. 380.

11. The Blake quotation is from Mary Hume Maguire, "The History of the Oath *Ex Officio* in England" (unpub. Ph.D. diss., Radcliffe, 1923), 143, quoting Lambeth MSS, Carta Miscellanea, XII, fol. 15. For Wigginton, his own statements, "A shorte sum of the hard dealing of Mr. John Whitgift now Archb: of Cant. against me," written Oct. 5, 1585, Morrice MSS, vol. C., Transcript, 759, and a second statement by Wigginton, dated Dec. 9, 1586, "A further report," in *ibid.*, 764. See also Peel, ed., I, 15–18, on Field's activities.

12. M. M. Knappen, *Tudor Puritanism, A Chapter in the History of Idealism* (Chicago, 1939), 284–8; J. B. Black, *The Reign of Elizabeth, 1558–1603* (Oxford, 1959, 2nd ed.), 200, 363, 376–82; J. E. Neale, *Elizabeth I and Her Parliaments* (New York, 1958), II, 15, 18–20, 31, 48–9, 60; Stuart Barton Babbage, *Puritanism and Richard Bancroft* (London, 1962), 18, 36–8; Neal, *History of Puritans*, I, 440.

13. Neale, *Elizabeth I and Her Parliaments*, II, 62–3; the first petition mentioned is "The Generall Inconveniences of the book of common prayer," 1584, Doc. 165, in Peel, ed., I, 257; the second petition is, "Means how to settle a godly and charitable Quietness in the Church," printed in Strype, *Whitgift*, I, 367.

14. "The humble petitions of the Commons of the Lower House of Parliament, to bee offered to the consideration of the Right Honourable the Lords spirituall and temporall of the Higher House," printed in Strype, *Whitgift*, III, 118–24; the quotation is from the eleventh petition, at p. 122.

15. Neale, II, 65–6; Whitgift's statements are in "The Answer of the Bishop of Canterbury to the petition of the Commons House," printed in Strype, *Whitgift*, I, 354–60 (quotations from pp. 358–9), and in his answer to similar petitions, in *ibid.*, III, 136; see also *ibid.*, I, 374–5, and III, 128.

16. "A Treatise made by a Burgess of the house to use in Parliament, manifestly proving that the proceedings of the L. Archbishop of Canterbury against poore ministers is unlawful," 1585, Br. Mus., Add. MSS, 48116, fols. 154 *recto* to 156 *recto*, 166 *verso* and *recto*.

17. *Ibid.*, 159 *recto* to 166 *recto*.

18. Neale, II, 69–71.

19. *Ibid.*, II, 72–5, 99–100.

20. Strype, *Whitgift*, I, 401–2; for the episode of 1579, *ibid.*, I, 164–8.

21. "A Declaration of the unjust Proceedings of the L. Bp. of London, against Edmond Allen and Thomas Carew, contrary to the Lawes of the Realme," Morrice MSS, Transcript, 651–2, and "A Note of the B. of L. dealing with Thomas Carew, Minister of the Parishioners of Hatfield Peverel," *ibid.*, 653–5. See also Strype, *Aylmer*, 78–9, and Neal, *Puritans*, I, 425–6.

22. Giles Wigginton, "A further report of the saide Jo: Cant: his further dealinge against me," Dec. 9, 1586, Morrice MSS, Transcript, 760, 763, 765, and Wigginton, "Certaine Probable Conjectures," Feb. 21, 1586/-87, *ibid.*, 766, 771.

23. John Udall, "Mr. Udall's Troubles," 1586, Morrice MSS, Transcript, 772–81; the quotations are from fols. 773, 781. The anecdote about James VI is from Sidney Lee's sketch of Udall in the *Dictionary of National Biography*, XX, 6.

24. "A generall Supplication made to the Parliament in Anno 1586. November," Morrice MSS, Transcript, 672–83, printed in Peel, ed., *Seconde Parte of a Register*, II, 70–87. The quotation from the manuscript is at fol. 679; it is at p. 82 in Peel.

25. Neale, II, 145–65, 223, 231–2.

26. The books that I found most useful on Browne, Barrow, and the early Separatists were Robert W. Dale, *History of English Congregationalism*, completed and edited by A. W. W. Dale (London, 1907, 2nd ed.); Champlin Burrage, *The True Story of Robert Browne* (London, 1906); F. J. Powicke, *Robert Browne, Pioneer of Modern Congregationalism* (London, 1910); Albert Peel, *The First Congregational Churches: New Light on Separatist Congregations in London, 1567–81* (Cambridge, Eng., 1920); Champlin Burrage, *The Early English Dissenters in the Light of Recent Research* (Cambridge, Eng., 1912, 2 vols.); F. J. Powicke, *Henry Barrow, Separatist* (London, 1900). Knappen, 306–16, and Jordan, I, 262–84, have good brief summaries.

27. "A Brief of the Examination of me. Henry Barrowe, the 19 of November, 1586" [misprint; should be 1587], "The Examinations of Henry Barrowe, John Grenewood, and John Penrie before the High Commissioners and Lordes of Counsel. Penned by the Prisoners Themselves before Their Deathes" [1593], printed in *Harleian Miscellany* (London, 1809), II, 10–41, and in Leland H. Carlson, ed., *The Writings of Henry Barrow, 1587–1590* (London, 1962), 91–100, which covers the examination of Nov. 19, 1587. Carlson, whose editing and scholarship are impeccable, estimates that the original rare tract was written in 1593 and published about 1595. The anonymous editor of the original edition noted, in his introduction, that Christ had never been imprisoned "for refusing to sweare to accuse him selfe." The material quoted from this first examination of Barrow is in Carlson, 96–8. Carlson tested Barrow's memory by comparing his account of one of his later examinations with an official record of the same examination, and found that Barrow was remarkably accurate and even objective. *Ibid.*, 203–4.

28. Barrow's second examination, Nov. 27, 1587, is in Carlson, 102–5. For

the document produced by Whitgift, see "A Breefe Sum of Our Profession," in *ibid.*, 81–5. For the trial and punishment of Barrow and Greenwood, see Leland H. Carlson, ed., *The Writings of John Greenwood, 1587–90* (London, 1962), 281, note.

29. "The True Coype of a Lamentable Petition delivered to the Queene's Majestye," March 13, 1589, in Carlson, *Greenwood*, 277–82. This document is in Harleian MSS, 6848 fols. 18 *verso* to 20 *recto*, Br. Mus. In the earlier stages of my research I read and examined a great many manuscripts on the Puritans, both Presbyterians and Separatists, in the State Papers Domestic, Elizabeth, P.R.O., and in the large collections in Harleian MSS, 6848, 6849, and 7042, to verify dates, citations, accuracy, and to supply omissions from various printed collections or documents printed in books by secondary authorities. When Carlson published his editions of *Barrow* and *Greenwood* in 1962, I found his work to be so accurate that I relied on him wherever possible, rather than on earlier printed collections or on my own manuscript work.

30. The "Pastoral Letter," which Barrow probably wrote in late 1587, is in Carlson, *Barrow*, 116. For some other Barrowist objections to the oath procedure, see "A Briefe of the Positions Holden by the Newe Sectorie of Recusants," in *ibid.*, 115, and Barrow's answer, "A Briefe Answeare to Certayne Sclaunderous Articles and Ungodlie Calumniations," in Carlson, *Greenwood*, 170–71. See also Barrow's fifth examination, on March 24, 1589, before the special commission, in Carlson, *Barrow*, 193–202, especially at p. 194. Barrow's book is *A Brief Discoverie of the False Church* (1590), reprinted in *ibid.*, 259–672; see pp. 648–53. The same special commission also examined Greenwood at about the same time as it examined Barrow in March 1589. Greenwood refused to answer an oath on the Bible although he offered to swear in God's name if necessary. The commission, not bothering to query him on what he meant by his condition, waived the oath altogether; his answers were very incriminating. See "The Answers of John Grenewood," in Carlson, *Greenwood*, 22–9.

31. "The Examination of John Wilson before the Bp. of Yorke High Commissioners at the manner of Bishopthrope," Morrice MSS, Transcript, 782–7, which includes the examinations of Jan. 9, 15, and 20, 1587; "A true Report of the B. of Londons proceedings by his Associates against Jo: Wilson, Preacher of Gods word, for a sermon preached by him at St. Michaels church in Cornhill the 16th of August," Aug. 24, 1587, in *ibid.*, 826–34. The first quotation is from fol. 782, the second from fol. 828.

32. "The whole processe of J. C. [John (Whitgift) of Canterbury] with G. W., the 6th day of December Anno. 1588," Morrice MSS, Transcript, 844–8.

33. Richard Cosin, *An Apologie for Sundrie Proceedings Ecclesiasticall* (London, 1593, 2nd ed.), S.T.C. #5821, Reel 210, Part III, 196–8.

34. *Ibid.*, III, 203–14, quotations at 210, 213–14.

35. *Ibid.*, III, 81–2, 215–18.

36. On Bancroft, see Roland G. Usher, *The Reconstruction of the English Church* (New York, 1910, 2 vols.), I, 22–38, 49–67, and Babbage's biography of Bancroft.

37. Strype, *Whitgift*, I, 551–3. William Pierce, ed., *The Marprelate*

Tracts (London, 1911), reprints the tracts. Edward Arber, *An Introductory Sketch to the Martin Marprelate Controversy, 1588–1590* (London, 1879), is really a collection of primary sources, some of considerable value. William Pierce, *An Historical Introduction to the Marprelate Tracts* (London, 1908), though sharing the fiercest Martinist prejudices, has long been the standard account and remains the most interesting account; see pp. 160, 177, 273–308, for material discussed in this paragraph. Pierce has been superseded in some respects by the recent account, Donald J. McGinn, *John Penry and the Marprelate Controversy* (New Brunswick, N.J., 1966). Albert Peel, ed., *The Notebook of John Penry, 1593* (London, 1944), Camden Third Ser., LXVII, has a discerning introduction on Penry's role in the controversy.

38. Mrs. Crane's statement is in "The Brief Held by Sir John Puckering, While Attorney General, against the Martinists," printed in Arber, 123, from Harleian MSS 7042, fol. 11, which I checked. See also Pierce, *Historical Introduction*, 197–205. For the documents, see Arber, 94–104, 121–2, 135–6.

39. Examinations of Udall by Puckering on Jan. 13 and July 13, 1590, are in Arber, 88–92. The principal source of Udall's examination and trial is *State Trials*, I, 1271–1310, which contains his own account. His report of the Jan. 13, 1590, examination is at pp. 1271–7; the comment by Puckering is at 1294.

40. The quoted material is from *State Trials*, I, 1274.

41. *Ibid.*, 1275–6.

42. *Ibid.*, 1276.

43. The act of 1581, 23 Eliz. ch. 2, sect. 9, is in G. W. Prothero, *Select Statutes and other Constitutional Documents Illustrative of the Reigns of Elizabeth and James I* (Oxford, 1894), 178. The quoted material is from *State Trials*, I, 1278.

44. 23 Eliz. ch. 2, sect. 13, in Prothero, 180; *State Trials*, I, 1280–81.

45. *State Trials*, I, 1286, 1289. For a discussion of the act of 1581, see Neale, *Elizabeth I and Her Parliaments*, I, 393–8.

46. *State Trials*, I, 1290–95.

47. *Ibid.*, 1297–1306.

48. *Ibid.*, 1306–10.

49. Quoted from an extract from the *Appellation*, printed in Arber, 73.

50. For the Star Chamber decree, see Prothero, 168–9. See also Frederick Seaton Siebert, *Freedom of the Press in England, 1476–1776* (Urbana, Ill., 1952), 61–2; Strype, *Whitgift*, I, 422–5, and III, 160–65. On Beale's manuscript of 1588–89, which does not seem to have survived, Strype, *Whitgift*, II, 30. The manuscript of 1589–90 is "A Collection shewinge what jurisdiction the clergie hathe heretofore lawfully used and maye lawfullye use in the Realme of Englande. Wherein it is manifestly proved, that the Prelates or Ecclesiasticall Judges never had anye authoritie to compell anie subjecte of the lande to an othe, unles it were in causes Testamentarie or Matrimoniall, or there to appertayninge," Cotton MSS, Cleopatra, F.I., fols. 1–49.

51. Beale, "A Collection," fols. 18 *verso* and *recto*. Beale declared that Otho's constitution of 1272, introducing the oath *de veritate dicenda*, violated Magna Carta. *Ibid.*, 21 *recto*. By "the olde lawes of this realm," Beale

meant, among others, the *Prohibitio Formata Super Articuli Cleri* of ca. 1315–16. *Ibid.*, fol. 22 *recto*—23 *recto;* see also 37 *verso* and *recto.* Mary Hume Maguire, "The History of the Oath Ex Officio" (unpub. Ph.D. diss., Radcliffe, 1923), transcribed in her appendix fols. 43–9 of Beale's "Collection," describing that section as "the most important part." See Appendix, 261–75, and the comment at p. 90 n. 1. The transcribed section is merely a summation to the whole argument; it does not include the arguments based on Magna Carta, which compose the most important part.

52. Strype, *Whitgift*, II, 28–31.

Chapter VI
Cartwright, Barrow, and Morice

1. A. Scott Pearson, *Thomas Cartwright and Elizabethan Puritanism, 1535–1603* (Cambridge, Eng., 1925), 227–31.

2. *Ibid.*, 257–63 and, for the quotations, 270–71. See also Roland G. Usher, *The Reconstruction of the English Church* (New York, 1910, 2 vols.), I, 60–63.

3. Pearson, 267–9, 315, 446; Thomas Fuller, *Church History of Britain* (Oxford, 1845, 6 vols.), III, 116–20; and, for Puritan co-operation with the authorities, see the depositions printed in John Strype, *The Life and Acts of John Whitgift* (Oxford, 1822, 3 vols.), II, 91–2, and III, 271–85. Whitgift's report to Burghley on the *classis* movement is in the latter, dated July 16, 1590, II, 6–13; the quoted remark is at p. 7. A companion report is in *ibid.*, II, 13–22.

4. The thirty-one articles are printed in Fuller, III, 105–11; the account of the examination is from Cartwright's letter to Burghley, Nov. 4, 1590, printed in the Appendix to Pearson, 455–6.

5. The interrogatories with Cartwright's answers are printed in Albert Peel and Leland H. Carlson, eds., *Cartwrightiana* (London, 1951), 21–7.

6. Pearson, 320.

7. "The truthe of that which the Ministers in prison hold touchinge the othe of office ministred by her Majesties high Commissioners," in *Cartwrightiana*, 28–30. The longer statement on the oath *ex officio* is printed in *ibid.*, 30–46. When the prisoners referred to the advice of "oure learned Councell in the lawe" not to take the oath, they must have meant advice received prior to their arrest, for elsewhere in the document they complain that they have not been permitted to have counsel.

8. Quotations are from *ibid.*, pp. 33, 37, 38.

9. *Ibid.*, 39, for the quotation.

10. *Ibid.*, 44, for the quotation.

11. Whitgift's comment is in Strype, *Whitgift*, II, 19. "Of oathes in Ecclesiastical Courtes," State Papers Domestic, Elizabeth, P.R.O. 907, P. 12/238, no. 47, dated Feb. 14, 1590 (1590/91). Another copy of this document is in Cotton MSS, Cleopatra F I, 76–7. A printed version is in Strype, *Whitgift*, III, 232–5; Strype incorrectly took it for an answer to a later treatise by James Morice, *ibid.*, II, 29–32.

12. "The doctrine, with some practices of sundry troublesome Ministers," etc., is printed in Strype, *Whitgift*, III, 235–42; see *ibid.*, II, 71,

where it is stated that Burghley received the document on Feb. 3, 1590/91. The quoted material is from *ibid.*, III, 241.

13. "A letter of the Puritan ministers imprisoned," printed in John Strype, *Annals of the Reformation and Establishment of Religion* (Oxford, 1824, 4 vols.), IV, 120–27; the quoted material is at pp. 120–21. The manuscript is dated April 1592, but Pearson, 327, and Peel and Carlson, *Cartwrightiana*, 28, agree that 1592 was a slip of the pen; the date should be 1591.

14. "Proceedings of certain unlawful Ministers, tending to innovation and stirrs," printed in Strype, *Whitgift*, II, 13–22; quoted material at p. 20.

15. The untitled report of the examination by an anonymous eyewitness, carrying the endorsement, "Mr. Cartwrightes aunsweres to the Commissioners," May 1591, is printed in Pearson, Appendix, 458–63. Internal evidence proves that Cartwright was not the author as Strype believed, *Whitgift*, II, 74.

16. For the trial of Vaux and Tresham, see above, ch. 2.

17. James Morice, *A briefe treatise of Oathes exacted by Ordinaries and Ecclesiasticall Judges, to answere generallie to all such Articles or Interrogatories, as pleaseth them to propound. And of their forced and constrained Oathes ex officio, wherein is proved that the same are unlawfull* (written 1590–92, published unlicensed in the Low Countries, 1598), S.T.C. #18106, Reel 480 (ed. of 1600), 38–9. Robert Beale also distinguished the oath proceeding in the High Commission from that in the Star Chamber; see Beale to Burghley, March 17, 1592/93, in Strype, *Whitgift*, II, 138.

18. My description of Star Chamber procedure is based on Sir William Holdsworth, *A History of English Law* (London and Boston, 1903–66, 16 vols.), V, 178–87; Edward P. Cheyney, "The Court of Star Chamber," *American Historical Review*, XVIII (July 1913), 737–41; and, especially, William Hudson, *A Treatise of the Court of Star Chamber* (*ante* 1635), printed in Francis Hargrave, ed. *Collectanea Juridica. Consisting of Tracts Relative to the Law and Constitution of England* (London, 1791–92, 2 vols.), II, 125–72, 181–231.

19. Strype, *Whitgift*, II, 71, 92. For the bill and answers by Cartwright and the others, see *ibid.*, III, 242–60. For the depositions of the nine ministers on behalf of the government, see *ibid.*, III, 271–82; for the depositions on behalf of the defendants, *ibid.*, III, 268–71, 282–5.

20. *Ibid.*, III, 243, 247, 257–8; Whitgift to Burghley, "The Effect of some of the principal Matters in the Bil and Complaint against Mr. Cartwright and the rest," endorsed by Burghley, June 23, 1591, in *ibid.*, II, 95. For Lord, *ibid.*, II, 86; for Johnson, III, 282.

21. *Ibid.*, II, 95.

22. For Fuller's interference in Udall's trial, *State Trials*, I, 1289.

23. Strype, *Whitgift*, II, 82–4.

24. *Ibid.*, Popham's report is at p. 83.

25. *Ibid.*, II, 73, for Knollys letter to Burghley, Jan. 9, 1592. See also, Pearson, 347–9, 352.

26. Champlin Burrage, *The Early English Dissenters in the Light of Recent Research* (Cambridge, Eng., 1912, 2 vols.), I, 136–42, 145, 152, and II, 43, 110; Leland H. Carlson, ed., *The Writings of John Greenwood, 1587–90* (London, 1962), 87; Benjamin Brook, *The Lives of the Puritans* (Lon-

don, 1813, 3 vols.), I, 397–400, and II, 90, 98–101; Strype, *Whitgift*, I, 567; and Strype, *Annals*, III, 117–22, and IV, 133–4.

27. "The humble most earnest, & Lamentable Complaint & Supplication, of the persecuted & proscribed Church & Servantes of CHRIST, falsely called Brownists: Unto the high Court of Parlament," March 1593, printed in Burrage, II, 109–13; another petition is in *ibid.*, 114–16. Burrage's transcriptions of these documents are accurate. Another petition, "The humble petition of many poor christians, imprisoned by the bishops in sundry prisons in and about London, to the lord treasurer," is in Strype, *Annals*, IV, 132–5.

28. "The humble petition," Strype, *Annals*, IV, 134. Burrage, *Early English Dissenters*, II, 31–61, prints Barrowist depositions of 1593 based on Harleian MSS, 6848 and 6849. I have used these manuscripts and find that Burrage's transcriptions are accurate. However, they are often condensed or incomplete; moreover, his citations are neither reliable nor complete. He frequently cited the *verso* side of a folio instead of the *recto*, and *vice versa*, and sometimes did not give the particular folio at all. He cited the source for Simkin's examination of April 5, 1593, as Harl. MSS, 6849, fol. 182; it should be 6848, fol. 33 *recto*. He omitted the second examinations of Collier, Settle, and Simkins, which are at 6848, fols. 49 *recto*, 67 *verso*, and 76 *recto*, respectively. Nevertheless, readers not having access to the manuscripts will find Burrage quite adequate. On Settle's troubles in 1586, see Albert Peel, ed., *The Seconde Parte of a Register . . .* (Cambridge, Eng., 1915, 2 vols.), II, 38–9.

29. For accurate if condensed transcriptions of Penry's examinations of March 26 and April 5, 1593, see Burrage, II, 37, 54–5. For his examination of April 10, when he incriminated himself, see "A brief Summe of the Examination of John Penrie," *Harleian Miscellany*, (London, 1809), II, 231–41. Johnson's examinations are in Burrage, II, 45, 56–7. See also William Pierce, *John Penry; His Life, Times and Writings* (London, 1923), 420–29.

30. The remarks by Burghley and Barrow are in Leland H. Carlson, ed., *The Writings of Henry Barrow, 1587–1590* (London, 1962), 183, 188.

31. Barrow's book of 1590, *A brief discoverie of the false church*, is reprinted in entirety in Carlson, *Barrow*, 263–673; the main section on the High Commission and its oath procedure is at pp. 647–73. See also pp. 284, 336, 511, 582, 602, 616.

32. Barrow recounted the story of the last-minute reprieve in a letter written a few days later, April 4 or 5, 1593, printed in Burrage, II, 105–6. If Penry's trial, as Daniel Neal, *The History of the Puritans . . .*, revised and corrected by Joshua Toulmin (Portsmouth, N.H., 1816, 5 vols.), I, 526, says of the trial of Barrow and Greenwood, was an artful contrivance by Whitgift to throw off the odium of death from himself to the civil magistrate, he succeeded beyond his expectations. The odium earned by the civil magistrate in the Barrow-Greenwood case was compounded in the Penry case. It was not clear then, nor is it clearer today, whether the indictment had any foundation. Penry expected to be indicted under 23 Eliz. ch. 2, like Barrow and Greenwood, and in anticipation wrote a first-rate argument proving that the statute could not be used against him. He was then indicted under the Act of Uniformity of 1559, 1 Eliz. ch. 2,

for contempt of the queen, the overthrow of religion, treason, and rebellion, preposterous charges founded exclusively on purely private papers found in his study in Scotland. He protested vehemently in a petition to Burghley. Then he was reindicted for felony under 1 Eliz. ch. 2, and this time extracts from one of his books, as well as from private papers, were cited against him. The felony consisted of "publishing scandalous writings against the Church," but the statute did not create any felony. The trial was a farce. Sir Edward Coke wrote that Penry was tried under 1 Eliz. ch. 2; Holdsworth remarked, "This is legally impossible." According to Holdsworth, the indictment could not have been founded on that statute; he claimed it "seems to be founded upon the 23rd of Elizabeth, chapter 2, section 4," but ended by adding, in confusion, that the indictment "was founded upon both statutes." For a discussion of Penry's indictment and trial, see William Pierce, *John Penry, His Life, Times, and Writings* (London, 1923), 433–9, 446–71, and Champlin Burrage, *John Penry, the So-Called Martyr of Congregationalism as Revealed in the Original Record of His Trial and in Documents Related Thereto* (London, 1913), 7–43; the latter, a pamphlet, contains the statements by Coke, Holdsworth's letter to Burrage, Penry's argument, and trial records. The quotations from Holdsworth are at pp. 13–14. See also Neal, I, 530–34; Strype, *Whitgift*, 181–5, which includes Penry's argument; and the selection of documents in Burrage, *Early English Dissenters*, II, 62–96.

33. The two letters from Morice to Burghley are quoted in Strype, *Whitgift*, 28 and 30. Morice made almost exactly the same explanation for writing his "Brief Treatise" in a later statement; see "A Remembrance of Certeine Matters concerninge the Clergeye and theire Jurisdiccion," 1593, Baker MSS, 40, Mm. 1. 51, fol. 105 (Cambridge U.). Strype gave 1590 as the date of the first letter to Burghley; more likely it was 1591. In the latter year, William Skinner wrote Burghley that he was expecting a copy of Beale's "collections" and of Morice's manuscript, which, Morice had told him, was written "last sommer vacacon"—*i.e.*, in 1590. But Morice also told him that the manuscript was "scribled so as there could not be use of it untill a transcript was new made." Morice intended, moreover, to expand his book to include "direct answering of the book sent from my L. Archbishop whereof he hath sene a copie"—Richard Cosin, *An Apologie for Sundrie Proceedings Ecclesiasticall* (London, 1591). Skinner to Burghley, March 14, 1590/91 State Papers Domestic, Eliz., 12/238, no. 75, P.R.O. 907. Cosin's 2nd ed., 1593, included the attack on "the Treatisour" and "the Note-Gatherer." Thus, Morice rewrote his "Brief Treatise" after seeing Cosin's book; it was then that Whitgift demanded a copy of his manuscript, Strype, *Whitgift*, II, 29. Cosin saw the revised manuscript and expanded his *Apologie*. Morice, on reading the second edition in 1593, revised his own manuscript again: "I have since that taken the paynes to justifie and mayntaine my said treatize, aunsweringe all the Shyftyge and deceiptfull Sophisticacions of this our cavellinge Civilian. . . ." "A Remembrance," cited above, this note, fol. 134. Morice's final revision was never published. Mary Hume Maguire, in "The History of the Oath *Ex Officio* in England" (unpub. Ph.D. diss., Radcliffe, 1923), made no use of the final revision in the text of her work, but she cited it in her bibliography as a manuscript volume, #234, dated 1594, in the library of

Lambeth Palace, consisting of 327 folios, under the title, "A just and necessarie defence of a Briefe treatise made against generall oathes exacted by Ordinaries and Judges Ecclesiasticall. . . ." I have not been able to obtain a microfilm copy. The book by Morice, cited in note 17, above, is based on a version of his manuscript completed in 1591 or 1592, before Cosin's assault on Morice and Morice's final revision.

34. Morice, *A briefe treatise of Oathes* . . . , 8–10, 11–18, 22, 26–31; the quotation is from p. 8.

35. *Ibid.*, 31, 32, 37, 47, and the quotation, 57–8.

36. Morice gave the text of his speech in "A Remembrance of Certeine Matters," cited in note 33 above. Mary Hume Maguire's unpublished dissertation includes in the appendix a complete and accurate transcription, 276–318, which I found easier to use than the manuscript. The quotation is from pp. 278–9 of Maguire's transcription.

37. *Ibid.*, 280, 284.

38. *Ibid.*, 287.

39. The first bill is in *ibid.*, 288–93; pages 289–91 concentrate on the issue of compulsory self-incrimination.

40. The second bill is in *ibid.*, 293–5; the same problem is dealt with in the main body of the speech, reported at pp. 280–82. Students of American constitutional history will find an extraordinary parallel between Morice's argument, that to deny a man the opportunity to practice his livelihood is a denial of due process of law, and the doctrine of due process which emerged in the United States in the last quarter of the nineteenth century.

41. The debate in Commons is reported in Morice, "A Remembrance," in Maguire's transcription, 296–7; Simonds D'Ewes, ed., *The Journals of All the Parliaments during the Reign of Queen Elizabeth* (London, 1682, rev. by Paul Bowes), 474–6; and, for secondary accounts, Strype, *Whitgift*, II, 122–30, and J. E. Neale, *Elizabeth I and Her Parliaments* (New York, 1958), II, 270–72.

42. Whitgift to Elizabeth, Feb. 28, 1592/93, British Museum, Additional MSS. 28571, fol. 139 (172); and, "An Inhibition from the Queen, not to read any Bill if it touched matter of State or reformation of the Churche," Feb. 28, 1592/93, P.R.O. 907, S.P. D., P. 12/244. For a slightly different version of the latter, see Neale, II, 274–5, citing other manuscript sources. See also Heywood Townshend, *Historical Collections: or, An exact Account of the Proceedings of the Four Last Parliaments of Q. Elizabeth* (London, 1680), 62–3.

43. Morice, "A Remembrance," 297–301, reports his examination by the Privy Council. Neale's remark is in his *Elizabeth I and Her Parliaments*, II, 269.

44. Beale to Burghley, March 17, 1592/93, in Strype, *Whitgift*, II, 130–41; the quoted matter is at p. 137. Neale stated that Strype, *ibid.*, I, 401–2, wrongly assigned to 1585 an undated manuscript in which Whitgift itemized various charges against Beale, presumably in the hope that the Privy Council would take disciplinary action against him. Neale claimed "there can be little doubt" that the document was framed by Whitgift shortly after the Parliament of 1593 ended. *Elizabeth I and Her Parliaments*, II, 277. I think there can be little doubt that Strype, who was often wrong

in dating manuscripts and who had little sense of chronology, was right this time. I have followed Strype in assigning the document to 1585; see above, ch. 4, pp. 148–9. A recitation of the various reasons for my rejection of Neale's assertion would be tedious and require more space than would be warranted. Two points must suffice. Whitgift said that Beale wrote a book against oaths "before the last Parliament," printed it abroad, and imported it via Scotland; moreover, that he subsequently wrote another book. If Neale is correct in his dating, the second book would be the "Collection," the first "Brief Notes." But we know that neither of these was published, though the book against oaths was published. Furthermore, Whitgift's comments about the second book do not fit the "Collection" of 1589–90, cited above, note 50, ch. 5. For the book of 1584, which does fit the description of Whitgift's comments, see above, note 8 of ch. 5.

45. "An Act against Popish Recusants," 35 Eliz. ch. 2 (1593), in J. R. Tanner, *Tudor Constitutional Documents, A. D. 1485–1603* (Cambridge, Eng., 1951), 159–62.

46. "An Act to Retain the Queen's Subjects in Obedience," 35 Eliz. ch. 1 (1593), 197–200. For the remarks by Wigginton and Udall, see above, ch. 5, pp. 158 and 165.

47. For the protest against the oath in 1597, see Strype, *Whitgift*, II, 375. Fuller, *Church History of Britain*, V, 107–12, prints a document which he dated as 1587, giving in parallel columns arguments for and against the High Commission and the oath *ex officio*. Fuller does not cite the source nor give the name of the author. The arguments are not only too sophisticated for 1587; they seem to rely on Cosin's *Apologie* for the *pro* position, rejecting the precedent of Hynde's case in the same manner as Cosin. The *con* position quotes chapter 29 of Magna Carta to prove that the High Commission cannot lawfully fine or imprison, and relies on the common law to rebut the legality of the oath *ex officio*. Among the interesting points made by the *con* position are the following: "And where loss of life, liberty, or good name, may ensue, the common-law hath forbidden such oath." "It is contrary to the fundamental law of liberty,—*Nemo tenetur seipsum prodere*." To these points, *pro* replied, "It is true, to give this oath to the defendant in causes of life and death, is contrary to the justice of the land," but in other cases the oath was legal; the *nemo tenetur* maxim applies only to the case of a secret crime. I would guess that this *pro-and-con* document belongs to 1593 or later. There is, however, a possibility that what appears to be Fuller's printing of an original manuscript is merely his own composition, summarizing the positions ca. 1587, as he understood them, taken by proponents and opponents of the High Commission's proceedings. It is often difficult to tell whether Fuller is quoting or composing.

48. "If a man plead in his answer Not Guilty, and will not answer the articles, it shall be held as a confession," Att. Gen. v. Johnes and Thomas, 1597, in John Hawarde, ed., *Les Reportes del Cases in Camera Stellata, 1593 to 1609*, ed. by William Paley Baildon (Privately printed, London?, 1894), 74; see also Att. Gen. v. Panter, 1579, where the defendant, having pleaded not guilty, refused to answer the interrogatories, "Whereupon it was ruled by the Court that, by the course of the Court, it is held as a

confession, and the cause may be judged immediately without other examination," *ibid.*, p. 72.

Chapter VII
James I, Bancroft, and Prohibitions

1. For general background on this chapter, I have found the following books to be most useful: Samuel Rawson Gardiner, *History of England from the Accession of James I. to the Disgrace of Chief Justice Coke, 1603–1616* (London, 1863, 2 vols.); J.R. Tanner, *English Constitutional Conflicts of the Seventeenth Century* (Cambridge, Eng., 1928); J.W. Allen, *English Political Thought, 1603–1660* (London, 1938, 2 vols.), vol. I (1603–1644); Margaret Atwood Judson, *The Crisis of the Constitution* (New Brunswick, N. J., 1949). For the incident of James's hanging the pickpocket, see Gardiner, I, 57, and Henry Hallam, *The Constitutional History of England From the Accession of Henry VII to the Death of George II* (London, 1867, 3 vols., 8th ed.), I, 295–6, where Hallam quotes the interesting remark of Sir John Harrington: "I hear our new king has hanged one man before he was tried; it is strangely done: now if the wind bloweth thus, why may not a man be tried before he has offended?"

2. The quotation from James I is from his "Speach, as It Was Delivered in the Upper House of the Parliament," March 19, 1603, in Charles Howard McIlwain, ed., *The Political Works of James I* (Cambridge, Mass., 1918), 275; McIlwain has a splendid introduction to James's works.

3. Tanner, *English Constitutional Conflicts*, 17–21. Quotations are from McIlwain's edition of James's works: *The Trew Law of Free Monarchies*, 62–3; "A Speach to the Lords and Commons," March 21, 1610, 307, 308, 310; and, "A Speach in Starr-Chamber," June 20, 1616, 332–3. McIlwain states, at p. xxxvii, that "throughout all the vicissitudes of his later struggle with the English Parliament, James held to all points of doctrine" laid down in his 1598 book.

4. J.W. Gough, *Fundamental Law in English Constitutional History* (Oxford, 1955), 52.

5. Judson, 17–67.

6. "Form of Apology and Satisfaction," June 20, 1604, the Commons to the King, in J.R. Tanner, ed., *Constitutional Documents of the Reign of James I* (Cambridge, Mass., 1930), 227. James's remark is quoted in Hallam, I, 308.

7. "No Bishops, no King," quoted in "Proceedings in a Conference at Hampton Court," 1604, in *State Trials*, II, 77 and 85. James's Edinburgh statement is quoted in Daniel Neal, *The History of the Puritans . . .* revised and corrected by Joshua Toulmin (Portsmouth, N. H., 1816, 5 vols.), II, 28, and Stuart Barton Babbage, *Puritanism and Richard Bancroft* (London, 1962), 42.

8. The Millenary Petition is printed in *State Trials*, II, 89–92, and in Tanner, *Constitutional Documents*, 56–60. For discussions of the Millenary Petition, see Babbage, 43–58; Roland G. Usher, *The Reconstruction of the English Church* (New York, 1910, 2 vols.), I, 288–309; and Robert W. Dale, *History of English Congregationalism*, completed and edited by A.W.W. Dale (London, 1907, 2nd ed.), 177–82, 188. For other petitions

against the oath *ex officio*, see Babbage, 51, 53; Usher, *Reconstruction*, II, 358; and Cartwright to Yelverton, Nov. 12, 1603, in A. Scott Pearson, *Thomas Cartwright and Elizabethan Puritanism, 1535–1603* (Cambridge, Eng., 1925), 481.

9. Babbage, 57–8; Usher, *Reconstruction*, I, 302–3, 306–9; and John Strype, *The Life and Acts of John Whitgift* (Oxford, 1822, 3 vols.), II, 485.

10. "Proceedings in a Conference at Hampton Court," in *State Trials*, II, 85–6. For secondary accounts of the Hampton Court Conference, see Usher, *Reconstruction*, I, 310–33, and Babbage, 62–71.

11. *State Trials*, II, 86.

12. *Ibid.*, 86, 87.

13. James is quoted in Strype, *Whitgift*, III, 408.

14. James is quoted in McIlwaine, 274. On the proclamation, Babbage, 72. The canons of 1604 are printed in Edward Cardwell, ed., *Synodalia, A Collection of Articles of Religion, Canons and Proceedings of Convocations* (Oxford, 1842, 2 vols.), I, 245–329; secondary accounts are in Babbage, 74–98, and Usher, *Reconstruction*, I, 334–41. The number of canons aimed against Puritanism is in Usher, I, 398.

15. For Bancroft's opposition to the oath, when framing the canons of 1604, see Usher, I, 348–9, and especially 398.

16. For the information on the Commons, see Babbage, 100, 101, 235. For Usher's statements, see his *Reconstruction*, I, 348, 349. James's proclamation is in Tanner, *Constitutional Documents*, 70–73. The best discussions on the number of deprived ministers are found in Babbage, 147–219, especially 147–8, 217, and Usher, *Reconstruction*, II, 3–19, especially 10.

17. Case of Richard Rogers and Others, March 1, 1604, in Benjamin Brook, *The Lives of the Puritans* (London, 1813, 3 vols.), II, 232. The quotation is from William Bradshaw, *English Puritanisme Containening the maine opinions of the rigidest sort of those that are called Puritanes* (London, 1605), S.T.C. #3516, Reel 627, pp. 29–30. See also, William Stoughton, *An Assertion for True and Christian Church-Policie* (London, 1604), 331–2, against the oath *ex officio*.

18. Francis Bacon, *Certaine Considerations Touching the Better Pacification and Edification of the Church of England*, 1604, in James Spedding, *The Letters and the Life of Francis Bacon, Including All His Occasional Works* (London, 1868, 7 vols.), III, 114.

19. F. W. Maitland, "English Law and the Renaissance," in Helen M. Cam, ed., *Selected Historical Essays of F. W. Maitland* (Boston, 1962), 144–5; see also Holdsworth, II, 493–509, and IV, 217–93.

20. Sir William Holdsworth, *A History of English Law* (London and Boston, 1903–66, 16 vols.), I, 228–9, 615, and II, 190–91, 193, 251, 266, 305.

21. Henry III's writs against Grosseteste and the act of Parliament of about 1316 are discussed above in ch. 2. The Statute of Praemunire is in Carl Stephenson and Frederick G. Marcham, eds., *Sources of English Constitutional History. A Selection of Documents from A.D. 600 to the Present* (New York, 1937), 227–8. See also William Stubbs, *The Constitutional History of England in Its Origin and Development* (Oxford, 1875, 2nd ed., 3 vols.), II, 410, 415, and III, 326–31.

22. Holdsworth, I, 459.

23. Roland G. Usher, *The Rise and Fall of the High Commission* (Oxford, 1913), 154–5.

24. *Ibid.*, 149–57.

25. Quotation from the Act of Supremacy, section 8, in Tanner, *Tudor Constitutional Documents*, 133.

26. Strype, *Whitgift*, II, 397; *Articuli Cleri*, 1605, Article 4, in *State Trials*, II, 136. Mary Hume Maguire, "Attack of the Common Lawyers on the Oath *Ex Officio* As Administered in the Ecclesiastical Courts in England," in *Essays in Honor of Charles H. McIlwain* (Cambridge, Mass., 1936), 222–23 cites the cases of Scroggs, Hynde, and Leigh as examples of prohibitions, but they were habeas corpus cases. See ch. 3, note 15, for citations.

27. Collier v. Collier is reported in 1 *Croke's King's Bench Reports* 201, under the name of Cullier v. Cullier, in 4 *Leonard's King's Bench Reports* 194, and in *Moore's King's Bench Reports* 906, available respectively in 78 *English Reports* 457, 74 *Eng. Rep.* 816, and 72 *Eng. Rep.* 987. See the preceding note for reference to the Leigh and Scroggs cases.

28. Dr. Hunt's case, 1 *Croke* 263 (1591), 78 *Eng. Rep.* 518. Anderson's statement is in *State Trials*, I, 1274.

29. Cawdrey's case is discussed in John Strype, *Historical Collections of the Life and Acts of the Right Reverend Father in God, John Aylmer, Lord Bishop of London* (Oxford, 1821), 84–97, and Brook, *Lives of the Puritans*, I, 433–41. Background documents are in Albert Peel, ed., *The Seconde Parte of a Register . . .* (Cambridge, Eng., 1915, 2 vols.), II, 203–7. The opinion of the King's Bench is in 5 *Coke's Reports* 1–41a (1591), 77 *Eng. Rep.* 1–47, and is conveniently abstracted in Tanner, *Tudor Constitutional Documents*, 372–3, and G. R. Elton, *The Tudor Constitution: Documents and Commentary* (Cambridge, Eng., 1962), 226–7.

30. 5 *Coke's Rep.* 8b, 9a, 40a, 40b, 77 *Eng. Rep.* 10, 11, 46.

31. The Register of Writs and Anthony Fitzherbert's *New Natura Brevium* were frequently cited by Beale, Morice, and Fuller. On the Register, see Percy H. Winfield, *The Chief Sources of English Legal History* (Cambridge, Mass., 1925), 286–302, and Holdsworth, II, 512–25; on Fitzherbert's book, which went through ten editions between 1534 and 1598, see Winfield, 302–3.

32. For Whitgift's objections to prohibitions, see the documents printed in Strype, *Whitgift*, III, 397–400 and 430–34. Strype dates the second as 1600, but it was prepared in conjunction with the first one, in 1598, as the manuscripts plainly show; Cotton MSS, Cleo. F. I., fols. 109 and 112.

33. Smith v. Smith, 1 *Croke Rep.* 741–2 (1600), 78 *Eng. Rep.* 974. On early prohibitions, see Usher, *Rise and Fall*, 159–64, and Usher, *Reconstruction*, II, 57–8, 70–73.

34. For Morice's argument, see above, ch. 6, note 40 and related text. For Bancroft's statement, see Babbage, 111, 264.

35. Babbage, 120–21. The questions, with the answers of the judges, are also in 2 *Croke* 37–8, 79 *Eng. Rep.* 30–31.

36. Babbage, 121–2. See also Usher, *Reconstruction*, I, 419–20.

37. *Articuli Cleri*, 1605, in *State Trials*, II, 131–60, reprinted from Coke's *Second Part of the Institutes of the Laws of England*, 601 ff. The quoted phrase is from *State Trials*, II, 136.

38. Articles 1, 2, 13, and 14, in *State Trials*, II, 134, 135, 143, 145.
39. *Ibid., passim;* the document gives the judges' answer to each article seriatim. For a discussion of the *Articuli Cleri,* see Usher, *Reconstruction,* II, 74–88; at p. 87 Usher refers to the king's reaction.
40. Faith Thompson, *Magna Carta, Its Role in the Making of the English Constitution, 1300–1629* (Minneapolis, 1948), 247, 257; the remarks of Hobart and Montague are given in Harold Spence Scott, ed., *The Journal of Sir Roger Wilbraham,* Camden Misc., 3rd ser. (London, 1902), 81–2. For Hobart, see also, David Harris Willson, ed., *The Parliamentary Diary of Robert Bowyer, 1606–1607* (Minneapolis, 1931), 127. See also, *Journals of the House of Commons,* ed. by T. Vardon and T. E. May (London, 1803 ff.), I, 286, 294, 296, 302–8, 387; and James Spedding, *The Letters and Life of Francis Bacon,* III, 263–6. Fuller's argument is cited in note 7 of the following chapter, where it is discussed at length.

Chapter VIII
Fuller and Coke

1. There is a long sketch of Coke in Sir William Holdsworth, *A History of English Law* (London and Boston, 1903–66, 16 vols.), V, 423–93. Catherine Drinker Bowen, *The Lion and the Throne: The Life and Times of Sir Edward Coke (1552–1634)* (Boston, 1956), is a splendid biography, a work of art somewhat impressionistic. Although Bowen's book is quite thin and sometimes unreliable on legal details, its faults are easily forgiven because it makes Coke come alive. Charles H. Randall, "Sir Edward Coke and the Privilege against Self-Incrimination," *South Carolina Law Quarterly,* VIII (Summer 1956), 417–53, is a useful though superficial introduction in which the mistakes derive from relying too heavily on secondary accounts.
2. Holdsworth, V, 426–7. F. W. Maitland, "History of English Law," in Helen M. Cam, ed., *Selected Historical Essays of F. W. Maitland* (Boston, 1962), 112. Coke's most notorious prosecution was in Raleigh's case, *State Trials,* II, 1–60 (1603). Sir James Fitzjames Stephen, *A History of the Criminal Law of England* (London, 1883, 3 vols.), I, 333, quoted by Holdsworth, wrote: "The extreme weakness of the evidence was made up for by the rancorous ferocity of Coke, who reviled and insulted Raleigh in a manner never imitated, so far as I know, before or since in any English court of justice, except perhaps in those in which Jefferies presided." See Bowen's discussion, 191–227, and Samuel Rawson Gardiner, *History of England from the Accession of James I. to the Disgrace of Chief Justice Coke, 1603–1616* (London, 1863, 2 vols.), I, 87–109. See David Jardine, *A Reading on the Use of Torture in the Criminal Law of England* (London, 1837), 46–7, 100, 105, for Coke's use of torture when he was attorney-general. See also John Campbell, *The Lives of the Chief Justices of England* (London, 1849–57, 3 vols.), III, 251–2.
3. 12 *Coke's Rep.* 19–20 (1607), 77 *Eng. Rep.* 1301–2.
4. "Of Oaths before an Ecclesiastical Judge Ex Officio," 12 *Coke's Rep.* 26 (1607), 77 *Eng. Rep.* 1308.
5. 12 *Coke's Rep.* 26–9, 77 *Eng. Rep.* 1308–11. The quoted phrases are

at p. 1309. Coke had used the phrase "invention of the devil" in connection with the oath, on an earlier occasion, Slade's case, 4 *Coke's Rep.* 92b, 95a (1602), 76 *Eng. Rep.* 1074, 1078, which Nicholas Fuller quoted in his *Argument* (1607), cited in note 7, below.

6. On Fuller's employment by the Puritans, see Stuart Barton Babbage, *Puritanism and Richard Bancroft* (London, 1962), 106. For Fuller in the Commons, see *Journals of Commons*, I, 276, 285, 286, 294, 334; David Harris Willson, ed., *The Parliamentary Diary of Robert Bowyer, 1606–1607* (Minneapolis, 1931), 102–3, 105, 265–6, 344–9. See also Roland G. Usher, "Nicholas Fuller: A Forgotten Exponent of English Liberty," *American Historical Review*, XII (1907), 743–5. Usher's indispensable article (pp. 743–60) was reprinted in his *The Reconstruction of the English Church* (New York, 1910, 2 vols.), II, 136–53. Bate's case is printed in "The Case of Impositions," *State Trials*, II, 371–91 (1606).

7. *The Argument of Master Nicholas Fuller, in the Case of Thomas Lad, and Richard Maunsell, his Clients. Wherein it is plainly proved, that the Ecclesiastical Commissioners have no power, by vertue of their Commission, to Imprison, to put to the Oath* Ex Officio, *or to fine any of his Majesties Subjects* (1607), 2–3.

8. Mary Hume [Maguire], "History of the Oath Ex Officio in England," (unpub. Ph.D. diss., Radcliffe, 1923), Appendix, 326–32, for a transcript of the articles against Fuller, "An Exact Copie of the Record of Nicholas Fullers case of Grayes Inne Esq. Termino Trin. Anno 5 Jac Regis," Lansdowne MSS 1172, fol. 101–4.

9. For Coke on Fuller's case, see 12 *Coke's Rep.* 41–4 (1607), 77 *Eng. Rep.* 1322–5.

10. Usher, "Nicholas Fuller," 747, 757.

11. Faith Thompson, *Magna Carta*, . . . (Minneapolis, 1948), 209; J. W. Gough, *Fundamental Law in English Constitutional History* (Oxford, 1955), 224, note C. Usher, "Nicholas Fuller," 758.

12. For the statutes of 1401 and 1534, see above, ch. 2, notes 23 and 35 and the related discussion in the text. *Argument of Fuller*, 5.

13. *Argument of Fuller*, 7–13, quotations at p. 10.

14. *Ibid.*, 14–18, quotations at pp. 14–15, 18.

15. Quoted in *ibid.*, 18, 21–2, 23.

16. Act of Supremacy, 1559, sections 6 and 21, in G. W. Prothero, *Select Statutes and other Constitutional Documents Illustrative of the Reignes of Elizabeth and James I* (Oxford, 1894), 5, 12. *Argument of Fuller*, 23, 26.

17. *Argument of Fuller*, 28–9.

18. The Latin writ of consultation is in Hume's Appendix, 332–4, "Consultation issued to Court of High Commission. Mich. 5 Jac. I.," Lansdowne MSS 1172, fol. 106. Usher, incorrectly translating the Latin, stated that the court also reserved for itself the interpretation of the letters patent and of the Act of Supremacy, "Nicholas Fuller," 751. The quotation from James is in *ibid.*, 750.

19. 12 *Coke's Rep.* 41–4, quotation at p. 42.

20. Usher, "Nicholas Fuller," 753–6.

21. Usher, *Reconstruction*, II, 206–7, for the quotations; see also Roland G. Usher, *The Rise and Fall of the High Commission* (Oxford, 1913),

181–2. Allan Ball's case, 12 *Coke's Rep.* 49–50 (1609), 77 *Eng. Rep.* 1329–30.

22. Excerpts from Cowell's *Interpreter* are in J. R. Tanner, ed., *Constitutional Documents of the Reign of James I* (Cambridge, Mass., 1930), 12–13; the 1606 quotation from Ellesmere is in John Hawarde, *Les Reportes del Cases in Camera Stellata, 1593 to 1609,* ed. by William Paley Baildon (London, 1894), 278, and the one from 1607 is in *State Trials,* II, 693–4.

23. *Prohibitions del Roy,* 12 *Coke's Rep.* 63–5 (1608), 77 *Eng. Rep.* 1342–3. Usher discusses this episode and prints the sources in "James I and Sir Edward Coke," *English Historical Review,* XVIII (Oct. 1903), 664–75; his narration of the episode is in *Reconstruction,* II, 213–16. The sources are confusing and not altogether reliable. It is difficult to synchronize them and reconstruct the sequence of remarks, let alone determine what was really said. My account seeks to strike a balance between Coke's and Usher's. It is not at all certain that Coke's final and famous retort, as well as other remarks which he credited to himself, were made on this occasion. But his report, which omits much of what James said and other details not favorable to him, fixed the record for posterity, making "under God and the law" a slogan of constitutionalism. Usher distrusted Coke's account to such an extent that he unwarrantably ignored it altogether in his narrative in *Reconstruction.* Coke reports the king's use of the charge of "treason," while Sir Julius Caesar's notes, in Usher, "James I and Sir Edward Coke," 669, contain the phrase "traiterous speech."

24. Usher, *Rise and Fall,* 190, describes an unnamed case for which he cites Stowe MSS 424, fol. 158. There is no case on that folio resembling the one described by Usher, nor is there any case in this manuscript, which Usher said was probably drawn up for Bancroft's use, bearing the date of Nov. 14, 1608. At fols. 160b–161a is the case of Thomas Rock, which fits perfectly the description and quotations in Usher's account; the case is dated Nov. 14, 1609. Bowen, *The Lion and the Throne,* 306, relies on Usher.

25. Case of Burneham and Stroude (1609), in Stowe MSS 424, fol. 162b. In *Rise and Fall,* 181, Usher inaccurately describes this case. Green, whom he calls the Puritan defendant, was the Church of England clergyman whom Burneham and Stroude attacked. Usher called Burneham "Burkham" and thought he was the place where the event occurred. Stowe MSS 424, fols. 158a–164b, describe all seventeen cases. For examples of Coke's interpretation of "enormities," see *ibid.,* William Prettyman's case (1609), fol. 164b; Arthur Lewes's case (1610), fol. 161a; Marmaduke Lang's case (1610), fol. 163a; Edmund Giles's case (1611), fol. 158b; and Darrington's case (1611), fol. 160a. For a published example, see Roper's case, 12 *Coke's Rep.* 47–8 (1608), 77 *Eng. Rep.* 1327–8, where Coke said that the High Commission could not "intermeddle" with all heresies, only "exorbitant" ones.

26. Case of Rochester and Mascall (1609), Stowe MSS 424, fol. 160b; see also "The L. Cook's Argument touching Rochester's case," Cotton MSS, Cleo. F. II, fols. 467–78. Case of Giles and Symonds (1611), Stowe MSS 424, fols. 158a–158b, misdated by Mary Hume Maguire, "Attack of the Common Lawyers . . . ," in *Essays in Honor of Charles H. McIlwain* (Cambridge, Mass., 1936), 226. Case of Richard, David, and

Joan Pierce (1611), Stowe MSS 424, fols. 158b–159a, and case of Edward and Anne Jenner (1611), in *ibid.*, fols. 159b–160a.

27. Edwards's case, 13 *Coke's Rep.* 9, at 10 (1609), 77 *Eng. Rep.* 1421, 1422. One of Wigmore's many errors is his statement that Coke said nothing in Edwards's case as to a privilege against a matter involving a penalty; Wigmore added that Coke did not declare the oath illegal either. John H. Wigmore, *A Treatise on the Anglo-American System of Evidence in Trials at Common Law* (Boston, 1940, 3rd ed., 10 vols.), VIII (rev. 1961 by J. T. McNoughton), 280 n. 53. The punishment for libel in the High Commission was fine and imprisonment, and this would be especially true of a libel against a bishop, which was the situation in Edwards's case. In Darrington's case (1611), Stowe MSS 424, fol. 160a, the defendant was imprisoned for libeling an archdeacon; he spent two years in jail until Coke freed him. The Pierces' case (1611), in *ibid.*, fols. 158b–159a, also involved imprisonment for libeling an ecclesiastical offical. It is true that Coke did not explicitly state in Edwards's case that the oath was illegal, but he did so in several other cases. He *was* inconsistent. In Edwards's case he implied that the oath might be exacted if the examination sought to force a confession of what Edwards said and did, rather than what he thought or believed. Coke sometimes left the impression that the oath was illegal when exacted without first making known the charges, or without giving a copy of the articles, to the accused. See the Coke-Popham statement of 1607 quoted above, pp. 230–31, and Cheekit's case (1611), discussed by Usher, *Rise and Fall*, 209, quoting Holkham MSS 677, fol. 327, which I have not used. According to Usher, the charge against Cheekit was "scandalous and factious speeches." He refused the oath and was imprisoned. Coke quoted Magna Carta and prohibited the High Commission from proceeding further "until they shall deliver unto him a true copie of the said articles." Yet there were many opinions by Coke, cited in preceding notes, in which he declared the oath to be illegal in any case, not testamentary or matrimonial, involving a layman as defendant. See also the discussion in note 43, below. Moreover, the crucial point is not whether he said the oath was illegal, but whether he said forced self-incrimination was illegal. That is, the oath was an issue only because it required a man to expose his guilt. Thus in Huntley v. Cage, 2 *Brownlow & Goldesborough* 14–16 (1611), 123 *Eng. Rep.* 787–8, Coke declared that the High Commission should not "examine any man upon his oath, to betray himself, and to incur any penalty pecuniary or corporal." He claimed that the oath was contrary to the common law even before the time of Edward II.

28. Babbage, 275–84, and Usher, *Reconstruction*, II, 223–45, summarize the various debates. See also Usher, *Rise and Fall*, 191–201, 210–18. Hobart's statement is in Sir Henry Hobart, "The Grounds of Prohibitions to the High Commission and the answers to them," Cotton MSS, Cleo. F. I., fol. 132. Coke's reply is spread through Cotton MSS, Cleo. F. I., fols. 116–26, 138–246, under five different titles, beginning with "A Preface to the Answeres of the Judges of the Courte of Comon Pleas unto the Objections and Arguments made (on behalfe of the Lorde Arch. B. of Canterbury) against Prohibicons." See also 13 *Coke's Rep.* 37–47 (1610), 77 *Eng. Rep.* 1448–57. In 1612, in a prosecution before the Privy Council and

the chief justices, including Coke, Hobart condemned the view that the king cannot, by commission or in his own person, meddle with the body, goods, or lands of his subjects except by indictment, arraignment, and trial, or by legal proceedings in the courts of justice in accordance with Magna Carta. This view, Hobart declared, with greater accuracy than Coke mustered, was "grossly erroneous and contrary to the rules of law." He also censured it as "dangerous and tending to the dissolving of Government." According to Hobart, the "law of the land" included the royal prerogative and the "absolute power" incident to the king's sovereignty. James Spedding, *The Letters and Life of Francis Bacon . . .* (London, 1868, 7 vols.), IV, 350.

29. [Henry Jacob], *To the right high and mightie Prince, James . . . An humble Supplication for Toleration* (London, 1609), 44, where Jacob, a Separatist leader, invoked Magna Carta, ch. 18—probably a misprint for ch. 28—and condemned the oath *ex officio,* "used in courts of popish inquisition," on ground that it compelled self-accusation and detection of others. The quotations from James are in Charles Howard McIlwain, ed., *The Political Works of James I* (Cambridge, Mass., 1918), 308, 311, 315.

30. The Petition of Right is in *State Trials,* II, 519–31, quotations at pp. 522–3; and also in Elizabeth Read Foster, ed., *Proceedings in Parliament, 1610* (New Haven, Conn., 1962, 2 vols.), II, 263–5. Commons also passed a bill, introduced by Fuller, against the oath *ex officio* on June 25, 1610; it did not receive the assent of the Lords. The bill declared that the oath *ex officio* violated both Magna Carta and the Act of Parliament of 1534, discussed above, ch. 2, note 38 and related text. The purpose of the bill was to prohibit ecclesiastical officers or the High Commission from administering the oath to compel subjects "to accuse themselves or to intrapp them by captious Interrogatories." Maurice F. Bond, ed., *Manuscripts of the House of Lords,* Historical Manuscripts Commission, New Series, vol. XI, *Addenda 1514–1714* (London, 1962), 125–6.

31. *State Trials,* II, 527, 524.

32. Coke on Proclamations is conveniently available in Tanner, *Constitutional Documents,* 187–8.

33. The prohibition against the oath was in Cheekit's case, discussed in note 27 above. The quotations from James and Salisbury are in Usher, *Rise and Fall,* 210, 218. The debate between Abbot and Coke is summarized in *ibid.,* 213–17. See also Coke, *The Fourth Part of the Institutes of the Laws of England* (London, 1817), ch. 74, "Of the High Commission," extracted in Tanner, *Constitutional Documents,* 156–64.

34. For the letters patent of 1611, see Prothero, 424–34, sections 3 and 11 for the oath provisions; *cf.* section 9 of the letters patent of 1559 and 1583, in *ibid.,* 230, 472e; only the 4th ed. of Prothero contains the document of 1583. Section 12 of the 1611 document made witnesses subject to the oath.

35. Section 11, letters patent 1611, in Prothero, 429. Not until the 1630's did the High Commission make a practice of finding obstinate persons *pro confesso.* See Usher, *Rise and Fall,* 247–8.

36. Coke's account is in 12 *Coke's Rep.* 88–9, 77 *Eng. Rep.* 1364–5.

37. The prohibitions referred to were in the Pierces' case, Nov. 21, 1611, and the Jenners' case, Nov. 28, 1611, cited in note 26 above. The

documents in Sayer's case are printed in Champlin Burrage, *The Early English Dissenters in the Light of Recent Research* (Cambridge, Eng., 1912, 2 vols.), II, 169–71. For Legate and Wightman, see *State Trials*, II, 727–34, and the discussion in W. K. Jordan, *The Development of Religious Toleration in England* (Cambridge, Mass., 1932–40, 3 vols.), II (1603–40), 43–52. Randal Bate, *Certain Observations of that Reverend, religious and faithful servant of God, and glorious Martyr of Jesus Christ, M. Randal Bate, which were part of his daily meditations in the time of his sufferings, whilst he was prisoner in the Gatehouse at Westminster* (1613?), S.T.C. #1580, Reel 873, pp. 170–74. 12 *Coke's Rep.* 93 (1612), 77 *Eng. Rep.* 1368–9, on the *Writ de Haeretico Comburendo*.

38. Quoted in Spedding, *Letters of Bacon*, IV, 381–2. See also Bowen, 338–41, and Holdsworth, V, 436–8.

39. Boyer's case, 2 *Bulstrode* 182–3 (1614), 80 *Eng. Rep.* 1052; Peacham's case is reported at length in Spedding, V, 90–129. The quotation on torture is at p. 94, the material on Coke at 100–101, 107–10, 120–21. See also Gardiner, II, 179–93.

40. Spedding, V, 223–5, 233–6, 272–5, 357–70. See also Bowen, 360–61, and Gardiner, II, 266–8, 272–8.

41. John Burrowes, Will. Cox, Dyton, and Other Plaintiffs v. The High Commission Court, 3 *Bulstrode* 48 (1616), 81 *Eng. Rep.* 42–7. Quoted matter at 81 *Eng. Rep.* 42–3.

42. *Ibid.*, 44–5.

43. *Ibid.*, 45–7. Wigmore, *Evidence*, VIII, 280 n. 54, cites this case as "Dighton v. Holt, 3 *Bulst.* 48." He jumped from the Edwards case of 1609 (see note 27, above, and related text), which he said was decided "on other points," to "Dighton v. Holt," which he described as Coke's "next" case. Coke, according to Wigmore, allowed the case to drag on for a year or more in order to induce either the accused or the High Commission to yield and thereby "to avoid the direct issue." In fact, however, Coke determined to meet the direct issue head on, as he plainly said. Moreover, Dighton and Holt were parties on the same side, against the Commission. Thomas Dighton is referred to as "Dyton" in *Bulstrode*. Maguire, who leaves the impression that Coke freed Burrowes and the others, says, "The judges followed the same line of reasoning in the case of Dighton and Holt . . ." as if the cases were different. Maguire, "Attack of the Common Lawyers," 227. See also "Dighton and Holt's Case," in 2 *Croke's King's Bench Rep.* 388, 79 *Eng. Rep.* 332, and the report in Henry Rolle, *Un Abridgement des Pleusieurs Cases et Resolutions del Comon Ley* (London, 1668, 2 vols.), ed. Sir M. Hale, 305, Prohibitions (T), case 3. Wigmore added that Coke's final decision was that the oath was improperly put by the ecclesiastical court, but that the objectionable thing was not that the accused should be compelled to answer; what was objectionable to Coke and the King's Bench, said Wigmore, was that the accused should be charged *ex officio* in a cause not testamentary or matrimonial but penal. Wigmore, VIII, 280; at p. 281 n. 64, Wigmore added that Coke, though opposing the oath *ex officio* in the High Commission, "appears as a consenting party to the enforcement of the even looser practice of the Court of Star Chamber." That is true. See the Countess of Shrewsbury's case, 12 *Coke's Rep.* 94, 95 (1613), 77 *Eng. Rep.* 1369, 1371. But Wigmore did

not know or did not mention that the oath in the Star Chamber was administered after a detailed indictment, the bill of complaint, was presented to the accused. It is true that the Star Chamber could be "loose" in its practices, that is, could act arbitrarily and at discretion—as could the High Commission—but the Star Chamber of Coke's time was not the infamous Star Chamber of Laud's. Wigmore finally concluded, *Evidence*, VIII, 281 n. 57, that in Spendlow v. Smith, there was a "plain ruling" in a case where the defendant had been put to his oath as to fraud. The oath was held illegal "for though the original cause belong to their cognizance, yet the covin and fraud is criminal; and . . . punishable, both in the Star Chamber and by the penal laws of fraudulent gifts, and therefore not to be extorted out of him by his oath." Spendlow v. Smith, *Hobart's King's Bench Rep.* 84 (1615?), 80 *Eng. Rep.* 234. Citations in Wigmore and Maguire to a wholly secondary source, *Jura Ecclesiastica: or the Present Practice in Ecclesiastical Courts*, by a Barrister of the Middle Temple (London, 1739–42, 2 vols.), are redundant.

44. Parson Mansfield's case (1610), Rolle, *Abridgement*, 305, Prohibitions (T), case 4; Parson Latters v. Sussex (1616?), *Noy's King's Bench Rep.* 151, 74 *Eng. Rep.* 1112–13.

45. Wigmore stated, as if he had never heard of Archbishop Laud, that after Coke carried his views to the King's Bench, "the matter seems to have been so far settled (in respect to ecclesiastical claims) that no more cases occurred, until in 1640, statute put an end, for the time, to further debate." *Evidence*, VIII, 281. To his statement Wigmore admitted one exception, Jenner's case, 1621, Rolle's *Abridgement*, 305, Prohibitions (T), case 5, where the ruling was that a man may not be compelled to answer on oath to matters of faith because there was a statute, under which he could be punished, against publishing false doctrine. On the High Commission's rules of procedure, see Usher, *Rise and Fall*, 244–5.

46. Marchant, *The Puritans and the Church Courts in the Diocese of York, 1560–1642* (London, 1960), 225, 231, 233, 235, 240, 251, 253, 254, 265, 271, 283, 286. Each of these twelve references to the oath exacted by the Commission from a Puritan minister between 1617 and 1632 appears in Marchant's long, biographical appendix, "List of Puritan Clergy," 222–318. Neither these nor similar cases are mentioned in the main body of the text. Marchant does refer to a few Chancery cases during this period in his text proper, but in the Chancery courts, like the Star Chamber, the oath was administered after the accused received a copy of the articles against him. Marchant is only slightly interested in procedure. Despite the dates in his title, 1560–1642, he deals mainly with the period 1633–42 and has very little information of any kind for the sixteenth century. He also referred at p. 78 to a case of 1633 before a "Visitation correction court" in which three church wardens took the oath and then refused to answer most of the questions, yet, "their opposition to the use of the *ex officio* oath was not challenged." Marchant has far more information on the lesser ecclesiastical courts than on the High Commission, yet in his discussion he referred to only one instance, during the period 1617–33, in which a lower ecclesiastical court tendered the oath. That case, in 1621, also involved a Puritan minister who swore the oath before a "Consistory

Court," *ibid.*, 184. The cases of the Separatists are reported in Samuel Rawson Gardiner, ed., *Reports of Cases in the Courts of Star Chamber and High Commission* (London, 1886), 279–80, 281, 284–6, 292–5, 300–302, 308–10, 315, and in Burrage, *Early English Dissenters*, II, 311–22, both transcribing Rawl. MS A. 128 in the Bodleian Library.

47. Burrage, II, 313, 317 for Lathrop's examination, and 313–14 for Eaton's. See also, *ibid.*, I, 320–25.

48. Quoted in Bowen, 530.

49. Bowen, 383, 389, 477–8; McIlwain, 333.

50. Wallace Notestein *et al.*, eds., *The Commons Debates, 1621* (New Haven, Conn., 1935, 7 vols.), VI, 471–3; III, 263. John A. Kemp, "The Background of the Fifth Amendment in English Law," *William and Mary Law Review*, I, (1958), 277 n. 102, stated that Coke was a member of a Parliamentary committee which demanded that the king be more diligent in the use of the oath against Catholic recusants. Kemp's source, *Commons Debates, 1621*, II, 26 n., does not refer to the oath. The committee merely petitioned the king to execute the laws against priests and recusants.

51. Bowen, 447–57, for Coke's activities in the Commons in 1621. *Ibid.*, 484, 496, for the quotations.

52. The Commission and Instructions for Raising the Forced Loan, Sept. 23, 1626, in Samuel Rawson Gardiner, ed., *The Constitutional Documents of the Puritan Revolution, 1625–1660* (Oxford, 1906, 3rd ed. rev.), 51–7; the oath procedure is specified at pp. 53, 55. The Petition of Right, June 7, 1628, in *ibid.*, 66–70; the oath procedure is condemned at pp. 67, 69. In a major case on the right against self-incrimination, the Supreme Court of the United States said that though the Petition of Right "insists upon the right secured by Magna Charta to be condemned only by the law of the land, and sets forth, by way of grievance, divers violations of it, [the Petition] is silent upon the practice of compulsory self-incrimination, though it was then a matter of common occurrence in all the courts of the realm." Twining v. N.J., 211 U.S. 78, 107–8 (1908). Wigmore, *Evidence*, VIII, 289 n. 98, was a little more accurate when he noted that the Petition of Right contained an objection against an oath procedure, but he was uncertain whether "a political promissory oath of conformity or obedience in connection with the refusal to pay ship money" was involved or "a really inquisitorial oath." Aside from the fact that "ship money" did not become an issue until 1634, Wigmore's mistake about the "political promissory oath" derived from his unfamiliarity with the king's instructions for raising the forced loan. For Lilburne's indentification of the oath in the Petition of Right with the oath *ex officio*, see the record of his trial of 1637 and related documents in *State Trials*, III, 1315, 1332, and his pamphlet, *A Worke of the Beast* (1638), reprinted in William Haller, ed., *Tracts on Liberty in the Puritan Revolution, 1638–1647* (New York, 1934, 3 vols.), II, 14–15.

53. The 1632 case is Geering's, in Gardiner, ed., *Cases in Star Chamber and High Commission*, 269.

54. "Proceedings against Sir Giles Mompesson," 1620, in *State Trials*, II, 1119, at 1123. On John Felton's case, see *State Trials*, III, 367, at 371, and

Jardine, *A Reading on the Use of Torture*, 11–12. For the statement of the judges in 1629, see "Proceedings against William Stroud and others," *State Trials*, III, 235, at 237.

55. Fitz-Patrick's trial, *State Trials*, III, 419, at 420 (1631), preceded by trial of Mervin Lord Audley, in *ibid.*, III, 401, at 413 (1631).

CHAPTER IX
Lilburne and the Abolition of the Oath

1. For background material I have relied mainly on Samuel R. Gardiner, *History of England from the Accession of James I. to the Outbreak of the Civil War, 1603–1642* (London, 1884–86, 10 vols.), vols. 6–9. W. K. Jordan, *The Development of Religious Toleration in England* (Cambridge, Mass., 1932–40, 3 vols.), II (1603–40), has also been very useful for church-state developments.

2. Roland G. Usher, *The Rise and Fall of the High Commission* (Oxford, 1913), 243, 251–2.

3. *Ibid.*, 243, 250–55, 330, 331; on Laud's visitations, see also Daniel Neal, *The History of the Puritans* . . . revised and corrected by Joshua Toulmin (Portsmouth, N. H., 1816, 5 vols.) II, 287–300.

4. Finch's letter is quoted in Usher, *Rise and Fall*, 318; see also, *ibid.*, 319–20. The "Root and Branch" Petition is in Samuel R. Gardiner, ed., *The Constitutional Documents of the Puritan Revolution, 1625–1660* (Oxford, 1906, 3rd ed. rev.), 137–44; see art. 28 at p. 143.

5. Usher, *Rise and Fall*, 247–8, 319–20, and 328, for the oath remaining the chief "bone of contention." *Ibid.*, 248, for the *pro confesso* theory. William Hudson, in his *Treatise of the Court of Star Chamber*, printed in Francis Hargrave, ed., *Collectanea Juridica* . . . (London, 1791–92, 2 vols.), II, 164, gives the *pro confesso* rule; at p. 168 he remarked that any one who refused oath or answer would be imprisoned and given time to reconsider; if still adamant he would be taken *pro confesso* "or sometimes he is kept with bread and water as young Booth was." For examples of refusal of the oath in 1634, see the cases of Granger, Botty, Norton, Westborne, Elkin, Bastwick, Ponder, Fox, Wells, Spencer, Yarrow, Blover and Rogers, in the manuscript notes of the Commission's records, P.R.O. 908, S.P.D. Car. I, P. 16/261, 1634. For additional examples in a published source, see the cases of Brandling (1633), Stocke (1635), Swinburne (1635), Greenwell (1635), Smirke (1637), Taylor (1637), Teasdale (1637), Smirke (1638), and Pearson (1638), in William H. D. Longstaffe, ed., *The Acts of the High Commission Court within the Diocese of Durham* (Durham and London, 1858), Publications of the Surtees Society, XXXIV, 53, 131, 140, 141, 172, 186.

6. Burton's discussion of the oath is in his *An apology of an appeale* (1636), S.T.C. #4135, reel 707, 11–15; the quotations are from pp. 12 and 15.

7. For Bastwick's refusal of the oath and the subsequent sentence, see P.R.O. 908, State Papers Domestic Car. I, P. 16/261, fols. 82b (Oct. 1634) and 183a (Feb. 1635). Usher, *Rise and Fall*, 326, claimed that Burton "was treated with leniency" and that the fine was only £100. See also, *ibid.*, 248, 312–13, 319. Fredrick Seaton Siebert, *Freedom of the Press in England,*

1476–1776 (Urbana, Ill., 1952), 61–2, 136–41. The case of Alexander Leighton (1630) illustrates the co-operation between the Commission and the Star Chamber and the latter's cruelty, *State Trials*, III, 383. Because Leighton was a minister "and this court [Star Chamber] for the reverence of that calling, doth not use to inflict any corporal or ignominious punishment upon any person, so long as they continue in orders, the court doth refer him to the High-commission, there to be degraded of his ministry; and that being done, he shall then also for further punishment and example to others, be brought into the pillory at Westminster, (the court sitting) and there whipped, and after his whipping be set upon the pillory for some convenient space, and have one of his ears cut off, and his nose slit, and be branded in the face with a double S S, for a Sower of Sedition; and shall then be carried to the prison of the Fleet, and at some other convenient time afterwards shall be carried into the pillory at Cheapside, upon a market-day, and be there likewise whipt, and then be set upon the pillory, and have his other ear cut off, and from thence be carried back to the prison of the Fleet, there to remain during life, unless his majesty shall be graciously pleased to inlarge him." *Ibid.*, at 385. Leighton remained in prison until freed by Parliament in 1640.

8. Gardiner, *History of England*, VI, 226–32; Samuel R. Gardiner, ed., *Documents Relating to the Proceedings against William Prynne, in 1634 and 1637* (London, 1877), Camden Society Publications, 75–6, 85–7, 90; *State Trials*, III, 711–70; William Prynne, *A New Discovery of the Prelates Tryanny* (London, 1641), 33–60. For the final decade of the Star Chamber, see Henry E. I. Phillips, "The Last Years of the Star Chamber, 1630–41," *Transactions*, Royal Historical Society, 4th ser., XXI (1939), 103–31.

9. There are two good biographies of Lilburne, both of which were invaluable to me. M. A. Gibb, *John Lilburne, The Leveller: A Christian Democrat* (London, 1947), and Pauline Gregg, *Free-Born John, A Biography of John Lilburne* (London, 1961). Gregg is more detailed; Gibb is more philosophical. Harold W. Wolfram's "John Lilburne: Democracy's Pillar of Fire," *Syracuse Law Review*, III (Spring 1952), 213–58, proved useful on legal points.

10. Trial of John Lilburne and John Wharton (1637), *State Trials*, III, 1315, at 1318. This account was written by Lilburne.

11. My account of Star Chamber procedure is based on Hudson, in Hargrave, *Collectanea Juridica*, II, 64, 127, 152.

12. *State Trials*, III, 1320.

13. *Ibid.*, 1321–3. Lilburne's remark that no one had ever before refused the Star Chamber oath is quoted in Gibb, 48, from Lilburne's *The Christian Mans Triall*, 6. Gregg, 57, stated that Lilburne had the distinction of being the first to refuse the Star Chamber oath. It seems most unlikely; indeed, in the account by Lilburne, printed in *State Trials*, 1315, at 1322, he stated that the Star Chamber compared him to "some that had harboured Jesuits and Seminary-priests (those traitors) who refused to be examined upon oath. . . ." Of course, the court's statement may have been untrue; it was certainly a tactic to shame the two Puritans by comparing them to those whom they despised and thereby persuade them to change their minds about refusing the oath. In any case, both Gregg and Gibb reflect naïve views about Star Chamber procedure. On Wharton's wars against the

High Commission, see *State Trials*, III, 1324; P.R.O. 908, S.P.D. Car. I, 16/324, fol. 4b; and a letter by Wharton, in *ibid.*, 16/373, dated Dec. 1637.

14. *State Trials*, III, 1323–8.

15. *Ibid.*, 1345 and 1349–50 for eye-witness accounts of Lilburne's punishment and physical condition; his speech in the pillory is reprinted in *ibid.*, III, 1329–40. His account of his punishment is also described in his *A Worke of the Beast* (1638), reprinted in William Haller, ed., *Tracts on Liberty in the Puritan Revolution, 1638-1647* (New York, 1933–34, 3 vols.), II, 3–24. For secondary accounts of his Star Chamber trial and punishment, see Gregg, 52–74, and Gibb, 45–56.

16. *State Trials*, 1350–52.

17. There is a chronological list of Lilburne's works in Gregg, 400–403. Clarendon's statement is in *State Trials*, IV, 1418.

18. On Trendall, see Jordan, II (1603–40), 165 n. 2, and Gregg, 76. For Foxely, see William Prynne, *Canterburies doom: or, The First Part of a Compleat History of the Commitment, Charge, Tryall, Condemnation, Execution of William Laud* (London, 1646), 387–8. Ward's book was *Theologicall Questions, Dogmaticall Observations, and Evangelicall Essays upon the Gospel of Jesus Christ, according to St. Matthew* (London, 1639); the censored passages appear in Prynne, *Canterburies doom*, 329–30.

19. Usher, *Rise and Fall*, 333; Gardiner, *History of England*, IX, 215.

20. Gregg, 83–4; Gibb, 77–8.

21. The "Root and Branch" Petition of London, referring to inquisitions reaching to thoughts, is in Gardiner, ed., *Constitutional Documents*, 143; it is also in *Speeches and Passages of this Great and Happy Parliament: From the third of November 1640, to this instant, June 1641* (London, 1641), which also includes the petition from Kent, p. 171, Bagshaw's speech against the oath, p. 347, and Peard's speech, 313–14. I used the manuscript version of Peard's speech, S.P.D. Car. I, vol. 450, no. 94.

22. On the inquisitions and Puritan ministers, see Neal, *History of the Puritans*, II, 297–300; *ibid.*, II, 270–90, on the émigrés to New England. See also Allen French, *Charles I and the Puritan Upheaval: A Study of the Causes of the Great Migration* (London, 1955), 283–99, 385–93. On Leighton see note 7 above, this chapter.

23. For Peard's speech, *loc. cit.*, note 21 above. Compare Sir James Fitzjames Stephen on the use of the oath by its opponents, *A History of the Criminal Law of England* (London, 1883, 3 vols.), I, 342–3.

24. French, 315–16; Lord's Bill on Church Reform, July 1, 1641, in Gardiner, ed., *Constitutional Documents*, 177.

25. Act for Abolition of the Court of Star Chamber, July 5, 1641, in *ibid.*, 179–86.

26. Act for Abolition of the Court of High Commission, July 5, 1641, in *ibid.*, 186–9; reconfirmed in 1661, 13 Car. II, ch. 12, sect. 4.

27. Trial of Fitzpatrick (1631), *State Trials*, III, 419, at 420.

28. Stephen, I, 358; see also 369–70, and *cf.* Stephen's remarks at p. 382. See also Sir John Pollock, *The Popish Plot: A Study in the History of the Reign of Charles II* (Cambridge, Eng., 1944), 296, 298.

29. On the oath of the accused at common law, see John H. Wigmore, *A Treatise on the Anglo-American System of Evidence in Trials at Common Law* (Boston, 1940, 3rd ed., 10 vols.), II, sect. 575(5), 681–2, and Sir

William Holdsworth, *A History of English Law* (London and Boston, 1903–66, 16 vols.), IX, 194.

30. J. R. Tanner, *English Constitutional Conflicts of the Seventeenth Century* (Cambridge, Eng., 1928), 105, 113, 115, and Clerical Disabilities Act, 1642, in Gardiner, ed., *Constitutional Documents*, 241–2. For the trial, see Proceedings against the Twelve Bishops (1642), *State Trials*, IV, 63, at 76.

31. For the Commons' censure of Lilburne's sentence, *State Trials*, III, 1342; for Clarendon, *ibid.*, IV, 1419; for the remark by Lilburne, Gibb, 93.

32. Jordan, III (1640–60), 42–57; Gregg, 113–14. For the number of newspapers, see Siebert, 203; for the number of pamphlets, see *ibid.*, 191, and Gregg, 94. Gregg and Siebert do not agree on the exact statistics, though both counted the pamphlets in the Thomason collection in the British Museum. For Siebert's remark on Lilburne, see pp. 198–9. See *ibid.*, 173–212, for a discussion of Parliament and censorship.

33. On the Levellers generally, see Joseph Frank, *The Levellers, A History of the Writings of Three Seventeenth-Century Democrats: John Lilburne, Richard Overton, William Walwyn* (Cambridge, Mass., 1955); Theodore Calvin Pease, *The Leveller Movement: A Study in the History and Political Theory of the English Great Civil War* (Washington, 1916); H. N. Brailsford, *The Levellers and the English Revolution*, ed. by Christopher Hill (London, 1961); the introduction by Don M. Wolfe in his edition of *Leveller Manifestoes of the Puritan Revolution* (New York, 1944); and the introduction by William Haller, in Haller and Godfrey Davies, eds. *The Leveller Tracts, 1647–1653* (New York, 1944), 1–50. For the information in my paragraph, see Gregg, 115, 117, 124; Gibb, 102, 103, 111, 122–3.

34. For Lilburne's examination before the committee, see his *A Copy of a Letter from Lieutenant-Colonel John Lilburne to a friend* (London, 1645), 2, 14. Italics added. The episode is recounted in Gregg, 119–21, and Gibb, 127–9.

35. Quoted in Gibb, 129, citing *Commons Journal*, IV, 235–7.

36. On Lilburne's reading, see Gibb, 130–33, and Gregg, 58, 94–5, 127, 133. Prynne's remark is in Gibb, 130. *Englands Birth-Right Justified* is reprinted in Haller, ed., *Tracts on Liberty*, III, 258–307; the quoted statement is at p. 263.

37. *Englands Birth-Right*, in Haller, III, 262–6.

38. *Englands Lamentable Slaverie* (1645) is reprinted in Haller, III, 311–35; the quoted matter is at p. 311. Cromwell's letter to Parliament is quoted by Lord Clarendon, in *State Trials*, IV, 1419.

39. Larner is quoted in Gregg, 136–7. See also William M. Clyde, *The Struggle for the Freedom of the Press from Caxton to Cromwell* (London, 1934), 109. On Lilburne, see Gregg, 137–42, and Gibb, 144–9.

40. Gibb, 150; Wolfe, 109, for the characterization of Overton's *Remonstrance;* Wolfe, 121, for the quotation from the document, which is reprinted at pp. 109–30.

41. Overton, *An Appeale, From the Degenerate Representative Body of the Commons of England Assembled at Westminster. To the Body Represented, The free people* (1647), reprinted in Wolfe, 156–95; quoted matter is at pp. 164–6, 192. Wolfe's description of the pamphlet as a "classic state-

ment" is at p. 155. Gregg, 145, quotes Lord Hunsdon's "Lilburne-like" comment. See Gregg, 144–51, for the episode involving Overton and his family. See also Overton's *The Commoner's Complaint* (1647), in Haller, *Tracts*, III, 393. In 1647 Nicholas Tew, the Leveller printer, also refused to answer questions before the Parliamentary committee on ground that he was not bound to accuse himself, *State Trials*, IV, 871, at 887.

42. Thomas Edwards, *Gangraena*, Part III (London, 1646), 169–70.

43. Gregg, 152–3.

44. G. P. Gooch, *Democratic Ideas in the Seventeenth Century* (Cambridge, Eng., 1926, 2nd ed.), 124, called Lilburne "the most popular man in England." Baxter and the anonymous newswriter are quoted in Gibb, 178.

45. Walwyn's *To the right honourable and supreme Authority of this Nation, the Commons in Parliament assembled. The humble Petition of many thousands* (1647) is reprinted in Wolfe, 135–41; the quoted lines are at p. 139. Gibb, 163. Margaret Atwood Judson, *The Crisis of the Constitution*, (New Brunswick, N.J., 1949), 381. For other Leveller documents demanding the right, see *The Case of the Armie Truly Stated* (1647), *To the Supream Authority* (1648), *To the Right Honorable, the Commons of England* (1648), *Foundations of Freedom* (the "2nd Agreement of the People," 1648), and *An Agreement of the Free People* (the "3rd Agreement of the People," 1649), in Wolfe, 38, 216, 266, 287, 301, 406. See also *Heads of the Proposals* (1647) and *Putney Projects* (1647), in A. S. P. Woodhouse, ed., *Puritanism and Liberty. Being the Army Debates (1647–49) from the Clarke Manuscripts with Supplementary Documents* (Chicago, 1951), 425 and 427. Additionally, see *A Declaration of Some Proceedings of Lt. Col. John Lilburn* (1648), *The Bloody Project* (1648), *Englands New Chains Discovered* (1649), *The Legall Fundamental Liberties of the People* (1649), *The Fountain of Slaunder* (1649), and *The Just Defense of John Lilburn* (1653), in Haller and Davies, *Leveller Tracts*, 109, 137–8, 163, 246, 410, 454, 457.

46. Theodorus Verax [Clement Walker], *Anarchia Anglicana: or, The History of Independency* (London, 1648), 53–60, quoted matter at pp. 55, 57.

47. J. Howldin [John Holden], *The Lawes Subversion: or, Sir John Maynards Case truly stated* (London, 1648), 6; at p. 16, Holden warned readers: "You may be imperiously commanded to fall upon the point of your own sword, i.e. to answer interrogatories propounded by degrees from a Command, to accuse yourselfe to an Oath *Ex Officio*."

48. *To the Right Honorable, The Commons of England In Parliament Assembled. The humble Petition of divers wel affected Persons* (1648), reprinted in Wolfe, 287. "We pray you . . ." is in *The Hunting of the Foxes* (1649), in *ibid.*, 371. The same pamphlet gives the soldier's reply to the General Council of the Army at p. 375; see also 372, 377, 378, 379. Lilburne's authorship of this pamphlet is uncertain. Gregg, 389 n. 2, attributes it to him; Wolfe, 356, attributes it to Overton. See Gregg, 269, for Parliament's condemnation of *Englands New Chains*, Part Two. Haller and Davies print *Englands New Chains*, 156–70, and the second part, 171–89.

49. For Bradshaw's remarks as Lilburne's counsel in 1645, see *State Trials*, III, 1349. The four prisoners co-authored an account of their arrest

and examination in *The Picture of the Councel of State* (1649), reprinted in Haller and Davies, 190–246. See also the accounts in Gibb, 256–8, and Gregg, 269–70.

50. *Picture of the Councel,* in Haller and Davies, 201–2, 204, 224, 237.

51. Gregg, 274–94; Gibb, 258–77.

Chapter X
The Right Secured

1. The report of Lilburne's trial in 1649, with related documents, is in *State Trials,* IV, 1269–1470. Quoted matter is at p. 1466.

2. *Ibid.,* 1281, 1283, 1386, 1294, 1299, 1306.

3. *Ibid.,* 1270–83.

4. *Ibid.,* 1281, 1286, 1293.

5. *Ibid.,* 1291, 1292, 1301, 1320–29.

6. *Ibid.,* 1292–6. In a treason case, refusal to plead to the indictment could be taken *pro confesso;* Sir James Fitzjames Stephen, *A History of the Criminal Law of England* (London, 1883, 3 vols.), I, 298.

7. *State Trials,* IV, 1295–1306; quoted matter at pp. 1297, 1298, 1300, 1305.

8. *Ibid.,* 1307, 1309–10.

9. *Ibid.,* 1310–14.

10. *Ibid.,* 1340–42. Extracts from Lilburne's pamphlets cover pp. 1352–72.

11. Lilburne's defense spreads over pp. 1373–95 in *ibid.*

12. *Ibid.,* 1377.

13. *Ibid.,* 1395, 1402.

14. *Ibid.,* 1405–6. See also the trial of Christopher Love (1651), *State Trials,* V, 43, who consciously emulated Lilburne, whose trial he had witnessed. At V, 76–7, the prosecutor complained that Love would not answer any questions to accuse himself.

15. Pauline Gregg, *Free-Born John, A Biography of John Lilburne* (London, 1961), 303–11; M. A. Gibb, *John Lilburne, The Leveller: A Christian Democrat* (London, 1947), 295–302.

16. Quoted in Gibb, 315.

17. Lilburne's trial of 1653 is reported poorly and incompletely in *State Trials,* V, 407–46. Clarendon's remark is in *State Trials,* IV, 1420. See also Gibb, 308–20; Gregg, 324–32.

18. The examination of the jury is reported in *State Trials,* V, 445–50.

19. Gibb, 321–45; Gregg, 333–46.

20. I have used only the selection from *Examen Legum Angliae: Or the Laws of England* (1656) as reprinted in Mark Howe, ed., *Readings in American Legal History* (Cambridge, Mass., 1949), 91–2. Howe states that the book is ascribed to A. Booth. The incident involving Holder is in the trial of the king, *State Trials,* IV, 989, at 1101. John H. Wigmore, *A Treatise on the Anglo-American System of Evidence in Trials at Common Law* (Boston, 1940, 3rd ed., 10 vols.), VIII (rev. 1961 by J. T. McNaughton) 289 n. 103, refers to this incident, giving Holder as "Holden," yet on the next page says incorrectly that the extension of the right against self-incrimination to a witness, rather than the accused party, "is for the first time made" in Reading's trial in 1679, *State Trials,* VII, 259, at 296.

That extension, made in 1649 to Holder, should be compared with the incident involving Scroop in 1642; his testimony was wanted by the Lords against the Duke of Richmond, raising the question whether his giving evidence under oath would require him to accuse himself. The Lords decided that a witness in court could be examined under oath and therefore ordered Scroop's testimony. Trial of James, Duke of Richmond, *State Trials*, IV, 111, at 120 (1642). See also the trial of Adrian Scroop, *State Trials*, V, 1034, at 1039 (1660).

21. Trial of John Crook, Isaac Grey, and John Bolton, *State Trials*, VI, 201, at 205, 206, 218, 222 (1662).

22. Trial of William Penn and William Mead, *State Trials*, VI, 951, at 957–8, 960 (1670).

23. *Ibid.*, 961–9. Penn added to his account of the trial an elaborate appendix, relying heavily on Magna Carta and Coke, in which he defended the freedom of the jury and religious and civil rights, *ibid.*, 970–92. For a secondary account see Catherine Owens Peare, *William Penn, A Biography* (Philadelphia, 1957), 109–22. Case of Edward Bushell, *State Trials*, VI, 999–1026 (1670).

24. Proceedings against Francis Jenkes, *State Trials*, VI, 1189, at 1191 (1676). See also Zechariah Chafee, Jr., *How Human Rights Got into the Constitution* (Boston, 1952), 57–62.

25. Sir John Pollock, *The Popish Plot: A Study in the History of the Reign of Charles II* (Cambridge, Eng., 1944), p. 265 and, for quoted material, 294–5.

26. Trial of Nathanael Reading, *State Trials*, VII, 259, at 296–7 (1679). On Reading's case, see Pollock, 335–8. Wigmore inaccurately stated that "Oates for the prosecution is not allowed to be asked questions to accuse himself," *Evidence*, VIII, 290 n. 105. The witness, William Bedlow, sometimes spelled Bedloe, was closely associated with Oates. See Stephen, I, 387, 388, 393, 400, and Pollock, 111–13.

27. In the late eighteenth century, American manuals for justices of the peace, after stating that a witness should not be asked any questions the answering of which might oblige him to accuse himself, added, "And lord Coke says, a witness alledging his own infamy or turpitude, is not to be heard. 4 *Inst.* 279." See, *e.g.*, Richard Starke, *The Office and Authority of a Justice of the Peace* (Williamsburg, Va., 1774), 146, and James Parker, *Conductor Generalis: Or the Office, Duty and Authority of Justices of the Peace* (New York, 1788), 169. See also Edward Wingate, *Maxims of Reason: or the Reason of the Common Law of England* (London, 1658), sect. 125, pp. 486–7. Treby's statement is in Peter Cook's trial, *State Trials*, XIII, 311 at 334–5 (1696). See also Jonathan Freind's trial, *ibid.*, XIII, 1, at 17 (1696), East India Co. v. Campbell, 1 *Vesey Sr.* 246 1748, 27 *Eng. Rep.* 1010, at 1011; Sir William Blackstone, *Commentaries on the Law of England* (Oxford, 1765–69, 4 vols.), III, ch. 23, p. 370. On a privilege against answers involving disgrace, see Wigmore, *Evidence*, III, sects. 984–6, pp. 561–71, and VIII, sect. 2255, p. 332. I find little basis for the proposition advanced by Wigmore that the privilege against disclosing facts involving disgrace or infamy, irrespective of criminality, began later than and independent of the right against self-incrimination. Reading's case of 1679, discussed above, shows the close relationship be-

tween the two and the fact that the one grew out of the other. Chief Justice Treby began his statement of the principle against self-infamation by declaring that questions making a man criminous could not be allowed. In Freind's case, cited in this note, he said, "no man is bound to answer any questions that will subject him to a penalty, or to infamy." The origin of such ideas belongs to the sixteenth century. Tyndale wrote that it was cruel to compel a man "to put either soul or body in jeopardy, or to shame himself," *The Obedience of a Christen Man* (1528), reprinted in *Doctrinal Treatises . . . By William Tyndale*, ed. Henry Walter (Cambridge, Eng., 1844), 335. In 1584 a statement by Whitgift revealed that someone had claimed that no man is obliged either to accuse himself or to disclose his own turpitude or infamy; see above, ch. 5, n. 6 and related text for the quotation and source. In Albert Peel and Leland H. Carlson, eds., *Cartwrightiana* (London, 1951), 30–46, especially 38 ff., there is a document by Cartwright and others, *circa* 1590, whose theme is that no man should destroy his reputation or infame himself by self-accusation or the accusation of others, or by self-incrimination. James Morice, in his book *A briefe treatise of Oathes* (1598), similarly condemned forcing men to accuse themselves "to the publique shame" or "reproach," quoted above, ch. 6, n. 34 and related text. In the Parliament of 1593 Morice had declared that ch. 29 of Magna Carta prohibited imposing an oath on anyone who is accused of "anye Crime or matter of disgrace," quoted above, ch. 6, n. 37 and related text. See also n. 47 to ch. 6, above, for the quotation from a document printed in Fuller, *Church History*, V, 107–12, where it was said, *circa* 1593, that an oath causing loss of good name is illegal. The act of 1534, so well known to opponents of the oath *ex officio*, was one of the several reconfirmations of Magna Carta that protected against the loss of good name without indictment. This act may have been the source for the later judicial doctrine against self-infamation. Or the source may have derived from the Star Chamber rule that witnesses should not be forced to incriminate themselves or even to answer a question that was prejudicial to themselves or revealed infamy that could not be the basis of prosecution, William Hudson, *Treatise of the Court of Star Chamber*, in Francis Hargrave, ed., *Collectanea Juridica . . .* (London, 1791–92, 2 vols.), II, 208–9.

28. Trial of Thomas White, *State Trials*, VII, 311, at 361 (1679). On Scroggs, see Stephen, I, 395, and Pollock, 354–5. Trial of Richard Langhorn, *State Trials*, VII, 418, at 435 (1679). Trial of Roger Palmer, Earl of Castlemaine, *State Trials*, VII, 1067, at 1096 (1680); Wigmore again misstated the facts, *Evidence*, VIII, 290 n. 105. See also the trial of William Viscount Stafford, *State Trials*, VII, 1293, at 1314 (1680).

29. Trial of Titus Oates, *State Trials*, X, 1079, 1099–100 (1685); also *ibid.*, 1123. See also trial of Thomas Rosewell, a Presbyterian minister charged with treason, *State Trials*, X, 147, at 169 (1684), where Jeffreys refused to permit an incriminating question to be put to witnesses and said, "Whether it be so, or no, you must not ask them, but prove it."

30. For extension of the right to civil cases, see Att. Gen. v. Mico, 1 *Hardres* 123, at 139–46 (1658), 145 *Eng. Rep.* 419, at 420–24; Trevor v. Lesguire, 1 *Finch* 72, at 73 (1673), 23 *Eng. Rep.* 39; Penrice v. Parker, 1 *Finch* 75 (1673), 23 *Eng. Rep.* 40; Bird v. Hardwicke, 1 *Vernon* 109

(1682), 23 *Eng. Rep.* 349; Firebrass's Case, 2 *Salkeld* 550 (1700), 91 *Eng. Rep.* 465; Att. Gen. v. Cresner, 1 *Parker* 279 (1710), 145 *Eng. Rep.* 779, at 780; Duncalf v. Blake, 1 *Atkyn* 52, at 53 (1737), 26 *Eng. Rep.* 35, at 35–6; Smith v. Read, 1 *Atkyn* 526, at 529 (1737), 26 *Eng. Rep.* 332; Earl of Suffolk v. Green, 1 *Atkyn* 450 (1739), 26 *Eng. Rep.* 286; Jones v. Meredith, 2 *Comyns* 661, at 672 (1739), 92 *Eng. Rep.* 1257, at 1263; Baker v. Pritchard, 2 *Atkyn* 387, at 389 (1742), 26 *Eng. Rep.* 634, at 635; Craig v. Earl of Anglesia, *State Trials*, XVII, 1139, at 1147 (1743); Boteler v. Allington, 3 *Atkyn* 453, at 457 (1746), 26 *Eng. Rep.* 1063; East India Co. v. Campbell, 1 *Vesey Sr.* 246, at 247 (1749), 27 *Eng. Rep.* 1010; Harrison v. Southcote, 2 *Vesey Sr.* 389, at 394–5 (1751), 28 *Eng. Rep.* 249, at 252–3; Brownsword v. Edwards, 2 *Vesey Sr.* 244, at 245–6 (1751), 28 *Eng. Rep.* 157, at 158–9. For sixteenth-century Chancery precedents, see Wigmore, *Evidence*, VIII, 288. For extension of the right to personal papers, see Rex v. Worsenham, 1 *Lord Raymond* 705 (1701), 91 *Eng. Rep.* 1370; Regina v. Mead, 2 *Lord Raymond* 927 (1704), 92 *Eng. Rep.* 119; Rex v. Cornelius, 2 *Strange* 1210, at 1211 (1744), 93 *Eng. Rep.* 1133, at 1134; Rex v. Purnell, 1 *Wilson K.B.* 239, at 242 (1744), 95 *Eng. Rep.* 595, at 597; Rex v. Heydon, 1 *Blackstone* 351 (1762), 96 *Eng. Rep.* 195; Roe dem. Haldane v. Harvey, 4 *Burrow* 2484, at 2489 (1769), 98 *Eng. Rep.* 302, at 305.

31. Coke's statement, from his 3rd *Inst.*, is quoted in James Bradley Thayer, *A Preliminary Treatise on Evidence at the Common Law* (Boston, 1898), 159. In Tyndal's case, for felony, "divers witnesses were produced by the defendant which were heard without oath," quoted in Thayer, 160, citing *Croke Car.* 291. But Sir William Holdsworth, *A History of English Law* (London and Boston, 1903–66, 16 vols.), IX, 195, said, "it was not till the latter half of the seventeenth century that the prisoner was allowed to call any witnesses on his behalf." For remarks disparaging unsworn testimony, see Hulet's trial, *State Trials*, V, 1185, at 1194 (1660); trial of Stephen Colledge *ibid.*, VIII, 541, at 638, 681 (1681). Scroggs's statement is in the trial of Thomas White, *ibid.*, VII, 311, at 359 (1679). For relaxation of the rule against permitting compulsory process for summoning the defendant's witnesses, see trial of John Twyn, *State Trials*, VI, 513, at 516 (1663), and trial of James Turner, *ibid.*, VI, 565, at 570 (1664); in the first case the judge promised to summon the witnesses, but in the second case the same judge said the law did not permit him to summon them. Reading's case, *ibid.*, VII, 259 (1619), cited by Wigmore, VIII, 685 n. 47, was not a felony case. On the acts of 1696 and 1701 see Stephen, I, 416; Wigmore, II, 685–86; and Thayer, 161. The acts are 7 Wm. III ch. 3, reprinted in Andrew Browning, ed., *English Historical Documents, 1660–1714* (New York, 1953), 89–91, and 1 Anne ch. 9.

32. For Whitelock, see *State Trials*, V, 469. In Twyn's case, *State Trials*, VI, 513, at 516–17 (1663), Chief Justice Hyde said, "Then I will tell you, we are bound to be of counsel with you, in point of law; that is, the court, my brethren and myself, are to see that you suffer nothing for your want of knowledge in matter of law . . . To the matter of fact, whether it be so or no: In this case the law does not allow you counsel to plead for you; but in matter of law we are counsel for you. . . ." Cf. Justice Holloway, in Rosewell's case, *ibid.*, X, 147, at 151 (1684): "We

cannot assign you counsel at present, for we have nothing to assign it upon. If there do any question of law arise in your case, then the court will (as they are bound to) take care of you, that you suffer no prejudice for want of the assistance of counsel; and in matters of fact upon your trial, the court are of counsel for you." In Colledge's case, *ibid.*, VIII, 549, at 570, Chief Justice North declared: "Now for those things that you demand, you cannot have them by law. No man can have a copy of the Indictment by law; for counsel you cannot have it unless matter of law arises, and that must be propounded by you; and then if it be a matter debatable, the court will assign you counsel, but it must be upon a matter fit to be argued: For I must tell you, a defence in case of High-Treason ought not to be made by artificial cavils, but by plain fact. If you propose any matter of law, the court will consider of it, and assign you counsel, if it be reasonable." Jeffreys's comment was made in the trial of Rosewell, *ibid.*, X, 147, at 267 (1684). In this case Jeffreys assigned counsel, *after* the trial was over and the jury had convicted, to argue exceptions to the indictment, yet denied a copy of the indictment to the defendant's counsel. But the indictment had been read aloud in court frequently. Counsel proved deficiencies in the indictment, and Rosewell was pardoned. It was a strange procedure. For Blackstone, see *Commentaries,* IV, 355.

33. Trial of Robert Mortimer, Lord Oxford, *State Trials,* XV, 1045, at 1 (1717). Stephen, I, 424. Blackstone, *Commentaries,* IV, 355–6.

34. Stephen, I, 417 n. 1, 440; Wigmore, VIII, 291 n. 108.

35. Stephen, I, 426–7; see also *ibid.*, 417–19.

36. On the incompetency of the accused to testify, see Holdsworth, IX, 193–6, and Wigmore, II, sect. 575, pp. 674–86, 701. Reform came earlier to America than England, beginning with enactments of the state of Maine in 1859 and 1864, followed by several other states and then a federal act of 1878. Before the English legislation of 1898, every state but Georgia had qualified criminal defendants to give sworn testimony if they wished. Georgia is presently the only common-law jurisdiction in the world to retain the old rule for accused persons. See Ferguson v. Ga., 365 U.S. 570 (1961). On extension of the right against self-incrimination to information merely *tending* to incriminate, which began in 1725, see Wigmore, IV, sects. 2260–61, especially p. 857 n. 1 and p. 863 n. 1, of the 2nd ed. of 1923, not the 3rd ed. which has been previously cited throughout. See Lord Chancellor Macclesfield's trial, *State Trials,* XVI, 767, 920, 1146, 1150 (1725), as cited by Wigmore.

37. Michael Dalton, *The Countrey Justice* (London, 1618), ch. 164, sect. 6, p. 273, citing Richard Crompton's 1606 ed. of Fitzherbert, *Office of the Justice of the Peace.* The same passage appeared in Dalton as late as the 1742 ed., 380. See also William Nelson, *The Office and Authority of a Justice of the Peace* (London, 1714), 253. Blackstone, when describing the preliminary examination, closely followed Lambard and Dalton: "For at common law, *nemo tenebatur prodere seipsum;* and his fault was not to be wrung out of himself, but rather to be discovered by other means and other men." *Commentaries,* IV, 296. The difference between the statement in Blackstone and those in the earlier works may have been merely verbal, but it was important. Dalton implied that the justices of the peace could wring a confession out of a suspect, but not on oath.

Blackstone made no mention of the oath and therefore stated the principle unequivocally. I have followed Stephen, I, 219–26, in assuming that the preliminary examinations were inquisitorial. The "third degree" was not a modern invention of the police. Cf. the statement of defense counsel in the trial of Charles Bembridge, *State Trials*, XXII, 1, at 143: "It is true he was examined in a mode of inquiry in which it was not improper perhaps, to examine him; but it cannot be doubted that the persons who did examine him saw that the questions that they put upon that occasion tended to criminate the person under that examination. What does your lordship do in that situation? *What does every judge do, even down to the lowest justice of the peace*, even to committee-men upon elections, whenever a question of that sort is asked of a witness? 'Stop; understand that you are at your own discretion whether you will answer that question or not; you need not accuse yourself.' The law of England is that no man is bound to accuse himself; and the man who administers that law always takes care to give that caution." (Italics added.) On the question of two witnesses validating a confession, see Kelyng's *Reports in Pleas of the Crown* 17, in 84 *Eng. Rep.* 1062, discussing Thomas Tonge's case, reported in *State Trials*, VI, 225, at 259–60 (1662), where the court ruled in favor of the admissibility of the evidence of Riggs and Tyler.

38. On *peine forte et dure*, see Thayer, 74–8; Luke Owen Pike, *A History of Crime in England* (London, 1873–76, 2 vols.), I, 210–11, 387, 468, 498; II, 194–5, 283–5, 346. See also the discussion in Blackstone, IV, 324–9, where there is a distinction between *peine* and torture. In 1772 *peine* was abolished by a statute which authorized the courts to take *pro confesso* anyone standing mute, as had been the rule in treason cases. In 1827 a new statute made standing mute equivalent to a plea of not guilty.

39. The old-fashioned treason sentence was used in America as late as 1766 against Prendergast, the leader of the rebels in the New York rent riots, but the sentence was not carried out. See Irving Mark, *Agrarian Conflicts in Colonial New York, 1711–1775* (New York, 1940), 147. See Leon Radzinowicz, *A History of English Criminal Law and Its Administration from 1750* (London, 1948, 3 vols.), I, ch. 7, on "Aggravated Forms of the Dealth Penalty," 206–27.

40. Samuel R. Gardiner, ed., *The Constitutional Documents of the Puritan Revolution, 1625–1660* (Oxford, 1906, 3rd ed. rev.), 183; trial of Thomas Tonge, *State Trials*, VI, 225, at 259 (1662); act of 1696, sect. 2, in Browning, ed., 90.

41. *State Trials*, I, xxv; Geoffrey Gilbert, *The Law of Evidence by a Late Learned Judge* (London, 1756), 139–40; for a broad statement of the general rule, see William Hawkins, *A Treatise of the Pleas of the Crown* (London, 1716), sect. 20, p. 433. Long before Gilbert's time, opponents of the oath *ex officio* claimed that it violated the law of nature; but they used the phrase in a different sense, meaning "unnatural." In 1656 a writer said, for example, that it was "against Nature, for him to be a means of his own punishment; a man ought to preserve himself, although to the hurt of another . . . if of necessity the one must needs be. Therefore to exact the Inquisition oath against a man['s] own self, is against the Law of Nature, and so against the Law of God," A. Booth, *Examen Legum Angliae*, in Howe, ed., *Readings in American Legal His-*

tory, 91. Similarly, in a 1658 case, Chief Justice Widdrington declared that the *nemo tenetur* maxim expressed the command of the law of Nature that every man should preserve himself from hurt, and concluded that a confession extorted by dread or compulsion could not be received in court, Attorney General v. Mico, 1 *Hardres* 137, at 139 (1658), 145 *Eng. Rep.* 419, at 420.

42. Trial of Matthew Mahoney, *State Trials,* XVII, 1003, at 1053 (1741); White's Trial, *ibid.,* 1079, at 1085 (1741). In the latter case, however, the judge ruled that because the prisoner had not alleged that his confession had been extorted, the question was an improper reflection on the examining magistrate. See also Rex v. Warickshall, 1 *Leach's Crown Cases* 263, at 264 (1783), 168 *Eng. Rep.* 234, at 235.

43. "Debate on a Motion for Indemnifying Evidence," May 20, 1742, in Samuel Johnson, ed., *Debates in Parliament* (London, 1787, 13 vols.), II, 121–3. The Duke of Argyle, in a speech favoring the bill, acknowledged "that no man is obliged to accuse himself, and that the constitution of Britain allows no man's evidence to be extorted from him to his own destruction." He described the right as one "of the first principles of English law." *Ibid.,* 142. Wigmore, *Evidence,* VIII, sect. 2226, p. 401, alleged that the rule against involuntary confessions and the right against self-incrimination, which he always called a "privilege" rather than a right, have been erroneously confused, the two being different in history, principle, and practice. He also claimed that the history of the two principles was "wide apart, differing by one hundred years in origin, and derived through separate lines of precedents." He added that if the "privilege, fully established by 1680, had sufficed for both classes of cases, there would have been no need in 1780 for creating a distinct rule about confessions." Although Wigmore's chronology was a bit casual, the "privilege" was indeed established by 1680, but it continued to grow in meaning. Examples of its expanding scope have been given in the text above. Wigmore assumed that its meaning was static. Connections between the two rules have also been indicated in the text above, showing how the one grew out of the other. That the two differed in principle, that is, had differing rationales, is partially correct, though proving little. Wigmore forgot that a rule of law may change not only in scope and meaning but in its rationale. The rule against swearing the accused in a criminal case, for example, originated, according to Wigmore, in the fact that the oath of the accused belonged to a different mode of proof or trial and had no place in trial by jury; later its rationale was placed on the ground that the accused's interest disqualified his testimony. The rationale of a rule of law is often an unreliable fiction; that two rules have differing rationales does not prove that they have "no connection." The phrase, "no connection," is Wigmore's, III, sect. 823, p. 249. There never was a single rationale of the right against self-incrimination. As a living principle of law its rationales changed from time to time as its meaning and application expanded. In any case that right and the rule on confessions shared at least one important rationale: the aversion of the common law to the coercion of the criminally accused. John M. Maguire, *Evidence of Guilt: Restrictions upon Its Discovery or Compulsory Disclosure* (Boston, 1959), 15, claimed, correctly, that Wigmore's differentiation of the two rules has

caused confusion. They differed in some respects, but the confessions rule was an offshoot and part of the self-incrimination rule in other, more crucial respects. Maguire noted that Wigmore made the "obviously inaccurate assertion that 'the privilege covers only statements made in court under process as a witness.'" Wigmore at that point was contrasting the privilege against incrimination with the confessions rule, which he said was the broader one because it might exclude statements obtained by promises as well as compulsion. But the contrast was possible only because Wigmore mistakenly shriveled the scope of the "privilege," which is in some respects broader than the confessions rule. The "privilege" covers, for example, the accused as well as witnesses, while the confessions rule covers only the person who is or may be the accused party. As Maguire indicated, Wigmore elsewhere acknowledged that the "privilege" was broader than he stated it to be in sect. 2266. In the same volume, for example, VIII, at sect. 2252(c) of the 3rd ed., 1940, he acknowledged that the "privilege extends to *all manner of proceedings* in which testimony is to be taken, whether litigious or not, and whether 'ex parte' or otherwise" (italics in original). Naughton, in his 1961 edition of Wigmore's vol. VIII, changed the phrase "in which testimony is to be taken" to "in which testimony is legally compellable," thereby retaining the error, in this instance, of overbroadness: the "privilege" does not apply when immunity or indemnity has been granted. Naughton caught the other error, which Maguire detected, changing it to the proposition that the privilege "covers only disclosures made under legal compulsion," 1961 ed., VIII, 401, thus introducing a new error of restrictiveness, for the "privilege" also covers disclosures made under illegal compulsion. Moreover, and once again, some disclosures made under legal compulsion, are not covered by the "privilege." Maguire, p. 16, noted that E. M. Morgan, *Basic Problems of Evidence* (Philadelphia, 1954), 129–31, "soundly rejects on practical grounds the line of thought launched by Wigmore, and in note 9 presents a considerable collection of cases." Maguire, pp. 16–17, also presents a considerable collection of cases against Wigmore's distinctions. The fact is that Wigmore relied mainly on nineteenth-century cases. The history of the confessions rule in the eighteenth century and the present state of constitutional law in the United States show the intimacy, not the opposition or differences, of the two rules. The most recent case is Miranda v. Arizona, 384 U.S. 436 (1966). See also cases there cited as well as those cited in Maguire and Morgan. For Wigmore's principal citations, see III, sect. 850(4), pp. 307–10, and VIII, sect. 2226, p. 402. In vol. III, sect. 823(c), pp. 249–50, Wigmore further elaborated on his proposition that "a confession is not rejected because of *any* connection with the *privilege against self-crimination.*" (The first italicized word is mine; the others are italicized in the original.) Here Wigmore introduced a new crop of errors and repeated others, buttressed once again by selected nineteenth-century citations. Grossly overstating his thesis, he claimed that "the theory of confessions has no connection with the theory of this privilege," a proposition which he "proves" by stating a tautological fact that is no proof at all, namely, that the "privilege" can protect only the person making the disclosure; in other words, that the rule against self-incrimination applies only to *self*-incrimination. But the rule against coerced confessions also protects only the person confessing against himself. Wigmore concluded that the "substance of the difference is that the confession-rule aims to exclude self-criminating statements which are *false,* while the privilege-rule gives the option of excluding those which are *true.*" III, 250. In fact, the confession-rule excludes all confessions extorted by promises or threats, whether the confession is true or not; it is the element of coercion that renders the confession suspect and therefore excludable. The "privilege-rule" is far broader than merely a privilege of refusing true statements, though it is accurate to imply that it does not protect false statements. The common element of both rules, basic to both, is involuntariness or coercion, a fact that Wigmore did not deny. Had he kept it in mind, his effort to clarify alleged confusion would not have been so confusing and erroneous. As McCormick said, "the kinship of the two rules is too apparent for denial. It is significant that the shadow of the rack and the thumbscrew was part of the background from which each rule emerged." Charles T. McCormick, *Handbook of the Law of Evidence* (St. Paul, Minn., 1954), 155.

44. Stephen, I, 220. *Cf.* the italicized statement in note 37 above.

45. *Picture of the Council of State,* 1649, in William Haller and Godfrey Davies, eds., *The Leveller Tracts, 1647–1653* (New York, 1944), 194.

46. Erwin N. Griswold, *The 5th Amendment Today* (Cambridge, Mass., 1955), 7, 73, 81.

Chapter XI
The American Colonies in the Seventeenth Century

1. Samuel Eliot Morison, ed., *Records of the Suffolk County Court, 1671–1680* (Boston, 1933), Colonial Society of Massachusetts, *Publications,* XXIX, unpaged preface. Twining v. N.J., 211 U.S. 78, 103, 108, 110 (1908), *per* Moody, J.; reaffirmed in Palko v. Conn., 302 U.S. 319, 323–4, 325 (1937), and Adamson v. Cal., 332 U.S. 46, 49–55 (1947), but overruled in Malloy v. Hogan, 378 U.S. 1, 6 (1964), and Miranda v. Ariz., 384 U.S. 436 (1966).

2. R. Carter Pittman's pioneering article, "The Colonial and Constitutional History of the Privilege against Self-Incrimination in America," *Virginia Law Review,* XXI (May 1935), 763–89, has been the standard work on the subject. His survey, though highly suggestive, is often inaccurate or misleading; one cannot rely on his data or his citations. Pittman was not only superficial. He left far more gaps than the sources, admittedly sparse, warranted. On the one hand he ignored the history of the right against self-incrimination in several colonies, including New York, for which the sources are ample, while on the other hand, he frequently found a recognition of the right where none existed in the evidence that he cited.

3. Julius Goebel, Jr., and T. Raymond Naughton, *Law Enforcement in Colonial New York: A Study in Criminal Procedure (1664–1776)* (New York, 1944), 656.

4. *Ibid.,* 657.

5. Among the leading works on English law in the colonies are Julius Goebel, Jr., "King's Law and Local Custom in Seventeenth Century New England," *Columbia Law Review,* XXXI (March 1931), 416–48; George

Lee Haskins, *Law and Authority in Early Massachusetts* (New York, 1960); Paul Samuel Reinsch, *English Common Law in the Early American Colonies* (Madison, Wis., 1890); Paul M. Hamlin and Charles E. Baker, *Supreme Court of Judicature of the Province of New York, 1691–1704* (New York, 1959, 3 vols.), I; George Athan Billias, ed., *Law and Authority in Colonial America: Selected Essays* (Barre, Mass., 1965); Arthur P. Scott, *Criminal Law in Colonial Virginia* (Chicago, 1930); Richard B. Morris, *Studies in the History of American Law: with Special Reference to the Seventeenth and Eighteenth Centuries* (New York, 1930); Francis R. Aumann, *The Changing American Legal System: Some Selected Phases* (Columbus, Ohio, 1940); Edwin Powers, *Crime and Punishment in Early Massachusetts, 1620–1692* (Boston, 1966).

6. For the Virginia charter of 1606, see Alexander Brown, ed., *The Genesis of the United States . . . A Series of Historical Manuscripts now first printed, Together with a Reissue of Rare Contemporaneous Tracts* (Boston, 1890, 2 vols.), I, 61. The charter of 1609 specified that "in cases capital and criminal, as civil, both marine and other . . . the said statutes, ordinances, and proceedings, as near, as conveniently may be, be agreeable to the laws, statutes, government, and policy of our realm of this England," *ibid.,* I, 236. Brown also reprinted the "Articles, Instructions, and Orders" of 1606 for the government of Virginia, *ibid.,* I, 69. The charters of Virginia are also in Francis N. Thorpe, ed., *The Federal and State Constitutions, Colonial Charters, and Other Organic Laws* (Washington, 1909, 7 vols.), VII, 3800, 3804–5. For a similar provision in other charters, see *ibid.,* III, 1839 (New England, 1620); III, 1856–7 (Massachusetts Bay, 1629); III, 1681 (Maryland, 1632); III, 1635 (Maine, 1639); I, 533 (Connecticut, 1662); VI, 3220 (Rhode Island, 1663); V, 2747 (Carolina, 1663); and II, 773 (Georgia, 1732). See also Charles M. Andrews, *The Colonial Period of American History* (New Haven, 1935–38, 4 vols.), I, 86 n. 1. For the Virginia Ordinance of 1621, see Thorpe, ed., *Federal and State Constitutions,* VII, 3812. For the Plymouth acts of 1623 and 1636, see Nathaniel B. Shurtleff and David Pulsifer, eds., *Records of the Colony of New Plymouth in New England, 1633–1691* (Boston, 1855–61, 12 vols.), XI, 3 and 12. For the Massachusetts Body of Liberties, see William H. Whitmore, ed., *The Colonial Laws of Massachusetts Reprinted from the Edition of 1660 . . . Containing also the Body of Liberties of 1641* (Boston, 1889), 32. See generally the chapters covering the colonial period in Rodney L. Mott, *Due Process of Law* (Indianapolis, 1926).

7. See works cited in note 5 above for references on early colonial law. See also Stefan A. Riesenfeld, "Law-Making and Legislative Precedent in American Legal History," *Minnesota Law Review,* XXXIII (January 1949), 103–44; Charles Warren, *A History of the American Bar* (Cambridge, Eng., 1912), Part I; Anton-Hermann Chroust, *The Rise of the Legal Profession in America* (Norman, Okla., 1965, 2 vols.), vol. I; Carroll T. Bond, ed., with the collaboration of Richard B. Morris, *Proceedings of the Maryland Court of Appeals, 1695–1729* (Washington, 1933), Introduction, v–li. For the Declaration of Rights and Grievances, see Worthington C. Ford *et al.,* eds., *Journals of the Continental Congress 1774–1789* (Washington, 1904–37, 24 vols.), I, 69.

8. Elizabeth Gaspar Brown, *British Statutes in American Law, 1776–*

1836 (Ann Arbor, Mich., 1964), 23–6, and Ford W. Hall, "The Common Law: An Account of Its Reception in the United States," *Vanderbilt Law Review*, IV, (June 1951), 791, at 799–800. For Coke on the common law, see Dr. Bonham's Case, 8 *Coke's Reports* 107, 115 (1610), and on Magna Carta, Catherine Drinker Bowen, *The Lion and the Throne: The Life and Times of Sir Edward Coke (1552–1634)* (Boston, 1956), 496. On the common law in American thinking, see Mark DeWolfe Howe, "The Sources and Nature of Law in Colonial Massachusetts," in Billias, ed., *Law and Authority*, 10–15; Benjamin F. Wright, *American Interpretations of Natural Law* (New York, 1962 ed.), 38, 58–61, 69, 88–9.

9. On Roger Williams, see Nathaniel B. Shurtleff, ed., *Records of the Governor and Company of the Massachusetts Bay in New England (1628–86)* (Boston, 1853–54, 5 vols.), I, 160, and Ola Elizabeth Winslow, *Master Roger Williams* (New York, 1957), 107–24. On William Pynchon, see Shurtleff, ed., *Records*, III, 215–16, 229–30; IV, 29–30, 48–9; and Clyde Augustus Duniway, *The Development of Freedom of the Press in Massachusetts* (New York, 1906), 32–3. On Henry Dunster, see Duniway, 34–5, and Samuel Eliot Morison, *Harvard College in the Seventeenth Century* (Cambridge, Mass., 1936, 2 vols.), I, 305–14. On the Quakers and Baptists, see Duniway, 35–7; Herbert L. Osgood, *The American Colonies in the Seventeenth Century* (Gloucester, Mass., 1957 reprint), I, 264–89; Brooks Adams, *The Emancipation of Massachusetts* (Boston, 1919, rev. ed.), 275–348; Rufus Jones, *The Quakers in the American Colonies* (New York, 1966 ed.), 63–89. The best survey of the suppression of freedom of expression in Massachusetts during the seventeenth century is in Duniway, 17–73. For other colonies, see Leonard W. Levy, *Legacy of Suppression: Freedom of Speech and Press in Early American History* (Cambridge, Mass., 1960), especially ch. 2. The cases of Anne Hutchinson, John Wheelwright, Peter Hobart, Robert Child, and Samuel Gorton are discussed below, this chapter, with appropriate citations.

10. Erwin N. Griswold, *The 5th Amendment Today* (Cambridge, Mass., 1955), 3. On Wheelwright, see Charles H. Bell, ed., *John Wheelwright, His Writings, Including his Fast-day Sermon . . . and a Memoir* (Boston, 1876); John Heard, *John Wheelwright* (Boston, 1930); Charles Francis Adams, *Three Episodes of Massachusetts History* (Boston, 1892, 2 vols.), I, 363–532, and II, 533–78; Brooks Adams, *Emancipation of Massachusetts*, 214–48; and for the most recent account, Emery Battis, *Saints and Sectaries: Anne Hutchinson and the Antinomian Controversy in the Massachusetts Bay Colony* (Chapel Hill, N.C., 1902).

11. John Winthrop, *Winthrop's Journal "History of New England"* *1630–1649*, ed. James Kendall Hosmer (New York, 1908, 2 vols.), I, 209, 211; C.F. Adams, *Three Episodes*, I, 366–8, 384, 432; and, for the theological controversy, Perry Miller, *The New England Mind: The Seventeenth Century* (Boston, 1961 ed.), 365–97.

12. The primary source for the trial of Wheelwright is *A Short Story of the Rise, Reign, and Ruine of the Antinomians, Familists and Libertines, that Infected the Churches of New England* (London, 1649), reprinted in Charles Francis Adams, ed., *Antinomianism in the Colony of Massachusetts Bay, 1636–1638. Including the Short Story and Other Documents* (Boston, 1894), 191–233. The authorship of *A Short Story* has been ascribed to

both Thomas Welde and John Winthrop. It was Winthrop who wrote the section dealing with the trial of Wheelwright. See Adams's Introduction to his *Antinomianism, passim,* but especially at pp. 37, 43, 57, 62. See also the note by Hosmer in *Winthrop's Journal,* I, 242. For the quotations from *A Short Story,* see Adams, *Antinomianism,* 194.

13. Adams, *Antinomianism,* 194.

14. *Ibid.,* 195.

15. *Ibid.,* 199–201.

16. Adams's characterization of the trial of Hutchinson is in his *Three Episodes,* I, 488. For original accounts of the trial, see his *Antinomianism,* 157–80, 217–33, 285–336; see also Franklin B. Dexter, "A Report of the Trial of Mrs. Anne Hutchinson before the Church in Boston, 1638," *Proceedings,* Massachusetts Historical Society, 2nd ser., IV (1889), 159–91, and Thomas Hutchinson, *The History of the Colony and Province of Massachusetts-Bay,* ed. Lawrence Shaw Mayo (Cambridge, Mass., 1936, 3 vols.), II, 366–91. The best secondary accounts are Adams, *Three Episodes,* I, 483–532; Battis, 176–289; and Edmund S. Morgan, "The Case against Anne Hutchinson," *New England Quarterly,* X (1937), 635–49. For the action against Aspinwall, Coggeshall, and other deputies, see Adams, *Antinomianism,* 136–8, 148–57, and *Winthrop's Journal,* I, 239–41.

17. The Body of Liberties is printed in Whitmore, ed., *The Colonial Laws of Massachusetts,* 32–61. A conveniently available reprinting is in Edmund S. Morgan, ed., *Puritan Political Ideas, 1558–1794* (Indianapolis, 1965), 177–203. For discussions of the Body of Liberties, see Haskins, *Law and Authority,* 36–7, 119–32, and Samuel Eliot Morison, *Builders of the Bay Colony* (Boston, 1930), 224–34. Winthrop's comment is in *Winthrop's Journal,* I, 151.

18. Liberty 45 is in Whitmore, *Colonial Laws,* 43. Liberty 3 in *ibid.,* 33. Cf. Haskins, *Law and Authority,* 202, on Liberty 3 as barring the oath *ex officio.*

19. [William Bradford], *Bradford's History "Of Plimoth Plantation." From the Original Manuscript* (Boston, 1898), 465.

20. *Ibid.,* 472–3.

21. *Ibid.,* 465–6.

22. *Ibid.,* 467.

23. James Savage, ed., *The History of New England from 1630 to 1649. By John Winthrop* (Boston, 1853, 2 vols.), II, 56. The Hosmer edition of *Winthrop's Journal,* II, 46, omits this passage.

24. Cf. Riesenfeld, "Law-Making and Legislative Precedent," 116, 130; Riesenfeld interprets Liberty 45 as a guarantee against compulsory self-incrimination and alleges that it was one of the rights of the Body of Liberties that "went, in some respects, noticeably beyond the traditional liberties of the Englishman." Haskins speaks of Liberty 45 as recognizing "a limited privilege against self-crimination" that "roughly paralleled English practice," p. 200. At another point Haskins adds that Riesenfeld "appears to be entirely accurate in the sense that a privilege against self-crimination, similar to that in effect in England after the prohibition of the *ex officio* oath, was recognized at this period of the colony's history," p. 283 n. 59.

25. On Gorton and his troubles, see Adelos Gorton, *The Life and Times*

of Samuel Gorton (Philadelphia, 1907), 11–51, and the sketch by James Truslow Adams in *The Dictionary of American Biography,* VII, 438–9. Perry Miller, *Orthodoxy in Massachusetts, 1630–1650* (Boston, 1959 ed.), 283–5, speaks of Gorton as belonging to a "lunatic fringe" against which the "machinery of Puritan inquisition was immediately put into action." There are also useful accounts in Hutchinson, *The History of . . . Massachusetts-Bay,* I, 102–6, and Samuel Greene Arnold, *History of the State of Rhode Island and Providence Plantations* (New York, 1859–60, 2 vols.), I, 169–72. Gorton's account of his trials is in his *Simplicities Defence against Seven-Headed Policy. Or Innocency Vindicated, being unjustly Accused, and sorely Censured, by that Seven-headed Church-Government United in New England* (London, 1646), reprinted in Peter Force, ed., *Tracts and Other Papers, Relating Principally to the Origin, Settlement, and Progress of the Colonies in North America* (New York, 1947 ed., 4 vols.), IV, tract VI, 56–75. The account of his trial in Portsmouth (Newport), Rhode Island, in 1642, is from Edmund Winslow, *Hypocracie Unmasked. A True Relation of the Proceedings of the Governor and Company of the Massachusetts (Bay) against Samuel Gorton of Rhode Island* (London, 1646), ed., by Howard Millar Chapin (Providence, 1916), 55.

26. The characterization of Gorton's remarks is in Winthrop's letter, reprinted in Gorton's *Simplicities Defense,* in Force, IV, 56. Gorton's account of his capture is in *ibid.,* 57–62.

27. *Winthrop's Journal,* II, 139–50, 160, tells the story of Gorton's capture and trial from the standpoint of the authorities.

28. Gorton, *Simplicities Defense,* in Force, IV, 63–4, 72–3.

29. *Winthrop's Journal,* II, 279.

30. *Winthrop's Journal,* II, 230, 244, 271 for the quotations concerning the Hingham Affair and William Vassall. Winthrop's discussion is at pp. 229–45, 264–6, 271. See also Miller, *Orthodoxy in Massachusetts,* 287–98. Liberty 94 of the Body of Liberties of 1641 specifies the capital crimes, in Whitmore, ed., *The Colonial Laws of Massachusetts,* 55.

31. The Child Remonstrance is printed in William H. Whitmore and William S. Appleton, eds., *The Hutchinson Papers* (New York, 1865, 2 vols.), I, 214–23. The trial of the remonstrants is reported in *Winthrop's Journal,* II, 296–309, 316.

32. The quotation from the indictment is in *Winthrop's Journal,* II, 299. See also Shurtleff, ed., *Records of the Governor and Company,* III, 90–91, 94, 97. Richard B. Morris, "Massachusetts and the Common Law: The Declaration of 1646," *American Historical Review,* XXXI (April 1926), 443–51, discusses the General Court's reply to the remonstrance. The definitive study of the episode is George Lyman Kittredge, "Dr. Robert Child the Remonstrant," *Publications of the Colonial Society of Massachusetts,* XXI (Transactions 1919), 1–146. Other worthwhile accounts are in Morison, *Builders of the Bay Colony,* 245–60, and Miller, *Orthodoxy,* 298–306.

33. Maverick's petition is quoted in Kittredge, "Dr. Robert Child," 58 n. 5, continued on 59, citing Massachusetts Archives (MS) B xxxviii, 228a, dated May 8, 1649. There were two trials of the remonstrants, the first in 1646, the second in 1647. It is not clear whether Maverick's statement applied to the preliminary proceedings of only the second trial, or of the

first, or of both; Kittredge inferred that Maverick referred to "the trial of 1647," but even if his date is correct, it passes belief that the General Court would have employed the oath *ex officio* in a public trial.

34. Kittredge, 37–40.

35. *Ibid.*, 40. See also Hutchinson, *The History of . . . Massachusetts-Bay*, I, 126–7, and *Winthrop's Journal*, II, 306–9. For the law of 1647 and the General Laws and Liberties of 1648, see Morison, *Builders of the Bay Colony*, 261–5. See also Max Farrand, ed., *The Book of the General Lawes and Libertyes Concerning the Inhabitants of Massachusetts* (Cambridge, Mass., 1929), p. 50 for the provision on torture, and p. 43 on oaths. For a discussion of the 1648 code, see Haskins, 118–20, 131–40, 201–2.

36. For the provision against torture in the Connecticut code of 1673, see *The Book of the General Laws for the People within the Jurisdiction of Connecticut* (1673) (Hartford, 1865), 65. Tharpe's case is in Franklin B. Dexter, ed., *New Haven Town Records 1649–1684* (New Haven, 1917–1919, 2 vols.), II, 184. The Massachusetts act of 1657 is in Shurtleff, ed., *Records of the Governor and Company*, IV, pt. i, 291. On oaths of purgation, see J. Hammond Trumbull and Charles J. Hoadley, eds., *The Public Records of the Colony of Connecticut* (Hartford, 1850–90, 15 vols.), II, 119; *The Book of General Laws . . . for Connecticut*, 41; Morison, ed., *Records of the Suffolk County Court*, I, 181, 328, 491, 559, and II, 1013; and Shurtleff and Pulsifer, eds., *Records of the Colony of New Plymouth*, XI, 234–5.

37. William Hand Browne *et al.*, eds., *Archives of Maryland: Proceedings of the Council of Maryland, 1636–1667* (Baltimore, 1883–in progress, 70 vols.), III, 176–7.

38. John Russell Bartlett, ed., *Records of the Colony of Rhode Island and Providence Plantations in New England (1636–1792)* (Providence, 1856–65, 10 vols.), I, 156, 181–2, 194; II, 238–9.

39. Hugh Hastings and Edward T. Corwin, eds., *Ecclesiastical Records. State of New York* (Albany, 1901–16, 7 vols.), I, 497; Frederick Zwierlein, *Religion in New Netherland* (Rochester, 1910), 230–32, 235–41.

40. Joseph H. Smith, ed., *Colonial Justice in Western Massachusetts (1639–1702): The Pynchon Court Record* (Cambridge, Mass., 1961), 146 n. 71, citing Hampton County Probate Court Records (MS), I, 152. In discussing criminal procedure generally, Smith states that the accused was not examined under oath, but adds: "Whether this was due to acceptance of the common law maxim given currency by Dalton, *Nullus tenetur seipsum prodere*, is not clear. There is some suspicion that John Pynchon and other magistrates upon occasion engaged in judicial browbeating of alleged defenders. . . . In no case did the accused claim privilege against self-incrimination." *Ibid.*, 146. It would be more accurate to have stated that the records used by Smith do not reveal whether an accused person claimed the right. If he "refused to confess against himself," it is not likely that he simply remained mute to the incriminating question; in the case of John Stewart, there was no challenge to the jurisdiction of the court nor any other basis for his refusal to answer except the right against self-incrimination. Even if Stewart did not expressly claim the right, the court must have construed his refusal to answer as being grounded on it, because there could have been no other basis for the court's acceptance of his refusal.

41. The act of 1677 is in William Waller Hening, ed., *The Statutes at Large Being a Collection of All Laws of Virginia* (*1619–1792*) (Richmond, 1809–23, 13 vols.), II, 442, and *ibid.*, II, 545–60, for the military trials. On Berkeley's suppression and trial of the rebels, see also Thomas J. Wertenbaker, *Virginia under the Stuarts* (Princeton, N.J., 1914), 193–4, 197–8, 203–4, 209, 241–2, and Wertenbaker, *Torchbearer of the Revolution: The Story of Bacon's Rebellion* (Princeton, N.J., 1940), 187, 198–205. In England, the right against self-incrimination was first extended to a witness in Holder's case, *State Trials*, IV, 989, at 1101 (1649).

42. For the Pennsylvania laws of 1682, framed in England, see Thorpe, *The Federal and State Constitutions*, V, 3059–63. See also George Staughton *et al.*, eds., *Charter of William Penn and the Laws of the Province of Pennsylvania* (Harrisburg, 1879), 99–154. On More and Robinson, see *Colonial Records of Pennsylvania, 1683–1790* (Philadelphia, 1852–60, 16 vols.), I (*Minutes of the Provincial Council*), 136, 140; and Gertrude MacKinney and Charles F. Hoban, eds., *Votes and Proceedings of the House of Representatives of the Province of Pennsylvania* (1682–1776), in *Pennsylvania Archives*, 8th ser., I, 66–9.

43. The Pennsylvania Charter of Liberties of 1682 and the Frame of Government of 1682 are in Thorpe, V, 3047–52, 3052–9. On Growdon, see *Colonial Records of Pennsylvania*, I (*Minutes of the Provincial Council*), 278.

44. The records of Bradford's examination do not appear in either the *Pennsylvania Archives* or the *Colonial Records of Pennsylvania*. Bradford's signed manuscript account of his examination is in the New York Historical Society, "The Examination of Wm. Bradford before Governour Blackwell att Philadelphia the 9th of the 2d Month 1689. concerning printing the Charter," Miscellaneous Bradford Papers, quoted by permission of the New York Historical Society. For general background on Pennsylvania politics of this period, see Edwin S. Bronner, *William Penn's "Holy Experiment": The Founding of Pennsylvania, 1681–1701* (New York, 1962).

45. Viola Florence Barnes, *The Dominion of New England* (New Haven, 1923), is the best work on the subject. See especially chs. IV and V on "Legislation and Taxation" and "The Administration of Justice." For the quotation on "ensnaring" examinations, see "A Narrative of the Proceedings of Sir Edmond Androsse and his Complices . . . by several Gentlemen who were of his Council" (1691), reprinted in Michael G. Hall *et al.*, eds., *The Glorious Revolution in America. Documents on the Colonial Crisis of 1689* (Chapel Hill, N.C., 1964), 33–4. For the act of 1692, see *Acts and Resolves, Public and Private, of the Province of Massachusetts Bay* (*1692–1786*) (Boston, 1869–1922, 21 vols.), I, 57 (ch. 20, sect. 4, 2nd sess.).

46. On Giles Cory, see Charles W. Upham, *Salem Witchcraft* (Boston, 1867, 2 vols.), II, 334.

47. Cotton Mather is quoted in George Lincoln Burr, ed., *Narratives of the Witchcraft Cases, 1648–1706* (New York, 1914), 363 n. 2. Thomas Brattle, "A Full and Candid Account of the Delusion Called Witchcraft" (1692), in Burr, 189. Robert Calef, "More Wonders of the Invisible World" (1700), in *ibid.*, 363, 364, 373, 374, 376. For illustrations of the claim of the right against self-incrimination in the witchcraft trials and judicial rebuffs,

see W. Elliott Woodward, ed., *Records of Salem Witchcraft Copied from the Original Documents* (Boston, 1864, 2 vols.), II, 33, and Peleg W. Chandler, ed., *American Criminal Trials* (Boston, 1841, 2 vols.), I, 88. *E.g.*, a defendant inquired, "would you have me accuse myself?" and the court replied, "yes if you be guilty."

48. [Thomas Maule] Theo. Philanthes, *New-England Persecutors Mauld With their own Weapons . . . Together with a brief Account of the Imprisonment and Tryal of Thomas Maule of Salem, for publishing a Book, entitled, Truth held forth and maintained* (New York, 1697), 62 pp. The remark about "divers Insnaring Questions" is at p. 55. On Maule, see Matt Bushnell Jones, *Thomas Maule, the Salem Quaker and Free Speech in Massachusetts Bay* (Salem, 1936), 42 pp., reprinted from Essex Institute Historical *Collections*, LXXII, No. 1, Jan. 1936.

49. Browne, ed., *Archives of Maryland: Proceedings of the Council of Maryland*, VIII (*1687/88–1693*), 499–500.

50. Browne, ed., *Archives of Maryland: Proceedings and Acts of the General Assembly of Maryland, 1693–1697*, XIX, 8–14, 89–90. See also Herbert L. Osgood, *The American Colonies in the Eighteenth Century* (New York, 1924, 4 vols.), I, 363–4.

51. Browne, ed., *Archives of Maryland: Proceedings of the Council of Maryland, 1698–1731*, XXV, 190–91, 234–5.

52. Case of David Leeds, 1693, in H. Clay Reed and George J. Miller, eds., *The Burlington Court Book: A Record of Quaker Jurisprudence in West New Jersey* (Washington, 1944), 151. The Connecticut statutes are in Trumbull and Hoadley, eds., *Public Records of Connecticut*, IV, 236, 410. The Pennsylvania Charter is in Thorpe, V, 3079.

53. "A Memoriall Concerning the Mal-administrations of His Excell^y Francis Nicholson, Esqr.," in "Charges Against Governor Nicholson," *Virginia Magazine of History and Biography*, III (1896), 378–9. Robert Beverley, *The History and Present State of Virginia*, ed. Louis B. Wright (Chapel Hill, N.C., 1947), 106–9, quoted matter at pp. 107, 109. For the date of the "Memoriall" see Richard L. Morton, *Colonial Virginia* (Chapel Hill, 1960, 2 vols.), I, 381. Letter of Philip Ludwell, Jr., undated, in *Calendar of State Papers, Colonial Series: America and West Indies, 1704–1705*, ed. Cecil Headlam (London, 1860 ff., 43 vols.), XXII, 105.

Chapter XII
Establishment of the Right in America

1. For the state of the colonial bar, see Charles Warren, *A History of the American Bar* (Cambridge, Eng., 1912), Part I; Anton-Hermann Chroust, *The Rise of the Legal Profession in America* (Norman, Okla., 1965, 2 vols.), vol. I; Paul M. Hamlin, *Legal Education in Colonial New York* (New York, 1939); and Edward Alfred Jones, *American Members of the Inns of Court* (London, 1924). On the use of Dalton and other law books by the colonial courts, see Edwin Powers, *Crime and Punishment in Early Massachusetts, 1620–1692* (Boston, 1966), 433; Carroll T. Bond, ed., with Richard B. Morris, *Proceedings of the Maryland Court of Appeals, 1695–1729* (Washington, 1933), xx, xxvii; George Athan Billias, ed., *Law and Authority in Colonial America: Selected Essays* (Barre, Mass., 1965),

13–14, 132 n. 5; Francis R. Aumann, *The Changing American Legal System: Some Selected Phases* (Columbus, Ohio, 1940), 43–8.

2. Julius Goebel, Jr., and T. Raymond Naughton, *Law Enforcement in Colonial New York: A Study in Criminal Procedure (1664–1776)* (New York, 1944), xxiii, xxvi, xxviii, 59, 556. Trial of Penn and Mead, *State Trials*, VI, 957–8 (1670).

3. Goebel and Naughton, xxviii, 56–7, 59–69, 284, 573. On Alexander and his library, see Hamlin, *Legal Education*, 76–8, 171–6. Appendix VII, in *ibid.*, lists the books in the libraries of several New York colonial lawyers. Smith's law books are enumerated at pp. 182–92.

4. Goebel and Naughton, 656–7.

5. On Gilbert, see above, ch. 10, n. 41 and related text. The fifth edition of Gilbert, *Law of Evidence by a Late Learned Judge*, was published in Philadelphia in 1788 and contained the identical passage, p. 137. Goebel and Naughton misstate that the book was used in New York "not long after publication," p. 628, n. 79, and wrongly give the date of publication as 1754. "A Treatise on Evidence," William Smith Papers, IX, 127–8, New York Public Library MSS. Smith's later relationship to the right against self-incrimination will be discussed below.

6. Giles Jacob, *A New Law-Dictionary* (London, 1732, 2nd ed.), under "Evidence." Jacob, *Every Man His Own Lawyer* (New York, 1768, 7th ed.), 93; the book was also published in Philadelphia in 1769. Henry Care, *English Liberties, or the Free born Subject's Inheritance* (London, 1691); I used the 5th edition (Boston, 1721), 198–9. There was a 6th edition published in Providence in 1774. Clinton Rossiter, *Seedtime of the Republic: The Origin of the American Tradition of Political Liberty* (New York, 1953), 457–8, n. 11. John Somers, *The Security of Englishmen's Lives, or the Trust, Power and Duty of the Grand Juries of England* (London, 1681; Boston, 1720; New York, 1773); I used the edition printed as the Appendix to [Anon.], *A Guide to the Knowledge of the Rights and Privileges of Englishmen* (London, 1757), 170. William Hawkins, *A Treatise of the Pleas of the Crown* (London, 1716), II, chap. 46, sect. 20, p. 433. William Nelson, *The Law of Evidence* (London, 1735), 51. See also Matthew Bacon, *A New Abridgment of the Law* (Savoy, Eng., 1731–59, 4 vols.), II, 288.

7. Michael Dalton, *The Countrey Justice* (London, 1618), 264; also in the London editions of 1619, 1677, and 1742, pp. 273, 411, and 380 respectively. William Nelson, *The Office and Authority of the Justice of the Peace* (London, 1714, 4th ed.), 253. [James Parker?] *Conductor Generalis, or the Office, Duty and Authority of Justices of the Peace* (Philadelphia, 1722), 83. In the 2nd ed. of *Conductor Generalis* (Philadelphia, 1749; also New York, 1749), an appendix on "Maxims and General Rules" included the following: "5. *Accusare Nemo se debet nisi coram Deo:* No man ought to accuse himself, unless it be before God. An Oath is not lawful whereby any Person may be compelled to confess, or accuse himself, &c. . . . The Law will not enforce any one to shew or say what is against him: for which Reason an Offender, tho' ever so culpable, may plead *Not Guilty*," *ibid.*, 434. The New York editions appeared in 1749, 1764 (two), 1787, 1788 (two), 1790, and 1794. "A List of Legal Treatises Printed in the British Colonies and the American States before 1801," ed.

Eldon Revare James, in Morton C. Campbell *et al.*, *Harvard Legal Essays Written in Honor of and Presented to Joseph Henry Beale and Samuel Williston* (Cambridge, Mass., 1934), 159-211, proved useful, but is not complete. For passages similar to those in *Conductor Generalis*, see also [Richard Burn], *An Abridgment of Burn's Justice of the Peace* (Boston, 1773), 123; Richard Starke, *The Office and Authority of a Justice of the Peace* (Williamsburg, Va., 1774), 145, 146; J. Davis, *The Office and Authority of a Justice of the Peace* (Newbern, N.C., 1774), 160; [John F. Grimké], *The South-Carolina Justice of Peace* (Philadelphia, 1788), 191; William W. Hening, *The New Virginia Justice* (Richmond, Va., 1795), 177, 286. Most of these manuals, like *Conductor Generalis*, also included the rule from Coke, "4 *Inst.* 279" or "*Coke Litt.* 158b," that a witness should not be examined to his own infamy or turpitude. William Wyche, *A Treatise on the Practice of the Supreme Court of Judicature of the State of New-York in Civil Actions* (New York, 1794), 156, citing Coke, said that a juror may be examined on oath "with regard to such causes of challenge, as are not to his dishonor or discredit, but not with regard to any crime, or any thing, which tends to his disgrace or disadvantage." The same rule was in Francis-Xavier Martin, *The Office and Authority of a Justice of the Peace . . . According to the Laws of the State of North-Carolina* (Newbern, N.C., 1791), 92.

8. J. J. Burlamaqui, *The Principles of Natural and Political Law*, trans. by T. Nugent (London, 1763, 2 vols.), II, 187-8. Baron Pufendorf, *The Law of Nature and Nations*, trans. by Basil Kenicott (London, 1729), 332, 353-4, 767.

9. Edward Wingate, *Maxims of Reason: or The Reason of the Common Law of England* (London, 1658), sect. 125, pp. 486-7. Hamlin, 173, 179, 181, 187, 194; Rossiter, 141, 217, 359, and related footnotes. Sir William Blackstone, *Commentaries on the Law of England* (Oxford, 1765-69, 4 vols.), III, ch. 7, p. 101, ch. 23, p. 370; IV, ch. 22, p. 296. Blackstone says nothing detailed or systematic about the right because he did not deal with the rules of evidence. At one point, when speaking of "established rules and maxims," he gave this illustration: "as 'that the king can do no wrong, that no man shall be bound to accuse himself' and the like," I, 68.

10. Goebel and Naughton, xxxi, 628-9, 641.

11. *Ibid.*, 654.

12. See above, ch. 10, notes 41-4 and related text.

13. Goebel and Naughton, 627, speculate that the swearing of defendant's witnesses was discretionary with the New York courts.

14. Chroust, I, 43-4, 130, 138, 296, 301; Arthur P. Scott, *Criminal Law in Colonial Virginia* (Chicago, 1930), 60, 79, 100; L. Kinvin Wroth and Hiller B. Zobel, eds., *Legal Papers of John Adams* (Cambridge, Mass., 1965, 3 vols.), II, 402-3 n. 40. Goebel and Naughton, 656, 659.

15. *Calendar of Council Minutes, 1668-1773*, ed. Berthold Fernow, New York State Library, *Bulletin 58* (March 1902) History 6 (Albany, 1902), 132; Philip L. White, *The Beekmans of New York in Politics and Commerce, 1647-1877* (New York, 1956), 87-8, 91-2; Lawrence H. Leder, *Robert Livingston, 1654-1728, and the Politics of Colonial New York* (Chapel Hill, N.C., 1961), 130-32; New York Council Minutes, June 25, 1698, VIII, 55-6, New York State Library MSS, Albany, N.Y.; John Key,

"Heads of Accusation against the Earl of Bellomont," March 11, 1700, in E. B. O'Callaghan and B. Fernow, eds., *Documents Relative to the Colonial History of the State of New-York* (Albany, 1853–87, 15 vols.), IV, 622; Commissioners of Statutory Revision, *The Colonial Laws of New York from the Year 1664 to the Revolution* (Albany, 1894, 5 vols.), I, 392–3; John Montague, *Arguments Offer'd to the Right Honourable the Lords Commissioners for Trade and Plantation Relating to Some Acts of Assembly Past* at New-York *in* America (London, 1701), in New-York Historical Society, *Collections* (New York, 1869), 180–83.

16. Proceedings of Lords of Trade, Jan. 20, 1699, in O'Callaghan and Fernow, eds., *Documents,* IV, 467.

17. *Ibid.,* IV, 648.

18. Rex v. Bayard, *State Trials,* XIV, 471–506 (1702); Leder, *Livingston,* 174–7.

19. Samuel Bayard to Adderly and Lodwick, Jan. 27, 1702, in O'Callaghan and Fernow, eds., *Documents,* IV, 945; New York Council Minutes, Jan. 21, 26, 1702, VIII, 302–3; Nicholas Bayard to Adderly and Lodwick, Jan. 28, 1702, in O'Callaghan and Fernow, eds., *Documents,* IV, 947; Sir Edward Northey to Board of Trade, April 25, 1702, in *ibid.,* IV, 954 (italics added).

20. "The Case of William Atwood, Esq." (1703), New-York Historical Society, *Collections,* XIII (New York, 1881), 269.

21. [Anon.], *A Narrative of a New and Unusual American Imprisonment of Two Presbyterian Ministers: and Prosecution of Mr. Francis Makemie. By a Learner of Law, and Lover of Liberty* (1707), in Peter Force, ed., *Tracts and Other Papers Relating Principally to the Origin . . . of the Colonies of North America* (New York, 1947 ed., 4 vols.), IV, No. 4, unpaged introduction "An Epistle to the Reader."

22. Leder, *Livingston,* 251–4; *Colonial Laws of New York,* II, 8–10, 98.

23. Journal of Board of Trade, May 5, 12, 1725, and Representation of Board of Trade, June 16, 1725, in O'Callaghan and Fernow, eds., *Documents,* V, 748, 750, 763; *Colonial Laws of New York,* II, 281–7.

24. *Colonial Laws of New York,* I, 454–5 (ch. 95, Oct. 18, 1701). Goebel and Naughton, 657, state that the first statute employing a purgatory oath was passed in 1709. For the acts after 1701, see *Colonial Laws of New York,* I, 657–8 (ch. 187, May 24, 1709), 678–9 (ch. 196, Sept. 24, 1709), 681 (ch. 197, Oct. 11, 1709), 764 (ch. 250, Dec. 10, 1712), 830 (ch. 282, Sept. 4, 1714), 889–90 (ch. 317, June 30, 1716); II, 245 (ch. 463, Nov. 10, 1725), 710 (ch. 568, Sept. 30, 1731), 954 (ch. 651, Dec. 16, 1737), 962 (ch. 655, Dec. 16, 1737); III, 243–4 (ch. 734, Oct. 29, 1742), 730–31 (ch. 869, July 1, 1748), 757–8 (ch. 881, Nov. 24, 1750), 1097–8 (ch. 979, July 5, 1755); IV, 349–50 (ch. 1086, Mar. 7, 1759). William Smith, *The History of the Late Province of New-York* (New York, 1829, 2 vols.), I, 139.

25. Benjamin Franklin, "Some Observations on the Proceedings against The Rev. Mr. Hemphill" (1735), in Leonard W. Labaree *et al.,* eds., *Papers of Benjamin Franklin* (New Haven, 1959 ff., 9 vols.), II, 37, 44, 45, 47, 49; Franklin, "A Defense of the Rev. Mr. Hemphill's Observations" (1735), in *ibid.,* II, 90, 99. See also, Merton A. Christensen, "Franklin in

the Hemphill Trial: Deism Versus Presbyterian Orthodoxy," *William and Mary Quarterly*, 3rd ser., X (July 1953), 422-40.

26. *Votes and Proceedings of the House of Representatives of the Province of Pennsylvania* (*1682-1776*), in Gertrude MacKinney and Charles F. Hoban, eds., *Pennsylvania Archives*, 8th ser. (n.p., 1931-35), VI, 4423 ff.; quotation at p. 4445.

27. The Smith-Moore case is reported in *ibid.*, VI, 4677-716.

28. *Ibid.*, VI, 4678-80, 4681-2, 4704. For a fuller discussion of the Smith-Moore case, see Leonard W. Levy, *Legacy of Suppression: Freedom of Speech and Press in Early American History* (Cambridge, Mass., 1960), 53-61.

29. *The Boston Post-Boy*, May 28, 1753. John Lovell, *Freedom, the First of Blessings* (Boston, 1754), 1; Samuel Cooper, *The Crisis* (Boston, 1754), 5-6. Shirley is quoted in John F. Burns, *Controversies between Royal Governors and Their Assemblies in the Northern American Colonies* (Boston, 1923), 132-3. See also John A. Schutz, *William Shirley, King's Governor of Massachusetts* (Chapel Hill, N.C., 1961), 177.

30. Daniel Fowle, *A Total Eclipse of Liberty* (Boston, 1755), 11-14, 16-20.

31. *Ibid.*, 15, 26, 27; *Journals of the House of Representatives of Massachusetts* (*1754-1755*), (Boston, 1956), XXXI, 63-4; *ibid.*, Part I, XXXII, 10, 23, 58-9.

32. Report of Committee of Council, Dec. 24, 1760, New York Colonial Manuscripts, LXXXIX, 54 (5), New York State Library; *State Trials*, XIV, 503.

33. "Note of Recognizances taken by Mr. Justice Horsmanden relating to illicit trade," John Tabor Kempe Papers, Box "B" (under Augustus Bradley), New York-Historical Society, N.Y.; Manuscript Brief, "The King agt. Waddell Cunningham and Thomas White," 1763, Pleadings, Pl. K 1023, pp. 8, 10, Hall of Records, New York County, N.Y.

34. MS Minute Book of the Supreme Court of Judicature, Oct. 19, 1762, to April 28, 1764, entries for Oct. 28, 1763, pp. 273, 289, Engrossed Minutes, Hall of Records, New York County, N.Y. Trammell v. Thomas, 1 *Harris & McHenry* (Maryland) 261 (1767); see also, Trammell v. Hook, *ibid.*, 259 (1767).

35. See cases cited above, ch. 10, n. 30. For the quotations, Rex v. Cornelius, 2 *Strange* 1210, at 1211 (1744), 93 *Eng. Rep.* 1133, at 1134; Roe dem. Haldane v. Harvey, 4 *Burrow* 2484, at 2489 (1769), 98 *Eng. Rep.* 302, at 305.

36. On the Wilkes case and related prosecutions, see Raymond Postgate, *That Devil Wilkes* (New York, 1929); George Nobbe, *The North Briton* (New York, 1939); George Rudé, *Wilkes and Liberty* (New York, 1962); Robert R. Rea, *The English Press in Politics, 1760-1774* (Lincoln, Neb., 1963); and Pauline Maier, "John Wilkes and American Disillusionment with Britain," *William and Mary Quarterly*, 3rd ser., XX (July 1963), 373-95.

37. [Anon.], *A Letter from Candor to the Public Advertiser* (London, 1764), signed, from "Grays-Inn." I used the third edition, of 1770, available in *A Collection of Interesting Political Tracts*, probably edited by John Almon (London, 1773, 8 vols), I, each tract separately paginated;

the quotation is at pp. 22–3. The first edition of the book by "Father of Candor" bears the title, *An Enquiry into the Doctrine, Lately Propagated, concerning Libels, Warrants, and the Seizure of Papers . . . in a Letter to Mr. Almon from the Father of Candor* (London, 1764). Although I used the first edition, my citations are to the more easily obtainable seventh edition, reprinted in vol. 1 of the same *Collection* in which Candor's book appeared. The seventh edition bears the title, *A Letter Concerning Libels, Warrants, the Seizure of Papers, and Sureties for the Peace of Behaviour* (London, 1771); the quoted matter is at pp. 66–7. *State Trials,* XVII, 726, ascribes the identity of Father of Candor to Lord Chancellor Camden or Lord Ashburton. See also, on the matter of identity, Rea, *The English Press in Politics,* 113, 246, notes 7 and 15. On Father of Candor's contribution to the theory of a free press, see Levy, *Legacy of Suppression,* 148–57.

38. Entick v. Carrington, *State Trials,* XIX, 1029 (1765). Boyd v. U.S., 116 U.S. 616, at 626 (1886).

39. *State Trials,* XIX, at 1038, 1041, 1063, 1073.

40. Boyd v. U.S., 116 U.S. 616, at 633. See also Bram v. U.S., 168 U.S. 532, at 543–4 (1897). For the recent cases joining the Fourth and Fifth Amendments, see Mapp v. Ohio, 367 U.S. 655, at 656–7 (1960), and Malloy v. Hogan, 378 U.S. 1, at 8–9 (1964).

41. See also editorial note in Wroth and Zobel, eds., *Legal Papers of John Adams,* II, 106–23, on the argument on writs of assistance, and Adams's Minutes of the Argument, 1761, in *ibid.,* 123–44. See also Oliver M. Dickerson, "Writs of Assistance as a Cause of the American Revolution," in Richard B. Morris, ed., *The Era of the American Revolution* (New York, 1939), 40–76, and Nelson Lasson, *The History and Development of the Fourth Amendment to the United States Constitution* (Baltimore, 1937), 51–78. The best work on the subject is the unpublished dissertation of Joseph R. Frese, "Writs of Assistance in the American Colonies, 1660–1776" (Harvard College, 1951).

42. Oliver M. Dickerson, *The Navigational Acts and the American Revolution* (Philadelphia, 1951), 230, quoting the *Pennsylvania Journal,* Oct. 19, 1769.

43. Quoted matter from David S. Lovejoy, "Rights Imply Equality: the Case against Admiralty Jurisdiction in America, 1764–1776," *William and Mary Quarterly,* 3rd. ser., XVI (Oct. 1959), 466–7.

44. On Laurens's troubles with the vice admiralty courts, see David Duncan Wallace, *The Life of Henry Laurens* (New York, 1915), 137–49; Dickerson, *Navigation Acts,* 224–31; Carl Ubbelohde, *The Vice Admiralty Courts and the American Revolution* (Chapel Hill, N.C., 1960), 105–14.

45. Henry Laurens, *Extracts from the Proceedings of the Court of Vice-Admiralty in Charles-Town, South-Carolina* (Philadelphia, 1768); I used the 2nd ed., published in Charlestown, 1769. The material on the oath is at pp. 31–3.

46. Sir Egerton Leigh, *The Man Unmasked: Or, the World Undeceived* (Charlestown, 1769), 77–9, 80–81, 86–8, for material on the oath; the line quoted is at p. 77.

47. The case of the *Liberty* is discussed in Dickerson, *Navigation Acts,*

231–45; Ubbelohde, *Vice Admiralty Courts*, 119–27; Wroth and Zobel, *Legal Papers*, II, 173–93. Oliver M. Dickerson, ed., *Boston under Military Rule (1768–1769) as Revealed in* A Journal of the Times (Boston, 1936), 43, 44, 46, 54, 56, 57, 64, 66, 67, 68, 72, 83, 98; the quotation on torture is at p. 72.

48. Adams's argument in "Sewal v. Hancock," in Wroth and Zobel, II, 194–207; the quotation is at p. 207.

49. The quotation is from Dickerson, *Navigation Acts*, 244.

50. Allen is quoted in *ibid.*, 246–7; Dickerson cites Report of John Swift, Collector at Philadelphia, to the Commissioners of Customs, P.R.O., Treasury Papers, I, Bundle 482.

51. Levy, *Legacy of Suppression*, 78–9.

52. Diary entry of Wed., Feb. 7, 1770, William H. W. Sabine, ed., *Historical Memoirs, from 16 March 1763 to 9 July 1776, of William Smith, Historian of the Province of New York* (New York, 1956), 74–5.

53. Levy, 81–2; [William Smith], "Copy of a late letter from an eminent Counsellor," *New-York Gazette: or, the Weekly Post-Boy*, March 19, 1770; William Smith, "Copy of a late letter from an eminent Counsellor," William Smith Papers, Folder #204-9, New York Public Library.

54. *Journal of the Votes and Proceedings of the General Assembly of the Colony of New York, 1769–1771*, P.R.O., Colonial Office Papers, Class 5, Vol. 1219, p. 8 (microfilm). The Assembly proceedings for Dec. 13, 1770, are also available in *New-York Gazette: and the Weekly Mercury*, Dec. 24, 1770.

55. Alexander McDougall, "To The Freeholders," *New-York Gazette: or, the Weekly Post-Boy*, Dec. 24, 1770; *ibid.*, March 25, 1771.

56. *Colonial Laws*, IV, 349–50.

57. Goebel and Naughton, 658, 659; *Colonial Laws*, V, 130, 621, 623; Brown v. Walker, 161 U.S. 591 (1896), and Ullman v. U.S., 350 U.S. 422 (1956).

58. *Colonial Laws*, V, 354, 583–4; III, 757–8.

59. *Ibid.*, V, 237–9, 458, 639, 642, 874; W. L. Grant and James Monroe, *Acts of the Privy Council of England, Colonial Series* (London, 1908–12, 6 vols.), V, 399–400.

Chapter XIII
The Fifth Amendment

1. Mason to George Mercer, Oct. 2, 1778, quoted in Kate Mason Rowland, *The Life of George Mason, 1725–1792* (New York, 1892, 2 vols.), I, 237. See also Robert A. Rutland, *The Birth of the Bill of Rights, 1776–1791* (Chapel Hill, N.C., 1955), 30–44.

2. Sect. 8, Virginia Declaration of Rights, in Francis N. Thorpe, ed., *The Federal and State Constitutions, Colonial Charters, and Other Organic Laws* (Washington, 1909, 7 vols.), VII, 3813 (italics added). William Waller Hening, ed., *The Statutes at Large Being a Collection of All the Laws of Virginia (1619–1792)* (Richmond, 1809–23, 13 vols.), II, 442, for the act of 1677. Richard Starke, *Office and Authority of a Justice of the Peace* (Williamsburg, Va., 1774), 141, 146. See also Hugh F. Rankin, *Criminal Trial Proceedings in the General Court of Virginia* (Charlottesville, Va., 1965), 99, and Arthur P. Scott, *Criminal Law in Colonial Vir-*

ginia (Chicago, 1930), 100. Parties in civil, as well as criminal, cases were incompetent by reason of "interest" to be witnesses in their own behalf, John H. Wigmore, *A Treatise on the Anglo-American System of Evidence in Trials at Common Law* (Boston, 1940, 3rd ed., 10 vols.), II, 681–2, 693–5.

3. Starke, *Office and Authority*, 145, 146. Sir William Blackstone wrote that "no man is to be examined to prove his own infamy" and said that not even a juror could be examined as to "any thing which tends to his disgrace or disadvantage," *Commentaries on the Law of England* (Oxford, 1765–69, 4 vols.), III, 364, 370.

4. In their descriptions of criminal procedure in colonial Virginia, neither Scott, 50–101, nor Rankin, 67–103, makes mention of the defendant's testifying, even unsworn, or being questioned by the prosecution, or saying anything.

5. Rowland, *Mason*, I, 239–41, 437; William T. Hutchinson and William M. E. Rachal, eds., *The Papers of James Madison* (Chicago, 1962 ff., 5 vols.), I, 170–78.

6. Julian P. Boyd *et al.*, eds., *The Papers of Thomas Jefferson* (Princeton, 1950 ff., 17 vols.), I, 341, 348, 359. In a proposed constitution for Virginia, drafted in 1783, Jefferson again omitted the right against self-incrimination, but again included a provision against torture, *ibid.*, VI, 298. He believed that the Declaration of Rights and Constitution of 1776 had the status of an ordinance only because not expressly declared to be superior to statutory law; yet his proposed constitution of 1783 contained no separate bill of rights and few rights that belong in such a document. In practice, the document of 1776 was regarded as fundamental and supreme law, *ibid.*, VI, 279–80.

7. On the committee draft, which is printed in Rowland, I, 436–8, see *The Papers of Madison*, I, 171. The final draft is in Thorpe, ed., *Federal and State Constitutions*, VII, 3812–14.

8. Thorpe, ed., III, 1688 (Maryland); III, 1891 (Massachusetts); IV 2455 (New Hampshire); V, 2787 (North Carolina), 3083 (Pennsylvania); VII, 3471 (Vermont). Thorpe did not include the Delaware Declaration of Rights of 1776; it is available in *Proceedings of the Convention of the Delaware State Held at New-Castle on Tuesday the Twenty-Seventh of August, 1776* (1776, reprinted Wilmington, Del., 1927), 19.

9. Thorpe, ed., V, 2594–8 (New Jersey); V. 2623–38 (New York). Julius Goebel, Jr., and T. Raymond Naughton, *Law Enforcement in Colonial New York: A Study in Criminal Procedure (1664–1776)* (New York. 1944) xvii; see also *ibid.*, 57, 325.

10. Thorpe, ed., II, 777–85 (Georgia); VI, 3248–57 (South Carolina).

11. Edward Dumbauld, "State Precedents for the Bill of Rights," *Journal of Public Law*, VII (1958), 323–44, includes a useful table, at pp. 343–4 showing the rights protected by state declarations of rights. But Dumbauld did not include those states that did not have a separate bill of rights, nor did he include rights guaranteed in the main body of the constitution of those that did have a separate bill. My figures include all states and Vermont. The "Table of Sources of the Provisions of the Bill of Rights" in Dumbauld's handy guide, *The Bill of Rights and What It Means Today* (Norman, Okla., 1957), 160–65, is also incomplete.

12. Thomas Jefferson, *Notes on the State of Virginia*, ed. William Peden

(Chapel Hill, N.C., 1955), 155. See also Leonard W. Levy, *Jefferson and Civil Liberties: The Darker Side* (Cambridge, Mass., 1963), ch. 2.

13. For the Rome case, see David S. Lovejoy, *Rhode Island Politics and the American Revolution, 1760–1776* (Providence, 1958), 174–6, 217 n. 11. For the Virginia incident, see the address of the House of Burgesses to Gov. Dunmore, March 13, 1773, in H. R. McIlwaine and J. P. Kennedy, eds., *Journals of the House of Burgesses of Virginia (1619–1776)* (Richmond, 1905–15, 13 vols.), XIII, 22. See also Rankin, 192–5. Although the Burgesses did not allude in any way to the right against self-incrimination, Pittman, "Colonial and Constitutional History of the Privilege," *Virginia Law Review*, XXI, 786, leaves a contrary impression. On Virginia's treatment of Tories during the Revolution, see Levy, *Jefferson*, ch. 2.

14. Victor Hugo Paltsits, ed., *Minutes of the Commissioners for Detecting and Defeating Conspiracies in the State of New York: Albany County Sessions, 1778–1781* (Albany, 1909, 3 vols.), I, 26. The volumes are filled, *passim*, with instances of individuals being examined under oath against themselves, but the examinations themselves are not given. The *Minutes* refer to "examinations on file," but they could not be located; they were probably burned in the fire of 1911. *The Minutes of the Committee and of the First Commission for Detecting and Defeating Conspiracies in the State of New York (1776–1778)*, New York Historical Society, *Collections* (New York, 1924–25, 2 vols.), contain similar instances. See also Claude H. Van Tyne, *The Loyalists of the American Revolution* (New York, 1902), 271. On André, see Peleg W. Chandler, ed., *American Criminal Trials* (Boston, 1841–44, 2 vols.), II, 168. On Deane, see Statement of Henry Laurens, April 21, 1779, in Edmund C. Burnett, ed., *Letters of the Members of the Continental Congress* (Washington, 1928, 5 vols.), IV, 166 n. 12, 168; *Freeman's Journal, or North-American Intelligencer* (Philadelphia), June 6 and 14, 1781. The *Journals of the Continental Congress* have nothing of relevance.

15. Max Farrand, ed., *The Records of the Federal Convention of 1787* (New Haven, 1911–37, 4 vols.), II, 587–8, 617–18, 628. Rutland, *Birth of the Bill of Rights*, ch. VI, contains a good account of the Convention in relation to civil liberties. On "parchment barriers," see Madison to Jefferson, Oct. 17, 1788, in Boyd, ed., *Papers of Jefferson*, XIV, 19. For illustrations of a similar sentiment among other Virginians, see Jonathan Elliot, ed., *The Debates in the Several State Conventions on the Adoption of the Federal Constitution* (Philadelphia, 1941, 2nd ed. rev., 5 vols.), III, 66, 70 (Randolph); 298 (Pendleton); 450–52 (Nicholas); 223, 561 (Marshall).

16. The quotation is from Hamilton in *The Federalist*, #84 (var. eds.). See also James Wilson, in Elliot, ed., *Debates*, IV, 435 ff., 453 ff. On protections in the main body of the Constitution, see Farrand, ed., *Records*, II, 340–42, 344–50, 375–6, 438, 617–18.

17. The Address of the Minority is in John Bach McMaster and Frederick D. Stone, eds., *Pennsylvania and the Federal Constitution, 1787–1788* (Philadelphia, 1888), 454–83; the duplication of Section 8 is at p. 461.

18. Elliot, ed., *Debates*, II, 111.

19. *Ibid.*, II, 166–70, 177.

20. *Ibid.*, III, 447–8, 451, 452, 593, 658.

21. *Ibid.*, I, 328, for the proposed amendment, and II, 400, 410–13.

22. George Mason to John Lamb, June 9, 1788; Patrick Henry to John Lamb, June 9, 1788; William Grayson to John Lamb, June 9, 1788; John Lamb to Governor Clinton, June 17, 1788; John Lamb to Joshua Atherton, June 6, 1788; Joshua Atherton to John Lamb, June 11, 1788; Rawlins Lowndes to John Lamb, June 21, 1788; Joshua Atherton to John Lamb, June 23, 1788; Timothy Bloodworth to John Lamb, July 1, 1788; Draft "Amendments to the New Constitution of Government" in the hand of Lamb's son-in-law, Charles Tillinghast: all in John Lamb Papers, Box 5, New-York Historical Society. Also, George Mason to John Mason, Sept. 2, Dec. 18, 1788, George Mason Papers, 1766–1788, pp. 245, 249, New York Public Library.

23. "Proceedings of the Convention of the State of New York in a Committee of the Whole," July 7, 1788, John McKesson Papers, Box 3, New-York Historical Society; Gilbert Livingston Papers, Box 2, New York Public Library. On the motives of the Anti-Federalists, see Levy, *Legacy*, 214–37 *passim*.

24. Elliot, ed., *Debates*, IV, 243 (North Carolina); I, 334 (Rhode Island, which ratified June 16, 1790).

25. For the exchange of letters, all in Boyd, ed., *Papers of Jefferson:* Jefferson to Madison, Dec. 20, 1787, XII, 439–40; Jefferson to Madison, July 31, 1788, XIII, 442–3; Madison to Jefferson, Oct. 17, 1788, XIV, 18–21; Madison to Jefferson, Dec. 8, 1788, XIV, 340; Jefferson to Madison, March 15, 1789, XIV, 659–61; Jefferson to Madison, Aug. 28, 1789, XV, 367–8. Speeches of Madison, June 8 and August 17, 1789, *Debates and Proceedings in the Congress of the United States* (Washington, 1834 ff.), 1st Congress, 1st Session, 431–42, 755; the quotation about judicial review is at p. 439. The latter source is commonly cited by its bookbinder's title, *Annals of Congress*.

26. Ames to Thomas Dwight, June 11, 1789, Seth Ames, ed., *The Works of Fisher Ames* (Boston, 1854, 2 vols.), I, 52–3, See also Levy, *Legacy*, 228–33.

27. Speech of Madison, June 8, 1789, *Annals of Congress*, I, 434. Madison's proposed amendment, "No State shall violate the equal rights of conscience, or the freedom of the press, or the trial by jury in criminal cases," was also original with him, *ibid.*, I, 435. Although no state had a "due process of law" clause in its constitution, several had a "law of the land" clause that was the equivalent.

28. In England, civil parties were not qualified to give testimony until an act of 1851; in the United States, Connecticut was the first state, in 1849, to abolish the incompetency of civil parties. Wigmore, *Evidence*, VIII, 695. For a different interpretation of Madison's proposed amendment that no person should be a witness against himself, see Lewis Mayers, *Shall We Amend the Fifth Amendment?* (New York, 1959), 201, 320 n. 41. Mayers assaults the policy of the right against self-incrimination and answers his title-question affirmatively. His historical background is skimpy and littered with factual errors; the American material is based mainly on Pittman's unreliable article (see above, ch. 11, n. 2) and the English mate-

rial mainly on Wigmore. Sometimes Mayers seems to base his historical background on thin air and perverse logic. His interest, however, is not in history but in the recent controversy surrounding the Fifth Amendment. Mayers admits that the "common law rule as it then existed, and as it continues to be applied to this day even in states in which the privilege enjoys no constitutional protection [only Iowa and New Jersey], covers a witness in every legal proceeding, civil as well as criminal." Yet Mayers alleges, without a shred of proof, that "to lawyers of that generation the words *against himself* applied only to a party and not to a witness. . . ." He is therefore able to argue, "The assumption is sometimes made that the use of the word 'witness' indicates that the witness was intended to be included. On the contrary, the exemption from being compelled to 'be a witness' is precisely the privilege of the accused, but *not* the privilege of the witness, who *can* be compelled to 'be a witness' but may not be compelled to 'give evidence' incriminating himself." See also Mayers, "The Federal Witness' Privilege against Self-Incrimination: Constitutional or Common Law?," *American Journal of Legal History*, IV (April 1960), 111–12. The error in Mayers's argument is that he either ignores the words "against himself" or assumes incorrectly and inconsistently that "against himself" meant one thing in the case of a party and another in the case of a witness. For early cases on the words "against himself," see note 35 below.

29. The amendments reported by the House Select Committee, July 28, 1789, are printed in *Documentary History of the Constitution of the United States of America, 1786–1870* (Washington, 1894–1905, 5 vols.), V, 186–9. In the appendices to his *Bill of Rights and What It Means Today*, Dumbauld has very conveniently brought together the amendments as proposed by Madison, as reported by the committee of the House, as passed by the House, as passed by the Senate, as agreed to after the deliberations of a joint conference committee and proposed by Congress to the states, 206–22. For Laurence's remarks, *Annals of Congress*, Aug. 17, 1789, I, 753. Mayers erroneously states that the motion to amend was adopted "by unanimous consent." The vote on the motion to amend is not given in the *Annals*. The members of the House Select Committee who had been members of the Federal Convention were Madison, Sherman of Connecticut, Abraham Baldwin of Georgia, Nicholas Gilman of New Hampshire, and George Clymer of Pennsylvania.

30. Charles Warren, "New Light on the History of the Federal Judiciary Act of 1789," *Harvard Law Review*, XXXVII (Nov. 1923), 111, 116, 118, 120, 122, 130 n. 177. [Edgar S. Maclay, ed.], *The Journal of William Maclay, United States Senator from Pennsylvania, 1789–1791*, intro. by Charles Beard (New York, 1927), 90–92, entries for June 29 and June 30, 1789. Richard Peters, ed., *The Public Statutes at Large of the United States of America* (Boston, 1861 ff.), I, 82, for the Judiciary Act of 1789, sect. 15.

31. Geyger's Lessee v. Geyger, 2 *Dallas* (Circ. Ct., Pa.) 332, at 333 (1795). On the non-compellability of the party opponent in a civil suit at common law and his compellability, by bill of discovery, to testify and produce documents in chancery cases, see Wigmore, *Evidence*, 168–74. The insight explaining Laurence's probable purpose in introducing the

motion to amend comes from an unsigned law note, "Applicability of Privilege against Self-Incrimination to Legislative Investigations," *Columbia Law Review*, XLIX (Jan. 1949), 87, at 92–3. For early precedents, see the cases cited, above, in ch. 10, n. 30. For a later case showing the rule applying the right against self-incrimination to the production of documents in civil cases, see Chetwind v. Marnell, 1 *Bosenquet & Puller's English Common Pleas Reports* 271 (1798). See also note 35, below, for cases extending the right against self-incrimination to civil witnesses whose answers could not incriminate them.

32. *Cf.* Mayers, "The Federal Witness' Privilege," *American Journal of Legal History*, IV, 116–17, who asserts that the Fifth Amendment was intended to protect the criminal defendant only, and argues that all of the clauses of the amendment that concern criminal proceedings, *"other than the self-incrimination clause"*—indictment by grand jury, no double jeopardy, and the due process clause—"protect the accused against executive oppression before the trial" (my italics). He adds that the only provision of the amendment not relating to criminal proceedings, the one guaranteeing just compensation in eminent domain cases, "is also a protection against *executive* action." But the power of eminent domain is essentially a legislative power; the due process clause applies to non-criminal proceedings; all of the Fifth Amendment rights were intended, primarily, to secure the people against legislative and judicial oppression; and none of the amendment's clauses, excepting the one relating to indictment by grand jury, are restrictive in operation to pre-trial proceedings. As for Mayers's main thesis, that the self-incrimination clause was intended to extend only to the criminally accused and not to a witness, early federal cases, cited in note 35, below, indicate otherwise, as does my argument at this point in the text above. Mayers sharply distinguishes, however, between the constitutional protection and that of the common law.

33. See Mitchell Franklin, "The Encyclopédiste Origin and Meaning of the Fifth Amendment," *Lawyers Guild Review*, XV (Summer 1955), 41–62. Franklin, on wholly different grounds, contends that the Fifth Amendment was intended to protect against self-infamy as well as self-incrimination. His article was cited approvingly by Justice Douglas, dissenting, in Ullmann v. U.S., 350 U.S. 422, 450–53 (1956). But Franklin's argument, that the Bill of Rights generally and the Fifth Amendment in particular is of French origin, a *précis* of Encyclopédiste theory, is a baseless concoction that defies the overwhelming evidence of English origins. He proves that Jefferson read Beccaria and then assumes that Jefferson had an influence in the framing of the Fifth Amendment, though he had none. The article is a tissue of presuppositions supported by a vast amount of irrelevant, anachronistic, and strained evidence.

34. Respublica v. Gibbs, 3 *Yeates* (Pa.) 429, at 437 (1802). See also Galbreath v. Eichelberger, 3 *Yeates* (Pa.) 515 (1803); Bell's Case, 1 *Browne* (Pa.) 376 (1811).

35. For state cases showing that the common-law right protected against self-infamy, as in the Pennsylvania cases cited in the note above, see State v. Bailly, 2 N.J. 396 (1807); Vaughn v. Perrine, 3 N.J. 299, at 303 (1811); Miller v. Crayon, 2 *Brevard* (S.C.) 108 (1806); and People v. Herrick, 13 *Johnson* (N.Y.) 82 (1816). The English courts at this time

were still applying the same rule; see Rex v. Lewis, 4 *Espinasse* 225, at 226 (1802), 170 *Eng. Rep.* 700, and Macbride v. Macbride, 4 *Espinasse* 242, at 243 (1802), 170 *Eng. Rep.* 706. However, an English treatise of 1801 cast doubt on the continuing validity of the broad proposition that compulsory self-infamation or self-disgrace was illegal. The author carefully defined the rule as having insured that "a witness shall not be rendered *infamous*, or even *disgraced* by his own examination, as to facts not connected with the cause in which he is examined," and added that the bench was divided on the point, Thomas Peake, *A Compendium of the Law of Evidence* (London, 1801), 129-30, and (London, 1813, 4th ed.), 143-4. The leading American case showing the subsequent repudiation of the claim that the Fifth Amendment protects against compulsory self-infamy is Brown v. Walker, 161 U.S. 591 (1892). See also Wigmore, *Evidence*, IV, sect. 2255, pp. 836-9, in the 2nd ed., and the same section in the 3rd ed., VIII, 332-3, and also, III, sects. 984-7; VIII, sect. 2215. For the earliest federal case applying the right against self-incrimination to a witness, see U.S. v. Goosley, Case No. 15,230 in 25 *Fed. Cases* (Circ. Ct., Va.) 1363, at 1364 (undated, but sometime in the 1790's; Iredell died 1799). Marbury v. Madison, 1 *Cranch* (U.S.) 137, at 144 (1803). See also, U.S. v. Burr, In re Willie, Case No. 14,692e, in 25 *Fed. Cases* (Circ. Ct., Va.) 38, at 39-41 (1807). See also, Zephaniah Swift, *A System of the Laws of the State of Connecticut* (Windham, Conn., 1795-96, 2 vols.), II, 239, and the references to the works by Martin, Hening, and Wyche, above, ch. 12, n. 7. There are dozens of early state cases in which the right against self-incrimination was extended to a witness even in civil suits where the questions asked might, if answered truthfully, "supply a link in the chain, which would lead to a conviction for a crime." See Grannis v. Branden, 5 *Day* (Conn.) 260, at 272-4 (1812), where the court quoted the *nemo tenetur* maxim. Some of the early state decisions in favor of the right were far-fetched, in effect taking literally the principle that a witness did not have to answer questions "against himself," whether or not his answers might incriminate him. That is, the right was illogically extended to witnesses in civil cases to protect them against answering questions that could not incriminate them but might injure their civil interests. One federal case was similar, Carne v. McLane, Case No. 2,416, in 5 *Fed. Cases* (Circ. Ct., D.C.), 89 (1806). In Simons v. Payne, 2 *Root* (Conn.) 406 (1796), the witness was "not obliged to testify against his interest as a bondsman." In Starr v. Tracy, 2 *Root* (Conn.) 528, at 529 (1797), the new rule was broadly given that "a witness is not obliged to disclose what will make against him." See also Connor v. Bradey, *Anthon's Nisi Prius Reports* (N.Y.) 135, at 136 (1809), extending the right to the witness though his answer to the question, revealing usury, would have exposed him "to civil injury only." In Tennessee the court acknowledged that the constitutional provision referred only to criminal cases, neglecting to notice that it also referred only to the "accused"; nevertheless the court declared, "but we think the principle existed previous to the Constitution" and applied it to a witness in a civil case who refused to answer on ground that his answer would be prejudicial to his interest civilly, Cook v. Corn, 1 *Overton* (Tenn.) 340, at 341 (1808). In Bell's Case, 1 *Browne* (Pa.) 376 (1811), the court said, "I have always overruled a question that would affect a witness *civilly*, or subject him to a *criminal prosecution:* I have gone farther; and where the answer to a question would cover the witness with infamy or shame, I have refused to compel him to answer it." But in Baird v. Cochran, 4 *Sergeant & Rawle* (Pa.) 397, at 400 (1818), the preceding case was in effect overruled on the point that the witness need not answer against his interest civilly; however, the court construed the constitutional provision, which referred only to the accused in criminal prosecutions, to apply to witnesses and to questions the answers to which "may degrade him in the public opinion" or reveal "something criminal, penal, or infamous, and not barely to matter of interest." For similar holdings, now the general rule, that the witness must answer questions against his interest though exposing himself to a civil suit, see Taney v. Kemp, 4 *Harris & Johnson* (Md.) 348 (1818), and Planters' Bank v. George, 6 *Martin O.S.* (La.) 670 (1819).

36. For the 1790 Pennsylvania formulation, see Thorpe, ed., V, 3100. Delaware also, in adopting a new constitution, in 1792, made the clause refer to "the accused," *ibid.,* I, 569. Abe Fortas, "The Fifth Amendment: *Nemo Tenetur Prodere Seipsum,*" Cleveland Bar Association, *The Journal,* XXV (April 1954), 91, at 98–100, *passim.*

37. The first quotation is from Chief Judge Calvert Magruder, in Maffie v. U.S., 209 Fed. 2nd 225, at 237 (1954); the second, from Justice Frankfurter, in Ullmann v. U.S., 350 U.S. 422, at 427 (1956). See also, to the same effect, Quinn v. U.S., 349 U.S. 155, at 161 (1955).

Appendix

1. I used the Soncino edition of *The Babylonian Talmud,* ed. by I. Epstein *et al.* (London, 1935 ff.). The volumes are not numbered consecutively. All editions of the Talmud contain the original folio references; the standard practice in Hebrew scholarship is to cite by abbreviated reference to "tractate" and folio. That can be a loose practice, because the tractate reference is useless unless one knows the "order" in which it belongs; moreover, the folio reference may spread over several printed pages. *E.g., Kethuboth* 18b, (tractate and folio) appears in a volume whose spine and title page give only the order, *Seder Nashim,* while *Baba Kamma* and *Baba Mezi'a* both appear in a volume whose spine and title page refer only to *Seder Nezikin.* For the benefit of those, like myself, who have never before used the Talmud, I give expanded citations. For a useful introduction to the Talmud, see the Forward by J. H. Hertz to *Nezikin: Baba Kamma,* xiii-xxviii. The first volume of each order also contains an introduction by the general editor, I. Epstein, and each tractate is introduced also by its own editor. Also helpful was Herman L. Strack, *Introduction to the Talmud and Midrash* (New York, 1959: authorized translation of the last revision of a book originally published in Germany, 1887); a pamphlet by Charles Auerbach, *The Talmud: A Gateway to the Common Law* (Cleveland, 1952); a superb book, George Horowitz, *The Spirit of Jewish Law* (New York, 1953); and Hyman E. Goldin, *Hebrew Criminal Law and Procedure* (New York, 1952). *Nezikin: Sanhedrin,* chs. 3–6, describes procedure. *Sanhedrin* 37b, p. 235, gives the quotation on "conjecture," or circumstantial evidence. On the need for certainty of guilt and exact consistency in the evidence, *ibid.,* 41a, p. 266.

2. The Hebrew maxim, for which I have given the English transliteration,

is the subject-entry of an indispensable, brief article in the Hebrew *Entsiklopediyah Talmudit (Talmudic Encyclopedia: On Matters of Law)*, eds. Mayer Berlin and Solomon Joseph Zevin (Tel Aviv, 1951, 3rd ed., 12 vols., in progress), I, 355-6. Mr. Sheldon R. Brunswick, formerly Semitics Librarian of Brandeis University, translated it for me. The phrase "no one can incriminate himself" appears in *Nezikin: Sanhedrin* 9b, p. 39; see also, *Nezikin: Baba Kamma* 44b, pp. 374, 375, and 75a, p. 429. On Anglo-American law, see John H. Wigmore, *A Treatise on the Anglo-American System of Evidence in Trials at Common Law* (Boston, 1940, 3rd ed., 10 vols.), VIII (rev. 1961 by John T. McNaughton), sect. 2276, pp. 456-62.

3. Talmudic references to the right against self-incrimination, with appropriate cases or illustrations, appear in *Nashim: Yebamoth* 25b, p. 154; *Nashim: Kethuboth* 18b, p. 102, and 41a, p. 228; *Nezikin: Sanhedrin* 9b, p. 39; *Nezikin: Baba Kamma* 64b, pp. 374-5, and 74b-75a, pp. 428-35; *Nezikin: Makkoth* 2b, pp. 5, 7. An example of the right being carried to an extreme is the case of a rabbi who accidentally blinded his heathen slave in one eye. The rabbi, who was prohibited by law from freeing the slave, rejoiced at the accident, because the law now required him to free the slave, as well as pay a fine, for harming him. But the court rejected the rabbi's confession of his guilt, and there being no witnesses for the slave, he was not set free. *Baba Kamma* 74b, p. 428. For the maxim that the admission of the civil defendant "is equal to the testimony of a hundred witnesses," *Nezikin: Baba Mezi'a* 3b, p. 9. On the questioning of the accused and double jeopardy, *Sanhedrin* 32b-33b, pp. 206-11.

4. *Baba Kamma* 75b, pp. 431-2; *ibid.*, 64b, pp. 374-5, and 75a, p. 429.

5. Goldin, *Hebrew Criminal Law*, 220-42, on "Refuted Witnesses." *Baba Kamma* 72b-75b, pp. 414-35; *Sanhedrin* 9b, p. 39, and 24b, p. 142 n. 4; *Nashim: Yebamoth* 25b, p. 154.

6. *Nashim: Kethuboth* 41a, p. 228; *Baba Kamma* 74b-75b, pp. 426-35. *Talmudic Encyclopedia*, I, 356.

7. *The Code of Maimonides: Book Fourteen, The Book of Judges*, trans. by Abraham M. Hershman (New Haven, 1949), 52-3.

8. Rosh (Asher ben Yihiel) is quoted in Simcha Mendelbaum, "The Privilege against Self-Incrimination in Anglo-American and Jewish Law," *American Journal of Comparative Law*, V (Winter 1956), p. 117, citing only *Responsae Rosh* (1250-1328). David Ibn Zimra is quoted in George Horowitz, "The Privilege against Self-Incrimination: How Did It Originate?," *Temple Law Quarterly*, XXXI (Winter 1958), at note 68, pp. 141-2, citing no authority; the same statement by David Ibn Zimra, again given without citation to the source, appears in paraphrase by Haim H. Cohn, "The Privilege against Self-Incrimination: Israel," *Journal of Criminal Law, Criminology and Political Science*, LI (July-Aug. 1960), pp. 177-8.

9. The remark by Wigmore appears in the 2nd ed. (1923) of his *Evidence*, cited above, IV, 819. The first quotation from the Supreme Court is from the opinion of Justice Moody in Twining v. New Jersey, 211 U.S. 78, at 91 (1908); the second is from the opinion of Chief Justice Warren in Miranda v. Ariz., 384 U.S. 436, at 458 (1966). Footnote 27 to Warren's statement also includes a reference to Norman Lamm, "The Fifth Amendment and Its Equivalent in the Halakhah," *Judaism: A Quarterly Journal*, V (Winter 1956), 53-9. Rabbi Lamm's article, which refers only to *San-*

hedrin 9b and *Kethuboth* 18b, is mainly a psychological analysis of Maimonides' statement, comparing his insights with those of Freud, Menninger, and Fromm. The same article, which praises Justice Douglas as "a great legal thinker," was quoted at length by Justice Douglas in Garrity v. N.J., 87 Sup. Ct. 616, at 619, note 8 (1967). Of the various articles which have appeared, showing the origin of the right in Talmudic law, Lamm's appears to be a quixotic choice for the Court to honor in splendid isolation. Any of the three articles cited in note 8, above, would have been more to the point, especially the one by Haim H. Cohn, a member of the Supreme Court of Israel and formerly both attorney-general and minister of justice. The pioneering article, in English, showing the origins of the right in the Talmud, is Louis N. Dembitz, "Accusatory and Inquisitorial Procedure," *The Jewish Encyclopedia*, ed. by I. Singer (New York, 1901 ff., 12 vols.), I, 163–4.

10. For a recent discussion of Old Testament influences on Massachusetts colonial law, see George Lee Haskins, *Law and Authority in Early Massachusetts* (New York, 1960), 124–6, 141–62. On the Hebrew requirement at Harvard, Samuel Eliot Morison, *The Intellectual Life of Colonial New England* (Ithaca, N.Y., 1956), 45; the quotation is from Morison, *Harvard College in the Seventeenth Century* (Cambridge, Mass., 1936, 2 vols.), I, 200.

11. The quotation is from Morison, *Founding of Harvard College* (Cambridge, Mass., 1935), 75. Sketches of the various English Hebraists appear in the *Dictionary of National Biography*. See also Horowitz, "Privilege against Self-Incrimination," 136–40, which includes Selden's quotations from Maimonides. The article by Horowitz, though very useful, is padded, misleading, and strains its evidence. He argues that the common-law right against self-incrimination derived from Hebraic sources. Curiously he offers for the Talmudic source of the right only a citation to *Baba Kamma* 74b. His proof that many of the Puritan leaders were so learned that they knew Latin "and even Greek" is quite irrelevant, as is their knowledge of Hebrew unless it also be proved that they read not only the Old Testament but the Talmud, particularly the sections referring to the right, and that they cited it. Only Selden did.

12. Horowitz, "Privilege against Self-Incrimination," 140.

BIBLIOGRAPHY

I. Manuscripts

Alexander, James. Papers. New-York Historical Society.

"Answer of the Judges." British Museum, Hargrave MSS, #237, folios 91–95b.

Bradford, William. "The Examination of Wm. Bradford before Governour Blackwell att Philadelphia the 9th of the 2nd Month 1689, concerning printing the Charter." Miscellaneous Bradford Papers, New-York Historical Society.

Burde, William. "A Treatise touching matters Ecclesiasticall." British Museum, Harleian MSS, #763, item 3, folios 172–96.

Cases in the Court of High Commission, 6 and 8 Jac. I. British Museum, Stowe MSS, #424, folios 158–64.

"Chronology of Eminent Persons, 1534–95." Dr. Williams Library, London.

"Collectanea de Potestate Ecclesiastica." British Museum, Cotton MSS, Cleopatra F. I, 32 items, 455 folios. Contains Beale's "A Collection," Morice's "Brief Treatise," several papers on the oath *ex officio* and others on prohibitions, some by Sir Edward Coke. Individual items are cited in footnotes.

"Collectanea de Potestate Ecclesiastica." British Museum, Cotton MSS, Cleopatra F. II (microfilm available in the Library of Congress), 90 items, 478 folios. Like the collection in Cleopatra F. I, this contains many papers on the jurisdiction and procedures of the ecclesiastical courts, including items by Coke and on the oath *ex officio*. Individual items are cited in footnotes.

Cotton, Isaac. "The Methodicall Prosecution of causes in the High Court of Star Chamber," 1622. British Museum, Stowe MSS, #418, 149 folios.

"An Exact Copie of the Record of Nicholas Fullers case of Grayes Inne Esq. Termino Trin. Anno 5 Jac. Regis." British Museum, Landsdowne MSS, #1172, folios 97–106.

Journal of the Votes and Proceedings of the General Assembly of the Colony of New York, 1769–1771. Colonial Office Papers, Class 5, vol. 1219, Public Records Office, London.

"The Judges answers to the severall Greevances against Prohibitions." British Museum, Hargrave MSS, #33, folios 112–16.

Kempe, John Taber. "The King agt. Waddel Cunningham and Thomas White." Pleadings, Pl. K 1023, Hall of Records, New York County, N.Y.

———. Papers. New-York Historical Society.

Lamb, John. Papers. New-York Historical Society.

Livingston, Gilbert. Papers. New York Public Library.
McKesson, John. Papers. New-York Historical Society.
Mason, George. Papers, 1766–1788. New York Public Library.
Minute Book of the Supreme Court of Judicature, Oct. 19, 1762 to April 28, 1764. Engrossed Minutes, Hall of Records, New York County, N.Y.
Minutes of the Governor and Council of New York Province, vol. VIII. New York State Library, Albany.
"Mr. Barrowe his examination," 1588. British Museum, Harleian MSS, #6848, item 3, folios 14–18a. Number 6848 is a large collection containing many items on the Separatists. Numbers 6849 and 7042 include many related documents.
Morice, James. "A Remembrance of Certeine Matters concerninge the Clergeye and theire Jurisdiccion," 1593. Cambridge University, Baker MSS, 40, Mm. 1. 51, folios 105–34.
Morrìce MSS, Vol. A ("Loose Papers"), Vol. B ("Seconde Parte of a Register"), and Vol. C ("Transcript"). Dr. Williams Library, London.
"A new Discovery of the singuler Jurisdiccion of the high Courte of Starre-Chamber," 1636. British Museum, Harleian MSS, #6448, 50 folios.
New York Colonial Manuscripts (103 vols.), LXXXIX. New York State Library, Albany.
"The Ordinary Course of Proceedings in causes pending in her Majesty's most honourable Court of Star Chambr." British Museum, Hargrave MSS, #482, folios 1–5.
"Remarques Upon History, 1546–1640." Dr. Williams Library, London.
Smith, William. Papers. New York Public Library.
State Papers Domestic, Charles I. Vols. 261, 324, 373, 434, and 450. Public Records Office, London.
State Papers Domestic, Elizabeth. Vols. 60, 71, 238, and 244. Public Records Office, London.
"A Treatise made by a Burgess of the house to use in Parliament, manifestly proving that the proceedings of the L. Archbishop of Canterbury against poore ministers is unlawful." British Museum, Additional Manuscripts 48116, folios 144–99. Folios 1–41 include Beale's "Book respecting Ceremonies."
"Treatise of Prohibitions with the Arguments pro and contra betweene the Lord Archbishop of Canterburie & Sir Edward Cooke." British Museum, Cotton MSS, Faustina D VI, 145 folios. Signed, Robert Wyseman, 6 April 1641.
Trial of Vaux and others before the Star Chamber. British Museum, Harleian MSS, #589, items 4 and 5, folios 44–51. See entry, below, for John Bruce, listing printed transcription.

II. Printed Primary Sources

To save space, the records of all court reports, both English and American, have been omitted. All English cases, including those by Bulstrode, Coke, Croke, Dyer, and many others cited in this book, are available in *English Reports*. Full Reprint Series (London, 1900–1930), 176 vols. American cases from the 1790's on are available in the various federal and state sets of reports cited in the footnotes. Colonial legal materials, whose location is not so obvious, are included in the following bibliography. References to "S.T.C." indicate a microfilm copy of an entry in A. W. Pollard, G. R. Redgrave, *et al.*, eds., *A Short-Title Catalogue* . . . , listed in Secondary Sources below.

Acts and Resolves, Public and Private, of the Province of Massachusetts Bay (1692–1786) 21 vols. Boston, 1869–1922.

Adams, Charles Francis, ed. *Antinomianism in the Colony of Massachusetts Bay, 1636–1638. Including the Short Story and Other Documents.* Boston, 1894.

Adams, George Burton, and H. Morse Stephens, eds. *Select Documents of English Constitutional History.* New York, 1929.

(Adams, John.) *Legal Papers of John Adams,* ed. by L. Kinvin Wroth and Hiller B. Zobel. 3 vols. Cambridge, Mass., 1965.

(Ames, Fisher.) *The Works of Fisher Ames,* ed. by Seth Ames. 2 vols. Boston, 1854.

(Anon.) "Applicability of Privilege against Self-Incrimination to Legislative Investigations," *Columbia Law Review,* XLIX (Jan. 1949), 87–96.

(Anon.) *A Collection of Interesting Political Tracts.* 8 vols. London, 1773.

(Anon.) *An Enquiry into the Doctrine, Lately Propagated, concerning Libels, Warrants, and the Seizure of Papers . . . in a Letter to Mr. Almon from the Father of Candor.* London, 1764.

(Anon.) *A Guide to the Knowledge of the Rights and Privileges of Englishmen.* London, 1757.

(Anon.) *A Letter Concerning Libels, Warrants, the Seizure of Papers, and Sureties for the Peace of Behavior* (London, 1771), in *A Collection of Interesting Political Tracts.* London, 1773. Vol. I.

(Anon.) *A Letter from Candor to the Public Advertiser.* London, 1764.

(Anon.) *A Narrative of a New and Unusual American Imprisonment of Two Presbyterian Ministers: and Prosecution of Mr. Francis Makemie. By a Learner of Law, and a Lover of Liberty* (1707), in Peter Force, ed., *Tracts and Other Papers,* IV.

Aquinas, Saint Thomas. *The "Summa Theologica" of St. Thomas Aquinas,* trans. Fathers of the English Dominican Province. 22 vols. London and New York, 1912–29.

Arber, Edward, ed. *The First Printed English New Testament. Translated by William Tyndale.* (Facsimile Text of the 1525 edition.) London, 1871.

——. *An Introductory Sketch to the Martin Marprelate Controversy, 1588–1590.* London, 1879.

Atkinson, E. G., ed. *Close Rolls of the Reign of Henry III, 1247–51.* London, 1922.

(Atwood, William.) "The Case of William Atwood, Esq." (1703), in *New-York Historical Society Collections.* New York, 1881. XIII, 263–81.

Augustinus, Saint Aurelius. *The City of God.* New York, 1945.

Babylonian Talmud, ed. I. Epstein *et al.* London, 1935 ff.

Bacon, Matthew. *A New Abridgment of the Law.* 4 vols. Savoy, Eng., 1731–59.

Bale, John. *Select Works, containing the Examination of Lord Cobham,*

William Thorpe, and Anne Askewe, ed. by Henry Christmas. Cambridge, Eng., 1849.

Bancroft, Richard. *Daungerous Positions and Proceedings, published and practised within this Iland of Brytaine, under pretense of Reformation, and for the Presbiteriall Discipline.* London, 1593.

(Barrow, Henry.) *The Writings of Henry Barrow 1587–1590,* ed. Leland H. Carlson. London, 1962.

Bartlett, John Russell, ed. *Records of the Colony of Rhode Island and Providence Plantations in New England (1636–1792).* 10 vols. Providence, 1856–65.

Barton, R. T., ed. *Virginia Colonial Decisions: Reports by Sir John Randolph and by Edward Barradall of Decisions of the General Court of Virginia, 1728–1741.* Boston, 1909.

Bate, Randal. *Certain Observations of that Reverend, religious and faithful servant of God, and glorious Martyr of Jesus Christ, M. Randal Bate, which were part of his daily meditations in the time of his sufferings, whilst he was prisoner in the Gatehouse at Westminster* (1613). S.T.C. #1580, Reel 873.

Bayne, C. G., and William H. Dunham, eds. *Select Cases in the Council of Henry VII.* (Selden Society Publications, vol. LXXV.) London, 1958.

Beverley, Robert. *The History and Present State of Virginia,* ed. by Louis B. Wright. Chapel Hill, N.C., 1947.

Blackstone, Sir William. *Commentaries on the Law of England.* 4 vols. Oxford, 1765–69.

Bond, Carroll T., ed., with Richard B. Morris. *Proceedings of the Maryland Court of Appeals, 1695–1729.* Washington, 1933.

Bond, Maurice F., ed. *Manuscript of the House of Lords, Addenda 1514–1714.* (Historical Manuscripts Commission, new series, vol. XI.) London, 1962.

The Book of the General Laws for the People within the Jurisdiction of Connecticut, ed. George Brinely. Cambridge, Mass., 1673. Reprinted; Hartford, 1865.

The Boston Post-Boy, 1753.

Bouton, Nathaniel, *et al.,* eds. *Documents and Records Relating to the Province of New Hampshire.* 34 vols. Concord, N.H., 1867 ff.

(Bradford, William.) *Bradford's History "Of Plimoth Plantation." From the Original Manuscript.* Boston, 1898.

(Bradshaw, William.) *English Puritanisme Containening the maine opinions of the rigidest sort of those that are called Puritanes* (1605). S.T.C. #3516, Reel 627.

Brown, Alexander, ed. *The Genesis of the United States . . . A Series of Historical Manuscripts now first printed, Together with a Reissue of Rare Contemporaneous Tracts.* 2 vols. Boston, 1890.

Browne, William Hand, *et al.,* eds. *Archives of Maryland.* 70 vols. Baltimore, 1883 ff.

Browning, Andrew, ed. *English Historical Documents 1660–1714.* New York, 1953.

Bruce, John, ed. *Letters of Queen Elizabeth and King James VI of Scotland.* (Camden Society Publications, XLVI.) London, 1849.

———. "Narrative of Proceedings in the Star-Chamber against lord Vaux, sir Thomas Tresham, sir William Catesby, and others, for a contempt in refusing to swear that they had not harbored Campion the Jesuit," *Archaeologia: or, Miscellaneous Tracts Relating to Antiquity*, XXX (London, 1844), 64–110.

Bruce, John and Thomas T. Perowne, eds. *Correspondence of Matthew Parker*. Cambridge, Eng., 1853.

Burlamaqui, J. J. *The Principles of Natural and Political Law*, trans. by T. Nugent. 2 vols. London, 1763.

(Burn, Richard.) *An Abridgment of Burn's Justice of the Peace*. Boston, 1773.

Burr, George Lincoln, ed. *Narratives of the Witchcraft Cases, 1648–1706*. New York, 1914.

Burrage, Champlin. *The Early English Dissenters in the Light of Recent Research*, 2 vols. Cambridge, Eng., 1912.

———. *John Penry, the So-Called Martyr of Congregationalism as Revealed in the Original Record of His Trial and in Documents Thereto*. London, 1913.

Burton, Henry. *An apology of an appeale*. London, 1636. S.T.C. #4135, Reel 707.

Calendar of Council Minutes, 1668–1783, ed. B. Fernow. New York State Library *Bulletin 58* (March 1902), History 6 (Albany, 1902).

Calendar of State Papers Domestic. 12 vols. London, 1856–72.

Candler, Allen D., ed. *Colonial Records of the State of Georgia*. 26 vols. Atlanta, 1905–16.

———. *Revolutionary Records of the State of Georgia (1769–1784)*. 3 vols. Atlanta, 1908.

Capes, W. W., ed. *The Register of John Trefnant, Bishop of Hereford, A.D. 1389–1404*. Hereford, Eng., 1914.

Cardwell, Edward, ed. *Documentary Annals of the Reformed Church of England (1546–1716)*. 2 vols. Oxford, 1839–44.

———. *Synodalia, A Collection of Articles of Religion, Canons and Proceedings of Convocations*. 2 vols. Oxford, 1842.

Care, Henry. *English Liberties, or the Free born Subject's Inheritance*. 5th ed. Boston, 1721.

"Charges Against Governor Nicholson," *Virginia Magazine of History and Biography*, III (1896), 373–82.

Coke, Sir Edward. *The Second Part of the Institutes of the Laws of England, Containing the Exposition of Many Ancient and Other Statutes Published with The Third Part . . . Concerning High Treason, and other Pleas of the Crown and Criminal Causes, and with The Fourth Part . . . Concerning the Jurisdiction of Courts*. 3 vols. London, 1817.

Colonial Records of Pennsylvania, 1683–1790. 16 vols. Philadelphia, 1852–60.

Commissioners of Statutory Revision. *The Colonial Laws of New York from the Year 1664 to the Revolution*. 5 vols. Albany, 1894.

Conductor Generalis, or the Office, Duty and Authority of Justices of the Peace (attributed to James Parker). Philadelphia, 1722. Various editions.

Cooper, Samuel. *The Crisis*. Boston, 1754.

Cosin, Richard. *An Apologie for Sundrie Proceedings Ecclesiasticall.* 2nd ed. London, 1593. S.T.C. 5821, Reel 210.

Dalton, Michael. *The Countrey Justice, Containing the Practice of the Justices of the Peace out of their Sessions.* London, 1618. Various editions.

Davis, C. H. *The English Church Canons of 1604, with Historical Introduction, and Notes.* London, 1869.

Davis, J. *The Office and Authority of a Justice of the Peace.* Newbern, N.C., 1774.

Debates and Proceedings in the Congress of the United States (Annals of Congress). Washington, 1834 ff. Vol. I.

D'Ewes, Simonds, ed. *The Journals of All the Parliaments during the Reign of Queen Elizabeth,* rev. by Paul Bowes. London, 1682.

Dexter, Franklin B., ed. *New Haven Town Records, 1649–1684.* 2 vols. New Haven, 1917–19.

———, ed. "A Report of the Trial of Mrs. Anne Hutchinson before the Church in Boston, 1638," *Proceedings,* Massachusetts Historical Society, 2nd ser., IV (1889), 159–91.

Dickerson, Oliver M., ed. *Boston under Military Rule (1768–1769) as Revealed in* A Journal of the Times. Boston, 1936.

Documentary History of the Constitution of the United States of America, 1786–1870. Derived from Records, Manuscripts and Rolls Deposited in the Bureau of Rolls and Library of the Department of State. 5 vols. Washington, 1894–1905.

Dow, George W., ed. *Records and Files of the Quarterly Courts of Essex County, Massachusetts.* 8 vols. Salem, Mass., 1911–21.

Duke of York's Book of Laws (1676–1682), and Charter to William Penn and Laws of the Province of Pennsylvania passed between 1682 and 1700, ed. by George Stoughton *et al.* Harrisburg, 1879.

Edsall, P. W., ed. *Journal of the Courts of Common Right of East New Jersey.* Philadelphia, 1937.

Edwards, Thomas. *Gangraena.* London, 1646.

Elliot, Jonathan, ed. *The Debates in the Several State Conventions on the Adoption of the Federal Constitution.* 2nd ed. rev., 5 vols. Philadelphia, 1941.

Elton, G. R., ed. *The Tudor Constitution: Documents and Commentary.* Cambridge, Eng., 1962.

Farrand, Max, ed. *The Book of the General Lawes and Libertyes Concerning the Inhabitants of Massachusetts.* Cambridge, Mass., 1929.

———, ed. *The Records of the Federal Convention of 1787.* 4 vols. New Haven, 1911–37.

Farrell, John T., ed. *The Superior Court Diary of William Samuel Johnson, 1772–1773.* Washington, 1942.

Figgis, J. N., and R. V. Lawrence, eds. *Selections from the Correspondence of the First Lord Acton.* London, 1917.

Fitzherbert, Anthony. *La Novel Natura Brevum* (1534), ed. by Wadham Windum. London, 1682.

———. *L'Office et Auctoritie de Justice de Peace,* ed. by Richard Crompton. London, 1588. Various editions.

Force, Peter, ed. *Tracts and Other Papers, Relating Principally to the*

Origin, Settlement, and Progress of the Colonies in North America. 4 vols. New York, 1947 edition.

Ford, Worthington C., *et al.*, eds. *Journals of the Continental Congress 1774–1789.* 24 vols. Washington, 1904–37.

Fortescue, Sir John. *De Laudibus Legum Angliae,* trans. by A. Amos. Cambridge, Eng., 1825.

Foster, Charles Wilmer, ed. *The State of the Church in the Reigns of Elizabeth and James I. As Illustrated by Documents Relating to the Diocese of Lincoln.* London, 1926.

Foster, Elizabeth Read, ed. *Proceedings in Parliament, 1610.* 2 vols. New Haven, Conn. 1966.

Fowle, Daniel. *Monster of Monsters.* Boston, 1754.

——. *A Total Eclipse of Liberty.* Boston, 1755.

Foxe, John. *The Acts and Monuments of John Foxe: A New and Complete Edition,* ed. by Stephen Reed Cattley, 8 vols. London, 1837–41.

(Franklin, Benjamin.) *Papers of Benjamin Franklin,* ed. by Leonard W. Labaree *et al.* 9 vols. New Haven, 1959 ff.

The Freeman's Journal, or North-American Intelligencer. Philadelphia, 1781.

Freidberg, Aemilius, ed. *Corpus Juris Canonici.* 2 vols. Leipzig, 1879–81.

(Fuller, Nicholas.) *The Argument of Master Nicholas Fuller, in the Case of Thomas Lad, and Richard Maunsell, his Clients. Wherein it is plainly proved, that the Ecclesiasticall Commissioners have no power, by vertue of their Commission, to Imprison, to put to the Oath Ex* Officio, *or to fine any of his Majesties Subjects.* London, 1607. 32 pp.

Gardiner, Samuel Rawson, ed. *The Constitutional Documents of the Puritan Revolution, 1625–1660.* 3rd ed. rev. Oxford, 1906.

——, ed. *Documents Relating to the Proceedings against William Prynne.* London, 1877.

——, ed. *Reports of Cases in the Courts of Star Chamber and High Commission.* London, 1886.

Gee, Henry, and William John Hardy, eds. *Documents Illustrative of English Church History.* London, 1921.

Gibson, Edmund, ed. *Codex Juris Ecclesiastica Anglicani: or the Statutes, Constitutions, Canons, Rubricks and Articles, of the Church of England.* 2 vols. Oxford, 1761.

Gilbert, Geoffrey. *The Law of Evidence by a Late Learned Judge.* London, 1756.

Grant, W. L., and James Monroe. *Acts of the Privy Council of England, Colonial Series.* 6 vols. London, 1908–12.

(Greenwood, John.) *The Writings of John Greenwood, 1587–90,* ed. by Leland H. Carlson. London, 1962.

(Grimké, John F.) *The South-Carolina Justice of Peace.* Philadelphia, 1788.

Hale, William. *A Series of Precedents and Processings in Criminal Causes, Extending from the Year 1475 to 1640; Extracted from Act-Books of Ecclesiastical Courts in the Diocese of London.* London, 1894.

(Hall, Edward.) *Hall's Chronicle; containing the History of England dur-*

ing the Reign of Henry the Fourth, and the Succeeding Monarchs, to the End of the Reign of Henry the Eighth. London, 1809.

Hall, Michael G., *et al.*, eds. *The Glorious Revolution in America: Documents on the Colonial Crisis of 1689.* Chapel Hill, N.C., 1964.

Haller, William, ed. *Tracts on Liberty in the Puritan Revolution, 1638–1647.* 3 vols. New York, 1934.

Haller, William, and Godfrey Davies, eds. *The Leveller Tracts, 1647–1653.* New York, 1944.

The Harleian Miscellany: or, a collection of scarce, curious, and entertaining Pamphlets and Tracts, ed. by William Oldys. 8 vols. London, 1744–46.

Hastings, Hugh, and Edward T. Corwin, eds. *Ecclesiastical Records. State of New York.* 7 vols. Albany, 1901–16.

Hawarde, John. *Les Reportes del Cases in Camera Stellata, 1593 to 1609,* ed. by William Paley Baildon. London, 1894.

Hawkins, William. *A Treatise of the Pleas of the Crown.* London, 1716. Various editions.

Haynes, Samuel, ed. *A Collection of State Papers relating to Affairs in the Reigns of King Henry VIII, King Edward VI, Queen Mary, and Queen Elizabeth. From the Year 1542 to 1570. Transcribed from Letters and other Authentick Materials Never Before Published, Left by William Cecil Lord Burghley.* 2 vols. London, 1740.

Hening, William W. *The New Virginia Justice.* Richmond, Va., 1795.

———. *The Statutes at Large Being a Collection of All the Laws of Virginia, 1619–1792.* 13 vols. Richmond, 1809–23.

Hoadly, Charles J., ed. *Records of the Colony and Plantation of New Haven (1638–1649).* Hartford, 1857.

———, ed. *Records of the Colony or Jurisdiction of New Haven (1653–65).* Hartford, 1858.

Hough, Charles Merrill, ed. *Reports of Cases in the Vice-Admiralty of the Province of New York and in the Court of Admiralty of the State of New York, 1715–1788.* New Haven, 1925.

Howe, Mark, ed. *Readings in American Legal History.* Cambridge, Mass., 1949.

Howell, Thomas B., comp. *A Complete Collection of State Trials and Proceedings for High Treason and Other Crimes and Misdemeanors from the Earliest Period to the Year 1783.* 21 vols. London, 1816.

Howldin, J. (John Holden). *The Lawes Subversion: or, Sir John Maynards Case truly stated.* London, 1648.

Hudson, William. *A Treatise of the Court of Star Chamber* (ca. 1635), in Hargrave, Francis, ed. *Collectanea Juridica. Consisting of Tracts Relative to the Law and Constitution of England.* 2 vols. London, 1791–92. I, 1–240.

Jacob, Giles. *Every Man His Own Lawyer.* 7th ed. New York, 1768.

———. *A New Law-Dictionary.* 2nd ed. London, 1732.

(Jacob, Henry.) *To the right high and mightie Prince, James . . . An humble Supplication for Toleration.* London, 1609.

Jefferson, Thomas. *Notes on the State of Virginia,* ed. by William Peden. Chapel Hill, N. C., 1955.

——. *The Papers of Thomas Jefferson*, ed. by Julian Boyd *et al.* 17 vols. Princeton, N. J., 1950 ff.

Johnson, Samuel, ed. *Debates in Parliament.* 13 vols. London, 1787.

Journal of the Legislative Council of New-York, 1691–1775. 2 vols. Albany, 1861.

Journals of the House of Commons. London, 1803 ff.

Journals of the House of Representatives of Massachusetts (1715–1756). 27 vols. Boston, 1919–57.

Lake, Sir Edward. *Memoranda touching the Oath* Ex Officio, *Pretended Self-Accusation Canonical Purgation.* London, 1663.

Lambard, William. *Eirenarcha.* London, 1581. Various editions.

Laurens, Henry. *Extracts from the Proceedings of the Court of Vice-Admiralty in Charles-Town, South-Carolina.* Philadelphia, 1768.

Leadam, I. S., ed. *Select Cases before the King's Council, 1243–1482*, intro. by J. F. Baldwin. (Selden Society Publications, XXXV.) Cambridge, Eng., 1918.

——, ed. *Selected Cases Before the King's Council in the Star-Chamber, commonly called the Court of Star Chamber, A.D. 1477–1509.* 2 vols. (Selden Society Publications, XV–XVI.) London, 1903.

—— and J. F. Baldwin. *Select Cases Before the King's Council, 1243–1482.* (Publications of the Selden Society, XXXV.) Cambridge, Mass., 1918.

Leigh, Sir Egerton. *The Man Unmasked: Or, the World Undeceived.* Charlestown, S.C., 1769.

Letters and Papers, Foreign and Domestic, of the Reign of Henry VIII. 21 vols. London, 1862 ff.

Libby, C. T., *et al.*, eds. *Province and Court Records of Maine, 1636–1718.* 5 vols. Portland, 1928–64.

Lilburne, John. *A Copy of a Letter from Lieutenant-Colonel John Lilburne to a friend.* London, 1645.

Longstaffe, William H. D., ed. *The Acts of the High Commission Court Within the Diocese of Durham.* (Publications of the Surtees Society, XXXIV.) Durham and London, 1858.

Lovell, John. *Freedom, The First of Blessings.* Boston, 1754.

Lovett, Richard. *A Collection of Early English New Testaments, Bibles and Other Books Illustrative Chiefly of William Tyndale and His Life-work.* Oxford, 1900.

Luard, Henry Richards, ed. *Roberti Grosseteste. Episcopi Quondam Lincolniensis. Epistolae.* London, 1861.

McIlwain, Charles Howard, ed. *The Political Works of James I.* Cambridge, Mass., 1918.

McIlwaine, H. R., ed. *Legislative Journals of the Council of Colonial Virginia.* 3 vols. Richmond, 1918–19.

——. *Minutes of the Council and General Court of Colonial Virginia, 1622–1632, 1670–1676.* Richmond, 1924.

——, and Benjamin Hillman, eds. *Executive Journals of the Council of Colonial Virginia.* 6 vols. Richmond, 1925–66.

——, and J. P. Kennedy, eds. *Journals of the House of Burgesses of Virginia (1619–1776).* 13 vols. Richmond, 1905–15.

MacKinney, Gertrude, and Charles F. Hoban, eds. *Votes and Proceedings of the House of Representatives of the Province of Pennsylvania*

(*1682–1776*), in *Pennsylvania Archives*, 8th ser., 8 vols. N.p., 1931–35.

Maclay, William. *The Journal of William Maclay, United States Senator from Pennsylvania, 1789–1791*, ed. by Edgar S. Maclay, intro. by Charles Beard. New York, 1927.

McMaster, John Bach, and Frederick D. Stone, eds. *Pennsylvania and the Federal Constitution, 1787–1788*. Philadelphia, 1888.

(Madison, James.) *The Papers of James Madison*, ed. by William T. Hutchinson and William M. E. Rachal. 5 vols. Chicago, 1962 ff.

(Maimonides.) *The Code of Maimonides: Book Fourteen, The Book of Judges*, trans. by Abraham M. Hershman. New Haven, 1949.

Martin, Francis-Xavier. *The Office and Authority of a Justice of the Peace, and of Sheriffs, Coroners, &c. According to the Laws of the State of North-Carolina*. Newbern, N.C., 1791.

(Maule, Thomas.) Theo. Philanthes, *New-England Persecutors Mauld With their own Weapons . . . Together with a brief Account of the Imprisonment and Tryal of Thomas Maule of Salem, for publishing a Book, entitled, Truth held forth and maintained*. New York, 1697.

The Minutes of the Committee and of the First Commission for Detecting and Defeating Conspiracies in the State of New York (1776–1778). (New-York Historical Society Collections.) 2 vols. New York, 1924–25.

Montague, John. *Arguments Offer'd to the Right Honourable Assembly Past at New-York in America* (London, 1701), in *New-York Historical Society Collections*. New York, 1869. 177–200.

More, Sir Thomas. *The apologye of syr Thomas More knyght* (1533). S.T.C. #18078, Reel 137.

———. *The Debyllacyon of Salem and Bizance* (1533). S.T.C. #18081, Reel 125.

Morgan, Edmund S., ed. *Puritan Political Ideas, 1558–1794*. Indianapolis, 1965.

(Morice, James.) *A briefe treatise of Oathes exacted by Ordinaries and Ecclesiasticall Judges, to answere generallie to all such Articles or Interrogatories, as pleaseth them to propound. And of their forced and constrained Oathes* ex officio, *wherein is proved that the same are unlawfull* (1600). S.T.C. #18107, Reel 480.

Morison, Samuel Eliot, ed. *Records of the Suffolk County Court, 1671–1680*. (Colonial Society of Massachusetts Publications, XXIX.) Boston, 1933.

Morris, Richard B., ed. *Select Cases of the Mayor's Court of New York City, 1674–1784*. Washington, 1935.

Nelson, William. *The Law of Evidence*. London, 1735.

New-York Gazette: and the Weekly Mercury. 1770–1771.

New-York Gazette: or, the Weekly Post-Boy. 1769–1771.

Noble, John, ed. *Records of the Court of Assistants of the Massachusetts Bay, 1630–1692*. 3 vols. Boston, 1901–1928.

Notestein, Wallace, *et al.*, eds. *The Commons Debates, 1621*. 7 vols. New Haven, 1935.

O'Callaghan, E. B., and B. Fernow, eds. *Documents Relative to the Colonial History of the State of New-York*. 15 vols. Albany, 1853–87.

Paltsits, Victor Hugo, ed. *Minutes of the Commissioners for Detecting and*

Defeating Conspiracies in the State of New York: Albany County Sessions, 1778–1781. 3 vols. Albany, 1909.

Paris, Matthew. *Chronica Majora,* ed. by Henry Richards Luard, in *Chronicles and Memorial of Great Britain and Ireland during the Middle Ages.* 7 vols. London, 1876.

Parry, J. H. *Register of John de Trillek, Bishop of Hereford, 1344–1361.* Hereford, Eng., 1910.

A Parte of a Register, contayninge sundrie memorable matters, written by divers godly and learned in our time. Middleburg, Germany, 1593.

Peake, Thomas. *A Compendium of the Law of Evidence.* London, 1801. Various editions.

Peel, Albert, ed. *The Notebook of John Penry, 1593.* (Camden Society, 3rd Ser., LXVII.) London, 1944.

———, ed. *The Seconde Parte of a Register: Being a calendar of manuscript under that title intended for publication by the Puritans about 1593, and now in Dr. William's Library, London.* 2 vols. Cambridge, Eng., 1915.

———, and Leland H. Carlson, eds. *Cartwrightiana.* London, 1951.

Peters, Richard, ed. *The Public Statutes at Large of the United States of America.* Boston, 1861 ff. Vol. I.

Pierce, William, ed. *The Marprelate Tracts.* London, 1911.

Pollen, John Hungerford, ed. *Unpublished Documents relating to the English Martyrs.* 2 vols. London, 1908.

Proceedings of the Convention of the Delaware State Held at New-Castle on Tuesday the Twenty-Seventh of August, 1776. First published, 1776; reprinted: Wilmington, Del., 1927.

Prothero, G. W. *Select Statutes and other Constitutional Documents Illustrative of the Reigns of Elizabeth and James I.* Oxford, 1894.

Provincial Records and Court Papers from 1680 to 1692. (New Hampshire Historical Society Collections, VIII.) Concord, N.H., 1866.

Prynne, William. *Canterburies doom: or, The First Part of a Compleat History of the Commitment, Charge, Tryall, Condemnation, Execution of William Laud.* London, 1646.

———. *A New Discovery of the Prelates Tyranny.* London, 1641.

———. *The Second Tome of an Exact Chronological Vindication and Historical Demonstration of our British, Roman, Saxon, Danish, Norman, English Kings Supream Ecclesiastical Jurisdiction.* 2 vols. London, 1665.

Pufendorf, Baron Samuel. *The Law of Nature and Nations,* trans. by Basil Kenicott. London, 1729.

Pusey, P. E., ed. *The Homilies of S. John Chrysostom, Archbishop of Constantinople, on the Epistle of S. Paul the Apostle to the Hebrews.* London, 1883.

Quincy, Josiah, Jr., ed. *Reports of Cases Argued and Adjudged in the Superior Court of Judicature of the Province of Massachusetts Bay, Between 1761 and 1772.* Boston, 1865.

Reed, H. Clay, and George J. Miller, eds. *The Burlington Court Book: A Record of Quaker Jurisprudence in West New Jersey.* Washington, 1944.

Registrum Brevium tam Originalium quam Judicialium. London, 1531; 4th ed., 1687.

Rhode Island Court Records. 2 vols. Providence, 1920–22.

Robinson, Hastings, ed. *The Zurich Letters, comprising the Correspondence of Several English Bishops and Others with some of the Helvetian Reformers, during the Early Part of the Reign of Queen Elizabeth.* Cambridge, Eng., 1842.

Rogers, Elizabeth Frances, ed. *The Correspondence of Sir Thomas More.* Princeton, 1947.

Rolle, Henry. *Un Abridgement des Pleusieurs Cases et Resolutions del Comon Ley,* ed. by Sir M. Hale. 2 vols. London, 1668.

Rotuli Parliamentorum; ut et petitiones, et placita in Parliamento tempore Edwardi R. I. (ad finem Henrici VII). 6 vols. London, 1767–77.

St. German, Christopher. *Dialogue betwixte two englyshemen, whereof one was called Salem, and the other Bizance* (1533). S.T.C. #21584, Reel 145.

———. *A Treatise concernynge the Division betwene the Spiritualitie and Temporalitie* (1532). S.T.C. #21587, Reel 145.

Saunders, William L., ed. *Colonial Records of North Carolina (1662–1776).* 10 vols. Winston, N.C., 1895–1906.

Scott, Harold Spence, ed. *The Journal of Sir Roger Wilbraham.* (Camden Miscellany, 3rd series, X.) London, 1902.

Shurtleff, Nathaniel B., ed. *Records of the Governor and Company of the Massachusetts Bay in New England (1628-86).* 5 vols. Boston, 1853–54.

———, and David Pulsifer, eds. *Records of the Colony of New Plymouth in New England, 1633-1691.* 12 vols. Boston, 1855–61.

Simpson, William. *The Practical Justice of the Peace and Parish-officer, of his Majesty's Province of South-Carolina.* Charlestown, 1761.

Smith, Joseph H., ed. *Colonial Justice in Western Massachusetts (1639–1702): The Pynchon Court Record.* Cambridge, Mass., 1961.

———, and Philip A. Crowl, eds. *Court Records of Prince Georges County, Maryland:1696–1699.* Washington, 1964.

Smith, Sir Thomas. *De Republica Anglorum,* ed. by L. Alston. Cambridge, Eng., 1960.

(Smith, William.) *Historical Memoirs, from 16 March 1763 to 9 July 1776, of William Smith, Historian of the Province of New York,* ed. by William H. W. Sabine. New York, 1956.

———. *The History of the Late Province of New-York.* 2 vols. New York, 1829.

Somers, John. *The Security of Englishmen's Lives, or the Trust, Power and Duty of the Grand Juries of England.* Boston, 1720.

Spedding, James, ed. *The Letters and the Life of Francis Bacon, Including All His Occasional Works.* 7 vols. London, 1868.

Speeches and Passages of this Great and Happy Parliment: From the third of November 1640, to theis instant, June 1641. London, 1641.

Stamp, A. E., ed. *Close Rolls of the Reign of Henry III, 1251-53.* London, 1927.

Starke, Richard. *The Office and Authority of a Justice of the Peace.* Williamsburg, Va., 1774.

Statutes of the Realm. ed. by A. Luders *et al.* 11 vols. London, 1810–28.

Staughton, George, *et al,* eds. *Charter of William Penn and the Laws of the Province of Pennsylvania.* Harrisburg, 1879.

Stephenson, Carl, and Frederick G. Marcham, eds. *Sources of English Constitutional History. A Selection of Documents from A. D. 600 to the Present.* New York, 1937.

Stoughton, William. *An Assertion for True and Christian Church Policie.* London, 1604.

Strype, John. *Annals of the Reformation and Establishment of Religion.* 4 vols. Oxford, 1824.

———. *Historical Collections of the Life and Acts of the Right Reverend Father in God, John Aylmer, Lord Bishop of London.* Oxford, 1821.

———. *The History of the Life and Acts of Edmund Grindal.* Oxford, 1821.

———. *The Life and Acts of John Whitgift.* 3 vols. Oxford, 1822.

———. *The Life and Acts of Matthew Parker, the First Archbishop of Canterbury, in the Reign of Queen Elizabeth.* 3 vols. Oxford, 1821.

Swift, Zephaniah. *A System of the Laws of the State of Connecticut.* 2 vols. Windham, Conn., 1795–96.

Tanner, J. R., ed. *Constitutional Documents of the Reign of James I.* Cambridge, Mass., 1930.

———. *Tudor Constitutional Documents, A.D. 1485–1603.* Cambridge, Eng., 1951.

Thorpe, Francis N., ed. *The Federal and State Constitutions, Colonial Charters, and Other Organic Laws.* 7 vols. Washington, 1909.

Towle, Dorothy S., ed. *Records of the Vice-Admiralty Court of Rhode Island, 1716–1752.* Washington, D.C., 1936.

Townshend, Heywood. *Historical Collections: or, An exact Account of the Proceedings of the Four Last Parliaments of Q. Elizabeth.* London, 1680.

Trumbull, J. Hammond, and Charles J. Hoadly, eds. *The Public Records of the Colony of Connecticut.* 15 vols. Hartford, 1850–90.

(Tyndale, William). *Doctrinal Treatises and Introductions to Different Portions of the Holy Scriptures. By William Tyndale,* ed. by Henry Walter. Cambridge, Eng., 1848.

———. *Expositions and Notes on Sundry Portions of the Holy Scriptures. By William Tyndale,* ed. by Henry Walter. Cambridge, Eng., 1849.

———. *The whole Workes of William Tyndale,* ed. by John Foxe (1573). S.T.C. #24436, Reel 340.

Usher, Roland G. *The Presbyterian Movement in the Reign of Queen Elizabeth as Illustrated by the Minute Book of the Dedham Classis, 1582–89.* (Camden Society, 3rd ser., VIII.) London, 1905.

Verax, Theodorus (Clement Walker). *Anarchia Anglicana: or, The History of Independency.* London, 1648.

Wallis, N. Hardy, ed. *The New Testament Translated by William Tyndale, 1534. A Reprint of the Edition of 1534 with the Translator's Prefaces and Notes and the Variants of the Edition of 1525.* Cambridge, Eng., 1938.

Ward, Richard. *Theologicall Questions, Dogmaticall Observations, and Evangelicall Essays upon the Gospel of Jesus Christ, according to St. Matthew.* London, 1639.

Webb, George. *The Office and Authority of a Justice of the Peace.* Williamsburg, Va., 1736.

(Wheelwright, John.) *John Wheelwright, His Writings, Including his Fastday Sermon, 1637, and His Mercurius Americanus, 1645, and a Memoir,* ed. by Charles H. Bell. Boston, 1876.

Whitehead, W. A., *et al.,* eds. *Archives of the State of New Jersey, 1631–1800.* 30 vols. Newark, 1880–1906.

(Whitgift, John.) *The Works of John Whitgift,* ed. by John Ayre. 3 vols. Cambridge, Eng., 1851–53.

Whitmore, William H., ed. *The Colonial Laws of Massachusetts Reprinted from the Edition of 1660, with the Supplement of 1672. Containing also the Body of Liberties of 1641.* Boston, 1889.

——, and William S. Appleton, eds. *The Hutchinson Papers.* 2 vols. New York, 1865.

Willson, David Harris, ed. *The Parliamentary Diary of Robert Bowyer, 1606–1607.* Minneapolis, 1931.

Wingate, Edward. *Maxims of Reason: or the Reason of the Common Law of England.* London, 1658.

Winslow, Edmund. *Hypocracie Unmasked. A True Relation of the Proceedings of the Governor and Company of the Massachusetts (Bay) against Samuel Gorton of Rhode Island* (London, 1646), ed. by Millar Chapin. Providence, R.I., 1916.

(Winthrop, John.) *The History of New England from 1630 to 1649. By John Winthrop,* ed. by James Savage. 2 vols. Boston, 1853.

——, *Winthrop's Journal "History of New England," 1630–1649,* ed. by James Kendall Hosmer. 2 vols. New York, 1908.

Wolfe, Don M., ed. *Leveller Manifestoes of the Puritan Revolution.* New York, 1944.

Woodhouse, Arthur A. S. P., ed. *Puritanism and Liberty, Being the Army Debates (1647–49).* 2nd ed. Chicago, 1951.

Woodward, W. Elliott, ed. *Records of Salem Witchcraft Copied from Original Documents.* 2 vols. Boston, 1864.

Wyche, William. *A Treatise on the Practice of the Supreme Court of Judicature of the State of New-York in Civil Actions.* New York, 1794.

III. Secondary Sources

Acton, Lord (John Emerich Dalberg). *Essays on Freedom and Power,* ed. by Gertrude Himmelfarb. New York, 1955.

——. *Lectures on Modern History,* ed. by Hugh Trevor-Roper. New York, 1961.

Adams, Brooks. *The Emancipation of Massachusetts.* Rev. ed. Boston, 1919.

Adams, Charles Francis. *Three Episodes of Massachusetts History.* 2 vols. Boston, 1892.

Allen, J. W. *English Political Thought, 1603–1660.* 2 vols. London, 1938.

Andrews, Charles M. *The Colonial Period of American History.* 4 vols. New Haven, 1935–38.

(Anon.) *Jura Ecclesiastica: or the Present Practice in Ecclesiastical Courts, by a Barrister of the Middle Temple.* 2 vols. London, 1739–42.

Anstruther, Godfrey. *Vaux of Harrowden, A Recusant Family.* Newport, Eng., 1953.

Arnold, Samuel Greene. *History of the State of Rhode Island and Provincial Plantations.* 2 vols. New York, 1859–60.

Auerbach, Charles. *The Talmud: A Gateway to the Common Law.* Cleveland, 1952.

Aumann, Francis R. *The Changing American Legal System: Some Selected Phases.* Columbus, Ohio, 1940.

Babbage, Stuart Barton. *Puritanism and Richard Bancroft.* London, 1962.

Baldwin, James Fosdick. *The King's Council in England during the Middle Ages.* Oxford, 1913.

Barnes, Viola Florence. *The Dominion of New England.* New Haven, 1923.

Battis, Emery. *Saints and Sectaries: Ann Hutchinson and the Antinomian Controversy in the Massachusetts Bay Colony.* Chapel Hill, N.C., 1902.

Beard, Charles Austin. *The Office of Justice of the Peace in England.* New York, 1904.

Beesly, E. S. *Queen Elizabeth.* London, 1892.

Bentham, Jeremy. *Rationale of Judicial Evidence* (1827), in *The Works of Jeremy Bentham,* ed. by John Bowring. 12 vols. Edinburg, 1843. Vol. VII.

Berkowitz, David Sandler, ed. *Bibliotheca Bibliographica Britannica: or, Bibliographies in British History.* 3 vols., plus addenda chapters separately printed. Waltham, Mass., 1963, privately printed.

Billias, George Athan, ed. *Law and Authority in Colonial America: Selected Essays.* Barre, Mass., 1965.

Black, J. B. *The Reign of Elizabeth, 1558–1603.* 2nd ed. Oxford, 1959.

Bowen, Catherine Drinker. *The Lion and the Throne: The Life and Times of Sir Edward Coke (1552–1634).* Boston, 1956.

Brailsford, H. N. *The Levellers and the English Revolution,* ed. by Christopher Hill. London, 1961.

Bronner, Edwin S. *William Penn's "Holy Experiment": The Founding of Pennsylvania, 1681–1701.* New York, 1962.

Brook, Benjamin, *The Lives of the Puritans.* 3 vols. London, 1813.

Brook, V. J. K. *Whitgift and the English Church.* London, 1957.

Brown, Elizabeth Gaspar. *British Statutes in American Law, 1776–1836.* Ann Arbor, Mich., 1964.

Bruce, John. "Outline of the History of the Court of Star-Chamber," in *Archaeologia: or, Miscellaneous Tracts Relating to Antiquity.* London, 1834. XXV, 342–93.

Burn, Richard. *Ecclesiastical Law.* London, 1763.

Burns, John S. *The Star Chamber, Notices of the Court and Its Proceedings, with a Few Additional Notes of the High Commission.* London, 1870.

Burrage, Champlin. *The True Story of Robert Browne.* London, 1906.

Campbell, John. *The Lives of the Chief Justices of England.* 3 vols. London, 1849–57.

Cantor, Norman F. *Medieval History.* New York, 1963.

Capes, W. W. *The English Church in the Fourteenth and Fifteenth Centuries.* London, 1903.

Chafee, Zechariah, Jr. *How Human Rights Got into the Constitution.* Boston, 1952.

Chambers, R. W. *Thomas More.* London, 1935.

Chandler, Peleg W. *American Criminal Trials.* 2 vols. Boston, 1841–44.

Cheyney, Edward P. "The Court of Star Chamber," *American Historical Review,* XVIII (July 1913), 727–50.

Christensen, Merton A. "Franklin in the Hemphill Trial: Deism Versus Presbyterian Orthodoxy," *William and Mary Quarterly,* 3rd ser. X (July 1953), 422–40.

Chroust, Anton-Herman, *The Rise of the Legal Profession in America.* 2 vols. Norman, Okla., 1965.

Clark, Andrew. *Lincoln Diocese Documents, 1450-1544.* London, 1914.

Clarke, John. *Bibliotheca Legum, or Complete Catalogue of the Common and Statute Law Books of the United Kingdom.* 2nd ed., 3 vols. London, 1819.

Clyde, William M. *The Struggle for the Freedom of the Press from Caxton to Cromwell.* London, 1934.

Cohn, Haim H., "The Privilege against Self-Incrimination: Israel," *Journal of Criminal Law, Criminology and Political Science,* LI (July–Aug. 1960), 175–8.

Connery, John R., S.J., "The Right to Silence," *Marquette Law Review,* XXXIX (Winter 1955–56), 180–90.

Conset, Henry. *The Practice of the Spiritual or Ecclesiastical Courts.* London, 1685.

Cooper, J. P., "The Supplication against the Ordinaries Reconsidered," *English Historical Review,* LXXII (October 1957), 616–41.

Dale, Robert W. *History of English Congregationalism,* ed. by A. W. W. Dale. 2nd ed. London, 1907.

Davies, Godfrey, ed. *Bibliography of British History, Stuart Period, 1603–1714.* Oxford, 1928.

Dawley, Powel Mills. *John Whitgift and the English Reformation.* New York, 1954.

De Pauw, Linda Grant. *The Eleventh Pillar: New York State and the Federal Constitution.* Ithaca, N.Y., 1966.

Dickens, Arthur Geoffrey. *The English Reformation.* New York, 1964.

———. *Lollards and Protestants in the Diocese of York, 1509-1558.* London, 1959.

Dickerson, Oliver M. *The Navigation Acts and the American Revolution.* Philadelphia, 1951.

———. "Writs of Assistance as a Cause of the American Revolution," in Richard B. Morris, *The Era of the American Revolution.* New York, 1939. Pp. 40–76.

Dumbauld, Edward. *The Bill of Rights and What It Means Today.* Norman, Okla., 1957.

———. "State Precedents for the Bill of Rights," *Journal of Public Law,* VII (1958), 323–44.

Duniway, Clyde Augustus. *The Development of Freedom of the Press in Massachusetts.* New York, 1906.

Elton, G. R. "The Commons' Supplication of 1532," *English Historical Review,* LVI (October 1951), 507–34.

Esmein, A. *A History of Continental Criminal Procedure, with Special Reference to France*, trans. by John Simpson. London, 1914.

——. *Le Serment des Inculpes en Droit Canonique* (Paris, 1896), reprinted in *Bibliothèque de L'Ecole des Hautes Etudes—Sciences Religieuses*, VII (1896), 231–48.

Farrand, Max. "The Delaware Bill of Rights of 1776," *American Historical Review*, III (July 1898), 641–9.

Fincham, Francis W.X. "Notes from the Ecclesiastical Court Records at Somerset House," *Transactions*, Royal Historical Society, 4th series, IV (1921), 103–39.

Fortas, Abe. "The Fifth Amendment: Nemo Tenetur Prodere Seipsum," Cleveland Bar Association, *The Journal*, XXV (April 1954), 91, 96–104.

Frank, Joseph. *The Levellers, A History of the Writings of Three Seventeenth-Century Democrats: John Lilburne, Richard Overton, William Walwyn*. Cambridge, Mass., 1955.

Franklin, Mitchell. "The Encyclopédiste Origin and Meaning of the Fifth Amendment," *Lawyers Guild Review*, XV (Summer 1955), 41–62.

French, Allen. *Charles I and the Puritan Upheaval: A Study of the Causes of the Great Migration*. London, 1955.

Frere, W.H. *The English Church in the Reigns of Elizabeth and James I.* London, 1904.

Frese, Joseph R. "Writs of Assistance in the American Colonies, 1660–1776." Unpublished Ph.D. dissertation, Harvard College, 1951.

Fuller, Thomas. *The Church History of Britain from the Birth of Jesus Christ until the year MDCXLVIII*, ed. by J.S. Brewer. 6 vols. Oxford, 1845.

Gairdner, James. *A History of the English Church in the Sixteenth Century, from the Accession of Henry VIII to the Death of Mary.* London, 1904.

——. *Lollardy and the Reformation in England.* 3 vols. London, 1908.

Galbraith, V.H. *The Making of Domesday Book.* Oxford, 1961.

Gardiner, Samuel Rawson. *History of England from the Accession of James I, to the Outbreak of the Civil War, 1603–1642.* 10 vols. London, 1886.

Gibb, M.B. *John Lilburne, The Leveller: A Christian Democrat.* London, 1947.

Goebel, Julius, Jr. "King's Law and Local Custom in Seventeenth Century New England," *Columbia Law Review*, XXXI (March 1931), 416–48.

——, and T. Raymond Naughton. *Law Enforcement in Colonial New York: A Study in Criminal Procedure (1664–1776).* New York, 1944.

Goldin, Hyman E. *Hebrew Criminal Law and Procedure.* New York, 1952.

Gooch, G.P. *Democratic Ideas in the Seventeenth Century.* 2nd ed. Cambridge, Eng., 1926.

Gorton, Adelos. *The Life and Times of Samuel Gorton.* Philadelphia, 1907.

Gough, J.W. *Fundamental Law in English Constitutional History.* Oxford, 1955.

Gregg, Pauline. *Free-Born John, A Biography of John Lilburne.* London, 1961.

Griswold, Erwin N. *The 5th Amendment Today.* Cambridge, Mass., 1955.

Hall, Ford W. "The Common Law: An Account of Its Reception in the United States," *Vanderbilt Law Review*, IV (June 1951), 791–825.

Hallam, Henry. *The Constitutional History of England from the Accession of Henry VII to the Death of George II.* 8th ed., 3 vols. London, 1867.

Haller, William. *The Elect Nation, The Meaning and Relevance of Foxe's Book of Martyrs.* New York, 1963.

———. *The Rise of Puritanism, 1570–1643.* New York, 1938.

Hamlin, Paul M. *Legal Education in Colonial New York.* New York, 1939.

———, and Charles E. Baker. *Supreme Court of Judicature of the Province of New York, 1691–1704.* 3 vols. New York, 1959.

Haskins, Charles Homer. *Norman Institutions.* Cambridge, Mass., 1925.

Haskins, George Lee. *Law and Authority in Early Massachusetts.* New York, 1960.

———. "Precedents in English Ecclesiastical Practices for Criminal Punishments in Early Massachusetts," in *Essays in Legal History in Honor of Felix Frankfurter*, ed. by Morris D. Forkosch. Indianapolis, 1966. Pp. 321–36.

Hilkey, Charles J. *Legal Development in Colonial Massachusetts, 1630–1686.* New York, 1910.

Hofstadter, Samuel H. *The Fifth Amendment and the Immunity Act of 1954: Aspects of the American Way.* Pamphlet distributed by the Fund for the Republic. New York, n.d., 45 pp.

Holdsworth, Sir William. *A History of English Law.* 16 vols. London and Boston, 1903–66.

Holt, J. C. *Magna Carta.* Cambridge, Eng., 1965.

Horowitz, George. "The Privilege against Self-Incrimination: How Did It Originate?," *Temple Law Quarterly*, XXXI (Winter 1958), 121–44.

———. *The Spirit of Jewish Law.* New York, 1953.

Hughes, Philip. *The Reformation in England.* 3 vols. London, 1950–54.

Hume [Maguire], Mary Ballantine. "The History of the Oath *Ex Officio* in England." Unpublished Ph.D. dissertation, Radcliffe College, 1923.

Hunard, Naomi D. "The Jury of Presentment and the Assize of Clarendon," *English Historical Review*, LVI (July 1941), 377–410.

Hunnisett, R. F. *The Medieval Coroner.* Cambridge, Eng., 1961.

Hutchinson, Thomas. *The History of the Colony and Province of Massachusetts-Bay*, ed. by Lawrence Shaw Mayo. 3 vols. Cambridge, Mass., 1936.

James, Eldon Revare, ed. "A List of Legal Treatises Printed in the British Colonies and the American States before 1801," in Morton C. Campbell *et al. Harvard Legal Essays.* Cambridge, Mass., 1934.

Jardine, David. *A Reading on the Use of Torture in the Criminal Law of England.* London, 1837.

Jones, Edward Alfred. *American Members of the Inns of Court.* London, 1924.

Jones, Matt Bushnell. *Thomas Maule, the Salem Quaker and Free Speech in Massachusetts Bay.* Salem, 1936. 42 pp. Reprinted from *Essex Institute Historical Collections*, LXXII (Jan. 1936).

Jones, Rufus. *The Quakers in the American Colonies.* New York, 1966 edition. First published in 1911.

Jordan, W. K. *The Development of Religious Toleration in England from the Accession of James I to the Convention of the Long Parliament (1603–1640)*. Cambridge, Mass., 1936.

———. *The Development of Religious Toleration in England from the Beginning of the English Reformation to the Death of Queen Elizabeth*. Cambridge, Mass., 1932.

———. *The Development of Religious Toleration in England from the Convention of the Long Parliament to the Restoration, 1640–1660; The Revolutionary Experiments and the Dominant Religious Thought*. Cambridge, Mass., 1938.

———. *The Development of Religious Toleration in England; Attainment of the Theory and Accommodations in Thought and Institutions (1640–1660)*. Cambridge, Mass., 1940.

Judson, Margaret Atwood. *The Crisis of the Constitution*. New Brunswick, N.J., 1949.

Keane, Morris. *The Outlaws of England*. Toronto, 1961.

Kemp, John A. "The Background of the Fifth Amendment in English Law," *William and Mary Law Review*, I (1958), 247–86.

Kenealy, William J., S. L., "Fifth Amendment Morals," *The Catholic Lawyer*, III (Autumn 1957), 340–55.

Kittredge, George Lyman. "Dr. Robert Child the Remonstrant," *Publications of the Colonial Society of Massachusetts*, XXI (Transactions, 1919), 1–146.

Klein, Arthur Jay. *Intolerance in the Reign of Elizabeth*. Boston, 1927.

Knappen, M. M. *Tudor Puritanism, A Chapter in the History of Idealism*. Chicago, 1939.

Lamm, Norman, "The Fifth Amendment and Its Equivalent in the Halakhah," *Judaism: A Quarterly Journal*, V (Winter 1956), 53–9.

Landynski, Jacob W. *Search and Seizure and the Supreme Court: A Study in Constitutional Interpretation*. Baltimore, 1966.

Lasson, Nelson. *The History and Development of the Fourth Amendment to the United States Constitution*. Baltimore, 1937.

Lea, Henry Charles. *A History of the Inquisition of the Middle Ages*. 3 vols. New York, 1955.

Lea, Homer C. *Superstition and Force*. 3rd ed. Philadelphia, 1878.

Leder, Lawrence H. *Robert Livingston, 1654–1728, and the Politics of Colonial New York*. Chapel Hill, N.C., 1961.

Le Van Baumer, Franklin. "Christopher St. German: The Political Philosophy of a Tudor Lawyer," *American Historical Review*, XLII (July 1937), 631–51.

Levy, Leonard W. *Jefferson and Civil Liberties: The Darker Side*. Cambridge, Mass., 1963.

———. *Legacy of Suppression: Freedom of Speech and Press in Early American History*. Cambridge, Mass., 1960.

———, and Lawrence H. Leder. "Exotic Fruit: The Right against Compulsory Self-Incrimination in Colonial New York," *William and Mary Quarterly*, 3rd ser. XX (Jan. 1963), 3–32.

Lingley, Charles R. *The Transition in Virginia from Colony to Commonwealth*. New York, 1910.

Lovejoy, David S. *Rhode Island Politics and the American Revolution, 1760–1776.* Providence, R.I., 1958.
———. "Rights Imply Equality: The Case against Admiralty Jurisdiction in America, 1764–1776," *William and Mary Quarterly,* 3rd ser. XVI (Oct. 1959), 459–84.
Lowell, A. Lawrence. "The Judicial Use of Torture," Parts I and II, *Harvard Law Review,* XI (1897–98), 220–33, 290–300.
Macaulay, Thomas B. *Critical and Historical Essays,* ed. by F. C. Montague. 3 vols. London, 1903.
McCormick, Charles T. *Handbook of The Law of Evidence.* St. Paul, Minn., 1954.
McGinn, Donald Joseph. *The Admonition Controversy.* New Bruswick, N.J. 1949.
———. *John Penry and the Marprelate Controversy.* New Brunswick, N.J., 1966.
McKechnie, William Sharp. *Magna Carta, A Commentary on the Great Charter of King John.* 2nd ed. Glasgow, 1914.
McKisack, May. *The Fourteenth Century, 1307–1399.* Oxford, 1959.
Maguire, John M. *Evidence of Guilt: Restrictions upon Its Discovery or Compulsory Disclosure.* Boston, 1959.
Maguire, Mary Hume. "Attack of the Common Lawyers on the Oath *Ex Officio* As Administered in the Ecclesiastical Courts in England," in *Essays in Honor of Charles H. McIlwain.* Cambridge, Mass., 1936. Pp. 199–229.
Maier, Pauline. "John Wilkes and American Disillusionment with Britain," *William and Mary Quarterly,* 3rd ser., XX (July 1963), 373–95.
Maitland, Frederic William. *Domesday Book and Beyond.* Cambridge, Eng., 1897.
———. "A Prologue to a History of English Law," in *Select Essays in Anglo-American Legal History,* ed. by a Committee of the Association of American Law Schools. 3 vols. Boston, 1907.
———. *Roman Canon Law in the Church of England.* London, 1898.
———. *Selected Historical Essays of F. W. Maitland,* ed. by Helen M. Cam. Boston, 1962.
Makower, Felix. *The Constitutional History and Constitution of the Church of England.* London, 1895.
Marchant, Roland A. *The Puritans and the Church Courts in the Diocese of York, 1560–1642.* London, 1960.
Mark, Irving. *Agrarian Conflicts in Colonial New York, 1711–1775.* New York, 1940.
Mayers, Lewis. "The Federal Witness' Privilege against Self-Incrimination: Constitutional or Common Law?," *American Journal of Legal History,* IV (April 1960), 107–41.
———. *Shall We Amend the Fifth Amendment?* New York, 1959.
Mendlebaum, Simcha, "The Privilege against Self-Incrimination in Anglo-American and Jewish Law," *American Journal of Comparative Law,* V, (Winter 1956), 115–19.
Merriman, Roger B. *The Life and Letters of Thomas Cromwell.* 2 vols. Oxford, 1902.

Meyer, Arnold Oscar. *England and the Catholic Church under Queen Elizabeth*, trans. by J. R. McKee. London, 1916.

Meyers, Denys P. *Massachusetts and The First Ten Amendments to the Constitution.* (74th Cong., 2nd sess., Sen. Doc. No. 181.) Washington, 1936.

Miller, Perry. *The New England Mind: The Seventeenth Century.* Boston, 1961.

———. *Orthodoxy in Massachusetts, 1630–1650.* Boston, 1959.

Morgan, Edmund M. *Basic Problems of Evidence.* Philadelphia, 1954.

Morgan, Edmund S. "The Case against Anne Hutchinson," *New England Quarterly,* X (1937), 635–49.

Moriarty, Eugene James. *Oaths in Ecclesiastical Courts.* Washington, 1937.

Morison, Samuel Eliot. *Builders of the Bay Colony.* Boston, 1930.

———. *Harvard College in the Seventeenth Century.* 2 vols. Cambridge, Mass., 1936.

Morris, Richard B. "Massachusetts and the Common Law: The Declaration of 1646," *American Historical Review,* XXXI (April 1926), 443–53.

———. *Studies in the History of American Law: With Special Reference to the Seventeenth and Eighteenth Centuries.* New York, 1930.

Morton, Richard L. *Colonial Virginia.* 2 vols. Chapel Hill, N.C., 1960.

Mott, Rodney L. *Due Process of Law.* Indianapolis, 1926.

Mozley, J. F. *John Foxe and His Book.* London, 1940.

———. *William Tyndale.* London, 1937.

Muscutt, Edward. *History and Power of Ecclesiastical Courts.* London, 1845.

———. *The History of Church Laws in England, from A.D. 602 to A.D. 1850.* London, 1851.

Neal, Daniel. *The History of the Puritans, or Protestant Non-Conformists from the Reformation to the Death of Queen Elizabeth,* rev. by Joshua Toulmin. 5 vols. Portsmouth, N.H., 1816.

Neale, J. E. *Elizabeth I and Her Parliaments.* 2 vols. New York, 1958. Vol. I: 1559–1581; Vol. II: 1584–1601.

Nevins, Allan. *The American States During and After the Revolution, 1775–1789.* New York, 1927.

Nobbe, George. *The North Briton.* New York, 1939.

Ogle, Arthur. *The Tragedy of the Lollards' Tower.* Oxford, 1949.

Osgood, Herbert L. *The American Colonies in the Eighteenth Century.* 4 vols. New York, 1924.

———. *The American Colonies in the Seventeenth Century.* 3 vols. New York, 1904.

Peare, Catherine Owens. *William Penn, A Biography.* Philadelphia, 1957.

Pearson, A. Scott. *Church and State; Political Aspects of Sixteenth Century Puritanism.* Cambridge, Eng., 1928.

———. *Thomas Cartwright and Elizabethan Puritanism, 1535–1603.* Cambridge, Eng., 1925.

Pease, Theodore Calvin. *The Leveller Movement: A Study in the History and Political Theory of the English Great Civil War.* Washington, 1916.

Peel, Albert. *The First Congregational Churches: New Light on Separatist Congregations in London, 1567–81.* Cambridge, Eng., 1920.

Phillimore, Sir Robert. *Ecclesiastical Law of the Church of England.* 2 vols. London, 1895.

Phillips, Henry E. I., "The Last Years of the Star Chamber, 1630–41," *Transactions*, Royal Historical Society, 4th ser., XXI (1939), 103–31.

Pierce, William. *An Historical Introduction to the Marprelate Tracts.* London, 1908.

————. *John Penry, His Life, Times and Writings.* London, 1923.

Pike, Luke Owen. *A History of Crime in England.* 2 vols. London, 1873–76.

Pittman, R. Carter. "The Colonial and Constitutional History of the Privilege against Self-Incrimination in America," *Virginia Law Review*, XXI (May 1935), 763–89.

————. "The Fifth Amendment: Yesterday, Today and Tomorrow," *American Bar Association Journal*, XLII (June 1956), 509–12, 588–94.

Plucknett, Theodore F. T. *A Concise History of the Common Law.* 5th ed. Boston, 1956.

Pollard, A. F. "Council, Star Chamber, and Privy Council under the Tudors," *English Historical Review*, XXXVII (July and Oct. 1922), 337–60, 516–39; XXVIII (Jan. 1923), 42–60.

Pollard, Alfred W., G. R. Redgrave, et al., eds. *A Short-Title Catalogue of Books Printed in England, Scotland, and Ireland, and of English Books Printed Abroad, 1475–1640.* London, 1946. Referred to as "S.T.C."

Pollen, J. H. *The English Catholics in the Reign of Queen Elizabeth.* London, 1920.

Pollock, Sir Frederick, and Frederic William Maitland. *The History of English Law Before the Time of Edward I.* 2nd ed., 2 vols. Cambridge, Eng., 1899.

Pollock, Sir John. *The Popish Plot: A Study in the History of the Reign of Charles II.* Cambridge, Eng., 1944.

Postgate, Raymond. *That Devil Wilkes.* New York, 1929.

Powers, Edwin. *Crime and Punishment in Early Massachusetts, 1620–1692.* Boston, 1966.

Powicke, F. J. *Henry Barrow, Separatist (1550–93), and the Exiled Church of Amsterdam.* London, 1900.

————. *Robert Browne, Pioneer of Modern Congregationalism.* London, 1910.

Powicke, Sir Maurice. *The Reformation in England.* London, 1961.

Radin, Max. *Handbook of Anglo-American Legal History.* St. Paul, Minn., 1936.

————. "The Myth of Magna Carta," *Harvard Law Review*, LXX (1947), 1060–91.

Radzinowicz, Leon. *A History of English Criminal Law and Its Administration from 1750.* 3 vols. London, 1948.

Randall, Charles H. "Sir Edward Coke and the Privilege against Self-Incrimination," *South Carolina Law Quarterly*, VIII (Summer 1956), 417–53.

Rankin, Hugh F. *Criminal Trial Proceedings in the General Court of Virginia.* Charlottesville, Va., 1965.

Rea, Robert R. *The English Press in Politics, 1760–1774*. Lincoln, Neb., 1963.

Read, Conyers, ed. *Bibliography of British History. Tudor Period, 1485–1603*. 2nd ed. Oxford, 1959.

———. *Lord Burghley and Queen Elizabeth*. London, 1960.

———. *Mr. Secretary Cecil and Queen Elizabeth*. New York, 1955.

———. *Mr. Secretary Walsingham and the Policy of Queen Elizabeth*. 3 vols. Cambridge, Mass., 1925.

Reed, H. Clay. "The Delaware Constitution of 1776," *Delaware Notes*, VI (1930), 7–42.

Reinsch, Paul Samuel. *English Common Law in the Early American Colonies*. Madison, Wisc., 1890.

Relf, Francis H. *The Petition of Right*. Minneapolis, 1917.

Richardson, H. G. "Heresy and the Lay Power under Richard II," *English Historical Review*, LI (1936), 1–28.

Richardson, H. G., and G. O. Sayles. *The Governance of Medieval England from the Conquest to Magna Carta*. Edinburgh, 1963.

Riesenfeld, Stephan A. "Law-Making and Legislative Precedent in American Legal History," *Minnesota Law Review*, XXXIII (Jan. 1949), 103–44.

Rogge, O. John. *The First and the Fifth with Some Excursions into Others*. New York, 1960.

Rossiter, Clinton. *Seedtime of the Republic: The Origin of the American Tradition of Political Liberty*. New York, 1953.

Rowland, Kate Mason. *The Life of George Mason, 1725–1792*. 2 vols. New York, 1892.

Rudé, George. *Wilkes and Liberty*. New York, 1962.

Rutland, Robert A. *The Birth of the Bill of Rights, 1776–1791*. Chapel Hill, N.C., 1955.

Scofield, Cora L. *A Study of the Court of Star Chamber*. Chicago, 1900.

Scott, Arthur P. *Criminal Law in Colonial Virginia*. Chicago, 1930.

Selsam, J. Paul. *The Pennsylvania Constitution of 1776*. Philadelphia, 1936.

Shannon, Albert C. *The Popes and Heresy in the Thirteenth Century*. Villanova, Pa., 1949.

Siebert, Fredrick Seaton. *Freedom of the Press in England, 1476–1776*. Urbana, Ill., 1952.

Sikes, Enoch W. *The Transition of North Carolina from Colony to Commonwealth*. Baltimore, 1898.

Silving, Helen. "The Oath," Parts I and II, *Yale Law Journal*, LXVIII (June and July 1959), 1329–90, 1527–77.

Simpson, Richard. *Edmund Campion, A Biography*. Edinburgh, 1867.

Stenton, Doris M. *English Justice between the Norman Conquest and the Great Charter, 1066–1215*. Philadelphia, 1964.

Stenton, Sir Frank. *Anglo-Saxon England*. 2nd ed. Oxford, 1947.

Stephen, Sir James Fitzjames. *A History of the Criminal Law of England*. 3 vols. London, 1883.

Stephens, W. R. W. *The English Church from the Norman Conquest to the Accession of Edward I*. London, 1904.

Strack, Hermann L. *Introduction to the Talmud and Midrash*. New York, 1959.

Stubbs, William. *The Constitutional History of England in Its Origin and Development.* 2nd ed., 3 vols. Oxford, 1875.

———. *Report of the Commissioners appointed to inquire into the Constitution and working of the Ecclesiastical Courts.* London, 1883. Appendix, vol. II.

Tanner, J. R. *English Constitutional Conflicts of the Seventeenth Century.* Cambridge, Eng., 1928.

Taylor, Telford. *Grand Inquest: The Story of Congressional Investigations.* New York, 1955.

Thayer, James Bradley. *A Preliminary Treatise on Evidence at the Common Law.* Boston, 1898.

Thompson, Faith. *Magna Carta, Its Role in the Making of the English Constitution, 1300–1629.* Minneapolis, 1948.

Thomson, John A. F. *The Later Lollards, 1414–1520.* New York, 1965.

Ubbelohde, Carl. *The Vice Admiralty Courts and the American Revolution.* Chapel Hill, N.C., 1960.

Upham, Charles W. *Salem Witchcraft.* 2 vols. Boston, 1867.

Usher, Roland G. "James I and Sir Edward Coke," *English Historical Review,* XVIII (Oct. 1903), 664–75.

———. "Nicholas Fuller: A Forgotten Exponent of English Liberty," *American Historical Review,* XII (1907), 734–60.

———. *The Reconstruction of the English Church.* 2 vols. New York, 1910.

———. *The Rise and Fall of the High Commission.* Oxford, 1913.

Van Caenegem, R. C. *Royal Writs in England from the Conquest to Glanville.* (Selden Society Publications, LXXVII.) London, 1959.

Van Tyne, Claude. *The Loyalists of the American Revolution.* New York, 1902.

Waddington, John. *John Penry, the Pilgrim Martyr, 1559–93.* London, 1854.

Wallace, David Duncan. *The Life of Henry Laurens.* New York, 1915.

Warren, Charles. *A History of the American Bar.* Cambridge, Eng., 1912.

———. "New Light on the History of the Federal Judiciary Act of 1789," *Harvard Law Review,* XXXVII (Nov. 1923), 49–132.

Wertenbaker, Thomas J. *Torchbearer of the Revolution: The Story of Bacon's Rebellion.* Princeton, N.J., 1940.

———. *Virginia under the Stuarts.* Princeton, N.J., 1914.

White, Philip L. *The Beekmans of New York in Politics and Commerce, 1647–1877.* New York, 1956.

Wigmore, John H. "Nemo Tenetur Prodere Seipsum," *Harvard Law Review,* V (May 1891), 71–88.

———. *A Panorama of the World's Legal Systems.* Washington, 1936.

———. *A Treatise on the Anglo-American System of Evidence in Trials at Common Law.* 3rd ed., 10 vols. Boston, 1940. Vol. VIII rev. 1961 by John T. McNaughton. (Also, 2nd ed., 5 vols. Boston, 1923.)

Wilkins, David. *Concilia Magnae Britanniae et Hiberniae.* 4 vols. London, 1737.

Williams, Edward Bennett. *One Man's Freedom.* New York, 1964.

Winfield, Percy, H. *The Chief Sources of English Legal History.* Cambridge, Mass., 1925.

Wing, Donald G., ed. *Short-Title Catalogues of Books Printed in England,*

Scotland, Ireland, Wales and British America 1641–1700. New York, 1945.

Winslow, Ola Elizabeth. *Master Roger Williams.* New York, 1957.

Wolfram, Harold W. "John Lilburne: Democracy's Pillar of Fire," *Syracuse Law Review,* III (Spring 1952), 213–58.

Worrall, John. *Bibliotheca Legum Angliae.* 2 vols. London, 1788.

Wright, Benjamin F. *American Interpretations of Natural Law.* New York, 1962.

Zwierlein, Frederick. *Religion in New Netherland.* Rochester, N. Y., 1910.

INDEX

Abbot, George, 249, 251-52, 257, 259, 260
Accusatio: procedure of, 22; discouraged, 25; used by High Commission, 129
Accusatorial procedures: origins, 5-7, 39; and inquest, 7-11; growth of jury, 11-16, 30-31; requirement of consent, 16-18; emergence of petty jury, 18-19; accusation, 29-30; role of judge, 31-33, 38-43; role of jury, 36-39; contrasted with inquisitorial procedures, 39-40; served needs of crown, 40-41; in Talmudic law, 433-34. *See also* Common law, Grand jury, Trial by jury, Magna Carta, Right to counsel
Act of Supremacy: 239; provisions of, 69; relation to High Commission, 233, 236-38, 240, 243, 247-48, 282
Acton, Lord: on Catholic persecution, 75-76
Adams, Charles Francis: on Wheelwright case, 340, 341; on Hutchinson case, 343
Adams, John, 398
Admiralty courts: procedures, 395, 398; Laurens case, 395-97; Hancock case, 397-99
Admonition controversy, 113
Adversary system, 6
Albigensian Crusade, 53
Allen, Andrew: on right against self-incrimination, 399
Allen, Edmond: refuses to incriminate self, 149
Allerton, Ralph: refuses oath *ex officio,* 79
Ames, Fisher, 422
Anabaptists, 76
Anderson, Edmond: and right against self-incrimination, 164; examines Udall, 164-65

André, John, 414
Andrews, Lancelot, 169
Andros, Edmund: inquisitorial tactics, 362
Anglican Church, 73, 91, 111-12, 122, 209, 266
Antinomianism, 340, 342-43, 344, 348
Appeal of felony, 7, 13, 30
Aquinas, Thomas: and heresy, 21; canon law, 96; against *nemo tenetur* maxim, 329; on self-incrimination, 446
Arundel, Thomas: tries Sawtre, 57; enforces oath *ex officio,* 59
Ashton, John: refuses oath, 55
Askew, Anne, 73
Attaint, 37
Atwood, William: 388; acknowledged right against self-incrimination, 379, 380
Audley, Lord: refuses to incriminate self, 264
Augustine, Saint, 21, 160
Axton, William, 132
Aylmer, John, 119, 138, 141, 149, 155, 173, 181

Bacon, Francis: 242, 246, 252, 253, 254, 260; on oath *ex officio,* 215, 396-97
Bainbrigg, Cuthbert: refuses oath *ex officio,* 189
Baldwin, J.F.: on oath *ex officio,* 50-51
Bancroft, Richard: 181, 188, 225, 246; on Cartwright, 112-13, 173; on High Commission, 126; anti-Puritanism, 162-163, 173-74; at Hampton Court conference, 211; on James I, 212; characterized, 213; as Archbishop of Canterbury, 213, 214; on prohibitions, 221, 226-27, 241-42
Barrow, Henry: 176, 189, 191; on Whitgift, 121; tried by High Commission,